Kashmir in the Aftermath of Partition

Kashmir remains one of the world's most militarized areas of dispute, having been in the grips of an armed insurgency against India since the late 1980s. In existing scholarship, ideas of territoriality, state sovereignty, and national security have dominated the discourses on the Kashmir conflict. This book, in contrast, places Kashmir and Kashmiris at the center of historical debate and investigates a broad range of sources to illuminate a century of political players and social structures on both sides of divided Kashmir and in the wider Kashmiri diaspora. In the process, it broadens the contours of Kashmir's postcolonial and resistance history, complicates the meaning of Kashmiri identity, and reveals Kashmiris' myriad imaginings of freedom. It asserts that "Kashmir" has emerged as a political imaginary in postcolonial era, a vision that grounds Kashmiris in their negotiations for rights not only in India and Pakistan, but also in global cultural and political spaces. This book further contends that the idea of territorial nationalism has failed to bring peace to the South Asian subcontinent. Instead, the trauma of partition continues to unfold in Kashmir, while Kashmiris struggle for dignity and rights.

Shahla Hussain teaches in the Department of History at St. John's University, USA.

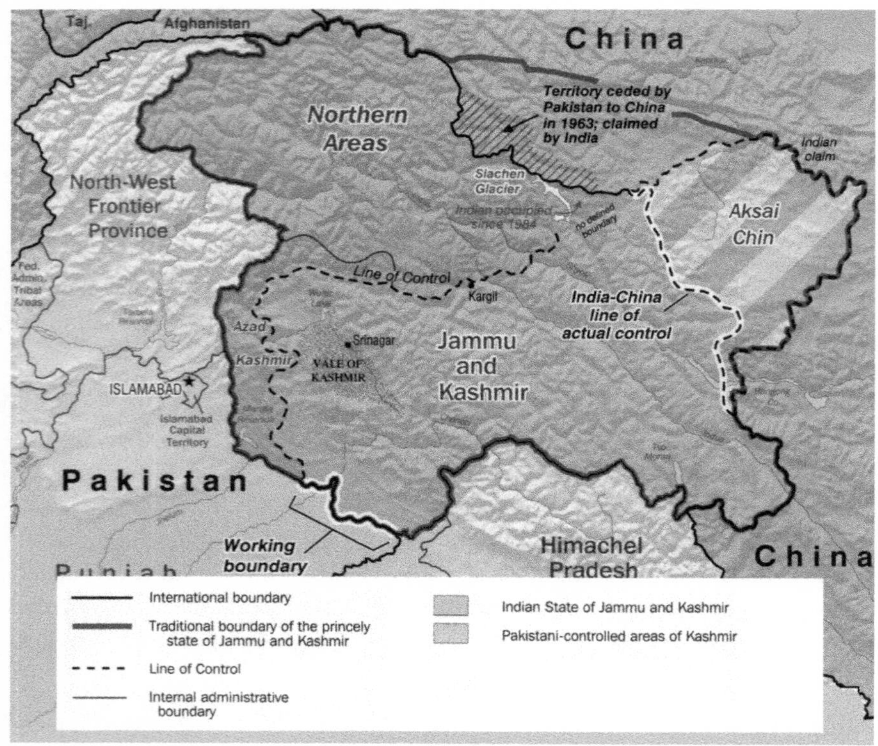

Map of the Disputed State of Jammu and Kashmir

Source: Based on map by US Central Intelligence Agency, 2002.

Note: In 2019 the Indian Parliament passed the Jammu and Kashmir Reorganization Act that stripped India-administered Kashmir of statehood and reconstituted it into two union territories: Jammu-Kashmir and Ladakh.

Map not to scale and does not represent authentic international boundaries.

Kashmir in the Aftermath of Partition

Shahla Hussain

Shaftesbury Road, Cambridge CB2 8EA, United Kingdom

One Liberty Plaza, 20th Floor, New York, NY 10006, USA

477 Williamstown Road, Port Melbourne, VIC 3207, Australia

314–321, 3rd Floor, Plot 3, Splendor Forum, Jasola District Centre, New Delhi – 110025, India

103 Penang Road, #05–06/07, Visioncrest Commercial, Singapore 238467

Cambridge University Press is part of Cambridge University Press & Assessment, a department of the University of Cambridge.

We share the University's mission to contribute to society through the pursuit of education, learning and research at the highest international levels of excellence.

www.cambridge.org
Information on this title: www.cambridge.org/9781009370202

© Shahla Hussain 2021

This publication is in copyright. Subject to statutory exception and to the provisions of relevant collective licensing agreements, no reproduction of any part may take place without the written permission of Cambridge University Press & Assessment.

First published 2021
First paperback edition 2023

A catalogue record for this publication is available from the British Library

ISBN 978-1-108-49046-7 Hardback
ISBN 978-1-009-37020-2 Paperback

Cambridge University Press & Assessment has no responsibility for the persistence or accuracy of URLs for external or third-party internet websites referred to in this publication and does not guarantee that any content on such websites is, or will remain, accurate or appropriate.

To Ahlay

Contents

Acknowledgments ix

Introduction 1

1. Meanings of Freedom in the Princely State of Jammu and Kashmir 24
2. Freedom, Loyalty, Belonging: Kashmir after Decolonization 77
3. Puppet Regimes: Collaboration and the Political Economy of Kashmiri Resistance 132
4. The Idea of Plebiscite: Discontent and Regional Dissidence 184
5. Mapping Kashmiri Imaginings of Freedom in the Inter-regional and Global Arenas 238
6. *Jang-i-Aazadi* (War for Freedom): Religion, Politics, and Resistance 292

Conclusion 349

Select Bibliography 361

Index 378

Acknowledgments

I would like to express my gratitude to numerous people and institutions. This book is an outgrowth of my doctoral dissertation at Tufts University. I am eternally grateful for the guidance and unwavering support that I have received from my former Ph.D. advisor, Ayesha Jalal. I am thankful for many constructive comments and feedback she provided that improved the clarity of my arguments. I also want to express my thanks to Kris Manjapra, Sugata Bose, Leila Fawaz, Reed Ueda, Annette Lazzara, and Steven Marrone for their guidance and encouragement during my time at Tufts.

The research for this book was made possible by generous grants and fellowships that I received from various institutions. I am grateful to the Tufts Provost Office and Tufts Institute of Global Leadership for providing me funds to travel to India for my fieldwork. The fellowship offered by the American Institute of Pakistan Studies allowed me to do research at the British Library and the National Archives, Kew. The Summer Support for Research received from St. John's University enabled me to dedicate my time to writing and completing this book.

I am indebted to several individuals who provided access to their priceless private collections and unpublished documents. In India-administered Kashmir, I owe my gratitude to Humaira Farooq, Bhushan Bazaz, Shabir Mujahid, and Mrs. Khan. They shared their archives, without which I would not be able to formulate critical arguments of my book. In England, I benefitted from the support of Daalat Ali, who was very hospitable and introduced me to a cross-section of British Kashmiri activists. I want to thank Masoom Ali, Shams Rehman, Wahid Siddiqi, Shabir Choudhry and Nazir Tabassum for sharing their archives with me. I am deeply appreciative of Agha Shabbar in Pakistan-administered Kashmir who arranged interviews on Skype with essential members of the Kashmiri community. I wish to record my gratitude to Dr. Abdul Basit, Ambassador Arif Kamal, Justice Abdul Majeed Mallick, Farooq Rehmani, Abdul Khaliq Ansari, and Maulvi Muhammad Ahmed for sharing their insights about Kashmir's politics and history.

My sincere thanks to the staff at the Jammu Archives, National Archives of India, Nehru Memorial Museum and Library, National Archives at Kew, and the British Library for accommodating my research requests. I am also grateful to Thomas Burbine for helping me acquire valuable documents from the Center for Research

Libraries at Chicago. The staff members of the Library of Congress at Washington DC and the United Nations Archives and Record Management were very helpful during my research visits.

I am fortunate to have a supportive department at St. John's University that reduced my teaching load so that I could dedicate my time to the completion of my book. My heartfelt thanks to my colleagues in the History department at St. John's for their friendship and support. I am grateful to all the people who read parts of the manuscript and offered valuable comments, especially Nerina Rustomji and Catherine R. Osborne. At Cambridge University Press, Qudsiya Ahmed, Aniruddha De, and Anwesha Rana provided support throughout the publication process.

Finally, I want to express my gratitude to my family, especially my parents who instilled in me the value of hard work and the importance of determination. My aunt and brother provided the needed moral support. I am especially grateful to my uncle for helping me translate literary works from Kashmiri to English. I dedicate this book to my daughter, Ahlay, whose love and support motivated me to take on and complete this project.

Introduction

From Zero Bridge
a shadow chased by searchlights is running
away to find its body.
On the edge
of the Cantonment, where Gupkar Road ends,
it shrinks almost into nothing, is
nothing by interrogation gates, so it can slip, unseen, into the cells:
Drippings from a suspended burning tire
are falling on the back of a prisoner,
the naked boy screaming, "I know nothing."
The shadow slips out, beckons *Console Me*,
"Rizwan, it's you, Rizwan, it's you," I cry out
as he steps closer, the sleeves of his *phiren* torn.
"Each night put Kashmir in your dreams," he says,
then touches me, his hands crusted with snow,
whispers, "I have been cold a long, long time."
"Don't tell my father I have died," he says,
and I follow him through blood on the road
and hundreds of pairs of shoes the mourners
left behind, as they ran from the funeral,
victims of the firing. From windows we hear
grieving mothers, and snow begins to fall
on us, like ash. Black on the edges of flames,
it cannot extinguish the neighborhoods,
the homes set ablaze by midnight soldiers.
Kashmir is burning:
I won't tell your father you have died, Rizwan
but where has your shadow fallen, like cloth
on the tomb of which saint, or the body
of which unburied boy in the mountains,
bullet-torn, like you, his blood sheer rubies

on Himalayan snow?
I've tied a knot
with green thread at Shah Hamdan, to be
untied only when the atrocities
are stunned by your jeweled return.

—Agha Shahid Ali,
"I See Kashmir from New Delhi at Midnight"[1]

The prominent Kashmiri-American poet Agha Shahid Ali's poem "I See Kashmir from New Delhi at Midnight," written in the 1990s, captures the violence and death embedded in Kashmiri bodies and minds as the Valley became embroiled in a full-fledged insurgency against the Indian state. Thousands of young Kashmiris, disillusioned with Indian democracy, found themselves enamored of the idea of *aazadi*, freedom. Because the mass upsurge took the form of a pro-independence movement, Indian security forces responded with aggression, failing to differentiate between insurgents and civilians as they protected their nation's territorial integrity. As pain, terror, and torture gripped almost every Kashmiri home, young Kashmiris were consumed with anger, resentment, and humiliation, and expressed frustration at their loss of human dignity. With teenage passions running high, some youth decided to trek the high mountain passes and cross into Pakistan-administered Kashmir to search for weapons and join the *tehreek-i-aazadi*, the "movement for freedom," unaware that death awaited them at the invisible, artificial border cutting through their ancient homeland.

Ali's poem is a eulogy for one such young Kashmiri. Rizwan, the eighteen-year-old son of the poet's family friend, had died, like thousands of other Kashmiris, while crossing the line of control. Deeply shaken, the poet imagines conversing with Rizwan's shadow, wandering through interrogation centers and sites of massacres in the Valley, searching for his body. The poet consoles Rizwan, referring to a green thread he has tied to the mesh of Shah Hamdan's shrine at Srinagar, an old Sufi practice for those seeking to have a specific wish granted: in this case, that atrocities in Kashmir end so that Rizwan's restless soul can find tranquility. But the green thread has not yet done its work. Twenty years have now passed since Rizwan's death, yet peace continues to elude the contested region of Kashmir, a contingent product of the postcolonial partition of the subcontinent that created the new states of India and Pakistan. The ongoing bloodbath in present-day Kashmir and Kashmiri Muslims' growing alienation from India stands in stark contrast to the historic year of 1947, when the popular leader Sheikh Muhammad Abdullah, hoping for a peaceful and prosperous Kashmir, tied its fate to India.

Since partition, Indian nationalists have obsessively viewed unrest in Kashmir through the lens of their fears about Pakistan, rather than as a result of the Indian state's abject failure to emotionally integrate Kashmiri Muslims into the rest of the nation. Because the Indian state views Kashmir from the perspective of "national security," individuals like Rizwan who challenge New Delhi's hegemony are consistently perceived as threats; the army feels justified in eliminating such citizens to protect its borders. In contrast, Kashmiri Muslim narratives portray young men like Rizwan as heroes, willing to sacrifice their lives to secure Kashmiri honor and dignity. What do these conflicting perceptions of Kashmiri resistance reveal about India's relationship with Kashmir? Why does the slogan "Freedom!" have such an appeal for Kashmiri Muslims? Why do thousands of Kashmiris turn up at the funerals of individuals the Indian state views as terrorists? The heart of this book is a search for the historical roots of this deepening estrangement between Kashmiris and the Indian state.[2]

The process of partition that created the states of India and Pakistan generated animosities as well. I argue that because, at the time of independence, India and Pakistan embraced the colonial construct of territorial nationalism, the retention of Kashmir—by any means necessary—came to seem indispensable to its national identity. In this context, "Kashmir" has been symbolically wedded to national pride, on both sides of the artificial border.[3] As both new nation-states set about integrating Kashmir into their respective bodies, the retention of its territory took precedence over the needs of its people. Both India and Pakistan therefore employed coercive instruments—the police, the army, and intelligence networks—to secure centralized authority over the now-divided princely state of Jammu and Kashmir and to suppress popular resistance. The concepts of "territoriality," "state sovereignty," and "national security" have dominated the nationalist discourses on the Kashmir conflict, while the Kashmiris' thwarted aspirations, which had built over decades of oppression under multiple empires, have seemed of little importance in Indian political discourse. This book, by contrast, investigates a broad range of sources to illuminate a century of political players and social structures in contested Kashmir, and to reveal Kashmiris' myriad imaginings of "freedom," transcending the borders of the nation-states between which the region is partitioned.

But the devastating postcolonial experiences of the territory's inhabitants have also been strangely marginal not just to political discourse but to the scholarly understanding of Kashmiri resistance. Scholarship on Kashmir, to date, has largely emerged from three disciplines. Political scientists and students of international relations, following the lead of Indian and Pakistani governing voices, have mainly seen the Kashmir question as an intractable territorial dispute or as a national security issue. In more recent times, political analysts have presented the Kashmir conflict as a manifestation of Islamist terrorism or jihad.[4] Anthropologists, meanwhile, have addressed the impact of violence perpetrated by the state and insurgents on Kashmiri society.[5] Finally, existing historical scholarship has primarily focused on the pre-1947 era of Kashmir.[6] This book brings together ideas, institutions, and political players that have shaped the postcolonial history of fragmented Jammu and Kashmir since the drawing of the artificial ceasefire line that cuts arbitrarily across the state. Placing the events of the last few decades in deep historical context allows us to view post-partition Kashmir not as the Indian or Pakistani states have seen it, but from a Kashmiri perspective.

Without ignoring the geopolitical currents which shape people's realities at any given moment, I take a bottom-up, people-centered approach that acknowledges the existence of conflicting and contradictory Kashmiri voices, braiding this history of internal diversity into the narrative of the Kashmir conflict. My hope is that this approach awakens readers to the larger historical currents within which real people today make decisions—and to the multiple moments in the past when those holding the levers of power at local, national, and international levels failed to prioritize Kashmiris' legitimate desires for what they later termed *aazadi*. My primary focus is on the Muslim community which includes the majority of the state residents, and whose thwarted aspirations have fueled Kashmiri resentment. However, since internal diversity is both a reality of Kashmiri life and an important theme of this work, I also investigate the views of the minority Buddhist and, especially, Hindu communities, which remain essential for understanding the seemingly intractable nature of the Kashmir conflict.

The core of this book is a close examination of the shifting postcolonial meanings of "freedom." The history of this multivalent concept reveals Kashmiris' changing worldviews as they negotiated the conflicting terrain of potential identities—Indian, Pakistani, and Kashmiri—each of which represented a different path to the freedom all claimed to seek. Instead of being passive spectators in the face of Indian and Pakistani power plays, I show that Kashmiris have consistently reinserted their own voices into local, national, and international narratives about the Kashmir conflict, and were and are active agents in the construction of their own sociopolitical identities. These identities have not always focused on gaining political freedom. Kashmiri political elites have often acted as mouthpieces for the nation-states, promoting their political agendas while simultaneously heightening Kashmiri misery. When their political legitimacy was in question, the collaborators' governance focused not on improving the situation of the masses but on creating networks of patronage to gain administrative acceptability.

Although the measures puppet regimes took won over certain social groups, the inhabitants of the former princely state of Jammu and Kashmir, the majority of whom suffered exclusion from structures of power and patronage, found themselves unrepresented by the political alliance between local elites and the nation-states. Conversely, the excluded Muslim majority (on both sides of divided Kashmir and within the wider British transnational community) employed the state's unique and disputed status to challenge the territorialization of state power and sovereignty by refusing to accept the ceasefire line as a permanent international border. They constructed a resistance discourse drawing inspiration from multiple international liberation movements to legitimize their own claims. The Kashmiri transnational activism enhanced feelings of political belonging, connecting even those who have never set foot in the physical territory to an imagined "homeland." In the process of charting these local, regional, and global Kashmiri connections, I map the contours of "Kashmiri-ness" in the postcolonial era.

Kashmir and Kashmiriyat: Identity, Freedom, and Self-determination

Contestations over "Kashmir" are not limited to cartographic representation and territorial boundaries; the debates extend into the validity of multiple definitions of "Kashmir," "Kashmiris," and "Kashmiri-ness." Does the term denote the occupants of the territory? Can the term "Kashmiri" be associated with only Koshur-speaking inhabitants of the state? Is it a legal term? What qualities, positive or negative, are associated with this identity? How have the answers to these questions changed with the political, economic, and social winds blowing through the province over the last century and a half?

According to a popular legend, the geographical entity of Kashmir emerged from a struggle for power between good and evil. The waters of a mighty lake covered the Kashmir Valley. It was a pleasure spot for gods and goddesses, until one day a demon came to inhabit it. The gods intervened and killed the demon; in the course of the battle water rushed out at the place where the Hindu god Vishnu struck the mountains with his trident, making the valley habitable.[7] The Muslim version of the same legend credits the Prophet Solomon for ordering a genie, Kashif, to drain the lake.[8] As Chitralekha Zutshi argues, this legend of divine intervention made the Valley a "sacred space" in Kashmiri oral traditions, an idea later embraced by the Muslim mystics who presented Kashmir as a "blessed landscape of Islam."[9]

As the inhabitants of the valley, called "Kashmiris" regardless of their religious affiliation, remained devoted to their sacred landscape dotted with shrines and temples, the valley and its surrounding areas were incorporated into various empires. Mughals, Afghans, and Sikhs in turn shaped and reshaped its geographical contours. While Kashmiris lamented the loss of their autonomy to these repressive foreign regimes, whose mismanagement reduced Kashmir to poverty, others' narratives denigrated Kashmiris as "worshippers of tyranny" (*zulumparast*) who lacked the will and courage to alter their deplorable situation.[10] These pejorative labels remained embedded in Kashmiri popular memory. Kashmiri discourses invoke such negative representations, dating from various stages of their turbulent history, creating a shared sense of lost dignity to mobilize the masses in a quest for *real* freedoms.

In the mid-nineteenth century, as British colonial domination spread to the frontiers of the South Asian subcontinent, the valley of Kashmir was mapped into the colonial landscape, and new borders and boundaries were created by outsiders once again. In 1846, the English East India Company assembled the diverse regions of the Kashmir Valley, Jammu, Ladakh, Gilgit, and Baltistan into the princely state of Jammu and Kashmir. Until partition the Dogra maharajas, based in Jammu, administered the state as one unit while accepting British paramountcy. The maharajas privileged their own Hindu community and excluded their majority Muslim subjects from power-sharing arrangements, a practice which generated deep resentment.[11] In the early twentieth century, however, a generation of Kashmiri Muslim community leaders, educated in new British and Muslim institutions and living both within and outside the princely state's territorial boundaries, tapped into the Kashmiris' feelings of injustice and oppression. These leaders contrasted these emotions with their supposed opposites, invoking "dignity" and "self-respect" to drive mass mobilization. As they gained momentum, the Muslim inhabitants of the princely state, although representing different sub-regional cultural and linguistic groups, claimed identification with "Kashmir" to legitimate their negotiations with the Dogra state. These trends underlay the Kashmiris' postcolonial stance toward both India and Pakistan, as well as their shared sense of identification with their homeland.

Much of the existing historiography confines Kashmiri identity to those who speak the Kashmiri language. In analyzing the early twentieth-century history of Kashmiri Muslim mobilization, scholars have focused on Kashmiriyat, a composite identity built around an imagined history where religious communities lived in peaceful coexistence, free from tensions and discord. Historian Chitralekha Zutshi has dismantled such definitions of Kashmiriyat, revealing that in the precolonial era regional political culture did not erase religious differences in favor of syncretism (the fusion of diverse religious beliefs and practices). Rather, Kashmiris defined their identity and sought to improve their society on the terms and via the practices of their distinctive religious belongings. In the early twentieth century, however, Kashmiri nationalists "denigrated religious affiliations in favor of an all-encompassing regional nationalism."[12] Zutshi's study shows how imbricated the links between regional and religious sensibilities were in Kashmiri political culture. Yet in the process of showing why and how Kashmiriyat was invented, she reduces its meaning to an instrumentalist political project that sought to emphasize religious syncretism in the Valley for nationalist purposes. A close study of the sociopolitical discourse of the early twentieth century reveals that the exponents of nationalism as a political strategy drew from indigenous traditions of regional and religious coexistence, in which the older mystical religious traditions of Kashmir built bridges across religiously defined communities. In other words, some Kashmiris had always held out the ideal of community coexistence, and religious affinities remained central to Kashmiriyat.

This book further contends that during the twentieth century the conception of Kashmiriyat was not monolithic. To begin with, "Kashmiri-ness," crucially, was never restricted to inhabitants of the Valley but included expatriates who retained an emotional attachment to Kashmir and called themselves Kashmiris.[13] The association of expatriate Kashmiris with their homeland in the colonial era, along with transnational interactions in the postcolonial period, complicate the category of Kashmiriyat. For expatriates the significance of belonging to Kashmir and being Kashmiri transcended prevalent cultural and territorial definitions of identity and referred primarily to an emotive attachment to a homeland. I emphasize that particularly in the postcolonial era, "Kashmir" has not been just a territorial space but a political imaginary, a vision that grounds Kashmiris in their negotiations for rights not only in India and Pakistan, but also in global cultural and political spaces.

I further differentiate between cultural and political identity in analyzing Kashmir's postcolonial history. Cabeiri Robinson focuses on the political strand of Kashmiri identity to examine Kashmiri refugees' identification with "Kashmir." She argues that Kashmiri Muslim refugees in Pakistan identified with "Kashmir" rather than with the new nation-state because of a pre-existing concept of territorial citizenship—the "state-subject" criteria introduced by the Dogra maharaja in 1927.[14] Postcolonial governments retained the policy, which allowed only residents of the state and recognized displaced Kashmiris to purchase land and seek employment in Jammu and Kashmir.[15] Many displaced Kashmiris hoped to return home and reclaim their lives and properties due to this state law. Patricia Ellis and Zafar Khan have asserted that "Kashmiri citizenship laws" even bind diasporic Kashmiris "psychologically and politically" with the homeland.[16] I build on these insights, and draw from my investigation of diverse linguistic and cultural communities in Pakistan-administered Kashmir, along with several diasporic communities who called themselves Kashmiris and claimed a shared belonging with the undivided territory of Jammu and Kashmir, although none had much connection to the Valley's culture or language. I agree with Robinson that the state-subject category not only reinforced Kashmir's unique position in relation to the central Indian and Pakistani states, but also enabled Kashmiri Muslims on both sides of the ceasefire line to claim a relationship with the undivided whole. These definitions of Kashmiri political identity allowed those living in Indian and Pakistan-administered Kashmir, as well as in the wider transnational community, to build a common identity around their "occupied" homeland.

The state-subject category, the basis of the political identity of Kashmiri Muslims (the most contentious issue in present-day Kashmir), is vehemently rejected by non-Muslim minorities who consider Kashmiriyat an Indian subculture. Ironically, this present-day Kashmiri Hindu political position is in sharp contrast to the "Kashmir for Kashmiris" movement initiated by their early-twentieth-century predecessors in response to outsiders' encroachment on their jobs. It was the Kashmiri Hindus' tireless agitation that forced the Dogra maharaja to introduce the state-subject category in the princely state of Jammu and Kashmir. However, the changing political dynamics of the postcolonial era, with much local power transferred to the Muslim majority, made state Hindus feel insecure about their minority status within the state. As early as the 1950s an organized agitation in Jammu supported by the Hindu nationalists demanded the abrogation of Kashmir's special status. Yet several non-Muslims within Jammu and Kashmir rejected this Hindu nationalist stance and supported Kashmir's autonomous position within the Indian union.

In the twenty-first century, however, as the Hindu right gained momentum in India, most, if not all, of the state's minorities have also demanded revocation of the state-subject category, considering it a hindrance to Jammu and Kashmir's complete merger with India. In the fall of 2019, as this book was being completed, the new Hindu-nationalist government's unilateral abrogation of Kashmir's special status, including Article 35A authorizing the state legislature to "make special provisions for permanent residents of the state," legally erased this special category. However, as this book reveals, the state-subject category is an important part of

Kashmir's history and is now engraved in the Kashmiri Muslim psyche as the essence of their political identity. It supports the idea of an undivided homeland free from occupation, binding Kashmiris across ideological and territorial divides. Kashmiri Muslims, jealously insistent on the state-subject category's retention, have long feared that the discontinuation of this category would alter Kashmir's demography and transform their community into a minority. These clashing identities and different understandings of Kashmiri political identity complicate the notion of "self-determination" which has been and remains central to Kashmir's resistance discourse, producing an acerbic debate in the public arena and in the sphere of print.

At a global level, the concept of "self-determination" gained popularity after the First World War, based on Woodrow Wilson's Fourteen Points statement of principles for global peace. Self-determination broadly refers to the right of people to shape their own political destiny, and this is how it is employed in the Kashmiri vernacular. But it is worth noting that at its contemporary geopolitical origins self-determination was understood to be for the "weaker sections of Europe"—Belgians, Poles, Czechs—rather than the peoples of the colonial world.[17] Mark Mazower contends that imperialists pushed for the "limited applicability" of self-determination to non-European nations. For them, mandates or international trusteeships remained essential to train certain races to become "democratic civilized nations."[18] As Timothy Mitchell argues, these structures allowed imperial powers to maintain indirect control by creating a new class of "native rulers," who presented themselves as nationalists but exercised only partial sovereignty. These puppet rulers lacked popular support, but the imperial powers interpreted their participation in governance as an expression of self-determination.[19] "Self-determination," then, was systematically utilized as an "instrument for domination and consent"—as indeed happened in postcolonial India, which appropriated such imperial understandings of the term to exercise its hegemony in Jammu and Kashmir. The support of local elites allowed India to claim legitimacy, delay the United Nations–mandated plebiscite, and interpret a series of farcical and rigged elections as Kashmiri expressions of "self-determination." Despite this ambiguous history, however, the language of self-determination captured the imagination of Kashmiris, who embraced it to seek rights initially from the Dogra monarchy, and later from the postcolonial states of India and Pakistan.

A formidable body of scholarship on Kashmir debates the 1949 United Nations resolution, which promised Kashmiris "democratic method of a free and an impartial plebiscite" to decide "the question of accession of Jammu and Kashmir state to India or Pakistan."[20] Some of this work foregrounds the pluralism of the state and highlights the contested allegiances that have complicated the long-promised granting of self-determination.[21] Others have suggested that the concepts of democracy and self-determination converge as the focal points of Kashmiri Muslim political aspirations.[22] Although these works correctly draw attention to the intractable fault lines that make self-determination more complex than it might seem, their limited political and territorial definition of self-determination does not address the emotional appeal this concept has had for Kashmiri Muslims across more than half a century. This book historicizes the meaning of "self-determination" to emphasize that Kashmiri imaginings of emancipation in different temporal frames were not confined to political freedom but also included concepts like human dignity, economic equity, and social justice.

These terms, contextualized in the regional environment of the Valley, reveal that Kashmiris' history of exploitative relations between social groups and of subjugation at the hands of ruling colonial dynasties shaped their visions of freedom. Kashmiris equated freedom with the concept of *insaaf*, or justice, the equitable distribution of resources for material development so that the disadvantaged were not mired in poverty; *haq*, or rights, meaning that rulers should practice political ethics and be accountable to the people; and *izzat*, human dignity. Throughout the twentieth century these terms dominated popular discourses on freedom as Kashmiris envisioned a society where they would not have to undergo humiliations at the hands of the ruling power. This study shows that these ideas gained significance in the postcolonial era as self-determination moved from fantasy to real possibility with the United Nations–mandated plebiscite, and informed popular resistance in the region. As the Indian state remained focused on retaining Kashmir's territory and denied Kashmiris freedom to shape their political future, Kashmiri imaginings of emancipation became intertwined with, but have never been confined to the limited territorial definition of self-determination (accession to either India or Pakistan). These developments politicized the meaning of "freedom," and revealed deep schisms between majority and minority communities' aspirations for "self-determination."

Territorialization, Borders, and Transnational Networks

The emergence of territorial nationalism in India during British colonial rule developed, after decolonization, into a "territory of sovereignty." Sumathi Ramaswamy traces the concept of territorialization to the sacredness associated with the anthropomorphic form of Mother India. As the colonial state fixed, measured, and mathematized the map of India with latitudes and longitudes, it became a "powerful emblem of anti-colonial nationalisms" and "penetrated deep into the popular imagination." Indian nationalists supplemented the map with the divine form of a Hindu mother goddess who "reaches for the map form in order to transform the geo body into a homeland and motherland to live and die for."[23] If India embodies a mother goddess, every inch of Indian territory is sacred, reinforcing territorialism but also excluding diverse religious and regional communities, especially peripheral ones like Kashmiri Muslims, who find it difficult to relate to the image of Mother India as the representative body of the Indian nation. However, such representations embed "Kashmir" in the nationalist imagination as an integral part of the nation-state's representation, the core of their identity and hence a non-negotiable issue.

The new South Asian nation-states produced territorial sovereignty in their peripheries through the coercive instruments of surveillance, mapping, and armed force, bringing together physical and cultural spaces with financial and social inequities that reinforced their marginality as compared to the "nation."[24]As India embarked on the territorialization of its peripheries, it provided Jammu and Kashmir with preferential treatment, primarily due to Kashmir's disputed nature as India, Pakistan, and China all laid claims to its territory. The ceasefire line, later renamed the line of control, is technically not a border, even though both India and Pakistan consider the territory of Jammu and Kashmir within their respective control as an integral part of their nation. In fact, the Indian state of Jammu and Kashmir is a different, more complicated entity than other Indian states in the sense that it is the only state that negotiated its relationship with India at the time of decolonization and partition. Article 370 of the Indian constitution guaranteed Kashmir's autonomy and allowed the state to have its own constitution, flag, and constituent assembly. It was agreed that any central power in Jammu and Kashmir state could only be implemented with the approval of the state's constituent assembly.[25]

Furthermore, India also provided special privileges and rights to the inhabitants of Jammu and Kashmir. Article 35A of the Indian constitution authorized state legislature to retain the state-subject category that only allows Kashmir's longtime inhabitants to purchase land or seek employment in the state. The Indian prime minister Jawaharlal Nehru included this article in the Indian constitution in 1954 to appease Kashmiri fears that "rich outsiders" might pay exorbitant prices to buy "delectable places," and reduce poor Kashmiris to a landless position. Such unique arrangements are not uncommon in federations.[26] India has also worked out different relations with states in the northeast. Articles 371 and 371A of the Indian constitution provide special rights and privileges to the residents of Sikkim, Nagaland, Manipur, and Arunachal Pradesh, and prohibit non-state residents from owning property in these states.[27]

While Kashmiri political elites collaborated with India to implement its development and centralization policies, Pakistan's bureaucracy established its complete hegemony in Pakistan-administered Kashmir, while theoretically accepting Kashmir's disputed status.[28] Pakistan's official policy of not integrating Azad Kashmir allowed the retention of its territorial claims over India-administered Kashmir, the source of the rivers Indus, Jhelum, and Chenab that flow from Jammu and Kashmir to Pakistan and sustain its economy.[29] As both nation-states, contrary to initial hopes, practiced overt and covert authoritarianism in their sides of Kashmir, Kashmiris' disappointment amplified. This book asserts that Kashmiri voices of resistance, aware of their unique and disputed status, have long challenged the territorialization of state power and state sovereignty by refusing to accept the ceasefire line as a permanent border. The inhabitants of Jammu and Kashmir have struggled to adapt to this artificial divide separating families, disrupting the environment, and destroying economic structures. In Kashmiri imagination, the new "border" is an aberration; exercising self-determination means in part erasing this line and roaming freely in their homeland without the constraints of its militarized landscape. In fact, the line of control remains fluid and porous, allowing a continuous flow of goods, peoples, and ideas.[30]

The internal diversity of Jammu and Kashmir adds significant complexity to Kashmiri resistance discourse. There are schisms and divisions within the Kashmiri resistance; individuals, groups, and sub-regions differ in their political visions. At different moments, both rival nations have manipulated the emotions of disenchanted Kashmiris and utilized some as pawns to promote nationalist agendas. Despite these challenges, dissenting Kashmiris have consistently attempted to find their own agency in shaping their resistance. Kashmiri voices of resistance forged regional connections across the two divided parts of Kashmir as they imagined and re-imagined Kashmir's political future. Studying this network broadens the contours of both postcolonial and resistance history, differentiates Kashmir's unique "border" experience from that of other states in South Asia, and reveals that many of those who traversed this arbitrary line did not always perceive their state as the periphery of a sovereign nation; instead, some contested the national territorialism of both India and Pakistan by creating their own notions of territorial integrity.

The Kashmiri challenge to "territorialization" has not only been posed within the confines of the subcontinent's political contestations but has also occurred in transnational space. The global dimension of the Kashmiri resistance shows the limitations of territorially bounded nationalist frameworks by addressing the ideological and political connections forged by Kashmiri transnational activists in the diasporic space.[31] Placing a marginalized region in a broader global history, my research investigates how transnational actors and the long-distance nationalism of Kashmiri emigrant groups made Kashmiris visible in the international arena and displaced perceptions of Kashmir as a peripheral region to be controlled and conquered.

Kashmiri imaginings of freedom in global arenas, especially during the eventful decades of the 1960s and 1970s, drew inspiration from anticolonial struggles across Africa, Asia, and Latin America that created transnational solidarity and conjured up new imaginaries of social justice, economic equity, and political freedom. These powerful ideas inspired transnational activists from Pakistan-administered Kashmir in Britain as they attempted to redefine the Kashmiri conflict while navigating the pressures of living on the margins of their host society. The British Kashmiri transnational community constructed its political claims in the image of the twentieth century's worldwide political movements for self-determination, placing the debate over Kashmir's freedom within an "anti-imperialist and anti-capitalist framework."[32] Reading transnational connections in this way gives new insight into postcolonial history, the meaning of Kashmiri identity, and the ways the transnational actors both challenged and replicated territorial nationalism with its claim that Kashmiris should have the right to choose independence.

Religion, Politics, and State Security

The role of Islam in Kashmiri resistance has fascinated politicians, journalists, and policymakers alike. As India tightened the noose of its centralization policy in the 1950s and attempted to fully integrate the disputed state of Jammu and Kashmir, Kashmiri Muslims invoked "self-determination" in protest. Many protestors calling for self-determination used religious slogans or expressed extra-territorial affiliations to convey dissent; the Indian government dismissed these as illegitimate demonstrations by a group of "separatist" Muslims. Indian nationalists today continue to interpret Kashmiri Muslim protests as a rejection of Indian secularism and an acceptance of Islamist ideology. Others depict Kashmiris' struggle for self-determination as a "long jihad" initiated by Pakistani intelligence agencies within weeks of the creation of India and Pakistan, with the end game of creating a larger Islamic state.[33] Such portrayals of Kashmiri resistance gained momentum in the aftermath of the armed insurgency of the 1990s, and a more recent trend delegitimizes Kashmiri protests as a "subset of the global Islamic terror game" in pursuit of an "Islamic Caliphate."[34]

However, analyzing Kashmiri resistance only through a religious lens is simply insufficient to explain the deeper roots of Kashmiri Muslims' sense of the political injustice and violation of individual liberties they have experienced as part of democratic India. Such arguments conveniently ignore the fact that in 1947 Kashmiri nationalists opted for India, going against their religious affinity with Pakistan. Presenting Kashmiri resistance as an "Islamist movement" is perhaps India's way of absolving itself of more than seven decades of actions that have alienated Kashmiris to the extent that they want nothing to do with New Delhi.

Religion and religious affiliation have been key components of Kashmiri Muslim identity throughout the twentieth century. "Religion" in this context, while not excluding matters of belief and ritual practice, has significant economic and social dimensions; for well over a century, community belonging has defined access to political, educational, financial, and social power. As Mridu Rai puts it, "the protest of Kashmiri Muslims" against the Hindu Dogra state, prior to Kashmir's accession to India, "represents not so much a defense of Islam but of the rights of a community defined as Muslims by ruling hierarchies minded to dole out patronage along religious lines." This religion-based neglect, in Rai's interpretation, became pivotal in mobilizing Kashmiri Muslims to fight for the material and cultural rights denied to them by the ruling regime.[35] In the postcolonial period, religious identity remained an important identification marker for Kashmiri Muslims, especially as independent India embraced "secular nationalism" both to define itself and to manage diversity and difference within the country. As Ayesha Jalal argues, India's conflation of secularism with nationalism misconstrued concern for one's religious community as disloyalty to the nation, delegitimizing minorities' fears and any aspirations that conflicted with the state's version of secular nationalism.[36] In Kashmir, when India's centralization policy created feelings of political injustice, Kashmiris appealed to religious differences as part of their resistance to complete integration.

I argue that Kashmiri Muslim assertions of religious identity to express political dissent do not lead directly to a fraught relationship with secularism, nor is it their religious identity as such that makes them oppose secular India. In the context of South Asia, "secularism" refers primarily to a political ideology, rather than alluding to "secularization," an open-ended historical process in which human beings "abandon otherworldly concerns and focus on the here and now."[37] Kashmiri political elites, in collaboration with India, spread the "doctrine of secularism" in the hope of bringing Kashmiris culturally closer to India through accelerated political and financial integration. Thus in Kashmir the secularism of the modern nation-state is a closed ideology imposed from above to bring

Kashmiris into the national mainstream whether they want to be there or not. Furthermore, the presence in Jammu of the Hindu right, clamoring for Kashmir's complete integration with or without popular support, bred insecurity among Kashmiri Muslims. Disaffected Kashmiris endangered by India's integrationist moves, constrained by economic resources, and excluded from political power have clung more tightly to their religious identity.

Most Kashmiri Muslims' expressions of attachment to religious identity are different from the articulations of an Islamist ideology by groups like the Jamaat-i-Islami of Jammu and Kashmir, a party that rejects Western-style democracy and secularism while claiming that absolute sovereignty resides with God.[38] In explaining the relatively recent appeal of such groups, who operated for a long time on the political fringes of the Valley before becoming more prominent, I trace the internal and external causes that gave the Jamaat political and social visibility. Indeed, the global resurgence of political Islam assisted such groups in establishing a ubiquitous presence in the 1980s. However, I also illuminate the economic transformations unleashed by India's development policies and the political blunders of Kashmiri nationalist leaders— developments that provided Islamist groups the space to develop their support base among middle-class Kashmiris and attempt to redefine self-determination.

Kashmiri Muslims' association with religious identity increased in intensity after India adopted a tough approach in the wake of the armed insurgency, arming its military with special powers to crush resistance. India's policies in Kashmir are largely in tune with its treatment of insurgencies in Assam and the northeast, yet there are some underlying differences. Kashmir's disputed nature and its Muslim-majority character add another layer of complexity in unraveling the severe responses of Indian soldiers to Kashmiri Muslim protestors. The involvement of Pakistan in the Kashmir dispute and its assistance to Kashmiri insurgents mean that the Indian army perceives Kashmiri resistance as a Muslim uprising in union with their archenemy, Pakistan, seeking to destroy India's territorial integrity.[39] But repression and terror have backfired, leading even apolitical Kashmiri Muslims more fully embrace their religious identity.

The present-day militarization of Kashmir has led to extensive human rights violations in the Valley. The treatment of Kashmir as an occupied territory turns the spotlight on the larger debate about the relationship between popular sovereignty and state legitimacy. Does the state have a responsibility to protect the human rights of its citizens to gain domestic legitimacy? To what extent have human rights abuses in Kashmir diluted India's legitimacy in the region? As Hallie Ludsin argues, the "concept of internal legitimacy flows from sovereignty in the people" and "sovereign rights can be lost" when governments, including democracies, commit "egragious human rights abuses."[40] However, India invokes the concept of state sovereignty that gives the state a monopoly on violence to protect its territorial integrity. Framing the Kashmir issue through a national security lens gives India flexibility on its constitutional commitment to protect the fundamental rights of its Kashmiri citizens, while also warding off moral condemnation from international organizations like the United Nations and Amnesty International, who draw global attention to extensive human rights violations in India-administered Kashmir. India dismisses such reports as a "selective compilation of largely unverified information" and a "violation of the country's sovereignty and territorial integrity."[41] Instead, India has sought international legitimacy for its actions by packaging Kashmiri civilian resistance as "Islamist terrorism." In a world threatened by radical Islamist groups and wary of any kind of resistance (whether civilian, military, or political) if it stems from Muslim communities or from Muslim-majority areas of the world, branding Kashmiri resistance as "Islamist" is a powerful tool for fending off international criticism of India's response.

Sources

Even though more than seventy years have passed since the partition of the South Asian subcontinent, most official documents in the Indian national archives regarding postcolonial Kashmir remain restricted, as Kashmir continues, from the point of view of the Indian state, to be a major national security issue. Furthermore, the ongoing conflict has taken a toll on the Jammu and Kashmir state archives, with administrators' attention being on "security" rather than on preserving the state's heritage. A substantial number of the state archive's relevant records have been left unprocessed; its dilapidated buildings leave rare documents and manuscripts immersed in dust and pigeon droppings, making access almost impossible.

To overcome the challenges posed by government archives in the subcontinent, I analyze a variety of vernacular sources in Urdu and Kashmiri to comprehend the political and social positioning of contemporary Kashmiri voices on both sides of the India–Pakistan divide as well as in the larger Kashmiri transnational community. Visiting Kashmiri community leaders and literati, I collected their unpublished memoirs, letters, and diaries, an alternative archive for reconstructing Kashmiri consciousness. I travelled to villages in India-administered Kashmir to meet with families that have been victims of the conflict and visited civil society groups to comprehend the impact of militarization on Kashmiri society.

Interactions with the Kashmiri transnational community in Britain made me re-examine the relationship between Kashmiri cultural identity and Kashmiri political identity. The extensive interviews I conducted with Kashmiris of various political orientations contributed significantly to my understanding of the issues of belonging, citizenship, and identity formation in one of the most contested regions of South Asia. Kashmiri literature, vernacular newspapers, and pamphlets capture the complexity of popular discourses and nationalist rhetoric, and bring together elite expression and excluded voices, while oral histories, social media posts, and political blogs illuminate the digital flavor of Kashmiri protest in the twenty-first century.

Complementing these diverse sources, archival repositories in India and England did yield some of the official sources necessary for a holistic understanding of the Kashmir conflict. I examined the legislative assembly debates of Jammu and Kashmir state to comprehend how Kashmiri political elites negotiated with India. Declassified Ministry of State files contain memos and legislation about the official Indian policy in the aftermath of partition and local police records document Kashmiri Muslim grievances against India in the early 1950s. The private papers of prominent Indian leaders and political parties provide insight into Indian policy debates about Kashmir, while the Dominion Office Files at Kew Archives in London contain files unavailable at the National Archives of India which illuminate Kashmir's internal dynamics in the 1960s and 1970s. I read these sources not only to get the state version of events, but also as a repository of popular voices: intercepted letters written by families or friends separated by the ceasefire line; petitions for repatriation sent to Indian and Pakistani officials by stranded Kashmiris desiring to return "home;" and letters written by ordinary Indian citizens requesting their political leaders to adopt a tough approach on Kashmir in the aftermath of partition. These people's voices within the official archives reveal how "Kashmir" is constructed and imagined in the nationalist imagination, while also uncovering the baggage of partition as contested postcolonial boundaries continue to disrupt peace in the South Asian subcontinent.

Organization and Layout

This book has six chapters, organized both chronologically and thematically. The first chapter examines Kashmiri understandings of freedom in an historical context, highlighting how Kashmiris engaged with pre-existing ideas of freedom for political mobilization in the late nineteenth and early twentieth centuries.

It teases out the tensions between secularly oriented nationalism and religiously informed universalism in the 1930s and 1940s to understand how Kashmiris defined and negotiated multiple meanings of religion and secularism prevalent in Kashmir. By focusing on the dissonance among Kashmiri voices, this chapter demonstrates the myriad visions the people of the princely state had for their state's future, visions that never found expression as both India and Pakistan laid claims to Kashmir's territory immediately after partition.

The second chapter addresses the themes of identity, belonging, and loyalty in the former princely state of Jammu and Kashmir in the aftermath of the sovereignty feud between India and Pakistan, which artificially divided Kashmir and dragged its people into an international dispute. Drawing on Kashmiri popular discourses, the chapter addresses resentment about how the promises of freedom actually unfolded in the region. It highlights the impact of decolonization on the divided state of Jammu and Kashmir and argues that the creation of the ceasefire line, which disrupted the natural environment and dismantled entire economic structures that had sustained the state prior to 1947, also shaped the question of Kashmiri Muslims' belonging to and their perceptions of India, Pakistan, and Kashmir. Ultimately, the sociopolitical processes and transformations set in motion at decolonization precipitated tensions between communities and subregions of Jammu and Kashmir, and with India on a larger scale.

In the third chapter, I examine the political economy of the Kashmiri resistance from 1953 to the 1980s, probing how India's development policies created a class of collaborators who transformed Kashmir's political processes and social structures. The chapter shows how integration with India ushered in cultural transformation in urban Kashmir, generating insecurities among Kashmiri Muslims while precipitating class differences and rural–urban tensions. It highlights social and economic discontent in postcolonial Kashmir, which initially fringe Islamist groups deployed to condemn the secularist and socialist ideologies propagated by the ruling elites, advocating an Islamic state as a solution to Kashmir's problems. As political elites monopolized all economic benefits in the decades following decolonization and partition, the excluded Kashmiri Muslim majority reacted and responded to their exclusion from networks of patronage, further alienating them from India.

The fourth chapter examines the resistance discourse fashioned by activists from diverse political leanings, especially that of the Plebiscite Front, which sought to mobilize the excluded majority and challenge Indian nationalist narratives' tacit assumption of Indian control over Kashmir. On a political level, the idea of a plebiscite and the conversations it inspired in the wider public arena brought competing definitions of self-determination into the dialogue. This chapter reveals that despite a fractured Kashmiri discourse, the plebiscite movement became popular in public arenas and in the sphere of print as activists connected self-determination with the concepts of *haq* (rights), *insaaf* (justice) and *izzat* (dignity) inherent in earlier Kashmiri discourses on freedom. It explores how the 1960s student activism pitted communities against each other and politicized the concept of self-determination, further driving a wedge between the majority Muslim and minority Hindu and Buddhist communities. The debates between plebiscite and autonomy shaped the post-1975 period; the Indian state met regional dissidence by undermining state governments to ensure that only parties or leaders who complied with New Delhi held power. This meddling intensified anti-India sentiments in the Valley and deepened regional divisions within the state of Jammu and Kashmir.

In the fifth chapter, I shift my attention to Pakistan-administered Kashmir and examine inter-regional connections across the ceasefire line as well as the transnational relationship between the expatriates and the homeland, both critical to Kashmiri understandings of sovereignty and territoriality. The hegemonic relationship of Pakistan with its part of Kashmir bred resentment and alienated large numbers of Azad Kashmiris. The chapter focuses on Kashmiri voices suspicious of both India and Pakistan, but inspired by a worldwide belt of twentieth-century insurgencies. Drawing inspiration from revolutionary movements in Vietnam, Algeria, and Palestine, these Kashmiris surreptitiously crossed the ceasefire line and advocated an armed struggle to liberate Kashmir. The second section of this chapter addresses the transnational dimension of postcolonial Kashmiri resistance to show how globally dispersed Kashmiris, pushed out by oppression, lack of economic opportunities, or physical displacement, engaged with the concepts of imperialism, socialism, and communism in shaping their myriad visions for Kashmir's freedom. It also examines diasporic tactics aimed at generating global support for Kashmiris physically trapped in the territorial dispute between India and Pakistan.

The last chapter unravels the role of Islam in Kashmiri resistance. It explores the significance of religious identity and symbolism in Kashmiri Muslim protests, while placing the articulation of an Islamist ideology by certain political groups in the context of Kashmiri disillusionment with their political elites, the rising power of the Hindu right, and the globalization of Islam. I draw upon novels, poetry, and short stories to reveal how state suppression made Kashmiri Muslims more aware of their religious identity in the post-insurgency era, while the power politics of India and Pakistan played a key role in shifting the image of Kashmiri resistance from a national freedom movement to Islamic jihad. As the insurgency crystallized religious identities, it created an impenetrable gap between Kashmir's Hindu and Muslim communities, revealing once more how the contested nature of "freedom" has helped to make the Kashmir dispute intractable. While Kashmiri Hindus lament the loss of their homeland, a new generation of Kashmiri Muslims use creative modes of protest including social media, music, paintings, and animation to challenge the militarization of Kashmir. The story of Kashmir in the late twentieth and early twenty-first century sheds light on the differentiation between popular and state sovereignty and the relationship between human rights and state legitimacy.

Notes

1. Extract from Agha Shahid Ali's poem "I See Kashmir from New Delhi at Midnight," in *The Country without a Post Office* (Delhi: Orient Longman, 2000), 10–12.
2. Brief sections of this manuscript have been published as the chapter "Kashmiri Visions of Freedom: The Past and the Present," in Chitralekha Zutshi (ed.), *Kashmir: History, Politics, Representation* (Cambridge: Cambridge University Press, 2018), 89–112.
3. Ananya Jahanara Kabir's *The Territory of Desire* argues that the "roots of Indian desire" for the Kashmir Valley are in its "symbolic capital." In the colonial period, the British photographers focused their lens on Kashmir's beautiful landscape, which enhanced its value. After decolonization, the Indian nation-state replicated this visual image of Kashmir in films and artworks, thus, embedding "Kashmir" in the national imagination. For details, see Ananya Jahanara Kabir, *The Territory of Desire: Representing the Valley of Kashmir* (Minneapolis: University of Minnesota Press, 2009).
4. Alastair Lamb, *Kashmir: A Disputed Legacy, 1846–1990* (Karachi: Oxford University Press, 1992); Sumit Ganguly, *The Crisis in Kashmir: Portents of War, Hopes of Peace* (Cambridge: Cambridge University Press, 1997); Robert Wirsing, *Kashmir in the Shadow of War: Regional Rivalries in a Nuclear Age* (London: Routledge, 2003); Praveen Swami, *India, Pakistan and the Secret Jihad: The Covert War in Kashmir, 1947–2004* (London: Routledge, 2006).
5. Haley Duschinski, "Destiny Effects: Militarization, State Power, and Punitive Containment in the Kashmir Valley," *Anthropological Quarterly* 82, no. 3 (2009): 619–717; Cabeiri Robinson, *Body of Victim, Body of Warrior: Refugee Families and the Making of Kashmiri Jihadists* (Berkeley: University of California Press, 2013).
6. Mohammad Ishaq Khan, *Kashmir's Transition to Islam: The Role of Muslim Rishis* (New Delhi: Manohar Publishers, 1994); Chitralekha Zutshi, *Languages of Belonging: Islam, Regional Identity and the Making of Kashmir* (New York : Oxford University

Press, 2004); Mridu Rai, *Hindu Rulers, Muslim Subjects: Islam, Rights and History of Kashmir* (Princeton, NJ: Princeton University Press, 2004).

7. Walter R. Lawrence, *Provincial Gazetteer of Kashmir* (repr., Delhi: Rima Publishing House, 1985), 21–2.
8. G. M. Mir, *Geographical Realities of Jammu and Kashmir* (Yorkshire: United Kashmir Publishers, 2000), 10.
9. Chitralekha Zutshi (ed.), *Kashmir: History, Politics, Representation* (Cambridge: Cambridge University Press, 2018), 5.
10. G. M. D. Sufi, *Kashir: Being a History of Kashmir*, Vol. 2 (New Delhi: Light and Life Publishers, 1974), 816; Walter R. Lawrence, *The Valley of Kashmir* (Srinagar: Kesar Publishers, 1967), 2–3.
11. Rai, *Hindu Rulers, Muslim Subjects*, 80–127.
12. Zutshi, *Languages of Belonging.*
13. Nasreen Ali in "Kashmiri Nationalism: Beyond the Nation State" has argued that the discourse of Kashmiriyat emerges from the displacement and resettlement of Kashmiris in the diasporic space. Nasreen Ali, "Kashmiri Nationalism: Beyond the Nation State," *South Asia Research* 22, no. 2 (September 2002): 145–60.
14. In 1911 the maharaja initiated a State Subject Definition Committee to probe complaints of Kashmiri Hindus against Punjabi Hindu domination in government services. They expressed concern that state policies have prevented Kashmiris from holding important positions in the government. To placate the disgruntled Pandit community, in 1927 Maharaja Hari Singh passed the Hereditary State Subject Act. According to this act, "all persons born or residing in the state before the commencement of the reign of Maharaja Gulab Singh and all persons who settled therein before the commencement of 1885 and have since been permanently residing in the country" were now considered state subjects. The law restricted state service to individuals who could produce a state-subject certificate. Additionally, non-state subjects could not purchase land in Jammu and Kashmir. Report of the Committee to Define the Term "State Subject," Political Department, 1935, File.No.199/RR-18, Jammu Kashmir Archives; Rai, *Hindu Rulers, Muslim Subjects*, 249–53. Robinson, *Body of Victim, Body of Warrior*, 37–9.
15. Robinson, *Body of Victim, Body of Warrior.*
16. Patricia Ellis and Zafar Khan, "The Kashmiri Diaspora: Influences in Kashmir," in Nadje Al-Ali and Khalid Koser (eds.), *New Approaches to Migration? Transnational Communities and Transformations of Home* (London: Routledge, 2002), 169–85.
17. Erez Manela, *Wilsonian Moment: Self-Determination and International origins of Anticolonial Nationalism* (New York: Oxford University Press, 2009), 17.
18. Mark Mazower, *No Enchanted Palace: The End of Empire and Ideological Origins of the United Nations* (Princeton, NJ: Princeton University Press, 2008), 44–5.
19. Timothy Mitchell, *Carbon Democracy: Political Power in the Age of Oil* (London: Verso, 2011), 92–9.

20. P. L. Lakhanpal, *Essential Documents and Notes on Kashmir Dispute* (Delhi: International Books, 1968), 158–9.
21. Navnita Chadha Behera, *Demystifying Kashmir* (Washington, DC: Brookings Institute Press, 2006).
22. Sumantra Bose, *The Challenge in Kashmir: Democracy, Self-Determination and a Just Peace* (New Delhi: Sage Publications, 1997).
23. For details, see Sumathi Ramaswamy, *The Goddess and the Nation: Mapping Mother India* (Durham, NC: Duke University Press, 2010); Sumathi Ramaswamy, "Maps and Mother Goddesses in Modern India," *Imago Mundi* 53 (2001): 97–114.
24. David Ludden, "Spatial Inequity and National Territory: Remapping 1905 in Bengal and Assam," *Modern Asian Studies* 46, no. 3 (May 2012): 483–525; Willem Van Schendel, *The Bengal Borderland* (London: Anthem, 2005).
25. For details, see A. G. Noorani, Article 370: *A Constitutional History of Jammu and Kashmir* (New Delhi: Oxford University Press, 2011).
26. Examples include Quebec's special status within Canada; the concessions to the east after German reunification in 1990; and the USA's Reconstruction after its Civil War. Dilip D'Souza, "India's Government Has Undermined the Very Essence of Federalism and Democracy," *The Nation*, August 15, 2019, https://www.thenation.com/article/india-kashmir-modi-bjp-federalism-and-democracy/, accessed November 15, 2019.
27. Article 371A prohibits non-residents from buying land in Nagaland. Article 371F grants special provisions to Sikkim which prohibit sale and purchase of land or property to outsiders. States under the Sixth Schedule of the constitution that include Assam, Meghalaya, Tripura, Mizoram, and the areas under the Gorkha Hill Council, Darjeeling, in West Bengal, impose restrictions on outsiders to buy land.
Subash Rajta, "Who Can and Cannot Buy Land in Himachal," *The Tribune*, October 30, 2019, https://www.tribuneindia.com/news/sunday-special/kaleidoscope/who-can-cannot-buy-land-in-himachal/819058.html, accessed October 30, 2019.
28. Christopher Snedden, *The Untold Story of the People of Azad Kashmir* (New York: Columbia University Press, 2012).
29. Anam Zakaria, *Between the Great Divide: A Journey into Pakistan-Administered Kashmir* (Delhi: Harper Collins, 2018, Kindle Edition). Zakaria draws from oral histories to explore the impact of the conflict on Azad Kashmiris from the tribal raid of 1947 to the rise of the armed insurgency in the 1980s.
30. Willem van Schendel's *The Bengal Borderland* examines how the political culture of borderlands is marked by continual struggles between the powers of territorial control and those of cross-border networking. Taking Bengal as an example, he presents borderland insurgencies as the machinations of rival nation-states in South Asia who aid and abet the insurgents to destabilize and dismember their neighbors. Instead of only seeing insurgencies as strategies of neighboring states, I also acknowledge the agency of "borderlanders" who resist marginalization and make themselves visible in the national arena.

31. Scholarship on South Asian historiography has studied the extraterritorial dimension of Indian nationalism. In *A Hundred Horizons* (Cambridge, MA: Harvard University Press, 2006), Sugata Bose argues that nationalist identity and imagination cannot be limited within a territorially delimited nation-state, while "oceanic dimensions of anti-colonialism may go some way in freeing the study of nationalism from its landlocked state." His study shows how the Indian Ocean served as an "inter-regional arena," carrying waves of laborers serving in mines and plantations outside India, soldiers serving overseas, and even expatriates who imagined and perceived an Indian homeland. Maia Ramnath's *Haj to Utopia: How the Ghadar Movement Charted Global Radicalism and Attempted to Overthrow the British Empire* (Berkeley: University of California Press, 2011) argues against viewing the anticolonial Ghadar movement in a nationalist framework; instead, she suggests that the Ghadar revolutionaries mediated local and transnational concerns across America, Europe, the Middle East, and East Africa.
32. Martin Sökefeld, "The Kashmiri Diaspora in Britain and the Limits of Political Mobilization," in Astrid Wonneberger, Mijal Gandelsman-Trier, and Hauke Dorsch (eds.), *Migration Networks Skills* (Hamburg: Transcript-Verlag, 2016), 23–46.
33. Jagmohan, *My Frozen Turbulence in Kashmir* (New Delhi: Allied Publishers, 1991); Praveen Swami, *India, Pakistan, and the Secret Jihad: The Covert War in Kashmir, 1947–2004* (London: Routledge, 2007), 2–3.
34. Vivek Sinha, "Yes, Kashmir Struggle Is a Subset of Global Islamic Terror Game," *Times of India*, June 6, 2017, https://blogs.timesofindia.indiatimes.com/between-the-lines/yes-kashmir-struggle-is-a-subset-of-global-islamic-terror-game/, accessed June 2017; Vivek Sinha, "Kashmir Struggle Is All about Establishing Islamic Caliphate and Sharia," Indiafacts.org, May 27, 2017, http://indiafacts.org/kashmir-struggle-is-all-about-establishing-islamic-caliphate-and-sharia/, accessed June 2018.
35. Rai, *Hindu Rulers, Muslim Subjects.*
36. Ayesha Jalal, *Democracy and Authoritarianism in South Asia: A Comparative and Historical Perspective* (Cambridge: Cambridge University Press, 1995), 161–83.
37. Ayesha Jalal, *Partisans of Allah: Jihad in South Asia* (Cambridge, MA: Harvard University Press, 2008), 12.
38. For details about the rise of Islamic revivalism in South Asia, see Seyyed Vali Reza Nasr, *Mawdudi and the Making of Islamic Revivalism* (New York: Oxford University Press, 1996).
39. Ahsan Butt, *Secession and Security: Explaining State Strategy against Separatists* (Ithaca: Cornell University Press, 2017).
40. Hallie Ludsin, "Returning Sovereignty to the People," *Vanderbilt Journal of Transnational Law* 46, no. 1 (January 2013): 97–169, https://www.vanderbilt.edu/wp-content/uploads/sites/78/Ludsin.pdf, accessed January 2019.
41. Indrani Bagchi, "India Slams UN Report," *Times of India*, June 14, 2018, http://theindiaobserver.com/india-slams-un-report-on-kashmir-calls-it-selective-compilation-of-largely-unverified-information/, accessed August 23, 2018.

1 Meanings of Freedom in the Princely State of Jammu and Kashmir

Come, gardener! Create the glory of spring!
Make flowers bloom and bulbuls sing—create such haunts!

Who will set you free, captive bird?
Crying in your cage, forge with your own hands
The instruments of your deliverance.

Wealth and pride and comfort, luxury and authority,
Kingship and governance—all these are yours!
Wake up, sleeper, and know these as yours.

Bid good-bye to your dulcet strains. To rouse
this habitat of flowers, create a storm,
Let thunder rumble,—let there be an earthquake!

—Ghulam Ahmad Mahjoor, "Come Gardener"[1]

In the early twentieth century rumblings of resistance against the despotic Dogra rulers of the princely state of Jammu and Kashmir gained momentum, and Kashmiris sought to alter the social injustices and economic inequities that defined their lives. New dreams, new aspirations, and new self-consciousness signaled an awakening, a rejection of subjugation and a deep desire to seek out freedom. This chapter explores Kashmiri imaginings of freedom in this historical context. Poetry, pamphlets, and literary works reveal how Kashmiris adapted pre-existing themes of freedom to fit the needs of their deteriorating economic and political landscape. While politicians and intellectuals made speeches, edited and wrote for newspapers and magazines, and organized study circles where discussion often spilled over into activism, Kashmiri poets profoundly affected by the revolutionary fervor of the 1940s wrote inspiring poems to spark courage and resilience in Kashmiris fighting for their rights. In constructing ideas about freedom, politicians and poets alike liberally borrowed from the ancient texts and mystical culture of Kashmir, but also remained open to new international ideas that could, they felt, improve human relationships and lay foundations for a strong society. Despite some shared culture and interests, however, I further argue that the definition of "freedom" was not universally constant; in the changing socioeconomic context of the late nineteenth and early twentieth centuries, Kashmir's social divisions and religious differences added complexities to this discourse.

In fact, broader regional relationships fueled Kashmiri narratives of "freedom," which were articulated not only by those within the princely state, but also by expatriates who had migrated to the plains of Punjab to escape poverty while retaining an emotional attachment to their homeland. In the early twentieth century, a new generation of educated, politically minded young Kashmiris, exposed to Western ideologies of nationalism, secularism, and socialism, adapted these concepts to fit the regional environment of the Valley. Their application of international discourses to the question of Kashmiri emancipation altered the feudal structures of the state, sharpening class conflicts and exposing social divisions. Ultimately, the political processes underway in the rest of the subcontinent informed the visions that inhabitants of Jammu and Kashmir had for their political future, especially in the critical decade before partition. While at the time of decolonization certain regions and sub-sections of the culturally diverse princely state identified with one or the other of the emerging political constructs of "India" and "Pakistan," others, including the critical figure of the maharaja, remained ambivalent about the future status of their princely state. Understanding the roots of the conflict that continues to wrack Kashmir today, I argue, requires understanding how Kashmiris' conflicting desires, developed in the decades before partition, left an open space in which the new nation-states could intervene, appropriating Kashmiri aspirations to suit their own political agendas.

"Freedom" from the Structures of the State in the Nineteenth and Twentieth Centuries

The concept of "freedom" has fascinated Kashmiris and dominated their sociopolitical discourses for centuries. The geographies, histories, and ethical treatises of pre-colonial Kashmir are replete with notions of freedom. Kalhana's *Rajatarangini*, or "River of Kings," believed by orientalist scholars to be the earliest recorded history of the Indian subcontinent, doubled as a treatise on efficient, ethical, and moral governance. The twelfth-century text sketches a picture of a good king: a man who ensures social peace, encourages agricultural productivity, and governs wisely, creating a harmonious society leading individuals toward freedom from injustice, ignorance, and selfishness.[2] Inspired by Buddhist philosophy, *Rajatarangini* compares the good ruler with a *bodhisattva*, endowed with piety and compassion to render service to humanity. The ideal king would consider justice and truth a part of his *dharma*, and set an example for others with his personal conduct.

The mystical traditions of Kashmir were infused with these concepts of ethics, humanism, and brotherhood; in a stratified society struggling against class and caste hierarchies, they attracted the disenfranchised. The first mystic poet of the Kashmir Valley, Laleshwari, popularly known as Lal Ded or Lalla, articulated a humanistic discourse intermeshing ethics and religious belief, and projected a universal vision of a good society. She exhorted rulers to endorse ethical behavior and end social disparities:

> I renounced fraud, untruth, and deceit;
> I taught my mind to see the one in all my fellow-men,
> How could I then discriminate between man and man,
> And not accept the food offered to me by brother man?[3]

The indigenous Muslim mystics of the fourteenth century, the Rishis, explained emancipation as a struggle to attain good social relations, end economic injustice, and understand all human beings as creations of God. The Rishis captured Kashmiris' imagination, making Islam comprehensible to ordinary people in ethical terms, as we can see in one of the verses of Sheikh Noor-ud-Din (or Nund Rishi), the patron saint of the Kashmir Valley. Noor-ud-Din defines the true Muslim as one who values the principle of righteousness:

> One who does not neglect one's daily duties,
> Who longs to live by the sweat of one's brow,
> Who controls the bestial anger of one's mind, who shows fortitude in provocation,
> May truly be called a Muslim.
> He will be among the people of paradise
> Who shares meal with the hungry,
> (who) is obsessed with the idea of removing hunger,
> Who humbly bows (in prayers) in all sincerity,
> Who scorns anger, greed, illusion, arrogance and self-conceit,
> May truly be called a Muslim.[4]

The Rishis defined "freedom" as an end to the exploitative character of Kashmiri society, which divided the rich from the poor and separated high and low castes. In their verses, they asked the rich to fulfill their social responsibilities and allow the less privileged to achieve a comfortable existence. These imaginings of freedom, transmitted from one generation to another via poetry and folklore, defined the way Kashmiris perceived emancipation by the early twentieth century: as a combination of personal and sociopolitical transformations.

Kashmiri aspirations for spiritual, economic, and political freedom were not much different from those of people across the globe; however, these ideas held special relevance in Kashmir due to a centuries-long pattern of repressive colonial dynasties. Afghans, Sikhs, and finally the British-supported Dogra Raj all prioritized high taxation over efficient governance to maintain their domination. Eighteenth- and nineteenth-century regional narratives and European travelogues alike document heart-wrenching stories of injustice and persecution which kept Kashmiris in constant terror. During his travels to Kashmir in the early nineteenth century, for example, the French naturalist Victor Jacquemont lamented the lack of value placed on human life in the poverty-stricken state. Jacquemont described the ruthlessness of the Afghan governors who employed collective punishments to create fear in people's hearts; their favorite tools of oppression included hanging political dissenters in public, then leaving their tortured bodies on display.[5] Other European travelers corroborated such stories of injustice, which continued after the Sikh conquest of 1819.[6] British explorer William Moorcroft exposed the disproportionate revenue demand that impoverished Kashmiri villages under Sikh rule. He described in detail the "ghastly picture of poverty and starvation" in "half deserted villages" as "wretched Kashmiris" struggled to survive under a regime that "looked upon [them] a little better than cattle."[7] As policies imposed by ruthless empires reduced ordinary Kashmiris to servitude, the ideas of "justice," "equity," and "truth" articulated by local saints and mystics under the banner of spiritual "freedom" provided hope that an oppressive society could be transformed.

In the late nineteenth century, regional political transformations ushered Kashmir into the "modern" era, creating conditions that ultimately resulted in Kashmiris' political mobilization in favor of "freedom." The Kashmir Valley became a part of the princely state of Jammu and Kashmir after the British East India Company put together several culturally diverse regions, taken from the Sikh kingdom of Punjab, and handed them over to Gulab Singh, a Dogra chieftain from Jammu, as a reward for his services during the Anglo-Sikh wars of 1846.[8] The Treaty of Amritsar transferred Kashmir and its surrounding areas to "Maharaja Gulab Singh and the male heirs of his body" for seventy-five thousand (Nanakshahee) rupees. Regional narratives later called this treaty a "sale-deed" that set a Hindu ruling house over the area without consideration for the wishes or interests of the vast majority of its people, who were Muslim.

In pre-colonial times, South Asian ruling dynasties had always prioritized their own religious communities, yet they never excluded public patronage of other communities, institutions, or places of worship. This patronage allowed them to retain legitimacy among religiously diverse subjects. Mridu Rai asserts the newly created Dogra maharajas, however, inaugurated a "territorially bound Hindu sovereignty," supporting only Hindu temples and neglecting the maintenance of Muslim shrines and mosques. [9] In some instances, Muslim religious places became storehouses for grains and ammunition, causing deep resentment. Furthermore, newly promulgated laws permitted Muslim converts to Hinduism to retain rights over their ancestral property and the guardianship of their children, while denying the same privileges to Hindu converts to Islam.[10]

Kashmiri Muslim alienation did not only stem from religious discrimination, however; unequal socioeconomic structures ensured the dominance of the ruling elite and created further discontent among the majority. While hierarchical social divisions already existed within Kashmiri society, the Dogra state created a new group of landed elites, mostly Hindus, who had land bestowed on them as compensation for both real and imaginary services rendered. This newly landed elite had exclusive rights over, and few obligations to, the mostly Muslim families who actually cultivated the land. Even though they were allotted only a certain amount of revenue from land grants, they exercised jurisdictional rights and could evict tenants at will, forcing the peasantry into complete submission.[11]

Lack of accountability encouraged Hindu revenue officials to use *begar*, or forced labor, a long-standing hierarchical Kashmiri institution of exploitation and expropriation, to compel peasants to perform various tasks for the state without compensation.[12] Some peasants avoided this degrading practice by bribing officials with gifts and money, while others sold their lands for a pittance to secure written exemption from all forms of forced labor.[13] Beyond forced labor, the peasantry was also exploited at harvest time, when their food grains were appropriated at half the original price. This practice subsidized urban populations like Srinagar's shawl weavers, whose product brought an approximate annual revenue of 600,000 rupees to the state.[14] Finally, the Muslim religious elite (*pir*s), especially shrine custodians, exerted their religious power to extract the remaining food grains and poultry left with the peasants for their personal consumption.[15] Traditional ties of obedience to these shrine custodians prevented an agrarian revolt, and the complicity of the Muslim elite with the Hindu bureaucracy ensured the continuing dominance of the upper classes.

Feeling powerless to alter this social system, the Kashmiri peasantry lamented the injustices which had befallen their community using culturally relevant forms of protest: folk theatre (*band-pathar*), satiric ballads (*ladishas*), and folk tales (*kath*). Bands and balladeers roamed the countryside, performing and singing at fairs and festivals, using humor to heal and replace sorrow with thoughts of happier times. Every street play addressed the social injustices faced by Kashmiri peasantry. In most plots, the king summons revenue officials to redress the wrongs suffered by the peasant. The peasant voices his grievances, but the revenue officials silence him. The bitter ironic end result finds the revenue officials innocent, while the peasant is held guilty.[16] One of these plays, *Raza-Pathar*, depicted peasants' contempt for the corrupt bureaucracy; its main character is a revenue official, Sagwan, who demands honey as a bribe from a potter. Instead of bringing the honey, the potter offers a pot full of mud as a bribe. When open criticism of the political elites' moral laxity risked reprisal, Kashmiri poetry and folklore used humor as resistance, publicly ridiculing corrupt officials and exposing inefficient governance while maintaining plausible deniability.[17]

Kashmiri misery was heightened by the natural calamities, including famines and epidemics, that engulfed the province periodically during the nineteenth and twentieth centuries. The unaccountable Dogra state's indifference to providing adequate relief to the victims of these unforeseen tragedies often led to starvation and death. A Kashmiri *ladisha*, or satiric ballad, sketched the pathos of the situation in these words:

> Oh dear, give a patient hearing to my woes!
> Famines and extreme poverty have made our lives miserable.
> The people who had little in store died mercilessly
> Even the wealthy traders were searching for a grain of rice.
> The hoarders were demanding exorbitant prices for a little handful of rice.
> Famines and extreme poverty have made our lives miserable.[18]

During the famine of 1877–8, the authorities set all grain apart for urban areas, leaving the agrarian population without food during the winter. The starving peasanty died in large numbers, but even the urban population (preserved at the cost of the cultivators) began to feel the pressure as the famine increased in severity in 1878. Storehouses which sold rice to the urban population at fixed rates remained closed for weeks; only the elites maintained access.[19]

The state's inability to provide adequate relief in this crisis forced the Dogra ruler to abolish the *rahdari* system, which had issued permits to subjects who wished to travel outside the state, allowing thousands of Kashmiris to leave their homeland to seek a better life. According to the 1891 Punjab census report, an extensive migration from princely Jammu and Kashmir led to 111,775 Kashmiri

Muslims resettling in the towns of Amritsar and Lahore in Punjab.[20] These migrants trudged through high mountain passes, risking their lives without adequate protection from the vagaries of weather, to seek a better future in the plains of India. Lacking language skills, they struggled in an unfamiliar environment, performing hard labor during the day and spending their nights in mosques, trying to save enough to return home and buy food for their families.[21] As these poor migrants lived on the margins in a foreign land, their host society looked down upon them, pejoratively labeling Kashmiris "cowards without dignity." With little understanding of the situation, these insults accused the migrants of lacking the courage to change their destinies and live respectably in their homeland.

Even European travelogues, while expressing more sympathy for Kashmiris, presented them as "mean spirited and inferior cowards." English missionary Arthur Brinckman wrote, for example, that "the poor Cashmere is like a mouse trying to drink milk with an army of cats in the same room with him. The Cashmere does everything slyly, lies constantly to save himself from oppression, from the suspicion of not having enough for himself and his family."[22] Other "sympathetic" reports, including one written by Settlement Commissioner Walter R. Lawrence, blamed inhuman living conditions in Kashmir on the peasantry's lack of initiative.[23] These widespread stereotypes created a sense of inferiority even among affluent Kashmiri families. Many migrant families preferred to "disown their Kashmiri origin or their long domicile in Kashmir" by calling themselves "Arabs, Turks, Iranians, or Afghans to escape the galling degradation and appalling humiliation of being called Kashmiri, with all that the expression connoted at one time."[24] In time, many of these migrant Kashmiri families would distinguish themselves in different fields; a new confidence would encourage future generations to embrace their homeland and contribute to the ferment of the 1930s.

Meanwhile, continued Dogra misgovernance in Kashmir provided an excuse for British intervention. The colonial state posted a British Resident in Jammu and Kashmir to ensure the Dogra state treated its subjects justly and redressed their grievances. The presence of a British Resident provided a mechanism for Kashmiri Muslims to express their grievances; they submitted petitions to the Resident in favor of reforms including revision of taxes; lighter assessment of revenue, preferably in cash; abolition of revenue farming; lifting restrictions on emigration; and the building of new roads and communications.[25]

The late-nineteenth-century construction of the Jhelum Valley Road, linking the princely state with Punjab, increased interactions between the state and expatriate Kashmiris, and generated wider sociopolitical awareness in the Valley, manifesting in renewed demands for "freedom." A number of expatriates became involved in efforts to transform the state's social structures and create a voice for excluded Kashmiri Muslims. These expatriate expressions of solidarity with Kashmir complicated Kashmiri identity; in fact, the significance of belonging to Kashmir and being "Kashmiri" began to transcend narrow cultural and territorial definitions and refer primarily to the emotive attachment self-identified Kashmiris had to their homeland, regardless of whether they resided in the state or not. In 1896, Kashmiri Muslims based in Punjab formed Anjumun-i-Kashmir-Mussalmanan-i-Lahore, an association to address their community's challenges; in 1901, it became the Muslim Kashmiri Conference, and in 1908, the All India Muslim Kashmir Conference.[26] As they renamed their organization in English, Kashmiri expatriates in Punjab sought legitimacy in the colonial politics and to expand the support base to include Kashmiris settled in different parts of India. This body of prominent individuals of Kashmiri descent engaged in activities on three different fronts: debating issues that confronted Kashmiri Muslims; presenting memorandums to the Dogra rulers on behalf of Kashmiri Muslims; and mobilizing Kashmiri Muslims to initiate social reform and to improve their social standing via education.[27]

Two prominent Kashmiri residents of Punjab, Munshi Muhammad-ud-din Fauq, the editor of the illustrated Urdu weekly *Kashmir Magazine*, and Muhammad Iqbal, the famed poet-philosopher, became the association's most active members and provided intellectual direction for the growing Kashmiri political awareness. Fauq and Iqbal emphasized the need to create a response of resistance, rather than hopelessness, in order to change Kashmiri Muslims' socioeconomic situation. Born in 1877, Fauq belonged to a middle-class Kashmiri family that had migrated to Sialkot from the Soebug district of the Valley. His literary skills drew him to journalism and he began publishing the *Kashmir Magazine* in Lahore in 1906, providing himself with the perfect medium for expounding his views on the social and economic issues confronting Kashmiris.[28] Intending to stir pride and self-confidence among his compatriots, he filled the weekly with stories of the glorious traditions of Kashmir's history along with his prescriptions for the future.[29]

Alongside his magazine, Fauq also penned a series of books which countered negative depictions of Kashmiris by emphasizing the greatness of Kashmir's past and explained Kashmiri servility as a consequence of foreign domination. *Shabab-i-Kashmir*, written in 1928, is an account of one of the most famous Muslim kings of Kashmir, Sultan Zain-ul-abidin (popularly known as the Bud Shah or "great king"), which sketched the glorious heritage of the king's reign and the contributions made by Kashmiris in the field of arts, literature, and architecture that had made Kashmir a centre of learning in the thirteenth century. According to Fauq, Zain-ul-abidin's policy of religious tolerance and inclusion set an example for other monarchs, especially those who privileged their own religious community while denying rights to other religious groups—a not-so-subtle comment on Dogra practices.[30]

Mashair-i-Kashmir, another of Fauq's books, assembled real-life stories about ordinary Kashmiris who had migrated to various parts of India and gained prominence due to their initiative: the Nawabs of Dacca, for example, had migrated from Kashmir as traders but through intelligence and hard work became the rulers of Eastern Bengal. Fauq aimed to convince the Kashmiri Muslim community that despite their disadvantages, with education and by taking advantage of opportunities they too could pull themselves up from a pitiable state and change their destinies. Fauq implored Kashmiri Muslim families to take pride in their Kashmiri identity instead of fabricating their genealogies to claim descent from Arabia, Iran, or Central Asia to fit in with more "honorable classes."[31] Fauq's discourse aimed to build confidence in Kashmiri identity and self-expression.

The other prominent early-twentieth-century literary figure of Kashmiri descent, Muhammad Iqbal, devoted his poetic faculties to providing Kashmiris with guidance. Although Iqbal's family had migrated from Kashmir to Lahore prior to the creation of the Dogra Raj, they had retained an emotional attachment to their homeland. Iqbal's poetry passionately appealed to Kashmiris to rise against oppression and cherish the concept of freedom. One poem, *Javid Nama*, written in 1932, describes a "spiritual journey made by the poet through the spheres of the moon, Mercury, Venus, Mars, Jupiter, Saturn, and beyond to the presence of God."[32] Iqbal adopted the theme of *miraj*, the Prophet Muhammad's spiritual journey across the seven heavens where he encountered and conversed with earlier prophets, to envision "Muslim regeneration and self-realization."[33] On his visit to and beyond the seven heavens, Iqbal comes across Kashmiris who had shaped the history of the region. In his conversations with them, Iqbal praises the dexterity and cleverness of Kashmiris, yet laments that lack of will has reduced them to a state of servitude: "Nation grazes upon another nation; my soul burns like a rue for the people of the Vale." In response, the great Kashmiri saint Sayyid Ali Hamdani refers to an inherent spark among Kashmiris that, once ignited, could "smite the rocks on its path and uproot the fabric of the mountains."[34] In the early decades of the twentieth century, individuals like Fauq and Iqbal voiced the grievances of Kashmiri Muslims in print media, hoping to build public opinion in favor of introducing reforms in the princely state of Jammu and Kashmir and improve Muslims' standard of living. In doing so, they meshed concepts of emotional and spiritual freedom and self-respect with calls to action for political freedom and self-determination.

Responding to Fauq's and Iqbal's calls, the Punjab-based expatriate Kashmiri intelligentsia established contacts with religious and urban elites in the princely state, initiating a joint effort to improve the status of their community.[35] Mirwaiz Rasool Shah, the religious preacher of the historic Jama Masjid and leader of a staunch support base in pockets of Srinagar city, emerged as an educational pioneer attempting to remove "Muslim backwardness."[36] In 1889, the Mirwaiz family set up the first primary school in Srinagar, which eventually became Islamia High School. In 1905, the family (in consultation with prominent Punjab-based Kashmiri intellectuals) established the first formal Muslim organization at Srinagar, the Anjumun-i-Nusrat-ul-Islam, with the goal of Kashmiri Muslim cultural regeneration.[37] Expatriate Kashmiris in various parts of India attended the Anjuman's annual conferences. Its monthly journal, *Halat-o-Rou-i-Dad*, published from Lahore, linked Kashmir's future prosperity to education, which would eliminate Kashmiri ignorance and inculcate self-worth. Seeking to end illiteracy among Kashmiri Muslims, the All India Kashmir Muslim Conference provided scholarships to deserving but impoverished Kashmiris. Between 1912 and 1929, the organization gave 123 students almost thirty-one thousand rupees.[38]

While practicing private charity, the conference also submitted memorandums to the maharaja requesting an increase in educational facilities for Muslims and appointing Muslims in state services. They further suggested that the maharaja recruit expatriate Kashmiri Muslims if he had trouble finding qualified Muslim candidates within the state.[39] Perhaps not surprisingly, the maharaja remained indifferent to the Conference's concerns.[40] In fact, he blamed the Kashmiri Muslim community for its backwardness, claiming that Muslims lacked the initiative to adopt English education, despite the equal opportunities theoretically provided to all communities. In 1916, the Dogra government appointed the Sharp Education Commission to inquire into Kashmiri Muslim grievances. The commission suggested making primary education both free and compulsory, to enable poverty-stricken Kashmiris to send their children to school. The minister of education, however, rejected this suggestion, arguing that implementing it would interfere with the economic sustenance of Muslims who relied on their children's labor to make ends meet.[41] Episodes like this increased Muslims' bitterness, as their protests and complaints within the current structures of the state evidently served no purpose; freedom from those structures would clearly be required for any more progress to occur.

The decade of the 1920s, a formative period for Kashmiris' awakening political consciousness, coincided with the aftermath of the First World War. The global war impacted the already deteriorating economic conditions in the Valley; a steep rise in rice paddy prices made it difficult for the urban poor to afford food grains.[42] Furthermore, the postwar recession decreased the demand for Kashmiri carpets, handicrafts, and shawls, affecting the manufacturing class. Distress and frustration among Kashmiri urbanites increased, eventually erupting in street protests. In 1924, workers in the government-owned silk factory struck to demand higher wages and an end to corruption. Instead of addressing their concerns, the Dogra state forcibly suppressed resistance, leading to the death of seven protestors and injuries to another forty.[43]

The regime's unsympathetic attitude convinced the Muslim clergy, landowners, and wealthy traders that they needed to step up external pressure on the maharaja. In 1924, these elites presented a memorandum to Lord Reading, the viceroy of British India, during his visit to the Valley, demanding government jobs, better educational facilities, ownership rights for the peasantry, and restoration of all mosques under Dogra control to the community. Once the viceroy left the Valley, however, the Dogra administration retaliated. Individuals who had signed the memorandum lost their jobs and land grants, and were debarred from attending the royal *durbar*s, or court sessions.[44] These repressive measures aimed at prominent Muslim families served their intended purpose as a warning to those contemplating resistance. However, they also united the elite Muslim community; rich merchant families donated to those arrested and the exiled, and the memorandum's signatories emerged as leaders of the Kashmiri Muslim community at home and abroad.[45]

While Muslims clamoring for rights from the Dogra regime saw "freedom" as both cause and consequence of the spread of education and social awareness in their community, the Kashmiri Hindus (Pandits), an educated but minority community, struggled to end discrimination from the Dogra administration. The state reserved its top-ranking jobs for Punjabi Hindus. Seeking equality in government employment, the community movement "Kashmir for Kashmiris" demanded that the state instead reserve employment for *mulki*s, or inhabitants of the state. In 1927, the Dogra maharaja, seeking to placate the disgruntled Pandits, passed the Hereditary State Subject Act, allowing only residents of the state to purchase land and seek employment in Jammu and Kashmir. This act entitled a rising segment of educated Kashmiri Muslims, smarting under the discriminatory policies of the Dogra state, to demand employment, including representation in state service jobs, according to their numbers.[46] (The act, retained in postcolonial Kashmir, would become a critical signpost in a long-running dispute over Kashmiri identity with both legal and emotional consequences, and will be discussed again in Chapter 2.)

By the late 1920s, the efforts of Kashmiri Muslim elites and their expatriate allies had succeeded in creating a new class of Kashmiri Muslims well versed in English education. These educated young Muslims, mostly from middle-class families, started a Reading Room at Fateh Kadal in Srinagar to discuss and debate their political future under the Dogra Raj. Some spoke directly against the regime. Molvi Muhammad Abdullah Vakil, originally from Shopian district in south Kashmir and a lawyer by profession, advised the educated community via lectures and sermons to wage a political resistance and demand equal rights. Even though the Dogra state had disallowed publication of newspapers in the Valley, Vakil used the Muslim press in Punjab to expose the state's discriminatory policies, secretly sending articles for publication to Munshi Muhammad-ud-din Fauq at Sialkot.[47] The articles published by the Muslim press in Punjab questioned the lack of employment opportunities for Kashmiri Muslims; restrictions on their employment in the army; and the imposition of the Seditious Meetings Act, which banned public meetings without prior approval from the government.[48]

Meanwhile, the middle-class Muslims of Jammu, culturally and socially closer to the Muslims of Punjab, witnessed growing religious tensions across the border. In the 1920s, the Arya Samaj, a Punjabi Hindu revivalist organization, initiated the Shuddi and Sangathan movements to bring non-Muslims into the Hindu fold, while Punjabi Muslims launched the Tabligh movement to counter the conversion drive. These religious tensions spilled into Jammu, making both Hindus and Muslims more aware of their religious identities. Muslim youth in Jammu set up the Young Men's Muslim Association (YMMA) along similar lines as Srinagar's Reading Room party, to protect their communitarian interests.[49]

No problem concerned middle-class Muslims in Jammu and Kashmir more than the question of unemployment. The growing number of educated Muslims and their claims to an equal share in government service-sector jobs created pressure on the Dogra regime; in 1930, in response, the government established an official Civil Service Recruitment Board. While the previous recruitment board had nominated scholarship candidates, new regulations made competitive tests a prerequisite for employment. The upper age limit for candidates was set at twenty, and only candidates belonging to "good and noble families" could apply for higher posts. Many Muslims believed the state had invented these conditions to provide a legal justification for denying them their legitimate share of employment in various sectors. Interestingly, by the 1930s most unemployed Kashmiri Muslim graduates were older than twenty-two, and as such were now debarred from any "respectable" service. Even if a candidate met all the criteria, however, the Dogra government reserved the right to deny him employment.[50]

Muslim youth contested the new recruitment rules; in September 1930, a Reading Room deputation to the government provided data on Muslim unemployment and warned that the state was accountable for its Muslim subjects' condition. Dogra representatives, however, rebuked the members of the deputation for their ungratefulness to the Dogra state, despite the maharaja's efforts to recruit a few Muslims in the administration. Although this meeting with the government representatives disappointed the activists, it reinforced their determination to prepare for a long political movement.[51] This new, educated middle-class Kashmiri Muslim leadership succeeded in forging contacts with the religious elites and the rich business classes, who had held the mantle of leadership in the previous decades. Growing political awareness among the Muslim community added a new tone to the Kashmiri discourse on freedom and brought into sharp relief various groups' conflicting visions of freedom.

The First Kashmiri Muslim Resistance: Muslim Reactions and Hindu Responses

Gathering discontent among Kashmiri Muslims, born out of decades of misgovernance, religious discrimination, and neglect, came to a boil in the summer of 1931.[52] As the first Kashmiri Muslim resistance gained ground, the inherent tensions between classes and communities surfaced, tearing at Kashmir's social fabric. Hindu and Muslim communities with different experiences as the subjects of the Dogra Raj perceived the political transformations of the early twentieth century through a communitarian lens. Simultaneously, the sectarian and class divisions within the Kashmiri Muslim community prevented the forging of a unified movement for rights. Although Kashmiri leaders and intellectuals attempted to bridge these inherent contradictions by weaving the Western ideas of nationalism and socialism into Kashmiri discourses of rights and freedoms, it proved a daunting task.

Kashmiri Muslim feelings of religious discrimination intensified after the news flowed into the Valley about the maharaja's officials' disrespect towards Islam, including incidents such as the refusal of the police to give permission to Muslims in Jammu to use a certain piece of land for prayers. The most provocative story concerned the behavior of a Hindu constable, who not only prevented an *imam* from reading his Friday sermon, but also showed disrespect to the Quran.[53] These reported events created an uproar among the Valley's Muslim community, where the political and economic climate was now ripe for a mass movement. Muslim leadership—composed of religious elites, rich merchants, and the landed gentry dominant in the 1920s, now joined by middle-class educated youth—decided to initiate a mass resistance against Dogra rule.

One individual who succeeded in making his presence felt among Muslim leaders during this first wave of open resistance was twenty-five-year-old Sheikh Muhammad Abdullah, who subsequently dominated Kashmiri politics for almost five decades. Born near Srinagar in 1905 to a middle-class family of shawl merchants, Abdullah received his early education in a traditional Muslim *maktab*, or religious school, where he learned to read the Quran. He resisted pressure to join the family business, instead dreaming of becoming a doctor. His first experience of anti-Muslim discrimination occurred when the state refused him a scholarship for medical school on religious grounds. Moving to Lahore to secure a Bachelor of Science degree, he became a frequent visitor to Muhammad Iqbal, the eminent poet and philosopher, and an active member of the Kashmir Muslim Conference, which profoundly shaped his political thought. From Lahore, Abdullah moved to Aligarh Muslim University, where he completed his Master of Science in chemistry in 1930. As one of the first Kashmiri Muslims to obtain a master's degree, he hoped to get a scholarship from the Dogra government to study abroad, but was unsuccessful. His personal experiences of marginalization convinced him to initiate a campaign, along with likeminded Kashmiris, to redress the grievances of the Muslim majority. As he later explained:

> I started to question why Muslims were being singled out for such treatment. We constituted the majority and contributed the most towards state's revenue, still we were continuously oppressed. Why? How long could we put up with it? Was it because majority of the government was non-Muslims? Or because most of the lower grade officials who dealt with the public were Kashmiri Pandits? I concluded that the ill-treatment of Muslims was an outcome of religious prejudice.[54]

As an active member of the Reading Room party, he became popular due to his powerful oratory and command of the Quran. His passionate speeches exhorted Kashmiris to cultivate a spirit of sacrifice, without which freedom would be a distant dream:

> The misery of Muslims can be alleviated only through sacrifice. So long as they fear imprisonment and persecution, there will be no end to their suffering. I would be the first individual to make sacrifice in our struggle.[55]

Abdullah's boldness and fearlessness made him extremely popular among Kashmiris, who fondly referred to him as the Sher-i-Kashmir, the Lion of Kashmir. In the 1930s the Mirwaiz of Jama Masjid, a prominent religious leader, introduced Sheikh Abdullah to the Kashmiri Muslim community as "our leader" and made an impassioned appeal for Kashmiris to act upon his orders and implement his proposed program. The Mirwaiz's support gave Abdullah not only political legitimacy, but access to the historic Jama Masjid platform for his political mobilization.[56]

Abdullah and other leaders, however, were not always the main drivers of events during the wave of resistance that rocked Kashmir in the summer of 1931. In June 1931, the Reading Room party organized a public rally at Khanqah-i-Mohalla, in the old city of Srinagar, to select another deputation of Muslim leaders to present their grievances to the maharaja. This event united all shades of Muslim opinion; religious leaders with different ideological orientations, rich elites, and the educated Muslim middle class came together on a common platform to voice their dissent against the regime. At the end of the meeting, when the main leaders had dispersed, Abdul Qadir, an ethnic Afghan Pathan and servant to a European vacationing in Kashmir, made an inflammatory speech imploring Kashmiri Muslims to rise in revolt against Hindu Dogra rule. Government spies reported this incident to the authorities, who arrested Qadir on charges of provoking communal strife. The disgruntled Kashmiri Muslim community, grateful for Qadir's bold stance, supported him by shouting anti-Dogra state slogans during his trial at the central jail in Srinagar on July 13, 1931.[57] In retaliation, the Dogra police opened fire, injuring hundreds and killing twenty-two. The crowd then rushed into the jail compound, took beds from the guards' quarters, and placed the dead bodies on them, carrying them in a procession toward Jama Masjid.[58]

Some of the protestors used this incident as an excuse for expressing their anger against Kashmiri Hindus, whom they perceived as inseparable from the Dogra government due to their dominant positions in the administration. These men targeted rich Hindu businesses, moneylenders, and landed elites, a move that shocked not only the Hindu community but also the Dogra police, who had never imagined a violent reaction from the supposedly "submissive" Kashmiri Muslims. The Maharaj Gunj market, in the heart of Srinagar city, emerged as the focal point of violence. Dominated by a large influx of Punjabi Hindu business groups, this new market had posed a serious challenge to the Muslim trading community in the localities of Jama Masjid and Nowhatta. A lack of capital combined with the state monopoly over trade prevented Muslims from competing with Punjabi Hindus, who had quickly established a monopoly.[59]

Some protestors, then, sought to re-establish their control over urban trading spaces, destroying Hindu shops, while others diverted their anger toward Hindu moneylenders' credit registers, destroying records so that no evidence of capital borrowed or interest accumulated by Kashmiri Muslim peasants or laborers was left.[60] The crowds' actions signal that their anger stemmed not only from the immediate incident of police violence, but also from the strains caused by the Great Depression, which had caused an unprecedented slump in the price of grain and a shortage of credit. The motivations of the 1931 riots were economic, social, and political, rather than being a mere expression of Muslim fanaticism against the minority Hindu community.

During these chaotic times, the All India Kashmir Committee at Lahore remained actively involved in Kashmiri resistance. Throughout India, members observed Kashmir Day on August 14, 1931, to show solidarity with Kashmiri Muslims, and worked with the Kashmiri Muslim leadership to reach a compromise with the Dogra administration. The two parties eventually reached an agreement, in which the regime promised to release on bail all prisoners accused of rioting and reinstate all Muslim government officials dismissed or suspended on charges of involvement in the protests. In return, Muslim leaders agreed to suspend the agitation and not indulge in anti-state activities.[61] Kashmiri Muslim workers and laborers, however, interpreted this agreement as a demonstration of weakness on the part of their supposed leadership. Those who had lost loved ones during the shooting and those who had suffered beatings, injuries, and arrests at the hands of the Dogra forces after the July 13 incident were unwilling to give up resistance. Gauging the public mood, elites and middle-class leaders realized it was imperative to continue the agitation despite the signed agreement, lest they lose public support.[62]

As the unrest continued, Kashmiri women from Maisuma and Gawkadal took the reins of protest and paraded the streets of the city, singing songs against the tyranny (*zulum*) of the Dogra Raj. Deeply affected by the arrests and even killings of their male relatives, the main economic providers in most families, the women's lyrics expressed their desire for a *just* government. Even the violence of police force did not dampen their spirits, although it had the capacity to turn fatal. A thirty-five-year-old woman, Freechi, whose husband had died in police firing, became a common sight at every procession. On one occasion, when policemen began to beat women protesters, Freechi physically assaulted an officer, hurling a fire pot (*kangari*) at his face and permanently disfiguring him. In retaliation, the police opened fire on the women, killing Freechi along with four other women and two children.[63]

There was no political space to express dissent, and the city's shrines and mosques emerged as points of congregation for the protestors. In September 1931, thousands of Kashmiris from Srinagar and its outskirts, tired of peaceful demonstrations, assembled at Khanyar's sacred shrine, the Dastageer Sahib, and paraded the streets of Srinagar with axes, spears, and lances to demonstrate their strength. To curb this defiance, the maharaja imposed an emergency ordinance, Notification No.19-L, drafted on the lines of the Burma Ordinance of 1818, which the British had used to put down an armed rebellion. It empowered any competent authority to arrest, without a warrant, any person who could reasonably be suspected of promoting or intending to promote disaffection against government authority. The government or its agencies, meanwhile, could take possession of any land or building, and even of moveable property. Non-compliance upon receipt of orders could lead to imprisonment extending up to three years, whipping not exceeding thirty stripes, and collective fines. This imposition of martial rule intensified state suppression and the Dogra army had many Kashmiris stripped naked and flogged at the exhibition grounds in full gaze of the public.[64] Instead of restoring peace, however, the military crackdown strengthened the Kashmiri Muslim challenge to Dogra domination.[65]

Kashmiri unrest did not remain confined to the princely state. In neighboring Punjab, two rival Muslim groups, the Ahrars and the Ahmadiyyas, vied to appropriate the Kashmir issue and therefore emerge as leaders of the wider Muslim community.[66] The All India Muslim Kashmiri Conference, reconstituted in 1931 as the All India Kashmir Committee under the leadership of Bashir-ud-din Mahmud Ahmad, the Khalifa of the Ahmadiyya community, saw Kashmir as an ideal location to win converts.[67] The Kashmir Committee, now mostly populated by Ahmadiyya members, championed civil rights for Kashmiri Muslims. The committee requested a meeting with the maharaja to resolve their differences and promote peaceful reconciliation, but the Dogra authorities invariably rejected such offers. The committee also established contact with Sheikh Abdullah in Srinagar and arranged to support Kashmiri political activists with propaganda and funds.[68]

Conversely, the Majlis-i-Ahrar, composed mostly of "anti-British urban Muslims and reformist members of the *ulama* with links to the Indian National Congress,"[69] adopted a more aggressive attitude toward securing Kashmiri Muslim rights. The Ahrars initiated the Kashmir Chalo movement, mobilizing almost 2,500 volunteers to infiltrate Jammu territory with *jatha*s, bands of supporters, who expressed dissent openly and courted arrest.[70] Inspired by the Ahrars, Muslim peasants in the border region of Jammu and Mirpur rose in revolt against the exploitative policies of the Dogra state that subjected them to heavy taxation.[71] Facing pressure on all fronts, the Dogra maharaja appealed to the British government for help and protection. In response, Britain compelled the maharaja to appoint an inquiry commission to probe the demands of his subjects, partly because his government had failed to suppress the popular revolt against it, and partly due to the highly effective agitation carried on in Punjab.[72]

The Glancy Commission, formed on November 12, 1931, included four members (two Muslims and two Hindus), each representing the regions of Kashmir and Jammu, yet failed to appease the minority community. The Muslim memorandum submitted to the commission, prepared in consultation with the members of the All India Kashmir Muslim Committee in Punjab, demanded a responsible government, a constitution, and the right to participate in elections. The Glancy Commission recommended restoration of Muslim religious shrines to the community. Another important clause in its final report related to issues of employment and education. It suggested "an increase in the number of Muslim teachers" and the appointment of a special officer for "promoting Muslim education." On the matter of distribution of government service, the commission argued against pitching minimum qualifications unnecessarily high, asking instead that the government advertise all vacancies and take effective measures to protect the interests of every community. Although the recommendations of the commission mostly protected the interests of the upper classes, peasants were ensured proprietary rights. These reforms largely satisfied the Muslim community.[73]

In October 1932, a representative body of upper- and middle-class Muslims formed their first political organization, the Muslim Conference, whose goal was to protect and promote the interests of the Muslim community. To make the Muslim Conference movement a success, Sheikh Abdullah sought an alliance with the Jammu Muslims organized under the banner of the YMMA and led by lawyer and political activist Chaudhry Ghulam Abbas. To begin with, the Muslim Conference professed its loyalty to the maharaja and claimed only to want to establish a responsible government under him. Although the organization passed resolutions demanding proprietary rights for the peasantry and a reduction in taxes for the labor class, for the most part it focused on constitutional reforms and sought a proportional share in service jobs for the Muslim community.[74] This longstanding goal united middle-class Muslims belonging to different sub-regions and with myriad ideological orientations.

The unity among Muslim Conference members did not last long. Personal egos and ideological differences soon led to a split within the party, as leaders disagreed on strategy around outside influences, especially from Punjab. Mirwaiz Yusuf

Shah wanted to disassociate Kashmir's freedom struggle from the influence of the Ahmadiyya-dominated All India Kashmir Committee at Lahore. His religious beliefs conflicted with the Ahmadiyyas' challenging of the finality of prophethood and, considering them heretics, he preferred not to associate with them politically. However, Abdullah wanted to work in close cooperation with them, considering their financial and moral support vital to the success of the movement.

Abdullah and Yusuf Shah also adopted contrary positions in an important intra-Muslim debate: the relationship between shrine worship and Islam. This issue had provoked sectarian quarrels between the two main religious leaders of Srinagar city, Mirwaiz Hamdani, who supported shrine worship, and Mirwaiz Yusuf Shah, who was against it. The conflict exploded into violence in July 1932 following Hamdani's eviction from the Jama Masjid by supporters of Yusuf Shah. In this battle Abdullah sided with Mirwaiz Hamdani, hoping to gain support from the custodians of shrines who held significant sway over Muslim public opinion.[75] Yusuf Shah retaliated by labelling Abdullah as an Ahmadiyya, a charge that had an impact on his popularity in the Valley. Vociferously denying this allegation, Abdullah was forced after all to distance himself from the All India Kashmir Committee.[76]

The tensions between the two leaders heightened after Mirwaiz Yusuf Shah expressed his loyalty to the Dogra ruler and accepted "an annual honorarium of Rs. 600, two rolls of English cotton, four rolls of China silk, a silver tray, and a shawl" in return for the maharaja's promise to consider Muslim demands.[77] His acceptance of this honorarium allowed his opponents to question Yusuf Shah's commitment to the Kashmiri movement. In 1933, he resigned from the Muslim Conference and formed his own political party, the Azad Muslim Conference.[78] Subsequently, the rivalry between these two leaders divided the urban Muslim community into "Shers," or Lions, after Abdullah's nickname "the Lion of Kashmir," and "Bakras," or Goats, in reference to the beards worn by Muslim *ulama* like the Mirwaiz.[79] The two groups could not reconcile their differences and often indulged in street fights. This rivalry prevented Muslim middle-class leadership from following up on the opening created by the mass uprising of the early 1930s.[80] Instead, Abdullah's Muslim Conference adopted a "moderate" practice of presenting memorandums and recommendations to the Dogra state.

In 1934, the maharaja established the Franchise Commission to give his disgruntled subjects some representation in a legislative assembly. Made up of thirty nominated and thirty-three elected members, it allowed the Muslim Conference to develop its organization as a political party. However, the franchise was restricted to men paying at least 20 rupees a year in land revenue, leaving out the poor among whom the Muslim Conference had been organizing. To win a majority in the assembly, they needed the support of affluent minorities as well as Muslim elites.[81] Therefore, Conference members considered it prudent to build bridges of understanding with groups of Hindus and Sikhs who were willing to work together on a "strategy of regional mobilization."[82]

Waging a united struggle for civil rights and bringing majority and minority communities onto a common platform posed new challenges. The minority Hindu community, comprising approximately 5 percent of the Valley's population, dominated the state services and viewed the political mobilization of the Muslim community with apprehension. They had expressed unhappiness with the 1931 Glancy Commission recommendation to increase the number of Muslims in government employment. Any concessions to Muslim demands, they argued, would come at the expense of their jobs. As such, Kashmiri Hindu organizations like the Sanatan Dharma Young Men's Association and the Yuvak Sabha initiated a "Roti Agitation," an "agitation for bread," that made preservation against Muslim encroachment its main priority and asked the Dogra state not to implement the Glancy Commission's recommendations.[83] Their hostility toward Kashmiri Muslim demands for equal rights caused some concern within the Hindu community; some Hindus believed that working with the majority community, rather than distancing themselves, was in the larger interests of Kashmiri Hindus. The minorities who sought cooperation with Muslims played an influential role in shaping Kashmiri discourses on freedom in the late colonial period.

For both Muslim and Hindu Kashmiris, ideas about "freedom" emerged in conversation with international ideologies popular during the 1930s and 1940s, that is, nationalism, communism, and socialism. Kashmiris well versed in English education sought to embed these sometimes conflicting ideas in the political fabric of Kashmir and thereby usher in an era of responsible government. One intellectual who reoriented Kashmiri Muslim resistance discourse was a prominent Hindu political activist who faced excommunication by his own community because he decided to support Kashmiri Muslim demands during the Glancy Commission era. Born in 1905 (the same year as Sheikh Abdullah) to a middle-class Pandit family, Prem Nath Bazaz graduated from Punjab University in 1927 and found employment as a supervisor of W.W. Trust Girls School at Srinagar. He began his political career as the president of the Yuvak Sabha, which worked to infuse a spirit of "patriotism" in favor of the Dogra ruler.[84] Bazaz was a prolific writer and established several newspapers like *Vitasta* (1932), *Hamdard* (1935), and *Voice of Kashmir* (1959) to address the political, economic, and social problems faced by Kashmiris.[85] Distressed by the Hindu–Muslim riots of the early 1930s, Bazaz attributed growing "communalism" in Kashmir to the support Kashmiri Muslims received from "pan-Islamic groups" in Punjab. Bazaz feared that alliance with Punjabi Muslims would ultimately lead to the formation of a theocratic state in Kashmir.[86] Additionally, however, he believed that the Pandit community's hostile attitude toward Muslim demands would endanger the interests of that minority community, writing that "the progress and prosperity of Kashmiri Pandits is synonymous with the complete political, social and economic freedom of Kashmir and liberation of the Muslim masses." His advice to his community was to take a leading role in Kashmiri resistance so as to direct it along a "saner path."[87] Bazaz established close friendships with Sheikh Abdullah and his associates, and advised them to make their movement broad-based rather than communitarian.[88]

Bazaz, along with other Kashmiri "progressives," created a new discourse on "freedom" that emphasized class differences rather than communitarian divisions. They promoted socialist ideas that could improve the indigent situation of the subordinate social classes, develop agriculture, and provide safeguards to the laboring classes. They believed that a strong focus on the economic issues that confronted poor Kashmiris could relegate religion to the background. Socialism fascinated Kashmiri Muslim leaders, who considered its economic basis identical with the teachings of the Quran emphasizing economic equity and social justice. The success of the socialist economic program, however, would be dependent on Kashmir's emergence as a unified entity.

To help Kashmiris conceive of their homeland holistically, Bazaz and Abdullah organized meetings and processions emphasizing unity as a prerequisite for economic justice and political liberty. In his presidential address at the annual session of the Muslim Conference in December 1933, Abdullah appealed to non-Muslims to wage a united struggle for the welfare of all "oppressed classes and communities."[89] Other members of the Muslim Conference also focused on the "unity" theme to mobilize all religious communities to usher real progress and prosperity.[90] However, Kashmiri Pandits expressed apprehensions about joining the Muslim Conference, as the party's name indicated that it was the representative body of Kashmiri Muslims exclusively. In 1934, Kashyap Bandhu, a prominent member of the Kashmiri Pandit community, submitted a memorandum to the Dogra prime minister, expressing fears about the Muslim political mobilization. He demanded safeguards for Kashmiri Pandits in state services, scholarships, and protection of their religious places.[91] Despite these concerns, in 1935, Abdullah and Bazaz jointly began to publish *Hamdard*, which romanticized Kashmir's past and made constant efforts to paper over the political, cultural, and religious differences between the communities. *Hamdard* asked Kashmiris to refrain from using terms like "Hindu" and "Muslim" in their political discourse, and instead use expressions like "oppressor" and "oppressed," as those roles could be found in any community.

Hamdard therefore implored all communities to struggle against "hunger, poverty, oppression and exploitation." Prem Nath Bazaz's 1936 article "Meaning of Nationalism" asked Kashmiri Muslims to keep away from religious parties that exploited religion to "bind the poor in the chains of slavery and ignorance."[92] Instead, Kashmiris should emulate countries like Egypt, Syria, and Iraq that prioritized secular nationalism over a theocratic state. Bazaz praised the Egyptian nationalist leader Saad Zaghloul for taking his country along the path of modernity and parliamentary democracy. Zaghloul not only excluded religion from politics, but also worked with diverse minority communities to build a strong Egyptian nation. Bazaz appealed to Kashmiri Pandits to model their politics along lines similar to Egypt's Christian Copts, who had defied British attempts to sow dissension, preferring to stand beside Egyptian Muslims. These actions had enabled them to emerge from the sidelines and play an important part in Egyptian politics.[93]

Kashmiri progressives like Bazaz worked tirelessly toward the secularization of Kashmir's politics and the promotion of Hindu–Muslim unity, a goal shared by many on the left. In 1936, Bazaz formed the Kashmir Youth League, representing "young elements from all communities, professing different religions," to struggle for a responsible government that would ensure economic, social, and cultural regeneration.[94] Placing the Kashmiri struggle in the context of the wider struggles for freedom taking place in other countries, the Youth League demonstrated solidarity with the 1936 Palestinian revolt against British colonial rule, criticizing its draconian imperialist suppression.[95] Youth League activists wanted Kashmiris to understand that resistance movements in other parts of the world stemmed not from religious differences, but from the forces of imperialism that curb the life prospects of the powerless.[96] With the support of various student bodies, the Youth League popularized the theory of class struggle and brought together individuals with leftist leanings from both Muslim and non-Muslim communities.

This period also coincided with the entry of communist leaders from India into the Valley, especially B. P. L. Bedi, Freda Bedi, and K. M. Ashraf. Communist activists established contacts with Kashmiri leaders and encouraged them to include workers and laborers in their movement. Although the Muslim Conference had rhetorically highlighted the challenges of the laboring classes, it had failed to bring about an organized labor movement. Credit for organizing laborers into trade unions went instead to Kashmiri communists who organized small associations representing occupations as diverse as drivers, boatmen, carpet-makers, and shawl weavers. In 1936, G. M. Sadiq, a Kashmiri communist political activist, brought these small unions under the banner of a single organization, the Mazdoor Sabha. Membership was open to all, and it emphasized respect for all religions.[97] The organization's goal was to end the disparities that existed between the capitalists and workers, rather than to claim a "fair share" of jobs for each religious community.[98]

The trade union movement appealed to workers suffering as a result of the Great Depression of the 1930s. The Depression meant adverse conditions for Kashmiri handicrafts industries like shawl and carpet weaving due to plummeting demand in the world market. Discontent grew among Kashmiri artisans, many of whom lost their jobs and found few alternative sources of employment. The Mazdoor Sabha emerged as their advocate and warned the government that no peace was possible in a country with high unemployment.[99] The Muslim Conference appropriated the rhetoric and organizational force of these labor movements and passed resolutions asking the government to improve labor conditions. Red banners and flags, the symbol of workers' revolutions, adorned the streets of Srinagar, and secular rather than religious slogans became the norm at every public gathering.

Secular progressive discourse was not confined to imploring Hindus and Muslims to unite around shared concerns. Many educated Kashmiris with leftist leanings, both Hindu and Muslim, wanted to mold their regional struggle on the secular-socialist ideas of the Indian National Congress. Prem Nath Bazaz, for example, participated in the annual Congress session at Lahore in 1930. He established contact with the prominent Congress leader Jawaharlal Nehru, who advised him that the local struggle in Kashmir "must be viewed in the light of the Indian struggle" as the "fate of Kashmir was bound up with India"—an ominous statement in light of the developments after partition.[100] Throughout the mid-1930s, Kashmiri activists debated the political role and impact of the two parties, the Congress and the Muslim League, operating at an all-India level. Most articles and editorials in *Hamdard* attempted to link Kashmir's politics with wider Congress goals. They presented Congress as a party focused on removing disparities between the rich and poor, and praised Congress leaders who sacrificed their lives for India's freedom from British imperialism.

Conversely, articles critical of the Muslim League, the party formed to protect the interests of Muslim minorities in India, represented the League as a party that only protected elite interests and demonstrated no efforts to bring economic freedom and social justice to the people at large. As the Muslim League distanced itself from popular movements for responsible government in the princely states, *Hamdard* advised Kashmiris to stay away from this party of "landed elites" and "rich business groups" with zero interest in bringing economic prosperity to downtrodden Kashmiris.[101] In 1937, Abdullah met Nehru at Lahore railway station, where the Congress leader insisted that a broad-based movement shaped by the ideals of secularism, socialism, and egalitarian society would be in the best interests of Kashmiris.[102] Impressed by Nehru, who was leading the All India States People's Conference, an organization that urged the princely states to introduce democratic representative governments, Abdullah took this advice to heart and decided to expand the Kashmiri rights movement.

This close contact between Abdullah and the Congress leaders came to fruition in the late 1930s, when the Sheikh wanted to emerge as a "nationalist" leader representing all communities. In his presidential address at the sixth annual session of the Muslim Conference, held in Jammu in March 1938, Abdullah emphasized that every subject of the maharaja—whether Hindu, Sikh, Buddhist, or Muslim—who had suffered under the present regime should get an opportunity to join in the struggle for a responsible government. He corrected the misconception among the Muslim community that all non-Muslims lived a life of comfort, providing examples of poor non-Muslims who also struggled against inequalities.[103] Despite his party's name, his demand for responsible government was not only on behalf of the majority of the Kashmiri population who were Muslims, but for all inhabitants of the state.

The Muslim Conference followed up this speech by issuing a manifesto entitled "National Demand." The document emphasized that their movement was one of peace and goodwill, aimed at securing elementary rights of citizenship. They wanted the maharaja to commit to a Jammu and Kashmir legislature that would consist entirely of members elected by all adults, with representation provided to workers and traders. Elections to the legislature would be based on joint electorates and minorities would be provided safeguards and weightages to ensure their representation. To ratify the manifesto, the Muslim Conference organized meetings and processions in various parts of Srinagar city. The Dogra state clamped down on these demonstrations and arrested top leaders of the Muslim Conference, including Sheikh Abdullah, provoking a renewed statewide agitation.[104]

An interesting dynamic of the new agitation was the Hindu community's decision to abstain from participating in strikes and demonstrations, despite efforts made by a few members of the community to show solidarity with the Muslim Conference. Eighteen non-Muslim members of the legislative assembly representing Jammu province issued a joint statement rejecting the National Demand manifesto since it did not represent the interests of the Pandit community. Acceptance of the Muslim Conference's "demand," they argued, would mean acceptance of Muslim rule.[105] Yuvak Sabha, the Kashmiri Pandit organization, considered the association of a few non-Muslims insufficient to give the movement a national character.[106] With most non-Muslims hesitating to support a political system that would transfer power to the Muslim majority, their aloofness created concerns among some Muslim Conference members that the minority community would always align with the Dogra state because their economic and political interests were protected under the status quo.[107]

Meanwhile, however, Abdullah continued to forge close contacts with the Indian National Congress, even presiding over one of the meetings held at the party's annual session at Tripura. In his speech, he assured the Congress that the Muslim Conference movement against the maharaja stemmed from economic issues, rather than "communal" motives.[108] In June 1939, a special session of the All Jammu and Kashmir Muslim Conference met at Pather Masjid, Srinagar, to change the name of the party from "Muslim" to "National," widening the scope of Kashmir's rights movement and including all religions and classes in its fold. Whereas the old Muslim Conference had demanded rights for Muslims from a Hindu government, the National Conference would couch its demands in terms of class.[109]

Not all Muslim Conference members were thrilled; some feared that it would become merely a local branch of the all-India party, although several acquiesced under pressure from Abdullah. Chaudhry Ghulam Abbas supported the resolution, but clarified that his support depended on an assurance that the National Conference would never submerge itself into the Congress.[110] Others were dead-set against this change and remained convinced that the name change would undermine Muslim interests, since the community was not yet politically mature enough to protect its own interests.[111] Chaudhry Hamidullah Khan, an important Muslim Conference member from Jammu, opposed the resolution on the ground that non-Muslims (who formed 20 percent of the population and held 90 percent of the government service positions) would not cooperate with Muslims. Hindu–Muslim unity was impossible, Khan felt, because Hindus held an advantageous position in the power structures. He added that those Kashmiri Pandits who had joined the Conference's ranks did not command the confidence of their community, saying:

> There can be no unity between the weak and the strong. They cannot march together. In Jammu we have Hindu money-lender while Muslims constitute

> the poor peasantry. Unity among them is impossible. Rajput's pride themselves to be rulers, they do not, therefore, feel any need for unity; that is why no other nation is coming forward by inch [*sic*]. How then are you going ahead by changing your own organization?[112]

Out of the 176 delegates of the Muslim Conference, 3 voted against and 3 walked out in protest. Despite Abdullah's hopes, the conversion of the Muslim Conference into the National Conference failed to bring Kashmiris together; ironically, it deepened the wedge within and between communities instead.

Failed Nationalism? Muslim Conference, National Conference, and the Minorities

Nationalist ideology was introduced into public debate in Kashmir as a way to ensure responsible government and proper representation of all communities in the state administration. Yet the demand for a responsible government failed to bridge conflicting political positions in the princely state of Jammu and Kashmir. Although Kashmiri nationalism drew on Western democratic ideals of responsible government, to popularize the concept outside the small circle of Western-educated elites, Muslim leaders continued to associate with religious festivals, shrines, and mosques. As Christopher Bayly has argued, Indian nationalism was widely rooted in society and "molded by ideologies, political norms and social organizations which derived from deeper indigenous inheritance."[113] Similarly, Kashmiri nationalism was built more from the region's social complexion than from discourses derivative of Western nationalism.

Abdullah not only used Quranic verses to mobilize popular support, but drew on older Kashmiri mystic religious traditions to spread his message, especially in rural areas. In one of his speeches, he linked the idea of "freedom" with ethics, humanism, and brotherhood, all concepts inherent in early Kashmiri texts and integral to a society greatly influenced by Islamic mystic traditions. Abdullah painted the Kashmiri struggle as a war between the forces of good and evil, which he defined as "all undesirable elements of human life such as slavery, poverty, ignorance, illiteracy and various other causes of human miseries."[114] The struggle for freedom, he wrote, could only succeed if ordinary men developed strong character, expressed love toward humanity, and endured suffering patiently. The spiritual struggle to be human remained the key component of Kashmiri freedom.

With Kashmiri society deeply aware of its religious sensibilities, Sheikh Abdullah and his political cohorts focused on religious terminology and other existing forms of speech and sentiment to mobilize the masses in support of Western concepts like nationalism. Maulana Masoodi, a close associate of Abdullah, explained that integrated national action to pursue a set political goal was in consonance with the tenets of the Holy Quran. The Quran imposes on Muslims the responsibility of cooperating with non-Muslims to attain a common goal—such as, Masoodi argued, a responsible government in Kashmir: "God had ordained Prophet Muhammad that those non-Muslims who sought to enter into an alliance with Muslims should be permitted to do so." He extensively quoted the Treaty of Hudaybiyyah, signed between Muslims representing the state of Medina and non-Muslims representing the Quraysh tribe of Mecca, which ended animosities between the two cities and allowed Muslims to return to Mecca to perform the annual pilgrimage.[115] These examples, and Abdullah's equation of "nationalism" with the mystical concepts of "unity and brotherhood," helped him convince his mostly illiterate Kashmiri Muslim base to support his efforts to unite majority and minority communities in pursuit of responsible government.

To make nationalism a success, Abdullah emphasized mutual tolerance between Hindus and Muslims, which he later claimed as evidence of his secularism. He refused, however, to consign religion to a private sphere. His essay "It Is Not Right to Subordinate Politics to Religion in the Light of Islam" did not deny the affinity between politics and religion, but, rather, gave an entirely different interpretation of this relationship. Abdullah argued that the fundamental aspect of Islam is *din*, the ethical side of religion, and not ritual practices. As the ethical side of religion teaches compassion, love, equality, and justice, the application of ethics to politics cannot create communitarian differences; on the contrary, it helps transcend divisions and works for the welfare of all. If religion in this sense is removed from politics, it would lead to anarchy and injustice. In Abdullah's perception, therefore, there was no contradiction between Muslim and nationalist identities. Being a nationalist did not mean that "Muslims should abandon their religious traditions," as every Muslim or Hindu could become a true nationalist or a perfect patriot without "turning their back on their religion."[116] Abdullah explained that movements of national struggles sometimes appear in the guise of religion because religion makes for the most effective appeal to human emotions.[117]

Nationalism and religious symbolism became intertwined in twentieth-century Kashmir. Abdullah used Friday services for political mobilization and participated in religious festivals like Milad-ul-Nabi, the birthday of the Prophet, and Miraj-ul-Alam, the day commemorating the heavenly journey in which the Prophet reached the presence of God, at the Hazratbal mosque, in order to establish ties with both urban and rural Kashmiris.[118] Abdullah's instrumental adaptation of nationalism to touch cultural and religious sensibilities was, as was typical for him at this time, aimed at reaching as wide an audience as possible.

Nationalist ideology, however, instead of uniting Kashmir and forging a responsible government, exposed the tensions within and between communities. Some members of the Kashmiri Pandit community, although apprehensive about Abdullah's motivations in creating the National Conference, did decide to join the party and take part in shaping the National Demand. Pandit Jialal Kilam, an important member of the minority community, tried to assuage its fears, promising that non-Muslim support of the National Demand would not lead to a transfer of power to Muslims; even after the creation of a responsible government, the Hindu maharaja would still exercise real power. The options before the Kashmiri Hindu community, he argued, were either to support the National Conference, which was closer to the Congress Party, or to let the Muslim League, a party that wanted the division of India, to establish a foothold in the Valley.[119]

The non-Muslim members of the National Conference, however, felt uncomfortable with Abdullah's continued association with Muslim symbols, mosques, and shrines. They questioned his commitment to secular nationalism and asked him to disassociate from the maintenance of shrines, as he was theoretically now leading a "National" organization and not a "Muslim" one. Abdullah rejected this criticism, questioning the double standards of Hindu party members who had no reservations about the Congress's use of Hindu symbols to mobilize the masses, but considered a similar strategy by Abdullah to be evidence of Muslim "communalism."[120] The tensions between Muslim and non-Muslim National Conference members disillusioned Prem Nath Bazaz, once an ardent Congress supporter, who now expressed dejection about how members of his own community had interpreted Congress "nationalism." He wrote:

> In trying to bring National Conference under the hegemony of the Congress leaders, the Hindu and the Sikh members were not prompted by any burning desire of freedom or even by wish to secularize state politics. They only felt happy that by doing so they were helping the cause of India nationalism, which despite the statements of Congress leaders to the contrary, was becoming another name for Hindu nationalism. Clearly it was the promoting of the communal mentality of the Hindus which was cleverly presented in a nationalist secular garb.[121]

Concepts like "nationalism" and "communalism" dominated the political discourse of the 1930s and 1940s. Ayesha Jalal has dismantled the misconception that these positions were binary opposites. The term "communal" was associated with those who did not belong to the Congress and articulated a politics of Muslim interest. Conversely, "unity of religion and politics at the level of discourse and pro-Congress national activity" was considered a nationalist position.[122] In the context of Kashmir both Hindus and Muslims considered the other "communal" for supporting their communitarian social, political, and economic interests. While Kashmiri Pandits considered Abdullah's articulation of "Muslim interests" in pursuit of power politics an expression of Muslim communalism, Kashmiri Muslims considered that their own politics, even when motivated solely by a desire to protect their communitarian interests, were an example of true nationalism, while labeling Kashmiri Hindus "communalists" for resisting the National Conference's political vision.

Distrust between the majority and minority communities in the Valley stemmed from fears and apprehensions about being dominated, politically and culturally, by the "other."[123] The Kashmiri Muslim community resented Kashmiri Hindus' resistance to their demands for equal rights and questioned their support for the maharaja; however, the minority community believed the "nationalism" of the National Conference was a façade for majority rule to their own detriment. As a member of the majority community and the leader of a nationalist party, the onus remained on Abdullah to find a way to gain the confidence of the minorities.

One missed opportunity for Abdullah to emerge as a representative of all communities came up during the Devanagari–Persian script controversy of the 1940s. Persian had been the state's official language for centuries and educated Kashmiris, both Hindu and Muslim, spoke and wrote it fluently. In 1898, Maharaja Pratap Singh "replaced Persian with Urdu as the official language, to benefit Punjabi Hindus" who held key posts in the administration and facilitate importing even more Punjabis. In the 1940s, the Dogra state decided to introduce the Devanagari script, in addition to the Persian script, for writing Hindustani. The official argument was that although Hindustani in Persian script was the state's official language, the state had to consider the reality that non-Muslims were more attracted to Sanskrit or Hindi. The government appointed a committee to consider the medium of instruction in state schools, which recommended against the introduction of two scripts on the grounds that this would encourage "separatist tendencies." The government went ahead regardless, issuing an order that the state language should be common Hindustani but written in two scripts. Students would have the option to choose either script, but teachers without knowledge of both scripts could not seek employment. Kashmiri Muslims resented this decision, as their representation in the education department had recently risen to 40 percent, but almost none of them were acquainted with the Devanagari script.[124]

The language question gave Muslim members of the National Conference an opportunity to gain minority trust by presenting a compromise solution acceptable to both communities. Prem Nath Bazaz suggested making knowledge of both scripts compulsory for all students and teachers; Abdullah rejected this suggestion, condemning it as ill-conceived. For Abdullah, taking a position on the language question contrary to the interests of the Muslim community meant damaging his support base. The National Conference organized protests and demonstrations in mosques and shrines against the decision to make Devanagari script necessary for employment in the education department. Extremely disappointed with the Muslim members of the National Conference, Bazaz, one of the Conference's main architects, saw this protest as "as a betrayal to the social, economic and spiritual emancipation of the motherland."[125] He distanced himself from both the National Conference and the Congress, both of which, he now believed, exploited religion for political ends.

After the language controversy, non-Muslims were convinced that they could not trust the National Conference to safeguard their cultural and linguistic interests. The National Demand had guaranteed protection of minorities' legitimate religious, cultural, and economic rights. An article in *The Tribune* stated: "Do the Muslim members stand by the National Demand? If so, may we enquire if their attitude on the script question is consistent with the assurance contained in the demand?"[126] Almost all Pandits disassociated from the National Conference, considering the Dogra ruler the protector of their community's interests. The inability of the National Conference's Hindu and Muslim members to put aside their fears of the other and arrive at a compromise power-sharing solution led to the failure of nationalism as a solution for Kashmir's problems.

Moreover, the criticism leveled against the National Conference was not the exclusive province of non-Muslims; some urban Muslims in the Valley and Jammu also disagreed with Abdullah's politics and offered a tough resistance to the "nationalist" creed. They saw its adoption as a step towards bringing Kashmiri politics into the wider orbit of the Indian National Congress, and felt that it would ultimately lead to Hindu domination. Some Muslims who had resisted the formation of the National Conference revived the old Muslim Conference in 1941, after Abdullah failed to unite the various religious communities within Jammu and Kashmir. Jammu Muslims, with a few exceptions, had not supported the formation of the National Conference in the first place. The idea of nationalism did not appeal to them; the prevalence of Hindu rightist organizations in Jammu and Punjab made them insecure, heightening their need for an explicitly Muslim party to protect their interests. Although Chaudhry Ghulam Abbas, an important leader from Jammu, had joined the National Conference, there was always pressure on him to leave the party; in 1940, Abbas resigned without offering any explanation, and in 1942 he lent his public support to the revival of the Muslim Conference.[127]

The leaders of the new Muslim Conference were landed elite and educated middle-class Kashmiris, with very few, if any, coming from the countryside. During the 1940s the party focused on protecting Muslim elite interests. Its grievances against the Dogra state included an increase in the percentage of Hindu representation in the cabinet and state services; the "lack of trust" shown toward Muslim employees; and the promulgation of the Arms Act, which allowed Rajput Hindus to keep firearms but placed restrictions on firearm possession for other communities. [128] The party also demanded the repeal of the penal code's cow-killing provision. Politically, the Muslim Conference decided to align with the Muslim League and offered its full support to the demand for the state of Pakistan.

Personal rivalries and diverging approaches to politics in Jammu and Kashmir caused conflicts between the Muslim Conference and the National Conference. Criticism and condemnation of the National Conference in the early 1940s made its leaders intolerant of any opposition. Street battles between supporters of Abdullah and Mirwaiz Yusuf Shah, who had broken with Abdullah in 1932, became a daily routine.[129] In Jammu province the popularity of the National Conference declined after members from the localities of Mirpur, Poonch, and Rajouri tendered their resignations and joined the Muslim Conference. In 1944, Chaudhry Ghulam Abbas even appealed to Abdullah to join the Muslim Conference, as the National Conference was still failing to emerge as a widely representative body.[130] Thereafter, Abdullah and his close associates established contact with Muhammad Ali Jinnah, the president of the All India Muslim League, hoping he could bring about a compromise between the two warring political parties in Kashmir.[131]

In the mid-1940s, the Muslim League under Jinnah emerged as a powerful organization demanding a Muslim state of Pakistan. Both rival parties from the princely state of Jammu and Kashmir extended invitations to Jinnah to visit the state, and provided him a warm welcome when he came. Abdullah offered to acknowledge the Muslim League's superiority over the Congress at an all-India level, but in return sought a policy of neutrality on the part of the League as far as the Muslim Conference and National Conference were concerned.[132] Jinnah refused to oblige. Instead, in his address at the annual session of the Muslim Conference, Jinnah criticized the inherent contradictions within the National Conference, claiming that it replicated Nehru's Congress Party. Both claimed to represent all communities, while in reality the National Conference remained a Muslim party, just as the Congress was a representative body of Hindus. He wanted the Muslim community in Jammu and Kashmir state to give up this "politics of deception," as it had only divided them into two camps.[133] Jinnah's complete support for the Muslim Conference caused an irreversible drift of the National Conference away from the Muslim League, with far-reaching repercussions on Kashmir's future history. However, due to its largely ineffective leadership, the Muslim Conference failed to capitalize on Jinnah's open support to build a mass base.[134] Instead Abdullah, challenged on all fronts, reached out to rural Kashmiris with a new "communist" vision to become a beacon of hope for the impoverished and politically disenfranchised.

Communists, Critics, and the Question of Self-determination in Agrarian Kashmir

In the 1940s, the agrarian question shaped the concept of emancipation. Under the influence of Indian communists, the National Conference presented an image of Kashmir free from social and economic hierarchies. Although the economic rhetoric of the nationalists allowed extension of their support base in rural Kashmir to counteract their falling popularity among educated urban Kashmiris, the elite classes and communities threatened by their radical vision for a free Kashmir launched a virulent critique. Here I trace how Kashmiri activists weaved socialist and communist ideas into their discourses on economic freedom, presenting a vision of a free and prosperous Kashmir, which mesmerized the ordinary peasantry.

Communist influence in Kashmir's politics had been visible since 1937 in the various trade unions later appropriated by the National Conference. However, communists found it difficult to penetrate religious Kashmiri society. Instead of starting a party branch in the state, it seemed prudent to infiltrate established student and political bodies like the Student Federation, Youth League, and the National Conference.[135] Communist activity in the Valley increased during the Second World War, especially after the Russo-German alliance against the Allies. The British government in India was suspicious of communist leaders' activities, forcing some to take refuge in the Valley. Niranjan Nath Raina, a Kashmiri Hindu trained at different communist centers in India, succeeded in organizing the "Study Circle" and the "Free Thinkers Association," a nuclei of local intellectuals who met to discuss and debate Marxism and Leninism in the context of Kashmir. The New Kashmiri Bookshop became a venue for the distribution of Marxist literature to educated Kashmiris.[136] In the mid-1940s, however, communist influence was most visible in the National Conference's *Naya Kashmir*, or "New Kashmir," manifesto. Abdullah presented a blueprint for a free Kashmir where peasants would be masters of their own lands and have the power to shape their own destinies. This vision, Abdullah hoped, would bring both peasantry and laborers into the fold of the National Conference.[137]

In the years leading up to 1947, the National Conference addressed economic issues faced by the masses, promised progressive social change, and proved itself a dynamic agent of political mobilization in rural Kashmir, as compared to the more stagnant and elitist Muslim Conference. In 1944, party delegates adopted the Bolshevist-inspired *Naya Kashmir* to explain the meaning of freedom to peasants and laborers. The manifesto provided a new vision for modern Kashmir. In its introduction, Abdullah paid tribute to Russia for demonstrating not merely theoretically but practically that "real freedom takes birth only from economic emancipation." The manifesto laid out the concept of popular sovereignty, noting that if sovereignty lies with the people, then states cannot ignore the aspirations of the masses. It then provided a constitutional framework for a free Kashmir: a representative legislature called the National Assembly, a cabinet government, and decentralized governance in the subregions.[138] However, its most significant points related to the abolition of feudal structures, especially land grants. It promised that land would be taken away from landlords without compensation and distributed among peasants. The concluding section elaborated on social schemes, including a charter for the rights of women. In sum, this document defined emancipation as political rights, economic freedom, and social justice.[139]

Socialist and communist currents seeped into the mainstream imagination of poets, writers, and intellectuals as they conceived a forthcoming revolution. Nationalists could explain the contents of *Naya Kashmir* to the peasantry in public forums organized for other purposes. Community gatherings around shrines or religious fairs became an important medium for making economic freedom part of the public dialogue. Literary discourse in Kashmir now centered on economic disparities and social discontent, imploring Kashmiris to end the feudal hierarchies that separated the rich from the poor. In one poem, Ghulam Mahjoor wrote:

Oh, workers and peasantry, unite
Seek rights, leave begging and praying to Jagirdars
Stand to break the chains of obsolete customs and conventions
Be not melancholic, brothers rejoice
We shall soon be free,
Freedom shall bring prosperity
We shall soon be free[140]

The idea of deeding land to its tiller made Abdullah extremely popular among the peasantry. He sought to make the National Conference a party of laborers and peasants, rather than of a rich elite. To ingratiate himself with this base, Abdullah adopted a red flag, signifying labor, with a plough representing the Kashmiri peasantry. The popular slogan "when the plough moves it tears the enemy apart" fired the imagination of the masses. In a 1945 speech, Abdullah rejoiced:

> An agitation is launched against the National Conference that it is supported only by the workers, the laborers, the peasants, and the poor. Its opponents claim that they are supported by the aristocratic classes and the big capitalists. I am extremely happy to know that our opponents have now realized the truth that we (National Conference) have hungry and naked peasants and toiling masses with us, while big capitalists feed themselves on the sweat and blood of these hungry and naked Kashmiris.[141]

The *Naya Kashmir* manifesto drew criticism from both Muslim Conference elites and Kashmiri Pandits, who each opposed the socialist promise of "land to the tiller." The Kashmiri Pandit community further rejected *Naya Kashmir* as a "communal" document prepared without consulting the state's minorities. They refused to accept any assembly or government in which one community, on the basis of its majority strength, could dominate the minority. Kashmiri Pandit leadership pointed out that Muslims had persistently demanded a change in the cow slaughter law and the Hindu law of inheritance. The National Conference's opposition to Hindi as a medium of instruction was another example of their "communal approach." Kashmiri Pandits, however, would support a government under the aegis of the maharaja, within which Muslims and non-Muslims would have equal power. The Kashmiri Hindu community continued to believe that a Muslim-majority government would jeopardize their cultural and economic interests.[142]

The *Naya Kashmir* manifesto faced its strongest challenge from individuals like Prem Nath Bazaz, who succeeded in organizing peasant resistance against the National Conference in 1945 and 1946. After his fallout with Abdullah over the scripts controversy, Bazaz distanced himself from the ideologies of nationalism and communalism, which he considered exclusionary and sources of division. Instead, M. N. Roy's radical humanism, which sought rationality and critical analysis of modes of domination, inspired Bazaz to seek to create a healthy society of morally and spiritually liberated individuals, as a fundamental requirement for Kashmir's progress.[143] Such a humanistic society would be a spiritual community "not limited by the boundaries of nationalism, capitalism, or fascism."[144]

Bazaz reached out to the literate classes in rural Kashmir, and in 1946 he formed the Jammu and Kashmir Kissan Conference to propagate "scientific education on politics"—free from the "taints of communalism and nationalism"—to the masses.[145] Presided over by Abdul Salam Yatu, a young educated Kashmiri peasant from Anantnag, its goal was to alter the existing social order.[146] Although the National Conference claimed to represent the "toiling masses," it was led by elites. On the contrary, the Kissan Conference claimed to be the true representative of the masses, drawing both its supporters and its leaders from the peasantry. The Kissan Conference emphasized the struggle to free Kashmiris from the bondage of "indigenous feudalism and capitalism." To usher in a new society, it was imperative to maintain distance from the elite-driven politics of the Muslim League and the Congress Party. Only when Kashmiris had attained the twin objectives of social equality and economic justice would they decide whether they wanted to "preserve the unity of the country or divide it."[147] The growing popularity of the Kissan Conference in certain areas of rural Kashmir made National Conference leaders bitter toward the new party. Notorious for their lack of tolerance for any opposition, the National Conference disrupted Kissan Conference meetings and harassed its supporters.

As challenges to the domination of the National Conference increased, Abdullah turned to revolutionary rhetoric to regain mass popularity.[148] In 1946, he submitted a memorandum to the Cabinet Mission sent by the British government to India to evolve a formula, with the consent of both the Congress and the Muslim League, for a transfer of power to Indians. The memorandum demanded not only the establishment of a responsible government in the state of Jammu and Kashmir, but the right to "absolute freedom from autocratic rule of the Dogra house."[149] It added that the Dogra ruler had no moral right to rule over the people of Kashmir because the East India Company had sold them, along with the territory of Kashmir, to Gulab Singh for seventy-five lakh rupees.[150] After the British withdrew from India, the memorandum insisted, "sovereignty must revert to the people and not to the state ruler." This rhetoric reappeared the same year in Abdullah's Quit Kashmir movement, which centered on the injustices suffered by Kashmiris at the hands of successive foreign dynasties that had treated them like slaves.[151] Every speech condemned Dogra rule as alien, comparable to that of the Sikhs, Pathans, and Mughals. Abdullah implored Kashmiris to break the chains of slavery and emerge free and victorious. This revolutionary rhetoric, representing the regional aspirations of Kashmiri-speaking Muslims, appealed to people's sentiments and turned the tide of public opinion in the Valley in favor of the National Conference. The Dogra government, less enthused, arrested Abdullah and curbed the Quit Kashmir resistance with arrests, injuries, and deaths.[152]

During this phase of repression, the Muslim Conference initially pursued a policy of outright opposition to the Quit Kashmir movement, asserting that the Congress Party was guiding the movement.[153] Ironically, the movement that the Muslim Conference was condemning as "Congress inspired" received complete support from the pro-Pakistan Muslim press of Punjab. Maulana Zafar Ali Khan, a prominent member of the Muslim League, wrote a poem in praise of the Quit Kashmir movement in the *Zamindar*, an Urdu newspaper published from Lahore.

> It is once again the season of arrests
> And once again, Kashmir's wound has become fresh
> The air is resonating once again with the clang of chains
> In which are drowned the shouts of "God is great!"[154]

To prove that the Muslim Conference was just as defiant against the Dogra regime as the National Conference, Chaudhry Ghulam Abbas conducted an annual session of the party at Srinagar in October 1946, despite a government ban on holding such meetings. This led to mass arrests of Muslim Conference leaders, removing them from the political stage at a critical time in Kashmir's history.[155] The state's Hindu community, meanwhile, also resisted the Quit Kashmir movement,[156] especially Abdullah's interpretation of the Treaty of Amritsar as a "sale deed" that allowed the Dogras to illegitimately control Kashmir's territory. The general secretary of the All State Kashmiri Pandit Conference, Shiv Narayan Fotedar, considered this a misstatement of historical facts. The sum paid to the English East India Company by Gulab Singh, he argued, was in the form of war indemnity, and thus could not be considered a sale deed. Fotedar emphasized that Pandits did not consider the maharaja an autocrat but in fact found the state of Jammu and Kashmir more progressive and constitutionally advanced than other Indian princely states.[157]

Even Congress leaders did not support the Quit Kashmir movement, since it aimed to remove a Hindu ruler from power. The press in India condemned the movement as reckless and ill-conceived.[158] The Congress Party distanced itself from Abdullah and pressed him to call off this "mischievous move" against the Dogra monarchy. Jawaharlal Nehru was the only Congress leader who condemned the repressive Dogra administration and offered complete support to the Quit Kashmir movement. But Nehru clarified that his support for Quit Kashmir stemmed from his emotional bonds with Kashmir due to his Kashmiri heritage, rather than from the Congress Party's policies.[159]

Clearly, though the Congress did not generally support him, Nehru was aware that in any future political agreement between Kashmir and India, Abdullah's support remained critical. Nehru addressed several letters and telegrams to the maharaja, impressing upon him the need to release Abdullah. He personally went to the Valley, despite a ban on his entry by state authorities, and in a symbolic gesture appeared in a trial court as a lawyer to defend Abdullah. Despite this robust defense, Abdullah was jailed for three years, and the National Conference remained a banned and suppressed organization until India's independence.[160] Events moved quickly, however. By the time of the Indian Independence Act, partition had become an imminent fact. While the creation of India and Pakistan consumed the South Asian subcontinent in a religious frenzy, Abbas and Abdullah, the two Kashmiri political rivals, remained incarcerated.

Revolt, Violence, and Tribal Invasion: The Beginning of the Sovereignty Dispute

The partition of the South Asian subcontinent enhanced tensions between the inhabitants of the princely state of Jammu and Kashmir divided along religious, linguistic, and regional lines, who claimed multiple visions for free Jammu and Kashmir. There was a great degree of ambiguity about the future status of Jammu and Kashmir; the leadership seemed uncertain whether to align with India, Pakistan, or remain independent. While the Valley's print media expounded the idea of freedom to include spiritual regeneration, social justice, and economic reconstruction, the violence and bloodshed that accompanied partition made it difficult for communities to ignore the new political constructs of India and Pakistan, both eyeing Kashmir's territory with vested interests.

In August 1947, the existence of 565 princely states, which covered 48 percent of India's territory and which despite lacking external sovereignty had enjoyed freedom to rule arbitrarily in their states during British rule, created a new set of complications. The Congress feared that the lapse of British paramountcy over the princely states could lead to the balkanization of India, as some princely states might assert their right to opt out of the union. India therefore decided to forego full independence and accept dominion status within the British Commonwealth, foreclosing the option of independence for the princely states.[161]

Lord Mountbatten, in a special session of the Chamber of Princes on July 25, 1947, explained to the princes that the Indian Independence Act released "the states from all their obligations to the crown," technically making them independent. However, he urged the princes to accede to either India or Pakistan on issues of defense, foreign affairs, and communications; maintaining national security and foreign relations would prove an arduous and financially crippling endeavor for the small princely states.[162] As most of these were landlocked within India, Mountbatten strongly suggested that the princes should accept the Congress's accession offer, which left the rulers "with great internal authority while divesting them of subjects they could not deal with on their own."[163]

Sardar Patel, the deputy prime minister of independent India, along with V. P. Menon, a secretary at the Ministry of States, worked tirelessly to persuade princes to integrate with India by providing them with large annual privy purses, permitting retention of titles and property, and appointing some as *rajpramukhs*—the equivalent of governors in the newly created Indian union.[164] Once all the princely states had acceded on defense, foreign affairs, and communication, India amended the instrument of accession and established direct control.[165] In most cases, the geographical location of the princely state predetermined the decision. In states that bordered both new countries, the princes took population composition into consideration.[166] However, the princely state of Jammu and Kashmir posed special challenges. It was the only princely state geographically contiguous with both India and Pakistan where a Hindu house ruled over a Muslim-majority population.

On the advice of his ministers, Maharaja Hari Singh agreed that the princely state of Jammu and Kashmir should be independent, as accession to either of the new nation-states would have cost him his throne. This vision of an independent Jammu and Kashmir created considerable apprehensions for Nehru and the Congress. Jammu and Kashmir had become a symbol of the Congress's secular ideal, a refutation of the two-nation theory of Jinnah and his Muslim League.[167] By showing that a Muslim-majority area was prepared to remain in India of its own free will, Nehru could demonstrate the validity of the Congress position; so he was very keen to mold the maharaja's thinking.[168] However, the maharaja avoided making any final decision. Instead, he signed a standstill agreement with Pakistan in August 1947, obligating Pakistan to supply food and other necessities. The maharaja's request for a "similar agreement with India was neither accepted nor rejected."[169] His subjects, however, representing different communities and sub-regions, expressed strong and differing desires about their political future after the termination of British paramountcy.

In defining their visions of freedom at the moment of independence, public discourse in the Valley focused on the concepts of social justice and economic equity, rather than political association with either India or Pakistan. Kashmiri poets wrote inspiring poems hoping for the transformation of exploitative feudal structures within Jammu and Kashmir and the creation of social justice for the downtrodden. Some poets equated freedom with an end to "religious bigotry" and asked Kashmiris to usher in a new society, where "religion" would not become a tool to create dissension and keep the poor subjugated. In a "crusade against religious fanaticism," the famous Kashmiri poet Abdul Ahad Azad wrote:

> In this vast expanse of oneness, who is my kin and who is stranger to me;
> A Muslim is to me as good as a Hindu
> My *deen* (religion) is fraternity, my *dharma* (faith) is oneness,
> My light is meant for one and all....[170]

At the same time, *Hamdard* urged Kashmiris to broaden their definitions of "freedom" beyond the limited notions of "nationalism" and "communalism" articulated by the rival Congress and Muslim League, since both ideologies had created discord, rather than unity.[171] Prem Nath Bazaz urged Kashmiris to strive for "human freedom," based on self-reliance and open mindedness. Real emancipation, Bazaz argued, would allow critical understanding of political issues and free Kashmiris from bias and prejudice. To gain real freedom, with equal rights for all communities, Kashmiris should demonstrate patriotism toward their homeland but distance themselves from any nationalism that breeds "inequality, excludes minorities, and deprives people of legitimate rights."[172]

Other *Hamdard* articles emphasized that political freedom, even if guaranteed constitutionally, could not last long without economic freedom. Despite natural resources like timber, water, and minerals which gave Kashmir immense development potential, the region suffered from economic backwardness. One editorial agreed that the abolition of land grants suggested by the National Conference's *Naya Kashmir* manifesto would reduce poverty. However, the author disagreed with the National Conference's plan to nationalize land and industries, which would concentrate power in fewer hands and create a totalitarian regime. Such experiments in Russia's industrial sector had not portended freedom, the author argued, but necessitated ruthless administration and the denial of political and democratic rights to dissidents. Nationalization had made the dictatorship of the proletariat into the dictatorship of the communist party. The author also, however, expressed his antipathy for capitalist economies that exploit workers and benefit the rich. Instead he suggested a "co-operative economy," with decentralized political and economic structures, to ensure equity and justice.[173]

The economic and social aspects of freedom also dominated *Khidmat*, the official mouthpiece of Abdullah's National Conference. Instead of taking a clear-cut position about the state's political future, Abdullah appeared ambivalent, asking Kashmiris to focus instead on economic freedom. Abdullah's political views on partition found expression in a series of articles he wrote in 1946. One of these, "Thoughts on Pakistan," considered the idea of a separate Muslim-majority area a fallacy; it would not rescue Muslims from Hindu domination. The creation of Pakistan would attenuate the Muslim minority problem, as "crores of Muslims living in the Hindu majority states of UP, CP, Bihar and Madras could not be forced to migrate to Pakistan." Internal differences within the South Asian Muslim community, based on regional differences of language and culture, Abdullah stated, would never allow Pakistan to emerge strong. He also expressed deep concerns about Pakistan's economic feasibility, arguing that "Pakistan would be poor compared to the inhabitants of Hindustan with less chances of betterment, living at best on religious ego." At the same time, he blamed "the Hindu cultural orientation of the Congress" for its insensitivity to Muslim cultural sensibilities and for excluding them from power-sharing arrangements, acts which had precipitated feelings of distrust and fear among Indian Muslims and led to the demand for Pakistan.[174]

During the immediate pre-partition period Abdullah was heavily influenced by communists and adopted their stated position of neutrality on the Congress and the Muslim League. The emphasis on compromise appealed to him. In another article, "Way Out," he laid out a "rational solution" that would not jeopardize the interests of India's minorities. He championed popular regional urges, emphasizing the importance of the right to self-determination for all nationalities inhabiting India. Granting this right would eliminate the possibility of a constitutional solution on communal lines. "This right can be conceded after territorial re-division of the provinces on scientific basis with due regard to linguistic and cultural homogeneity of each unit," he wrote. Overall, Abdullah was not in favor of partition, and considered the best solution to be a loose federation within which provinces would be able to retain their autonomy.[175] Once Pakistan became a reality, however, he faced a dilemma about which course of action to adopt in Muslim-majority Kashmir. Abdullah had a friendly relationship with the Congress, but he understood many Kashmiri Muslims were hesitant about a close association with Nehru's India. Abdullah's personal animosity for Jinnah, who had criticized Abdullah's National Conference during his visit to the Valley in 1942, added to his concerns, as he was unsure how their relationship would unfold if Kashmir became a part of Pakistan. Most significantly, Abdullah remained skeptical about whether the Muslim League, a party dominated by landed elites, would ever allow *Naya Kashmir*'s promise of "land to the tiller" to become a reality.

This ambiguity was reflected in Abdullah's famous speech at Hauzari Bagh in September 1947. Abdullah laid three options before Kashmiris: India, Pakistan, and independence. The right to decide the future status of Jammu and Kashmir,

Abdullah vociferously argued, rested with the people. "If Jammu and Kashmir State is bypassed," Kashmiris would raise a "banner of revolt and we shall face a struggle." At the same time, he advised the masses to support whichever nation-state would recognize Kashmir's "sovereignty." [176] While the thrust of his speech was clearly pro-India, he disagreed with the Congress's centralizing impulse and supported the right of the people to choose independence, if accession appeared unattractive to them. Abdullah's hesitation in adopting a clear-cut approach on the question of accession stemmed from the insecurities that gripped Kashmiri Muslims about their fate in Hindu-majority India in the aftermath of the bloodbath accompanying partition. Abdullah wanted these raw emotions and fears to abate before making any "practical" decision about Kashmir's future.

During these uncertain times, *Khidmat* proved an effective platform for Abdullah. One editorial, "Choosing the Alternative," impressed upon all three powers—the Congress, the Muslim League, and the maharaja—that voices of Kashmiris needed to be heard on the question of accession. Abdullah appealed to Kashmiri Muslims to unite in their basic demand: the right to self-determination to mold their own destiny. He even expressed a desire for an "independent" Kashmir to prevent rich Indian and Pakistani capitalists from taking over Kashmir's territory. "National Conference would resist Kashmir being parceled into *Mamdot* estates and *Noon* zamindaris [capitalist families in Pakistan] or its rich resources being exploited by *Birlas* or *Dalmias* [capitalist families in India]," Abdullah wrote.[177] He called for a transitional stage of political development, in which the state would, at least temporarily, accede to neither India nor Pakistan.

Abdullah subtly used his slogan "freedom before accession" as a bargaining chip to secure autonomous status for Kashmir. He expressed a willingness to think about Kashmir's accession to Pakistan if it were guaranteed complete internal autonomy. However, Muhammad Ali Jinnah's indifference to the National Conference leaders at this critical time convinced Abdullah that Pakistan would never grant Kashmir autonomous status.[178] On the other side of the equation, the close personal and political relationship between Nehru and Abdullah convinced the National Conference leader that Nehru's India would provide Kashmir with greater autonomy within the Indian Union than Pakistan would. However, these were Abdullah's personal views, which did not necessarily reflect the viewpoint of the entire Muslim community. In general, Abdullah's supporters lacked a clear sense of belonging to either India or Pakistan, though most were willing to follow his lead due to the respect he had derived from enduring long prison sentences for resisting Dogra autocracy.

Some Kashmiris who supported the Muslim Conference had a different vision for Kashmir's political future, preferring accession to Pakistan, but as before the party lacked leadership to give it a cohesive voice or direction. In the Valley, the Muslim Conference support base remained primarily in urban Srinagar, while in Jammu the party had a powerful presence.[179] The inability of the Muslim Conference to create a grass root movement in the larger Valley reinforced Nehru's conviction that Abdullah's National Conference was the dominant party in the state. Furthermore, the Muslim League's policy of non-interference in the internal affairs of the princely states hampered the growth of the Muslim Conference, in contrast with the Congress's active involvement with the National Conference. In a letter to K. H. Khurshid, the private secretary to the president of the Muslim League, a member of the Muslim Students Union at Srinagar complained, "Kashmiri Muslims long for the guidance of the League but they are dismayed. Pakistan needs Kashmir and we need Pakistan. But the fight for it must begin now. Thus, the policy of non-interference is beyond my understanding."[180] Despite these complaints, the Muslim League continued the same policy in Kashmir as it had adopted in the other princely states, possibly confident that Muslim-majority Jammu and Kashmir would inevitably accede to Pakistan.

The Muslim Conference had always supported the Pakistan movement of the Muslim League, yet in May 1947 its leadership seemed strangely uncertain about the state's political future. In a press release on May 10, 1947, Chaudhry Hamidullah, the president of the Muslim Conference, urged the maharaja "to declare Kashmir independent." The Muslim Conference offered the maharaja full cooperation in establishing a separate constituent assembly to frame the state constitution according to the wishes of the people. The maharaja would be the first constitutional ruler of the new independent and democratic Kashmir.[181] Only when it seemed that the Congress was putting pressure on the maharaja to accede to India, rather than remain independent, did the Muslim Conference veer to the viewpoint that Kashmir should accede to Pakistan in matters relating to defense, communications, and foreign affairs.

While Valley Muslims were ambiguous about their sense of belonging, whether to India, Pakistan, or an independent Kashmir, Muslims living in the western parts of Jammu province, closer to the borders of Punjab, had different political experiences. The violence unleashed by partition led to killings and mass migrations on both sides of the India–Pakistan border. In Jammu armed groups representing Hindu rightist organizations like the Rashtriya Swayamsevak Sangh (RSS) retaliated against Muslims after Punjabi Hindu refugees arrived in Jammu with harrowing accounts of murder and rape. The presence of armed Sikh and RSS bands in Jammu gave credence to theories that the maharaja wanted to eliminate the state's Muslims to ensure accession to India.[182] Indeed, starting in

September 1947 violence against Jammu Muslims quickly led to migrations to Pakistan. Some Jammu Muslims fled to Poonch and Mirpur, creating another communal backlash—this time by Muslims against Hindus and Sikhs. The communal situation in Jammu was exacerbated by repressive measures adopted by the maharaja, including arrests of local politicians, censorship, and the general stifling of debate. However, it was the *jagir* of Poonch, a Muslim-majority district in western Jammu, which became the focal point of resistance toward the Dogra state.[183]

The Dogra state's turbulent relationship with Poonch began in the 1830s, when Gulab Singh imposed Dogra rule by eliminating the local Muslim ruler, along with his family and supporters, and handing over the district to one of his close relatives. In 1925, the Dogra maharajas established direct control over Poonch and increased taxation, making life unbearable for ordinary people. No measures were taken to improve the condition of the peasantry, since the entire region was held as a land grant, while the land's actual cultivators were reduced to the position of serfs. The unproductive nature of the land, along with heavy taxes, forced Poonchis to search for work outside their *jagir*.[184] Its location, close to major military recruiting regions in Punjab such as Sialkot, encouraged them to enlist in the army. During the First World War, 31,000 men from Poonch and Mirpur served in the British Indian army. In the Second World War, almost 50,000 Poonchis served in the British army. In 1947, Muslim men in Poonch with military experience and training outnumbered the maharaja's armed forces.[185] After the Second World War, the discharged soldiers had returned home, but could not serve in the Dogra army due to laws against Muslim enlistment. The experience of Muslim Poonchis in the battlefields of Europe and West Asia provided them with both military training and access to firearms. The maharaja, fearing their military capabilities, asked Poonchis to disarm; although they complied with the order, Poonchis felt betrayed when the same weapons appeared in the hands of Hindus and Sikhs during the riots of 1947.[186]

In June 1947, the people of Poonch initiated a no-tax campaign: a civil disobedience movement in response to the maharaja's imposition of numerous taxes on the already overburdened peasantry. The Dogra Raj's use of force to suppress this agrarian revolt proved unwise. A peasant revolt against feudal control rapidly developed into a Hindu–Muslim conflict, and the revolt assumed a "definite pro-Pakistan character." The Dogra state lost control over Poonch and its population, while the tribesmen of the North West Frontier Province, aided by Pakistan, entered the princely state to "liberate" Kashmir.[187] The October 1947 tribal invasion forced the maharaja to appeal to the Indian government for help. India reiterated that its military support would be forthcoming only if the princely state acceded to India.[188] On October 26, Maharaja Hari Singh signed an instrument of accession which was formally accepted by the Indian government.

The instrument spelled out the extent to which sovereignty was transferred from the state to the central government. While Jammu and Kashmir relinquished its control over defense, foreign affairs, and communication, it was to remain autonomous in all other respects. Moreover, Lord Mountbatten, the Governor General of India, added a proviso while accepting the instrument of accession. "It is my Government's wish," Mountbatten wrote, "that as soon as law and order has been restored in Kashmir and its soil cleared by the invaders the question of the state's accession should be settled by reference to the people."[189] Nehru also promised that the Indian government would withdraw its troops from Kashmir after restoring peace in the region, providing an opportunity for Kashmiris to decide their political future.[190] These events set the stage for the opening of India and Pakistan's still-unresolved dispute over Kashmir.

Conclusion

Due to their long struggles under autocratic regimes which granted them few rights, the concept of freedom fascinated Kashmiris throughout the decades before independence. Although Kashmiris articulated a variety of visions for exactly how "freedom" would or should transform their social and economic structures, they generally sought a free society that valued good social relations, human dignity, religious tolerance, and compassion for the poor. Local adaptations of international ideologies shaped their emancipation movements to fit their regional environment, and plunged a range of Kashmiri voices into fierce debates over the concepts of socialism, communism, and nationalism. However, as I will explore in the next chapter, in the aftermath of partition, as Kashmir became embroiled in the sovereignty dispute between the newly created states of India and Pakistan, Kashmiri aspirations took a backseat as both new nations focused on territorial nationalism and strengthening their borders. India perceived Kashmiri self-determination as a threat to its territorial integrity, while the ideals of freedom conceived by Kashmiris prior to accession to India remained a distant dream. Instead of creating a society that could improve human relationships and lay the foundation for a strong future society, Kashmiris were confronted with a sociopolitical system that not only failed to redress their economic, political, and cultural grievances, but went out of its way to suppress free expression. Despite these challenges, Kashmiri yearnings for freedom remained strong; local poets penned verses expressing their deep desire to shape their own political destiny. Mirza Arif Beg wrote in 1947:

> Ourselves shall we set up a nation free;
> Ourselves shall we refashion the nation's fate!
> Our hearts have cherished the dreams of democracy!
> We have to turn Kashmir into a real paradise!
> We have to wash away the bolt of servility!
> Lo, there appears the sun of truth;
> And the ghost of falsehood melts away![191]

Notes

1. Extract from Ghulam Ahmad Mahjoor's poem "Come Gardener," in Triloki Nath Raina (ed. and trans.), *The Best of Mahjoor: Selections from Mahjoor's Kashmiri Poems* (J&K Academy of Art, Culture and Languages, Srinagar, 1989), http://www.koausa.org/Poets/Mahjoor/75&76.htm, accessed January 15, 2018.
2. Kalhana, *Rajatarangini*, Vol. 1, trans. M. A. Stein (Westminster: Archibald Constable and Company, 1900).
3. M. I. Khan, *Kashmir's Transition to Islam*, 74.
4. M. I. Khan, *Kashmir's Transition to Islam*, 124.
5. For details see Victor Jacquemont, *Letters from India, 1829–1832; Being a Selection from the Correspondence of Victor Jacquemont* (London: Macmillan and Co., 1936).
6. Robert Throp, *Cashmere Misgovernment*, in S. N. Gadru, *Kashmir Papers: British Intervention in Kashmir* (Srinagar: Freethought Literature Company, 1973); G. T. Vigne, *Travels in Kashmir, Ladakh and Iskardo*, 2 vols. (New Delhi: Sagar Publications, reprinted in 1981); Baron Erich von Schonberg, *Travels in India and Kashmir*, Vol. 2 (London: Hurst & Blackett, 1853).
7. William Moorcroft, *Travels in the Himalayan Provinces of Hindustan and the Panjab, in Ladakh and Kashmir, in Peshawar, Kabul, Kunduz, and Bokhara from 1819 to 1825*, Vol. 1 (London: William Clowes and Sons, 1841), 293–4.
8. Lakhanpal, *Essential Documents and Notes on Kashmir Dispute*, 28–32.
9. Rai, *Hindu Rulers, Muslims Subjects*, 80–127.
10. Mirza Shafiq Hussain, *Kashmiri Musalmanon ki Siyasi Jad-o-Jahad: Dastawaiz 1931–1939* (Srinagar: Gulshan Publishers, 1991), 89–96.
11. A. Wingate, *Preliminary Report of Settlement Operations in Kashmir and Jammu* (Lahore: W. Ball & Co., 1888), 27–9.
12. Lawrence, *The Valley of Kashmir*, 411.
13. Lawrence, *The Valley of Kashmir*, 414–16.
14. Yusuf Saraf, *Kashmiris Fight for Freedom*, Vols. 1 and 2 (Lahore: Ferozsons Publications, 1977), Vol. 1, 282.

15. Zutshi, *Languages of Belonging*, 77–8.
16. Farooq Fayaz, *Kashmir Folklore: A Study in Historical Perspective* (Srinagar: Gulshan Books, 2008), 129–41. For details, see Lawrence, *The Valley of Kashmir*, 256; Gulshan Majeed, *Aspects of Folklore with Special Reference to Kashmir* (Srinagar: Centre of Central Asian Studies, 1997).
17. Fayaz, *Kashmir Folklore*, 134–5.
18. Fayaz, *Kashmir Folklore*, 54.
19. "The Famine in Kashmir; A Government Report," Foreign and Political Department (Progs. December 1879, Nos. 250/289), 16–18, National Archives of India, New Delhi.
20. Saraf, *Kashmiris Fight for Freedom*, Vol. 1, 298.
21. Sheikh Muhammad Abdullah, *The Blazing Chinar: An Autobiography*, translated from Urdu by Mohammad Amin (Srinagar: Gulshan Books, 2013).
22. Arthur Brinckman, "Wrongs of Cashmere," in S. N. Gadru (ed.), *Kashmir Papers: British Intervention in Kashmir* (Srinagar: Freethought Literature Company, 1973), 1–46.
23. Lawrence, *The Valley of Kashmir*, 2–3.
24. Sufi, *Kashir*, Vol. 2, 683.
25. Rai, *Hindu Rulers, Muslims Subjects*, 136–7.
26. M. S. Hussain, *Kashmiri Musalmanon ki Siyasi Jad-o-Jahad, 1931–1939*, 7–9.
27. M. S. Hussain, *Kashmiri Musalmanon ki Siyasi Jad-o-Jahad, 1931–1939*, 7–9; "Submission of Resolution Passed by the Muslim Kashmir Conference Held at Lahore and the Orders of His Highness regarding the Proposed Preference to Non-state Subjects Hindus and Muslims over State Subjects," Old English Records, 254/P-127, 1912, Jammu Kashmir State Archives.
28. "Muhammad-ud-din Fauq: Remembering First Journalist of Kashmir," *Kashmir Dispatch*, January 5, 2012, https://kashmirdispatch.com/2012/07/05/mohammad-ud-din-fauq-remembering-first-journalist-of-kashmir/108557/, accessed June 14, 2019.
29. Muhammad-ud-din Fauq, *Mashir-i-Kashmir* (Lahore: Zafar Brothers, 1911), 113.
30. Muhammad-ud-din Fauq, *Shabab-e-Kashmir* (Srinagar: Gulshan Publishers, 1984), 2–9.
31. Muhammad-ud-din Fauq, *Tarikh-i-Aqwam-i-Kashmir* (Srinagar: Chinar Publishing House), 3.
32. Iqbal, *Javid Nama*, translated by Arthur J. Arberry (London: George Allen, 1966), 3.
33. Iqbal, *Javid Nama*, 3.
34. Iqbal, *Javid Nama*, 117–18.
35. M. S. Hussain, *Kashmiri Musalmanon ki Siyasi Jad-o-Jahad, 1931–1939*, 7–9.
36. G. H. Khan, *Freedom Movement in Kashmir: 1931–1940* (Delhi: Light and Life Publishers, 1980), 60–5.

37. Molvi Atiqullah Shah, *Serat-ul-Waizeen* (Lahore: Rifai Aam Press, 1910), 24, cited in G. H. Khan, *Freedom Movement in Kashmir*, 60–1.
38. M. S. Hussain, *Kashmiri Musalmanon ki Siyasi Jad-o-Jahad, 1931–1939*, 8.
39. "Invitation by the Honourable Secretary, Kashmir Muslim Conference to His Highness, the Maharaja Bahadur on the Occasion of the Annual Meeting of the Conference at Rawalpindi," Old English Records, 226-p-81/1918, Jammu and Kashmir Archives.
40. *Roudad*, Annual Session of All India Muslim Kashmir Conference (Lahore: Steam Press, 1925), 9–15; Muslim Kashmir Conference Lahore, R1/1/1974, British Library, London.
41. *Roudad*, Annual Session of All India Muslim Kashmir Conference, 9–15.
42. Hafiz Muhammad Ismaili, "Personal Diary 1907–1950, May 28, 1918 Item 5," cited in G.H. Khan, *Freedom Movement in Kashmir*, 80.
43. Telegram sent to the Viceroy of India from Musalmaans of Kashmir, in Labour Strike in Silk Factory, Foreign and Political Department, F. No. 19 (2)-P/1924.
44. "Apology of Khwaja Hasan Shah Naqshbandi of Khanyar, Srinagar," File 540, 1925, General Records, Jammu Kashmir State Archives, Jammu.
45. Saraf, *Kashmiris Fight for Freedom*, Vol. 1, 335–9.
46. Report of the Committee to define the Term "State Subject," Political Department, 1935, File. No. 199/RR-18, Jammu Kashmir Archives; Rai, *Hindu Rulers, Muslim Subjects*, 252–3.
47. Fida Hassnain, "Reading Room Was Brainchild of Molvi Abdullah Vakil," *Greater Kashmir*, July 13, 2009.
48. For details, see "Muslam-i-Kashmir ki Halat-i-Zar," *Inqilab*, April 11, 1929, in General Department, File No. 1328, P-47, 1929, Jammu Archives; "Kya Kashmir ki Muslmanoon ki Faryad Suni Jayeegi," *Kashmir Muslamaan*, May 1, 1931, in General Department, File No. 39, 87–88, 1931, Jammu Archives.
49. Saraf, *Kashmiris Fight for Freedom*, Vol. 1, 351.
50. Saraf, *Kashmiris Fight for Freedom*, Vol. 1, 355.
51. Prem Nath Bazaz, *The History of Struggle for Freedom in Kashmir* (Srinagar: Gulshan Publication, 2003), 143.
52. For a detailed account of Kashmiri Muslim mobilization in the early 1930s, see Rashid Taseer, *Tehreek-i-Hurriyat-i-Kashmir*, Vol. 1 (Srinagar: Ali Brothers, 1973).
53. "Khutba Eid ki Bandish," *Kashmiri Musalmaan*, May 17, 1931, in General Department, File 39/87-88, Jammu Archives.
54. Sheikh Mohammad Abdullah, *Flames of the Chinar: An Autobiography*, translated from Urdu by Khushwant Singh (New Delhi: Penguin Books, 1993), 12–13.
55. S. M. Abdullah, *The Blazing Chinar*, 61.
56. Saraf, *Kashmiris Fight for Freedom*, Vol. 1, 364.
57. M. S. Hussain, *Kashmiri Musalmanon ki Siyasi Jad-o-Jahad, 1931–1939*, 12–14.
58. Saraf, *Kashmiris Fight for Freedom*, Vol. 1, 373–8.

59. Ishaq Khan, *Perspectives on Kashmir: Historical Dimensions* (Srinagar: Gulshan Publishers, 1983), 135.
60. "Kashmiri Hindus and the Recent Disturbances Published by Santam Dharma Youngmen's Association," 15–16, in Foreign and Political Department, File No. 133-P, 1932, National Archives of India, New Delhi.
61. "Letter written by the President of All India Kashmir Committee to the Maharaja on 25 September 1931," Foreign and Political, 1932 File No. 133-P, National Archives of India, New Delhi.
62. Saraf, *Kashmiris Fight for Freedom*, Vol. 1, 400.
63. Saraf, *Kashmiris Fight for Freedom*, Vol. 1, 404.
64. For details, see the Middleton Report, "Inquiry into the Disturbances in Kashmir in September 1931," Foreign and Political, 1932, File No. 140-P (Secret), National Archives of India, New Delhi.
65. Saraf, *Kashmiris Fight for Freedom*, Vol.1, 388–400.
66. For a fuller discussion of the politics of Ahmadiyyas and Ahrars, see Ayesha Jalal, *Self and Sovereignty: Individual and Community in South Asian Islam since 1850* (New Delhi: Oxford University Press, 2001), 351–70.
67. The Ahmadiyya sect was founded in British India near the end of the nineteenth century in Qadiyan, Punjab. It originated with the life and teachings of Mirza Ghulam Ahmad (1835–1908), who claimed that he was the *mujaddid* (divine reformer), the promised messiah and *mahdi* awaited by Muslims. Ian Copland, "Islam and Political Mobilization in Kashmir, 1931–34," *Pacific Affairs* 54, no. 2 (Summer, 1981): 228–59.
68. "Letter written by the President of All India Kashmir Committee to the Maharaja on 25 September 1931," Foreign and Political, 1932 File No. 133-P, National Archives of India, New Delhi.
69. Rai, *Hindu Rulers, Muslim Subjects*, 262.
70. Ahrar Party and the Jammu Disturbances, in Foreign and Political, 1932, File No. 141P (Secret), National Archives of India, New Delhi; Saraf, *Kashmiris Fight for Freedom*, Vol. 1, 438.
71. P. N. Bazaz, *The History of Struggle for Freedom in Kashmir*, 152.
72. Saraf, *Kashmiris Fight for Freedom*, Vol. 1, 438–9.
73. Memorandum of the Jammu and Kashmir Muslims presented to the Maharaja on October 19, 1931, in Khan, *Freedom Movement in Kashmir, 1931–1940*, 439–51; P. N. Bazaz, *The History of Struggle for Freedom in Kashmir*, 177.
74. For Muslim Conference resolutions, see M. S. Hussain, *Kashmiri Musalmanon ki Siyasi Jad-o-Jahad.*
75. Copland, "Islam and Political Mobilization in Kashmir, 1931–34."
76. S. M. Abdullah, *The Blazing Chinar*, 114–5.
77. Saraf, *Kashmiris Fight for Freedom*, Vol. 1, 488.
78. M. S. Hussain, *Kashmiri Musalmanon ki Siyasi Jad-o-Jahad*, 23–4.
79. Lamb, *Kashmir: A Disputed Legacy, 1846–1990*, 93.

80. "Kashmir Disturbances: Activities of S. M. Abdullah in Connection with the Political Situation in the State," File No. IOR/ R/1/1/2531, 1934, Jammu Archives.
81. Rai, *Hindu Rulers, Muslim Subjects*, 274.
82. Rai, *Hindu Rulers, Muslim Subjects*, 275.
83. Memorandum presented by the Sanatan Dharm Youngmen's Association to the Maharaja, October 24, 1931, in Khan, *Freedom Movement in Kashmir, 1931–1940*, 463–73.
84. G. H. Khan, *Freedom Movement in Kashmir*, 59.
85. Prem Nath Bazaz, *Kashmir Pandit Agitation and Its Aftermath* (New Delhi: Pamposh Publications, 1967), 40.
86. Bazaz's letter to Gandhi, May 8, 1934, cited in Prem Nath Bazaz, *Kashmir in Crucible* (New Delhi: Pamposh Publications, 1967), 174.
87. P. N. Bazaz, *The History of Struggle for Freedom in Kashmir*, 154–5.
88. S. M. Abdullah, *The Blazing Chinar*, 156.
89. "Sheikh Muhammad Abdullah's Presendential Address at the Second Annual Session of the Muslim Conference," Mirpur, December 15–17, 1933, in M. S. Hussain, *Kashmiri Musalmanon ki Siyasi Jad-o-Jahad*, 291–307.
90. "Muhammad Akbar Khan's Welcome Address at the Second Annual Session of the Muslim Conference," Mirpur, December 15–17, 1933, in M. S. Hussain, *Kashmiri Musalmanon ki Siyasi Jad-o-Jahad*, 279–87.
91. "Memorial Presented to the Prime Minister of Jammu and Kashmir by Kashyapa Bandhu," cited in G. H. Khan, *Freedom Movement in Kashmir*, 417–25.
92. "The Responsibility of Muslims, Hindus and Sikhs," *Hamdard*, Srinagar, May 9, 1936.
93. "The Meaning of Nationalism," *Hamdard*, Srinagar, August 15, 1936.
94. P. N. Bazaz, *The History of Struggle for Freedom in Kashmir*, 160; G. H. Khan, *Freedom Movement in Kashmir*, 328–9.
95. *Hamdard*, Srinagar, October 3, 1936.
96. *Hamdard*, Srinagar, April 13, 1937.
97. "The Mazdoor Sabha," *Hamdard*, Srinagar, October 23, 1936.
98. G. H. Khan, *Ideological Foundations of Freedom Movement in Jammu and Kashmir* (Delhi: Bhavana Prakashan, 2000), 335–43.
99. "Memorandum Presented by the Laborers of the Silk Factory to the Government of Kashmir," *Hamdard*, Srinagar, September 4, 1937.
100. Letter from Bazaz to Nehru, June 24, 1936, cited in Bazaz, *Kashmir in Crucible*, 178.
101. "Why Kashmiris Cannot Benefit from the Muslim League Politics?" *Hamdard*, Srinagar, May 7, 1938; "Congress and Pandit Jawahar Lal Nehru," *Hamdard*, Srinagar, May 7, 1938.
102. S. M. Abdullah, *The Blazing Chinar*, 166–7.
103. P. N. Bazaz, *The History of Struggle for Freedom in Kashmir*, 160–1; "Presidential Address of Sheikh Muhammad Abdullah in the Sixth Annual Session of All Jammu

and Kashmir Muslim Conference, 1938," in M. S. Hussain, *Kashmiri Musalmanon ki Siyasi Jad-o-Jahad*, 443–72.

104. "National Demand," *Hamdard*, Srinagar, May 7, 1939; G. H. Khan, *Ideological Foundations of Freedom Movement in Jammu and Kashmir*, 96.
105. Pandit Shiv Narain Fotedar, "Kashmir Situation and After," *The Tribune*, Lahore, December 16, 1938; G. H. Khan, *Freedom Movement in Kashmir*, 350–1.
106. Fotedar, "Kashmir Situation and After."
107. Chaudhry Ghulam Abbas, *Kashmakash* (Srinagar: Kashmir Studies Foundation, 2001), 176–7.
108. Syed Taffazull Hussain, *Sheikh Abdullah: A Biography: The Crucial Period, 1905–1939* (Srinagar: Woodclay, 2009), 288–9.
109. P. N. Bazaz, *The History of Struggle for Freedom in Kashmir*, 165.
110. P. N. Bazaz, *The History of Struggle for Freedom in Kashmir*, 163–4.
111. For details, see Chaudhry Ghulam Abbas, *Kashmakash*.
112. Saraf, *Kashmiris Fight for Freedom*, Vol. 1, 535.
113. C. A. Bayly, *Origins of Nationality in South Asia* (New Delhi: Oxford University Press, 1998), 116–19.
114. Sheikh Muhammad Abdullah, *Elan-i-Haq*, No. 3 (Srinagar: Nishat Press, 1942), 3–6; G. H. Khan, *Ideological Foundations of Freedom Movement in Jammu and Kashmir*, 168.
115. "Speech by Mualana Masoodi," *The Khalid*, Srinagar, June 21, 1939, cited in G. H. Khan, *Ideological Foundations of Freedom Movement in Jammu and Kashmir*, 153–4.
116. Sheikh Muhammad Abdullah, "Siyasat ko Mahzab Kay Tabih Karna Islam ki Roo Say Durust Naheen," *Hamdard*, July 9, 1939.
117. S. M. Abdullah, *The Blazing Chinar*, 179; G. H. Khan, *Ideological Foundations of the Freedom Movement*, 163–5.
118. Mohammad Ishaq Khan, "The Significance of the Dargah of Hazratbal in the Socio-Religious and Political Life of Kashmiri Muslims," in Christian W. Troll (ed.), *Muslim Shrines in India* (Delhi: Oxford University Press, 1992), 172–87.
119. "Kashmir Hindus Have to Decide Whether They Want to Be with the Congress or the Muslim League," *Hamdard*, Srinagar, July 9, 1939.
120. S. M. Abdullah, *The Blazing Chinar*, 179.
121. P. N. Bazaz, *The History of Struggle for Freedom in Kashmir*, 167–8.
122. Ayesha Jalal, "Exploding Communalism: The Politics of Muslim Identity in South Asia," in Sugata Bose and Ayesha Jalal (eds.), *Nationalism, Democracy and Development* (New Delhi: Oxford University Press, 1997), 76–103.
123. For details, see "The Minority Question in Kashmir Politics," *Hamdard*, Srinagar, July 31, 1938; "The Future of Kashmiri Pandits," *Hamdard*, Srinagar, September 24, 1943.
124. Saraf, *Kashmiris Fight for Freedom*, Vol. 1, 564–66.
125. P. N. Bazaz, *The History of Struggle for Freedom in Kashmir*, 178–80.
126. Saraf, *Kashmiris Fight for Freedom*, Vol. 1, 556–66.

127. Abbas, *Kashmakash*, 184–91.
128. A free rendering of a pamphlet issued by the Muslim Conference, Publicity Department, File No. M/15/43/N, 1943, Jammu Archives.
129. P. N. Bazaz, *The History of Struggle for Freedom in Kashmir*, 184–5.
130. For a detailed account of Abbas's role in pre-1947 Kashmir politics, see Abbas, *Kashmakash*.
131. P. N. Bazaz, *The History of Struggle for Freedom in Kashmir*, 202–7.
132. Saraf, *Kashmiris Fight for Freedom*, Vol. 1, 627.
133. P. N. Bazaz, *The History of Struggle for Freedom in Kashmir*, 189–207.
134. Saraf, *Kashmiris Fight for Freedom*, Vol. 1, 627–41.
135. Balraj Puri, *Communism in Kashmir* (Calcutta: Institute of Social and Political Studies, 1961), 1–4.
136. Puri, *Communism in Kashmir*, 1–4.
137. For details, see Sheikh Muhammad Abdullah, *New Kashmir* (New Delhi: Kashmir Bureau of Information, 1951).
138. Sumantra Bose, *Kashmir: Roots of Conflict, Paths to Peace* (New Delhi: Vistaar Publications, 2003), 25–6.
139. Sheikh Muhammad Abdullah, *New Kashmir* (New Delhi: Kashmir Bureau of Information, 1951), 1–44.
140. Manzoor Fazili, *Socialist Ideas and Movements in Kashmir* (New Delhi: Eureka Publications, 1980), 145.
141. G. H. Khan, *Ideological Foundations of Freedom Movement in Jammu and Kashmir*, 243.
142. *The Tribune*, Lahore, October 15, 1945.
143. For a detailed discussion on the life and works of M. N. Roy, refer to Kris Manjapra, *M. N. Roy: Marxism and Colonial Cosmopolitanism* (Delhi: Routledge, 2010).
144. B. K. Mahakul, "Radical Humanism of M.N. Roy," *The Indian Journal of Political Science* 66, no. 3 (2005): 607–18.
145. P. N. Bazaz, *The History of Struggle for Freedom in Kashmir*, 221–38.
146. Prem Nath Bazaz, *Jammu Kashmir Kissan Mazdoor Conference: A Short History* (Rawalpindi: Kissan Mazdoor Publishing Bureau, 1946), 3–16.
147. P. N. Bazaz, *Jammu Kashmir Kissan Mazdoor Conference*, 3–16.
148. Ian Copland, "The Abdullah Factor: Kashmiri Muslims and the Crisis of 1947," in D. A. Low (ed.), *Political Inheritance of Pakistan* (Basingstoke: Macmillan, 1991), 218–47.
149. G. H. Khan, *Ideological Foundations of the Freedom Movement*, 99.
150. Lakh is a unit of value in South Asia; 1 lakh is equal to 100,000.
151. S. M. Abdullah, *The Blazing Chinar*, 257–8.
152. Saraf, *Kashmiris Fight for Freedom*, Vol. 1, 673–6.
153. Saraf, *Kashmiris Fight for Freedom*, Vol. 1, 685.
154. S. M. Abdullah, *The Blazing Chinar*, 264–5.

155. Saraf, *Kashmiris Fight for Freedom*, Vol. 1, 669–77.
156. "Lachmi Narayan Dhar, the President of All Kashmir Hindu Students Conference, 14–16 October 1945," in Private Papers of S.P. Mookerjee, 11-1V Installment, Subject File, 223, Nehru Memorial Museum and Library, New Delhi.
157. "Statement Issued by Shiv Narayan Fotedar, President All India Kashmir Pandit Conference, 1946," in Private Papers of S. P. Mookerjee, 11-1V Installment, Subject File, 223, Nehru Memorial Museum and Library, New Delhi; *The Tribune*, Lahore, May 13, 1946.
158. *The Ranbir*, Jammu, December 1, 1946.
159. G. H. Khan, *Ideological Foundations of the Freedom Movement*, 102–3.
160. *Kashmir on Trial: State vs. Sheikh Abdullah* (Lahore: Lion Press, 1947), 14; Ajit Bhattacharjea, *Kashmir: The Wounded Valley* (New Delhi: UBS publishers, 1994), 80–1.
161. Jalal, *Democracy and Authoritarianism in South Asia*, 32.
162. Lakhanpal, *Essential Documets and Notes on Kashmir Dispute*, 41–3.
163. Ramchandra Guha, "What Mountbatten Really Did for India," *The Hindu*, October 12, 2003.
164. Mohan Krishen Teng, *Kashmir: Article 370* (New Delhi: Anmol Publishers, 1990), 6–21.
165. Sisir Gupta, *Kashmir: A Study in India–Pakistan Relations* (London: Asia Publishing House, 1966), 16–20.
166. Lakhanpal, *Essential Documents and Notes on Kashmir Dispute*, 40–5.
167. Rai, *Hindu Rulers, Muslim Subjects*, 296.
168. For details, see Lamb, *Kashmir: A Disputed Legacy, 1846–1990*, 109–13; Bhattacharjea, *Kashmir: The Wounded Valley*, 102–35.
169. Lakhanpal, *Essential Documets and Notes on Kashmir Dispute*, 45; Michael Brecher, *The Struggle for Kashmir* (New York: Oxford University Press, 1953), 33.
170. Fazili, *Socialist Ideas and Movements in Kashmir*, 179.
171. Prem Nath Bazaz, "Gandhism, Jinnaishm and Kashmir," *Hamdard*, Srinagar, April 19, 1947; Prem Nath Bazaz, "Communalism and Nationalism: Two Sides of Same Coin," *Hamdard*, Srinagar, April 18, 1947.
172. "Crush Fascism," *Hamdard*, Srinagar, April 12, 1947.
173. "Economic Planning and Kashmir," *Hamdard*, April 23, 1947.
174. Sheikh Muhammad Abdullah, "Thoughts on Pakistan," *Khidmat*, Srinagar, December 23, 1946.
175. Sheikh Muhammad Abdullah, "Way Out," *Khidmat*, Srinagar, April 24, 1946.
176. "Freedom Before Accession: Speech of Sheikh Abdullah at Hauzari Bagh," *Khidmat*, Srinagar, September 30, 1947.
177. Sheikh Muhammad Abdullah, "Choosing the Alternative," *Khidmat*, Srinagar, October 15, 1947 (emphasis mine).
178. S. M. Abdullah, *The Blazing Chinar*, 278–9.

179. Letter written by Mir Abdul Aziz, General Secretary of Muslim Students Union, to K. H. Khurshid, March 14, 1947, in Z. H. Zahid (ed.), *Jinnah Papers: Quaid-i-Azam Mohammad Ali Jinnah Papers: Prelude to Pakistan, 20 February–2 June 1947* (Islamabad: National Archives of Pakistan, 1993), Doc. 128, 249.
180. Letter written by Mohiuddin, member, Muslim Students Union, to K. H. Khurshid, March 11, 1947, in Z. H. Zahid, *Jinnah Papers*, Doc. 220, 114.
181. Saraf, *Kashmiris Fight for Freedom*, Vol. 1, 707–8.
182. Sardar Ibrahim Khan, *Kashmir Saga* (Lahore: Ripon Printing Press, 1965), 40–9.
183. For details, see S. I. Khan, *The Kashmir Saga*.
184. Lamb, *Kashmir: A Disputed Legacy, 1846–1990*, 122–6.
185. Snedden, *The Untold Story of the People of Azad Kashmir*, 30–2.
186. Lamb, *Kashmir: A Disputed Legacy, 1846–1990*, 123.
187. P. N. Bazaz, *The History of Freedom Struggle in Kashmir*, 323–4.
188. V. P. Menon, *The Story of Integration of Indian States* (London: Longman, 1955), 274–5.
189. Lakhanpal, *Essential Documents and Notes on Kashmir Dispute*, 57.
190. Lakhanpal, *Essential Documents and Notes on Kashmir Dispute*, 62.
191. P. N. Pushp, "The Reflection of Freedom Struggle in Kashmiri Verse," in Mohammad Yasin and Abdul Qaiyum Rafiqi (eds.), *History of the Freedom Struggle in Jammu & Kashmir* (New Delhi: Light and Life, 1980), 236–7.

2 Freedom, Loyalty, Belonging
Kashmir after Decolonization

O golden oriole, winter's gone,
Gay spring has come again!
Step out and feast your weary eyes
On the myriad flowers a bloom.
Flowering plants have spread their arms;
Perch on the bough your fancy takes;
But with an alien as your gardener,
This freedom won't remain.
The Wular Lake is still in flood,
The North Wind howling strong;
The shore is far away, and you
Must steer your course with care!

—Ghulam Ahmad Mahjoor, "O Golden Oriole!"[1]

For the inhabitants of the former princely state of Jammu and Kashmir, freedom came at a price. The Indian–Pakistani battle for sovereignty over the territory turned the Kashmir question into an international dispute and led to the drawing of an arbitrary ceasefire line dividing the province. War, violence, and displacement led Kashmiris to believe that their much-awaited freedom still eluded them. Kashmiri society battled this turmoil during the 1950s as it tried to come to grips with not only the presence of the Indian and Pakistani states, but also Kashmiris' own place within these new political constructs.

This chapter explores the immediate aftermath of decolonization, during which India and Pakistan, aided by local political elites, sought to legitimize their rule over their respective sides of Kashmir. Meanwhile, the United Nations' promise of a plebiscite to resolve the area's disputed status created ambiguity about Kashmir's future, making Kashmiris question whether they had a place in either of the newly created nation-states. For over seventy years, questions of belonging and loyalty for various communities living on both sides of the ceasefire line and how they imagined their role in the politics of postcolonial Kashmir have sparked a debate. To what extent is their belonging rooted in a political, regional, or cultural sense of identity? Some have argued that the loyalty of Kashmiri Muslims lay with Pakistan because of their supposedly shared religious sensibilities. This view has been bolstered not only by Pakistani nationalist writings, but also by devotees of India's Hindu right.[2] Indian and Kashmiri nationalist discourses, in contrast, have characterized Kashmir as a land devoid of religious discord.[3] This articulation of Kashmiriyat emphasizes the secular spirit of Kashmiris to justify the decision of the National Conference to support Kashmir's accession to India.[4] Research on the present political turmoil in Kashmir draws from these two classifications of Kashmiri identity as well. In effect, scholars have reinforced the legitimacy of these two irreconcilable nationalist narratives.

Here, I demonstrate that Kashmiri belonging in the immediate aftermath of partition did not seamlessly merge into the national identities of India and Pakistan. Kashmiri imaginings of "freedom" transcended the artificial "borders" sketched by the nation-states. I contend that the creation of the ceasefire line itself, which cut arbitrarily through the natural environment and dismantled the structures that had sustained the state's economy prior to 1947, shaped Kashmiri Muslims' perceptions of India, Pakistan, and Kashmir. Decolonization and war set in motion social and economic transformations, along with larger political structures, that altered relationships within and between communities and complicated questions of identity, belonging, and loyalty. Ultimately, conflicting communitarian interests in postcolonial Kashmir strained the relationship of the region with the Indian state, leading to a crackdown against Kashmiri nationalist leaders who opposed complete integration and shattering any illusion of shared ideals and emotional bonds between Kashmir and India.

Decolonization, Failed Freedom, and the Question of Belonging

The close partnership forged between the Indian National Congress and Sheikh Abdullah's National Conference during the 1930s and 1940s came to fruition during the Indo-Pakistani War of 1947–8. As Pakistani-backed tribal raiders from the North-West Frontier Province, now renamed Khyber Pakhtunkhwa, caused mayhem in the Valley, the Dogra administration collapsed, and the maharaja escaped to Jammu in the dead of the night. The National Conference stepped in to fill the vacuum, organizing local volunteers to maintain calm amid news of brutalities committed by raiders. On October 30, 1947, four days after signing the instrument of accession, the Dogra maharaja, on India's direction, put in place an Emergency Council, headed by Sheikh Abdullah and consisting of thirteen Muslim and ten non-Muslim members.[5] National Conference militias provided intelligence to the Indian Army and joined it in protecting important bridges. They even constructed roads enabling Indian troops to reach far-flung areas occupied by the tribal invaders.[6] The National Conference's support legitimized India's presence in Kashmir at a time when the international community was debating the Kashmir question at the United Nations. Grateful to Abdullah, Indian prime minister Jawaharlal Nehru constantly pledged to consult the Kashmiri people about their wishes once peace prevailed in the region.[7] Abdullah interpreted this assurance as Nehru's support for a conditional accession, to be fully confirmed only after securing the state's autonomy.

Indian nationalist narratives from this era portray Indian and National Conference leaders forming a strong bond to save Kashmir from anarchy and gain its freedom. These narratives contain not only a tremendous outpouring of praise for Abdullah's secular outlook, but an insistent presentation of Abdullah as Kashmir's sole representative, despite the existence of different visions for Kashmir's political freedom. In a November 1947 letter to the maharaja, for example, Nehru described Abdullah as a man with "integrity" without whose support "no satisfactory way out" to the Kashmir issue was possible.[8] Mohandas Gandhi, the preeminent Indian nationalist leader, called Abdullah the "real maharaja" of Kashmir, which under his guidance set an example of communal amity while the rest of the subcontinent reeled in religious frenzy.[9] In exchange for this support, Abdullah himself refrained during this period from invoking the slogan of "self-determination." Instead, he expressed his complete faith in India and assured the public of a forthcoming new era of rights, democracy, and freedom.

While certain sections of Kashmiri Muslim society and other political groups in Jammu and Kashmir disagreed with Abdullah's politics, thousands of Kashmiris held him in deep reverence as a result of his courage in mobilizing resistance against the autocratic Dogra regime since the 1930s. Social groups including laborers and peasants believed Abdullah's promises that India would allow the *Naya Kashmir* manifesto, a program that pledged social justice and economic equality, to serve as the basis for democratic governance in the region. Clearly, this moment in Kashmir's immediate postcolonial history presented Indian and Kashmiri nationalist leadership with an opportunity to deliver the benefits of real democracy and win the hearts and minds of Kashmiris, even their opposition, by demonstrating the difference between autocratic regimes and democratic governments. But this moment was not seized; instead, one vision for Kashmir's freedom rode roughshod over other imaginings to secure its political agenda, denying Kashmiris a voice in shaping their future.[10]

Kashmiri and Indian nationalists' rhetoric of "freedom" conflicted with the narratives penned by Kashmiris of alternative political leanings (even those who had once supported Abdullah) during the early days of the Awami Raj, or "People's Rule." The diaries of Mahmood Hashmi, a lecturer at Amar Singh College in Srinagar, published in the 1950s, provide a detailed account of the new political culture ushered in by the National Conference as it established its so-called people's rule in strife-torn Kashmir. Like many patriots, Hashmi initially joined Sheikh Abdullah's Peace Army to protect his homeland from the tribal invasion; however, his experiences of "freedom" under National Conference rule left him disillusioned. Hashmi witnessed how "nationalist gangs" in red armbands used the frenzy created by the tribal invasion and the breakdown of law and order as cover to beat members of the opposition, ransack the homes of Muslim Conference members, and break radios and transistors that broadcast "enemy propaganda" from Pakistan-administered Kashmir. While the National Conference leadership worried that broadcasts giving the viewpoint of the Pakistani-supported Muslim Conference about partition violence against Jammu's Muslim community could arouse the public in favor of Pakistan and make it difficult for nationalists to control Kashmir, Hashmi saw that Abdullah's supporters were destroying any space for consensus policy.[11]

Kashmiri nationalists countered voices like Hashmi's with a liberal use of counter-propaganda to sustain the impression that most Kashmiris supported Sheikh Abdullah's political vision. The atrocities committed against all Kashmiris, regardless of their religious denominations, during the tribal invasion became a key talking point as nationalists sought popular support. Nationalist-arranged theatrical shows and concerts highlighted Kashmiris' "unbounded fervour" to protect their homeland from tribal "savagery." One elaborate production included a battalion of women armed with wooden guns, marching and chanting slogans in support of Kashmir's accession to India.[12] These images, broadcast both in India and globally, created an image of a progressive Kashmir eager to tie its destiny with secular India. According to Qureshi, however, the reality was far more complicated. Indeed, stories of tribal brutalities, committed in the interest of looting and plunder, had motivated thousands of Kashmiris to join auxiliary forces in defense of their families and communities. At the same time, many of those Kashmiris who fought alongside the Indian armies to repel the tribal invasion were driven by financial, not ideological, considerations. When factories faced closure due to war conditions in the Valley, the National Conference's Home Guard provided temporary employment.[13]

An extensive intelligence network worked zealously to suppress opposition. B. P. L. Bedi, the chief of the National Conference propaganda department and a close associate of Abdullah, hired two hundred informers. Every day, these spies interacted with locals in the streets and bazaars of Srinagar, gathering information about political perceptions. A committee of writers, poets, and artists analysed this incoming information and, in response, published propaganda posters with striking poetry and captions. Put up all over the city, the posters signalled to the opposition that the "government was aware of their statements and police could any time come and arrest them."[14] Propagandists also strove to build the National Conference's image as the protector of Kashmiri peasantry and an instrument for restoring Kashmiri dignity. One image popular in nationalist print media depicted a peasant carrying a plough, the party symbol of the National Conference, emphasizing the socialist ideals of the party as a representative of the working classes.[15] Nationalist propaganda aimed to gain a popular mandate for the view that broadly shared Kashmiri prosperity could only become a reality within Nehru's socialist India.

Although Kashmiri nationalist leaders had spent decades fighting the oppressive Dogra regime, once in power they emulated the authoritarian maharajas, defeating the very purpose of the long struggle for rights and representative democracy. Kashmiris living a nightmare in this situation of "freedom" were disappointed by a National Conference they had once held in high esteem for its vision of democratic ideals and socialist program. Some Kashmiri political activists, expelled to India due to their opposition to Abdullah's policies, wrote scathing pamphlets exposing nationalist repression under one-party rule. In his 1949 pamphlet *Behind the Iron Curtain in Kashmir*, for example, Jagannath Sathu, born in a middle-class Pandit family in Shopian, provided a graphic account of conditions in India-administered Kashmir to "stir the world conscience to provide justice to Kashmiris."[16] India, however, banned Sathu's pamphlet for "carrying pro-Pakistan propaganda," claiming that it had been published "by some agencies in Pakistan with a view to secure the accession of Kashmir to Pakistan."[17]

Soon after the nationalists assumed power, Sathu wrote, the political parties that existed prior to Kashmir's accession to India—the Muslim Conference, the Kissan Mazdoor Conference, the Kashmir Socialist party, the State Kashmir Pandit Conference, and Praja Parishad—became "non-existent and organizationally weak" as the so-called people's government arrested prominent opposition members. As political detainees exceeded available prison space, nationalists "improvised to accommodate them," creating jail cells out of "shops and homes." Before being assigned to these makeshift jails, prisoners were brought to Kothi

Bagh Police Station, known as the "slaughterhouse," and endured extreme torture at the hands of the notorious police officer Ghulam Qadir Ganderbali, a close associate of the deputy prime minister of Kashmir, Bakshi Ghulam Muhammad. Ganderbali's methods included beating with *lathis* and whips, pulling whiskers, and dragging prisoners across pavements with their hands and feet tied together. He hoped to extort confessions and label detainees as "state enemies" collaborating with Pakistan to disrupt law and order.[18]

New ordinances promulgated by the state under cover of the emergency also curbed free expression. The government stopped publication of all journals and periodicals advocating independent policy. In 1948, the administration prevented political opposition groups from approaching the United Nations team visiting the Valley; a contingent of intelligence agents shadowed the international visitors to ensure that they received only state-sponsored information. Laws also restricted processions and gatherings. The judiciary readily implemented these arbitrary ordinances and declared countless Kashmiris potential "suspects" either for invoking anti-government slogans or for disagreeing with National Conference ideology. Punishments varied depending on the severity of the offense: anti-government slogans could land a person in prison for four to six months,[19] while individuals perceived as "greater threats" were declared "enemy agents" and deported to Pakistan. The Indian press, according to Sathu, considered it a patriotic duty to whitewash the oppressive political climate in the Valley, ensuring that the Indian public and the outside world did not possess truthful information.

Although India had embraced the mantle of "democracy" at independence, the new state struggled to apply this concept in conflict-ridden Kashmir. As territorial considerations overshadowed democratic principles, the Indian government allowed the National Conference to build "monolithic control without any checks and balances."[20] India believed it needed Abdullah's support to legitimize its claim to Kashmir, especially in the United Nations, so it assisted the suppression of voices disagreeing with the Conference's political outlook. The oppressive climate in the Valley, however, as exposed by Sathu and other pamphleteers, debunked the Indian government's stance that its support for the National Conference stemmed from the party's commitment to democracy and secularism. India's disregard for "civil liberties and human rights" convinced some Kashmiris that India planned to retain Kashmir against the will of the people.[21]

While nationalist suppression of opposition political thought made a mockery of "freedom," the drawing of an arbitrary ceasefire line disrupted social networks and separated families from each other, making it mentally agonizing for Kashmiris to adapt to the new reality of the Indian and Pakistani states. A short story, "The Neutral Zone," written in the 1960s by an anonymous author, sketches the uncertainty and pain partition caused for ordinary people living close to the new ceasefire line. The story concerns an engaged couple from a remote village in Poonch. Living simple lives, the pair are oblivious to the political transformations taking place in the South Asian subcontinent. They wake up on their wedding morning stunned by the presence of armed personnel in their village, claiming to represent the new nation-states of India and Pakistan. The armies occupy opposite banks of a river flowing through their village. The river becomes the "border" and guards prevent people from moving freely across it. Since families and businesses are spread across both sides of the river, this event separates parents from their children, breaks old friendships, and affects economic interactions. The engaged protagonists, separated by the river, refuse to accept this demarcation. In the dead of night, each secretly crosses the river to reunite, but are arrested by the opposing armies and branded as "spies" and "enemy agents."[22] This story resonates with the pain of countless families separated by an artificial divide, revealing the struggle of communities as this partition, like many others in South Asia, infringed on social, economic, and interpersonal relationships.

Cabeiri Robinson has asserted that a new category of displaced Kashmiris, referred to as "refugees" and trapped on either side of the ceasefire line, now lived in a liminal space, unsure where they belonged.[23] While some displaced people were victims of the violence that accompanied the partition in 1947, others had been expelled from their homes due to their political opposition to the Valley's ruling government. Another group included laborers and merchants who worked in West Punjab and found themselves on the other side of the "border" at the time the conflict broke out. By 1949, almost seven hundred and fifty thousand people were displaced.[24] For these Kashmiris, the ceasefire line was an aberration, a temporary feature to be removed once Kashmiris exercised their promised self-determination and erased artificial "borders" to reconnect communities.

Displaced Kashmiris struggled to adapt to these new demarcations and could not differentiate between their new and old home. The new nation-states, however, treated "the ceasefire line as a frontier of political as well as military control."[25] The war frenzy accompanying the division of Kashmir led India to limit even postal communication; telegrams between the two parts of Kashmir ceased, while letters were censored and sometimes never reached families on the opposite side.[26] Both rival countries restricted movement, required Kashmiris to seek permits to move within their own state. Though people sometimes crossed the ceasefire line for regular social and economic interactions, India and Pakistan saw them as infiltrators and they became primary surveillance targets for state intelligence officials.[27] In 1948, the state government passed the Jammu and Kashmir Ingress Control Act, intended to keep foreigners out of the state on security grounds. These "foreigners," however, also included Kashmiris; a considerable number of the original residents of Jammu and Kashmir had either migrated or been trapped in Pakistan after the drawing of the ceasefire line.[28] Many wished to return to their homes to visit or resettle, but the Indian Ministry of Defence issued no permits for residents of Azad Kashmir to pay a temporary visit, fearing they might be spies of the enemy country. Citing security reasons, the government only gave permits for permanent resettlement to "Kashmiris stranded in Pakistan."

The procedure for resettling in India-administered Kashmir was also very complex, requiring clearance from the state governments as well as from both India and Pakistan. After the state verified the travelers' credentials, the Indian High Commission at Lahore could issue a permit. But Pakistan did not allow Kashmiris to leave on a permanent resettlement permit unless they had also obtained a "no objection" certificate, which were rarely distributed due to "Pakistani insecurity about a projected plebiscite." If a Kashmiri succeeded in securing a no-objection certificate in Pakistan, he then had to obtain another certificate, this time from the state government in India-administered Kashmir. This documentation was then sent to the Ministry of States, which forwarded it to the Deputy High Commissioner for India, who finally issued a repatriation certificate for the individuals concerned.[29]

If a resident of India-administered Kashmir only wished to visit Pakistan-administered Kashmir temporarily, he had to obtain a "No Objection Return Certificate" from the state government, valid for a specified period. Once equipped with this certificate, he applied to the Pakistan High Commission for a permit to Pakistan. He did not show the certificate, however, because the government of Pakistan did not recognize Kashmir either as a part of India or as a legal state government. For the lucky few issued a travel permit, checkpoints allowed entry by virtue not of Indian citizenship but of Jammu and Kashmir residency. When the traveler wished to return to Kashmir, however, he had to use the certificate obtained from the state government to apply to the Indian mission at Lahore for a return permit.[30]

In the early 1950s, as India embarked on integrating Kashmir, "Indian passports" served as a means to stamp Indian identity on Kashmiri residents and to compel Pakistan to acknowledge Kashmiris as Indian citizens. Some Indian officials believed that the introduction of passports could alienate Kashmiris by making it harder for them to connect with their families across the ceasefire line, jeopardizing votes for accession to India in the still-looming plebiscite. They pointed out that Pakistan would reject such passports and not grant Kashmiris visas, as they did not recognize India's rights over Kashmir. The deputy home minister, however, brushed aside these concerns and clarified: "If Pakistan refuses to grant visas, the Kashmiri authorities would in no way feel unhappy since their policy has been to discourage such visits to Pakistan."[31]

These complex legal procedures made it difficult, if not impossible, for "trapped" Kashmiris to return home or to maintain basic connections with their kith and kin. Several repatriation cases placed before the Indian Ministry of States during the 1950s related to separated Kashmiri families stranded in Pakistan and Azad Kashmir.[32] These applicants requested that India and Pakistan take a humanitarian approach and allow family units to stay together. Justifications for their requests to travel home included desire to be with dying parents, a need to care for minor children, or participation in the weddings and funerals of loved ones. In May 1953, one old gentleman, Sheikh Abdul Samad, originally a resident of Handwara district but now "trapped" in Rawalpindi, requested a permit due to his failing health; he wished to "die in his village." Concerned that it would take a longer time to reach Kashmir via India, Samad, unaware of the new laws, requested permission to enter the Valley through Tetwal, a border village on the line of control.[33] Meanwhile, the family members of Muslim Conference activists who had either willingly left the Valley or been expelled requested permission from the Indian government to bring their families to the other side.

Despite these requests on humanitarian grounds, state officials granted clearance only to those individuals attached to their own political ideology. Others were considered "dangerous security threats" and denied permits. In some cases, the only way to obtain permits was through bribes or political influence, and, as a result, the permit system became a tool of harassment against Kashmiris. In many cases those who disagreed with the policies of the state government were declared suspects and illegally detained after they applied for a permit.[34] These bureaucratic procedures—defined by nationalist agendas and devoid of human considerations—made Kashmiris apprehensive about the motivations of the state governments and both nation-states.

As Kashmiris dealt with the humanitarian ramifications of the ceasefire line, the environmental and economic chaos created by partition added to their insecurities, further complicating their sense of belonging. The division of Kashmir dismantled entire economic structures that had sustained the state's trade and commerce, affecting the Muslim trading class the hardest. Prior to the war, all the major highways and waterways had connected Kashmir with West Punjab, which became a part of Pakistan after partition. Exports from

Kashmir, especially fruit and other products with a very short life span, were originally transported speedily to Rawalpindi via the Jhelum Valley Road.[35] In the new postwar political scenario, trade along these roads came to a standstill. Merchants suddenly overstocked with artistic products stopped procuring goods from Kashmiri Muslim artisans, wood-carvers, coppersmiths, carpet weavers, and papier-mâché workers, whose economic lives were in turn adversely impacted. For Muslim timber merchants, it became impossible to use the three main rivers (Indus, Jhelum, and Chenab) that flowed from the state of Jammu and Kashmir to Punjab and had previously carried millions of tons of timber to important rail junctions such as Jhelum and Wazirabad, free of charge.[36]

These urban Kashmiri Muslims, artisans, traders, businessmen, and government servants, the politically conscious minority in the Valley, struggled to contemplate a future accession to India under these conditions. The economic situation worsened as drawn-out debates in the United Nations Security Council prevented political conditions in the state from stabilizing. Tensions between India and Pakistan kept visitors out of the Valley, greatly affecting the economic status of the Muslim houseboat owners who survived on tourism.[37] The sudden lack of imports to the Valley also created an acute shortage of essential commodities, especially food grains, kerosene oil, and salt. Although the Indian government invested in a new highway connecting the Valley with Jammu and East Punjab, the road failed to improve the state's finances; it cut through high mountain passes and did not remain functional during winter, isolating the Valley from the rest of India.[38] This economic insecurity posed a challenge to the National Conference leadership; how could they increase revenue and balance the budget? Budget estimates between 1948 and 1950 demonstrate that the state struggled to deal with its deficit. In 1948–9, revenue was at 300 lakh rupees and expenditures were 641 lakh rupees. The next year, revenue was estimated at 355 lakh rupees and expenditures were up to 726 lakhs.[39] Partition of Kashmir drove deteriorating standards of living, and administrative inefficiency in dealing with these economic challenges made Kashmiris sullen and resentful about Abdullah's decision to align with India.

Kashmiris' economic misery increased after the National Conference government, intending to generate more revenue, "nationalized" trade, transport, and supplies. To stall competition from independent traders, imports and exports could only take place through government emporiums set up in various cities. Many private transport businesses closed after the state established full control over the transport department.[40] Business families' autonomy was curtailed and their dependence on government syndicates increased; the state granted the syndicates power to confer permits for private trade. Kashmiris watched helplessly as the policy of nationalization conferred power on this select group. Furthermore, to ensure supplies of essential commodities, the National Conference government established full control over procurement and distribution of salt, sugar, cotton, yarn, and edible oils. The government assigned each region of the state a fixed quota of supplies, later transferred to cooperative societies for distribution.[41] But corrupt administrative officials, in most cases, hoarded supplies and sold them on the black market at exorbitant rates.[42] Trade and commerce in the state suffered a shock, while Kashmiris became poorer and lost purchasing capacity.[43]

Some of Sheikh Abdullah's policy decisions, especially his insistence on retaining the state's financial autonomy from India while running a deficit in the state budget, created serious challenges for the nationalist government. A significant rise in the price of commodities during the late 1940s and early 1950s was primarily caused by disruption of the old routes directly connecting Kashmir with the rest of India via West Punjab, which became a part of Pakistan; most commodities now had to be transported over long distances and difficult routes. The government's decision to maintain customs duties on goods coming from outside the state generated revenue but also further increased commodity prices. The Indian government offered grants and loans to help the state balance its budget but attached conditions. From 1947 to 1950, the state received 59,555,000 rupees as cash loans, and this amount advanced as "Aid to Kashmir" was "treated in principle as recoverable loan."[44] However, Abdullah was concerned that if Kashmir became dependent on grants and subsidized food from Delhi, it would reduce Kashmiri self-sufficiency, and allow New Delhi the power to interfere in Kashmir's political matters.[45] With this mindset, the state government refused to abolish customs duties, one of its main ways of raising independent revenue.

Despite Abdullah's fears, economic realities in Jammu and Kashmir forced the National Conference to ask the Government of India to provide subsidized salt in October 1948. Initially, the Ministry of Finance considered it unfair for the state government to impose a customs duty on subsidized salt. After considerable deliberations, however, the Indian government decided to provide the subsidy, "purely for political reasons." As rock salt was readily available in Pakistan, Kashmiris smuggled it across the ceasefire line, and the general feeling prevailed that had the ceasefire line not been drawn, people would have been able to procure salt and other goods at cheap rates. To counter the perception that the current boundary was an economic disadvantage to residents, the Indian government decided to bear the cost of lowering the price of salt to a reasonable level, hoping to win Kashmiri support in case there was a plebiscite.[46]

The rising prices of essential commodities made it extremely difficult for underpaid government officials, mostly from the Kashmiri Hindu community, to make ends meet. *Martand,* the community's official newspaper, suggested salary increases to bridge the discrepancy between income and prices. As the state exchequer refused to honor this request due to lack of funds, *Martand*'s editorials recommended that the government should provide a temporary allowance instead.[47] However, the government responded, "Where can we get more money? Until and unless the economic conditions of the country improve it is not possible to redeem that pledge."[48] Instead, trying to balance its budget, it imposed new taxes, angering Kashmiris who believed the government was making no effort to provide financial relief in times of inflation.

The chaotic sociopolitical scenario was clearly visible in Kashmiri poetry, which highlighted the broken promises of its leaders. Renowned poet Ghulam Ahmad Mahjoor (1887–1952), who had strongly supported the progressive ideas of the National Conference prior to 1947, expressed his disappointment at the failures of "freedom." He was arrested for his poem "Azadi" ("Freedom"), a satire of Kashmir's political culture:

> Freedom being of heavenly birth
> Cannot move from door to door
> You will find her camping in the homes
> Of a chosen few alone
> There is restlessness in every heart,
> But no one dare speak out—
> Afraid that with free expression
> Freedom may be annoyed.[49]

Equating freedom with unfulfilled aspirations, many Kashmiri Muslims also expressed disappointment with the National Conference's misgovernance. An extract from an intercepted letter written by a Kashmiri Muslim captures a bit of how "freedom" was understood in the early 1950s:

> We just live but prefer death to such a life. Businessmen are greatly worried and men in services have no peace of mind and physical comfort. Yes, only two hundred or three hundred men live well. God only knows how the people in general pass their days. Nobody has the courage to speak and arrests have become a daily routine. Only those men who play to their [National Conference] tune are prosperous. The people are not happy.[50]

Kashmiris suffering the ramifications of the first India–Pakistan War held Abdullah's Awami Raj, and his political partnership with India, responsible for unfulfilled promises, the suppression of their rights, and their economic misery.

Many Kashmiri community leaders who had once actively participated in the movement against the Dogra autocracy implored both their leaders and ordinary Kashmiris not to allow their hard-won freedom to slide into chaos and anarchy. Munshi Muhammad Ishaq (1901–69), a Kashmiri freedom activist and a close associate of Abdullah, wrote *Fourteenth Century* in the 1950s, a scathing critique of the shortsightedness that had made a charade of "freedom." Those who had participated in the resistance against the Dogra regime, Ishaq wrote, demanded a "price" for their sacrifices. They thronged ministers' offices seeking government jobs for their kin. To appease their political base, the ministers spent a substantial part of the budget maintaining an expanded government, even creating new posts without job descriptions. In Ishaq's opinion, this practice was not a solution to growing unemployment. The best incentive the state could provide was to increase the salaries of low-grade officials and instill accountability among politicians. At the same time, Ishaq advised Kashmiris not to be overly critical of their leaders but to understand the difficulties of administering a state under war-like conditions and without adequate finances. To curb misuse of power, he advised Kashmiris to develop strength of character and realize that real freedom could only be attained through integrity. It was clear to Munshi Ishaq that Kashmiris themselves had to take responsibility if conditions were to improve, while their leaders needed to be honest and tolerant and not lose track of what "freedom" was supposed to mean.[51]

Growing Kashmiri restlessness over Abdullah's political partnership with India was not lost on Abdullah, who saw his support base erode as economic discontent increased in the late 1940s. Abdullah's speeches requested Kashmiris to understand his administration's policies and decisions in the context of the conditions created by the India–Pakistan War. Poet Ghulam Ahmad Mahjoor versified Abdullah's speech "The Oath and Covenant of Hazratbal," delivered on January 14, 1949:

> We are at present facing difficulties
> Kashmir was caught up in the war
> It is not we who are to blame, but the prevailing situation
> Why do you complain and mourn?
> Go pray to God, he will remove your difficulties
> If you criticize us, it would be an exercise in futility

I agree we are not totally blameless,
But why do you not judge justly
And make allowances for our difficulties? [52]

The "speech" goes on to express the administration's sincere effort to "steer the Kashmiri boat, trapped in a whirlpool, to calmer waters." Although Abdullah claimed his goal was to secure peace and prosperity for Kashmir, his speeches failed to abate Kashmiri resentment. As the National Conference continued its authoritarian policies, the desire for real freedom gained intensity.

In the early years after accession, Abdullah did not harp on self-determination. His contention, rather, was that "he alone represented Kashmir and whatever he decided was good enough for Kashmiris."[53] During this period Abdullah supported Kashmir's accession to India at various national and international forums; in March 1948, Abdullah in a press conference at Delhi reiterated, "the people of Jammu and Kashmir" support India "because India is pledged to the principle of secular democracy in her policy and we are also in pursuit of the same objective."[54] Despite these promises made to India by the Kashmiri nationalist leadership, many Kashmiri Muslims remained skeptical about India's democratic credentials and their potential future place within a theoretically secular, but in reality, Hindu-dominated, Indian state.

Kashmiri Muslims and the Question of Loyalty

In the aftermath of decolonization, the Indian state chose to define itself as a "secular" country where people of all castes and creeds enjoyed equal freedoms. India celebrated Kashmir's accession to India at every national and international forum; that the Muslim-majority state of Jammu and Kashmir preferred to tie itself with secular India, rather than Islamic Pakistan, bolstered India's secular credentials. However, the Indian state failed to establish a relationship of trust with Kashmiri Muslims. The Muslim-majority character of Jammu and Kashmir, and Pakistan's disputed claim to the territory, created endless Indian doubts about Kashmiri Muslim loyalty. Many feared that in the event of a plebiscite, Kashmiri Muslims would vote for Pakistan. As a politics of fear gripped the subcontinent in the aftermath of partition, the Kashmiri Muslim community also became apprehensive about their minority status in a Hindu-majority India. They keenly observed how "secular" India was planning to define the position of minorities and manage difference, which significantly influenced their sense of belonging and loyalty.

The partition of the subcontinent in 1947 along ostensibly religious lines pitted communities against each other. The accompanying violence led to mass migrations of Hindus and Sikhs eastward and Muslims westward. Some Punjabi refugees found their way to Jammu province, carrying with them harrowing accounts of murder and rape; the presence of Hindu and Sikh refugees intensified backlash by their co-religionists against the Muslim inhabitants of Jammu.[55] The communal situation worsened as armed bands representing Hindu rightist organizations like the RSS (Rashtriya Swayamsevak Sangh) formed. Incidents of violence against Jammu's Muslims increased, forcing many to attempt migration to Pakistan. In November 1947, Dogra officials instructed the Muslims of Jammu to congregate at the state grounds known as the "police lines." They promised safe passage to Pakistan under the protection of the Dogra army. However, their convoy was redirected to a secluded area where the Muslim evacuees were executed.[56]

While interreligious violence in Jammu province affected all communities, the inability of the Hindu Dogra ruler to prevent the violence against the Jammu Muslim community had a profound impact on Kashmiri Muslims. In September 1947, the *Civil and Military Gazette* reported that "Jammu will almost be free of Muslims if the present speed of evacuation continues unchecked. It is estimated that 500,000 Muslims have migrated to West Punjab [in Pakistan]."[57] Riot-driven migration substantially decreased the number of Muslims in eastern Jammu, and precipitated Kashmiri Muslim fears that the Hindu right might alter the Valley's demography to make them a minority even within the province if Kashmir became a part of Hindu-majority India.

When, in the aftermath of partition, the Congress Party professed secular nationalism as its creed to build a strong unitary center, it was also papering over regional, religious, and linguistic differences. This conflation of secularism with nationalism in effect delegitimized any minority fears and aspirations that conflicted with the state's version of nationalism.[58] The new Indian state showed no sensitivity toward internal cultural differences and demanded unquestioning and total allegiance to the nation-state. The government placed Muslims in an undifferentiated category of people that sympathized with Pakistan. The attachment of Hindus to the Indian nation was beyond doubt, but Muslim citizens had to demonstrate their sincerity and prove that they were worthy of Indian citizenship.[59]

Indian Muslims were strongly encouraged to integrate into the Indian secular and democratic framework, but to do so they had to stop openly drawing on the religious and cultural strands of their identity. The linguistic controversy of the colonial era had made Hindus consider Hindi symbolic of their cultural identity, while Urdu was identified as the language of Muslims. Prior to independence, the Congress Party reiterated that Hindustani, written in both Devanagari and Persian script, would be the official language. However, in 1949 the Indian Constituent Assembly adopted Hindi as India's only official language, despite pleas for reconsideration by Muslim Congress Party members.[60] Having failed to secure all-India status for Urdu, Muslim Congress members attempted to at least have it recognized as a regional language. Although their petition contained more than two million signatures, the new government denied the request, arguing that it would be impossible to have Urdu as an official language due to administrative complications.[61] Even though many prominent Muslim Congress members were disappointed by this decision, they felt unable to take any further concrete step, fearing they would be labeled "anti-nationalists." In fact, Indian leaders reminded Muslims who pointed to the discrepancies between India's secular constitution and its implementation that "to win the confidence of their fellow countrymen" and the government, they had to "make India's culture [meaning Hindu culture] their own."[62]

In this context, with cultural assimilation now the highest official value, selling Kashmiri Muslims the idea of a limited accession to India proved a daunting task for Abdullah and his National Conference. The treatment afforded to Indian Muslims by the Indian state had a profound impact on how Kashmiri Muslims perceived their own potential future in India. The public discourse of Kashmiris expressed concern about moves to erase the cultural identity of Indian Muslims. They highlighted contradictions within the Congress Party, which claimed to be a secular body but directed efforts to revive Brahmanism in India. The decision of the Indian government to include cow slaughter as one of the Directive Principles of State Policy, renovate temples at state expense, and inaugurate national projects with Hindu rituals created apprehensions among Kashmiri Muslims about India's secular credentials.[63] It appeared to them that the Congress was conflating Indian culture with Hindu culture, excluding minorities in defining the new nation's identity. Ironically, while Hindu citizens of India could assert their religious identity and still claim to be "secular," the only way for Muslim citizens to be considered secular was to disassociate from their religiously informed cultural identity. Congress leaders thus, while they continually invoked the concept of "secularism," failed to earn the confidence of Kashmiri Muslims.

Partition had a psychological effect on Indians, who were frightened by the thought of losing any more territory. Under these circumstances Kashmir became the crown of India's national pride, to be retained at any cost. Public opinion in India was therefore strongly in favor of an aggressive Kashmir policy to preempt the possibility of a plebiscite. Some went even further, suggesting forcibly converting Kashmir into a Hindu-majority belt. Proposals to the Home Ministry of India argued for the resettlement of Hindu refugees in Kashmir. In October 1948, Himat Ram Guru of Jaipur suggested that fifty lakh Hindu refugees from Pakistan should be settled in the "thousand acres of land lying barren and useless."[64] He considered this action imperative for ensuring that "Kashmir remains with India for good," if ever a referendum were to take place. Indians like Himat Ram Guru saw Kashmiri Muslims as suspects to be kept under surveillance.[65] Another letter from an annoynomous "well-wisher" to the Home Ministry went so far as to label Kashmiri Muslims as the "internal enemy" of the Indian state. It proposed to

> treat [Kashmiri Muslims] the same way as we [India] have treated the raiders [from Pakistan]. The external enemies cannot harm the country so much as their associates and sympathizers within state territories can disrupt the management and aid the enemy. The key posts are held by Muslims and they can betray the Hindu population anytime.[66]

The author suggested that these "internal enemies" be ousted from the state.

Congress leaders also expressed fears about Kashmiri Muslim loyalty. In his first report on Kashmir, B. N. Mullik, the deputy director of the Intelligence Bureau, mentioned Kashmiri Muslims' intense disappointment with Pakistan and Abdullah's ideological commitment to India. But Sardar Vallabhbhai Patel, the Home Minister of India, repudiated this part of the report, convinced that Kashmiri Muslims could not be trusted and that their antipathy to the Dogra ruler was in reality an aversion to India.[67] Linking Kashmir to the broader question of Muslims in India, Patel criticized Indian Muslim silence on "Pakistan's interference in Kashmir."[68] This background explains a 1951 memorandum submitted by Indian Muslims to Frank P. Graham, a United Nations representative to India and Pakistan, which strongly advocated Kashmir's integration to "secure interests of forty million Indian Muslims."[69] During these years, eager to be accepted as India's loyal citizens, Indian Muslims formed organizations that attempted to mobilize Kashmiri Muslim public opinion in India's favor.

Kashmiris, however, disagreed that their self-determination could endanger Indian secularism. Coming from a disputed region with a Muslim majority, a Kashmiri Muslim had the leverage to question India's national integration policy of centralization and homogenization. During the early 1950s, the Praja Parishad agitation in Jammu reinforced Kashmiri Muslim insecurities and had a profound impact on the community's thought. Directed by Hindu right-wing elements and supported in India, the agitators demanded forcible integration of the state into India. Even the position adopted by the Congress Party against the Praja Parishad agitation convinced Kashmiri Muslims that the Congress and the Hindu rightist organizations were united in their desire to retain Kashmir. As Bazaz argued, the difference was only that the Congress wanted to woo Kashmiris through generous treatment and the widest possible autonomy in internal administration, while the Hindu rightist parties wanted to integrate Kashmir into India with or without the support of Kashmiri Muslims.[70]

Articulations of betrayal, anger, and resentment became particularly prevalent during the early 1950s as it became apparent that Jawaharlal Nehru's pledge to consult residents' wishes on the state's accession, made only a few years earlier, would not be upheld. Confiscated pamphlets and intercepted letters written by Kashmiri Muslims to their friends and relatives across the ceasefire line provide insight into the mood of the times and the writers' deep sense of resentment against attempts at integration.[71] An intercepted letter written to the editor of *Daily Milap* by an anonymous Kashmiri directly addressed its north Indian audience, expressing bewilderment at threats of expulsion made by various Indian leaders against citizens who kept symbols of their Muslim cultural identity. "Can democracy be established with threats and by causing fear in the hearts of minorities?" the writer wondered. He refused to accept that India was a democratic secular country; to the contrary, he was convinced that Hindu nationalism was on the rise. The letter argued that Kashmiri Muslims would resist complete accession to India if they were convinced that abrogation of Kashmir's special status was the first step toward converting Kashmir into a Hindu-dominated region.[72] The pamphlet *Three Questions*, also anonymous, critiqued the "imperialistic designs" of India that moved to "grab the land of Kashmir." According to the author, Kashmiris understood that India's promise of self-determination was only a front to gather world support and emerge as an Asian leader. Instead of allowing Kashmiris to decide their political future, India and the National Conference had collaborated to put Kashmir behind the "iron curtain"—a phrase calculated to evoke Western support in a larger Cold War context.[73]

Some prominent Hindu political activists from the Valley also strongly disagreed with India's heavy-handedness in the region. One individual who raised his voice against democratic suppression was Prem Nath Bazaz, a political adversary of Abdullah who had vocally disagreed with his politics since the 1940s, and consequently was banished to Delhi after accession.[74] Through his writings, Bazaz reminded his fellow Hindus that in a Muslim-majority state, the

Hindu-dominated center would not guarantee their security. Although it sounded plausible to control the Muslim Valley with India's help, in reality, suppression of Kashmiri Muslim democratic aspirations for any length of time would breed hostility. He predicted that India would have to have an "army of occupation" in order to retain Kashmir. This would widen divisions between communities and precipitate a struggle that would jeopardize the future and safety of Hindus in Jammu and Kashmir.[75] Bazaz implored Hindus to support the Kashmiri Muslim call for self-determination. Only then, he emphasized, would it be possible to envision a future where Hindus and Muslims could work together to set up social and political democracy in Kashmir.[76]

Bazaz articulated his vision for Kashmir's future in a 1950 pamphlet entitled *Azad Kashmir* (Free Kahmir).[77] He imagined a utopian Kashmir that would accede to Pakistan, because of the Muslim character of the state, but retain its autonomous status. To ensure feelings of security for Hindus, Sikhs, and Buddhists, this theoretical Azad Kashmir would provide substantial safeguards and reserve representative seats for minorities in proportion to their populations.[78] Although Bazaz's suggestion clearly drew from the National Conference's concept of *Naya Kashmir*, it differed significantly in both form and content. He connected the idea more overtly with rationalism, humanism, and social justice, and focused on myriad forms of freedom, decoupling it from limited notions of independence.

The end of colonialism in the subcontinent, Bazaz argued, brought *independence* but limited *freedom*; Congress leaders in India and Muslim League leaders in Pakistan alike failed to accept differences and treat minorities equally—a setback to "real freedom." Azad Kashmir, in Bazaz's vision, would set an example by providing its entire population with civil liberties, social justice, and economic emancipation. The main goal of the pamphlet was to inspire self-reliance and encourage critical thinking among Kashmiris. These traits would help replace hero worship with independence, blind faith with intelligent understanding, and ignorance with critical determination—all important facets of real democracy.[79] But although it was a brilliant idea, the Azad Kashmir movement was unrealistic. National Conference repression, and the denial of free expression, continued to generate resentment and strengthen the resistance movement in Kashmir.

Many Kashmiri Muslims from the Valley imagined a better future as part of Muslim Pakistan, which they considered sympathetic to their demands for self-determination. With no scope for democratic expression, some Kashmiris decided to adopt a more aggressive attitude and seek help from Pakistan to challenge India's undemocratic style of administration. Pakistan was more than happy to comply with such requests, especially in light of its frustrations at the United Nations' failed attempts to resolve the Kashmir conflict. Pakistan desperately wanted jurisdiction over the Valley in order to control the waters of the Indus, Jhelum, and Chenab rivers flowing from Jammu and Kashmir to Pakistan.

The people trapped in this international territorial dispute perceived themselves as powerless. A few Kashmiris believed that the only way to restrain a powerful adversary was to seek help from an equally strong force, so an underground organization, formed in 1948, planned subversive activities against what they considered the forced occupation of Kashmir by India. A conspiracy was hatched to overthrow the nationalist regime, leading to arrests of prominent lawyers, professors, and government officers. One group even succeeded in planting a bomb in the secretariat building, where a meeting of the cabinet was to take place. The state foiled the plan and the perpetrators were arrested, although they ultimately escaped to Pakistan-administered Kashmir.[80]

Those Kashmiris who imagined a better future with Pakistan and left the Valley, either of their own free will or through forced expulsion, soon felt disappointed with their new reality. Kashmiris arriving in Pakistan-administered Kashmir (Azad Kashmir) for the first time were shocked at how Pakistani bureaucracy also smothered democracy in the region. Although Pakistan maintained that Azad Kashmir was independent, and allowed the territory to have the trappings of its own constitution, prime minister, president, and flag, all real power remained with the Pakistani bureaucrats in the Ministry of Kashmir Affairs.[81] A memoir written by displaced Kashmiri lawyer Khawaja Ghulam Naqui (1925–2002) narrates the frustrations of Kashmiri Muslims during this period as they sought political space within Pakistan while simultaneously holding on to their regional identity. An ardent supporter of accession to Pakistan, Naqui had suffered "tribulations and hardships" in India-administered Kashmir due to his extreme political ideology. Having escaped to Azad Kashmir after his arrest in connection with the 1948 anti-state activities, Naqui became disillusioned shortly after crossing the ceasefire line. The Ministry of Kashmir Affairs, he wrote, treated "Azad Kashmir's territory [as] a colony of Pakistan" and strengthened its power by "manipulating one Kashmiri group against the other." It seemed to him that an "honorarium from Pakistani exchequer" made most politicians and refugee families subservient and economically dependent on Pakistan. His refusal to accept such an "honorarium" made him suspect in the eyes of the Ministry of Kashmir Affairs, which quickly labeled him a "possible agent of Abdullah's regime." These experiences shattered his previous political beliefs.[82]

The doubts cast on the "loyalty" of any Kashmiri who expressed dissent against the ruling government on either side of the ceasefire line complicated Kashmiri feelings of belonging. Disappointment increased due to the deteriorating political and economic conditions of Azad Kashmir and the indifference of the Pakistani administration to resolving people's issues. In his contemporary notes, F. P. Mainprice, a British citizen who worked for the Ministry of Kashmir Affairs after partition, elaborated how the Indian–Pakistan War of 1948 left the villages close to the "border" uninhabitable: bombs destroyed homes, while tribal fighters looted property and slaughtered cattle. Fear of shelling prevented cultivation, leading to scarcity of food grains. Traditional sources of income that sustained these far-flung villages were destroyed, while Pakistan used their manpower as "unpaid labor" for the "defense of the country." Mainprice expressed concern that the Ministry of Kashmir Affairs paid more attention to power politics, propaganda, and a distant and still entirely theoretical plebiscite than to the immediate practical problems of food, transport, housing, and rehabilitation. They deliberately restricted visits by foreign journalists and United Nations delegates to "accessible areas where civil administration was effective," creating a misleading picture about the real conditions in Pakistan-administered Kashmir.[83] Mainprice believed that these hardships demoralized Kashmiris and created a feeling of bitterness toward Pakistan.

Kashmiri discontent is corroborated by letters written back and forth across the ceasefire line. While elite Kashmiri Muslim families integrated relatively easily into Pakistani society, poorer Kashmiris found it difficult to survive in Azad Kashmir. A 1951 intercepted letter from Muhammed Shafi, originally a resident of Gojwara, Srinagar, narrates his difficulty in finding employment and making ends meet in Azad Kashmir. Shafi's letter provides insight into the desperation of Kashmiris eager to return to the "mother country" at any cost, as he refers to an incident involving approximately one hundred Kashmiri Muslims who decided to secretly cross the ceasefire line after Pakistan's government denied them permits to return home. A battalion of the Pakistani Army stopped them close to the line near Moji village, forcing them to return to Muzaffarabad. A few of them, nevertheless attempting to run toward the forest, were killed by the soldiers. Shafi's letter advised Kashmiris in the Valley to develop a realistic understanding of the conditions in Pakistan and not attempt to cross the "border."[84]

Stories of economic hardships and smothered democracy in Pakistan-administered Kashmir made Kashmiris question whether that region was free to shape its destiny any more than India-administered Kashmir was. Another intercepted letter, written by a displaced Kashmiri to his friend in Jammu, provides a glimpse into emerging Kashmiri Muslim apprehensions about Pakistan:

> The intentions of Pakistan in respect to Kashmir are not honest. These Pakistani *nawabs* [princes] want beautiful Valley of Kashmir— They have neither any sympathy for Muslims nor any idea for the welfare of Pakistan. We have seen their working in the small area of Azad Kashmir where they have deprived locals of their internal freedom. Our leaders are not capable of introducing present day reforms nor are they in a position to appreciate their value [*sic*]. It will not be an act of wisdom to get out of India's grips and fall into that of the Pakistani roguish *nawabs* [*sic*].[85]

Kashmiris' frustration increased through the early 1950s as they struggled to locate themselves within the new context of the nation-states "India" and "Pakistan." The international community, as represented by the United Nations, failed to resolve the conflict and bring the two competing parties to the table to develop a consensus on Kashmiri self-determination.[86] It gradually dawned on Kashmiris that India and Pakistan, with utter disregard for their aspirations, saw their homeland as a piece of land to be gained and retained. The rich complexity of Kashmiri Muslim belonging flowers in Saadat Hasan Manto's 1951 short story "Tetwal ka Kutta," about a dog subjected to political brutality by Indian and Pakistani forces. Tetwal is a border area in the state of Jammu and Kashmir, and the dog—called Jhunjhun by the Indians and Sunsun by the Pakistanis—finds it hard to distinguish the arbitrary ceasefire line. He, like the Kashmiris he represents, "does not know whether he is a Pakistani or an Indian, and is eventually killed in crossfire between the two."[87]

Throughout this period, Kashmiris lamented the division of Jammu and Kashmir as a result of the war, but even more, they wanted stability and a definite end to the bitter feud between India and Pakistan. Peace in the region, they believed, would end poverty, promote tourism, and allow Kashmir to trade with both countries.[88] There was no general sense of identity with India or Pakistan; the overwhelming majority of Kashmiris, if free to choose, would probably have voted for an independent Kashmir.[89] Ghulam Mahjoor's poem "An Appeal" is a lament on the impending fate of Kashmir as it faced the immense, disempowering trials that ushered in perennial conflict instead of long awaited freedom:

> O morning breeze when you reach America
> Go to the Council in Lake Success and describe our plight in detail
> A wrestling match started in our home and we got trampled underfoot
> One says Pakistan, and another says Hindustan
> Meanwhile this country has become a Dakistan [a ruined country]
> Let them leave us that would be best for us

Let these wise people be thrown out of this land
We will ourselves rule our own country, this is our only plea![90]

While the nation-states wanted to establish territorial control, ordinary Kashmiris affected by the arbitrary drawing of a line that divided their families and disrupted economic interactions wanted prosperity for their homeland. Mahjoor's poem pleaded not only with India and Pakistan but with the world community to recognize Kashmir's plight and allow Kashmiris to control their own land.

This ambiguity was further reinforced by Kashmiri Muslim leadership, especially Sheikh Abdullah, who dabbled with the idea of independence while officially maintaining that he sought an autonomous Kashmir within India. Speaking to British correspondents Michael Davidson and Ward Price in 1949, Abdullah expressed his interest in a united Jammu and Kashmir, its independence guaranteed not only by India and Pakistan but also by Britain, the United States, and other members of the United Nations, as a possible solution to lingering territorial disputes.[91] India saw Abdullah's statement as a challenge to the finality of Indian accession. Although Abdullah backtracked to appease his Indian backers, he nevertheless worked feverishly to ensure that Kashmir's accession to India would be limited, while also exploring the option of an independent Kashmir, backed by foreign powers and having treaty relations with both India and Pakistan.

Kashmiri "Particularism" and the State-subject

Although Jammu and Kashmir state acceded to India in 1947, because it was the only state negotiating its relationship with Delhi, that relationship was distinctive compared to other Indian states.[92] At the time of independence, the princely states signed an instrument of accession limiting the jurisdiction of India's central government to three subjects: defense, foreign affairs, and communication. Subsequently, they were integrated completely into the Indian Union. Almost all of the 565 princely states within India's new territorial boundaries followed this pattern, but the disputed nature of Kashmir's territory, and the United Nations resolutions that called for a plebiscite there, made Jammu and Kashmir an exception.[93] Even the government of India clarified as early as 1948 in its official publication about the provisional nature of Kashmir's accession, "until such a time as the will of the people of the state could be ascertained."[94] Furthermore, the Kashmiri leadership that legitimized India's presence in Kashmir had also insisted that its support for Kashmir's accession to India was conditional on India allowing Kashmir to retain its autonomous status. These complications confronted the Indian Constituent Assembly when it began debating the position of princely states within the Indian Union in the spring of 1949.

Kashmiri–Indian negotiations for an acceptable settlement dominated local political discourse in 1949. The Kashmiri leadership, led by Abdullah, met with Indian prime minister Jawaharlal Nehru and his deputy, Sardar Patel, to deliberate on "the subjects in respect of which the state should accede to the Union of India." On October 17, 1949, the Indian Constituent Assembly, aware of the international implications of the Kashmir question, inserted Article 306A into India's constitution, affirming the provisional accession of Jammu and Kashmir pending final settlement of the dispute with Pakistan.[95] After India became a republic in January 1950, "Article 306A became the basis of Article 370 of the Indian constitution," which asserted Jammu and Kashmir's autonomy within the Indian union.[96] A wide range of provisions of the Indian constitution pertaining to other Indian states therefore did not apply to Jammu and Kashmir. The state was entitled to its own constitution and to set up its own constituent assembly to determine the sphere of the central government's jurisdiction over the state. Parliament's legislative powers under this article were again restricted to defense, foreign affairs, and communication.[97] Article 370 specifically stated that if other union powers were extended to Jammu and Kashmir, the prior approval of the state government was required. Most importantly, the consent provided by the state government was strictly provisional and had to be ratified by the state constituent assembly.[98]

Even though the Indian parliament had approved a special status, clearly its leadership saw Article 370 as a temporary feature that would eventually be removed to ensure a strong center. The principal drafter of Article 370, N. Gopalaswami Ayyangar, explained Kashmir's special status in these words: "…it is one of our commitments to the people and the government of Jammu and Kashmir that no such additions should be made except with the consent of the state constituent assembly which may be called in the state for the purpose of framing its constitution." At the same time, he expressed hope that "in due course even Jammu and Kashmir will become ripe for some sort of integration" akin to other Indian states.[99]

In the early 1950s, the Indian government consented to both the formation of a constituent assembly in Jammu and Kashmir and a self-framed state constitution. This arrangement was based on India's understanding that the constituent assembly would ratify Kashmir's accession to India, thus avoiding the necessity of complying with the United Nations–mandated plebiscite.[100] In early 1951, the

National Conference government began preparations to convene the constituent assembly. Concerned with this new turn of events, Pakistan raised the matter at the United Nations, whose Security Council "reminded the governments and authorities concerned that future status of the state could only be decided through the democratic method of free and impartial plebiscite."[101] It also made clear that any decision reached by the constituent assembly to determine the state's future affiliation would not be binding on any party. Nevertheless, Abdullah went ahead with his plans, as he wanted the assembly to decide the issue of accession. All the opposition parties either boycotted or were barred from participating in the elections, so National Conference members dominated the assembly.[102]

Once the constituent assembly was formed in October 1951, it did not immediately adopt the Indian constitution, but laid out three options for Kashmir's future: integration with India, accession to Pakistan, and complete independence.[103] Although in his opening speech Abdullah established his preference for autonomy within India, New Delhi and Kashmir differed in their definition of "autonomous status." Indian leadership saw Article 370 as temporary, but Abdullah's viewpoint was that any dilution of the terms of Article 370 over time would lead to an obliteration of Kashmir's relationship with India. These perceptions of Abdullah manifested in the *Report of the Basic Principles Committee*, which imagined Jammu and Kashmir as "an autonomous republic within the Indian Union, with a separate president, national assembly, judiciary, regional autonomy, and separate citizenship."[104] The assembly also adopted a separate state flag to be "flown on all normal occasions and restricted the use of the Indian national flag to formal functions."[105]

Several Kashmiri Muslims, however, expressed disappointment with Abdullah's decision to form the constituent assembly to decide the accession issue, rather than a free and fair plebiscite. Anti-Abdullah posters appeared at several localities of Srinagar city criticizing Abdullah for his failure to translate his vision of freedom, which had mobilized countless Kashmiris to offer sacrifices during the Quit Kashmir movement against the Dogra monarchy. Intelligence reports from this period reveal a growing desire even among the Kashmiri government officials to "sabotage the formation of the Constituent Assembly" and hold Abdullah accountable. While voices of dissent rejected Abdullah's leadership, the National Conference continued with its agenda of securing autonomy and special privileges for Kashmiris.[106]

Another debate consuming the Kashmir constituent assembly related to the question of citizenship for Kashmiris. This debate was intimately connected with a concept developed as a legal category only recently: the state-subject. During the first decades of the twentieth century the Kashmiri Hindu community, equipped with modern education, had begun to feel threatened by the rising numbers of Punjabi Hindus in government employment. They initiated a movement, "Kashmir for Kashmiris," claiming their superior rights as *mulki*s ("people of the land") as opposed to "outsiders." In 1912 the Dogra ruler adopted criteria for defining a "Kashmiri," including residency in Jammu and Kashmir "for not less than twenty years" and "intention to live in the said territories for an unlimited time." The possession of immovable state property was another qualification to secure a *rayat-nama*, or state-subject certificate. In reserving appointments for state subjects, however, the maharaja included employees from other parts of India who had been in service for ten years.[107] The Kashmiri Hindu community, unhappy with this extension of the state-subject category, organized an agitation, pressuring the maharaja to grant the title of "state-subject" only to persons who could prove hereditary residence in the state for five generations. In 1927, the Dogra ruler instituted another definition: "all persons born and residing in the state before the commencement of the reign of Maharaja Gulab Singh and all the persons who settled therein before the commencement of 1885 and have since been permanently residing in the country" were now considered state-subjects. The maharaja also decreed that people from outside the state who lacked this designation could neither own land nor seek employment in the princely state of Jammu and Kashmir.[108]

The state-subject category thus came to define Kashmiri political identity, which further twisted the ambiguity about Kashmiri Muslim belonging in the postcolonial era. As India-administered Kashmir was autonomous, its constituent assembly exercised its exclusive right to define and regulate the rights and privileges of state residents by retaining the Dogra maharaja's state-subject category to define "citizens" of Jammu and Kashmir state. In his 1952 address to the constituent assembly, Sheikh Abdullah defined a "natural" citizen of Jammu and Kashmir as an "inhabitant of Kashmir whose father has been living on this land since times immemorial." He extended the privileges and obligations of state citizenship to those "stranded Kashmiris" in Pakistan-administered territories who wished to return home once peace prevailed. Even the constitution of Jammu and Kashmir reserved almost twenty-five seats in the legislative assembly for displaced Kashmiris.[109] Mirza Afzal Beg, a prominent member of Abdullah's cabinet, advocated "double citizenship," common under federal governments. Separate citizenship for Kashmiris, Afzal Beg argued, was a necessity to ensure that the "backward" region, steeped in poverty, would have the "unhindered opportunity to progress" by "reserving services for the indigenous inhabitants of the state."[110]

However, in negotiations with Delhi, Abdullah agreed that permanent residents of Jammu and Kashmir had no citizenship distinct from Indian citizenship.

The Indian prime minister in a statement to the parliament in July 1952 reiterated India's commitment to respect the special privileges granted to citizens of Jammu and Kashmir that "barred non-state subjects from acquiring immovable property and applying for jobs in the state."[111] Nehru emphasized that the "state legislature shall have the power to define and regulate" the rights of the permanent residents of the state.[112] Later, the Presidential Order of 1954 embedded these special privileges in Article 35A of the Indian constitution. Across the ceasefire line, the government of Azad Jammu and Kashmir also kept the category of state-subject, reserving state employment and property ownership to them and recognizing all displaced state-subjects as Kashmiris.[113] In postcolonial Kashmir, the state-subject category became a key marker of Kashmiri Muslim political identity and reinforced Kashmiri affiliation with the territory of Jammu and Kashmir as it existed before the drawing of the ceasefire line in 1949.[114]

While in the early 1950s the various decisions by the state constituent assembly in India-administered Kashmir were in complete conformity with Article 370, the central government concurrently pressed for a personal settlement with Abdullah. These negotiations culminated in the Delhi Agreement, made between Nehru and Abdullah on July 24, 1952, and understood as a first step toward integration. According to the terms of this agreement, Jammu and Kashmir would be part of India, although retaining a high degree of autonomy. The state would have its Sadar-i-Riyasat, or governor, chosen by the state assembly rather than appointed by the Indian president as in other states. Additionally, Kashmiris would be classified as citizens of India, and their flag would fly beneath the Indian tricolor. However, no definite agreement was reached with regard to "citizenship, fundamental rights, the jurisdiction of the Supreme Court of India, financial integration and application of emergency provisions to the state."[115]

Abdullah had surrendered various other matters in the instrument of accession to India. However, he found it difficult to reconcile the ideals of the National Conference with the provisions of the Delhi Agreement. The constituent assembly debated the agreement and some of its members expressed apprehensions about any modifications to the current Delhi–Kashmir relationship. Some worried that applying the fundamental rights of the Indian constitution to Kashmir would impact the "revolutionary agrarian reforms" that confiscated land without compensation and provided it to the peasants.[116] Others expressed unwillingness to accept the jurisdiction of the Supreme Court as the "conservative constitution of India" would not accommodate "people-friendly measures, like the abolition of the *jagirdari* [land grant] system" and would involve Jammu and Kashmir in the "labyrinth of the Supreme Court," wasting both time and money.[117] The assembly expressed its willingness to create fundamental rights and duties for "citizens" according to the *Naya Kashmir* manifesto, rather than the Indian constitution. The National Conference also strongly resented an attempt made by the central government to bring about financial integration by extending the jurisdiction of the central comptroller and auditor general to the state.[118] The Delhi Agreement of 1952 thus failed to provide a permanent resolution to the question of Jammu and Kashmir's precise relationship with India, instead starting Jammu and Kashmir down a conflicting path with the Indian state and exposing simmering regional divisions.

Agrarian Reforms and Minority Voices in Kashmir, Jammu, and Ladakh

Kashmir's postcolonial political dynamics cannot be understood without considering emerging sub-regional tensions within the state of Jammu and Kashmir. The accession of the state to India brought the Valley into prominence for the first time since the princely state's creation in 1846. This shift had a decisive bearing not only on the continuing interplay between region and center, but also on communitarian interactions. A large share of religious minorities in Jammu, Ladakh, and the Valley expressed reservations about the National Conference's administrative policies that they considered a deliberate ploy to alter their socioeconomic status and ensure the domination of the Muslim majority. The fears and insecurities gripping minorities in the aftermath of the sovereignty dispute shaped their sense of belonging and their relationship with the Muslim majority community.

Several factors precipitated interregional tensions and placed the Valley on a collision course with other subregions as well as the Indian state.[119] During the tribal invasion of 1947, Abdullah, as head of the Emergency Administration, reached most decisions without consulting Maharaja Hari Singh even though constitutional authority still technically rested with him.[120] Relations between Abdullah and the maharaja further deteriorated after Abdullah's administration held Hari Singh responsible for the communal riots in Jammu that converted the subregion into a Hindu-dominated belt.[121] National Conference leaders accused the maharaja's prime minister of distributing arms received from India for the Home Guards, the local militia resisting the tribal invasion, to the Hindu right-wing activists of the RSS to eliminate Jammu's Muslim population.[122]

The extermination of Muslim evacuees transported from Jammu and surrounding areas toward Pakistan, while under the supposed protection of the Dogra state army, raised deep concerns within and outside the state. Mohandas Gandhi, the preeminent leader of the Congress Party, called for the maharaja's abdication since he had failed to protect his subjects.[123] Abdullah, meanwhile, suggested curtailing the rights of the maharaja and reducing his powers as the titular head of state.[124] Hari Singh's frustrations increased as political initiative and power slipped from Dogra hands. He observed his irrelevance to the Indian government, which insisted on appeasing Abdullah's demands and whims while advising the maharaja to embrace a "spirit of accommodation, forbearance, and statesmanship."[125] Indian leadership, in other words, was unwilling to side with the maharaja while Abdullah's support remained critical to its presence in Kashmir.

The minority Hindu community in the Valley, which had held most positions of power during Dogra rule, struggled to adapt to the changing political dynamics of independence. Prior to 1947, the loyalty of Kashmiri Hindus (Pandits) lay with the maharaja. After the state's accession to India, many in this community began to identify their religious and political interests with India, where Hindus were a majority. Although Sheikh Abdullah's politics had been criticized by Pandits during the Dogra regime, many of them embraced him in 1947 as a beacon of Hindu–Muslim unity, because his support ensured that Kashmir would remain with India rather than acceding to Pakistan.[126]

In the early 1950s some of Abdullah's policy decisions, motivated primarily by his desire to implement the *Naya Kashmir* manifesto, and stem the loss of his social base among the Muslim community, generated resentment among minorities. The official mouthpiece of the Kashmiri Hindu community, *Martand*, highlighted the contradictions in Abdullah's supposed "secularism," and pointed out the discrepancies in his administrative policies geared to the interests of the Muslim community.[127] Kashmiri Pandits accused the government of catering to its Muslim voting base by creating a separate Muslim-majority district of Doda, thereby dividing and weakening the Hindu-majority district of Udhampur in Jammu province. Minorities' cries about discrimination increased after the government decided to grant college scholarships on the basis of need rather than merit.[128] Highly educated non-Muslims felt this policy excluded meritorious Hindu students and gave undue preference to the Muslim community. In the government sector, Kashmiri Pandits now had to share jobs with the Muslim community; in some cases, corruption and nepotism allowed less qualified Muslims to hold important government positions.[129]

These post-independence shifts in local power structures provoked a strong reaction from Kashmiri Hindus; they struggled to comprehend how Kashmiri

Muslims could secure such an advantageous position in such a brief time. This was not what they had "bargained for or expected under India; it added to their ill will against Muslims and the Kashmir government."[130] Fear of Muslim political domination led some insecure Pandits to portray Kashmiri Muslims as unreliable and untrustworthy in their reports to the Indian government.[131] Claiming to be the only true "secular nationalists" from the Valley, they doubted the sincerity of the National Conference's proclaimed ideals, and questioned the secular credentials of their Muslim neighbors.[132]

None of the new state policies transformed communitarian relations as much as the decision of the state constituent assembly to transform rural Kashmir by implementing revolutionary agrarian reforms abolishing absentee landlordism.[133] As most of the land available for redistribution was in the possession of Hindus, they interpreted agrarian reform as a deliberate move to alter the entire social organization of the state to the disadvantage of the minority community. In October 1950, the National Conference government passed the Big Landed Estate Abolition Act, transferring land ownership in excess of 22.75 acres (excluding orchards, fuel, and fodder resources) to its tillers.[134] From 1950 to 1952, about 700,000 of Jammu's landless peasants, including 250,000 low-caste Hindus, became peasant proprietors.[135] The state took over untenanted land and the property of evacuees to set up collective or cooperative farming for landless laborers.[136]

The most revolutionary aspect of these reforms was that no compensation was paid to the now former landlords, the case against such compensation having been made by the commission set up by the constituent assembly to deliberate implementation of the agrarian reform. Even though the Indian constitution guaranteed payment for the acquisition of property for public purposes, the commission argued that Kashmir's autonomous nature allowed it to abolish landlordism without compensation.[137] Their report stated that the government lacked the resources to pay the market value for the land. Further, it claimed that the land had originally belonged to the tiller, while the princely-era proprietors of the land were descendants of rent collectors, leaseholders, and government servants who had manipulated records and claimed ownership rights even though their tenants had done all the work of reclaiming and improving the land. The commission held that as "sleeping partners," landlords had no right to own land beyond certain limits and would have to be content with what the act allowed them to retain. It concluded that there was no moral, economic, or social basis for compensation, which would only perpetuate the inequitable distribution of wealth.[138]

Kashmiri peasants, who benefited economically and socially from these agrarian reforms, held Abdullah in deep reverence and emerged as his core base of support. However, these reforms did not benefit all Kashmiri peasants equally. Gains were defined by one's place in the rural hierarchy, with the top tier of the peasantry profiting more than the landless. Peasants who rented from holders of more than 22.5 acres acquired 1 acre to 6 acres for themselves. Conversely, many peasants that rented from landlords with holdings of 12.5 acres or less not only remained landless even after the reforms but, worse, continued to pay half of their produce as rent.[139] Particular villages also certainly benefitted more than others. A case study conducted by Daniel Thorner in the 1950s investigated a single *halqa*, or administrative zone, to study the impact of Kashmir's agrarian reforms. In one particular village, there were two kinds of land: 300 acres of *marusi* (ancestral) land, which peasants owned and tilled themselves, and about 650 acres held by an absentee landlord based in Srinagar city. Under the Big Estate Abolition Act, the absentee landlord lost almost all of his land. Peasants had cultivated about 500 acres of this land; 120 acres had been underwater since the floods of 1950. The government turned over the cultivated 500 acres to its tenants, who in most cases already held *marusi* land. On the other hand, landless laborers from nearby villages received patches of submerged land ranging in size from one quarter to one half acre. In order to make this soggy wasteland yield crops, landless laborers borrowed money from *sarmayadars* (moneylenders) for seeds, cattle, and ploughs. Out of 1,800 villagers, only ten families now had enough land for subsistence. The rest migrated to cities as laborers.[140]

While these laws aimed at ameliorating the position of the peasantry, their implementation only added to many tenants' problems. The Distressed Debtors Relief Act of 1950 was another measure in this mold. This law intended to free the peasantry from the clutches of the usurious *sarmayadars*. If the debtor proved he had repaid the original principal "one and a half times through cash or kind" the remaining debt would be written off. The implementation of these reforms was outside the purview of the judiciary; instead, the "Debt Reconciliation Board decided such issues with no provision for the lawyers" to avoid legal intricacies.[141] Between July 1950 and the end of 1951, the debt board "examined 41,000 and settled 35,000 cases. These cases had a total debt of an estimated 10 million rupees which was scaled down to 2.3 million rupees."[142] The passing of the Debtors Relief Act, however, created a new problem: proprietors created by agrarian reforms found it difficult to borrow money to improve their land. There were no "reliable credit societies" created by the government to meet the monetary needs of peasants.[143] Distressed by the new law, moneylenders refused to give loans to peasants for purchasing seed, cattle, and agricultural implements until they signed a legal document in the presence of magistrates. Instead of improving the conditions of landless peasants, these reforms forced some to work for free on the fields of moneylenders to pay off their debts.

Meanwhile, the bureaucracy in charge of land distribution extorted money from gullible peasants by making them deposit a fee for transferring land. In many cases, a tenant had to pay a sum equal to the market price of the land allotted to him.[144] The "*sarmayadars* (moneylenders), *sarpanches* (village officials) and *khadpanches* (people who surround village officials in hope of gaining influence or wealth), in connivance with village officials," manipulated revenue records and rewarded themselves and their friends with the best land.[145] Many landowners declared their estates "orchards" because the agrarian law exempted fruit farms from the acreage ceiling. In other cases, they saved their lands by dividing the property among family members.[146] Certainly, Kashmiri nationalist narratives' picture of a prosperous rural Kashmir, where peasants were freed from bondage and landed elites lost their power, were a bit overstated.

Agrarian reforms did, however, negatively affect former landowners, the majority of whom belonged to the Hindu community. Dogra *zamindars* considered the compulsory acquisition of land without compensation an infringement on their fundamental rights, deliberately designed to benefit the Muslim community of Kashmir. Muslim peasants, they complained, gained a "double advantage" by gaining proprietary rights without making any payment. The Hindu community, on the other hand, was deprived of their "only means of livelihood," leaving them with no option but to migrate to other parts of India.

Jammu's *zamindars* petitioned the state to differentiate between categories of landlords as it decided about compensation. They complained that about 30 percent of the land owned by their community had not been received as a *jagir*, or land grant, but had been secured in the late nineteenth century when the maharaja allowed people to cultivate barren lands. In the case of landlords who had purchased their own lands and made huge investments, the *zamindars* argued, nonpayment of compensation was unjust. They pointed to disparity of implementing socialist principles on the land while allowing "capitalists" like businessmen, contractors, and traders to accumulate money: "Our ancestors labored hard, earned money and purchased lands, while others utilized their earnings in gold, silver, houses and shops. The government should not interfere with our legal rights."[147] The land being taken away from them without compensation had been purchased with their hard-earned money, in the hope that it would yield good returns for future generations. The community emphasized that it was not against agrarian reforms in theory but wanted equal and just treatment in practice to preserve their community from economic ruin and future migrations. They suggested, furthermore, that the state "dispose of the properties of evacuees and raise funds to pay compensation to the landlords" since the government lacked pre-existing resources for this.[148]

The maharaja complained to the Home Ministry of India about the revocation of *jagirs*. He interpreted this policy as a deliberate move by the National Conference to estrange him from the landlords who had pledged loyalty to his family.[149] Under Sardar Patel, the ministry was sympathetic to the maharaja's position, and asked Abdullah to reconsider abolishing the *jagirdari* system without compensation on constitutional grounds. This measure, the home ministry feared, would create ill feelings within Kashmir's minority community.[150] However, Abdullah considered these reforms an internal matter, outside the jurisdiction of New Delhi. In no mood to compromise at this moment, Abdullah reminded Sardar Patel that National Conference support for the provisional accession had been given on the promise that the socialist principles enshrined in the Conference's New Kashmir manifesto would become a reality within independent India.[151]

The National Conference's increasing hold on state power in the post-independence period thus created deep resentment in Jammu. The inhabitants of Jammu complained Abdullah only "catered to his Kashmiri Muslim political base." Jammuites felt ignored and underrepresented in the state's political structure.[152] The Dogra community considered Abdullah a representative of Kashmiri Muslims, while non-Muslims regarded the maharaja as a "symbol of their safety." In July 1949, the maharaja, under pressure from both the Congress Party and the National Conference, abdicated in favor of his son, Karan Singh. This was an interim arrangement, however, since in June 1952 the constituent assembly of Kashmir abolished the institution of the monarchy altogether. In the future, a democratically elected state constituent assembly would choose the constitutional head of the state because "sovereignty resides in the people" and all "power and authority must flow from the expression of their free will."[153]

However, this decision was made by an assembly dominated by members of the National Conference, which had won all seventy-five seats in the state's first-ever elections. This overwhelming victory was not, however, due to equally dominant popular support. The government had barred many members of the opposition in Jammu to contest elections, especially the Praja Parishad. They had rejected the nomination papers of at least thirteen candidates.[154] The Praja Parishad felt locked out of democratic participation, considered the abolition of the monarchy a ploy to remove all traces of Hindu power. One contemporary letter complained that Kashmir's Muslims were "infatuated and intoxicated with unbridled power. They terrorize the minorities, to an extent, that they [minorities] feel that the Congress has created a Pakistan in Kashmir in order to wipe out the name of Hinduism from this state. They [Kashmiri Muslims] look forward to the day when they could find their way out of the homeland [India]." In this connection, "we would assure you and warn you that the Muslims are and will be for Pakistan however, India may try to placate them."[155] The crux of his letter was that Kashmiri Muslims are not to be trusted. Even Abdullah, who had advocated accession to India, was now branded as the worst enemy of India and Hindus.

Ladakh, a sparsely populated region with a mountainous terrain, had a majority Buddhist population, which was equally discontented with the National Conference. Ladakhi Buddhists perceived the agrarian reforms as an attack on their monasteries, since much land was the property of the *gompas*, though rented to peasants at extortionate rates.[156] The new state budget also did not allow any funds for the construction of canals, improvement of roads, or betterment of communication in the subregion.[157]

Marginalized within the new state structures, Ladakhi Buddhists claimed a separate national identity and decided to break away from "Kashmiri rule." In 1949, the "Buddhist Association of Ladakh" submitted a memorandum to Jawaharlal Nehru, requesting that Ladakh not be bound by the plebiscite decision should the state's Muslim majority decide in favor of Pakistan.[158] In 1952 the abbot of Spituk monastery, Kushok Bakula, challenged the legality of the state government's jurisdiction over Ladakh, claiming that with the transference of sovereign power from the maharaja to the National Conference, the constitutional link that tied the subregion to the Valley was shattered. A separate treaty, signed in 1834, had governed Ladakh's relationship with the Dogra Raj, and as a result, Bakula claimed the moral and juridical right to shape the future of Ladakh independent of the rest of the state.[159] Without directly demanding secession from the Indian union, the *lama* hinted at political union with Tibet if India failed to ensure Ladakh's prosperity. In 1952, Bakula sought federal status for Ladakh, including a legislative assembly with sole authority to make laws for the region. If this plan was not acceptable to the Indian state, Bakula suggested the formation of a fifteen-member statuary advisory committee based on joint electorates to deliberate on Ladakh's economic, political, and religious matters.[160] However, the state ignored his demands, and Ladakhi resistance against the Valley's political and economic dominance continued.

Overall, Kashmir's minority communities were apprehensive about their future in a Muslim-majority state that had introduced reforms and legislations placing them, as a group, at significant disadvantage. The fear visible in their discourse was attenuated by the disputed nature of Jammu and Kashmir and the United Nations' promise of self-determination; in the event of a plebiscite, Muslim-majority Kashmir might vote for Pakistan and jeopardize their future. Hindu rightist groups in Jammu played up these fears and launched a virulent campaign against the National Conference's demand for autonomy, which was the basis of Kashmir's political partnership with India.

Praja Parishad's Response to Kashmir's Autonomy and the Plebiscite Question

In the 1950s, a Jammu-based Hindu rightist political party, the Praja Parishad, launched a powerful and aggressive campaign to integrate Jammu and Kashmir into the Indian union.[161] The Praja Parishad agitation was focused on the ambiguous concepts of belonging and loyalty I have previously explored, and brought the presence of a minority community identifying with India, and a majority community torn between India, Pakistan, and Kashmiri independence, into sharp relief, while also precipitating the downfall of Sheikh Abdullah and his National Conference. Although the Praja Parishad articulated the needs of the Jammu subregion, it drew its roots from the RSS, a Hindu nationalist organization dedicated to the protection of Hindu cultural, political, and religious interests.[162] The Praja Parishad party interpreted the socioeconomic transformation in Jammu and Kashmir as the result of a Muslim administration bent on destroying Hindu culture.[163]

The Praja Parishad accused Sheikh Abdullah of preaching the "cult of Kashmiri nationalism," which it considered contrary to "Indian nationalism." Textbooks portraying Kashmir as an independent nation sharing its boundaries with neighboring India seemed dangerous to India's integrity. The party found the idea of an autonomous Kashmir with a separate flag, a separate constitution, and a separate president unacceptable because these elements would deliberately create a separatist mentality among Kashmiri Muslims.[164] Most members of the Hindu community who were former supporters of the National Conference resented Abdullah's resistance to complete integration and came to doubt his patriotism.

The Praja Parishad drew its main support base from the urban middle class of Jammu city. In February 1952, students from Jammu's Gandhi Memorial College protested the hoisting of the National Conference party flag alongside the Indian flag at an event where Abdullah was a guest of honor.[165] When state authorities decided to expel the students, Jammu became a scene of continuous protests. The slogan "one nation, one constitution, and one president" became the Parishad battle cry.[166] The agitation moved from demonstrations towards extremism, with occasional incidents involving sabotage against factories, bridges, and government buildings. Constant clashes between the police and demonstrators led to large-scale arrests, while the state government's stern measures to curb agitators created a public uproar in India about the denial of civil liberties to Jammu and Kashmir's Hindu minority.

In June 1952 the Praja Parishad submitted a memorandum to Dr. Rajendra Prasad, the president of India, expressing its desire to completely integrate. Claiming that the Indian nation was one and its constitutional principles applicable to all its citizens, with no exceptions on the basis of distinctive communal identity,[167] the party argued that the Delhi Agreement was an appeasement of Kashmiri Muslims and a betrayal of Indian soldiers and citizens who had endured physical and economic privations to retain Kashmir for India. Kashmiri Muslims did not deserve special treatment, the memo argued, on account of the "psychological and religious pulls of Pakistan." If "thirty-five million Muslims in India are living as equal and free citizens," Kashmiri Muslims could also live as an integral part of India and accept the Indian constitution.[168] Throughout this period, Parishad activists toured different parts of India, reaching a national audience and widening their support base beyond Jammu.

The Praja Parishad agitation received moral, material, and political support from Hindu rightist parties all over India, including the Jan Sangh, the Hindu Mahasabha, and the Akali Dal of Punjab. In its 1952 Kanpur session, Jan Sangh authorized its president, Syama Prasad Mookerjee, to organize a *satyagraha*, or civil disobedience movement, in support of the Jammu agitation.[169] Mookerjee entered into an elaborate correspondence with both Nehru and Abdullah to discuss the viewpoint of the agitators. He emphasized the failure of both the Congress and the National Conference to satisfy the aspirations of Jammu and Ladakh, which had led to the agitation. For peace to prevail, Mookerjee suggested to "both parties to reiterate that the unity of the state would be maintained and the principle of autonomy would apply to the province of Jammu as a whole and of course, also to Ladakh and Kashmir Valley."[170] This position contradicted Mookerjee's support of the movement for full integration.

The finalization of Kashmir's accession to India without holding a plebiscite in the Valley remained a key demand of Hindu nationalists. Although Mookerjee considered Kashmir's constituent assembly to be unrepresentative of the state's citizens, he still wanted it to ratify Jammu and Kashmir's final accession to India.[171] Within the party, however, not all the agitators agreed with a statewide accession. Some of the Parishad leaders in Jammu wanted a "zonal plebiscite" to integrate only Jammu and Ladakh with India.[172] This vision of plebiscite, however, created problems. While it aimed to grant the right of self-determination to every region, in Jammu three of the six districts (Doda, Rajouri, and Poonch) were Muslim-majority. They would refuse to be "bracketed with Dogra Hindus and preferred to stay with Valley Muslims."[173] The Indian prime minister rejected the idea of a zonal plebiscite, assuming it would lead to further partition along religious lines.

As Mookerjee's correspondence with Nehru and Abdullah failed to yield any result, in March 1953 the Hindu nationalist parties defied the government's ban on public meetings to organize demonstrations, court arrests, and demand Kashmir's full integration with India. This agitation led to an outcry in the Indian parliament against the arrest of Hindu nationalist leaders, and several members expressed unhappiness with Nehru's administration by walking out in protest. Accusing Abdullah of creating a "new sovereignty for Jammu and Kashmir," Mookerjee intensified the agitation by marching, with a band of volunteers, in defiance of a Jammu and Kashmir ordinance requiring every person entering or leaving the Valley to get prior approval from the central defense department.[174]

In May 1953, Mookerjee set out for Jammu to investigate the real conditions in Kashmir. Abdullah's government detained Mookerjee for violating the permit requirements, although it placed him under house arrest at a cottage near the famous Mughal gardens of Srinagar, rather than imprisoning him. This action was widely criticized in the Indian press, but the political situation became worse when Mookerjee fell suddenly ill and died in a state hospital. His death while in detention at Srinagar led to violent demonstrations in various parts of India, during which agitators burned effigies of Abdullah in protest.[175]

The Indian public wondered if Abdullah's government had hatched a plan to murder Mookerjee. Even members of the Congress Party who were unhappy with the Praja Parishad agitation now accused the National Conference of criminal negligence for failing to provide adequate health care.[176] One inflammatory poster, which showed the Kashmiri leader wielding an axe dripping with blood while the severed head of the late president of Jan Sangh lay beside him, reflected the public mood.[177] To appease growing anger, the state government withdrew its charges against Parishad leaders. Although their well-orchestrated movement lost its momentum after Mookerjee's death, the party clung to its demand of full integration of Kashmir with the Indian union. The religious affiliation of Jammu and Kashmir's minorities with Hindu-majority India made it convenient for many of them to embrace an identity of loyal citizenship and demand closer ties with India. While integration promised attractive avenues for minorities in the state, it conflicted with Abdullah's support of provisional accession to India.

An Independent Kashmir? Sheikh Abdullah amid the Political Winds of the 1950s

The early 1950s were a trying time for Abdullah and his National Conference. Abdullah realized that his influence among Kashmiri Muslims was ebbing, and was shaken by the altered attitudes of his erstwhile Indian allies who now wanted complete integration of Kashmir with India. During his first few years in office, he had suppressed every voice that challenged Kashmir's accession to India and repeatedly justified National Conference policies.[178] In public meetings, he claimed that Kashmir had an honorable place in democratic India. The decision to tie Kashmir's fate with India had been reached because of India's commitment to the principle of "secular democracy," ideals in tune with the "agenda of the National Conference."[179] Throughout this period, Abdullah seemed to support delaying self-determination, expressing concerns that Pakistan would not allow a fair plebiscite and would impose its two-nation theory on Kashmiris. His ultimate hope remained that his constituent assembly would make the final determination about Kashmir's future.

Early on, Abdullah firmly believed that so long as the National Conference endorsed Kashmir's accession to India he was destined to rule the state. However, the strength of Hindu nationalism in India plagued Abdullah's mind; as time went on, he became less confident that Hindu nationalists would allow an autonomous Kashmir. Reports submitted to him by advisors like G. M. Ashai, the registrar of Kashmir University, in 1949 pointed to the challenges Indian Muslims faced as they struggled to hold on to their cultural symbols of identity in secular India. The "second-class treatment" given to Muslims in India at large caused Abdullah to fear that Kashmiri Muslims might receive similar treatment if Kashmir's complete integration with India occurred.[180]

The presence of Indian intelligence agencies that not only monitored the actions of Kashmiri Muslims, but doubted the loyalty of Abdullah, whose support had provided legitimacy to India's claim on Kashmir, also alienated the leader.[181] The lack of trust in Abdullah and his supporters by individuals like Sardar Patel convinced him that India would not allow Kashmir to remain autonomous. Under the circumstances, he began to consider the possibility of a sovereign Kashmir whose territorial integrity was recognized and guaranteed not only by India and Pakistan, but also by world powers and the United Nations. This concept, rather than a straight choice between India and Pakistan which might result in accession to the latter, would continue to ensure Abdullahs dominance; as a tactical move, the demand for independence might also force India into a binding agreement regarding the state's autonomy. As recounted earlier, when Abdullah expressed this idea in April 1949 in an interview with a British newspaper, his remarks raised a great alarm in Delhi; while he recanted the statements, he retained an attachment to the concept of an independent Kashmir.[182]

Abdullah's fears about Kashmir's political future grew in the 1950s as the Hindu rightists' demand for complete integration merged into the Congress policy of centralization. This placed Abdullah in an embarrassing position, because he had promised his supporters an autonomous Kashmir as a condition of accession to India. He was well aware that any kind of compromise on state autonomy would lead to further loss of social support, allowing his critics to gain the upper hand in the state. Abdullah adoped an uncompromising stance on accession after the Praja Parishad agitation gained steam. "The Parishad agitation," he claimed, "literally poured cold water on the efforts of the National Conference to rally Muslim support for India all these years."[183] To protect his position, Abdullah adopted an aggressive attitude toward the erosion of Kashmir's autonomous status, and attempted to crush the agitation in Jammu just as he had suppressed dissident Muslim voices in the Valley.

In December 1952 Acharya Kripalani, the leader of the Socialist Party of India, had accused Abdullah and his administration of exhibiting prejudice in the treatment of Hindu minorities. In March of the following year the Jammu agitators, who had the complete support of Indian public opinion, presented a memorandum to Nehru accusing the state police of molesting female activists and using ruthless force to suppress free expression.[184] In response, members of the Indian parliament protested Abdullah's administration and intervened to seek the release of Praja Parishad leaders.[185] These Indian politicians worried that Abdullah's autonomy from the Indian constitution had allowed him to make policy detrimental to the minority community in his state.

Prior to the Praja Parishad agitation, the National Conference had used dictatorial policies to crush alternative voices in the Valley. The Indian press had willingly blacked out reports of these atrocities, and New Delhi had even assisted in suppressing Abdullah's Kashmiri Muslim opposition. However, a similar exercise of unrestricted power in Hindu-dominated subregions of the state created a backlash throughout India. Abdullah now realized that "Nehru was not leading India towards the goal of secularism and democracy;" instead, "Hindu India was dragging an idealist prime minister on the path of Brahmanism."[186] This thought filled his mind with fears and doubts about the future of an autonomous Kashmir within India.

Beginning in 1952, Abdullah's frustration against integrationist forces spilled out in a series of speeches questioning India's secularism and expressing doubts about the Congress' intentions and integrity vis-à-vis Kashmir. In one of his most controversial speeches, delivered at Ranbirsinghpura on April 10, 1952, Abdullah questioned the reality of Indian secularism: "If there is a resurgence of communalism in India—how are we to convince Muslims of Kashmir that India does not intend to swallow up Kashmir?"[187] He made it clear that Kashmir could not lose its independent identity; the state's relationship with India should be confined to the three provisional subjects of defense, foreign affairs, and communications. He asked the Indian press to respect Kashmiri desires for autonomy, warning that constant criticism would "destroy bonds of kinship between India and Kashmir."[188] The reaction in India to these outspoken statements, regardless of religious affiliation, was sharp and strong. Acharya Kripalani's *Vigil* published a scathing critique after the Ranbirsinghpura speech:

> We thought Abdullah knew what he owed to the Indian press. What made him forget the debt? Has not the Indian press done its utmost to build him up as Kashmir's savior? Has it not been a polite convention with the main Indian press to avoid all mention of some of the props on which Sheikh Abdullah's authority in Kashmir and his prestige outside rest?[189]

The more hostile India grew toward the National Conference, the more bitter Abdullah's rhetoric became, driving him away from the Indian government and closer to Kashmiri Muslims. In large public gatherings, he confessed that he had committed "mistakes and blunders in [the] past" but he was not "prepared to betray his people." He candidly admitted that "Hindu communalists want to merge Kashmir with India by force" but "how far they succeed ... is for the state people to decide."[190] He openly complained that Muslims were not getting a fair deal in recruitment to central departments. He lamented his failure to keep his promise that Kashmiri interests would be safe in India. Educated unemployed Muslims, he commented, were forced to look toward Pakistan because while their Hindu compatriots found avenues in India open to them, Muslims were debarred from the central service. He made it clear that instead of serving as a satellite to either Pakistan or India, Kashmir should follow an independent path that would lead the state to prosperity. He now felt that "duty is not to merge Kashmir with India or Pakistan but to keep the ideal of freedom alive."[191] Although he never directly defined what he meant by "freedom" nor gave a definite plan for true independence, his pointedly vague statements allowed people to draw their own conclusions. His way out of the impasse of the early 1950s was to establish a Kashmir living in friendship and economic cooperation with both India and Pakistan.[192] This rhetoric was very much in tune with Kashmiri Muslim sentiments and experiences: finally expressing popular perceptions and openly challenging India to consider Kashmiri Muslims an important voice helped Abdullah regain his lost popularity.

Weekly reports received by the Indian government described Kashmiri Muslims' support for Abdullah after he began openly resisting Indian attempts to move toward integration. Confiscated posters put up in the localities of Maharajganj, Nowhatta, Zainakadal, and Nawakadal in 1952 expressed satisfaction with Abdullah's attempts to severe all connections with India and protect Kashmir's freedom. The posters asked Kashmiri Muslims to resist if India were to use force to integrate Kashmir. The intercepted letters of politically minded Kashmiris questioned the one-sided coverage of the Jammu agitation by the Indian press, while ignoring Kashmiri opinion. A letter written to the editor of *Daily Milap* expressed surprise at the hostile attitude of Indian politicians who wanted to impose the Indian constitution on Kashmiris, despite the "agreement arrived with Sheikh Abdullah" that the "Indian government will know the will of the people before permanent accession." The author clarified that Kashmiri resistance to integration stemmed from the belief that full accession would nullify the state-subject category and lead to the resettlement of Hindu refugees—the first step to convert the state's Hindu minority into a Hindu majority.[193]

During the 1950s, Abdullah flirted with the idea of independence with the help of Western powers. He had two secret discussions with Loy Henderson, the US Ambassador to New Delhi. Abdullah briefed him that a majority of the population in Jammu and Kashmir desired an independent Kashmir. He even suggested that the United Nations should include independence as one of the possible solutions to Kashmir.[194] In Abdullah's opinion, an independent Kashmir could only exist if India and Pakistan established friendly relations and if the United States, through the United Nations, provided investments or other economic assistance. The United States was thinking along the same lines as Abdullah, according to a report published in the *New York Times* on July 5, 1953. The article envisioned a "special status for the Kashmir Valley, possibly independence guaranteed by both countries and partition of the rest of the state along lines occupied by the opposing armies under the cease-fire agreement" as a solution to the Kashmir dispute. Along with the report, the *Times* published a map partitioning Jammu and Kashmir.[195]

Although Abdullah apparently had detailed discussions about Kashmir's independence with foreign dignitaries, there was no organized conspiracy to attain independence for Kashmir. Even as late as April 1953 Abdullah was looking for a compromise solution, sending clear signals to Jammu and Ladakh that he wanted to develop consensus. The constituent assembly's Basic Principles Committee envisaged multitiered autonomy, mutual accommodation, the preservation of Kashmir's autonomous setup, and the devolution of powers to groups in Jammu and Ladakh.[196] In a message broadcast on Radio Kashmir on April 17, 1953, Abdullah announced his decision to give autonomy to the different cultural units in the state, so that every unit would receive equal opportunities for development.[197] He planned to incorporate appropriate provisions into the state constitution to ensure cooperation among various cultural groups in Jammu and Kashmir. However, in this federal plan, the Valley would still be a dominant power. The Praja Parishad activists and their supporters rejected Abdullah's compromise plan. They were interested in the complete integration of Jammu and Kashmir with India.

Abdullah believed that the key cause of prolonged popular turmoil was the climate of uncertainty surrounding the future of Jammu and Kashmir state. The best course for the National Conference administration, in his opinion, was to concentrate on bringing about a final settlement to this larger question. The National Conference appointed a subcommittee to examine constitutional options for Jammu and Kashmir as a whole. Abdullah expressed his disillusionment with the state's relationship with India and declared his interest in all possible forms of independence.[198] In June 1953 the Basic Principles Committee suggested four possible options for Kashmir's future: (i) an overall plebiscite for the whole state to decide whether or not to accede to India or Pakistan; (ii) independence for the whole state; (iii) independence for the whole state with joint Indian and Pakistani control of foreign affairs and defense; and (iv) the Dixon Plan, with independence for the plebiscite area.[199] These options were approved as constitutional in the subcommittee but a few members of the National Conference expressed concern. They thought the independence option would lead to anarchy and widespread disturbances, and "turn Kashmir into a cockpit of international intrigue."[200] As diverging views within the party created a political split, Abdullah summoned the working committee of the National Conference to ratify his new line and decided to make his decision public on August 21, 1953, during the Muslim festival of Eid.[201]

Abdullah's ideas about a possible "independent Kashmir" were perceived by Nehru to be "very dangerous" to India's security. Nehru reminded Abdullah that there were "middle courses," but added, "nobody can guarantee the distant future."[202] Maulana Abdul Kalam Azad, another prominent Congress leader, expressed India's willingness to make Kashmir's special position permanent, without any conditions.[203] Yet this assurance failed to narrow the widening gap between Kashmir and India. In a candid response, Abdullah stated that India's offer was not sufficient to appease agitated Kashmiri Muslims, who doubted whether the Congress would be able to resist Hindu rightist parties both within and outside the state of Jammu and Kashmir clamoring for complete integration with India.[204] Abdullah's uncompromising stance made Indian leaders rethink their relationship with him.

The Indian government's worries were intensified by the tense political atmosphere in the Valley. Dissident groups, emboldened by the Hindu rightist parties' agitation, came out in defense of their rights. People marched in the streets chanting pro-Pakistan and "Azad Kashmir" slogans. Although the state government took prompt action and arrested the protestors, New Delhi was alarmed by these reports from the Valley. Acharaya Kriplani, an important Congress leader, visited the Valley in June 1953 to feel the pulse of the public and expressed bewilderment about the open expression of anti-India sentiment and the "lack of appreciation" shown by Kashmiri Muslims for the "services rendered by India." He lamented that even government employees had no hesitation in expressing their support for an independent Kashmir. He firmly believed that the only way India could retain Kashmir was to "displace Abdullah" by creating a split within the National Conference.[205]

Working under B. N. Mullik, the intelligence agencies succeeded in dividing Abdullah's cabinet. Motivated primarily by personal ambition, Bakshi Ghulam Muhammad, the deputy prime minister of Kashmir, acknowledged Abdullah's leadership, yet worked surreptitiously with the dissident faction to maneuver for his dismissal.[206] On August 9, 1953, the nominal head of state, Karan Singh, signed an order for Abdullah's arrest under the Public Security Act. As India embarked on its policy of retaining Kashmir's territory, it conveniently removed the individual who had provided legitimacy to their presence in Jammu and Kashmir. The arrest was celebrated triumphantly in Jammu, while the Valley witnessed hostile demonstrations on an unprecedented scale, ruthlessly suppressed by the Indian army. Jeeps carrying militias patrolled the streets and police, fearing retaliation, guarded banks and post offices.[207]

This postcolonial episode set the tone for Kashmir's future relationship with India. Kashmiri Muslims interpreted the undemocratic dismissal of Abdullah, who had challenged Indian might, as an assault on their identity. It was a painful reminder that hopes for "freedom" had failed and that India's covert authoritarianism had replaced Dogra despotism. In the collective memories of ordinary Kashmiris, this incident was a replay of 1931, when Abdullah, the Sher-i-Kashmir (Lion of Kashmir), had stood up to the autocratic Dogra rule. It allowed Abdullah to reemerge not as the authoritarian ruler he had appeared in the aftermath of the first India–Pakistani War, but as a courageous leader who resisted Indian might to protect Kashmir's unique identity and inspired Kashmiri Muslims of different political orientations to organize united protest movements against the new regime. For weeks the Valley remained completely shut down, and the resistance showed no signs of slackening. Kashmir was simmering with anger against what its residents called Indian imperialism, and Abdullah's arrest provided an opportunity to vent their emotions.[208]

Conclusion

The dawn of independence ushered in the Awami Raj, the "people's rule," in India-administered Kashmir, as Kashmiri nationalists assumed political power under the banner of "democracy" and expressed their support for Kashmir's provisional accession to India while simultaneously suppressing groups with different visions for Kashmir's future. In this chapter I have argued that Kashmiris' initial experiences with the concept of "democracy" made them equate the term with authoritarianism. These policies also created disquiet and dissatisfaction with India and the National Conference's collaborative politics, which furthered each other's political agenda but denied real freedom to ordinary Kashmiris. The unresolved nature of Kashmir's status and the possibility of a plebiscite also shaped Kashmir's evolving relationship with India during the 1950s.

Instead of neatly separating the two divided parts of Kashmir, the arbitrary ceasefire line drawn at the end of the first India–Pakistan War created a humanitarian and economic crisis. Kashmiris resisted this artificial partition of their formerly unified social and economic world, while struggling to find a sense of belonging in both India and Pakistan. The territorial nationalism and centralized structure inherited by the Indian state from its former colonial masters made the physical retention of Kashmir's territory a priority, rather than gaining popular sovereignty by winning the hearts and minds of Kashmiris. Kashmiris' ideals of freedom, conceived prior to accession to India, remained a distant dream as the Indian state embarked on a policy of complete integration during the 1950s. The next chapter illuminates the deep social fissures created by the transformation of Kashmir's political economy, which had an impact on all Kashmiris, regardless of their regional and religious background.

Notes

1. Extract from Ghulam Ahmad Mahjoor's poem "O Golden Oriole!" in Triloki Nath Raina (ed. and trans.), *The Best of Mahjoor* (Srinagar: J&K Academy of Arts, Cultures and Languages, 1989), Poem no. 77. These are selections from the poem, which has not been quoted here in entirety.
2. For details, see *White Paper on Jammu and Kashmir Dispute* (Islamabad: Ministry of Foreign Affairs, Govt. of Pakistan, 1977); "Political Note on Kashmir Problem," *Azad Kashmir Government Documents*, MSS.Eur.D.704, India Office Library; "Various suggestions received from the public on the Kashmir issue," Ministry of States, 10(3)-K/1948, National Archives of India, New Delhi.
3. Zutshi, *Languages of Belonging*, 2–4.
4. For details, see Sheikh Muhammad Abdullah, *Aatish-i-Chinar* (Srinagar: Ali Muhammad and Sons, 1985); Government of Jammu and Kashmir, *Kashmir's Relationship with India* (Srinagar: 1948).
5. Nasir A. Naqash and G. M. Shan, *Kashmir: From Crisis to Crisis* (Delhi: APH Publications, 1997), 91.
6. S. M. Abdullah, *The Blazing Chinar*, 289–90.
7. Lakhanpal, *Essential Documents and Notes on Kashmir Dispute*, 62–3.
8. S. Gopal (ed.), *Selected Works of Jawaharlal Nehru*, Vol. 4 (New Delhi: Jawaharlal Memorial Fund, 1986), 324–5.
9. Mahatma Gandhi, "Speech at Prayer Meeting" on 1 November 1947, in *The Collected Works of Mahatma Gandhi*, XC (New Delhi: Ministry of Information and Broadcasting, 1984), 206–10.
10. Chitralekha Zutshi, in *Languages of Belonging*, has stated that "the organization [the National Conference] that had first demanded political and social rights on behalf of Kashmiris became its greatest repressor." Zutshi, *Languages of Belonging*, 313–15.
11. Mehmood Hashmi, *Kashmir Udas Hai: Report* (Lahore: Al-Faisal, 1994), 25–44.
12. Hashmi, *Kashmir Udas Hai*, 25–7.
13. Hashmi, *Kashmir Udas Hai*, 27.
14. B. P. L. Bedi, *Transcripts of Interview* (New Delhi: Nehru Memorial Museum and Library), Accession No. 270, 334.
15. Bedi, *Transcripts of Interview.*
16. Jagannath Sathu, *Behind the Iron Curtain in Kashmir* (Delhi: Kashmir Democratic Union, 1952), 2–3.
17. "Ban on the Entry into India of the Booklet, Behind the Iron Curtain in Kashmir," No (8), (22)-K/49, 1949, Ministry of States, National Archives of India, New Delhi.
18. Sathu, *Behind the Iron Curtain in Kashmir*, 34–5.
19. Most judicial files pertaining to 1947–8 are no longer available; however, a few files existed in the Record Room of the District Court Complex, Jammu and Kashmir. For example, Cr. Appeal No: 128 of 2004 (1948). Session Judge of Kashmir Province

Mr. M. A. Shahmiri sentenced an accused to four months in prison on the charge of making a statement that the government may last few months only; *Khizar Ganai vs State.* He was charged with raising anti-government slogans and was put in prison for six months.

20. Balraj Puri, "Jammu and Kashmir," in Myron Weiner (ed.), *State Politics in India* (Princeton University Press, 1968), 215–246.
21. Prem Nath Bazaz, *Does India Defend Freedom or Fascism in Kashmir?* (New Delhi: Kashmir Democratic Union, 1952), 15–17.
22. Hasan Raheel and Ghulam Mustafa Khawaja, *Soont Kaal*, Vol. 1 (Mirpur: True Kashmir, 1989), 114–19.
23. Robinson, *Body of Victim, Body of Warrior*, 46–8.
24. Robinson, *Body of Victim, Body of Warrior*, 47.
25. Robinson, *Body of Victim, Body of Warrior*, 45–7.
26. "Discontinuance of telegrams between Azad Territory and rest of Kashmir state," File No 4(11)-K/48, Ministry of States, National Archives of India, New Delhi.
27. Judicial files at the District Sessions Court (1947–53) pertaining to Kashmiris convicted for crossing the LOC were prosecuted under S.3 of Egress and Ingress Internal Movement Ordinance of 1948.
28. "Control of Movements in Kashmir State," *The Indian Civil Liberties Bulletin*, no. 79 (April 1956).
29. "Legal basis of Kashmir Permit System"; "Arrangments relating to the Jammu and Kashmir State," Ministry of States, 7/10 (15)-K/52, 1952, National Archives of India, New Delhi; "Kashmir Entry Permits: Decision That Temporary Permits Should Not Ordinarily Be Issued to Kashmir Nationals Coming from Pakistan with Visas to Visit This Country," F.10 (10)-K /53, 1953, Ministry of States, National Archives of India, New Delhi.
30. "India–Pakistan Passport System: Arrangments relating to the Jammu and Kashmir State," 7/10 (15)-K/52, 1952, Ministry of State, National Archives of India, New Delhi.
31. "India–Pakistan Passport System: Arrangments relating to the Jammu and Kashmir State," 7/10 (15)-K/52, 1952, National Archives of India, New Delhi.
32. "Entry of Kashmiri Laborers from Pakistan to India without Permits," 10(4)-K/50, 1950, Ministry of States, National Archives of India, New Delhi; "Unauthorized Ingress into J&K State of Certain Muslim Civilians," 1 (34)-K/50, 1950, Ministry of States, National Archives of India, New Delhi.
33. "Repatriation of Kashmiris from Pakistan," File No. 7(9)-K/53 (Secret) 1953, Ministry of States, National Archives of India, New Delhi.
34. Mridula Sarabhai, "Jammu and Kashmir Ingress Control Act," 1956, All India Congress Committee Papers, S. No. 2054, 2nd Installment, Nehru Memorial Museum and Library, New Delhi.
35. "Political Note on Kashmir Problem," Mss.Eur.D.704, India Office Library, London.

36. For details, see Prem Nath Bazaz, *Economic Chaos in Kashmir* (New Delhi: Kashmir Democratic Union, 1952).
37. P. N. Bazaz, *Economic Chaos in Kashmir*, 6–7.
38. P. N. Bazaz, *Economic Chaos in Kashmir*, 3–10.
39. "Political Situation in Sheikh Abdullah's Kashmir," DO 142/370, National Archives, Kew, UK.
40. P. N. Bazaz, *Economic Chaos in Kashmir*, 21–2.
41. Government of Jammu and Kashmir, *A Report: Four Years* (Srinagar, 1951), 10.
42. H. Sarwaria, *Inside Kashmir: Nepotism and Bribery in the State*, Ministry of States, 16(4)-K/49, National Archives, New Delhi, India.
43. P. N. Bazaz, *Economic Chaos in Kashmir*, 18.
44. "Grants and Loans to J&K," Ministry of States, No. 15 (23)-K/54, National Archives of India, New Delhi.
45. S. M. Abdullah, *The Blazing Chinar*, 345–6.
46. "Request from the Jammu and Kashmir Government for a Subsidy to reduce the price of salt in the state," Ministry of States, 6(25)-K/1948 4-5, National Archives of India, New Delhi.
47. "Price Rise and Scarcity," *Martand*, December 23, 1949.
48. P. N. Bazaz, *Economic Chaos in Kashmir*, 15.
49. Extract from Ghulam Ahmad Mahjoor's poem "Azadi" ("Freedom"), in Triloki Nath Raina (ed. and trans.), *An Anthology of Modern Kashmiri Verse* (1930–1960) (Poona: Sangam Press, 1972), 74–7. These are selections of a poem which have not been quoted here in entirety.
50. Extract from "A letter from Ghulam Hasan Buch Srinagar Kashmir to Mian Aziz Ahmed Khan, 1528 Agar Mall Road Rawalpindi, September 1951," in "Reports regarding Muslim Affairs in Jammu and Kashmir," Ministry of States, 8(12)-K/1951, National Archives of India, New Delhi.
51. Munshi Muhammad Ishaq, *Choudhveen Sadi* [Fourteenth Century], pamphlet in Urdu, my translation (Srinagar: Self published, 1950) (personal collection of Munshi Ghulam Hasan, Srinagar).
52. Extract from Mahjoor's poem "The Oath and Covenant at Hazratbal," in Syed Taffazull Hussain (ed. and trans.), *Topical Poems of Mehjoor* (Srinagar: Self-published, 2016), 68–9.
53. B. N. Mullik, *Kashmir: My Years with Nehru* (New Delhi: Allied Publishers, 1971), 23.
54. Satish Vashishth, *Sheikh Abdullah: Then and Now* (Delhi: Maulik Sahitya Prakashan, 1968), 49.
55. Pyarelal describes Gandhi's views about riots in Jammu. "Following upon the Punjab upheavals, in October 1947, Muslim evacuee convoys going out of Jammu were attacked and massacred by non-Muslims who at times were directed by RSS. The state army played a very discreditable part in these massacres. When Gandhi

came to know about it, he said that Maharaja as an absolute ruler could not be absolved from responsibility." Pyarelal, *Mahatma Gandhi: The Last Phase*, Vol. 2 (Ahmedabad: Navajivan, 1958), 498–9. Lal Khan, *Kashmir Ordeal: A Revolutionary Way Out* (United Kingdom: Arc Publications, 2005), 45.

56. Saraf, *Kashmiris Fight for Freedom*, Vol. 2, 824–7.
57. "Exodus of Muslims from Jammu," *Civil and Military Gazette*, September 26, 1947, in Snedden, *The Untold Story of the People of Azad Kashmir*, 51.
58. See Jalal, *Democracy and Authoritarianism in South Asia*, 208.
59. See Gyanendra Pandey, "Can a Muslim Be an Indian?" *Comparative Studies in Society and History* 41, no. 4 (October 1999): 608–29.
60. "Constituent Assembly Debates: 14 September 1949, Part 2," Indiankanoon.org, https://indiankanoon.org/doc/173426/, accessed May 25, 2019.
61. P. N. Bazaz, *The History of Struggle for Freedom in Kashmir*, 352–3.
62. P. N. Bazaz, *The History of Struggle for Freedom in Kashmir*, 346.
63. P. N. Bazaz, *The History of Struggle for Freedom in Kashmir*, 354–7.
64. "Letter from Himat Ram Guru of Jaipur to Sardar Patel on 6 October 1948," in "Various Suggestions Received from the Public on the Kashmir Issue," Ministry of States, 10(3)-K/48, National Archives of India, New Delhi.
65. "Letter from Himat Ram Guru of Jaipur to Sardar Patel on 6 October 1948."
66. "Letter from a well wisher to Sardar Patel on 11 November 1948," in "Various Suggestions received from the Public on the Kashmir Issue," Ministry of States, 10(3)-K/48, National Archives of India, New Delhi.
67. Mullik, *Kashmir: My Years with Nehru*, 14–15.
68. Omar Khalidi, "Kashmir and Muslim Politics in India," in Raju G. C. Thomas (ed.), *Perspective on Kashmir: The Roots of Conflict in South Asia* (Boulder, CO: Westview Press, 1992), 279.
69. Zakir Hussain, *Indian Muslim Leaders Memorandum on Kashmir* (New Delhi: Aligarh Muslim University, 1951), 2.
70. P. N. Bazaz, *The History of Struggle for Freedom in Kashmir*, 572.
71. For details, see "Reports regarding Muslim affairs in Jammu and Kashmir, Ministry of States," File No. 8(12)-K/51, National Archives of India, New Delhi; "Intelligence Reports regarding Muslim Affairs in J&K," Ministry of States, File No. 8 (4)-K/52, National Archives of India, New Delhi; "Extract from Part V of the Daliy Summary of Information on Kashmir," Ministry of States, No. 29, dated 28-2-51, National Archives of India, New Delhi.
72. "Letter addressed to editor of *Daily Milap* from a person (name illegible), President, Independent Kashmir," Srinagar, 1952, 8(4)-K/1952, National Archives of India, New Delhi.
73. "Reports Regarding Muslim Affairs in Jammu and Kashmir," File No. 8(12)-K/51, Ministry of States, National Archives of India, New Delhi.

74. P. N. Bazaz, *The History of Struggle for Freedom in Kashmir*, 536–7.
75. P. N. Bazaz, *The History of Struggle for Freedom in Kashmir*, 569–70.
76. Prem Nath Bazaz, *Azad Kashmir: A Democratic-Socialist Conception* (Lahore: Ferozsons Publications, 1950), 49–50, 60–4.
77. P. N. Bazaz, *Azad Kashmir*, 62–3.
78. P. N. Bazaz, *Azad Kashmir*, 92–4.
79. For details, see P. N. Bazaz, *Azad Kashmir*, 141–60.
80. P. N. Bazaz, *The History of Struggle for Freedom in Kashmir*, 532.
81. Snedden, *The Untold Story of the People of Azad Kashmir*, 87.
82. An unpublished autobiography of Khawaja Ghulam Naqui (private collection of Mahboob Ali, Srinagar).
83. Documents Belonging to the Late F. P. Mainprice, DO/35/3049, National Archives, Kew, UK.
84. "A letter from Mohammad Shafi to Ghulam Sarwar, Editor, *The Rozana Hind*. Report on the General Conditions in Pakistan and Azad Kashmir," Ministry of States, 8(20)-K/51, 1951, National Archives of India, New Delhi.
85. "A letter addressed to Abdul Rahim, Secretary Majlis-Auqauf-Islamia, Jammu from a displaced Kashmiri," Ministry of States, 8(20)-K/51, 1951, National Archives of India, New Delhi (italics mine).
86. For details, see Lakhanpal, *Esential Documents and Notes on Kashmir Dispute*, 146–283.
87. *Greater Kashmir*, "Bloodbath by Dogs," April 24, 2012; Saadat Hassan Manto, "Tetwal Ka Kutta," http://urduadab4u.blogspot.com/2010/08/tetwal-ka-kutta-afsaana-by-manto.html, accessed January 2019.
88. "A letter from A. A. Scott, H. B. Badami Srinagar to Mr. and Mrs. D. H. Lewis, 9 Canning Street Liverpool England, A letter addressed to Miss Helen Edwards, 117 Hannerstack Hill London, N.W 3 England from (name) illegible in Dal Lake," Srinagar, Ministry of States, 8(22)-K/51, National Archives of India, New Delhi.
89. "Political Situation in Sheikh Abdullah's Kashmir," 1952–1953, DO 142/370, National Archives, Kew, UK.
90. Ghulam Ahmad Mahjoor, "O Morning Breeze," in Syed Taffazull Hussain (ed. and trans.), *Topical Poems of Mehjoor* (Srinagar: Self published, 2016), 99–102.
91. J. N. Dogra, "The Great Betrayal: Independent Kashmir Demanded" (New Delhi: Hind Union Press, 1949), in Ministry of States, 16(4)-K/49, National Archives of India, New Delhi; Durga Das (ed.), *Selected Correspondence of Sardar Patel 1945–50*, Vol. 1 (New Delhi: Navajivan Publishing House, 1971), 266–7.
92. Noorani, *Article 370*, 1.
93. In the case of Jammu and Kashmir, the Instrument of Accession which the Dogra maharaja signed on October 26, 1947, was accompanied by a letter written by the Governor General of India, Lord Mountbatten, which stipulated that "as soon as law and order has been restored in Kashmir and her soil cleared of the invader;

the question of the state's accession would be settled by a reference to the people." Noorani, *Article 370*, 3.

94. Noorani, *Article 370*, 3.
95. Noorani, *Article 370*, 1–28.
96. Sumantra Bose, *Kashmir: Roots of Conflict, Paths to Peace*, 59.
97. Article 306A, Constituent Assembly of India Debates (Proceedings) – Vol. X, Monday, 17 October, 1949, http://164.100.47.194/loksabha/writereaddata/cadebatefiles/C17101949.html, accessed July 7, 2019.
98. Noorani, *Article 370*, 5–6.
99. Noorani, *Article 370*, 64–6.
100. S. Gopal (ed.), *Selected Works of Jawaharlal Nehru*, Second Series, Vol. 15, Part II (New Delhi: Jawaharlal Nehru Memorial Fund, 1993), 307–13.
101. For text of the resolution, see "Resolution 91 (1951) Concerning the India–Pakistan question submitted by the Representatives of United Kingdom and United States and adopted by the Security Council on March 30, 1951" (Document No. S/2017/Rev. 1, dated March 30, 1951), https://www.mtholyoke.edu/acad/intrel/kashun91.htm, accessed June 30, 2020.
102. Sumantra Bose, *Kashmir: Roots of Conflict, Paths to Peace*, 55.
103. Sheikh Mohammad Abdullah, Ghulam Mohammad Sadiq, and Mridula Sarabhai (eds.), *Sheikh–Sadiq Correspondence: August to October 1956* (New Delhi: Mridula Sarabhai, 1958), 7.
104. Teng, *Kashmir: Article 370*, 61.
105. Mullik, *My Years with Nehru*, 27.
106. "Extract from Part V of the Daily Summary of Information of Kashmir, No. 29, dated 28-2-51," Ministry of States, National Archives of India, New Delhi; "Intelligence Reports regarding Muslim Affairs in J&K," File No. 8(4)-K/52, Ministry of States, National Archives of India, New Delhi.
107. "Report of the Committee to define the Term 'State Subject,'" Political Department, 1935, File.No.199/RR-18, Jammu Kashmir Archives, cited in Rai, *Hindu Rulers, Muslim Subjects*, 252–3; Robinson, *Body of Victim, Body of Warrior*, 31–45.
108. "Report of the Committee to define the Term 'State Subject,'" cited in Rai, *Hindu Rulers, Muslim Subjects*, 252–3; Robinson, *Body of Victim, Body of Warrior*, 31–45
109. Jammu and Kashmir Constituent Assembly Debates: Part 1, 558.
110. Jammu and Kashmir Constituent Assembly Debates: Part 1, 566.
111. Burhan Majid, "Why Article 35 A Matters?" *The Wire*, April 13, 2019, https://thewire.in/law/why-article-35a-matters, accessed November 25, 2019. The Jammu and Kashmir Constitution adopted in 1956 defined a permanent resident as those who had been a state subject since May 14, 1954, or who has been a resident of the state for ten years and has lawfully acquired immovable property.
112. Noorani, *Article 370*, 141.

113. "AJ&K Interim Constitution, 1974" – Law Department AJ&K, https://law.ajk.gov.pk/assets/lawlibrary/2019-02-13-5c645034ade141550078004.pdf, accessed March 15, 2020.
114. Cabeiri Robinson has elaborated how the state-subject criteria defined the political identity of Kashmiri Muslim "refugees" displaced during the India–Pakistan wars. For details, see *Body of Victim, Body of Warrior*, 45.
115. Noorani, *Article 370*, 157.
116. Jammu and Kashmir Constituent Assembly Debates: Part 1, 541–5.
117. Jammu and Kashmir Constituent Assembly Debates: Part 1, 541–5.
118. Noorani, *Article 370*, 158–72.
119. For details, see Balraj Puri, *Jammu and Kashmir: Triumph and Tragedy of Indian Fedralism* (New Delhi Asia Book Corp., 1981).
120. Das, *Sardar Patel's Correspondence, 1945–50*, Vol. 1, 116–21.
121. S. M. Abdullah, *Flames of the Chinar*, 97.
122. Das, *Sardar Patel's Correspondence, 1945–50*, Vol. 1, 134–7.
123. Pyarelal, *Mahatma Gandhi: The Last Phase*, Vol. 2 (Ahmedabad: Navajivan Press, 1958), 499.
124. Puri, *Jammu and Kashmir*, 82.
125. Puri, *Jammu and Kashmir*, 75.
126. For details, see P. N. Bazaz, *Kashmir Pandit Agitation and Its Aftermath* (New Delhi: Pamposh Publications, 1967).
127. "Qanoon Ka Wiqar Aur Hakoomat ka Faraz," *Martand*, October 27, 1948.
128. *Secularism in Kashmir* (Delhi: Kashmir Democratic Union, 1952), 7–15.
129. *Secularism in Kashmir*, 7–15.
130. P. N. Bazaz, *Kashmir Pandit Agitation and Its Aftermath*, 9.
131. "Letter written by Prem Nath Misri to Indian Prime Minister," October 1952, Ministry of States, F 19(67)-K/1952, National Archives of India, New Delhi.
132. Mullik, *Kashmir: My Years with Nehru*, 12.
133. "Jammu and Kashmir Government Proposal to Abolish the Zamindari System," 1(38)-K/50 1949, Ministry of States, National Archives of India, New Delhi.
134. *Land Reforms: A Review of the Land Reforms with Special Reference to Big Landed Estate Abolition Act for the Period Ending July 1952, in the Jammu and Kashmir State* (Land Reforms Officer, J&K State, 1953), 7–10.
135. Brecher, *The Struggle for Kashmir*, 161.
136. "Land Reforms in Jammu and Kashmir," Department of Information, Jammu and Kashmir, 1–12.
137. For details, see *Report of the Land Compensation Committee* (Srinagar: Government of Jammu and Kashmir, 1952).
138. Wolf Isaac Ladejinsky, "Land Reform Observations in Kashmir," in Louis J. Ladejinsky (ed.), *The Selected Papers of Wolf Ladejinsky, Agrarian Reforms an Unfinished Business* (New York: Oxford University Press, 1977), 178–89.

139. Daniel Thorner, "The Kashmir Land Reforms: Some Personal Impressions," *The Economic Weekly* (September 1953): 999–1002.
140. Thorner, "The Kashmir Land Reforms," 999–1002.
140. S. M. Abdullah, *The Blazing Chinar*, 341.
142. Ladejinsky, "Land Reform Observations in Kashmir," 187.
143. P. N. Bazaz, *Economic Chaos in Kashmir*, 43.
144. P. N. Bazaz, *Economic Chaos in Kashmir*, 37.
145. Thorner, "The Kashmir Land Reforms," 999–1002.
146. Nisar Ali, *Agricultural Development and Income Distribution in Kashmir* (New Delhi: Rima Publishing House, 1985), 5.
147. "Letter from Zamindars of Jammu to Prime Minister of Jammu and Kashmir Sheikh Muhammad Abdullah," Ministry of States, F.1(2)-K/1948, National Archives of India, New Delhi.
148. "Letter from Zamindars of Jammu to Prime Minister of Jammu and Kashmir Sheikh Muhammad Abdullah."
149. "Letter from Maharaja Hari Singh to Sardar Patel, Home Minister of India," Ministry of States, F.1(3)K(S)/1948, National Archives of India, New Delhi.
150. Bhattacharjea, *Kashmir: The Wounded Valley*, 175.
151. For details, see S. M. Abdullah, *The Blazing Chinar*.
152. Gurcharan Singh Bataia, "Sheikh Abdullah and Praja Parishad: Striking Similarities in Approach," *Kashmir Affairs* 2, no. 3 (January–February 1959): 18–21.
153. *Constituent Assembly Debates* (Srinagar: Government of Jammu and Kashmir, 1955), 425.
154. Sumantra Bose, *Kashmir: Roots of Conflict, Paths to Peace*, 54–5.
155. "A letter written by Jagan Nath Dhar to Sardar Vallabhai Patel, Deputy PM of India, 13 September 1948," Ministry of States, 10(3)-K/48, National Archives of India, New Delhi.
156. Behera, *Demystifying Kashmir*, 109.
157. Shridhar Kaul and H. N. Kaul, *Ladakh through the Ages: Towards a New Identity* (New Delhi: Indus, 1992), 183.
158. Balraj Madhok, *Jammu, Kashmir and Ladakh: Problem and Solution* (New Delhi, 1987), 68–71.
159. Kushak Bakula, as cited in Kaul and Kaul, *Ladakh through the Ages*, 185.
160. P. N. Bazaz, *The History of Struggle for Freedom in Kashmir*, 564–7.
161. Madhok, *Jammu, Kashmir and Ladakh*, 29–30.
162. "Intelligence Reports: Praja Parishad and other Hindu and Sikh parties in J & K State," 8(3)-K/53, Ministry of States, National Archives of India, New Delhi. For details, see Balraj Puri, *Jammu: A Clue to Kashmir Jammu—A Simmering Tangle* (New Delhi: Photoflash Press, 1966).
163. All Jammu and Kashmir Praja Parishad, *Jammu Fights against Separatism, Communalism, and Totalitarism* (New Delhi: All Jammu and Kashmir Praja

Parishad, 1952), 2–4; "Complaints regarding Discrimination against Hindi in Jammu and Kashmir State," 16(10)-K/50, Ministry of States, National Archives of India, New Delhi.

164. For details, see All Jammu and Kashmir Praja Parishad, *Jammu Fights against Separatism, Communalism, and Totalitarism.*
165. Reeta Chowdhari Tremblay, "Jammu: Autonomy within an Autonomous Kashmir?" in Raju G. C. Thomas (ed.), *Perspectives on Kashmir: The Roots of Conflict in South Asia* (Boulder, CO: Westview Press, 1992), 161.
166. Tremblay, "Jammu: Autonomy within an Autonomous Kashmir?" 160–1.
167. P. N. Bazaz, *The History of Struggle for Freedom in Kashmir*, 586.
168. Bhartiya Jana Sangh, *Kashmir Problem and Jammu Satyagraha* (Delhi, 1952), 2.
169. P. N. Bazaz, *The History of Struggle for Freedom in Kashmir*, 595.
170. Full Text of Nehru–Mookerjee–Abdullah Correspondence, January–February 1953, https://archive.org/stream/in.ernet.dli.2015.63380/2015.63380.Nehru-mookerjee-Abdullah-Correspondence_djvu.txt, accessed December 1, 2019.
171. For details, see *Integrate Kashmir: Nehru–Mookerjee–Abdullah Correspondence* (New Delhi: Kashmir Bureau of Information, 1953); P. N. Bazaz, *The History of Struggle for Freedom in Kashmir*, 603.
172. N. L. Gupta, *RSS and Kashmir* (New Delhi: Sampradayikta Virodhi Committee, n.d), 8.
173. Sumantra Bose, *Kashmir: Roots of Conflict, Paths to Peace*, 64.
174. Tremblay, "Jammu: Autonomy within an Autonomous Kashmir?" 160–2.
175. David Lockwood, "The 'Lion of Kashmir': Sheikh Mohammed Abdullah and the Dispute over the Relationship between Jammu & Kashmir State and the Indian Union," Ph.D. dissertation submitted to Johns Hopkins University, 1971, 212–17.
176. P. N. Bazaz, *The History of Struggle for Freedom in Kashmir*, 604.
177. Lockwood, "The 'Lion of Kashmir,'" 217.
178. P. N. Bazaz, *The History of Struugle for Freedom in Kashmir*, 671–2.
179. Vashishth, *Sheikh Abdullah*, 49–50.
180. Mullik, *Kashmir: My Years with Nehru*, 11.
181. Mullik, *Kashmir: My Years with Nehru.*
182. Dogra, *The Great Betrayal*; Sumantra Bose, *Kashmir: Roots of Conflict, Paths to Peace*, 60.
183. Ashutosh Varshney, "Three Compromised Nationalisms: Why Kashmir Has Been a Problem," in Raju G. C. Thomas (ed.), *Perspectives on Kashmir: The Roots of Conflict in South Asia* (Boulder, CO: Westview Press, 1992), 191–234, 213.
184. P. N. Bazaz, *The History of Struggle for Freedom in Kashmir*, 595.
185. Mridula Sarabhai's Correspondence and Notes relating to the Kashmir Dispute, 1951–1953 (Microfilm) MS/18. Nehru Memorial Museum and Library, New Delhi.
186. P. N. Bazaz, *The History of Struggle for Freedom in Kashmir*, 678.
187. P. N. Bazaz, *The History of Struggle for Freedom in Kashmir*, 676.

188. "Sheikh Abdullah's Kashmir, 1947–1953," DO 35/6631, Dominion Office Files, National Archives, Kew, UK.
189. P. N. Bazaz, *History of Struggle for Freedom in Kashmir*, 585.
190. "Sheikh Abdullah's Kashmir, 1947–1953," DO 35/6631, Dominion Office Files, National Archives, Kew, UK.
191. "Sheikh Abdullah's Kashmir, 1947–1953," DO 35/6631, Dominion Office Files, National Archives, Kew, UK.
192. "Sheikh Abdullah's Kashmir, 1947–1953," DO 35/6631, Dominion Office Files, National Archives, Kew, UK.
193. "A letter addressed to the editor of Daily Milap from the President of Independent Kashmir, Srinagar, May 1952," Intelligence Reports Regarding Muslim Affairs in Jammu and Kashmir, Ministry of State, 8(4)-K/52, 1952.
194. Varshney, "Three Compromised Nationalisms," 205.
195. Robert Trumbull, "India and Pakistan near Pact to Split Kashmir, Avoid War," *New York Times*, July 5, 1953.
196. Suresh K. Sharma and S. R. Bakshi, *Sheikh Abdullah and Kashmir* (New Delhi: Anmol Publications, 1995), 159; P. N. Bazaz, *The History of Struggle for Freedom in Kashmir*, 597; Sumantra Bose, Kashmir: *Roots of Conflict, Paths to Peace*, 62.
197. P. N. Bazaz, *The History of Struggle for Freedom in Kashmir*, 597.
198. G. M. Sadiq, an important member of the National Conference, in a letter to Sheikh Abdullah, written in October 1956, reminded him that prior to his dismissal in August 1953, Abdullah had advocated for Jammu to be integrated with India; Pakistan–administered areas to be made a part of Pakistan; and the Valley to be declared independent. For details, see Abdullah, Sadiq, and Sarabhai, *Sheikh–Sadiq Correspondence*, 28.
199. For details, see "Sheikh Sadiq Correspondence," All India Congress Committee Papers, F. No 3589, 2nd Installment, Nehru Memorial Museum and Library, New Delhi.
200. For details, see "Sheikh Sadiq Correspondence," All India Congress Committee Papers, F. No 3589, 2nd Installment, Nehru Memorial Museum and Library, New Delhi.
201. Sumantra Bose, *Kashmir: Roots of Conflict, Paths to Peace*, 65.
202. Noorani, *Article 370*, 230.
203. Lakhanpal, *Essential Notes and Documents on Kashmir Dispute*, 247.
204. Lakhanpal, *Essential Notes and Documents on Kashmir Dispute*, 245–8.
205. Private Papers of J. B. Kriplani, F. No. 184. 1953, Nehru Memorial Museum and Library, New Delhi.
206. On July 29, 1953, Bakshi Ghulam Muhammad in a public gathering at Kulgam stated, "Islam ordains that every Mussalman, must cherish faith in five cardinal principles, but I have a sixth principle as well. I have complete faith in leadership of

Sheikh Muhammad Abdullah. If I have to go to the gallows for it, I am prepared." P. N. Bazaz, *The History of Struggle for Freedom in Kashmir*, 687.

207. For details, see Sadiq Ali and Madhu Limaye, *Report on Kashmir* (Bombay: Praja Socialist Party, 1954), 1–34.
208. "Impressions of Visitors to Kashmir," Dominion Office, DO 35/ 6632, National Archives, Kew, UK.

3 Puppet Regimes
Collaboration and the Political Economy of Kashmiri Resistance

The liar ascends the throne,
And the truth is hanged on the gibbet;
Out of jealousy, honours are
Bestowed on the unworthy.
What can be in store for society?
Where illiterates wield the pen
And eunuchs wield the sword!

—Mirza Arif Beg, "Ten Quatrains"[1]

Written in the wake of the imposition of a New Delhi–sponsored puppet regime in the early 1950s, prominent Kashmiri poet Mirza Arif Beg's "Ten Quatrains" laments a lost society that has compromised its morality, political ethics, and sense of justice for quick riches and worldly power. The unrepresentative and corrupt administration put in place after the unceremonious dismissal of Kashmir's prime minister, Sheikh Abdullah, for resisting Kashmir's complete integration with India, wreaked havoc on Kashmiri society, creating new social groups who repeated the sins of the past, monopolizing power and excluding the majority from networks of patronage. As India attempted to bring Kashmir closer to itself, its imposition of puppet regimes transformed Kashmir's political economy, producing social fissures between and within classes and religious communities.

Prior to Kashmir's accession to India the political economy was designed to create social and economic inequalities, with the rich reaping all benefits at the cost of the poor. The landed class created and nurtured by the Dogra state in rural Kashmir exercised domination. Meanwhile, in the urban centers the elites, both Hindu and Muslim, lived a life of comfortable existence and the state subjected ordinary artisans, shawl weavers, and laborers to heavy taxation. As Kashmiri nationalists led the movement for rights in the mid-twentieth century, they articulated a vision for economic freedom that promised to eradicate the hierarchical relations of exploitation and expropriation in Kashmiri society. Their economic vision of ending the dominance of landed elites who exercised complete hegemony over the peasantry mobilized agrarian Kashmir to imagine emancipation as equity and justice in economic dealings. However, these imaginings remained unfulfilled in the aftermath of partition. Even though Kashmiri nationalists implemented their promise of *Naya Kashmir* by abolishing absentee landlordism and distributing land to its tillers, the reforms failed to bridge the disparity of wealth between social classes. The economic status of certain sections of agrarian Kashmir improved, yet a new class of rural elites retained land privileges, ensuring that the now well-to-do peasantry remained closely aligned with existing power structures. Economic and social disparities in Kashmir widened along both axes after the arbitrary drawing of the ceasefire line divided Kashmir and dismantled economic structures that had sustained the region's trade and commerce. As the resentment in urban centers, especially among petty traders, shopkeepers, and artisans increased, it enhanced political instability.

The political tensions in the Valley amplified after the Indian state committed to a policy of centralization and introduced an era of repressive and unrepresentative government in Kashmir to facilitate the state's integration,[2] even while theoretically Kashmir remained a disputed region awaiting the implementation of its promised self-determination. This chapter focuses on India's integration policy to examine the social and economic re-definition of Kashmiri society which shaped its postcolonial political culture. Because the pliant regime put in power by New Delhi in 1953 required legitimization, the central government stepped up economic development in the region to demonstrate the benefits of a close relationship with India. It provided numerous grants and subsidies to win over Kashmiris—but these funds, while seemingly endless, did not flow equally to all, or even to the many. Wealth became concentrated in the hands of few, while ordinary Kashmiris felt the brunt of income inequality and social segregation. This chapter asserts that India's development policies created a vision of economic prosperity but failed to ensure redistributive justice. The corrupt state regime, in its zeal to financially integrate, limited Kashmir's economic freedom. Free-flowing funds from New Delhi created a dependent mentality and destroyed Kashmiri initiative and self-reliance. Instead, the pliant regime created a new Kashmiri social group who not only collaborated to integrate the state with India but also introduced a new "modern" culture alien to traditional Kashmiri society.

Further, I argue here that the postcolonial transformation of Kashmir's political processes and economic structures during the era of the puppet regimes reshaped the boundaries of its majority Muslim community. Fierce internal debates broke out over the importance of religious identity, and Muslim religious institutions emerged as spaces where Muslims could address their conflicts over the definitions of modernity, secularism, and democracy. As political integration drove the cultural transformation of urban Kashmir, Islamist groups used political and social discontent among the excluded Muslim majority to condemn the ideologies of secularism and socialism propagated by the ruling elites. Instead, they advocated for an Islamic state as a solution to Kashmir's socioeconomic problems. Ultimately, economic policies—whether initiated by the Indian state, Kashmir's puppet leaders, or as a compromise between the two—led to changes in the political economy of the Valley that had a far-reaching impact not only on political and social structures, but on the tumultuous relationship between Kashmir, Kashmiris, and India.

Integration, Collaboration, and Economic Mismanagement

Indian nationalist narratives portray the period after 1953 as a golden era in which poverty-stricken Kashmir miraculously transformed into a land of prosperity and plenty. Their primary focus is on the economic advancement of Kashmir under the new administration, with the goal of creating an egalitarian society with high living standards for everyone. The Indian media that had once promoted Sheikh Abdullah as Kashmir's savior now carved a populist image of the new prime minister: Bakshi Ghulam Muhammad. According to this narrative, Bakshi symbolized Kashmiri aspirations; he sought to lift Kashmiris from a "morass of poverty, ignorance and squalor."[3] This populist image, however, clashed with the waves of protest demonstrations that swept Kashmir after Abdullah's dismissal, conveniently overlooked by the Indian press. Aware that Bakshi lacked legitimacy and hoping to appease the populace, the Indian state stepped up economic development in the region. Central funds poured into Jammu and Kashmir as the Indian government aimed to win over Kashmiris while using its pliant government to integrate the state with India.

Bakshi Ghulam Muhammad, a prominent member of the National Conference, emerged as the face of Kashmir's "modernization." He had played a significant role during the movement against the autocratic Dogra rule and had suffered imprisonment several times. Bakshi's humble beginnings had enabled him to connect with the masses, and he had succeeded in mobilizing the students and workers in their quest for a responsible government. Due to his strong grassroots support, Bakshi earned the trust of Abdullah, who appointed him as his deputy prime minister after Kashmir's accession to India.[4] The highly ambitious Bakshi, however, desired more than just being second in command. He took advantage of New Delhi's displeasure with Abdullah, convincing the center of his dependability and assuring them of his complete loyalty.

India was thrilled to replace Abdullah with Bakshi, as he had risen from the ranks in the National Conference due to his organizational skills and could connect to ordinary Kashmiris. A pragmatic politician, Bakshi worked to subdue Kashmiri discontent on three fronts: strengthening his support base by addressing basic economic needs; converting Kashmir into a police state to suppress dissenters; and offering secret financial aid to political groups that opposed Abdullah.[5] He further consolidated his position by arranging regional conventions of National Conference workers throughout the Valley. This party had failed to emerge as a democratic body due to the autocratic disposition of its past leaders. Most of these leaders had equated "freedom" with power for themselves, making the party an "abode of power-hunters, careerists, flatters and parasites." Lacking much distinct ideology other than the thirst for power, most of the National Conference seamlessly shifted its loyalties from Abdullah to the new state-sponsored regime.[6]

Despite Bakshi's combination of bribery and suppression, many Kashmiris refused to sell their allegiance and endured immense hardships, sometimes suffering imprisonment for years.[7] Bakshi's government expanded the police department, creating new battalions trained in torture methods. The new law allowed the government to detain citizens for up to five years without informing them of the grounds. A mafia-style group of thugs called, with bitter irony, the "Peace Brigade," assisted the police in their inhumane interrogations of the political opposition.[8] While the state treated political dissenters as subversive agents, the network of intelligence agencies created a shadow of uncertainty over every Kashmiri whose loyalty to Bakshi's government was in doubt.[9]

The new administration balanced its harsh policies by offering individual Kashmiris a series of political and economic rewards in exchange for their support of Kashmir's accession to India. Struggling to gain legitimacy after it usurped power from Sheikh Abdullah, the Bakshi regime tried to convince the public that aligning Kashmir's interests with those of India was in their best interests. In public gatherings, Bakshi promised Kashmiris necessities like jobs, roads, and water, while in private he pressured community leaders to convince the masses that a pragmatic attitude toward the new political situation would lead to economic prosperity. Instead of focusing on the plebiscite question, Bakshi believed that people should take advantage of the new economic development policies to secure business benefits, government services, and scholarships for children, arguing that these steps would free Kashmiris from the clutches of poverty and provide a better future for their children.[10]

The new prime minister also reached out to political groups like the Muslim Conference, which had been marginalized after 1947 due to its support of Kashmir's accession to Pakistan. Most of its members had migrated to Pakistan-administered Kashmir, yet the party still commanded a support base in the old city of Srinagar, especially among the followers of the Mirwaiz family, the chief preachers of the historic Jama Masjid. State bureaucrats and politicians met secretly with Muslim Conference members, with the former attempting to expand the new administration's support base, while the fragmented Mirwaiz group sought a space in the new postcolonial religious–political milieu of Kashmir. At one August 1954 meeting, well away from the public glare, the chief secretary of Jammu and Kashmir accused Abdullah of risking the lives and security of Kashmiri Muslims, forcing Bakshi to align with India to prevent massacre: "Indian army officers would have slaughtered the entire civilian population as was done in Hyderabad."[11] He implored Muslim community leaders to dispel Bakshi's image as a traitor and present him instead as an emancipator, one who had taken grave risks to secure the future of Kashmiri Muslims. A number of clerics present endorsed this image, enabling Bakshi to use the joint influence of religious leaders and Abdullah's opponents to gain legitimacy among the common people.[12]

The state discourse highlighted the unsatisfactory performance of Abdullah's government in resolving the economic crisis generated by the India–Pakistan War of 1948, which had created an acute shortage of commodities along with inflation. As Abdullah rejected economic dependence on India to maintain Kashmir's autonomy, he resisted taking subsidies from New Delhi, even though there was a shortage of food grains in the Valley. In his speeches he implored Kashmiris to eat potatoes rather than accept subsidized rice, as it would mean compromising their dignity and freedom.[13]

To ensure that limited food grains were also available to urban Kashmiris, Abdullah continued the Dogra policy of *mujawaza* (grain procurement), the main cause of peasant resentment. Official publications circulating in the 1950s and 1960s traced discontent to poverty and a low standard of living, promising Kashmiris economic reconstruction and a corruption-free government. The new administration tapped into the economic grievances of the masses to provide monetary concessions to Kashmiris included the abolition of *mujawaza*; reorganization of cooperative stores manned by corrupt officials; the creation of alternative credit societies; and the formation of cottage industries. In villages, procurement was now on a voluntary basis. The government removed restrictions on the movement, sale, and purchase of rice paddies. Urban areas benefited from generous concessions including reduced grain prices and higher government salaries.[14]

The decision to abolish *mujawaza* created a shortage in rations at Food Control Department granaries, but the government managed this potential crisis with India's help. The central government hugely subsidized rice, with Punjabi imports guaranteeing abundant food at cheap prices.[15] Government statistics show this considerable reduction in price: prior to August 1953, the Ministry of Food sold six *seers* of rice for 7 rupees, but during Bakshi's tenure, the price dropped to 1 rupee.[16] Significantly, the state provided the rich and the poor with food at the same rates, resulting in an abrupt increase in the standards of living, but failed to shrink the gap between the rich and the poor. Besides these concessions, the government made free education at all levels a priority and even established its own medical and engineering colleges. Infrastructure projects, meanwhile, changed the landscape; as new roads and bridges connected rural and urban areas, they created the image of a prosperous Kashmir.[17]

The development projects introduced by the state government to enhance its legitimacy required large cash flows unavailable in poverty-stricken Kashmir. India, therefore, funded the state regime, but the influx of capital came with a price: the erosion of Article 370 in its constitution, which guaranteed Jammu and Kashmir's autonomy. The constituent assembly of Kashmir had ratified accession to India and accepted the jurisdiction of the Indian constitution and the Indian Supreme Court over Jammu and Kashmir.[18] The constituent assembly gave the central government the right to legislate in Jammu and Kashmir on most subjects on the union list, including part XI of the Indian constitution over which the center has the exclusive power to legislate.[19]

Financial integration placed Jammu and Kashmir on an equal footing with other Indian states. Prior to 1953, Abdullah's government had resisted falling under India's economic control, insisting that central government assistance comes in the form of loans rather than grants. Even though the central government advanced cash under the description "Aid to Kashmir," it treated these sums as loans recoverable from the state government.[20] In 1954, Bakshi's government removed customs barriers between Kashmir and the rest of India and accepted the central government's control over federal revenue and expenditure.[21] The state lost control over interstate transit duties that had fetched a revenue of approximately 120 lakh rupees per year.[22] An agreement reached in January 1956 allowed India to collect 55 percent of net proceeds of income tax; 4 percent of duties on matches, tobacco, and vegetable products; and 100 percent of estate duties.[23]

On November 14, 1957, the state constituent assembly accepted constitutional provisions regarding the auditor and comptroller general; thereafter, revenues and expenditures were subjected to scrutiny by the auditor general of India.[24] India began to provide financial assistance to the state in the form of grants and subsidies not repayable to New Delhi.

To appease the collaborators essential for Kashmir's political integration, the Indian state gave preferential economic treatment to Jammu and Kashmir, as compared to other Indian states. Statistics on Kashmiri state assistance show that compared to other Indian states, Kashmir received a larger share of central assistance, especially in the 1950s and 1960s, when the center was working to erode Kashmir's autonomous status (see Table 3.1). After financial integration, Kashmir's share in the divisible pool of central taxes also increased, even though it was the least-taxed state in India. While the average Indian state in 1958–9 received "less than 30 percent of their tax revenue, Kashmir's share in the tax pool was about 56 percent of its total revenue." The finance commission provided Jammu and Kashmir with development grants and "special" grants to offset "economic backwardness" in the region. Although Jammu and Kashmir state made no effort to generate more taxes, the second finance commission recommended a grant of 300 lakh rupees to Jammu and Kashmir under Article 275.[25] The central ministers even provided state development grants not governed by the recommendations of the finance commission, such as one of 265.24 lakh rupees to "ensure minima in the standard of social service."[26]

Table 3.1 Comparative statistics of the central assistance (as percentage of total outlay) provided to Indian states in the first three five-year plans

	Plan 1	*Plan 2*	*Plan 3*
Andhra Pradesh	56	62	66
Assam	75	85	73
Bihar	54	70	65
Kerala	55	55	66
Madhya Pradesh	65	77	69
Madras	49	60	65
Punjab	87	70	58
West Bengal	73	63	64
Jammu and Kashmir	77	96	83

Source: State Outlay, Central Assistance and State Resources: Plan 1, Plan II, and Plan III, cited in Balraj Puri, "Kashmir in the Economic and Budgetary Map of India," *Kashmir Affairs* 9 (January–February 1961): 36–8.

Despite these extensive development funds from the center, Jammu and Kashmir also continued taking huge low-interest loans from New Delhi.[27] However, the state government not only failed to pay installments, but in most cases also avoided interest payments. In 1965, the state government asked the Indian Finance Commission for a loan modification. In a memorandum submitted to the commission, the state requested that India "lighten the burden of debt" by either writing off liabilities or making a substantial grant to enable the government to pay the interest that had accumulated on the accounts.[28] Total cash loans from the central government between 1953 and 1962 significantly increased, of which neither the principal nor the regular interest was typically paid (see Table 3.2).

Table 3.2 Loans from India to the Jammu and Kashmir government, 1951–60

Year	*Amount (Rupees in Lakhs)*
1951–2	50.80
1952–3	90.00
1953–4	182.25
1954–5	124.00
1955–6	167.27
1956–7	510.64
1957–8	251.35
1958–9	391.82
1959–60	718.50

Source: Balraj Puri, "Kashmir's Indebtedness to the Center," *Kashmir Affairs* 4, no. 11 (May–June 1961): 10–11.

Cash flow from grants and loans alike presented the potential for explosive economic growth. The standard of living improved among certain sections of Kashmiri society. There was an increasing demand for consumer goods in the late 1950s. The number of radio licenses increased by more than eight times the previous decade, and the need for motorcycles jumped tenfold. Businesses flourished; restaurants, bars, and cinema houses emerged in every town. Yet the rate of growth in the state domestic product remained at 7–8 percent.[29] The new economy failed to generate higher revenue, as the state's own resource generation, even after financial integration with India, was almost non-existent.[30] In the first three five-year plans, central assistance solely drove economic growth.[31] The state government's obsession with its own security made it impossible to use these funds to truly develop the local economy. To win popular support, the state administration provided subsidies in lieu of collecting taxes, reducing the revenue available for investment or loan repayment. And instead of investing Indian funds in industrial growth or agricultural production, the state expanded the police and intelligence departments to curb political discontent.

Kashmiri visions of economic freedom and prosperity for all were shattered due to the state's inability to drive consistent economic growth. The Plebiscite Front, the party formed by disgruntled supporters of Abdullah who were now leading the movement for self-determination, expressed concern over the state government's fiscal policy, which they believed crushed economic self-reliance and made Kashmir dependent on India. G. H. Shah, the general secretary of the Plebiscite Front, wrote an article in *Minorities Views* in May 1968, debunking the myth of Kashmir's economic growth under Bakshi's administration, instead highlighting the soaring cost of living, stagnant incomes, and increasing unemployment in Kashmir. He pointed out that the prices of rice, sugar, cloth, pulses, vegetables, and fuel had increased by more than 300 percent, while the income of wage earners had remained stagnant since 1953. This had created an "unbridgeable gap between the real and actual income," with "83% of the state's population" earning an average monthly income of "less than Rs.16.35 per head."[32]

Another article in the *Mahaz*, the official newspaper of the Plebiscite Front, suggested that instead of pouring money into the state, India should focus on creating jobs that would generate income and tax revenue alike. These activists lamented that, in the name of progress and prosperity, Bakshi had created a dependent economy geared to make Kashmiris the slaves of India.[33] Bakshi always denied what he called "absurd accusations," arguing that, as an "integral and indivisible part of India," Kashmir was right to seek central assistance. He reprimanded his critics for equating slavery with "a younger brother [Kashmir]" seeking help from an "elder brother [India] who was rich and prosperous."[34]

The close relationship between Bakshi and his sponsors in India left the new prime minister with complete freedom to build a new class of collaborators loyal to India and protected against popular condemnation. This desire found fertile soil in several economic and social groups in the Valley. Many urban Kashmiris wanted to improve their economic standing after the ceasefire line rendered old trade routes inaccessible, while the petty shopkeepers, peddlers, and laborers resented rising prices and commodity shortages that made it difficult to make ends meet. Although some of the Kashmiri peasantry who had benefitted from Abdullah's agrarian reforms remained die-hard supporters during his days of incarceration, others, who had suffered his administration's forced procurement of food grains that hardly left enough for their families' sustenance, supported the new regime. Reeling from the economic chaos of the postcolonial years, these disgruntled Kashmiris readily offered support to the puppet regime. As money flowed in from New Delhi, the poverty-stricken Kashmiris hoped that money appropriated at the top would trickle down to the needy and alter their economic situations. Bakshi believed his populist measures would buy people's support and ensure Kashmiri silence. As he expanded his network of collaborators, Bakshi asserted his legitimacy in various forums, claiming that forty lakh (4 million) Kashmiris (the total population of the Valley in the 1950s) supported him, even though they might silently sympathize with Abdullah.[35]

Riyaz Punjabi has argued that the close nexus between bureaucrats, businessmen, and politicians created an exclusive social group, a nouveau riche who reaped maximum benefits from financial integration with India.[36] I further explore how the patronage politics of this period, in reality, benefited the supporters, friends, and relations of political elites. Prior to 1953, many political elites had abused their power, but had cherished autonomy and resisted integration. The new class of collaborators accepted liberal financial aid as the price of integration; the generous central funds available after 1953 created a rich business class with close economic ties to India. In turn, this group created a broad support base using a new machinery of political and economic rewards. A highly subsidized economy and discretionary sanctions of permits, licenses, and contracts created this new social group.[37]

The *Ayyangar Committee Report* published in 1967 to probe corruption at the state level scrutinized the rise of this business class. The report traces the emergence of the "Bakshi Brothers Corporation," a powerful family of traders who monopolized political power for ten years, using their connections to become wealthy. It states in 1947, the family of Bakshi Ghulam Muhammad owned a small fur business in Srinagar, generating a total income of 800 rupees per month, along with all immovable property worth 10,000 rupees. Once Bakshi became prime minister of Kashmir, however, he established a monopoly over three main government departments: transport, forests, and public works. As per the report, the value of his property increased to 1.45 crore[38] rupees approximately within ten years.[39]

The new administration's patronage politics also created a support base among Kashmiris who received government contracts. This top-down network of corruption reached an unprecedented level in the 1960s, when almost every administrative department was involved in shady dealings. Sustained with a flow of funds from New Delhi, many contractors, forest lessees, and transporters now supported Kashmir's integration with India. Although most were illiterate, the benefits and rewards they received for this support helped them rise economically and socially alike. Even individuals opposed to Bakshi's policies often found it impossible to avoid the whirlpool of corruption.

After 1953, the Forest Department and the Public Works Department (PWD) became lucrative avenues for corruption and exploitation of government funds. Kashmir's forests represented some of its most attractive and potentially lucrative natural resources. The Bakshi regime reserved the best contracts for its loyal supporters, allowing them to siphon government funds without concern for the renewability of Kashmir's natural resources. While the executive body placed advertisements inviting tenders for cutting and removing trees, this procedure was a formality; the government already knew who would receive the lease. In theory, the forest lessees paid a royalty to the state and were required to complete the task on time.[40] However, with the support of bureaucrats and politicians, the lessees devised ingenious ways to avoid honoring these contracts. Meanwhile, the PWD presented another avenue for creating a Kashmiri nouveau riche. The ruling elite hired carpenters, masons, and plumbers to build their mansions. Construction workers were not paid in cash; instead, they were rewarded with PWD contracts for government buildings and development projects.[41] In many cases, the government allotted several contracts to one individual against a single tender, or deliberately avoided advertising notices for tenders, denying those without political contacts a fair chance to compete.[42]

The state administration also created loyalists through the distribution of route permits. As per the Jammu and Kashmir Motor Vehicles Act of 1941, the government had the right to grant permits and lay conditions on carrying capacity and routes. The transport authority, after objective appraisal of traffic, determined how many vehicles were invited to apply for permits; then the government issued permits to those who could render efficient service. Trafficking of permits was contrary to the spirit and purpose of the Motor Vehicles Act, and in some cases could entail penalties or lead to cancellation. However, under Bakshi's government, trafficking in permits ensured an easy and comfortable living and became a reward for past or present political and social service. Most people who applied for permits owned no vehicle but leased or sold these permits to others. A deliberate policy not to issue adequate public carrier permits created a scarcity value.[43] The few permit holders enjoyed a virtual monopoly, which increased the price of permits; their black-market value ranged from 16,000 to 30,000 rupees.[44] The corrupt transport business gave rise to a number of millionaires who in turn generously funded the ruling party.

Nepotism and cronyism was a major component of the selection process for government positions, while to succeed at any economic enterprise in the state required official favors, corruption, and humiliation. The groups that collaborated with the government and provided political support received the best jobs. Most, if not all, of the appointed government servants lacked objective qualifications, with some even lacking primary education; the only qualification that mattered was a relationship with a bureaucrat or minister, or the office they held in National Conference committees.[45] Unfortunately, while scions of the new elites had a guaranteed future, impoverished Kashmiris without political connections struggled to find even menial jobs in the administration.[46] The deepening wedge between the rich and the poor in Kashmir became more visible after the emergence of this new class which amassed "fortunes through dubious means."[47]

The Kashmir legislative assembly discussed the rising corruption which created immense hardships for common Kashmiris and alienated them from the government. In the mid-1960s, some members even demanded the creation of a high-power board to eradicate corruption, along with an amendment to the Jammu and Kashmir Preventive Corruption Act to hold ministers and assembly council members, not just government servants, accountable.[48] The corruption of the Forest Department, in particular, was a popular topic. Some members of the assembly worried about the exploitation of Kashmir's "national wealth."[49] Others suggested ending the privatization of forest leases; instead, they proposed a state corporation with 33 percent government shares. In response to this criticism, the minister of forests emphasized that rebates were only provided on humanitarian grounds, to save poor lessees from heavy losses. However, he promised that in the future his department would survey forests to check the quality of timber before leasing them for extraction. Ironically, the corrupt ministry based its argument on social equality, rejecting the suggestion to set up a corporation as "it would allow some individuals to dominate these corporations and negate their socialist ideals."[50]

As "integration" remained India's primary interest, the state was largely indifferent to popular grievances and the patronage politics that alienated many Kashmiris. As early as 1957, prominent Congress leader Mridula Sarabhai worried that India would allow the Kashmiri government to destroy its cherished principles of socialism. In a letter to the members of the Indian parliament, she cautioned that allowing the few to gain at the cost of the many would breed discontent.[51] She critiqued the Indian Administrative Services officers posted in Kashmir, who hoarded money and resisted transfer to any other Indian state.[52] Balraj Puri, a prominent political activist from Jammu, expressed similar concerns to the Indian prime minister about the corrupt and oppressive political climate of Kashmir. Puri quoted Prime Minister Nehru as saying that "India's case [on Kashmir] revolved around him [Bakshi] so despite all his shortcomings, Bakshi's government had to be strengthened. We are there [Kashmir] at the point of a bayonet. Till things improve democracy and morality can wait [in Kashmir]."[53]

Although the Indian government collaborated throughout the 1950s with Bakshi's regime to consolidate Kashmir's integration with India, by the early 1960s Indian leadership felt confident that Kashmir had become an impregnable and inseparable part of India and decided to rein in the puppet administration. The money pumped into the state had successfully created a class of Indian supporters and had, Indian officials believed, resolved the issue of Kashmiri self-determination.

New Delhi shifted its focus to addressing the absolute impunity of the local regime. The Indian press, previously silent about the free hand given to the pliant regimes in the interest of national security, published editorials and articles pressuring the Indian state to hold the Kashmiri government responsible. The publication of the Audit Report of 1962 exposed irregularities in the Jammu and Kashmir administration, building momentum for the removal of Bakshi Ghulam Muhammad. Press outrage over the "wastage of Indian taxpayers' money" led to a commission of inquiry, the Ayyangar Commission, to probe the misuse of power that had helped Bakshi and his family gain riches. The commission authenticated fifteen out of thirty-eight allegations.[54] Clearly, Bakshi had become a source of embarrassment for the central government; realizing that he had outlived his usefulness, he reluctantly offered his resignation in October 1963.

India may have moved too soon, however. The regime that followed from 1964 to 1972, headed by prominent leftist Kashmiri leader G. M. Sadiq, who had played an active role during Kashmiri mobilization against the Dogra rule, continued the Indian policy of integration but failed to win popular support. Kashmiri Muslims excluded from structures of power and frustrated with the decade-old repressive policies of the state-sponsored regime supported the renewed movement for self-determination led by Sheikh Abdullah's Plebiscite Front. Sadiq's administration, concerned about growing Kashmiri Muslim resentment, promised the emotional integration of Kashmir with India with a policy of "restoring civil liberties, providing clean administration and introducing democratic practices, thus retrieving the good name of the Indian Union."[55] Sadiq freed political prisoners and allowed freedom of expression and freedom of the press. To ensure social justice and equal opportunities for all, the state appointed a cadre of officials based on merit, honesty, and integrity. An obligatory "code of conduct" for state ministers required the disclosure of property details before taking the oath of office. The state administration's new mantra of a healthy respect for laws and norms aimed to bring Kashmiris closer to India in a different manner than had Bakshi's program of tying a Kashmiri elite to India through corruption.[56]

The rhetoric of good governance, however, could not dislodge the networks of corruption that had become deeply entrenched in the sociopolitical fabric of Kashmir. A committee to recruit honest officials for the Kashmir Civil Services provided a private list of "notorious officials" to the government to prevent them from holding important positions. Unfortunately, this list was publicly disclosed, providing an opportunity for corrupt officers to use their political connections to obtain positions.[57] The anti-corruption organization only prosecuted five officials in nine years (1963–72), revealing its ineptness at bringing bureaucrats and politicians to justice.[58]

Sadiq's government did succeed in further eroding the autonomous status of Kashmir to satisfy Indian public opinion. In March 1965, Article 356 of the Indian constitution was applied to Jammu and Kashmir, empowering India to replace the legislatively appointed head of state (Sadar-i-Riyasat) with a New Delhi-appointed "governor." This official had extraordinary powers, previously exercised by the Sadar-i-Riyasat, to assume any or all functions of the government under Section 92 of the Jammu and Kashmir constitution.[59] In a move toward political integration, the working committee of the National Conference, a Sadiq faction, dissolved itself and merged into India's ruling Congress Party as a provincial branch. This angered Kashmiri Muslims, who despite their grievances with the National Conference saw the regional party as a symbol of their "political achievements, cultural advancement, and national existence."[60] Throughout the late 1960s, the mood in the Valley was volatile, especially among students, who firmly believed that their leaders were stooges of the Indian government that had hampered the cause of Kashmiris.[61] Kashmiri youth searched for any and every excuse to express their resentment of the state-sponsored regimes.

The spirit of discontent also spread among the Kashmiri intelligentsia, unhappy with state's economic policies that had crippled individual initiative and created dependency through incurring ruinous debts from the center. *Mahaz*, the official newspaper of the Plebiscite Front, ran editorials about the party's economic vision for Kashmir's prosperity. G. Lone, a prominent member of the Plebiscite Front, believed that the reopening of old routes and rivers that connected the state to the rest of the world would revive Kashmiri self-sufficiency. He drew attention to how the ceasefire line had dismantled the major waterways, highways, and railheads that had sustained Kashmir's trade prior to partition.[62] Five major trade routes had previously connected Jammu and Kashmir to the plains of Punjab; the most important was the Jhelum Valley Road that joined the Valley to the North-Western Railways at Rawalpindi.[63] Lone believed that the closure of the Jhelum Valley Road, the easiest route connecting the mountainous Valley with the rest of the subcontinent throughout the year, had hampered the export of Kashmiri handicrafts on a large scale. In fact, prior to 1947, these trade routes carried goods not only to other regions of the subcontinent but also to Europe and Britain. The princely state exported approximately 9,441,500 *maunds* of timber, fruits, wool, silk, and hides and imported almost 1,923,000 *maunds* of cotton, sugar, and salt through these routes.[64] Trade with foreign countries yielded a revenue of 1.25 crore rupees. However, after accession to India most of these routes were eliminated and hit the Kashmiri business community hard.

Kashmiri intellectual debates centered on how to create industrial growth. G. H. Khan, a prominent Kashmiri bureaucrat, also argued against complete dependence on the Banihal Road. This road connected Kashmir with India but remained closed for six months during winter. Without any access to railways or to the Jhelum Valley Road, the yearly closure destroyed old markets, raised transportation costs, and prevented the development of small-scale industries that required raw materials. The fruit industry, for example, would have a wider market if Kashmiris could access the wholesale market at Rawalpindi, 200 miles away, as opposed to Delhi, a distance of about 600 miles. The free movement of services, goods, capital, and labor across the artificial ceasefire line, Khan believed, would restore Kashmir's economic prosperity and reduce the line to a mere geographical demarcation.[65] The Kashmiri intelligentsia debunked the statist perspectives that connected Kashmir's prosperity with economic aid flowing from India by providing an alternative vision for Kashmir's self-sufficient economic growth; in doing so, they challenged the artificial line of demarcation that disastrously separated peoples, communities, and cultures, along with markets.

Kashmiri visions of creating a prosperous state by opening trade routes across the ceasefire line rather than by relying on grants from New Delhi failed to materialize as the regional balance of power shifted in India's favor after the India–Pakistan War of 1971, leading to the dismemberment of Pakistan and the creation of the new nation-state of Bangladesh.[66] Thereafter, India and Pakistan agreed to rename the ceasefire line the "line of control," and promised that neither side "shall seek to alter it unilaterally" irrespective of mutual differences and legal interpretations.[67] Even Sheikh Abdullah, who had opposed integration with India and mobilized Kashmiris on the plank of self-determination, took steps to reconcile with New Delhi. In 1975 he signed an accord with Indira Gandhi, accepting Kashmir as an integral part of India, and returned to power in Jammu and Kashmir. His supporters, however, interpreted the accord as a betrayal of trust by a leader whom they had revered.[68]

Feeling disillusioned with Abdullah's politics, people protested and demonstrated against his new government. After Abdullah resumed the reins of administration, he promised Kashmiris a corruption-free society, hoping to win back popular support. However, instead of offsetting preexisting networks of institutional patronage, Abdullah's administration became an extension of these entrenched power structures. The Saxena *Crusade against Corruption* report published in 1984 revealed that state employees engaged in acts of rent-seeking, documenting 3,330 cases of corruption from 1975 to 1981.[69] Abdullah's opponents secretly circulated a pamphlet entitled *Lal Kitab* (Red Book) during the 1980s to harm him politically. The book claimed that "assets, properties, illegally occupied government land, [and] palatial buildings" were constructed with "money and material obtained from all sorts of dubious sources, especially from contractors working with government departments." The anonymous writer emphasized that Abdullah's administration was no different from the recent puppet regimes.[70]

The depth of corruption in Kashmir becomes evident through the tales of tax evasion by some of the richest business families. A series of income tax raids in 1981 on Kashmiri business elites, motivated by New Delhi's need to subdue regional dissidence, struck at some of Abdullah's staunchest supporters and exposed the nefarious connections between politicians, bureaucrats, and businessmen. Some families reluctantly admitted that they had cemented firm links with the National Conference through trusts headed by the party's leadership. Five of the seven families raided, for example, comprised the fifteen-member National Conference. The central government announced that officials had seized gold and jewelry worth more than 20 lakh rupees, and uncovered tax evasion in the staggering amount of 5 crore rupees—more than the state's entire income and corporate tax revenue (4.1 crore rupees) in 1979–80.[71] The raid even yielded hashish in one office, implicating the owner in smuggling. While many Kashmiris understood that these raids were politically motivated, they were extremely disappointed with their leaders and felt that "honest practices and laws were meant only for un-influential poor people."[72]

The lack of transparency and accountability eroded people's trust in their own leaders, leaving a negative impact on Kashmir's political structures and economic institutions. Corruption even damaged Kashmir's natural resources. Besides exploiting the forests for debt servicing, in the mid-1980s the National Conference chief ministers G. M. Shah and Farooq Abdullah initiated several projects that polluted Kashmir's air, water, and soil. The administration allotted influential business owners plots at cheap rates to construct hotels and commercial complexes along the Dal Lake, the largest lake in the Valley. Sewage from the construction flowed into the lake, and silting reduced its size from 24 square kilometers to about 10.[73] Although the state government set up commissions of inquiry to probe corruption cases, Kashmiris remained skeptical.[74] Administrative anti-corruption campaigns, many people believed, could not succeed unless the political structures were cleansed of dishonest politicians and bureaucrats.

Indian nationalist narratives often blame the widespread corruption in Kashmir on Article 370, which allowed the autonomous state government to practice misgovernance without accountability. Jagmohan, the India-appointed governor of Kashmir from 1984 to 1989, argued that "Article 370 acquired a thicker and malevolent texture," allowing corruption to acquire "new fangs and depth in Kashmir."[75] Nevertheless, the blame placed on state leaders ignores the issues that compelled the central government to inundate Kashmir with funds and allow political elites to practice misgovernance. The center used state-sponsored governments to erode Article 370 and create a supporting structure of Kashmiris whose economic interests were tied with India. Without absolving political elites of stealing government funds, the center refused to address the economic discontent that strengthened the networks of corruption. It set a trend that continued throughout the 1970s and 1980s. As their basic freedoms were being denied, Kashmiris became convinced that every government was hollow, organized solely to benefit the wealthiest class and bring the state closer to India. The ruling elites lived in "palatial houses, provided the best education for their children," and manipulated their way into top government jobs. Excluded Kashmiris, on the other hand, had little access to political power, lived in "dilapidated houses," and struggled to find employment for their children.[76] Meanwhile, the new social groups, intoxicated with political power and greed, transformed Kashmiri society; their actions generated a strong reaction from underprivileged sections and affected Kashmiri perceptions of secularism, modernity, and religion.

Social Transformations in Urban Kashmir: Modernity and Responses to Secularism

As the postcolonial Indian state professed secular nationalism as the creed justifying centralization and homogenization, papering over regional, religious, and linguistic differences, it misconstrued concern for one's religious community as disloyalty to the nation.[77] Conflating secularism with nationalism shaped debates over the definition of modernity, especially after the pliant regimes reformulated Kashmir's social structures and altered old values. The state regime, in collaboration with India, spread the "doctrine of secularism" in the hope of bringing Kashmiris culturally closer to India through accelerated political and financial integration. Thus, in Kashmir, the secularism of the modern nation-state was a closed ideology imposed from above to bring Kashmiris into the national mainstream. The Kashmiri Muslim community responded in diverse ways to the socialeconomic transformations that altered older ethical values based on their class status. While many of the nouveau riche in urban Srinagar, who benefitted from closer political ties with India, embraced "secularism" and showed disdain for religious beliefs, values, and ethics, a section of the rural elite and the lower middle classes, excluded from networks of patronage during the era of the pliant regimes, embraced an Islamist ideology that brought them closer to political Islam.

The regimes that followed Abdullah's 1953 dismissal from power diverted attention from political matters and convinced many Kashmiris that modernization required cultural and political integration with India. Bakshi Ghulam Muhammad introduced a series of cultural festivals (Jashan-i-Bahar) to showcase the accomplishments of both Indian and Kashmiri poets, artists, and musicians.[78] Every year, thousands of Indian tourists, including special invitees, visited the Valley to participate in literary readings, folk dances, and concerts. The festivals boosted tourism overall, and rest houses, clubs, and hotels sprang up across the Valley. Additionally, the government demanded that bars, cinemas, and nightclubs be established to make Kashmir more attractive to tourists. These measures improved the region's economy, but unleashed major cultural changes as drugs, drinking, and gambling became common among political elites.

As Kashmiris came into greater contact with the cultures of both India and the outside world, some modernization took place naturally. In particular, Kashmiri women began to renegotiate patriarchal authority, especially after the introduction of women's educational institutions. Education outside their homes empowered Kashmiri women and transformed family relations and traditional patterns of marriage. Young women not only sought economic independence, but also often defied social boundaries; intercommunity marriages became a possibility.[79] Older Kashmiris universally considered such marriages "undesirable socialization" and blamed "modernization" for women's new autonomy and challenge to parental authority.[80] Newspaper editorials advised parents to allow their daughters to seek education, but to monitor their interactions so as to avoid bringing "shame to the family" by making wrong choices about their life partners.[81] Traditional

Kashmiri society struggled to adapt to modernization. At the same time, fears and insecurities increased as Bakshi's regime embraced the mantle of India's secular nationalism to bring Kashmiris into the national mainstream.

The collaboration between pliant regimes in Kashmir and the Indian state benefited the ruling elite and the nouveau riche, who readily embraced Indian culture and the mantle of secular nationalism. Claiming to be secular and modern, many new urban elites derided religious values, idealism, and hard work, the ethics that had sustained Kashmiri society, in exchange for quick riches and power. Kashmiri social life now revolved around "acquisition of wealth and its vulgar display."[82] Most Kashmiris, however, equated the secularism and modernity propagated by the ruling elites with a culture of urban degradation, and considered secularism a threat to their religiously informed cultural identity.

Kashmiri novels and short stories provide insight into the perceived moral degradation and urban decadence connected with the rise of new social groups that supported integration with India. To a poor, urban Kashmiri in the postcolonial era, politicians, bureaucrats, businessmen, and police officials were not objects of respect or emulation. They were contemptible figures who exploited the poor and disrespected human values. Consider the following story from Akhtar Mohiuddin, the most eminent Kashmiri novelist of postcolonial Kashmir. Mohiuddin's novel *Jahnamuk Panun Panun Naar* (To Each According to His Own Hell), written in 1975, is dedicated to "the first young man who will pick up a gun to clean this mess."[83] The story critiques modern Kashmiri elites who wanted to build a new world on the edifice of secularism. The novel highlights the decadence of ruling elites, the exclusion and exploitation of the poor, and how different classes negotiated the complex terrain of modernity. Set in a city where democracy has derailed, the book's characters still hope for an era of civil rights and liberty. When a "charlatan" promises them democracy and becomes their chief executive, he saves the outer structure of democracy at the expense of its very soul.[84] The author emphasizes that this new form of democracy is "secular and amoral," dominated by drug addicts, thieves, and criminals who scorn ethics and morality. In this new society, religious values are reviled as obscurantism and wealth defines an individual's status. In their keenness to appear "modern," ruling elites copy the Western lifestyle, at odds with their traditional religious society. Ordinary Kashmiris compromise their values to fit in with the new social order, which lauds equality for women while exploiting them in practice.

The main character is a beautiful girl from a poor family who falls in love with the chief executive's son, Madanwar. Madanwar's family disapproves of this relationship because of the girl's poor background and inability to bring a big dowry. The family decides to end the relationship and send their son abroad for higher education. Madanwar convinces his father to arrange a match for the girl, who might have difficulty finding another husband in these circumstances. The chief executive induces Mr. X, a poor clerk in his administration, to marry the girl by offering him a promotion, a plot of land, and a beautiful bungalow in a posh colony. Mr. and Mrs. X's new wealth and status lead powerful bureaucrats and ministers to befriend them, and they are sucked into the valueless society of the elites. As they strive to become "respectable citizens," the couple embraces immorality, dishonesty, and exploitation: they indulge in a narcotics business, exploit young girls, and even compel their own daughter to have illicit relations with powerful individuals they could later blackmail for favorable business deals. This story contends that in Kashmir the very definition of "respectability" had undergone a massive transformation and that the secular modernity practiced by some ruling elites, created and nurtured by Indian money, lacked human values, excluded the poor, and exploited women.[85]

The excluded majority, instead of revolting against this oppressive environment, either remained complacent or compromised with the new system. Many Kashmiris saw this moral compromise as the "psychological moment" of their defeat by a system "deliberately set in motion to destroy their identity."[86] The well-known Kashmiri writer Amin Kamil's short story "Infernal Creature" written in 1958 provides insight into how immorality became the norm.[87] The main character is a thief who strips dead bodies of shrouds. In the beginning, this heinous practice fills the villagers of Zaji Pathir with shame and anger. They start doubting and questioning each other, which affects relationships within society and divides neighbors and families. Ultimately, people realize that paying the costs of finding and confronting the thief is not in their best interest. Although they keep on hurling curses at the unknown shroud thief, they do not try to change the deplorable situation. Robbing the dead of their shrouds becomes a custom of that village, akin to giving the last bath and burying the body. After twenty years, the thief is finally revealed, and begs for forgiveness on his deathbed. People forgive him; however, they soon discover that there is a new thief, more ruthless than the last, who not only robs the shrouds but also leaves naked bodies exposed. The "pious inhabitants" of Zaji Pathir now shower blessings on the former thief, "an individual with a conscience" because he hesitated to expose dead bodies, as compared to the new thief, a target of verbal curses.[88] The story is a social criticism of Kashmiris who, while claiming to be pious and free from all vices, remain indifferent to the moral chaos engulfing society.

Kashmiri intellectuals engaged in considerable soul searching over the relationship between modernity and secularism, and their respective uses and purposes, benefits, and limits. What, they asked, is modernity? Why should religion be an important part of secular education? Intellectuals attributed what they saw as a moral decline in Kashmiri society to political elites' deliberate indoctrination of secular values for national integration, which many believed aimed to eliminate their religious identity. A new reframing of the state's educational policy, in turn, would stem this moral decline. The state's educational system, according to the well-known Kashmiri scholar Ghulam Hassan Khan's 1968 indictment, was designed to "create a sense of integration, unity, and solidarity" with the "secular and nationalist ideals" of India. Educational policy focused on creating a new generation of Kashmiris free from "obscurantisms, superstition and other evils" and willing to embrace "modernity." Any association with "religious values" and "traditional education" was considered a move backward. The state's educational system also focused on Indian culture and traditions, refraining from educating Kashmiris about their own history or language.[89]

The Indian state, according to this critique, wanted to create a new generation of Kashmiris immersed in the "ancient culture of India" but disconnected from Kashmir's past. In 1966 the Indian parliament deemed certain passages in Kashmir's history books a challenge to the sovereignty and the territorial integrity of India. The textbook in question contained a chapter on the New Kashmir Manifesto, interpreted as "advocating [the] idea of a separate Kashmir" and deliberately indoctrinating Kashmiri children to consider themselves separate from the Indian Union. Members of the Indian parliament accused the Kashmiri government of indulging in "anti-national" activities. Even though the minister of home affairs emphasized that most of the book referred to "secularism" and the "Vedic culture" of India, his statements failed to appease angry politicians. The state government withdrew the textbook from the curriculum and appointed a textbook inquiry committee to remove "objectionable content" from elementary and middle school textbooks. The textbook committee received strict direction to frame the curriculum in a manner that would encourage Kashmiri children to emerge as "good members of democratic, secular, and socialist India."[90]

Many Kashmiri intellectuals debated the state's educational policy, which they believed eroded not only their religious identity but also their uniqueness as Kashmiris. Ghulam Hassan Khan, in his unpublished pamphlet "Kashmir's Educational System," blamed the educational policy for creating an unethical society. Khan disagreed with the government's decision to exclude religious education from the curriculum, arguing that ethical education created a society free from greed, deceit, and slander. Focusing on religion as a faith rather than as a political identity, Khan argued that a religious-minded person, whether a "Sikh, a Hindu or a Christian" would have "right values" and live in amity with members of other faiths.[91] He emphasized that modernity was attainable without divorcing it from religious values. Kashmiris could embrace modernity's true spirit by focusing on scientific knowledge, which would enable technological and economic progress. He urged Kashmiris to take charge of their own destiny and appoint honest and upright individuals as religious leaders. Khan asked the Indian state to provide legal protections for Muslim educational institutions that propagated ethical teachings to future generations. This would assure Kashmiri Muslims that their culture and heritage were safe as part of secular India.

Simmering discontent among Kashmiri Muslims due to the integration policy of the state-sponsored regimes, acting at the behest of the Indian state, reached a tipping point in the winter of 1963, when their most treasured relic, the Moe-e-Muqaddas, the Sacred Hair of the Prophet, went missing from the Hazratbal shrine at Srinagar. The theft of the relic provoked intense public indignation throughout the Valley. Streams of Kashmiris defied the freezing weather and gathered at the historic Lal Chowk, or the Red Square, to express their outrage. As the people wept and wailed, the general secretary of the ruling National Conference, Bakshi Rashid, whose family had been instrumental in integrating Kashmir with India, attempted to appease the crowds, but only further infuriated them. To the protesters, he symbolized the Kashmiris who had sold their homeland to India for monetary benefits. Emotions ran high and the mob retaliated against the Bakshi family, targeting their property and setting fire to their cinema houses and automobile firms. The government suppressed their demonstrations with force, opening fire on protesters, killing three and injuring nearly 300 people. Even a fourteen-hour curfew failed to calm the people.[92]

The protests provided Kashmiri Muslims an opportunity to resist their state's integration and express resentment against a tyrannical regime that suppressed "any dissent with police interrogation, secret informers, and sadistic peace brigades."[93] The demonstrations brought the entire community together; free kitchens sprang up and people opened their homes to protesters. Unable to control the mass upsurge, the administration collapsed. The government operated only a few closely guarded offices, as the situation spiraled beyond the control of Indian authorities.[94] The demonstrations took a political turn when the pro-plebiscite groups united to form a central action committee that not only sought recovery of the holy relic but also launched an agitation, simultaneously demanding a plebiscite and the release of Sheikh Abdullah.

The effects of this agitation reverberated throughout the subcontinent. The Hindu rightist organizations in Jammu, eager to divert attention away from the Kashmiri revolt, presented the Holy Relic agitation as a "communal" movement. This event sparked a wave of communal riots all over the subcontinent and claimed the lives of hundreds of minorities: Hindus in East Bengal (then East Pakistan) and Muslims in Calcutta, the capital of West Bengal province in India.[95] In the Valley, no communal riots occurred; the Action Committee leaders warned against violence. Yet these events outside the Valley intensified Kashmiri Muslim insecurities about the rising power of the Hindu right in India. Shortly thereafter, the government restored the holy relic to the Hazratbal shrine, although they never disclosed how it had been recovered, claiming a secret "intelligence operation."[96] The open rebellion of Kashmiri Muslims exposed the weakness of India's hold on the state and revealed its inability to win Kashmiri hearts and minds despite pouring unlimited funds into the region. As the agitation brought India to the edge of losing Kashmir, the national leadership realized it had misread the political conditions in the Valley. This event shattered India's perceptions about Kashmir's successful integration.

The agitation also exposed the general unpopularity of the India-sponsored prime minister of Kashmir, Bakshi Ghulam Muhammad, both despite and because of his scattering of Indian largesse among a new collaborator class. Aware of the challenges the agitation posed to his political legacy, Bakshi issued a lengthy statement to explain the "real mind of [the] Kashmiri Muslim," trying to shift the focus of popular conversation to Kashmiri Muslim apprehensions about Hindu-majority India. He had tried to turn Kashmiris into loyal Indian citizens by making them realize their best interests lay in being a part of a democratic and secular India, but, he claimed, he had failed because of the growing Hinduization in India.

Bakshi blamed his failure to win Kashmiri hearts and minds on not only communal culture, but the rising power of India's Hindu right parties.[97] In Jammu, the Jan Sangh leader Balraj Madhok endorsed the idea of Hindu superiority and promoted "nationalizing the Muslims." The party claimed that in a Hindu nation Muslims should have "no privileges, or any preferential treatment, not even citizen rights."[98] Hindus were the only loyal citizens; Muslims needed to adopt Hindu culture and language to be "naturalized" as true citizens of India. In this context, Kashmiri Muslims were anxious after the state's 1965 decision to replace Urdu and Kashmiri terms like *sadr-i-riyasat* (governor) and *wazir-i-azam* (chief minister) with Sanskritized terms such as *rashtrapati* and *pradhanmantri*. The Hinduization propagated within the state of Jammu and Kashmir made Kashmiri Muslims contemplate ways to protect their cultural and religious identity.

The Kashmiri religious organizations that emerged on the political scene after the Holy Relic agitation took the lead in addressing these Kashmiri Muslim concerns. The Auquaf-i-Islamia, a body formed in 1963 to preserve Muslim mosques and shrines, focused on the challenges faced by the Muslim community in a detailed memo. They proposed establishing private schools to provide both religious and secular education. Lacking sufficient funds to establish their own schools, some members of Auquaf suggested assisting organizations like the Jamaat-i-Islami and the Anjuman-i-Tabligh-ul-Islam to spread religious education among Muslims. Within these Muslim educational spaces, Kashmiris tussled over social influence and political power, and engaged in debates over Islam's relationship with ideas about secularism and modernity.

Many Kashmiri Muslims adhered to the beliefs of the Anjuman-i-Tabligh-ul-Islam, which had been founded in 1932 by a group of Muslim theologians to propagate the Hanafi sect of Islam, ideologically tied to various shrines in the province. This organization committed to creating a just and righteous social order that not only reflected an Islamic world-view but promoted world peace, human fraternity, and universal friendship.[99] In the context of Kashmir, the Anjuman perceived two major threats to the "value systems of Islam": Western materialism that eroded human values and Islamic theocratic universalism that encouraged authoritarian tendencies. Comparing the "two evils," the chief of the organization, Maulana Qasim Bukhari, believed that the theocratic state posed the greater threat because it "negated true Islam based on [the] Quran and lifestyle of Prophet and his companions." The Anjuman claimed that religion and politics contradicted each other: politics was subject to temporal considerations, but the "principles of Islam are eternal and cannot be abrogated."[100] Politically, the party supported the dismissed prime minister of Kashmir, Sheikh Abdullah, especially during the years he led the movement for self-determination. As the controllers of local shrines and mosques, their support enabled Abdullah to reach a wider audience. Confident of its popularity among the public, the organization did not initiate an educational policy that would strengthen its ideology.

Conversely, another group of Islamic scholars, inspired by the Islamic and political ideals of Maulana Mawdudi, the founder of the Jamaat-i-Islami, came together in 1945 to create a branch of the party in Kashmir and promote the creation of an explicitly Islamic state. In the aftermath of partition, the Jamaat emerged in Kashmir as an independent body with its own constitution. It made the crucial decision not to align with Jamaat-i-Islami Hind, the Indian branch of the party, which considered Kashmir an integral part of India and limited itself to safeguarding personal law, language, religious endowments, and the cultural identity of Indian Muslims. Instead, the Jamaat in Kashmir was drawn toward the political stance of the Jamaat-i-Islami branch in Pakistan, which advocated for the preservation of the place of Islam in Pakistani society and politics.[101] The party had no preexisting social or political base in the Valley, yet it grew in popularity among Kashmiri Muslims because of the deteriorating socioeconomic conditions and lack of democratic accountability in the region.

The rising power of the Hindu rightist groups in Jammu who preached an exclusionary discourse spurred the Jamaat to echo their rhetoric and project themselves as defenders of Islamic identity in the Valley.[102] The Jamaat-i-Islami blamed "selfish mullahs" for the marginalization and powerlessness of Kashmiri Muslims, and considered rituals associated with Sufi-based Islam as un-Islamic. Yet they did not launch a direct attack on such religious practices. Instead, the ideologues of the Jamaat, aware of the popularity of Sufi saints and shrines in the Valley, "operated from within existing Sufi frameworks" to present the "true monotheistic teachings of the Sufis."[103] Editorials in their newspaper *Azan* asked Kashmiris to see Islam as a complete ideology and code of life, covering all aspects of the collective and personal experience. They believed that a correct implementation of Islam was impossible to attain under a corrupt political regime. The Jamaat-i-Islami's rhetoric addressed issues of poverty, arguing that the secular nationalism practiced by ruling Kashmiri elites allowed the rich to amass wealth and exploit the poor. A political system governed by Islamic rules, they argued, would ensure accountability, an equitable system of distribution, the elimination of immorality, and the reconstruction of society.[104] The Jamaat's politics aimed to dislodge the power of the National Conference, which drew its support from followers of Kashmir's Sufi-based Islam. Instead of immediately posing a direct challenge to the National Conference in the political arena, the Jamaat considered the social reformation of Kashmiri society essential to weaken its opponents' support base.

The Jamaat intended to transform the state's educational system, hoping to advance their beliefs in schools, colleges, and government offices, and create supporters who would view every social and political issue through the prism of their brand of Islam. The party played on Kashmiri Muslim fears that the new "secular" style of education was in reality a carefully planned conspiracy to spread immorality and vice among the youth. The Jamaat's primary, middle, and even high schools taught modern disciplines as well as Islamic subjects, so their students could make a seamless transition to professional colleges and occupy different branches of administration.[105] By 1974, the party sponsored 120 schools (3 high schools, 54 middle schools, and 61 primary schools) with a total of 13,000 students, including 4,000 girls.[106] Through its study circles and libraries, the Jamaat also established a substantial presence among lecturers and students in colleges in the Kashmir Valley.

The middle and lower classes became enamored with the ideology of the Jamaat after the 1970s.[107] The events of the post-partition decades and the activities of the Indian puppet regimes, followed by the disappointments of Abdullah's second administration, had led the lower middle classes of Kashmir to feel economically excluded and socially deprived. Poorer Kashmiris had benefited from the schools that had cropped up all over the Valley but found it difficult to find good jobs or promotions. Many found it impossible to arrange their daughters' marriages without paying huge dowries. Weddings and associated costs drained the lower middle classes, forcing them into debts they found difficult to repay.[108] Although community leaders tried to impose restrictions on food and guest lists to lower costs, the poor and middle classes still struggled to live under this oppressive system. To many in this sector of society, the Islamist alternative proposed by the Jamaat seemed more viable, as governmental policies had failed to provide equitable justice to date. Excluded from the networks of patronage, these deprived groups believed political Islam could fill the vacuum and provide them better and more just lives. As such, the Jamaat succeeded in widening its social base among the lower middle classes in urban Kashmir and drew supporters from disaffected Kashmiris who felt threatened by integration with India, constrained by economic resources, and excluded from political power.

Rural–Urban Tensions: Commercialization of Agriculture and Rural Elites

Rural Kashmiris, who had been inspired by the economic vision for emancipation prior to Kashmir's accession to India, did not benefit equally from Kashmir's "modernization," and felt economic freedom had eluded them. Although certain urban sectors had benefited from the influx of money from India, rural Kashmiris generally remained mired in large-scale poverty. During the postcolonial decades many migrated to urban areas, a move that further strained rural–urban relationships and stressed the state's economic resources. Rural Kashmir, a hierarchical society with religious elites at the top and landless laborers at the bottom, became further divided after the commercialization of agriculture in the 1970s. Economic stratification created a new rural elite, the rich and middle-class orchardists, many of whom collaborated with political elites to establish their dominance by embracing an Islamist ideology in contrast to the peasantry, who mostly practiced traditional Sufi-based Islam.

Economic development projects after the 1953 deposition of Sheikh Abdullah, whose support base and principle economic reforms had been in rural areas, focused mostly on Kashmir's cities. Although Jammu and Kashmir's population was only 17 percent urban and 83 percent rural, the state divided expenditures equally between rural and urban areas, a mismatch evident in state rural development projects.[109] For example, the community projects and national extension blocks undertaken in the late 1950s and 1960s only focused on developing certain pockets of a village. Development in the villages merely provided a "window dressing to screen off the backwardness" and create a sense of "artificial prosperity."[110] Additionally, the urban population benefited from subsidies for food grains, power, and drinking water, while the rural population secured only a small portion of these benefits.

During the 1960s, the state legislative assembly engaged in countless debates on rural poverty and economic disparity which highlighted the challenges faced by people living in the far-flung villages of Kashmir. These discussions raised questions about how to create policies that would allow Kashmiris to sustain themselves with their own food production and stop the importation of food grains from India. Shamim Ahmed Shamim, a prominent journalist and a member of the state legislative assembly, exposed the urban bias of the state government in his speeches and writings. He challenged the supposed socialist principles of a government that aimed to establish a classless society but treated villagers as second-class citizens. "How can a government decide on its own that urban areas should receive subsidized food grains, towns should get one-fourth of what major cities get, while villagers should be denied everything?" he asked in one 1970 speech.[111] Shamim argued that constant import of food grains from Punjab and elsewhere, without any concrete steps to improve productivity within the state, created a dependent mentality among Kashmiris. Even plans to improve food production, he argued, primarily benefited the urban rich. For example, the Krishi program, designed to improve fertility with better seeds and fertilizers, only succeeded in making the land unproductive. To make money from this program, government agents forced peasants to buy these fertilizers. Anyone who refused to comply was harassed, and in some cases even beaten or arrested, while the agents dumped triple the amount of fertilizers needed on small areas of land. The uncontrolled use of fertilizers made almost 500 acres of land unsuitable for food grains, but soon after, large hashish farms cropped up on this same land. Shamim considered these government initiatives a "ploy to make [an] entire generation of young Kashmiris addicted to drugs, killing their spirit and initiative."[112]

Women, in particular, felt the burden of the state's failure to provide peripheral villages with the necessities of life, like potable water; instead they carried heavy containers of water to their mountaintop hamlets. These challenges in the outskirts shaped the villagers' political psyches and they grew disappointed with the indifference of their political leaders. During elections, candidates showed up at their doorsteps, making promises that they never honored. For these villagers, projected Kashmiri political futures that were deeply meaningful to urban intellectuals and businessmen—Indian, Pakistani, autonomous, independent—held no meaning. All they wanted from the state was good governance: any leader who would provide them with water, roads, health, and sanitation. Shamim believed that the wide gap in sympathy between government ministers and rural Kashmiris stemmed from stark differences in their lifestyles; those in power could not comprehend the worldview of the poor villagers.[113]

To resolve urban–rural disparities, legislative assembly members tried to limit the expanding wealth of the urban class. But land continued to increase in cost, which meant that poor people could not purchase it. The new urban elite had large properties, while the poor in rural Kashmir found it difficult to construct even one house.[114] The government eventually amended the 1962 Urban Moveable Property Tax to limit the expanding real estate portfolios of the urban elite. Originally, any individual who owned a house worth two lakh rupees or more had had to pay this tax. However, the amended act lowered the limit to one lakh, forcing the urban elite to think twice before acquiring more properties. This move decreased the cost of land by one-tenth, in turn lowering prices of commodities and making it easier for the poor to survive.[115]

The various initiatives introduced by the state to empower rural Kashmiris and improve agricultural productivity did not always yield positive results. In its first three five-year plans, the Indian government focused on increasing production: improving irrigation facilities, consolidating holdings, improving market intelligence, and creating an Intensive Agricultural Area Programme (IAAP).[116] Food production in Kashmir increased from 3.53 lakh tonnes in 1951–2 to 6.76 lakh tonnes in 1964–5,[117] but still could not feed a growing population.[118] The state continued to import food grains from India; the net import of food grains increased from 56,000 tons in 1961–2 to 95,000 tons in 1964–5.[119] Faced with a persistent food shortage, the government embarked on a Green Revolution in

Kashmir as well as in other parts of India. Starting in 1968, the new agricultural strategy introduced fertilizers and High Yielding Variety (HYV) seeds. However, these modern techniques failed to solve Kashmir's problems.[120]

Understanding the challenges that confronted rural Kashmir requires returning two decades prior, to the aftermath of the Big Estate Abolition Act of 1950. This act had set out to transfer ownership from an unproductive landlord class to the land's tillers, but had failed to completely transform rural Kashmir. This reform had replaced some old elites, but created a new agrarian power structure populated by National Conference affiliates, retaining the old class privileges and social divisions within Kashmiri society with new personnel. Both old and new elite classes exploited loopholes in the law.[121] As the reforms had limited individual holdings, the elite among the peasantry collaborated with village officials to manipulate revenue records by dividing their properties among family members. The number of smallholdings increased, making efficient modernized farming difficult. Furthermore, the uniform ceiling on land without due consideration to the fertility of the soil and terrain hampered agricultural productivity. The "protected tenants" also exploited the flaws in the reforms to their advantage. As there was no ceiling on their holdings, sometimes the tenants would "illegaly sublet their lands violating the spirit of land reforms."[122]

To ensure that the land reforms worked for everyone, the Land Commission Committee, set up in 1963, recommended amendments to the agrarian laws of the 1950s. The amendments made the rights of the protected tenants "inheritable but not transferable." In case a tenant failed to "cultivate his land without sufficient cause for more than one year, his right of occupancy or protected tenancy extinguished from the end of the year."[123] Despite the Tenancy Amendment Acts passed in 1955 and 1962 to give more rights to tenants, loopholes in the laws still guaranteed power to absentee proprietors. Meanwhile, the commercialization of agriculture in the 1970s created orchardists as a new power group. A provision of the Big Landed Estates Abolition Act in 1950 had exempted orchards from appropriation, thus paving the way for big landholders to escape the ceilings on property ownership by converting cereal acreages into orchards. Some farmers who found the existing system of cropping patterns unprofitable also converted farms on hill slopes, cultivable wastes, pastures, or forestlands into orchards.[124] Economists M. L. Misri and M. S. Bhat attribute an increase in fruit production to the incentives government provided to the orchardists, like input subsidies and marketing facilities that contributed to a favorable cost–benefit ratio.[125] As a result, food grain production remained stagnant, but the horticulture sector exploded. In fact, the agrarian reforms of 1972, meant to remedy the failure of the Big Estate Abolition Act of 1950, further strengthened the position of the orchardists.

In 1971, Syed Mir Qasim became the chief minister of Jammu and Kashmir state. As Abdullah had done two decades earlier, Qasim aimed to confer ownership rights on tillers and abolish absentee landlordism. His government passed the Jammu and Kashmir Agrarian Reforms of 1972, which conferred ownership rights on any person who held land in his personal cultivation.[126] The law lowered the ownership ceiling from 22 ¾ acres to 12 ½ acres. Peasants had to pay a levy to gain ownership rights, but at rates lower than the prevailing market rates for landowners. Additionally, the law allowed absentee landowners with an income of less than 500 rupees per month to keep 3 acres of land for self-cultivation if they resided in the same village. If smallholders had given land to tenants for farming, the tenant could retain 2 acres, for which the landowner would get compensation at market value. Bigger landed elites, on the other hand, were provided compensation at a fixed rate. In a major advance, the new agrarian act fixed the ceiling by family, not on an individual basis, unlike the other states of India where holdings were divided among individual members of families. This prevented the emergence of smallholdings like those that cropped up after the land reforms of the 1950s, when the elite distributed land among family members to escape the ownership limit.[127]

Despite the laudable intent to change Kashmir's agrarian structures, this new round of reforms generated debates in media and government circles. Some argued that these reforms lacked proper planning. The reforms did not specify how the government planned to disburse surplus land. Kashmiris did not know whether the landless or farmers with very smallholdings (about half of whom lived below the subsistence level with less than 1 acre of land) would receive land as part of the recent reforms. In addition, people worried about the unlimited power of the government to set compensation rates, which they feared could lead to arbitrary decisions. Even landowners expressed skepticism about the right of absentee property owners to resume ownership rights. Although the land reforms of the 1950s had provided them with the option to reclaim 17 *kanal*s (about 2 acres) of *abi* (water) land for personal cultivation, the government had found excuses to keep their cases in revenue courts rather than releasing the land.[128]

The most striking feature of the new act was that the state retained the exemption of orchards from the ceiling, although the government now did charge rent on orchards in excess of the ceiling area on a scale not exceeding 800 rupees a year. Furthermore, as this law further reduced the ceiling from 22 ¾ acres to 12 ½ acres, even more landowners now converted their land into orchards to circumvent confiscation. The legislative assembly demanded a ceiling on orchard ownership as well to prevent the rise of a new capitalist class in Kashmir. One orchardist in Anantnag district owned 1,902 acres of land, immensely above the ceiling, while others owned apple farms spread over 200 and 300 *kanals* (about 25 and 37.5 acres, respectively).[129] Newspaper editorials implied that the government had excluded orchards from the new reforms to appease a powerful lobby of bureaucrats and politicians who owned fruit farms throughout the state. The opposition groups were not happy with this development. The government suspended the act and created a committee to probe the shortcomings of these reforms.

In 1976, the government passed the Jammu and Kashmir Agrarian Reforms Act, which placed a ceiling of 12 ½ acres on all land ownership and, for the first time, included orchards.[130] However, those who converted inferior lands unsuitable for cereal production into orchards could possess another 200 *kanals* (approximately 25 acres) of land.[131] In the 1970s, the government's policy to exempt orchards from ceiling limits and encourage farmers to grow fruit crops, especially apples, almonds, walnuts, and saffron, gave agriculture a commercial orientation. Orchards generated substantial income and had a high remunerative value. In a span of ten years from 1968 to 1978, orchards recorded a fourfold increase from 7,769 to 31,595 hectares.[132] The export of fruit also increased from 16.89 lakh quintals in 1973–4 to 55.17 lakh quintals in 1985–6.[133]

Commercialization made certain towns and districts in the Valley extremely prosperous, especially the apple town of Sopore, popularly known as Chhota London, or Small London, Anantnag, and Shopian. A powerful lobby of orchardists emerged from these districts and monopolized power at the village, block, and district levels; the same men dominated *panchayats*, cooperatives, and credit institutions. Their power structure within the village was not an isolated phenomenon; this rural elite had links with state assemblies and major political parties.[134] By 1987, many elected legislators came from rural orchardist backgrounds, and had their "political base and traditional sources of livelihood" in villages. They controlled the vote in their respective districts, meaning that the Congress and the National Conference drew maximum support from rural constituencies. The "apple tycoons" and "saffron princes" parlayed their connections to the political–administrative apparatus of the state into a fortune. As orchards were exempted from ceiling limits, they largely remained outside the tax net and, like the forest lessees, contractors, and transporters detailed earlier, accumulated tens of millions of rupees.[135]

Many of these rich orchardists, conscious of their new-found economic, social, and political status and eager to maintain it, searched for a religious ideology different from the beliefs of the ordinary peasantry, the "devotees of shrines" or *ahl-i-itiqadi*s. They took actions to identify themselves as a separate class, for example, refusing to celebrate shrines and saints to clarify their distance from the "un-Islamic" practices of the rural Muslim majority. Some of the rural elite supported the Jamaat-i-Islami as a link with the wider international Muslim community and supported Jamaat's mission to create a Nizam-i-Mustafa or Islamic state in Kashmir. They participated in social welfare schemes and doled out donations for the construction of Sunni mosques and madrasas as competitors to the Sufi shrines. To gain respectability, they began to display several outward symbols of Islamic adherence, from fulfilling the basic obligations of faith to flaunting dress codes popular in Islamic countries but relatively foreign to Kashmir. Any aspect of life that conflicted with these rigid interpretations of Islam was "publicly decried and declared un-Islamic."[136]

Although the Jamaat established a foothold among the rich orchardists of the Valley, not all orchardists were extremely wealthy. The commercialization of agriculture and the agrarian reforms of the 1970s also created a rural middle class. Most orchard owners belonged to this class, owning marginal or small orchards. They depended on commission agents to channel their produce in markets, enabling "agents," mostly rich orchardists, to skim off their surplus.[137] Although the commercialization of agriculture failed to ensure equitable justice, the middle-class peasantry dreamed of better opportunities and used education to gain social advancement. The rural middle classes, in their efforts to climb the social ladder, willingly imitated the new religious practices of the rural rich to establish their superiority over laborers, artisans, and service providers, whom they could in turn stigmatize as irreligious. The support from these new groups allowed the Jamaat to expand its base from lower-middle-class urban Kashmiris to rural Kashmir, especially among the members of wealthy families from Sopore and Anantnag.[138]

The Jamaat's popularity among orchardists became apparent once the party emerged as a force on the political spectrum. In 1970, Sheikh Abdullah's Plebiscite Front made a strategic decision to contest elections to India's parliament in 1971 and the Jammu Kashmir legislative assembly in 1972. Mir Qasim, the chief minister of the state and a representative of the Congress Party, allied with the Jamaat despite their pro-Pakistan stance to undercut the popular Plebiscite Front.[139] The Jamaat and Congress worked together to win the Jamaat five seats in the 1972 assembly elections.[140] While in the 1977 elections the Jamaat was able to win only one seat, party candidates continued to do well in Kashmir's fruit belt, enabling the Jamaat to share power and privilege with the larger Congress and National Conference parties.

While a section of the rich and middle-class orchardists alike increasingly inclined toward the Jamaat's politics and Sunni Islam, most small farmers and landless laborers at the bottom of the social ladder, the poorest Kashmiris, continued to profess their commitment to shrines. Landless laborers, the lowest strata of Kashmiri rural society, lived in poverty and had not benefited from the land reforms of the preceding decades. The land reforms had fragmented larger estates and increased the number of smallholdings. When the rural elite purchased these smallholdings and later converted them into horticultural land, there was a sharp rise in the share of landless households, from 1 percent in 1971 to 6.8 percent in 1980–1.[141] The rise in commercial crop prices benefited farmers, but increased the cost of living for poor rural households that did not own and farm their own land. Rural poverty was a source of concern for the state's government.[142]

Sheikh Abdullah's administration, which had regained power after accepting Kashmir as an integral part of India in the 1975 accord, saw the ability for the state to support itself as a critical component of eradicating poverty and ushering in real prosperity. Abdullah promoted self-sufficiency to reduce the crippling financial burden of subsidizing food grains, water, and electricity. Food subsidies imposed an annual burden of 23.61 crore rupees on the exchequer at a time when the entire tax revenue of the state was only 18.51 crore rupees.[143] In contrast to the puppet governments, which had paid the subsidies anyway to avoid political uprisings, Abdullah withdrew them to "end economic dependence on Delhi" and bring food prices on a par in urban and rural areas.[144] The state argued that subsidized food grains helped urban dwellers but did not benefit farmers, who found it impossible to make a profit selling their crops to the state at very low prices. Ultimately, the pricing policy killed farmers' incentive to produce, resulting not only in low profitability but in a failure to invest in scientific technology for improving production. In addition, the subsidy policy often required the government to purchase food at high prices from markets in Delhi and sell it at low prices in Kashmiri cities, draining the state's exchequer.[145] The first budget proposed by Abdullah's government increased power charges by 10 per cent and the drinking water tariff by 25 per cent. Abdullah admitted in the legislature and in public meetings that his new economic policy would strain the average family's budget, but he argued that the government's savings would be spent on development projects, providing legitimate employment instead of passive subsidies and ultimately increasing families' income and purchasing power.[146]

The subsidy withdrawal did not, however, lead as directly to self-sufficiency as Abdullah had hoped. During India's fifth five-year plan, Jammu and Kashmir met only 42 percent of its expenditures from internal resources. The state's revenue did increase from 47 crore rupees in 1976 to 100 crore rupees in 1980, but at the same time its financial dependence on the center increased. During the first six years of Abdullah's new regime, the state's debt increased from 364 crore rupees in 1975 to 670 crore rupees in 1981.[147] The source of the internal revenue increase was also a serious problem, as it came primarily due to the sale of forests and liquor. Revenue from forests increased from 9.5 crore rupees in 1974–5 to 28 crore rupees in 1981–2, and constituted more than half of the non-tax revenue of the state. Throughout the 1960s, Abdullah's Plebiscite Front had criticized the exploitation of forest resources by previous governments, but once in power, they too eagerly depleted the state's forest wealth.[148] In the same period, excise revenue from alcohol increased from 5.5 crore rupees to 13 crore rupees, the sales tax yield from 4 crore rupees to 16 crore rupees. The liquor shops that appeared all over the Valley during this period increased state revenue, but generated resentment among the disenfranchised. Calls for a ban on the sale of liquor became popular, with proponents arguing that it turned Kashmiri youth into addicts with crippled mental faculties.[149]

Sheikh Abdullah's attempts to strengthen his support base among the Kashmiri peasantry with poverty elimination programs mostly failed. Programs like the Integrated Rural Development Programme (IRDP), meant to "alleviate the poor above the poverty line," and the National Rural Employment Programme (NREP), designed to provide employment by strengthening economic infrastructure, had limited benefit for the poor.[150] Officials failed to utilize the allocated funds at both district and divisional levels. Corruption and misuse of funds followed a similar pattern to other state poverty-alleviation programs.

Village poverty increased in both the 1970s and 1980s, forcing many rural families to leave their hereditary occupations and migrate to cities in search of government jobs and a better life. Failure to bring any concrete change to the villages therefore eroded the rural base of the National Conference by the mid-1980s. Gradually, rising unemployment, coupled with political disenfranchisement, created resentment in the hearts of both urban and rural Kashmiris against the center and their own leadership. Many disillusioned Kashmiris shifted their loyalties to political groups like the Jamaat who tapped into political and economic grievances to reframe Kashmiri self-determination in Islamist tones, while convincing Kashmiris to embrace an "Islamic" model as a path to removing social inequalities and ushering in overall economic prosperity.

Unemployment, Economic Dependence, and Kashmiri Resentment in the 1980s

In the 1980s, to counter rising regional dissidence around India, the Congress began to centralize the government; it demanded complete subordination of regional parties that threatened its electoral prospects. These expectations clashed with the reality in Kashmir, as the National Conference maintained a separate Kashmiri identity while the Congress increasingly appealed to India's Hindu majority by embracing the traditional themes of Hindu rightist parties. Kashmiris also struggled to differentiate between the politics of Hindu rightists who wanted to abrogate Article 370 and those of the Congress Party, which claimed secularism but simultaneously overtly mobilized the majority Hindu community to win mass support.

Kashmiri Muslims resented New Delhi's interference in the state government, as it appointed and dismissed governments to maintain Indian influence. Instead of bringing Jammu and Kashmir closer to India, the centralization policy had the opposite of its intended effect. Manipulation of voting lists, the arrest of opposition candidates, and ballot-box rigging marred every election. India's throttling of postcolonial democratic aspirations in the Valley weakened its hold over the people.[151] The middle classes and the poorer strata of society had worked hard to gain an education in order to improve their living conditions, but economic freedom still seemed a distant dream in a state with limited opportunities. Educated but unemployed youth clamored to change the patron–client relationship between New Delhi and Kashmir.

The educated middle classes in Kashmir had many reasons for discontent. In 1947, the literacy rate in the state of Jammu and Kashmir was only 5 percent.[152] After the government dismissed Abdullah from power in 1953, it began providing free education from primary to university, even in far-flung areas of the state. The number of elementary schools increased from 1,305 in 1950–1 to 10,483 in 1996–7, while the number of students enrolled in primary and middle schools went up from 1.04 lakhs to 8.23 lakhs during the same period.[153] The state also granted educational loans to students selected or nominated for training and technical courses, both in and outside the state. Scholarships were awarded to members of Scheduled Castes, "backward" classes, and those who belonged to lower income groups.[154] Widespread education did not, however, translate to an equally widespread opportunity. Although education now reached remote areas of Jammu and Kashmir due to the state's increased investment in the construction of schools, corruption and nepotism practiced by the political elites ensured that its economic fruits were reaped by only a few.

Most students, without political influence and connections, faced discrimination in admission to professional colleges, since the number seeking admission exceeded capacity. In 1963, the state adopted a "proper system of selection for eligible candidates." The Public Service Commission, an organization formed to make appointments in the government service sector, submitted a merit list of candidates to the chief minister, who had the discretion to add or drop selected candidates.[155] The administration sometimes modified the merit list for political purposes, adding new candidates to reward supporters even when they lacked academic qualifications.

Realizing the need to bring further transparency, in 1966 the state government modified the selection procedure; the Public Service Commission now held a written test or interview to select candidates. Despite these laws and procedures, many selections continued to be made in an arbitrary and discriminatory manner. Some rejected students filed writ petitions before the High Court of Jammu and Kashmir, and in many cases the court made "critical comments" on the selection procedures: "It appears that the selection has been made by the committee either consciously or unconsciously in such a way as to discriminate between candidates even belonging to the same class as citizens."[156] In the service sector, the state government openly flaunted the Jammu and Kashmir Civil Services Rules in recruitments and promotions. Annual reports indicated that the government did not maintain seniority lists to decide promotion on a fair basis.

Public education created a new force of informed individuals who both sought economic betterment and were able to understand how political elites and their collaborators benefitted from every government policy—a state of affairs leading to deep resentment when graduates from the new schools failed to find jobs.[157] Throughout the 1960s, the public blamed the government for using service sector jobs as a source of political gain. Political leaders gave unqualified people jobs in exchange for votes, leaving administrative departments infested with an incompetent and corrupt workforce. The education department, in a painful irony, suffered the most; it became, in reformer Shamim Ahmed Shamim's phrase, "the store-house of arbitrary appointments," an "easy medium to provide employment to beneficiaries."[158] In some cases, political candidates wrote appointment orders on matchboxes if they were canvassing and had no access to official paper. Such actions created an "army of [unqualified] teachers" and lowered Kashmiri educational standards, hindering students in later competitive examinations.[159] In turn, low educational standards created unproductive workers who failed to contribute to the development and progress of Kashmir. As the number of graduates who made their way through this system only to lose jobs to unqualified political operatives kept increasing, the failure of the state to satisfy their socioeconomic expectations came to be seen as a deliberate denial of opportunity.

Meanwhile, the spread of education even among rural Kashmiris encouraged competition between rural and urban populations for government jobs. Rural residents resented how recruiting boards appointed individuals from the urban areas of Srinagar and Jammu to rural postings. Some complained about deliberate delays in posting interview invitations, which prevented villagers from competing with city dwellers.[160] Additionally, while the selection boards claimed to emphasize candidates' intrinsic merit, rural members of the state legislative assembly demanded the abolition of recruitment boards that ignored the affirmative-action claims of certain "backward" villages.

The Jammu and Kashmir Civil Service Rules of 1956 introduced reservation in jobs for "backward classes" not adequately represented in the government services. Until 1968, the government of Jammu and Kashmir did not have a clear-cut classification of "backward" classes or a provision for special benefits for them.[161] While some government notifications listed certain classes as "backward," the state continuously amended the list to suit "particular situations." In 1967, a working rule emerged from an affidavit filed by the state government in response to a writ petition submitted by two teachers to the Supreme Court. The affidavit stated that 50 percent of posts were to be filled by Kashmiri Muslims, 40 percent by Jammu Hindus, and 10 percent by Kashmiri Hindus.[162] The state government justified this distribution to the Supreme Court on the grounds that the Muslim community as a whole, in addition to Hindus from Jammu, formed a backward class of citizens, as they were not adequately represented in the service sector.

The court, examining this position, ruled that the "backward class" was not synonymous with "backward caste" or "backward community." The two designated groups formed 94.2 percent of the total state population; the court emphasized that the government could not treat the entire population as "backward," due to considerable differences in the degree of "backwardness" within any community or caste. To consider an entire community "backward" would place affluent members on a par with "genuinely backward" groups in need of protection. This placed unfair pressure on socially and economically disadvantaged groups to compete with their coreligionists who had had better opportunities, creating a scenario that "shuts out backward classes from services."[163]

Under the recommendation of the Gajendragadkar Commission, the government formed a committee to define "backward classes" on the basis of income level, occupation, and place of habitation.[164] Despite these clear-cut recommendations, the rural elite in Kashmir manipulated "backward" certificates to their advantage, illegally issuing certificates to rich peasants, including religious elites like *pir*s and *mufti*s, who had sufficient income not to need affirmative action.[165] The rural elite preferred possession of a 'backward' certificate to open competitions for places in professional colleges, judicial services, and other prestigious government positions, and their ability to manipulate the system meant that once again, the poor were left at a disadvantage.

The issue of employment also generated tensions between Hindu and Muslim communities, as both claimed discrimination. Kashmiri Hindus who had dominated the government service sector for generations complained that Muslims now received most jobs, forcing many Pandit families to migrate to different parts of India. At the same time, Muslims bemoaned that Hindus had a much larger share in central departments and more seats in government training institutions than should be based on population share. Kashmiri Pandits were "roughly 1 ½ percent of the total population" in 1967 but held 638 gazetted posts out of 2,252 positions. Non-gazetted appointments the same year stood at 44,529, of which Pandits held 7,136, or more than 18 percent.[166] The Pandit community's grievances stemmed from the corruption and nepotism of the state regimes that allowed less qualified Muslim candidates to secure jobs over more brilliant Hindu candidates. The Pandit community believed that most Muslims secured jobs not on the basis of merit but due to personal connections. One prominent Kashmiri Pandit political activist, Prem Nath Bazaz, explained, however, that the sentiments of his community were directed less by the "injustice done to [the] community," and more by the "the rapid rise of Muslims in all occupations during past two decades" that had ended their monopoly over the service sector.[167]

The competition for jobs created ongoing animosity between the two communities. In 1968, Kashmiri Muslims submitted a memorandum to the home minister, Y. B. Chavan, complaining that state departments, including telecommunications, insurance, income tax collection, the accountant general's office, and the Indian Airlines Corporation, discriminated against Kashmiri Muslims.[168] The Staff Selection Commission appointed about twenty thousand people in Class C to central government positions every year, but a negligible number of Kashmiris received such appointments.[169] Of the 14,743 central government employees in Jammu and Kashmir in 1989, Hindus comprised 83.66 percent in the officer category, while only 6.89 percent were Muslim. In the "clerical and non-gazetted category," Hindus comprised 79.27 percent and Muslims were 12.98 percent. In the Class IV service category, Hindus held 72.87

percent of central government posts, while 15.70 percent were Muslims.[170] The Indian administrative service was supposed to recruit 50 percent of its personnel from within the state, yet during the 1980s it only drew 25 percent of its candidates from Kashmir.[171] Of the twenty-two government secretaries in Kashmir, only five were Kashmiri Muslims. Kashmiri Muslims believed that they were not treated as equal citizens, and that despite their educational qualifications they would not find jobs in the central departments or even in India.

Even the Kashmiri Muslim elite felt aggrieved by the "political caste system" that prevented them from holding high positions within the central departments. In *The Kashmiri Mussulman*, a book about the challenges confronting Kashmiri Muslims in the postcolonial era, G. H. Khan lamented that although no caste system existed in a religious or social sense, since 1947 Kashmiri Muslims had remained political "untouchables of the first degree" because the Indian state always doubted their credibility and loyalty. The second, third, and fourth category of "political untouchables" depended on the party in power and how closely they adhered to the center's line. High-caste Muslims were, in the eyes of the Indian state, political opportunists, willing to deride their Islamic faith for political rewards. All Kashmiri Muslims, including both elites and excluded, saw a bleak future for themselves in the Indian administration and central bureaucracy.[172] This feeling of hopelessness compounded in the 1980s with a boom in educational levels. College graduation rates increased by 50 percent, and there was an 18 percent increase among postgraduates (Table 3.3). Kashmiri Muslim graduates felt frustrated. Within their own state, they could not find employment if they lacked political contacts, while they believed that as Muslims they stood no chance of being hired in India.

Table 3.3 Educational enrollments in Jammu and Kashmir, 1950–85

Year	*Primary*	*Middle*	*Secondary*	*Colleges*	*Universities*	*Engineering*	*Medical*	*Agriculture*
1950	78,000	20,000	5,600	2,779	–	–	–	–
1960	216,000	60,000	22,000	8,005	174	171	182	
1968	362,000	105,000	51,000	16,718	1,285	1,280	848	80
1980	537,800	167,200	83,600	15,828	3,351	1,286	1,072	294
1985	663,700	232,700	132,800	20,089	4,139	2,784	1,110	312

Source: *Jammu and Kashmir: An Economic Profile* (New Delhi: Government of India, 1995), 18; Sumit Ganguly, *Crisis in Kashmir: Portents of War, Hopes to Peace* (Cambridge: Cambridge University Press, 1997), 33.

Rising unemployment in the state stemmed from the slow pace of industrial development projects. An analysis of the first few five-year plans reveals limited expenditures to establish industries in Kashmir, as industrialization was never an integral part of the overall development strategy. The first five-year plan (1951–6) allocated 103.50 lakh rupees to the army and a mere 35.61 lakh rupees to industry. The second (1956–1) allotted 8.4 percent of the planned expenditure to industrial development. The third five-year plan (1961–6) aimed to establish basic industries, such as sheep and wool development centers.[173] New Delhi showed no interest in developing industries in Kashmir. During the period of economic centralization, India refused to set up industry in Kashmir due to a lack of raw materials and high transportation costs.[174] While the rest of India benefited from the investments made in the industrial sector, Kashmir failed to reap similar benefits, which hindered its development.

The lack of industrial development in the state made government services almost the only option for college graduates' employment, which increased accordingly (Table 3.4). Pressure on the service sector affected its absorption capacity, however. In 1985, there were 2.10 lakh registered unemployed Kashmiris; the number rose to 2.55 lakhs in 1990.[175] The actual number of unemployed workers may have been much larger, as registration in employment exchanges was not compulsory.[176] Growing unemployment created a class that looked for other avenues to become rich. Drug trafficking, for example, could generate quick money; shady deals between smugglers, bureaucrats, and politicians allowed money to flow among the Kashmiri nouveau riche.[177] Drug trafficking also led to increased associated criminal activity; criminals later penetrated the insurgent movement of the 1990s, ran a parallel government, and amassed wealth through extortion.

Table 3.4 Number of government employees in Jammu and Kashmir, 1978–88

Year	*Number of government employees*
1978	138,040
1979	140,352
1980	145,120
1981	150,608
1982	156,804
1985	232,600
1987	233,780
1988	235,930

Source: Government of Jammu and Kashmir, *Report of the Committee of Economic Reforms* [*Godbole Committee Report*] (Srinagar: Government of Jammu and Kashmir, 1998), 85.

The state's inability to attain economic autonomy stemmed not only from theft and power play by corrupt elites, but also from the political complexities associated with Jammu and Kashmir's unique status within India. From 1953 to 1970, the center funded 90 percent of the state's five-year plans, creating a class of collaborators who would support Kashmir's accession to India. The state economy became dependent on the center as Kashmiris grew used to its spending far exceeding its income. Bureaucrats, politicians, and rich business owners took the money doled out by the center, but nothing reached the masses. The center knew about this rampant corruption and nepotism but remained indifferent. Most importantly, these regimes had little legitimacy, and accordingly, their "willingness to pursue rational economic management in terms of either raising resources or pruning expenditure was extremely limited."[178] In fact, the level of expenditure and any desire to raise taxes was "determined by [the] need to take populist measures to gain administrative acceptability if not political legitimacy."[179]

However, in 1970, New Delhi shifted its financial relationship with Kashmir after successful encroachments against Article 370 had brought Jammu and Kashmir more firmly within India's grip. Providing Kashmir with "preferential treatment" now served no purpose. As such, India placed Jammu and Kashmir with other "special category" Indian states, including Arunachal Pradesh, Assam, Himachal Pradesh, Manipur, Meghalaya, Mizoram, and Nagaland. The Fifth Finance Commission, while devising a formula to share central assistance among states, accorded special status to some states based on harsh terrain, "backwardness," and social problems. A "special category" state received federal assistance, tax breaks, and excise duty concessions to establish manufacturing facilities within their territories.[180] However, while all other "special category" states received 90 percent grants and 10 percent loans, Jammu and Kashmir received 30 percent grants and 70 percent loans.[181] Although this kind of aid was what Abdullah had sought in the immediate aftermath of accession to avoid financial dependence on Indian grants, since that time the economic policies unleashed in Kashmir had prevented economic growth and increased the state's debt burden. Kashmiris now considered the preponderance of loans over grants to be "discriminatory," because their state was treated differently from other special category states. The center justified its policy by citing the benefits already incurred by the state after the discretionary transfer of money from the center following Abdullah's dismissal from power.[182] Between 1980 and 1990, central loans went up steeply from 683.49 crore rupees to 2,396.67 crore rupees.[183] The state government was forced to divert its resources to debt service, rather than to productive investments and industrial growth. Meanwhile, the ongoing dispute over Kashmir has had dire consequences for the state's economy. Even Indian loans are used by Jammu and Kashmir for security-related expenditures, instead of for its own economic development. A major portion of central funding is spent on maintaining the Jammu-Srinagar highway, the only road link between Kashmir and India, enabling Indian armed forces to maintain a substantial presence in Kashmir.[184]

Since partition, the flow of funds from New Delhi into Kashmir, whether in the form of loans, grants, or subsidies, has produced an acerbic debate at the regional and national levels. Indian nationalist narratives sketch a picture of an "ungrateful" Kashmir, disgruntled and unhappy with India, searching for any opportunity to protest, despite the immense monetary contributions India has made to bring prosperity to the state. These narratives often emphasize that the state has made zero contributions in return, along with its persistent inability to pay its share of income tax.[185] Many Kashmiris refute such arguments, presenting India as a colonial power intent on exploiting Kashmiri resources, especially its water and forests, to erode the state's wealth and keep the region subjugated.[186]

To generate more revenue for debt repayment, the state has long supplied forest resources to the Indian railways, leading to extensive deforestation. As a potentially high-value resource was "sold at a throwaway price," deforestation not only failed to bring substantial financial gain, but also "eroded the potential for future income that could make the state self-reliant."[187] The state's rivers and streams have also remained outside the orbit of Kashmiri control. The central government took control of vital state water resources. The Committee on Economic Reforms in its report published in 1998 highlighted the abundant potential of Jammu and Kashmir's water resources. The four main river basins of Chenab, Jhelum, Indus, and Ravi provided Kashmir with opportunities for "hydropower development unequaled in any other state." Despite this situation, only one major hydropower project commissioned by the state sector existed—the 1978 Lower Jhelum Hydroelectric Project (LJHP) with an installed capacity of 105 MW. As per the report, the state used to purchase 80 percent of its power requirements as high-cost thermal power from the central sector.[188] Furthermore, the state's two spells of appointed "governor rule" (in 1986 and 1990) had provided the National Hydel Power Corporation (NHPC) control over the Sawalkot and Baghlihar projects on the Chenab.[189] The NHPC controlled not only the generation but also the distribution system.

The 1960 Indus Waters Treaty, meanwhile, saw India bartering the water resources of Jammu and Kashmir to Pakistan without paying any heed to Kashmiri interests. Under the treaty, India controlled three rivers, the Sutlej, Beas, and Ravi, which flow through Himachal Pradesh and Punjab, for irrigation and power. Pakistan controlled the waters of the remaining three rivers, namely the Chenab, Jhelum, and Indus, that flow through Jammu and Kashmir. The treaty created a restriction on the total storage capacity for these three rivers.[190] As a result, the state of Jammu and Kashmir could undertake only one electricity project, which meant reduced power generation in the Valley during the winter months due to the low discharge of water. In the late 1990s power generation went down to 25 to 30 percent of the installed capacity between October and March, "resulting in recourse to high-cost gas generation or a larger import of costly power from the central power stations."[191] Kashmiris continue to demand compensation for losses sustained due to restrictions that prevented the state from generating income from hydroelectricity. Overall, the water situation contributes to the economic dependence of Jammu and Kashmir state on India.

Conclusion

Kashmiri understandings of economic emancipation became further obscured after India embarked on a mission to integrate Jammu and Kashmir. The new state-sponsored regimes created and nurtured by India's money created an aura of economic prosperity over Kashmir, modernizing its landscape and providing subsidies to win Kashmiri loyalties. In practicing patronage politics, however, the puppet regime misused government funds for personal enrichment, while awarding jobs, economic deals, and business tenders to their political supporters. As this culture of corruption swamped the region, it eroded economic freedom and introduced insecurity in economic relationships. The ability to fulfill their dreams and aspirations remained out of reach for most Kashmiris, as the elite abused their power to enrich themselves.

The Indian state, for its part, allowed corruption and nepotism as long as Kashmir remained economically dependent and politically quiescent. Although the patronage politics of the state-sponsored regimes succeeded in creating a class of loyalists who monopolized all economic benefits, this class by definition excluded most Kashmiris. Economic transformations created by successive government policies in post-1953 Kashmir generated new rents in Kashmir's social fabric and pitted both old and new classes against each other. These new economic arrangements also precipitated rural–urban tensions, creating new rural elites and rich orchardists who collaborated with urban political elites in exploiting the poor. As democracy derailed, Kashmiri voices of resistance drew inspiration from pre-existing ideas about economic freedom, invoking concepts of economic equity and social justice to inform political debates and instances of popular resistance.

Although the middle classes in both urban and rural Kashmir received free education, they failed to secure jobs or promotions without political connections or bribes. Marginalized within political structures and excluded from networks of patronage, their narratives equated the "secularism" and "modernity" promoted by the ruling elites with the degradation of Kashmiri society and saw these concepts as a threat to their religiously informed cultural identity. Governments in both Jammu and Kashmir and India failed to address popular discontent. Meanwhile, the pliant regimes of the 1950s and 1960s lacked legitimacy and only remained in power through bribes and subsidies funded largely by grants and loans from India. A silent understanding between the state regimes and the Indian government allowed corrupt political elites to erode the state's autonomous status. The marginalization of the least privileged strata of society created a feeling that despite their efforts to rise through education they had been deliberately excluded due to their religion and their lack of political connections. Economic deprivations, the erosion of Kashmir's autonomy, and the ongoing denial of democratic rights all alienated Kashmiris from Indian democracy, setting the stage for Kashmiris' renewed demand for self-determination.

Notes

1. Extract from Mirza Arif Beg's poem "Ten Quatrains," in T. N. Kaul (ed.), *Gems of Kashmiri Literature* (New Delhi: Sanchar Publishing House, 1996), 143.
2. Riyaz Punjabi, "Kashmir: The Bruised Identity," in Raju G. C. Thomas (ed.), *Perspectives on Kashmir: The Roots of Conflict in South Asia* (Boulder, CO: Westview Press, 1992), 131–52.
3. U. S. Rao, "Brave New Kashmir in the Making," *Times of India*, New Delhi, September 15, 1957.
4. S. M. Abdullah, *Flames of the Chinar*, 103.
5. For details, see Mridula Sarabhai, "The Role of Communalists and Their Patrons in Jammu and Kashmir State since 9th August 1953," 1956, All India Congress Committee Papers, F. No. 3589, 2nd Installment, Nehru Memorial Museum and Library, New Delhi.
6. P. N. Bazaz, *The History of Struggle for Freedom in Kashmir*, 700.
7. For details, see Prem Nath Bazaz, *Democracy through Intimidation and Terror: The Untold Story of Kashmir's Politics* (New Delhi: Heritage, 1978) and Sanaullah Butt, *Kashmir in Flames* (Srinagar: Ali Mohammad and Sons, 1981).
8. P. N. Bazaz, *Kashmir in Crucible*, 69–70.

9. The families of detained individuals suffered financial hardships; in many cases, the legitimate allowance promised by the state never reached them. The government twisted the rules to deny allowance, sometimes releasing the detainees on parole before six months, then immediately arresting them again and considering it fresh detention. "The Problem of Detunes and Political Prisoners in J&K State," 1955, All India Congress Committee Papers, F. No. 2054, 2nd Installment, Nehru Memorial Museum and Library, New Delhi.
10. Sarabhai, "The Role of Communalists and Their Patrons in Jammu and Kashmir State since 9th August 1953."
11. Sarabhai, "The Role of Communalists and Their Patrons in Jammu and Kashmir State since 9th August 1953."
12. Sarabhai, "The Role of Communalists and Their Patrons in Jammu and Kashmir State since 9th August 1953."
13. S. M. Abdullah, *The Blazing Chinar*, 345.
14. Directorate of Information and Broadcasting, *Five Months: Account of the Work Done by the Jammu and Kashmir Government under Prime Minister Bakshi Ghulam Mohammad* [August 9, 1953 to January 9, 1954] (Jammu and Kashmir State: Government Press, 1954).
15. Letter from V. Narayan, Joint Secretary, Government of India, to Bakshi Ghulam Muhammad, November 29, 1954, 3(38)-K/54, Ministry of States, National Archives of India, New Delhi.
16. Directorate of Information and Broadcasting, *Five Months*, 2–3.
17. Directorate of Information and Broadcasting, *Five Months*, 6.
18. Noorani, *Article 370*, 264–74.
19. Teng, *Kashmir: Article 370*, 93–4.
20. From 1947 to 1954, India provided 98,345,000 rupees as loans and 62,059,034 rupees under the heading "Aid to Kashmir." "Aid to Kashmir," Ministry of States, No. 15 (23)-K/54, National Archives of India, New Delhi.
21. "Grants to Kashmir," Ministry of States, No. 3(11)-K/54, National Archives of India, New Delhi.
22. "Grants to Kashmir," Ministry of States, No. 3(11)-K/54.
23. Teng, *Kashmir: Article 370*, 78.
24. Teng, *Kashmir: Article 370*, 78.
25. Balraj Puri, "Central Aid to Kashmir," *Kashmir Affairs* 3, no. 9 (January–February 1961): 29–35.
26. Puri, "Central Aid to Kashmir," 29–35.
27. Balraj Puri, "Kashmir's Indebtedness to the Center," *Kashmir Affairs* 4, no. 11 (May–June 1961): 10–11. Ranging from interest rates of 2.75 to 4 percent, these loans were to be repaid in twenty years.
28. Puri, "Kashmir's Indebtedness to the Center," 10–11.
29. Balraj Puri, "A General View of Galloping but Lopsided Economy," *Kashmir Affairs* 3, no. 9 (January–February 1961): 8–17.

30. Haseeb A. Drabu, *J&K Economy: Reform and Reconstruction* (New Delhi: Asia Development Bank, 2004), 4.
31. Balraj Puri, "Budgets of the First and Second Five Year Plans: Revenue Receipts and Expenditure," *Kashmir Affairs* 3, no. 9 (January–February 1961): 18–23.
32. G. M. Shah, "Kashmir: Political Instability and Economic Strangulation," *Minorities Views* 1, no. 1 (Kashmir Special Number, May 1968): 19–22.
33. "Kashmir's Economy," *Mahaz*, Srinagar, August 12, 1964.
34. Bakshi Ghulam Muhammad, *Aid from India* (Srinagar: Ministry of Information and Broadcasting, 1955), 1–3.
35. Mohammad Ashraf, "Shrinking Political Space in Kashmir!" *Cross Currents*, November 15, 2018.
36. For details, see Riyaz Punjabi, "Corruption: A Factor of Kashmiri Alienation," *Mainstream* 29, no. 21 (March 16, 1991), 23–4.
37. Punjabi, "Corruption."
38. Crore is a unit of value in South Asia; 1 crore is equal to 10 million.
39. *Report of the Commission of Inquiry to Enquire into Charges of Misconduct against Bakshi Ghulam Muhammad* [*Ayyangar Committee Report*] (Srinagar: Home Department, J&K Government, 1967), 52–5, 100.
40. Government of Jammu and Kashmir, *Jammu and Kashmir Legislative Assembly Debates* (June–July 1962), 65–6; *Ayyangar Committee Report*, 358–74, 703–5.
41. One such case that received publicity in local press related to a certain block officer and contractor. The contractor, Abdullah Butt, had received a PWD contract of 18,000 rupees for the construction of a dam in a village. However, the contractor in liaison with the block officer usurped government funds. Instead of building a dam in the village, the contractor built a brick wall in the house of the block officer. In the official records, the block officer showed that the contractor accomplished his work and constructed a dam. "Community Projects and National Extension Service: Development or Punitive," 1957, All India Congress Committee Papers, 2nd Installment, F. No. 3589, Nehru Memorial Museum and Library, New Delhi.
42. For details, see *Ayyangar Committee Report.*
43. *Ayyangar Committee Report*, 300–3.
44. Puri, "A General View of Galloping but Lopsided Economy," 8–17.
45. "Community Projects and National Extension Service: Development or Punitive."
46. Examples published in the *Ayyangar Committee Report* highlight how political elites maneuvered their influence to ensure a bright future for their children. *Ayyangar Committee Report*, 132–6.
47. Punjabi, "Corruption"; Peer Giyas-Ud-Din, *Understanding the Kashmiri Insurgency* (New Delhi: Anmol Publications, 1992), 69–70.
48. Government of Jammu and Kashmir, *Jammu and Kashmir Legislative Assembly Debates* (Jammu: Government Press, March–April 1964), 55–7.
49. For details, see Government of Jammu and Kashmir, *Jammu and Kashmir Legislative Assembly Debates* (Jammu: Government Press, February–March 1963), 38–74;

Government of Jammu and Kashmir, *Jammu and Kashmir Legislative Assembly Debates* (Jammu: Government Press, February–March 1964).

50. Government of Jammu and Kashmir, *Jammu and Kashmir Legislative Assembly Debates* (Jammu: Government Press, June–July 1962), 65–9.
51. "Who Gets Economic Benefits: Drainage of Resources," 1957, All India Congress Committee, 2nd Installment, F. No. 2054, Nehru Memorial Library and Congress, New Delhi.
52. "Who Gets Economic Benefits: Drainage of Resources."
53. Balraj Puri, *Kashmir towards Insurgency* (New Delhi: Orient Longman, 1993), 43–7.
54. For details about corruption charges against Bakshi Ghulam Muhammad, see *Report of the Commission of Inquiry* (Srinagar: Home Department, 1967).
55. P. N. Bazaz, *Kashmir in Crucible*, 73.
56. "Transformation of Kashmir," *The Tribune*, Ambala, August 15, 1969.
57. Shamim Ahmed Shamim, "Kashmir Administrative Services: A Sad Tale of Corruption and Nepotism," *Aina*, June 17, 1965.
58. Punjabi, "Corruption," 23–4.
59. P. N. Bazaz, *Kashmir in Crucible*, 83.
60. P. N. Bazaz, *Kashmir in Crucible*, 91.
61. W. L. Allinson, *Kashmir: A Report*, October 15, 1965, Kashmir Internal Situation, DO 133/173, 1965, National Archives, Kew, UK, 82.
62. G. Lone, "Making Kashmir Economy Self Reliant," Srinagar, *Mahaz*, August 1964.
63. "Political Note on Kashmir Problem," Mss.Eur.D.704, 2–3, India Office Library, London.
64. "Political Note on Kashmir Problem," 4.
65. G. H. Khan, *Kashmiri Muslaman ki Iqhtisadi, Mahasharti aur Deeni Zarrorraten* (Srinagar: Self-published, 1968) (personal collection of M. Khan, Srinagar).
66. Sumantra Bose, *Kashmir: Roots of Conflict, Paths to Peace*, 89.
67. "Simla Agreement," http://www.stimson.org/research-pages/simla-agreement/, accessed March 15, 2018.
68. "Kashmir Accord," *Azan*, Srinagar, February 5, 1973.
69. Siddhartha Prakash, "The Political Economy of Kashmir since 1947," *Contemporary South Asia* 9, no. 3 (2000): 315–37.
70. *Lal Kitab* (Srinagar: n.d.) (private collection of Syed Nazir Ahmed Shah, Kashmir).
71. "Tax Raids: Shaking the Sheikh," *India Today*, New Delhi, May 16–31, 1981.
72. Muhammad Farooq Rehmani, *Sheikh Abdullah ke Naqoosh* (Srinagar: Gulshan Publications, 1988), 20, cited in Jagmohan, *My Frozen Turbulence in Kashmir*, 205.
73. Jagmohan, *My Frozen Turbulence in Kashmir*, 211.
74. Jagmohan, *My Frozen Turbulence in Kashmir*, 206–7.
75. Jagmohan, *My Frozen Turbulence in Kashmir*, 204.
76. Punjabi, "Corruption," 23.
77. Jalal, *Democracy and Authoritarianism in South Asia*, 157–62.

78. Government of Jammu and Kashmir, *Kashmir Festival* (Srinagar: Press Information Bureau, 1956), 3.
79. "Education and Women," *Martand*, Srinagar, May 12, 1958.
80. "New Values," *Martand*, Srinagar, June 7, 1957.
81. "New Values."
82. Punjabi, "Corruption."
83. Akhtar Mohiuddin, *Jahanumukh Panun Panun Naar* (Srinagar: Nishat Publications, 1975), translated here by Syed Taffazull Hussain, Srinagar.
84. Mohiuddin, *Jahanumukh Panun Panun Naar*.
85. Mohiuddin, *Jahanumukh Panun Panun Naar*.
86. Shamim Ahmed Shamim, "Tazleel ke Dag," *Aina*, Srinagar, November 5, 1967.
87. Amin Kamil, "Infernal Creature," in *Kathi Manz Kath* (Srinagar: Sheikh Ghulam Mohammed and Sons, 1958), 85.
88. Amin Kamil, "Infernal Creature," in M. Siddiq Beig, *Kashmiri Short Stories* (Srinagar: Crown Printing Press, 1997), 58–66.
89. Ghulam Hassan Khan, "Kashmir's Educational System," unpublished pamphlet, Srinagar, 1968 (personal collection of Mrs. Khan, Srinagar).
90. "The Text Book Controversy," Ministry of Home Affairs, File No. 2/21/1966, National Archives of India, New Delhi.
91. G. H. Khan, "Kashmir's Educational System."
92. *The Kashmir Revolt*, pamphlet published by the Muslim Action Committee of Kashmir, Srinagar, 1964, Internal Affairs in Indian Held Kashmir, DO 88/5/2A, National Archives, Kew, UK.
93. *The Kashmir Revolt*.
94. For details, see Mullik, *Kashmir: My Years with Nehru*, 128–37; Giyas-Ud-Din, *Understanding the Kashmiri Insurgency*, 33–9.
95. "Toll in Calcutta Put at Sixty in the Riots," *New York Times*, January 12, 1964, https://www.nytimes.com/1964/01/12/archives/toll-in-calcutta-put-at-60-in-riots-hindu-mob-kills-3-policemen.html, accessed January 1, 2019; Sumantra Bose, *Roots of Conflict, Paths to Peace*, 91.
96. Mullik, *Kashmir: My Years with Nehru*, 142–3.
97. "Statement of Bakshi Ghulam Muhammad," Internal Affairs in Indian Held Kashmir, DO 88/5/2A, National Archives at Kew, UK.
98. Nafis Ahmad, *The Jan Sangh and the Muslims* (New Delhi: Sarmodhya Virodhyi Committee, 1964), 17–18.
99. *Anjumun-i-Tablighul Islam Jammu wa Kashmir Kaa Nasbul Ain aur Agraz-wa-Maqasid* (Constitution, Aims, and Objectives of Anjumun-i-Tabligh-ul Islam) (personal collection of Showkat Hussain Keng, Srinagar); Mushtaq Ahmad Wani, *Muslim Religious Trends in Kashmir in Modern Times* (Patna: Khuda Bakhsh Oriental Public Library, 1997), 51.
100. M. A. Wani, *Muslim Religious Trends in Kashmir in Modern Times*, 52–3.

101. Yoginder Sikand, "The Emergence and Development of the Jama'at-i-Islami of Jammu and Kashmir (1940s–1990)," *Modern Asian Studies* 36, no. 3 (July 2002): 705–51.
102. Chapter 6 addresses in detail the political role played by the Jamaat in Kashmir's postcolonial history. Jalal, *Democracy and Authoritarianism in South Asia*, 179.
103. Sikand, "The Emergence and Development of the Jama'at-i-Islami of Jammu and Kashmir (1940s–1990)."
104. Directorate of Education, *Jamat-i-Islami: Jammu wa Kashmir ki Talimi Sagarmiyan* (Srinagar: Education Department, Srinagar), 4–5; M. A. Wani, *Muslim Religious Trends in Kashmir In Modern Times*, 62–6.
105. M. A. Wani, *Muslim Religious Trends in Kashmir in Modern Times*, 70–2.
106. Government of Jammu and Kashmir, *Jammu and Kashmir Legislative Assembly Debates* (Srinagar: Government Press, October–November 1974), 54.
107. Sikand, "The Emergence and Development of the Jama'at-i-Islami of Jammu and Kashmir (1940s–1990)."
108. Ghulam Hassan Khan, "Social Problems of Kashmiri Muslims," unpublished articles, Srinagar, 1972 (personal collection of Mrs. Khan, Srinagar).
109. Shamim Ahmed Shamim, "Gharibon ki Haqtalfi," speech delivered in State Legislative Assembly, September 1968, reprinted in Qurrat-ul-Ain, *Aina Numa: Collection of Shamim Ahmed Shamim's Speeches in the State Legislative Assembly and Indian Parliament* (Srinagar: TFC Publications, 2004), 64–8.
110. "Community Projects and National Extension Service: Development or Punitive."
111. Shamim, "Gharibon ki Haqtalfi," 64–8.
112. Shamim Ahmed Shamim, "Corruption and Financial Bungling of Funds," speech delivered in State Legislative Assembly, September 1970, in Qurrat-ul-Ain, *Aina Numa*, 25–6.
113. Government of Jammu and Kashmir, *Jammu and Kashmir Legislative Assembly Debates* (Srinagar: Government Press, September–October 1970), 42.
114. Government of Jammu and Kashmir, *Jammu and Kashmir Legislative Assembly Debates* (Jammu: Government Press, March–April 1971), 44–7.
115. Government of Jammu and Kashmir, *Jammu and Kashmir Legislative Assembly Debates* (March–April 1971), 44–7.
116. N. S. Gupta and Amarjit Singh, *Agricultural Development of States in India*, Vol.1: *Jammu and Kashmir* (New Delhi: Seema Publications, 1979), 224–337.
117. National Council of Applied Economic Research, *The Techno-Economic Survey of Jammu and Kashmir* (New Delhi: National Council of Applied Economic Research, 1969), 162.
118. Gupta and Singh, *Agricultural Development of States in India*, Vol. 1: *Jammu and Kashmir*, 229–31.
119. National Council of Applied Economic Research, *The Techno-Economic Survey of Jammu and Kashmir*, Table 18, 189.

120. M. L. Misri and M. S. Bhat, *Poverty, Planning and Economic Change in Jammu and Kashmir* (Delhi: Vikas Publishing House, 1994), 78.
121. Thorner, "The Kashmir Land Reforms," 999–1002.
122. For details, see M. S. Bhat, "A Profile of Agrarian Science in Jammu and Kashmir," in Madan Lal Sharma and R. K. Punia (eds.), *Land Reforms in India: Achievements, Problems, and Prospects* (New Delhi: Ajanta Publications, 1989), 98–112; Prakash, "The Political Economy of Kashmir since 1947."
123. *Report of the Land Commission* (Srinagar: Government of Jammu and Kashmir, 1968), 11–12.
124. Misri and Bhat, *Poverty, Planning and Economic Change in Jammu and Kashmir*, 250–1.
125. Misri and Bhat, *Poverty, Planning and Economic Change in Jammu and Kashmir*, 251.
126. Government of Jammu and Kashmir, *Jammu and Kashmir Legislative Assembly Debates* (Srinagar: Government Press, October 1972), 4–8; K. S. Khosla, "Kashmir Pioneer in Radical Reforms," *Times of India*, New Delhi, November 4, 1972.
127. Government of Jammu and Kashmir, *Jammu and Kashmir Legislative Assembly Debates* (October 1972), 4–8; Khosla, "Kashmir Pioneer in Radical Reforms."
128. Khosla, "Kashmir Pioneer in Radical Reforms."
129. Government of Jammu and Kashmir, *Jammu and Kashmir Legislative Assembly Debates* (October 1972), 45; Khosla, "Kashmir Pioneer in Radical Reform."
130. Department of Information, *Jammu and Kashmir Agrarian Reforms Act of 1976* (Srinagar: Government of Jammu and Kashmir, 1976).
131. Bhat, "A Profile of Agrarian Science in Jammu and Kashmir," 98–112.
132. Misri and Bhat, *Poverty, Planning and Economic Change in Jammu and Kashmir*, 77.
133. Misri and Bhat, *Poverty, Planning and Economic Change in Jammu and Kashmir*, 77.
134. P. S. Verma, *Jammu and Kashmir at Political Crossroads* (New Delhi: Vikas Publishing House, 1994), 188.
135. Verma, *Jammu and Kashmir at Political Crossroads*, 192.
136. K. Warikoo, *Religion and Security in South and Central Asia* (London: Routledge, 2014), 70.
137. Misri and Bhat, *Poverty, Planning and Economic Change in Jammu and Kashmir*, 252.
138. Giyas-Ud-Din, *Understanding the Kashmir Insurgency*, 80.
139. Qasim, *My Life and Times*, 132.
140. Verma, *Jammu and Kashmir at Political Crossroads*, 121–8.
141. Misri and Bhat, *Poverty, Planning and Economic Change in Jammu and Kashmir*, 209–10.
142. Misri and Bhat, *Poverty, Planning and Economic Change in Jammu and Kashmir*, 331–74.

143. Janak Singh, "Kashmir Reduces Subsidy Burden: Some Bold Measures," *Times of India*, New Delhi, April 16, 1976.
144. Department of Information and Broadcasting, *"My Blood Your Sweat," Text of Speech by Chief Minister Sheikh Muhammad Abdullah on 14 May 1975* (Srinagar: Government of Jammu and Kashmir, 1975), 1–3.
145. Prakash, "Political Economy of Kashmir since 1947."
146. J. Singh, "Kashmir Reduces Subsidy Burden."
147. Balraj Puri, "What Is Wrong with Kashmir's Finances," *Economic and Political Weekly* 16, no. 19 (May 9, 1981): 845–6.
148. Puri, "What Is Wrong with Kashmir's Finances."
149. Muhammad Farooq Rehmani, *Azadi ki Taalash* (Srinagar: Aflak Publishers, 1982), 279–81.
150. Misri and Bhat, *Poverty, Planning and Economic Change in Jammu and Kashmir*, 331, 333–6.
151. For details, see Jalal, *Democracy and Authoritarianism in South Asia*, 175–81; Sumantra Bose, *Kashmir: Roots of Conflict, Paths to Peace*, 88–94; Puri, *Kashmir towards Insurgency*, 31–8.
152. *Report of the Committee of Economic Reforms* [*Godbole Committee Report*] (Srinagar: Government of Jammu and Kashmir, 1998), 245.
153. *Godbole Committee Report*, 245.
154. *Report of the Jammu and Kashmir Commission of Inquiry* [*Gajendragadkar Committee Report*] (Srinagar: Government of Jammu and Kashmir, 1968), 66.
155. For details, see *Gajendragadkar Committee Report*, 49–72.
156. *Gajendragadkar Committee Report*, 49–72.
157. Sumit Ganguly, "Explaining the Kashmir Insurgency: Political Mobilization and Institutional Decay," *International Security* 21, no. 2 (Fall, 1996): 76–107.
158. Shamim Ahmed Shamim, "Problem of Unemployment," March 29, speech in the Legislative Assembly of Jammu and Kashmir, in Qurrat-ul-Ain, *Aina Numa*, 18–19.
159. Shamim, "Problem of Unemployment," 18–19.
160. Government of Jammu and Kashmir, *Jammu and Kashmir Legislative Assembly Debates* (Jammu: Government Press, March 1967), 25–8.
161. "Backward class" is a collective term used by the Government of India for educationally and socially disadvantaged castes. This typically includes Scheduled Castes, Scheduled Tribes, and Other Backward Classes.
162. On April 1, 1967, the population in the Valley was 53.3 percent of the total population of the state, while its share in services was 60.9 percent. Jammu's population was 44.2 percent of the total population of the state but its share in services was only 36.1 percent. The recruitment in the thinly populated Ladakh region had declined from 2.5 percent in 1961–2 to 1.4 percent in 1965–6. Community-wise, the report stated, "the position of Muslims has shown an improvement though their share in the services on 1 April 1967 was appreciably less than it should be on the basis of

population. The position of Hindus has shown a decline though their share in the services as on 1 April 1967 was substantially higher than what was due to them according to their population." *Gajendragadkar Committee Report*, 54–6.

163. *Gajendragadkar Committee Report*, 54–8.
164. *Gajendragadkar Committee Report*, 56–63.
165. Government of Jammu and Kashmir, *Jammu and Kashmir Legislative Assembly Debates* (Srinagar: Government Press, October 1970), 72–3.
166. P. N. Bazaz, *Kashmir Pandit Agitation and Its Aftermath*, 10–11.
167. P. N. Bazaz, *Kashmir Pandit Agitation and Its Aftermath*, 10–11.
168. *"Real Side of the Picture," Memorandum Presented by the Muslim Citizens of Kashmir to Mr. Y.B. Chavan, the Home Minister of India* (Srinagar: Nishat Press, 1967), 3–4.
169. *"Real Side of the Picture,"* 3–4.
170. Tapan Bose, Dinesh Mohan, Gautam Navlakha, and Sumanta Banerjee, "India's Kashmir War: A Report," *Economic and Political Weekly* 25, no. 13 (March 31, 1990): 650–62.
171. Bose, Navlakha, and Sumanta Banerjee, "India's Kashmir War."
172. Ghulam Hassan Khan, *The Kashmiri Mussulman* (Srinagar: Faleh-E-Eam Press, 1973), 24–5.
173. Prakash, "The Political Economy of Kashmir since 1947."
174. DN, "Kashmir and India," *Economic and Political Weekly* 26, no. 34 (August 24, 1991): 1959–61, 1956.
175. Prakash, "The Political Economy of Kashmir since 1947."
176. *Godbole Committee Report*, 256–61.
177. "Postal Staff in *Charas* (Hashish) Racket," *Times of India*, June 8, 1973.
178. Drabu, *J&K Economy*, 3–5.
179. Drabu, *J&K Economy*, 3–5.
180. R. Ramalingom and K. N. Kurup, "Plan Transfers to States: Revised Gadgil Formula—An Analysis," *Economic and Political Weekly* 26, nos. 9–10 (March 2–9, 1991): 501–6.
181. *Godbole Committee Report*, 13–14.
182. *Godbole Committee Report*, 13–14.
183. *Godbole Committee Report*, 85.
184. DN, "Kashmir and India."
185. Sushant Pandey, "Money Spent by India on Jammu and Kashmir," *Knowledge of India*, July 20, 2016.
186. DN, "Kashmir and India."
187. DN, "Kashmir and India," 1956.
188. *Godbole Committee Report*, 192.
189. DN, "Kashmir and India," 1956.
190. *Godbole Committee Report*, 194.
191. *Godbole Committee Report*, 194.

4 The Idea of Plebiscite
Discontent and Regional Dissidence

Young and old cry everywhere,
We will have a plebiscite!
They talk about it everywhere,
Rich and poor desire it,
We will have a plebiscite!
Everyone hates falsehood,
They want justice to prevail,
If you do not believe us, listen to the refrain all around,
We will have a plebiscite!
In streets and bazaars people say,
We will have a plebiscite!
Being morally right, that is our strength;
We will have a plebiscite!
We do not hate anyone,
We only demand a plebiscite!

—"We Will Have a Plebiscite"[1]

During the 1950s and 1960s, the concept of "plebiscite" caught the imagination of Kashmiri Muslims living under oppressive state regimes and excluded from the networks of patronage by the Kashmiri political elites who collaborated to integrate Jammu and Kashmir with India. Demanding "self-determination," these excluded voices expressed their discontent against a hegemonic power by organizing a plebiscite movement that challenged Indian nationalist narratives' tacit assumption of Indian control over Kashmir. While local bands and balladeers integrated "self-determination" into their songs, making the term a part of popular memory, activists and writers mobilized the excluded majority to generate global support for Kashmiris trapped in the territorial dispute between India and Pakistan.

The right to self-determination, as per the United Nations Security Council resolution of 1948, promised the inhabitants of Jammu and Kashmir the option of joining India or Pakistan. This political and territorial definition of self-determination does not address the passionate emotions and responses that this concept evoked among Kashmiri Muslims. The term encapsulated Kashmiri desire for a voice not only in shaping their political destiny, but also in creating a society that valued freedom of expression, respected individual dignity, and was free from social and economic inequality. In postcolonial Kashmir, the slogan of self-determination emerged as a nonviolent demand for all communities struggling to attain rights and liberty under India-sponsored puppet regimes. The plebiscite demand appealed to the sentiments of ordinary Kashmiri Muslims, while activists broadened its meaning from simple political emancipation to encompass ethical concepts of human dignity, justice, and truth—ideas inherent in the earlier discourses of Kashmiri freedom. Most significantly, the slogan of self-determination provided supporters with psychological space to question the hegemony of the nation-states treating Kashmiri destiny as a mere territorial dispute. "Self-determination" projected Kashmiris themselves as the main actors shaping the future of their homeland.

At the same time, this resistance discourse, fashioned by leaders and activists of various political leanings, brought competing definitions of self-determination into the dialogue, while also revealing the fractures within Kashmiri discourse. The concepts of "majority" and "minority," a primary marker of the complexities of Kashmir's turbulent past, politicized "self-determination;" it became a battle cry for Kashmiri Muslims denied a share in power structures, but one strongly opposed by most non-Muslims, who supported Kashmir's complete integration with India. The meaning of "self-determination" evolved along with the changing geopolitical realities of the South Asian subcontinent.

Finding a Voice: The Evolution of Self-determination

The concept of "self-determination" became popular in the Kashmiri political discourse prior to the internationalization of the Kashmir dispute. Kashmiri nationalists led by Sheikh Abdullah, first demanded self-determination for Kashmiris in 1945, during the Dogra rule.[2] At this time the National Conference called for basic political rights for Kashmiris, along with a responsible and representative government.[3] In a 1946 memorandum to the Cabinet Mission, Abdullah clarified that sovereignty resided with the people: all political, economic, and social relationships derive their authority from the collective will.[4] Despite the fact that Kashmiris did not get a chance to decide their own future when the accession to India occurred, the imprint of promises made by Indian leaders remained in their memories. In the postcolonial era, Kashmiri attachment with self-determination gained momentum after Kashmiri nationalists in collaboration with India crushed dissenting voices to impose their political vision. In retaliation, Kashmiri activists, both Hindus and Muslims, invoked self-determination to challenge state authoritarianism and regain their political agency.

Kashmiri resistance discourse is replete with instances of India's promises to allow the inhabitants of Jammu and Kashmir the right to self-determination. On November 2, 1947, as India and Pakistan were battling over Kashmir, the Indian prime minister declared his government's pledge, given not only to "the people of Kashmir but also to the world," to "hold referendum under international auspices such as the United Nations" to determine whether the people of the state preferred to join India or Pakistan.[5] In public gatherings, press conferences, and international forums, Nehru reiterated this commitment various times over the next few years. In August 1952, for example, Nehru in a note to Sheikh Abdullah stated that if the people of Jammu and Kashmir decided to "part company from India, there the matter ends, however we may dislike it or however disadvantageous it may be to India."[6] But these promises remained unfulfilled because India remained unsure about the outcome of a plebiscite in Muslim dominated Kashmir and stymied every effort to resolve this issue at the United Nations. India's insistence on "integration" to retain territorial control in Kashmir led to rigged elections, suppressed democracy, and denial of basic civil liberties. On their part, Kashmiri political activists highlighted India's unfulfilled commitments to legitimize their demand for self-determination and present it as a struggle for "truth" and "justice."

In the immediate aftermath of the first India–Pakistan war, Sheikh Abdullah's ambiguous stance on the question of self-determination further entangled this issue. As his relationship to Delhi and his belief in the promise of state autonomy shifted, the preeminent Kashmiri leader sometimes reiterated his faith in accession to India, while at other moments he questioned the finality of accession. Abdullah's critics on all sides—Kashmiris, Indians, and Pakistanis—attribute his vacillating positions on accession to his political ambition to be "autonomous" and create a *sheikhdom* where he and his henchmen could practice authoritarian politics without accountability. Abdullah's supporters, meanwhile, consider his changing political positions a tactical move to ensure Kashmir's autonomy in a context of Kashmiri Muslim apprehension about growing Hindu nationalism in

India. Regardless of Abdullah's ultimate motives, as India embarked on a policy of centralization and integration of Jammu and Kashmir with India, Abdullah resisted, leading to his dismissal as prime minister and his subsequent arrest. On October 5, 1953, the India-sponsored regime, led by Bakshi Ghulam Muhammad insistent on ratifying Kashmir's accession to India, convened a constituent assembly to accept Kashmir as India's integral part.[7]

At a global level, Cold War politics provided India with an official reason to withdraw from its plebiscite offer. India raised concerns about Pakistan's 1954 decision to ally with the United States by joining the South-East Asia Treaty Organization (SEATO) and the Baghdad Pact in exchange for military assistance. The Soviet Union, meanwhile, adopted a pro-India posture on the Kashmir question, referring to the state of Jammu and Kashmir as "one of the constituent states of the Republic of India."[8] Nehru, convinced that the Soviet Union would veto any resolution the United Nations made on Kashmir, backtracked from his international commitment to Kashmir. In 1956 Nehru, believing that Pakistan's alignment with the United States put India at risk, asked the Indian parliament to withdraw the offer of the plebiscite.[9] Thereafter, the collaboration of local elites to integrate Kashmir provided India a space to conflate plebiscite with "self-rule," and present Kashmiri participation in rigged elections as Kashmiri exercise of self-determination.

In the early 1950s, the winds of change blowing in India-administered Kashmir convinced both supporters and detractors of Abdullah of India's intention to impose its political will on Kashmiris by denying them a voice in shaping their political future. As their feelings of political injustice and disempowerment crystallized, Kashmiris felt frustrated. They had endured political suppression since Kashmir's accession to India and considered self-determination essential to take back their agency. Sensing the growing Kashmiri Muslim disenchantment, individuals and groups who had disagreed with Abdullah's support for provisional accession to India emerged from the shadows to reorient Kashmiri resistance. The main opposition party to Abdullah's politics in the late 1940s, the Muslim Conference, had disintegrated in the Valley after accession: most of its members either voluntarily moved to Pakistan-administered Kashmir or were deported due to their political differences with Abdullah's administration. In response to India's policy of centralization, those party affiliates who had remained in the Valley organized secret meetings to challenge Kashmir's complete integration with India.[10]

Meanwhile, several non-Muslim critics of Abdullah (Prem Nath Bazaz, Pitambar Nath Dhar Fani, D. N. Bhan, and J. N. Sathu), expelled from Kashmir, had taken refuge in India. In Delhi, they formed the Kashmir Democratic Union (KDU) to question the partition of Jammu and Kashmir, which separated families and uprooted Kashmiris, while "non-Kashmiri" armies occupied Kashmir's territory against the people's will. The KDU demanded an end to despotic governance and freedom for Kashmiris to choose their own destiny by exercising self-determination. The official newspaper of the KDU, *Voice of Kashmir*, also served as a forum for "suppressed" Kashmiris with different perspectives to express their aspirations. These individuals stirred up quite a controversy with their sarcastic and frequently biting critiques of Kashmir "nationalist" leaders, the Indian state, and the political stance of their own community of Kashmiri Hindus.[11] Severe condemnation by the Kashmiri Hindu community, including being branded "pro-Pakistan," did not deter them from expressing the importance of providing Kashmiris a free will to decide their political future.

Prem Nath Bazaz, in particular, provided an intellectual direction to the Kashmiri demand for self-determination. In a series of articles in the *Voice of Kashmir*, Bazaz lamented the lack of a clear conception of "self-determination" in different Kashmiri communities. Kashmiri Hindus and Muslims, he wrote, understood self-determination from a narrow communitarian perspective, rather than as a united stance to bring freedom and prosperity to Kashmir as a whole. Kashmiri Hindus, despite a deep-seated resentment against the state's land reform policies that shook the foundations of their economic life and forced nearly 30,000 Kashmiri Hindus to migrate to India, were eager to declare the Indian part of Kashmir "free and democratic." Similarly, Kashmiri Muslims claimed that Pakistan-administered Kashmir had attained liberation, yet they could not justify the economic deterioration and political suppression in "Azad" Kashmir that motivated Muslim refugees from Jammu to return home. Immersed in religious prejudices and fears of being dominated by the "other," both communities were oblivious to the reality that "progress and prosperity are indivisible" and needed to be shared jointly in Jammu and Kashmir state. One community could not have freedom without the other.[12]

Bazaz's argument was not only about political and economic freedom, but also about moral goodness. He lamented that Kashmiri Muslim leaders on both sides of the divide believed freedom meant replacement of the Dogra Raj with self-glorification and positions of prestige for their supporters. "Freedom" in Kashmir had degenerated into an unseemly scramble for power in which lying, deceit, faithlessness, and treachery were on full display. The exercise of self-determination would only be effective if Hindus and Muslims united to create a progressive and free Kashmir, focusing on character development, moral regeneration, and intellectual growth before political and social freedom. Bazaz's concern for the national character also shaped his anger that India and Pakistan had made Kashmir a "national prestige" issue rather than prioritizing the aspirations of the people who inhabited that land. He expressed disbelief at the hypocrisy of Indian leadership who condemned imperialism in any shape and form on the world stage, yet vehemently denied their policy of political suppression and military domination in Kashmir. The Indian leaders who had struggled against British colonial rule for decades, Bazaz argued, were now amnesiac regarding their own experiences in bondage. India claimed to contribute to the economic prosperity of Kashmir, but denied self-determination and imposed pliant regimes that ensured Kashmir's moral degeneration. The "oppressed Kashmiris," with no space to express "true feelings," resorted to falsehood and treachery, which destroyed the "national character" of Kashmiri society and crushed its spirit of freedom.[13]

Elevating the issue of Kashmiri self-determination to the international level, Bazaz submitted a memorandum to the 1955 Asian–African conference at Bandung that defined India as an "imperialistic power that has turned Kashmir into a colony." Although he differentiated old and new colonialism, Bazaz argued for its eradication in "every form and content." Even though countries like India and Russia only acknowledged the "old type, practiced by European powers," the experiences of decolonized nations proved that a new kind of nation-state colonialism was taking root: one that subjugated other nationalities and suppressed local cultures. Pointing out the discrepancies in India's high moral stance that condemned imperialism in Algeria and Cyprus, yet ignored the claims of self-determination emanating from the disputed state of Jammu and Kashmir, Bazaz asked the assembled nations to pressure India to allow Kashmiris to decide their own future. India's intransigence in resolving the Kashmir dispute, Bazaz argued, prevented it from taking its rightful international station as a democratic country.[14]

The KDU was often dismissed by its critics as a party of intellectuals with no political foothold to maneuver Kashmir's complex politics, but this did not discourage its members from expressing their views, hoping to bring a positive change. Kashmiri voices of resistance also came together in public arenas, even prior to Abdullah's imprisonment, to challenge India's insistence on full integration. In June 1953 Ghulam Mohiuddin Karra, the "legendary hero of the Quit Kashmir movement," formed the Political Conference, a party that advocated Kashmir's accession to Pakistan.[15] Karra belonged to a family of pashmina traders with business links in Calcutta (now known as Kolkata). The family returned to the Valley in the 1920s to participate in the growing Muslim political mobilization against the Dogra Raj.[16] After completing his education at the Aligarh Muslim

University, Karra returned home to join Abdullah's National Conference and fight Dogra autocracy. As a prominent figure in nationalist politics, Karra supported Abdullah in every political initiative against the princely state. However, after Kashmir's accession to India, Abdullah denied Karra an appropriate position in the new government, leaving him frustrated. He resigned from the National Conference and aligned with Pandit Raghunath Vaishnavi, Sham Lal Yachu, Mirwaiz Ghulam Nabi Hamdani, and others alienated by the dictatorial approach of the National Conference leadership.[17]

The Political Conference published posters and pamphlets and organized demonstrations to mobilize Kashmiris.[18] The stifling of political dissent and economic dislocation caused by the drawing of the ceasefire line increased Kashmiri resentment of India. Meanwhile, Kashmiri Muslim insecurities about the rise of Hindu nationalism in India were multiplied by the Praja Parishad agitation, which, led by the Hindu right, demanded Kashmir's complete integration. In these conditions, thousands of Kashmiris chanted pro-Pakistan slogans at the demonstrations organized by the Political Conference, whose leadership was subsequently jailed. To appease Karra's political base, the India-sponsored administration of Bakshi Ghulam Muhammad offered to release him from prison and give him a cabinet position; Karra refused the offer and instead continued to build momentum for self-determination.[19] After the passing of the Preventive Detention Law in 1955 allowing the arrest of political dissenters without due process, several leaders of the Political Conference shifted their activities to Delhi and established contacts with the KDU to build support for self-determination.

The Political Conference published two newspapers, *Naya Payam* in Urdu and *Free Thinker* in English, to reach audiences both in and outside Jammu and Kashmir. Besides publishing articles demanding a plebiscite, the editors also devoted space to the philosophy of radical humanism advocated by M. N. Roy, a prominent Indian revolutionary who emphasized that rationalism, individual freedom, and morality, not dogma, should shape political views. The editors, as interested in cultural regeneration as the KDU's chief theorist Bazaz, considered Roy's views essential to the project of self-determination.[20]

Meanwhile, in Kashmir, Kashmiris watched helplessly as Bakshi's administration unleashed suppressive policies, crushing opposition and denying voices of resistance due legal process and fundamental rights enshrined in the Indian constitution. During the 1950s, illegal arrests and beatings in police stations were regular features of life for political protestors. The seemingly perpetual repression embittered Kashmiris toward India and its handpicked regime. The police used third-degree torture methods to silence opposition, branding the chests of dissenters with red hot irons or stuffing hot potatoes down their mouths. The notorious "Peace Brigade," a group of police henchmen, harassed the opposition, making life unbearable for those with different political views.[21]

In a society steeped in violent political suppression, literary work provided an outlet for Kashmiris to express their views with relative freedom from persecution. For example, Akhtar Mohiuddin's "My Lips Are Sealed," a short story, provides an insight into how manipulative state regimes exploit the insecurities of individuals, transforming them into pawns of the security apparatus. The story concerns a henchman, Qadir Chaan, who spends his days harassing ordinary people with different political persuasions. The narrator, curious to understand Chaan's motivations, visits his home and establishes a relationship of trust. He is surprised to see that Chaan is a family man, living in poverty and raising three unmarried daughters, with dreams for their prosperous future. Cognizant of his unethical behavior, Chaan worries the hand of divine justice might visit unhappiness on his children to punish him for his misdeeds.

Unburdening his heart, Chaan reveals how one wrong act, committed in the heat of the moment on the day of Sheikh Abdullah's arrest, changed his life forever. Chaan, it develops, held the administration of Sheikh Abdullah responsible for inflation and economic hardship that made it impossible for him to provide medicine for his sick mother, leading to her death. Angry and hurt, he failed to understand people protesting the arrest of Abdullah. Enraged, Chaan lashed out at a protestor, killing him on the spot. He dreaded the ramifications of his actions but was surprised when the new administration expressed pride at his "brave" act and hired him to beat political dissenters and instill terror among opponents deemed "anti-national." Feeling trapped, Chaan accepted the offer; however, as he tells the narrator, his mental anguish deepens every day as he sees no escape from his personal hell.[22] The repressive state machinery that crushed political opposition heightened feelings of political injustice and made the idea of self-determination very appealing to excluded Kashmiri Muslims.

Left-wing Indian opposition groups like the Praja Socialist Party (PSP) worried that repression of civil liberties in the Valley would crystallize pro-Pakistan sentiments and lead to a Kashmiri Muslim revolt against "secular" India. The PSP leaders Jayaprakash Narayan, Dr. Ram Manohar Lohia, and Asoka Mehta complained about the "prevalence of political terrorism" in Jammu and Kashmir and the need to restore democracy and civil liberties.[23] In 1953 the PSP formed a Kashmir branch of their party, the Awami Socialist Conference, led by Khawaja Omar Bhat, with an objective of good governance and social justice. The PSP's "enlightened policy" urged Kashmiris to demand political rights, rather than self-determination. Prem Nath Bazaz of the KDU, however, took PSP leadership to task for their "ivory tower" mentality and indifference to the inhumane policies of both nation-states that made it impossible for separated families divided by an arbitrary ceasefire line to reconnect or even communicate with their kith and kin. For these "lacerated [Kashmiri] hearts," Bazaz argued, exercising self-determination was the only way forward.[24]

While Hindu and Muslim Kashmiri voices tried to shape the demand for self-determination in both the print media and public arenas, Sheikh Abdullah, incarcerated in the Kud jail at Jammu, wrote a detailed letter to the United Nations Security Council interpreting India's withdrawal of the offer of plebiscite as a "fraud upon the people" and "breach of international commitments and promises."[25] He made it clear that the decision to consider Kashmir an integral part of India was an imposition on Kashmiris, made by a pliant regime that governed Kashmir through "monstrous laws" stifling all civil liberties. Abdullah questioned India's stance on the plebiscite, which "penalized Kashmiris for Pakistan's alliances and pacts." While refuting the arguments made by the Indian prime minister (who had expressed apprehensions that if a plebiscite went in favor of Pakistan, it would arouse religious passions in India and endanger the Indian Muslim minority), Abdullah questioned the strength of an Indian secularism that required Kashmiri "enslavement" as the basis of Indian Muslim security. "Is India's secularism skin deep, that it will collapse like a pack of cards as soon as Kashmiris exercise their right of self-determination?" The letter appealed to the world community to stand by the ideals of freedom and peace and allow "four million downtrodden Kashmiris to shape their political future."[26] Abdullah's prison-cell attempt to restore Kashmiri self-determination was received warmly by his loyalists, who rejected India's Cold War decision not to hold a plebiscite.

The Plebiscite Movement: Mobilization and Popular Support

The supporters of Sheikh Abdullah, sidelined from politics after his arrest, considered it prudent to embrace self-determination. They popularized the idea of the plebiscite to put pressure on Delhi to end centralization or face a full-fledged resistance. Within the plebiscite movement there were multiple visions for Kashmir's future. The suffocating political atmosphere created by the India-sponsored regime united all strands of Kashmiri resistance to build a momentum for self-determination.[27] Although the Plebiscite Front framed self-determination as a political choice between India and Pakistan, they drew upon the people's simmering resentment against an oppressive state apparatus to explain "self-determination" as a struggle against political injustices and hegemonic domination.

In 1955, therefore, Abdullah's supporters formed the Plebiscite Front, which posed a challenge to complete integration with India, rather than allow their opponents, like the Political Conference, to take the lead in shaping Kashmiri political discourse. Its main architect, Mirza Afzal Beg, a lawyer and a close lieutenant of Sheikh Abdullah, along with thirteen other signatories, including seven of the seventy-five members of the Kashmir Constituent Assembly, demanded peaceful settlement of the Kashmir dispute according to the free will of the people through an impartial agency of the United Nations.[28] The Plebiscite Front's membership was open to every citizen of the state, irrespective of caste, creed, or religion, provided they accepted Kashmir's provisional accession to India. The party strove to establish a democratic way of life through peaceful means, aiming to restore the self-respect and self-confidence of Kashmiris. Abdullah himself never joined the Plebiscite Front, but he remained its chief patron.[29]

The political actors who shaped the Plebiscite Front represented different ideological persuasions. Each strand tried to steer the party in a direction aligned with their political vision for Kashmir. Maulana Masoodi, a teacher by profession and a founding member of the National Conference, desired greater autonomy for Kashmir within the political and constitutional ambit of India. Sofi Akbar from Sopore and Munshi Ishaq from Srinagar joined the Plebiscite Front hoping to bring about Kashmir's accession to Pakistan, convinced that Kashmiri Muslims were not safe in Hindu-dominated India.[30] Behind closed doors, Mirza Afzal Beg gave assurances to pro-Pakistani activists that the Plebiscite Front supported their stance. However, in the public arena Beg and Abdullah refused to take a clear-cut stand, giving the impression that they would flow with popular tide after Kashmiris exercised the right of self-determination.[31] The Plebiscite Front's wavering position was in sync with Abdullah's political stance in 1947 when he pushed for "freedom before accession" without expressing complete support for either India or Pakistan.

The support base of the Plebiscite Front was made up of poor and middle-class Kashmiri peasantry, laborers, custodians of shrines, and a few urban families, mostly from old Srinagar city, that had been die-hard supporters of Sheikh Abdullah. The party's main challenge was to make the plebiscite call broad-based, mobilizing villages and towns in support of their cause. This proved a daunting task as the state regime adopted a harsh approach toward individuals sympathetic to the Plebiscite Front. Mridula Sarabhai, a prominent Congress leader who disagreed with New Delhi's decision to remove Abdullah from power, documented different techniques used by the state regimes to demoralize supporters of the Plebiscite Front. The punishments ranged from dismissal from government services to denial of monthly food rations to towns that showed allegiance to the Plebiscite Front.[32] The worst abuse suffered by dissenters was "push back"—the police, without informing the families of political prisoners about their whereabouts, took them to the ceasefire line and physically pushed them to other side.[33]

To mobilize Kashmiri resistance in this early phase, Plebiscite Front activists tapped into concepts inherent to earlier Kashmiri freedom discourses: *haq* (rights), *insaf* (justice), and *izzat* (dignity). Self-determination was equated with demands for civil liberties, the value of human life, and the restoration of Kashmiri dignity. These ideas resonated for the majority of those that, despite state suppression, joined the plebiscite movement to support an ideology that promised them rights and an end to the inhuman living conditions created by the pliant regime. A pamphlet titled *Taqdeer-i-Kashmir* (Fate of Kashmir), written by an anonymous author and published by the Plebiscite Front a few years after its creation, lamented that Kashmiris shackled in the chains of "slavery" had been living without dignity, denied to them by the powerful state. Self-determination, the author believed, was the only way to attain freedom. As a very precious commodity, freedom is not "given" but "gained" through united movements infused with individuals of strong character willing to sacrifice. However, the author cautioned, the path of freedom was treacherous as the Indian puppet regime used "terror" and "desire" to crush such Kashmiri aspirations. While some Kashmiris worried that demanding "truth" in an anti-democratic state would lead to a severe backlash, others, mesmerized by the wealth and riches bestowed by new networks of patronage, remained complicit and indifferent to freedom. This moment in history, the author emphasized, was a test of Kashmiri character; the suppression of dissent and democracy made self-determination not a political option but a life and death struggle for truth and justice.[34]

Kashmiri poets who contributed to the literature of the Plebiscite Front aimed to create among their audience, steeped in Sufi based Islam, an emotional connection to the political demand of "self-determination." They drew from spiritual ethics to present the political resistance in the Valley as a war between forces of *haq* (truth) and *batil* (falsehood). Habib Kaifi's poem "Maarka-i-Haq Wa Batil" (The War between Truth and Falsehood) published in the *Mahaz* during the 1960s emphasized the importance of faith to defeat the powers of "injustice"—a clear reference to the undemocratic puppet regime in power.

Truth and falsehood have been enemies since time immemorial
Pharaoh has always warred with Moses
While the true believer has always worn a crown of thorns
Although falsehood has raised a lot of dust (to hide the truth)
The signs of providence are not dulled and shine brightly
Those who search for God reach their destination
While the worshippers of Satan, forever wander aimlessly [35]

The pro-plebiscite leaders also formed branches in various parts of the state to popularize their ideology. In a 1958 speech to almost a thousand activists in Sopore district, Sofi Muhammad Akbar, the president of the Plebiscite Front, presented "self-determination" as the birthright of every individual. He dismissed the rhetoric of editorials published in *Khidmat*, the official newspaper of the state, that demonized plebiscite activists as "state enemies." Instead he reminded his audience about the "truth" behind their demands, referring to the letter of Lord Mountbatten, attached to the accession document, that had made accession conditional until Kashmiris exercised their right of self-determination. Akbar's speech also activated the concept of "justice" as he invoked another theme that consumed plebiscite activists: the torture unleashed against political dissenters and the denial of Kashmiris' human dignity and self-respect. Akbar drew parallels between the treatment of Kashmiris under despotic Dogra rulers and the present "democratic" state regime, reminding Kashmiris to remain firm in their quest for justice, without which their long-cherished dream of freedom would remain unfulfilled.[36]

The plebiscite activists questioned the legitimacy of the ruling regime that had crushed democracy to retain Kashmir for India. However, Bakshi's regime dismissed the Plebiscite Front's claims that India denied Kashmiris a voice in shaping their future by pointing to the state elections, an opportunity for the masses to participate in the political process. The free and fair elections, an essential component of a democratic state, had no space in Kashmir as the New Delhi-sponsored establishment effectively monopolized elections. In 1957 the state government dissolved the constituent assembly after adopting the constitution, and ordered fresh elections to build the new legislative assembly. To disfranchise voters, a defective and incomplete voters list excluded political dissenters and included bogus names. The regime filed criminal litigation against workers in opposition parties and rearrested political dissenters on parole. The henchmen of the ruling party declared invalid the nomination papers filed by opposing candidates. As a result, these so-called elections saw most candidates "returning unopposed," while the opposition groups in the legislature had zero representation.[37] Dismayed, plebiscite activists questioned India's stance that elections were a substitute for a plebiscite; farcical "elections" under anti-democratic conditions did not represent the real voice of Kashmiris.[38]

Meanwhile, domestic pressure from the Indian opposition parties unhappy with the Congress's Kashmir policy, along with international criticism, became a source of embarrassment for India. In January 1958, Sheikh Abdullah was released from prison and received a warm reception from Kashmiris. Abdullah's popularity had waned when he held political power; however, his dismissal and arrest for resisting complete integration made him a hero even among critics who disagreed with his politics. He dedicated his post-prison time toward reconnecting with the masses and retaking control of the Hazratbal mosque, the platform he had used during his resistance to the Dogra state.

As in the pre-partition era, Kashmiri activists and leaders denied a place within formal political structures shifted to alternative arenas, like the mosques and shrines, to gain legitimacy and mobilize mass support. The language of religion, too, became a tool for mobilization, just as it had when Abdullah was waging a nationalist campaign against the Dogra princely state. In the winter of 1958, Abdullah attended Friday congregations, visited shrines, and quoted the Quran in his political discourses to explain the meaning of the political struggle for self-determination. In a speech at the Hazratbal shrine to commemorate the death of the first caliph, Abdullah drew comparisons between the hardships of Kashmiris and the resilience shown by the Prophet and his companions when faced with countless challenges. Claiming to draw inspiration from the path of "truth" chosen by Imam Hussain, the grandson of the Prophet, in the field of Karbala, who preferred to sacrifice his family rather than accept a corrupt and illegitimate regime, Abdullah promised to follow the same path.

As in Akbar's speech the same year, Abdullah equated the concept of "truth" with the promises of self-determination made to Kashmiris by Indian leadership and the international community; the religious emphasis reminded listeners that holding on to faith (*din*) would provide the people with courage in their search for "justice."[39] This speech invited Kashmiris to offer "sacrifices" to attain freedom, warning them not to be enticed by the material rewards offered by the state regimes who had "sold Kashmiri honour and dignity" for power. Abdullah equated the subsidized rice and other benefits offered to poor Kashmiris by the state regime as a ruse to compel Kashmiris to "accept slavery at the cost of freedom."[40] He questioned the assertion of the state regimes that Kashmiris had accepted accession to India, pointing to the presence of large battalions of the Central Reserve Police and the Peace Brigade at every nook and cranny to suppress dissent. Abdullah's speech, like his countless other elocutions, drew from religious idioms not only to explain his motivations, but also to legitimize his political actions.

The Indian press, upset with Abdullah's rhetoric, labeled demands for self-determination as "anti-India" and branded Abdullah's politicization of religion as "fanatically communal."[41] Abdullah responded in a pamphlet entitled *Why Self-Determination?*[42] The label of "disloyalty" conferred on him by the Indian press, Abdullah argued, was not on firm ground. The Indo-Kashmir relationship was based on mutual agreements and promises. The Congress's support for self-determination at the time of partition had encouraged the National Conference to endorse provisional accession to India. However, with time, India's intransigent position on self-determination "hurt [Kashmiri] sentiments of friendship and love towards India."

Abdullah also dismantled allegations of an imperialistic conspiracy with the United States to convert Kashmir into another Korea and perpetuate war in the region. Since the government found it impossible to prove these allegations against him, Abdullah retorted, they labeled him "communal" to delegitimize his party's demand for self-determination. He emphasized that this label was not a new one—since the 1931 agitation against the Dogra Hindu ruler, the Hindu press had labeled him as a leader of Kashmiri Muslims. Yet at the time of partition, when the entire subcontinent was reeling under religious frenzy, Abdullah's party had made it their top priority to protect Hindu minorities. Taking credit for preventing violence against these minorities, Abdullah reiterated that even in the postcolonial era, "Hindu–Muslim unity" was his basic stance. His aim was to ensure that, despite provocations from Hindu right organizations in Jammu or other parts of India, the Valley would remain safe. This policy was his expression of secularism.

Abdullah's instrumental use of religion to popularize "self-determination," then, was meant to reach a wider Kashmiri audience by tying the plebiscite demand to their religious sensibilities. References to his religious beliefs in speeches, he argued, helped him explain the true nature of Kashmir's political culture to a wider audience without contradicting his policy toward religious minorities. Offering prayers at mosques or reciting verses from the Quran, Abdullah emphasized, was not communalism; rather, he was simply fulfilling religious obligations. He expressed a desire that "every Hindu, Muslim, or Sikh follow their own religious precepts, as every religion teaches the path of truth." If people would truly follow their religions, in fact, they would use a "just approach" in dealing with the Kashmir problem.[43]

Public support for Abdullah and the Plebiscite Front generated anxiety within the ruling regime and they began contemplating ways to curb the situation before it reached a point of no return. Four months after Abdullah's release, the state government, in collaboration with Indian intelligence officers, drafted a case to arrest Abdullah and keep him in prison indefinitely. In 1959, Abdullah and other leaders of the Plebiscite Front faced trial in the Kashmir Conspiracy Case for allegedly "conspiring with Pakistan to bring about the secession of the state from India."[44] The prosecution claimed that Abdullah's close links with a militant group, the "War Council," indicated a desire to subvert the state government and create hostile feelings against India. Abdullah, they alleged, had egged on the War Council to commit violent acts and hosted secret meetings furthering Kashmir's merger with Pakistan, which, in turn, supposedly supplied him and his associates with financial aid, arms and ammunition.[45] Abdullah's wife (Begum Abdullah) was accused of being in league with Pakistan to overthrow the state government; she had allegedly accepted money from Pakistan and used it for "anti-national" activities. Trials related to these accusations continued for five years, with Abdullah spending much of this time behind bars; however, there was no evidence directly linking Abdullah with any conspiracy, either to overthrow the state government or to take Kashmir out of the Indian union by force.

India's policy to stifle political dissent with the assistance of Bakshi regime produced popular resistance in the fateful winter of 1963, when Kashmiris gathered at the historic Lal Chowk (Red Square) to express outrage at the theft of a relic of the Prophet Muhammad housed at the Hazratbal mosque and held in deep reverence by the Kashmiri Muslim community. The Muslim Action Committee, a conglomeration of religious groups and plebiscite parties, united to lead a movement for the recovery of the holy relic. They politicized the agitation, converting the movement for the restoration of the relic into a demand for self-determination. Even after Indian intelligence agencies restored the relic under cover of a "secret operation," the Action Committee refused to yield, demanding Abdullah's release from prison.[46] To curb growing resistance, the state government arrested leaders of the Action Committee, further infuriating Kashmiris.

Kashmiri resistance in this case was clearly not a mere expression of anguish at the mysterious disappearance of the relic, but an outlet for Kashmiri Muslim anger against an India-sponsored state regime created primarily to curb free political expression and integrate Kashmir with India. Although India officially portrayed the holy relic agitation as a religious affair directed against the local administration, it forced India to reconsider the basic premise and structure of its Kashmir policy.[47] The Indian prime minister, in an emergency meeting of the central cabinet, expressed bewilderment at Kashmiri anger, as he believed India had done "so much for the people of Kashmir."[48] Pandit Raghunath Vaishnavi, a prominent member of the Political Conference, wrote to Indian president Dr. S. Radhakrishnan and implored India to take a bold decision on Kashmir and release Sheikh Abdullah, since the "corrupt ruling clique stands discredited, dishonoured and demoralised."[49] Nehru also believed that India's only chance of getting Kashmiri Muslims to accept accession and integration lay in winning over Abdullah, as no political solution was possible without his participation. As a result, India withdrew the case against Abdullah in 1964 due to a lack of credible evidence; Abdullah, for his part, resolved to work with Nehru to find a lasting solution to the Kashmir problem.

The Politics of Plebiscite: New Solutions and Internal Schisms

In the 1960s, the international community proposed slicing Kashmir into two parts, accepting the ceasefire line as a border between India and Pakistan.[50] The plebiscite leadership, concerned by such proposals, linked self-determination with the reunification of the old princely state of Jammu and Kashmir. They aimed to foster an understanding with India and Pakistan to erase the ceasefire line which disrupted economic and social relations and separated families from each other. This section focuses on the strategies adopted by the top brass of the plebiscite leadership on making their voices heard in the international corridors, while navigating internal divide and outside challenges.

The Plebiscite Front emphasized that no permanent solution of the Kashmir dispute was possible without taking into consideration the voices of Kashmiris across the ceasefire line.[51] The division of Kashmir, the Plebiscite Front activists believed, would permanently bifurcate the state's economic resources, ultimately leading to Kashmir's economic strangulation. They demanded reopening Kashmir's "natural road links," which, like the Jhelum Valley road, connected the mountainous Valley with rest of the subcontinent throughout the year. These roads would promote trade and revive Kashmiri self-sufficiency.[52] At the same time, the Plebiscite Front refused to accept the decision of the Kashmir constituent assembly on accession because the assembly failed to consult representatives from Pakistan-administered Kashmir, who formed a third of the population of Jammu and Kashmir. Sheikh Abdullah, too, considered the reunification of Kashmir impossible without involving Pakistan, which controlled half of the former state of Jammu and Kashmir. The official newspaper of the Plebiscite Front, *Mahaz*, focused on bridging the differences between India and Pakistan to end the suspicion and distrust that prevented cooperative and collective efforts for peace. The salvation of Kashmiris was dependent on the friendship between India and Pakistan—if the conflict remained, Kashmiris would be the worst sufferers. Peace in Kashmir, on the other hand, would improve the economy of the entire region and lower the costs of external defense.[53]

Abdullah's insistence on reaching an India–Pakistan understanding irked the public in both countries. In India, many read into it a predilection for Pakistan. Abdullah refuted allegations that he wanted to create discord within India by promoting amity with Pakistan. Any conflict between these two countries, in his words was, "suicidal" for Kashmiris.[54] Other Indians considered Abdullah's release a gamble that might cause India to lose face and territory. They firmly believed that Kashmir's integration with India was non-negotiable, and that any discussion with Pakistan or the United Nations was contrary to nationalist interests.[55] The Pakistani press, meanwhile, unhappy with Abdullah's reticence in his criticism of India, criticized in turn Abdullah's new political stance: trying to be an "apostle of peace between India and Pakistan" rather than a leader working to free "Kashmiris from bondage." [56]

During his negotiations with Nehru, Abdullah came up with the formula of an India–Pakistan–Kashmir confederation. He traveled to Pakistan to convince President Ayub of his new vision for Kashmir.[57] However, President Ayub dismissed the idea of a confederation as an "absurd move" to extend Indian hegemony, which if pursued would lead to the "enslavement" of Pakistan.[58] The concept could "generate pressures in East Pakistan to merge with West Bengal, and in Bengal as a whole to join the confederation as an independent member," destabilizing again the entire region.[59] Abdullah, however, insisted on a meeting between the heads of India and Pakistan, emphasizing that any genuine effort would require negotiation and compromise from all parties. Although Ayub Khan agreed to visit India, the meeting never occurred due to the death of Nehru on May 27, 1964.[60]

Nehru's death changed the situation completely, giving new prominence to those who argued for Kashmir's complete integration with India. Nehru had relied on provincial and district Congress committees, dominated by the landowning castes allied with urban middle-class businessmen and merchants, to strengthen the support base of the Congress. This group succeeded in gaining the upper hand after his death. These representatives of the regional Congress committees had often used Hindu symbolism at the time of elections "to blunt the edge of caste and class conflicts."[61] They maintained that the accession of

Jammu and Kashmir was final and argued for the abrogation of Article 370, a special clause within the Indian constitution that allowed Kashmir to retain its autonomous status. This group demonstrated their political dominance within the Congress not only in their refusal to negotiate with Pakistan, but also in their drive to integrate the Kashmir state with India.

In this climate denuding Article 370 of all powers became the top priority for the Indian administration. G. M. Sadiq, the new prime minister of Jammu and Kashmir, tried to appease Indian leadership by further eroding Article 370 in March 1965. Sadiq's government extended Article 356 of the Indian constitution to Jammu and Kashmir, replacing the legislatively appointed head of state (Sadar-i-Riyasat) with a New Delhi–appointed governor, invested with powers to assume any or all functions of the government under Section 92 of the Jammu and Kashmir constitution.[62] Legally, "any change to Article 370" needed the approval of the state constituent assembly; since that body no longer existed, "the right reverted to the Kashmiris who had elected it." However, the "elected Kashmiri candidates" had, as previously mentioned, come to power through undemocratic "elections." A. G. Noorani, a prominent Indian constitutional expert, stated that legally union powers could not be extended to Jammu and Kashmir without prior concurrence of the state government; even this was strictly provisional and had to be ratified by the state constituent assembly. However, as Kashmir's constituent assembly dispersed in November 1956 after adopting the constitution of Jammu and Kashmir, the authority that could extend the Indian constitution to the state also vanished.[63] New Delhi disagreed with this interpretation and considered "Article 370 not a wall but a tunnel," meaning that the Indian government had eroded Kashmir's special status in the past, and would continue to do so in the future.[64] Notably, neither India nor the state government took the reaction of the state's people into consideration.

In 1965, New Delhi encouraged the state government to merge the National Conference, a regional political party, into a provincial branch of India's ruling Congress Party. Instead of bringing Kashmiris nearer to India, this decision to destroy a regional party that had been a symbol of Kashmiri aspirations during the Dogra period augmented hostility, making any emotional integration all the more difficult. Abdullah challenged the disbandment and replacement of the National Conference as a threat to Kashmiri Muslim identity. He asked Kashmiri Muslims not to join the Congress party and cease social interaction with those individuals who supported this move.[65] The call for a social boycott (*tarqi mawalat*) of individuals associated with the Congress affected Kashmiri Muslims who had joined the party; the excluded majority refused to take part in any celebration or mourning associated with Congress families, causing further divisions.[66]

The schisms in the Kashmiri political discourse of the mid-1960s amplified after Abdullah failed to achieve an India–Pakistan–Kashmir confederation. Abdullah, feeling insecure about the rise of new political actors in the Valley, decided to revitalize his position within plebiscite politics. His primary target was a young leader, Mirwaiz Farooq, who had a strong political base in interior Srinagar city and emerged as an effective leader during the Holy Relic agitation. Abdullah's rivalry with Farooq stemmed from political and ideological differences with the Mirwaiz family dating to the mid-1930s, when Mirwaiz Yusuf Shah (uncle of Mirwaiz Farooq) broke off from Abdullah's Muslim Conference to form the Azad Muslim Conference. To undermine Mirwaiz Farooq, Abdullah refused to recognize his Action Committee for the right of self-determination. Mirwaiz Farooq considered this a personal affront and an effort to curtail his rising power.[67]

Old animosities between these two opposing political ideologies in Kashmir (the Mirwaiz group and Abdullah's supporters) rekindled as both tried to establish their monopoly over the movement for self-determination. In June 1965, Mirwaiz Farooq broke away from the Action Committee, a party which contained members of both the rival groups, and set up his own Awami Mahaz to press for "self-determination of Kashmiris who had only two choices open for them—India or Pakistan—independence or greater autonomy was not an option."[68] Both ideological disagreements and internal personal rivalries hampered unity within the plebiscite movement. Yet they united on one idea: India and Pakistan should accept that sovereignty lay with the people and allow Kashmiris to decide their own political future. Political activists implored all Kashmiris to put aside their petty differences and pursue a quest for human dignity denied to them by India and its pliant regimes.[69]

The plebiscite leadership, extremely disappointed with India and Pakistan's failure to take any positive step toward the resolution of the Kashmir dispute, decided to once again bring the Kashmir issue to the world forum and compel the international community to take initiative. In 1965, Sheikh Abdullah visited various foreign countries, including the United Kingdom, France, Algeria, and Saudi Arabia, appealing for the support of Kashmiri self-determination.[70] At a press conference in Cairo he presented Kashmir's status as a "human problem and a moral issue" that called for sympathy and understanding. In an emotional tone, he stated that the artificial line of control "cuts the land into two, piercing through the hearts of its people, leaving one part of the body on one side and the other on the other side. It separates daughters from mothers, fathers from sons, as they are denied a share in each other's joys and sorrows."[71] He added that uncertainty had paralyzed Kashmiris and prevented the region from attaining economic self-sufficiency. Focusing on the "human sufferings," however, Abdullah implored the world community to analyze this problem from the point of view of Kashmiris who were living this conflict, rather than through the eyes of Indian and Pakistani politicians. Portraying Kashmiris as the "victims" of the conflict, Abdullah emphasized that the "desire of the people of Kashmir is and has always been that the future of the homeland should be left in their hands."[72]

On this same trip, Abdullah's meeting with the Chinese premier Chou En-lai in Algeria, where he welcomed Chinese support for self-determination and accepted an invitation to visit China, profoundly irked the Indian leadership and launched him into new political trouble.[73] In 1962, China had challenged India's sovereignty by claiming Aksai Chin on Ladakh's border, a part of the disputed territory of Jammu and Kashmir. In a new set of Cold War developments, the India–China conflict had encouraged the United States to supply weapons to the Indian armed forces, offending their former ally Pakistan, who then initiated diplomatic and military ties with China.[74] In March 1963, Pakistan ceded a sizeable chunk of territory from northern Jammu and Kashmir to China, exacerbating India's suspicions about the emergence of a Sino-Pakistani alliance.[75] Chinese support to Abdullah, therefore, became a cause of concern for India, which feared another alliance between China and Pakistan to support Kashmiri self-determination, posing a threat to India's national security and containing India's desire for regional hegemony over South Asia. India cancelled Abdullah's passport after his arrival at New Delhi and arrested him for violating the Defence of India Rules.[76]

Abdullah's arrest once again united different strands of the plebiscite movement to express anger against India. Pakistan used Kashmiris' seething anger to its advantage by initiating "Operation Gibraltar," a two-stage military plan to infiltrate Kashmir with armed personnel and incite locals to revolt, providing them with arms and ammunition. In the second stage, with the region already in chaos, regular Pakistani forces would cross over into Kashmir.[77] Pakistan launched this attack on August 9, 1965, the anniversary of Sheikh Abdullah's most recent arrest, and expected "fullest co-operation of the local Muslims."[78]

Despite this confidence, most members of the plebiscite leadership worried about Pakistan's plans to send guerilla forces into the state to "free Kashmir from bondage." Although committed to "self-determination," these leaders believed that change through bloodshed was not in the interest of Kashmiris. It would draw the wrath of the Indian security forces and put at risk the lives of everyone in the territory, including women, children, and the elderly.[79] Leaders from pro-plebiscite political groups like the Action Committee, the Plebiscite Front, the Awami Action Committee, and the Political Conference advised Kashmiris to be neutral. However, a strand of the plebiscite leadership strongly disagreed with their counterparts. The president of the Plebiscite Front, Munshi Ishaq, accused some plebiscite leaders of "sabotaging this event for personal security." In September 1965, he resigned his office in protest, expressing regret that due to the "selfishness and cowardice" of Kashmiri leaders "we missed a golden opportunity to liberate Kashmir."[80]

Despite the neutral stance of most of the plebiscite leaders, some Kashmiris did cooperate with the guerillas, especially in the districts of Baramulla, Budgam, and Srinagar, by providing food and shelter and acting as guides.[81] In the heart of Srinagar city, the locality of Batamaloo emerged as a battleground between the Indian army and Pakistani guerillas, both professional soldiers and Kashmiri volunteers, causing loss of life and property.[82] Ultimately, Pakistan's ambitious operation failed. It involved India and Pakistan in another major war in which neither side was successful in attaining its military objectives. However, it did provoke pro-Pakistan sentiments in the Valley, and a strand of the Kashmir resistance adopted extremist tones in demanding self-determination.

Student Activism: Growing Schisms between the "Majority" and "Minority" over Self-determination

During the mid-1960s, Kashmir's college campuses became hotbeds of resistance and the students chaffed at the existing political authority and displayed displeasure with India and their state-sponsored regime. The India–Pakistan War of 1965 lasted only seventeen days, but helped trigger the unrest. The January 10, 1966, Tashkent Agreement which ended open hostilities put "Kashmir in cold storage" while both countries agreed to continue negotiations during this time toward resolving the Kashmir dispute.[83] The Valley subsequently experienced an increase in student activism on college campuses and in cities, due to the students' frustration with the suffocating political atmosphere in the Valley, which made self-determination very appealing.

The student activists held demonstrations throughout the state and experimented with a more forceful approach to demanding self-determination, hoping to effect fundamental changes in India's Kashmir policy. Often these protestors invoked extraterritorial affiliations and expressed support for Pakistan to counter the unmatched power of the state's forces. Kashmiri Muslim student activism therefore also brought into sharp relief the Hindu minority community's growing dissatisfaction with the Kashmiri demand of self-determination; the Hindu community felt secure in Kashmir's complete accession to India and dismissed student protests as the handiwork of Kashmiri "separatists" who could not relate to India's secular traditions. These conflicting perspectives on "self-determination" led to deepening polarization of the state's majority and minority communities.

In the aftermath of the 1965 war, India declared the slogan of "plebiscite" illegal and New Delhi instructed the state regime to arrest individuals advocating self-determination. It proved difficult for the state government to implement this order, however, as the plebiscite had become an emotive issue supported by a large group of Kashmiris. As the chief minister G. M. Sadiq found it impossible to detain large sections of the Muslim population, the Indian government doubted his credibility as a "nationalist."[84] Instead, India reposed complete faith in the home minister of Jammu and Kashmir, D. P. Dhar, a prominent Kashmiri Hindu member of the state Congress Party. Since 1947, Dhar had been an influential advisor to Indian intelligence in Srinagar, consulted by New Delhi on all vital matters concerning the state.[85] He advised a tough stance and, invoking the same aspirational terms as the plebiscite movement with a totally different end in mind, considered "stringent laws a must to maintain integrity, freedom, and democracy in Kashmir."[86]

In 1966, the Indian government declared the Plebiscite Front and other organizations challenging India's sovereignty illegal. The next year, parliament adopted the "Prevention of Unlawful Activities Bill," which provided the government with sweeping powers to outlaw organizations or detain individuals found guilty of questioning India's sovereignty over any of its territory.[87] The immediate purpose of this bill was to curb any agitation aimed at changing the status of Kashmir. Additionally, the state government introduced scores of arbitrary laws specific to Kashmir, arming the executive with unlimited powers. These laws were not new to Kashmir; previous state governments had also introduced such notifications (Enemy Agents Act, Security Act, and Preventive Detention Act) "for the security of a border state."[88] After the 1965 war, however, they were made more stringent. The network of intelligence agencies developed to such an extent that almost anyone could be suspected of being a police informer. Expenditures on maintaining the Central Intelligence Department (CID) increased from 3 lakh rupees (1963–4) to 48 lakh rupees (1968–9).[89]

Members of the state legislative assembly advised restraint in imposing laws to curtail civil liberties. One especially vocal member, Shamim Ahmed Shamim, in a virulent critique of "black laws," held the Indian government responsible for turning the Valley into one big interrogation center. After the war, he claimed, India had faced a major "psychological crisis"—the trauma of war causing the government to imagine that every Kashmiri was an enemy bent upon destroying state security.[90] Draconian laws rooted out individual freedom and allowed the state the liberty to arrest any individual who expressed a view contrary to state policies. Shamim considered it a grave injustice that the government could label any citizen a Pakistani spy and deny them the opportunity to prove their innocence. The "black laws" invalidated the ruling elite's claim that Kashmir was an integral part of India; if the Indian constitution provided fundamental rights to its citizens, then it was the duty of the government to provide Kashmiris with those same rights.[91]

A section of the Indian intelligentsia also considered a harsh approach toward Kashmiris detrimental to Indian interests. An Indian intellectual, J. J. Singh, considered Kashmiri resentment stemming from the "cruel face India has put before Kashmiris," which forces Kashmiris to see India as a "colonial power." Even though India spent enormous amounts of money providing Kashmir with economic development, he argued, the denial of basic civil liberties deepens the wedge between Kashmir and India.[92] In a scathing critique of India's Kashmir policy, J. P. Narayan, the Indian opposition leader, emphasized that there was no credible proof that the people of the Valley accepted the legal fact of accession. To hold a sizeable chunk of the population against their will, he argued, would cause India to lose credibility in the world arena. He warned such actions would symbolize the "enthronement of aggressive Hindu communalism" and that "communalism is bound in the end to turn upon the Hindu community itself and destroy it."[93] However, the new prime minister of India, Indira Gandhi, who had come to power in January 1966, ignored voices that cautioned restraint. Instead, she focused on consolidating her position within her party and continuing with a tough stance on Kashmir to appease her political base.

In this oppressive political climate, arrests and detentions of pro-plebiscite voices became routine again. The state considered every individual who raised a voice for self-determination a traitor. [94] These harsh methods cowed the older generation, who had been active supporters of Abdullah in his struggle against the Dogra regime; however, the younger generation of Kashmiris, who came of age during the era of pliant regimes and had witnessed exclusion from networks of patronage, expanded their resistance despite state repression. The student movement, led by the Youth League and dominated by middle-class students in professional and degree colleges, reacted against the denial of civil liberties in the

Valley. Students who joined the self-determination movement routinely risked arrest and physical harm, thus putting their academic futures in jeopardy, but gained converts on campuses across the Valley.

Srinagar city emerged as the focal point of demonstrations as students from different colleges came together to protest at the historic Lal Chowk (Red Square) in October 1965. The state ordered the closure of all schools for six months, greatly affecting the academic future of the student community. When schools opened again, the government posted large contingents of the Central Reserve Police Force (CRPF) to intimidate students and prevent demonstrations. This phase saw the movement for self-determination turning into what Cyril Dunn, a British journalist working for *Observer*, called a "children's revolt" that was "terrifying in its innocent determination."[95] Reporting from Kashmir, Dunn clarified that the student movement in the Valley should not evoke images of young men who sought Western libraries in West Asia, but of a generation of children who had witnessed the denial of basic liberties. Even the older generation of Kashmiris, he wrote, seemed in awe of these teens who addressed mass meetings with greater fire than Abdullah. The journalist narrated an incident where a "petite girl aged sixteen" commanded the stage and roused the male students to struggle for rights and justice. She gave a fiery speech, oblivious of any danger, drawing parallels between the policies of the regime and an era of suppression unleashed in nineteenth-century Germany by Chancellor Bismarck against the Catholic Church (the infamous *Kulturkampf*).[96]

Several of the student organizations that cropped up in the mid-1960s submitted memorandums and resolutions to the United Nations expressing their disappointment with the international community, which had debated Kashmir for eighteen years without resolving the conflict. A common theme in student speeches was the denial of basic civil liberties. Comparing the atrocities committed at interrogation centers with the reign of terror unleashed in Nazi Germany by the Gestapo, Kashmiri student narratives highlighted the cruel and repressive methods used to break their spirits.[97] In their documents for the international community, students foregrounded state repression and government indifference toward peaceful protests for rights and liberty.[98] Instead of addressing their concerns, the students wrote, the state accused anyone protesting against its policies either of collaborating with infiltrators or of being infiltrators themselves. Kashmiri youth questioned the logic of security agencies that branded them "infiltrators" in their homeland.

Imploring the world community to see Kashmiri struggles from their eyes, the students lamented that the present state of civil liberties provided them no choice but to contemplate countering violence with violence. One of the resolutions handed to the United Nations by a group of Kashmiri Muslim students stated:

> We have a life in us and we are not dumb-driven cattle [*sic*]. If blood is the language of justice we shall give it.... If India calls us "infiltrators" then it must know that our number is five million. The five million people of Jammu and Kashmir are fighting a just war and all freedom-loving people are on our side. This war has been fought in Cuba and Algeria. It is a people's war against colonialism and imperialism, the war of oppressed against the oppressors and war of justice and truth.... Long live the Revolution![99]

The younger generation expressed extreme disappointment with their elders, accusing them of acting as stooges of the Indian government and directing the self-determination movement to fit Indian interests. During a massive public rally in October 1965 organized by the Plebiscite Front, the students took command of the movement, shouting pro-Pakistan slogans and forcing moderate leaders to take a back seat.[100] They reiterated their commitment to an undivided Kashmir, emphasizing their refusal to accept internal autonomy for India-administered Kashmir as a solution to the Kashmir problem.

The student demonstrators' open expression of support for Pakistan was an expression of desperation by an excluded majority struggling against an oppressive environment, as the students' self-identification with revolutionaries in Cuba and Algeria makes clear. Prominent longtime political activist Prem Nath Bazaz described this emotional state in an October 1965 letter to the Indian prime minister, writing that it was imperative to understand the deeper causes of "pro-Pakistan sentiment," rather than simply equating it with common religious affiliation. He advised Indian leaders to take responsibility for this growing alienation caused by their own repressive policies; placing blame on others would not help. Pakistan would continue to create chaos if Kashmiri Muslims remained unhappy.[101] According to Bazaz, politically mature Kashmiri Muslims, aware of the anti-democratic tendencies and deteriorating economic situation in Pakistan-administered Kashmir, did not support accession to Pakistan. Kashmiris would have forgotten the accession issue, Bazaz argued, if New Delhi had kept a vigilant eye on state regimes and allowed good governance. Giving state regimes a free hand to practice unbridled power had led Kashmiri Muslims to equate democracy with authoritarianism. He implored Indian leaders to understand that the Kashmir problem stemmed from India's failure to convince Kashmiri Muslims that they could live peacefully in India. Although India stated *ad nauseam* that Kashmir was legally a part of India, this stance "loses all moral force when the majority of people cease to have any respect for it or are opposed it."[102] The use of state violence to curb peaceful protests, especially after 1965, created a feeling of powerlessness among Kashmiri Muslims, who ridiculed Indian ideals of democracy and secularism, and instead identified India with repression, persecution, and hooliganism.

The year 1967 witnessed the further politicization of self-determination and communalization of Kashmir's political culture, with deteriorating conditions in the Valley leading to violence, curfews, and arrests. Growing Kashmiri Muslim demands for self-determination made a large section of the Kashmiri Hindu community (Kashmiri Pandits) insecure and increased tensions between the two communities. In August 1967, a seemingly minor incident in Srinagar city provoked a major period of unrest, which pitted Hindu and Muslim communities against each other and came to be known as the Kashmiri Pandit Agitation. Tensions erupted when a Hindu woman (Parmeshwari Handoo) married a Muslim man (Ghulam Rasool Kanth) and converted to Islam. The leaders of the Hindu community labeled this marriage as an "abduction" and convinced the girl's mother to file a police case alleging that she was a minor. However, police investigations revealed that Handoo was, at eighteen, a legal adult and had married of her own free will. Despite family and community pressure, she refused to buckle and end her marriage.

Unhappy with the police investigation, the leaders of the Hindu community organized a Hindu Action Committee to take the issue to court, arguing that Handoo "had no right to enter wedlock as she was a minor."[103] While the case was pending, the agitators demanded that Sadiq's government use its discretionary power to hand the girl over to her mother, with or without her permission. The Muslim chief minister, G. M. Sadiq, expressed his inability to take any steps while the matter was before the High Court. The Hindu Action Committee then demanded the dismissal of the state government and the imposition of governor's rule in Kashmir. The Hindu right politicized the incident, encouraging Kashmiri Hindus to use it as a focus for their wider grievances against the government and the Muslim community.

The educated Kashmiri Pandit community had deep-seated complaints against the state government.[104] Although Hindus had dominated the service sector in the colonial era, the spread of education among Muslims in postcolonial Kashmir ended the Hindu monopoly and made the service sector a source of competition between the two communities. Additionally, corruption and nepotism within the state government excluded many deserving Hindus from promotions and jobs. Kashmiri Hindus wanted to widen the network for service-sector jobs and ensure their community's rightful share of central positions. They resented the push for self-determination; if the majority Muslim community exercised this right to vote for accession to Pakistan, it could jeopardize their security as a part of the larger Hindu majority in India. The Pandit Agitation helped them to establish political distance from the Muslim majority and emphasize that despite their minority status, they were not powerless—they had the support of the entirety of Hindu India. These events complicated the relationship between the two communities and even caused a split within the ruling Congress Party; barring a few exceptions, Hindu and Muslim members took contrary positions on the Kashmiri Pandit Agitation.

India's Hindu right encouraged the Kashmiri Hindu community to express resentment about the preferential employment of Kashmiri Muslims through public demonstrations. Their rhetoric addressed the injustice of a state government that sacrificed the economic interests of the Hindu minority to appease "pro-Pakistani Kashmiri Muslims."[105] Their provocative statements went to the extent of asking Kashmiri Muslims to leave India if they wanted to harp on self-determination. Although the anti-Muslim essence of the agitation stemmed from feelings of anger and insecurity, in their zeal to express political dissent agitators indulged in acts that widened the gulf between the two communities. Most Kashmir Muslims considered armed personnel a symbol of oppression, while the Kashmiri Hindu community felt that the presence of Indian armed forces was essential for their security in a Muslim-dominated state. During the agitation over the Handoo incident, the Hindus "deliberately fraternized" with the Indian army and the CRPF, offering gifts and sweets in the presence of "Muslim onlookers" and generating resentment.[106] Furthermore, Hindu right parties exhorted Kashmiri Hindus to be courageous, assuring them that any untoward incident against the Hindu community in Kashmir would provoke a violent reaction against Indian Muslims.[107]

The Muslim community was "neutral" in the initial stages of the Kashmiri Pandit Agitation; however, the threatening statements of Hindu right groups and violent demonstrations in Jammu provoked a strong counterreaction. In a massive demonstration at Srinagar, Kashmiri Muslims burned effigies of Hindu rightist leaders, expressing anger against their threats of expulsion and calling for self-determination. The protests took on a political color: the Hindu community considered any demand for self-determination to be anti-national and a threat to India's sovereignty, while the Muslim students, disillusioned with Indian policies and figurehead regimes, deliberately shouted pro-Pakistan slogans to express dissent with Kashmir and India.[108] The verbal clashes created a volatile political situation that could have erupted into major riots. To control the situation in the city, the government clamped down with a sixty-hour curfew, ordered press censorship, and deployed armed contingents of the CRPF.

Many Kashmiri intellectuals expressed extreme disappointment with the supporters of the Kashmiri Pandit Agitation. Journalist and politician Shamim Ahmed Shamim considered the agitation responsible for destroying the spirit of tolerance that had prevented major communal riots in 1947.[109] He argued that the Pandit agitation added a "new dimension" to Kashmiri identity, making Kashmiris focus more on religious identity than regional oneness. The agitation, he believed, set the wrong tone; it failed to address the larger issues faced by Kashmiris, irrespective of their religious denomination. The Hindu community complained of discrimination, yet forgot to include the excluded majority of Kashmiri Muslims who shared similar grievances against a corrupt government. Shamim admitted that the Pandit community had raised important points about the challenges faced by Kashmiri minorities; however, he believed, their voices would have carried more weight had they won the support of the Kashmiri Muslim community and widened their definition of minorities to include Indian Muslims, who not only faced discrimination but also lived in constant fear of riots in Hindu-majority India.[110]

While the politicization of "self-determination" pushed the majority and minority communities away from each other, the Indian government watched with concern the radicalization of student plebiscite activists who began contemplating armed resistance to stop the violation of their civil liberties. Many activists considered armed might their only option to force India to grant Kashmiris self-determination. In the 1960s a network of local "resistance cells" emerged among the student body; most members came from middle-class families and were studying in professional colleges, but in some cases they even included government employees. These groups organized strikes and demonstrations, circulated pro-plebiscite posters, and worked on securing arms and ammunition. In 1966 one such cell, the Students' Revolutionary Council, caught the attention of the administration in the Valley as they circulated "Red Kashmir" posters "bearing a map of India with Jammu and Kashmir marked as a separate entity in red ink." A year later this group assaulted a Border Security Force (BSF) sentry and snatched his rifle.[111]

The key leaders of the Students' Revolutionary Council (Ghulam Rasool Zehgeer, Fazal Haq Qureshi, and Nazir Ahmad Wani) stirred what they called a "revolution" by organizing Al-Fatah. This organization, based at Awantipora (south Kashmir), intended to operate an armed movement to gather international attention.[112] The preamble of the radical organization's manifesto used the metaphorical descriptors of "elephant" and "mosquito" to explain the Kashmiri struggle against India, an unequal battle in which the elephant, despite its obvious advantage, is unsuccessful against the "stealth" of the mosquito. The Al-Fatah activists, aware of anti-colonialist guerilla movements around the globe, borrowed this analogy from American journalist Walter Lippmann, who, writing about another global power and another guerilla force in South East Asia, predicted the defeat of the greatest military in the world by the guerillas of the Vietcong, "not because the mosquitoes are too brave or too fanatical, but because mosquitoes do not surrender to elephants."[113] Likewise, the leaders of Al-Fatah believed that guerilla warfare in Kashmir could defeat the sophisticated mechanized war machinery of the Indian state. The modus operandi of Al-Fatah activists involved seizing weapons from unaware policemen or indulging in armed bank robberies like the notorious Hazratbal Robbery Case, with the money looted from the banks used to secure weapons.[114]

Indian intellectuals and political leaders viewed the growing Kashmiri Muslim extremism in the Valley with apprehension, especially as they realized that Muslim alienation was combined with a lack of legitimate leadership to negotiate with. A series of Indian writings after the 1965 war argued that this event had foreclosed the option of plebiscite in Kashmir. Further, these voices refused to consider Pakistan a party to the Kashmir dispute after its "unprovoked aggression." As a result, they emphasized direct negotiations with legitimate Kashmiri leaders.[115]

In these new circumstances, the best solution was to restore a "moderate" Kashmiri voice (that is, Sheikh Abdullah) to power and grant Kashmir autonomy and "self-government" within the ambit of the Indian constitution. These political leaders made it clear to Abdullah that no Indian government could ever put the issue to the vote in Kashmir in a form that would offer an alternative to accession. However, a "new autonomy arrangement" could be a possibility. Kashmiris would have to be satisfied with elections; however, unlike in previous elections, Abdullah would have a chance to advocate for a novel approach.[116] Opposition leaders presented a memorandum to the Indian parliament with almost 163 signatures demanding Abdullah's release.[117] Ironically, this "new" Indian stance on Kashmir bore a striking resemblance to the position India had adopted in 1947. Faced with tribal raids that year, the Indian government had considered it sufficient to ascertain Abdullah's support and consider it binding for all Kashmiris, without providing an opportunity for the people themselves to decide their future.

A group of Kashmiri intellectuals aware of the political feelers put out by India about a possible reconciliation with Abdullah decided to organize the State People's

Convention in October 1968. The convention invited intellectuals, politicians, journalists, and students from every region of the state and with diverse opinions, hoping to build a consensus on possible solutions.[118] The convention brought sub-regional and communal differences on the question of self-determination into sharp relief, while also highlighting that the Indian government and Kashmir's excluded majority had perhaps irretrievably opposing stances on Kashmir. The inaugural address of Indian opposition leader Jayaprakash Narayan emphasized that the government of India "cannot accept a solution that places Kashmir outside the union of India," thus contradicting Abdullah's discourse of self-determination.[119]

Convention debates on the future status of Jammu and Kashmir also exposed the ways categories of "minority" and "majority" played into understandings of self-determination. Some Kashmiri Muslims demanded a plebiscite to erase an artificial ceasefire line that divided Kashmiri families and turned the entire region into a military cantonment, denying Kashmiris free movement within their own state. While many Kashmiri Muslim voices called for a free and sovereign Kashmir, some rejected the idea of independence in favor of accession to Pakistan.[120] The ideas from the Valley, meanwhile, clashed with the solutions suggested by participants from Jammu who suggested a federal setup, a kind of regional autonomy that decentralized political power and ensured an equitable distribution of resources across the three regions of the state.[121] Most Hindus from both Jammu and the Valley rejected the idea of plebiscite and asked Kashmiris to find a solution within the confines of the Indian constitution—in other words, rejecting the demand of the self-determination movement, a vote in which Kashmiris could determine whether accession to India was acceptable. Due to these essential contradictions, the State People's Convention failed to arrive at a consensus on ways to negotiate a solution that was acceptable to all communities and sub-regions.[122]

This new challenge demanded that Abdullah balance two extremes: India was adamant that accession was a closed issue, while Kashmir's excluded majority, mobilized on the plank of self-determination for twenty-two years, was unwilling to compromise. Abdullah's public speeches continued emphasizing the right of self-determination to generate mass support; however, behind closed doors, he was planning a compromise with New Delhi. A strand of the Plebiscite Front, tired of resistance and eager to embrace power, denounced the party's "unproductive political stance," encouraging Abdullah to choose the parliamentary path.[123] This "moderate" faction influenced the Plebiscite Front to participate in the *panchayat* and assembly elections, despite a party ban on participation in elections until the right of self-determination was accepted. Many plebiscite activists considered the decision to participate in elections to be a deviation from the party's basic objectives and subsequently distanced themselves from the Plebiscite Front.[124]

Sheikh Abdullah, aware of the growing discontent among youth and plebiscite activists against any compromise with New Delhi on the question of self-determination, called a second session of the State People's Convention in June 1970. He put forward the new policies of the Plebiscite Front. Its main proposal was for a federal government arrangement consisting of one supreme and several regional bodies. The regions listed included Pakistan-controlled Azad Kashmir and northern areas. The Front envisaged a reunited Jammu and Kashmir that "would either be independent or join Pakistan."[125] Although this stance allowed Abdullah to regain popularity, it caused apprehension among the state Congress Party.

Rather than deal with the Plebiscite Front democratically and allow them to participate in the 1971 parliamentary elections, Prime Minister Indira Gandhi declared that India would not allow any party to undemine the validity of Kashmir's accession to India.[126] The state Congress Party enlisted the services of the Jamaat-i-Islami, an Islamist political party, to develop an alternative power structure and undermine the appeal of the Plebiscite Front in Jammu and Kashmir. The Indian government accused the Plebiscite Front of associating with the extremist student group Al-Fatah.[127] Although Abdullah strongly denied these allegations, the government banned him from Jammu and Kashmir for three months under the Indian Maintenance of Public Order Act. In Jammu and Kashmir, itself, "at least 350 officials and members of the Front were arrested under the Jammu and Kashmir Preventive Detention Act in a series of police raids."[128] In January 1971, the Plebiscite Front was declared an "unlawful association," on the grounds that it had tried to bring about the secession of Jammu and Kashmir from India.[129] These steps eliminated any Plebiscite Front involvement in the March 1971 elections and allowed the state Congress Party to win uncontested.

The political climate of the subcontinent transformed once more with the India–Pakistan war of 1971, which led to the dismemberment of Pakistan and changed the dynamics of power in South Asia, with India emerging as a dominant power.[130] After these events, the Plebiscite Front believed that "the only course open to them was to sincerely declare their fidelity to India" and to regard the "limits set by [the Indian constitution] as unassailable frontiers and move accordingly."[131] The primary issue now became not whether accession was final, but what the status of Jammu and Kashmir would be within India. The best bargain for Abdullah, given these wider conditions, was to secure as much autonomy as possible. Abdullah modified the tone and content of his self-determination discourse: from the political choice between India, Pakistan, and independence, self-determination now became a "right to secure a place of respect and honour for peasants, workers and all other communities."[132]

Negotiations between the Indian government and Mirza Afzal Beg, the representative of the Plebiscite Front, ultimately culminated in the Indira–Abdullah Accord of 1975.[133] The accord marked a substantial compromise on the part of Abdullah, who not only accepted the finality of Jammu and Kashmir's accession to India, but acknowledged the amendments made in Article 370 of the Indian constitution, the article which had given Jammu and Kashmir autonomous status. Although the accord emphasized that Article 370 would govern relations between New Delhi and Kashmir, between 1954 and the mid-1970s nearly 30 constitutional orders "integrating" Jammu and Kashmir with India had been issued from New Delhi and 262 union laws had been made applicable to the state.[134] The only substantial difference between Jammu and Kashmir and other Indian states now related to the rights of permanent residents. Abdullah's insistence on retaining the language of Article 370 during his negotiations with New Delhi was motivated by his need to convince his followers that he had not compromised with India over Jammu and Kashmir's autonomy.

Following the accord, Abdullah disbanded the Plebiscite Front and re-created the National Conference, a new party acceptable to all three sub-regions of Jammu and Kashmir state. Mirza Afzal Beg joined Abdullah in emphasizing that a plebiscite was not the only method of ascertaining the people's wishes: "other honourable courses to know the will of the people could be explored."[135] A significant gap now developed between the political elite of the plebiscite movement and the Kashmiri Muslim public opinion. While the former accepted the reality of Indian sovereignty over Jammu and Kashmir, the latter found it difficult to compromise with the "new situation." Abdullah's conciliatory stance created a backlash; during his negotiations with New Delhi, pro-plebiscite activists strongly objected to any settlement with India. After decades of fiery rhetoric and real political suppression, ordinary Kashmiris' feeling of betrayal was intense; they failed to comprehend this political shift, blaming their leaders for compromising in pursuit of power.[136]

Deep unrest erupted in protest demonstrations in the districts of Baramulla and Anantnag, home to several dissenting Plebiscite Front members. The district of Anantnag organized a grassroots movement against the accord. The localities of Sarnal and Kadipora, inhabited by *gaba* (rug) makers and crewel embroiders who were not dependent on government employment, expressed political dissent without dread of economic reprisal. Searching for any excuse to protest, resistant voices in Anantnag organized a major uprising in May 1973 that spread to other towns and districts of the Valley.[137] Students at Anantnag Degree College discovered Arthur Mee's *Book of Knowledge: Children's Encyclopedia*, containing a drawing of the Prophet Muhammad, in their college library.[138] As representations of the Prophet are strictly forbidden in Islam, the students started demonstrations against the government which had permitted the import of such publications to Kashmir. Although the book was immediately banned, the incident sparked more general protests, leading to four deaths and over a hundred arrests. The unrest gained momentum in November when students at Srinagar objected to the government's decision to change the name of Women's College to Nehru Memorial College, forcing the government to rescind the change.[139]

In the old city of Srinagar, Abdullah's political compromise met with criticism from his old rival Mirwaiz Farooq, the leader of Awami Mahaz, who still interpreted Kashmiri self-determination as accession to Pakistan. As an anti-accord proponent, Mirwaiz used his platform at the Jama Masjid to organize rallies and protests. He saw the accord as a reflection of Abdullah's duplicity after decades during which excluded Kashmiris had supported him, and his stance on self-determination, despite immense hardships. Abdullah's dictatorial behavior, Mirwaiz argued, was in tune with his past actions as when he had imposed his views on Kashmiris in 1947. Then and now, Abdullah had chosen to ignore voices of dissent and rule with an iron fist, throwing democratic norms to the winds. Prior to the accord, he reminded Abdullah that Kashmir was at the "crossroads of history." Any wrong decision would not only cost Abdullah his place in Kashmir's body politic, but also wash away his sacrifices and services from the past. Mirwaiz Farooq emphasized that his party would resist any decision arrived at with New Delhi by any individual, however important, unilaterally.[140]

Meanwhile, another group, the Jamaat-i-Islami, with a strong foothold in Sopore district, labeled the accord as a "sell-out." Although the Jamaat had aligned with the Congress during the 1971 assembly elections to undercut the Plebiscite Front, the Jamaat considered Kashmir a disputed issue and missed no opportunity to question India's legitimacy in Kashmir. As such, the Jamaat too questioned Abdullah's wisdom in making people undergo years of privations, bloodshed, and continuous restlessness if his party still eventually had to affirm the reality of Kashmir's accession to India. The accord's critics also complained that negotiations were carried on secretly, with Kashmiris not taken into confidence until the deal was struck early in 1975.[141]

Although a pragmatic move, Abdullah's compromise with New Delhi had tarnished his image as a self-sacrificing Kashmiri leader who put the interests of Kashmiris before his own. To appease the radicalized student community, Abdullah's new administration considered it prudent to withdraw cases against the Al-Fatah student activists; some of the radicals were co-opted and given important positions within the administration.[142] However, large sections of Kashmiris, especially the young, continued to reject the finality of Jammu and Kashmir's accession to India. The anti-accord forces suspended revolutionary activity, acknowledging the new geopolitical realities of the subcontinent, but continued to organize protests and demonstrations. The older generation of Kashmiris, however, was willing to give Abdullah a chance to provide them with democratic rights and good governance.

Delhi versus Kashmir: Autonomy, Centralization, and Regional Dissidence

In the 1970s and 1980s, in the aftermath of the accord, the idea of "self-determination" largely ceased to be relevant: the new slogan of "autonomy" now dominated state politics. Despite National Conference claims of "exceptionalism," the accord made Kashmir a constituent unit of India: an integral and inseparable part of India. However, granting political rights to Kashmiris proved insufficient to abate the bitterness accumulated over decades of misgovernance. Although many Kashmiris were willing to give Abdullah's compromise a chance, the scars of mental and physical trauma endured during the Plebiscite Front movement remained. However, Abdullah went ahead with re-establishing his authority and securing political power for his kin, but found it a challenge to resist New Delhi's centralization.

Abdullah realized that the maintenance of his political base in the Valley depended on taking a posture of autonomy to compensate for abandoning the slogan of self-determination. However, this new position placed Kashmir in conflict with New Delhi again as the growing strength of regional parties in the rest of India eroded the social base of the Indian National Congress, increasing its feeling of insecurity.[143] In the 1980s, the Congress moved toward centralization and demanded the complete subordination of regional parties, while the National Conference was keen to retain a distinctive Kashmiri identity. As the opposing ideologies of integration and autonomy fought for dominance in Jammu and

Kashmir, the tensions between sub-regions and communities prevented real peace from taking hold despite the 1975 accord.

To offset a presumed adverse reaction to the accord within Kashmir, Abdullah asserted his political independence from New Delhi at the beginning of this period. In February 1975, the Congress Party which controlled the state legislature unanimously elected Sheikh Abdullah as leader, hoping that he would join the ruling state Congress Party. Abdullah refused to oblige; instead he invited the Congress members to join his old party, the National Conference.[144] In 1977 the Congress Party suffered a debacle in the general elections in India. At this point the Congress members of the Jammu and Kashmir legislative assembly withdrew their support from Abdullah, hoping to form a Congress government in the state. However, Abdullah persuaded the state governor, L. K. Jha, to dissolve the assembly and order fresh elections, intending to democratically oust the state Congress Party and take complete control.[145]

Most Indian narratives consider that the "free and fair" elections of 1977 brought Kashmir a step closer to emotional integration with India. The fairness of the elections, the story goes, allowed a regional party to rout a ruling national party and made Kashmiris realize the benefits of being a part of democratic India. Others consider this moment a public approval for Kashmir's integration with India.[146] Such assessments ignore the strategies that helped the National Conference win the 1977 elections. Abdullah's popularity had reached an unprecedented low after the accord; to mobilize votes he now made the restoration of Kashmir's autonomy his campaign platform. His opponents in the Janata Party, an uneasy alliance with clashing political ideologies, united around "fighting National Conference fascism" and preventing a reemergence of "authoritarian rule in Jammu and Kashmir."[147] The Janata Party promised an era of good governance and democratic rights, yet the central Janata leadership stood for the complete abrogation of Article 370. This contradiction within the Janata Party, attacked by Abdullah in his political campaign, prevented it from emerging victorious.

The National Conference, meanwhile, reiterated that any attempt to abrogate Article 370 would shake the basis of Kashmir's accession to India and presented the election as a referendum on Kashmiri self-respect.[148] The anti-Muslim rhetoric of Hindu right groups within the Janata Party was freely highlighted to turn Kashmiris against them. A close associate of Abdullah, Mirza Afzal Beg, even declared the 1977 elections a plebiscite over the issue of Kashmir's international sovereignty. He showed a green handkerchief, a symbolic reference to Pakistan, at various public gatherings, to express National Conference support of the Muslim community.[149] In other words, the electorate in Kashmir voted not for emotional integration with India, but for internal autonomy. As Noorani asserts, "the 1975 accord had collapsed."[150] However, this election highlighted the polarization between Kashmir and Jammu. Abdullah's support was confined to the Valley, while Jammu voted for the parties advocating complete integration.

Abdullah's second tenure failed to offset the networks of corruption and nepotism of previous regimes; instead, it became an extension of these entrenched power structures. A new educated generation of politically aware Kashmiris, unwilling to accept any form of misgovernance and disappointed with Abdullah, supported the anti-accord groups who emerged as voices of resistance to Abdullah's political ideology. They expressed dissent through demonstrations, challenging the image of Sheikh Abdullah as the sole representative of Kashmiri Muslims.[151] Ironically given his extensive career of resistance and imprisonment, in 1977 Abdullah promulgated the Public Safety Ordinance Act, giving the state power to detain individuals in the interests of "state security" for two years without providing grounds for the detention.[152] *Azan*, the official mouthpiece of the Jamaat, questioned Abdullah's authoritarianism, which they interpreted as a political crutch used by an unpopular leader with a dwindling support base to control belligerent voices.[153]

In the waning years of his life, Abdullah remained committed to restoring Kashmir's autonomy, despite shrinking political space for regional assertation within India and despite his law directed against political dissidents who questioned his accord. Abdullah's "autonomy" rhetoric frustrated Indira Gandhi, the other partner in the controversial accord, who after resuming power in January 1980 focused primarily on subordinating the states. Abdullah refused to be cowed and asserted his own autonomy by challenging New Delhi's authority whenever he could. The issue that finally ruptured relations between New Delhi and Kashmir was the question of the "state-subject" category, introduced by the Dogra maharaja in 1927 and retained by the postcolonial governments. The Jammu and Kashmir constitution defined a permanent resident "as a person who is a citizen of India and was a state subject on 14 May 1954." This law allowed only residents of Jammu and Kashmir to purchase land and seek employment in the state. It also provided a provision for displaced state subjects in "territory now included in Pakistan" to return under the "permit of resettlement" and become Indian citizens and permanent residents of the state.[154] The state legislature was legally and constitutionally competent to make laws for the resettlement of its permanent residents living in Pakistan. This law, implemented for the first time in 1955, allowed 646 people from Pakistan-administered Kashmir to resettle in the state.[155]

Although India had been successful in eroding Article 370, the special privileges granted to state residents had remained intact. The presence of almost fifty thousand refugees from West Pakistan along the border in Jammu province, however, complicated this matter. The West-Pakistani Refugees Action Committee, created in the 1950s, agitated intermittently for permanent resident status and proprietary rights over evacuee lands. In 1957, the constituent assembly expressed concern that granting permanent citizenship to people from "outside" the state would render safeguards for state subjects useless. It would encourage individuals from outside the state to claim "state domicile" and seek the rights of permanent subjects.[156] Instead of taking any action, the assembly left this issue to future governments. In 1979, the Refugees Action Committee again took up this issue with the state government, demanding that the legislature alter the legal definition of the state subject. However, the state government decided only to solve the problem of Kashmiri state subjects located across the ceasefire line, for whom there was a clear-cut provision in the state constitution.[157]

As the "refugee question" gained visibility in India, Abdullah decided to use it to reassert Kashmir's autonomy. In March 1980, a National Conference legislative assembly member introduced the Permanent Resettlement Bill, enabling state subjects who had migrated to Pakistan-administered Kashmir before 1954 to resettle permanently in the state. The bill stated that applications for such permits could come from the persons directly or through their relations living on the Indian side of the border. The bill, based on humanitarian considerations, sought the "reunion of hard-pressed blood relations who were separated by the crucial circumstances of 1947."[158] Although the state legislature passed the bill, Governor B. K. Nehru withheld his consent on constitutional grounds, arguing that "the state cannot confer Indian citizenship on those who choose to accept Pakistani nationality. Since it is the central government alone which controls the entry of foreigners into India, the state legislature was not, therefore competent to enact a bill providing for the return from Pakistan of those persons who have desired to come back and resettle in the state."[159] However, the legislative assembly criticized the governor's judgment, which bypassed the state constitution and undermined the state's political autonomy.

The bill precipitated tensions not only between New Delhi and Kashmir but also within regions and communities in the state. The most vocal reaction came from West Pakistani refugees in Jammu, who launched into a period of agitation. All political forces in India, moreover, vehemently opposed the bill; many argued that it would pose a threat to India's security by letting hundreds of Pakistanis operate as spies in India. Describing it as a "mischievous piece of legislation," they questioned the logic of allowing people who had "*deliberately* migrated to Pakistan" and acquired Pakistani citizenship to return to Indian Kashmir.[160]

The Indian press once again labeled Abdullah a "Muslim communalist," while Abdullah in turn denounced critics of the bill as "Hindu communalists" out to convert the Muslim-majority state of Jammu and Kashmir into one with a Muslim minority. Abdullah considered the demand of his critics to grant state-subject rights to refugees from West Pakistan a determined effort to change the demographic composition of the state. Why should Indians support rights for Hindus who had migrated to Jammu and Kashmir from Pakistan, but resist the rights of Kashmiri Muslims in Pakistan-administered Kashmir to return to their homeland? Furthermore, he disagreed that the Indian citizenship act was applicable to Jammu and Kashmir, as that would violate Article 370. The state, he added, had its own citizenship act and the right to enact legislation on the subject belonged to the state government.[161] The Resettlement Bill, if passed, would have allowed Kashmir to decide on citizenship, and even make decisions about the "residents of Azad Kashmir," which might have made the ceasefire line irrelevant.[162] This was Abdullah's last attempt to defy New Delhi in pursuit of real autonomy. He died in October 1982, passing the mantle of restoring Jammu and Kashmir's political autonomy to his son, Farooq Abdullah.

With the transfer of power from father to son, the National Conference faced new challenges. Farooq Abdullah, a doctor by profession, had spent most of his youth in London while his father was leading the plebiscite movement, and had no political experience in the Valley. Eager to assert his authority and eliminate potential rivals, old party elites and family members who had steered National Conference during rough times, Farooq Abdullah exiled them from the party. These policies deepened schisms within the National Conference and these disgruntled politicians became Farooq Abdullah's enemies, eventually collaborating with New Delhi to bring about his downfall.[163]

Farooq Abdullah's tenure as chief minister of Jammu and Kashmir in the 1980s coincided with a period during which New Delhi sought strong centralized governance against rising regional assertion in Punjab, Assam, Tamil Nadu, and the North East. As the Congress Party grew more insecure in the face of this regional dissidence, it showed no patience toward the assertion of political will by mainstream Kashmiri leadership. Farooq Abdullah's decision not to sign an electoral alliance with the Congress Party during the 1983 elections frustrated Indian prime minister Indira Gandhi. Farooq considered that an alliance with the Congress would not only dilute the separate identity of the National Conference, but also enhance resentment among Kashmiris still seething about the Indira–Abdullah accord of 1975.[164] Instead, Farooq Abdullah considered it prudent to expand his base by aligning with his father's old rival Mirwaiz Farooq (Awami Majlis Amal), putting an end to decades of bitterness.[165] Mirwaiz Farooq, as previously noted, a vocal advocate of self-determination, did not directly participate in the elections, but offered unconditional support for Abdullah. The slogan "Long Live Double Farooq" became common, while the flags of both parties were hoisted side by side at street crossings.[166]

During the elections of 1983, both New Delhi and Kashmiri politicians legitimized religion's politicization and utilized majoritarian mobilization techniques for electoral ends.[167] The Congress Party considered any regional opposition "anti-nationalist" and labeled individuals who challenged the centre's domination "disloyal." True "nationalist" groups, according to this rhetoric, supported Indira Gandhi.[168] Gandhi's electoral strategy, which promised to protect the nation from anti-national Muslim minorities, deliberately vilified Muslims as "unpatriotic" and "secessionist." In an explicit appeal to the base of the Hindu right, the Congress Party openly sided with Jammu, promising to remove "regional imbalances" and assuring them that they were "a part of Hindu India that has been neglected by Muslim Kashmir."[169]

Playing up the threat of Kashmiri Muslim domination, Gandhi emphasized that the Resettlement Bill would further enhance the minority status of Hindus and Sikhs by admitting displaced Muslims who had fled their homes in 1947. The National Conference, for its part, also played the majoritarian mobilization card, expressing suspicions of Hindu domination and demanding the preservation of Article 370 to ensure power would not be transferred from Srinagar to New Delhi. The elections polarized around issues of region and religion, with Muslim-dominated areas of Jammu voting for National Conference candidates, just as Hindus voted for the Congress.[170] In the end, the National Conference won 46 of 75 seats, while the Congress Party led the opposition with 26.[171]

Farooq Abdullah's success in the 1983 elections encouraged him to seek recognition at a national level—a decision that ultimately cost him severely. After joining a nationalist alliance against the Congress Party that included other states clamoring for more autonomy from New Delhi, Farooq Abdullah arranged an opposition conclave at Srinagar attended by fifty-nine opposition leaders representing seventeen regional parties.[172] New Delhi interpreted this as a renewed Kashmiri challenge to centralized power and decided to discredit Abdullah's reputation and pave the path for his dismissal. Farooq Abdullah was accused of collaborating with political groups like the Jammu and Kashmir Liberation Front, an England-based Kashmiri nationalist group fighting for

Kashmir's independence; he had participated in their meetings in the 1970s when his father was leading the plebiscite movement.[173]

However, it was an October 1983 cricket match between India and the West Indies played at Srinagar that provided New Delhi with the opportunity to remove Farooq Abdullah from power. During the match, a representative of the People's League, a party that stood for self-determination and refused to accept the accord of 1975, mobilized Kashmiris to show their resentment against India. A large section of the crowd cheered the West Indies and booed the Indian team. As the match was broadcast live in different parts of the world, India felt embarrassed about this open demonstration of dissent and the continued international presence of the Kashmir issue. Indira Gandhi maneuvered to topple Farooq Abdullah's government in alliance with G. M. Shah, his brother-in-law, who had always wanted to inherit Sheikh Abdullah's role. On July 1, 1984, twenty-six members of the Congress Party, along with thirteen National Conference supporters, withdrew support from Farooq Abdullah and pledged their confidence in G. M. Shah. Delhi feared retaliation from Kashmiris against this illegal and undemocratic action. The governor brought in many paramilitary personnel from India to maintain law and order.[174]

The ease with which India subverted the democratic process crystallized Kashmiri Muslim apprehensions about their irrelevance for India. Farooq Abdullah's unconstitutional dismissal sent a message to Kashmiris that even when their mainstream leaders professed loyalty to India, they were neither trusted nor free to express any opposition. G. M. Shah, the new chief minister, lacked popular support and had no political influence of his own, either organizational or legislative; he relied totally on New Delhi. He only remained in power through silencing dissidents, imposing a continuous curfew in the valley and deploying massive parailitary forces.[175]

The center–state dynamic increased Kashmiri anger directed not only at India but at their own leaders. Once again, the themes of justice, rights, and dignity that defined Kashmiri understandings of self-determination dominated Kashmiri narratives of resistances. Kashmiri voices of dissent considered the abandoning of self-determination by their leaders a betrayal of faith that plunged the future Kashmiri generations into chaos and turmoil. They were convinced that justice (*insaf*) had eluded them, while their leaders had been unsuccessful in restoring Kashmiri dignity (*izzat*). Farooq Rehmani, a prominent member of the anti-accord People's League, expressed disdain for the Indian government's definition of "patriots" as those who neither acknowledged their Kashmiri identity nor embraced their Muslim distinctiveness, but only expressed loyalty to Congress. An ideal patriot would have no morality but would be willing to succumb to the lure of power and money.[176] Kashmiris expressed unhappiness with leaders who, they felt, allowed themselves to be pawns of New Delhi because of personal vendettas or the desire for political power.

Corruption, nepotism, and regional dissidence compounded the chaos and confusion that marked G. M. Shah's government. New Delhi took direct control, withdrew their support of Shah's government, and declared governor's rule over Kashmir after the 1986 communal riots in Jammu.[177] The sub-regions of Jammu and Ladakh, whose majority Hindu and Buddhist populations, respectively, felt politically ignored and economically marginalized by Kashmiri Muslims from the Valley, welcomed New Delhi's direct control over Kashmir.

Sub-regional Tensions and the Conflicting Understandings of Self-determination in Jammu and Ladakh

Self-determination took on a different meaning in Jammu and Ladakh. The religiously and ethnically diverse regions of Jammu, Ladakh, and Kashmir had long and rival ambitions and aspirations. After the accession of the princely state of Jammu and Kashmir to India and the abdication of the maharaja, political power within the state shifted from Jammu to Srinagar. The National Conference government, dominated by Kashmiri Muslims from the Valley, introduced agrarian reforms in the 1950s that confiscated large tracts of land from mostly Hindu landowners, generating criticism that the reforms were a deliberate attempt to alter the socioeconomic power of the Hindu community. In the 1950s these dispossessed social groups, uncertain about Kashmir's political future due to its disputed nature, feared that in the event of a plebiscite the Muslim majority of Kashmir would vote for Pakistan and jeopardize their political future. Hindu rightist groups, with a strong presence in Jammu, played up these fears and launched a powerful and aggressive campaign to integrate Jammu and Kashmir. Although their agitation led to the dismissal of Sheikh Abdullah and to the emergence of India-sponsored regimes which played a critical role in the abrogation of Article 370, these outcomes did not abate resentment in Jammu.

The spectre of a United Nations–mandated plebiscite made many Jammuites feel at a disadvantage. There was a growing feeling among them that the Valley always received preferential treatment as compared to other sub-regions of the state because New Delhi wanted to appease Kashmiri Muslim majority, and win over local elites. The India-sponsored regimes based in the Valley misused endless funds provided to them by New Delhi in lieu of constitutionally integrating Kashmir. The residents of Jammu complained about discrimination in state services and the lack of development activity in their sub-region. In 1968, the state administration tried to appease Jammu by setting up a commission of inquiry to investigate these sub-regional imbalances.[178] Its report showed that even though development expenditures during the second and the third five-year plans were almost equally shared between the sub-regions of Jammu and Kashmir, in the employment sector the Kashmir Valley showed an increase compared to Jammu. Kashmir's population was 53.3 percent of the total population of the state, but its share of service jobs in April 1967 was 60.9 percent. Jammu's population was 44.2 percent of the total population of the state, but its share of service employment was only 36.1 percent.[179] Furthermore, the Valley had a majority share of professional institutions, industrial plants, state-owned corporations, and banks, while the same level of investment had not been made in Jammu. This uneven economic development and discriminatory recruitment policies caused deep resentment in Jammu.

Intellectuals from Jammu debated these sub-regional disparities and suggested numerous ways to overcome them. Balraj Puri, a prominent voice from Jammu, in his 1958 *Debate on Jammu Problem*, blamed the centralization of political power in the Valley, which excluded Jammu from power-sharing arrangements, for creating discontent. The position of chief minister invariably belonged to the Valley, as it was the most populous sub-region of the state. India, he wrote, needed to address the genuine resentments of Jammuites, instead of appeasing Kashmir, due to its international importance.[180] He expressed concern that India's policy of placing "politically corrupt and morally bankrupt" regimes in power to integrate the region, while asking Jammuites to remain silent about misgovernance for the sake of larger national interests, only widened the gulf between the two regions. He also took issue with labeling every valid grievance of Jammu "communal," just because linguistically and religiously Jammu was different from the Muslim-majority Valley.[181]

In 1966, Balraj Puri and his allies (including Ved Bhasin, the editor of leading daily newspaper *Kashmir Times*) formed the Jammu Autonomy Forum, seeking an equitable share of political power along with internal autonomy for all three sub-regions of the state. These "regional autonomists" supported Article 370 and autonomy of the state within India, but at the same time demanded autonomy for sub-regions of Jammu and Kashmir. They considered that the "militant nationalism" of the Hindu rightist parties had "undermined Jammu's unique role as a geopolitical bridge between Kashmir and the rest of India."[182] Although the autonomists never supported the idea of Kashmiri self-determination, they insisted on the restoration of democracy and civil liberties in Kashmir.

In the late 1960s, Sheikh Abdullah also supported sub-regional autonomy as the best solution for the inter-regional tensions. The Jammu and Kashmir State People's Convention, presided over by Abdullah in 1968 and 1970 and attended by almost the entire spectrum of Kashmir politics, adopted a five-tier internal constitution that suggested maximum regional autonomy subject to the unity of the state, as well as further devolution of political power to the district, town, and *panchayat* levels. Under Abdullah's leadership, the revived National Conference also proposed in a 1976 policy statement "to reorganize constitutional set up of the state which would provide regional autonomy and further decentralize power."[183] Yet, once in power, Abdullah's government never implemented these promises, substantiating the feeling among Jammu Hindus that the Valley wanted to retain its political domination.

Conversely, another group within Jammu rejected the idea of both regional autonomy and self-determination and demanded the state's complete integration with India. This group's support base stemmed from the urban middle classes, the rural upper castes, and students who leaned toward the Hindu right. The integrationists rejected Kashmiri Muslim demands for autonomy and claimed Kashmir for India due to its being a site of ancient Hindu culture and heritage, visible throughout the Valley's landscape which was dotted with Hindu temples and pilgrimage sites. Balraj Madhok, a prominent voice from Jammu's Hindu right, reminded his audience about the Hindu holy places like "the caves of Amarnath, the springs of Mattan and Kheer Bhawani and the temples of Martanda and Shankaracharya" that attract pilgrims to Kashmir from all over India.[184] He blamed Kashmiri Muslim leadership for denuding the cultural and religious links that tied Kashmir with India while projecting Kashmiri Muslim identity as different from Indian identity. Madhok also leveled criticism at Indian leadership for providing liberal economic aid and raising the per capita income of Kashmiris, but making no effort to connect Kashmir "culturally and emotionally with its pre-Islamic past." The more affluent Kashmiri Muslims became, Madhok argued, the deeper their religious awareness grew, making them "fanatical" and "intolerant" toward India. The only solution was to alter the Valley's demography and make the region a Hindu-majority area.[185] To implement this long-standing policy, Hindu nationalists pushed for the resettlement of Hindu refugees from West Punjab with rights to buy and own land in Kashmir, despite Article 35A which restricted such privileges only to state-subjects.

Hindu rightist groups in Jammu consistently and vehemently opposed any suggestion of decentralized internal government and equitable power sharing between regions. In 1965 the Hindu rightist groups in Jammu offered a solution to trifurcate Jammu and Kashmir, which would lead to union territory status for Buddhist-majority Ladakh and the reconstitution of Hindu-majority Jammu either as a separate state or as a part of the neighboring Indian state of Himachal Pradesh.[186] This meant fragmenting and partitioning Jammu and Kashmir "on essentially communal lines," while the fate of the Valley was left unspecified, "apart from emphasizing the need to crush 'secessionism' and 'fundamentalism' without mercy and quarter."[187]

After the 1980s, the Congress Party, as the principal opposition party in the state, also found it politically viable in Jammu to divert the regional urge for autonomy into an integrationist slogan. The underlying reason for the Congress and the Hindutva[188] communalists' vehement opposition to decentralized internal governance, according to Sumantra Bose, was that "tiered, organic devolution of power leading to an autonomous Jammu" would have meant "Jammu Kashmir as a whole was an autonomous unit governing its own affairs, with only residual authority over key matters vested in Delhi. Only a democratically-constituted, substantively autonomous Jammu and Kashmir government can possibly delegate authority to lower levels, including the constituent regions."[189] New Delhi's resistance to the idea of autonomy for Jammu merged with the stance of the Hindu rightist groups. Within the sub-regions, a culture of fear grew as an increased focus on religious identities brought regional disparities into sharp relief.

In October 1987, pent-up regional discontent spilled into the massive Durbar Move agitation, consuming both the Valley and Jammu. The state of Jammu and Kashmir had two capitals, Jammu in winter and Srinagar in summer, a tradition since the Dogra Raj. The cause of the unrest was a state government order reducing the number of offices moved to Jammu for the winter.[190] The official reasoning was that the Durbar move (the name of the twice-yearly shift) was a costly enterprise, and the government needed to save money. However, the inhabitants of Jammu interpreted the order as an attempt to downgrade their status, and a first step toward permanently shifting the capital to the Valley. The Jammu Bar Association organized intense agitation, forcing the government to rescind the order. The order's withdrawal, however, instantly sparked counter-agitation in Kashmir Valley, led by the Bar Association of Srinagar, against the "abject surrender of National Conference government before the Jammu agitators."[191] Although the agitation failed to achieve much of substance, it reinforced political differences, creating a volatile situation.

Ladakh, another sub-region with a vast territory but a small population, evenly divided between Buddhists in Leh district and Muslims inhabiting Kargil, also had grievances against the Valley-dominated administration.[192] Like the Hindus of Jammu, Ladakhi Buddhists distrusted the state government due to the feeling that they were discriminated against in the service sector and in the allocation of funds for development. Ladakhis demanded the distribution of government funds on the basis of area, rather than population. The Sikri Commission of 1979, set up by the government to report on regional imbalances, suggested giving Ladakh greater weight in fund allocation, but rejected some of Ladakh's funding demands. In the 1980s, Ladakhi Buddhists unhappy with the recommendations of the Sikri Commission demanded to opt out of Jammu and Kashmir state. They wanted New Delhi to directly administer the region, even though this demand clashed with the aspirations of the 47 percent Ladakhi Muslims living in the Kargil district, who did not want to opt out of Muslim-majority Kashmir. As a compromise in the 1980s, the Ladakhi Buddhists laid out new demands for regional autonomy and Scheduled Tribe status. The Jammu and Kashmir government expressed no reservations against Ladakh being granted a Scheduled Tribe status by New Delhi; however, the autonomous status for Ladakh remained unresolved, causing deep resentment.[193]

These simmering tensions between the Kashmir Valley and Ladakh morphed into a religious conflict after the 1987 elections. Since the 1960s, the Hindu right organizations based in Jammu had supported Ladakhi grievances against Kashmiri domination at every forum. In 1969, the Hindu nationalist party, the Rashtriya Swayamsevak Sangh (RSS) in its official newspaper, *Organizer*, covered Ladakhi resentment, "citing a memorandum by the Buddhist Action Committee of Leh listing allegations of Muslim aggression against the Buddhist population."[194] The Ladakhi Buddhist Association developed a close relationship with the Hindu right parties in India. They interpreted Ladakhi political and economic discontent in cultural and religious terms, arguing that the cultural identity of Ladakhis was unsafe in a Kashmiri-dominated Muslim government.[195] In the late 1980s, the association began a social boycott of the Muslim community, forcing Ladakhi Muslims to close their businesses and move to the Valley. The contacts forged with Hindu rightist forces, especially the Bharatiya Janata Party (BJP), enabled them to raise awareness at a national level of their demand for a union territory status, directly ruled by New Delhi.[196] In the late 1980s, then, while the Hindu and Buddhist minorities felt insecure in a Muslim-dominated Kashmir and sought identification and integration with India, the Valley went the opposite way and adopted a militant posture against India's denial of democracy and liberties in Kashmir. While a large section of the minorities in Jammu and Ladakh resented the political dominance of the Valley-based Muslims and wanted to integrate with India completely, they were less passionate about giving the same right of self-determination to the majority community.

Conclusion

Kashmiris' conflicting understandings of "self-determination" in different temporal and spatial frames reveal the many adjustments, compromises, and confrontations made as different communities and regions within India-administered Kashmir negotiated for rights. The indiscriminate repression of Kashmiris, whether done directly by India or at the behest of state-sponsored regimes, made self-determination appealing for a vast majority of Kashmiri Muslims. As a nonviolent demand, self-determination drew on concepts of justice, truth, and rights inherent in the earlier discourses on freedom, to combat organized state suppression. Kashmiris imagined self-determination to usher in freedoms and liberties, while also erasing artificial barriers and "borders" created by the nation-states that separated families from each other. This understanding of self-determination informed political debates and instances of popular resistance against oppressive state policies in India-administered Kashmir. However, as some political ideologues framed self-determination as accession to India or Pakistan, the minorities in heterogenous Jammu and Kashmir state with their own political visions challenged the majority's demand for self-determination and presented it as "anti-national." In their perceptions, Kashmiri Muslim participation in elections held under the auspices of the Indian constitution, even if rigged, was a sufficient expression of self-determination.

Across the line of control, the concept of self-determination also fascinated the inhabitants of Pakistan-administered Kashmir (Azad Kashmir) as they struggled to end the domination of Pakistani bureaucracy that controlled Azad Kashmir by propping up regimes that remained subservient and toed Pakistan's political line. Pakistan remained focused on gaining the territory on the Indian side of Kashmir and made very little effort to improve the economic and political conditions of Azad Kashmir, causing discontent and large-scale migrations to Britain. The demand for self-determination on the Pakistani side of the ceasefire line manifested from demands for autonomy to complete independence. The next chapter traces the political imaginary of Kashmiris living in Pakistan-administered Kashmir and the wider transnational community as they reframed "self-determination" in the international arena in several important ways.

Notes

1. Extract from a folk song cited in Aisha Begum's article "We Will Have a Plebiscite," *Mahaz*, Srinagar, October 13, 1964.
2. Behera, *Demystifying Kashmir*, 106.

3. S. M. Abdullah, *The Blazing Chinar*, 238–9.
4. B. P. L. Bedi and Freda Bedi, *Sheikh Abdullah: His Life and Ideals* (Srinagar: 1949), 18; F. M. Hassnain, *Freedom Struggle in Kashmir* (New Delhi: Rima, 1988), 140.
5. Lakhanpal, *Essential Documents and Notes on Kashmir Dispute*, 72.
6. Noorani, *The Constitutional History of Jammu and Kashmir*, 202.
7. P. N. Bazaz, *The History of Struggle for Freedom in Kashmir*, 704.
8. Lamb, *Kashmir: A Disputed Legacy, 1846–1990*, 230; Sumantra Bose, *Kashmir: Roots of Conflict, Paths to Peace*, 71.
9. Lamb, *Kashmir: A Disputed Legacy, 1846–1990*, 230; Sumantra Bose, *Kashmir: Roots of Conflict, Paths to Peace*, 71.
10. Balraj Puri, "Pakistani Movement in Kashmir," *Kashmir Affairs* 2, no. 8 (November–December 1960): 17–25.
11. Prem Nath Bazaz, "Spokesman of the Oppressed," *Voice of Kashmir* 1, no. 1, Delhi: Kashmir Democratic Union (November 1954): 1–4.
12. Prem Nath Bazaz, "Thoughts on Kashmir in Bondage," *Voice of Kashmir* 2, no. 1, Delhi: Kashmir Democratic Union (January 1955): 12–17.
13. P. N. Bazaz, "Thoughts on Kashmir in Bondage."
14. Prem Nath Bazaz, "Bandung Brings Kashmir's Freedom Nearer," *Voice of Kashmir* 11, no. 5, Delhi: Kashmir Democratic Union (May 1955): 1–5.
15. "Formation of the New Political Party Called the Kashmir Political Conference," File No. 1(10)-K/53, 1953, Ministry of States, National Archives of India, New Delhi.
16. R. S. Gull, "Man of the Match," *Kashmir Life*, May 26, 2014.
17. Puri, "Pakistani Movement in Kashmir," 17–25.
18. "Formation of the New Political Party Called the Kashmir Political Conference."
19. Sarabhai, "The Role of Communalists and Their Patrons in Jammu and Kashmir State since 9th August 1953."
20. Puri, "Pakistani Movement in Kashmir," 17–25.
21. P. N. Bazaz, *Kashmir in Crucible*, 87.
22. Akhtar Mohiuddin, *Looking into the Heart of Life* (Srinagar: Book Bank, 2010), 163–76.
23. Ali and Limaye, *Report on Kashmir*, 21–33.
24. Prem Nath Bazaz, "Praja Socialist Party and Kashmir," *Voice of Kashmir* 2, no. 1, Delhi: Kashmir Democratic Union (January 1955): 1–5.
25. Sheikh Muhammad Abdullah, *Former Prime Minister of Kashmir Appeals from Behind the Prison Walls* (Washington, DC: Information Division, Embassy of Pakistan, 1957), 6.
26. S. M. Abdullah, *Former Prime Minister of Kashmir Appeals from Behind the Prison Walls.*
27. For details, see *Mahaz-i-Raishumari Ka Ehlan Haq*, No. 1 (Star Press, Srinagar, 1956).

28. Interview with Ghulam Ahmed Bukhari, District President (Budgam branch), Plebiscite Front, Srinagar, May 2009.
29. B. Mirza Muhammad Afzal Beg, *White Paper on Constitutional Relationship of Kashmir with India* (Srinagar: Jammu and Kashmir Plebiscite Front, 1964), 6–7.
30. For details, see Munshi Muhammad Ishaq, *Nidai-i-Haq* (Srinagar: Kashmir Book Foundation, 2014).
31. P. N. Gunjoo, *Portrait of Sheikh Muhammad Abdullah* (Srinagar, 1964), 41–2.
32. "Resumption of Repression by National Conference Office Bearers," 1957, All India Congress Committee Papers, 2nd Installment, F. No. 3589, Nehru Memorial Museum and Library, New Delhi.
33. Sarabhai, "Jammu and Kashmir Ingress Control Act."
34. *Taqdeer-i-Kashmir*, Srinagar, August 7, 1956 (personal archives of Syed Ghulam Ahmed Bukhari, Beerwah, Kashmir).
35. Extract from Habib Kawifi's poem "The Struggle between Truth and Falsehood," *Mahaz*, October 3, 1964, translated here by Syed Taffazull Hussain, Srinagar.
36. Sofi Muhammad Akbar, *Mahaz-i-Raishumari: Ehlan-i-Haq* (Srinagar: Star Press, February 1956), 2–15 (from the personal archives of Syed Ghulam Ahmed Bukhari, Beerwah, Kashmir).
37. Mridula Sarabhai, "Free and Fair Electioneering?" 1957, All India Congress Committee Papers, 2nd Installment, F. No. 3589, Nehru Memorial Museum and Library, New Delhi.
38. Recommendations made by the Special Convocation, All Jammu and Kashmir Plebiscite Front, 1965 (notes from the personal archives of Syed Ghulam Ahmed Bukhari, Beerwah, Kashmir).
39. "Call for Justice: Sheikh Muhammad Abdullah's Speeches," 1958, All India Congress Committee, 2nd Installment, F. No. 3589, Nehru Memorial Museum and Library, New Delhi.
40. "Call for Justice: Sheikh Muhammad Abdullah's Speeches."
41. "Call for Justice: Sheikh Muhammad Abdullah's Speeches."
42. Sheikh Muhammad Abdullah, *Why Self-Determination?* (Srinagar: Jammu and Kashmir Plebiscite Front, 1959), 5–9.
43. S. M. Abdullah, *Why Self-Determination?* 5–9.
44. For details, see Mirza Muhammad Afzal Beg, *The Kashmir Conspiracy Case: Reports* (Srinagar: Legal Defense Committee, 1961); "Kashmir Conspiracy Case: Correspondence between Sheikh Abdullah and Others," Home Ministry, 18/11/59, 1959, National Archives of India, New Delhi.
45. Mullik, *Kashmir: My Years with Nehru*, 72–6.
46. Giyas-Ud-Din, *Understanding the Kashmir Insurgency*, 36.
47. For details, see Mullik, *Kashmir: My Years with Nehru*.
48. Mullik, *Kashmir: My Years with Nehru*, 133–5.
49. Mona Bhan, *Pandit Rughonath Vaishnavi Annual Lecture* (Srinagar, July 2016), 19–30.

50. *Studies for Kashmir Solution Based on Functional Arrangement*, SEA 70/1 (Kew, UK: National Archives, 1963).
51. Ghulam Nabi Khayal, "Eak Manhoos Lakheer," *Mahaz*, Srinagar, July 25, 1964.
52. G. Lone, "Making Kashmir Economy Self-Reliant," Srinagar, *Mahaz*, August 1964.
53. Pandit Rughonath Vaishnavi, "Hind-Pak Dosti ki Sharat-i-Muqqadam," *Mahaz*, Srinagar, August 15, 1964.
54. Sheikh Muhammad Abdullah, *Jammu and Kashmir: A Human Problem* (Srinagar: Jammu and Kashmir Plebiscite Front, 1965), 2–3.
55. *Times of India*, New Delhi, May 3, 1964.
56. "Sheikh Abdullah's Tour of Pakistan," *Times of India*, New Delhi, May 27, 1964.
57. Y. D. Gundevia, *The Testament of Sheikh Abdullah* (New Delhi: Palit & Palit, 1974), 127-131.
58. Mohammad Ayub Khan, *Friends Not Masters* (London: Oxford University Press, 1967), 128.
59. Inder Malhotra, "Rear View: Difficulty of Coming Together," *Indian Express*, June 13, 2018.
60. Gundevia, *The Testament of Sheikh Abdullah*, 130.
61. Jalal, *Democracy and Authoritarianism in South Asia*, 207.
62. P. N. Bazaz, *Kashmir in Crucible*, 83.
63. Noorani, *Article 370*, 15.
64. P. N. Bazaz, *Kashmir in Crucible*, 83.
65. Mir Qasim, *My Life and Times* (New Delhi: Allied Publishers, 1992), 106.
66. P. N. Bazaz, *Kashmir in Crucible*, 99–100.
67. P. N. Bazaz, *Kashmir in Crucible*, 70–84.
68. "Rift within the Plebiscite Front: A Note," Kashmir Internal Situation, DO 133/175, 1967, National Archives, Kew, UK.
69. Muhammad Noor-ud-din, "Freedom Is Our Birth Right," *Mahaz*, Srinagar, October 17, 1964.
70. "Sheikh Abdullah's Statements during His Visit Abroad—March–April 1964," Ministry of Information and Broadcasting, Kashmir Publicity, 1964, File No: 426/vi (20)/1964/KP, National Archives of India, New Delhi; Vashishth, *Sheikh Abdullah*, 134–8.
71. S. M. Abdullah, *Jammu and Kashmir*, 2–3.
72. "Sheikh Abdullah's Statements during His Visit Abroad—March–April, 1964," Ministry of Information and Broadcasting, Kashmir Publicity, 1964.
73. "Sheikh Abdullah's Statements during His Visit Abroad—March–April, 1964," Ministry of Information and Broadcasting, Kashmir Publicity, 1964; Gundevia, *The Testament of Sheikh Abdullah*, 132–7.
74. Sumantra Bose, *Kashmir: Roots of Conflict, Paths to Peace*, 76–7.
75. Lamb, *Kashmir: A Disputed Legacy, 1846–1990*, 240–3.
76. Gundevia, *The Testament of Sheikh Abdullah*, 90.

77. Lamb, *Kashmir: A Disputed Legacy, 1846–1990*, 258.
78. P. N. Bazaz, *Kashmir in Crucible*, 94–102.
79. P. N. Bazaz, *Kashmir in Crucible*, 94–7.
80. Munshi Muhammad Ishaq, *Nidai-i- Haq* (Srinagar: Self-published, 1969) (personal archives of M. Ishaq, Srinagar), 9–10.
81. Rao Farman Ali Malik, *Kashmir under the Shadow of Gun* (New Delhi: Uppal Publishing House, 2012), 36–8.
82. P. N. Bazaz, *Kashmir in Crucible*, 102–3.
83. Lamb, *Kashmir: A Disputed Legacy, 1846–1990*, 270–1.
84. S. Butt, *Kashmir in Flames*, 122–7.
85. Lamb, *Kashmir: A Disputed Legacy, 1846–1990*, 281.
86. Government of Jammu and Kashmir, *Jammu and Kashmir Legislative Assembly Debates* (Srinagar: Government Press, August–September 1967), 64–5.
87. "Letter from the Permanent Representative of Pakistan Addressed to the President of the Security Council, 28 December 1967," Kashmir Internal Situation, DO 133/175, 1968, National Archives, Kew, UK.
88. P. N. Bazaz, *Kashmir in Crucible*, 203–12.
89. Government of Jammu and Kashmir, *Jammu and Kashmir Legislative Assembly Debates* (Jammu: Government Press, February–March 1970), 58.
90. Government of Jammu and Kashmir, *Jammu and Kashmir Legislative Assembly Debates* (Srinagar: Government Press, August–September 1967), 64–5.
91. Government of Jammu and Kashmir, *Jammu and Kashmir Legislative Assembly Debates* (August–September 1967), 64–5.
92. J. J. Singh, "Kashmir: A Garland of Razors around India's Neck," October 1966, in Private Papers of J.P. Narayan, 3rd Installment, Sub. F. No. 90, Nehru Memorial Museum and Library, New Delhi.
93. J. P. Narayan, "Constitutional Integration without Emotional Integration Meaningless," in Balraj Puri, *J. P. on Jammu and Kashmir* (New Delhi: Gyan Publishing House, 2005), 61–4.
94. "Anti-India Propaganda through "Sada-i-Kashmir," Ministry of External Affairs, Kashmir Section, P-V/102/13/66, 1966, National Archives of India, New Delhi.
95. Cyril Dunn, "Bayonets to Crush a Children's Revolt," *Observer*, 25 October 1965, Kashmir Internal Situation, DO 133/173, 1968, National Archives, Kew, UK, 367.
96. Dunn, "Bayonets to Crush a Children's Revolt."
97. Anti-India Propaganda through "Sada-i-Kashmir," Ministry of External Affairs, Kashmir Section, P-V/102/13/66, 1966, National Archives of India, New Delhi.
98. "Full Text of the Kashmir Student Resolution Handed Over to the United Nations Headquarters Srinagar, on 10 October 1965," Kashmir Internal Situation, DO 133/173, 1965, National Archives, Kew, UK, 362.
99. "Full Text of the Kashmir Student Resolution Handed Over to the United Nations Headquarters Srinagar, on 10 October 1965," 362.
100. Allinson, *Kashmir: A Report*.

101. "Letter from Prem Nath Bazaz to the Indian Prime Minister Lal Bahadur Shastri, October 1965" (personal archives of Bushan Bazaz, Delhi).
102. "Letter from Prem Nath Bazaz to the Indian Prime Minister Lal Bahadur Shastri, October 1965."
103. "Memorandum Presented to the Union Home Ministry by the Hindu Action Committee," Home Department, IS-112-A/ 67, 1967, Jammu Archives.
104. For details about grievances of Kashmiri Hindus, see P. N. Bazaz, *Kashmir Pandit Agitation and Its Aftermath*, 6–12.
105. P. N. Bazaz, *Kashmir Pandit Agitation and Its Aftermath*, 20.
106. P. N. Bazaz, *Kashmir Pandit Agitation and Its Aftermath*, 18.
107. P. N. Bazaz, *Kashmir Pandit Agitation and Its Aftermath*, 14.
108. For details, see P. N. Bazaz, *Kashmiri Pandit Agitation and Its Aftermath.*
109. Shamim Ahmed Shamim, "Kashmir Pandit Agitation Has Weakened the Roots of Kashmir's Accession with India," in Qurrat-ul-Ain, *Aina-Numa*, Part 4 (Srinagar: TFC Centre, 2004), 69–81.
110. Shamim, "Kashmir Pandit Agitation Has Weakened the Roots of Kashmir's Accession with India," 69–81.
111. Malik, *Kashmir under the Shadow of Gun*, 55–7, 85–7.
112. Malik, *Kashmir under the Shadow of Gun*, 55–7, 85–7.
113. Walter Lippmann, "Elephants Can't Defeat Mosquitoes," *Tonawanda News*, New York, December 4, 1967.
114. Malik, *Kashmir under the Shadow of Gun*, 55–7, 85–7.
115. R. K. Patil, "Future Trends of the Political Situation in Kashmir," 1968, Private Papers of J. P. Narayan, 3rd Installment, Sub. F. No. 91, Nehru Memorial Museum and Library, New Delhi.
116. Patil, "Future Trends of the Political Situation in Kashmir," 1968, Private Papers of J. P. Narayan.
117. Vashishth, *Sheikh Abdullah*, 142–3.
118. P. N. Bazaz, *Democracy through Intimidation and Terror*, 18–20.
119. Jayaprakash Narayan, "Inaugural Speech," in Manzoor Fazili, *Kashmir Predilection* (Srinagar: Gulshan Publications, 1988), 77–87.
120. For detailed proposals submitted to the convention, refer to Fazili, *Kashmir Predilection*.
121. Fazili, *Kashmir Predilection*, 125–43, 198–204.
122. Balraj Puri, "State People's Convention: An Assessment," *Economic and Political Weekly* 5, no. 37 (September 12, 1970): 1524–6.
123. Ishaq, *Nidai-i-Haq* (1969), 8–10.
124. Ishaq, *Nidai-i-Haq* (1969), 8–10.
125. Lamb, *Kashmir: A Disputed Legacy, 1846–1990*, 285.
126. Lamb, *Kashmir: A Disputed Legacy, 1846–1990*, 285.
127. "Letter by Sheikh Abdullah to J.P. Narayanan, January 1970," Private Papers of J.P. Narayanan, Nehru Memorial Library, New Delhi.

128. *Times of India*, New Delhi, January 9, 1971; Lamb, *Kashmir: A Disputed Legacy, 1846–1990*, 286.
129. Gundevia, *The Testament of Sheikh Abdullah*, 141.
130. Sumantra Bose, *Kashmir: Roots of Conflict, Paths to Peace*, 89.
131. Ghulam Nabi Hagroo, "Fidelity Call to Muslims," *Motherland*, New Delhi, September 12, 1971.
132. *Motherland*, New Delhi, September 15, 1972.
133. G. R. Najar, *Kashmir Accord 1975: A Political Analysis* (Srinagar: Gulshan Publishers, 1988).
134. Sumantra Bose, *Kashmir: Roots of Conflict-Paths to Peace*, 88.
135. *Motherland*, New Delhi, June 2, 1975.
136. For details, refer to Rehmani, *Azadi ki Talash*; Sanaullah Butt, *Uhad-Nama-Kashmir* (Srinagar: Ali Muhammad and Sons, 1996).
137. Altaf Hussain, *Shabir Shah: A Living Legend in Kashmir History* (Srinagar: Noble Publishing House, 1994), 66–7.
138. Lamb, *Kashmir: A Disputed Legacy, 1846–1990*, 304–5.
139. S. Butt, *Kashmir in Flames*, 176–7.
140. *Indian Express*, New Delhi, September 2, 1974.
141. *Azan*, Srinagar, February 5, 1973; P. N. Bazaz, *Democracy through Intimidation and Terror*, 28.
142. "Al-Fatah: The Biggest Espionage Group in Kashmir," *India Today*, February 29, 1984, available at https://www.indiatoday.in/magazine/cover-story/story/19840229-al-fatah-is-biggest-espionage-groups-unearthed-in-jammu-kashmir-802836-1984-02-29, accessed January 21, 2018.
143. For details, see Atul Kholi, *Democracy and Discontent: India's Growing Crisis of Governability* (Cambridge: Cambridge University Press, 1990).
144. Lamb, *Kashmir: A Disputed Legacy, 1846–1990*, 309.
145. Lamb, *Kashmir: A Disputed Legacy, 1846–1990*, 313.
146. For details, see M. J. Akbar, *Kashmir: Behind the Vale* (New Delhi: Viking Publishers, 1991); Puri, *Kashmir towards Insurgency*.
147. P. N. Bazaz, *Democracy through Intimidation and Terror*, 40–1.
148. Saraf, *Kashmiris Fight for Freedom*, Vol. 2, 1279–82.
149. Victoria Schofield, *Kashmir in Conflict: India, Pakistan and the Unending War* (London: I.B. Tauris, 1998), 125.
150. Noorani, *Article 370*, 17.
151. For details, see Rehmani, *Azadi ki Talash*.
152. Ghulam Hassan Khan, *Government and Politics of Jammu and Kashmir* (Srinagar: Self-published, 1988), 158–60.
153. *Azan*, Srinagar, September 10, 1980.
154. G. H. Khan, *Government and Politics of Jammu and Kashmir*, 157–62.
155. Ram Krishen Kaul, *Political and Constitutional Development of Jammu and Kashmir* (Delhi: Seema Publications, 1984), 226.

156. Government of Jammu and Kashmir, *Constituent Assembly Debates* (Srinagar: Jammu and Kashmir Government, 1956), 154–5.
157. For details, see G. H. Khan, *Government and Politics of Jammu and Kashmir.*
158. Balraj Puri, "Implications of the Settlement Bill," *Kashmir Times*, Jammu, April 27, 1982.
159. G. H. Khan, *Government and Politics of Jammu and Kashmir*, 111.
160. Kuldip Nayyar, "Kashmir's Search for Identity," *Kashmir Times*, Jammu, May 13, 1982 (emphasis mine).
161. Speech delivered by Sheikh Muhammad Abdullah at Hazratbal Shrine on May 28, 1982, *Kashmir Times*, Jammu, May 29, 1982.
162. Lamb, *Kashmir: A Disputed Legacy, 1846–1990*, 320.
163. *Democracy a Casualty in Jammu and Kashmir*, pamphlet published by the General Secretary, Jammu and Kashmir National Conference (personal archives of Shabir Mujahid).
164. Farooq Abdullah, *My Dismissal* (New Delhi: Vikas Publishing House, 1985), 21.
165. F. Abdullah, *My Dismissal*, 28.
166. Tavleen Singh, *Kashmir: A Tragedy of Errors* (Delhi: Viking 1995), 33.
167. Sumantra Bose, *Kashmir: Roots of Conflict, Paths to Peace*, 90–1.
168. F. Abdullah, *My Dismissal*, 28–9.
169. "Mrs. Gandhi in a New Role: As CPI Leader Sees It," *Times of India*, New Delhi, June 22, 1983
170. Balraj Puri, "Congress I: Short Sighted Game," *Economic and Political Weekly* 18, no. 49 (December 3, 1983): 2051–2.
171. Sumantra Bose, *The Challenge in Kashmir*, 42.
172. Puri, "Congress I," 45; F. Abdullah, *My Dismissal*, 45–61.
173. F. Abdullah, *My Dismissal*, 30–1, 36–9.
174. Bhattacharjea, *Kashmir: The Wounded Valley*, 248–50.
175. Balraj Puri, "Driving the People to Extremism: Logic of Centre's Policies," *Economic and Political Weekly* 19, no. 35 (September 1, 1984): 1509–10.
176. Interview with Farooq Rehmani, Islamabad, 2010.
177. Puri, *Kashmir towards Insurgency*, 36.
178. *Gajendragadkar Committee Report*, 42.
179. *Gajendragadkar Committee Report*, 54.
180. Balraj Puri, "Jammu's Quest for Identity," *Economic and Political Weekly* 19, no. 41 (October 13, 1984): 1772–3.
181. Balraj Puri, "Debate on Jammu Problem," *Kashmir Affairs* 6, no. 2 (May–June 1959): 33–6.
182. Puri, "Jammu's Quest for Identity."
183. Puri, "Jammu's Quest for Identity."
184. Balraj Madhok, *Kashmir: Centre of New Alignments* (New Delhi: Deepak Prakashan, 1963), 160.

185. Madhok, *Jammu, Kashmir, and Ladakh*, 3–18.
186. Sumantra Bose, *The Challenge in Kashmir*, 92–3.
187. Sumantra Bose, *The Challenge in Kashmir*, 92. To quote Bose:

    Of the six districts in Jammu, Poonch has a massive Muslim majority of close to 90 percent, and Doda and Rajouri have substantial Muslim majorities of between 60 and 65 percent. Udhampur has a substantial Hindu majority of 65 percent, while Jammu and Kathua have massive Hindu majorities of between 80 and 90 percent.

188. V. D. Savarkar, a leading ideologue of Hindu nationalism, popularized Hindutva (Hindu-ness), an ideology that seeks to establish the cultural and political hegemony of Hindus.
189. Sumantra Bose, *The Challenge in Kashmir*, 90.
190. Balraj Puri, "Stir in Jammu and Kashmir Not Communal," *Times of India*, New Delhi, November 26, 1987.
191. Puri, "Stir in Jammu and Kashmir Not Communal."
192. The previous chapter elaborates in detail Ladakhi grievances and demands in the aftermath of decolonization. *Gajendragadkar Committee Report*, 43.
193. Balraj Puri, "Route of Ladakh's Integration," *Economic and Political Weekly* 17, no. 8 (February 20, 1982): 273–5.
194. Martijn van Beek, "Beyond Identity Fetishism: 'Communal' Conflict in Ladakh and the Limits of Autonomy," *Cultural Anthropology* 15, no. 4 (November 2000): 525–69.
195. Behera, *Demystifying Kashmir*, 116–17.
196. Puri, "Route of Ladakh's Integration."

5 Mapping Kashmiri Imaginings of Freedom in the Inter-regional and Global Arenas

Many do not know where you are buried
There is no news, there is no grave
But for the millions you inspired
You live in their hearts and minds[1]

Written by M. Yameen, these verses capture Kashmiris' emotions about their most prominent voice of resistance during the 1960s, 1970s, and 1980s, Maqbool Butt (1938–84). Branded a "traitor" by the Indian state and labeled a "double agent" by the Pakistani military establishment, both of whom saw him as a citizen of one or the other nation-state, Butt cuts a complex figure in the subcontinent's postcolonial history. This chapter attends to these interpretations, but argues that to see Butt as a potential traitor to either nation-state was to miss his basic political point. Throughout Kashmir's postcolonial history, as I have recounted, Kashmiri Muslims transgressed the ceasefire line for social, economic, and political interactions, even though both India and Pakistan considered the flow across this "border" as unauthorized and illegal. Butt and his fellow resistance members openly rather than covertly challenged the hegemony of India and Pakistan by refusing to accept the ceasefire line as a permanent border, seeing it as an aberration. For them, "freedom" meant not the option to choose India or Pakistan in a plebiscite they had little evidence would ever occur, but rather the reunification of the entire historical territory of the state of Jammu and Kashmir and thus the healing of the social, economic, and political wound caused by the illegitimate ceasefire line.[2] Butt's actions were directed against India and Pakistan only incidentally; they were undertaken rather in pursuit of his nationalist vision of a free Kashmir.

While much of the rest of this book focuses on events in India-administered Kashmir, especially in the Valley, this chapter concentrates on two other key spaces where a postcolonial Kashmiri nationalist identity developed and where new ideas about what freedom would look like, and how best to obtain it, were propagated:

Pakistan-administered Kashmir, and the transnational spaces, especially in the industrial cities of Great Britain, where exiles, expatriates, and refugees both debated events in their homeland and attempted to exert influence on them. These spaces were isolated neither from each other nor from India-administered Kashmir, although interactions between Kashmiri writers, leaders, and activists, split by the ceasefire line and living in separated territories administered by rival and sometimes outright warring nation-states, have remained marginal in the history of postcolonial Jammu and Kashmir. Scholars have assumed that Kashmir's divided parts were disconnected and isolated from each other. On the contrary, throughout Kashmir's postcolonial history voices of resistance in the Valley forged networks across the line of control, despite its being patrolled, fenced, and land-mined, and across the oceans and land masses which also physically separated Kashmiris from their homeland. The reunification of the old princely state, which would reconnect separated families, open old roadways, and link Kashmir with other parts of the world, has embedded itself in Kashmiri dreams.

Dreams and imagination, however, bear a complex relationship to reality. Political dissidents from India-administered Kashmir considered the "other" side a place of refuge against the unjust policies of the India-sponsored puppet regimes that denied them a voice in shaping their political future. They considered Pakistan an ally in their quest for self-determination and perceived Pakistan-administered Kashmir as a "free" land, with its inhabitants allowed to pursue an autonomous future. In reality, the inhabitants of the so-called Azad Kashmir were not as free as the territory's name proclaimed. Instead, they lived in tension with the Pakistani bureaucracy, an outside authority that dominated the region, creating schisms and divisions between Kashmiri political and social groups. Regional discontent in Pakistan-administered Kashmir, no less than in India-administered Kashmir, manifested in protests ranging from demands for autonomy to calls for complete independence.

In this chapter I explore the theme of resistance as Kashmiri Muslims from across both sides of the India–Pakistan divide, disheartened by the intolerable conditions imposed by ruling regimes and frustrated at being unheard in the international corridors of power, challenged the sovereignty of both nation-states. As the conventional approach of popular protests exemplified by Sheikh Abdullah's peaceful plebiscite movement failed, one strand of Kashmiri Muslim resistance began to call for an armed rebellion—at first with limited success, but with more and more credibility as both nation-states and the international community seemed impervious to Kashmiri misery, and as other nationalist postcolonial armed struggles like those in Palestine, Algeria, and Vietnam met with different forms of success. In Azad Kashmir some Kashmiri activists, inspired by these movements, sought radical political and social change, harnessing the feelings of "injustice" and "lost dignity" inherent in earlier Kashmiri discourses on the freedom to create grassroots resistance.

But far from being limited to the territorial area of the projected free state of Jammu and Kashmir, politically disenfranchised Kashmiris crafted strategies of protest and claimed an active role in shaping their future well beyond the subcontinent. Globally dispersed by a lack of economic opportunities or political displacement, the Kashmiri transnational community also dissented. Decades before India and Pakistan laid claims to their homeland in 1947, itinerant Muslim laborers from the princely state of Jammu and Kashmir had migrated to Britain and East Africa. Relocation provided an escape from the poverty and political suppression that engulfed Kashmir during the Dogra Raj. Some found employment in the port city of Bombay as lascars on the British merchant fleets, where they worked as stokers in coal rooms. These early Kashmiri migrants pioneered the chain of migration to Britain that increased after decolonization, especially from the eastern part of the old Jammu province, which later came under the control of Pakistan.[3]

Over the course of the late twentieth century British expatriates from Pakistan-administered Kashmir, in particular, changed international attitudes about political exclusion in their homeland and shaped their political claims and strategies in the image of worldwide movements for self-determination. They expressed solidarity with other liberation movements and created transnational activism that linked them to their homeland. As the transnational community challenged the territorial nationalism of the nation-states, it claimed that Jammu and Kashmir was part of neither India nor Pakistan but instead belonged to the people of the state, who possessed the inherent right to shape their future in accordance with their collective aspirations, including as an independent state.

Tools of Territorial Control: Accommodation and Resistance in Azad Kashmir

The eastern parts of the former princely state of Jammu and Kashmir that came under the control of Pakistan after the United Nations–negotiated ceasefire on January 1, 1949, acquired the nickname *Azad*, or "free," Kashmir, from the movement that initially liberated the area from the control of the Dogra Raj. This Muslim-dominated region, comprised of the three principal areas of Poonch, Muzaffarabad, and Mirpur, is home to diverse linguistic and cultural communities including the Sudhan-dominated areas around Bagh and Rawalakot, the Jat-dominated area around Mirpur, the Gujjars of Muzaffarabad, and the Rajputs spread across the territory. Many of these communities had little connection to the Valley's culture.[4] The region's social fabric was defined by *biradaris*, "clans" or kinship networks.[5] Ethnic and linguistic diversity determined power relationships within Azad Kashmir's postcolonial political landscape as the *biradaris* vied for political control based on their views on Kashmir's relationship with Pakistan.[6]

Though the loyalties of Azad Kashmiris lay primarily with their own clans, these diverse communities also identified as Kashmiri. Their affinity with the old princely state of Jammu and Kashmir stemmed from the "state-subject" category, introduced by the Dogra maharaja in 1927 and retained by the postcolonial governments. This legal designation differentiated *mulki*, "people of the land," from *gairmulki*, "people not of the land," and prevented the latter from purchasing land and seeking employment in Jammu and Kashmir. Although Pakistan-administered Kashmir adopted a constitution in the 1970s, the Rules of Business of the Azad Kashmir Government (1950) reserved the state-subject category for all inhabitants of the former princely state, included displaced Kashmiris.[7] The residents of Pakistan-administered Kashmir held Pakistani passports for international travel. However, a stamp in the citizenship column identified a Kashmiri as a "native subject of the former state of Jammu and Kashmir."[8] This definition of Kashmiri identity united diverse cultural and linguistic groups in Azad Kashmir and in the wider transnational community in a sense of shared belonging with the undivided territory of Jammu and Kashmir. Azad Kashmiris embracing a Kashmiri, rather than Pakistani, political identity is due to an increasing disillusionment with Pakistan over its policies in the region, which denied residents democratic rights, ignored economic development, and focused primarily on gaining and retaining territorial sovereignty. A Kashmiri identity allowed Azad Kashmiris to establish emotional and political distance from Pakistan and to claim political, economic, and social rights as Kashmiris.[9]

Prior to Jammu and Kashmir's accession to India, the Azad Kashmir movement emerged in Poonch and in the eastern districts of Jammu province against the autocratic and discriminatory policies of the Dogra ruler. Sardar Muhammad Ibrahim Khan, a scion of a landed family from Poonch and an active member of the Muslim Conference who later became the first president of Azad Kashmir, organized the Poonch uprising. Under his leadership, the "rebels" formed an "Azad Kashmir Army" with the goal of liberating Kashmir from the Dogra Raj. Ordinary Poonchis supported the rebels with food and rations. By October 1947, the "rebels" controlled the eastern part of the Jammu district from their base at

Murree, near the Poonch border. They even formed a de-facto Azad Jammu and Kashmir government as early as October 4, 1947, but this step failed due to a lack of planning and coordination.[10]

The tribal invasion of October 1947, supported by Pakistan, however, changed the course of the Azad Kashmir movement. An undisciplined band of tribal fighters from Khyber Pakhtunkhwa arrived to assist the Poonch "rebels," but attacked and rendered homeless the non-Muslims in the eastern part of the Jammu province, while also looting, raping, and pillaging the Muslim communities.[11] Furthermore, the Azad Kashmir movement failed to retain its autonomous nature once Kashmir became an issue primarily about India's and Pakistan's disputed sovereignty. Many in Azad Kashmir interpret the tribal incursion as Pakistan's "meddling" that took away "the political agency of Kashmiris" and provided India "legitimacy" to send its army into the region.[12]

Meanwhile, the "rebels" had successfully formed the Azad Kashmir provisional government, at Pulandri on October 24, 1947, to end "Dogra tyrannies" and secure "self-government" for all inhabitants regardless of religious affiliation.[13] They had the support of the All Jammu and Kashmir Muslim Conference, and the "progressives among the non-Muslim communities."[14] However, the provisional government lacked capital, resources, and experienced staff, and struggled to establish rudimentary administrative branches.[15] Pakistan's military and financial support of the Azad Kashmir movement, especially after Kashmir's accession to India, allowed Pakistan's army to control some of Kashmir's territory. As Pakistan's control over the Azad Kashmir significantly increased, large parts of the "Azad Army were disbanded and amalgamated into Pakistani army."[16] However, the United Nations Security Council's resolutions on the Kashmir dispute, which stipulated a free and impartial plebiscite to allow Kashmiris to determine their political fate, also created ambiguity about Kashmir's status. Political elites, mostly representatives of the Muslim Conference, debated the desirability of either integrating Azad Kashmir with Pakistan or maintaining its "independent status" until the completion of the promised plebiscite.

Sardar Ibrahim Khan, the leader of the Azad Kashmir movement, demanded an international legal status for the provisional government of Jammu and Kashmir and recognition of their government as the only constitutional and legal authority that could decide Kashmir's future.[17] The Indian government and the National Conference, the nationalist party supporting Kashmir's accession to India, however, challenged Khan's ambition to be the sole arbiter of Kashmir's political future. Aware of the conflicting demands, the United Nations gave the Azad Kashmir government the status of a "local authority" with full powers to manage internal matters, but with Pakistan retaining administrative control, until the promised plebiscite.[18] Pakistan did not legally integrate Azad Kashmir, considering the entire state, including those portions under the control of India, as disputed territory. Pakistan depended on the rivers flowing from the Valley to sustain its agricultural sector and provide electricity to millions. It relied on an eventual victory in the future plebiscite, counting on the territory's Muslim majority to choose accession to Pakistan for all of Kashmir. Integrating Azad Kashmir would have meant accepting the ceasefire line as a permanent boundary and hence demolishing Pakistani claims to India-administered Kashmir. Azad Kashmir, then, found itself in a state of limbo. It was neither a Pakistani province with constitutional rights and powers nor a sovereign state.[19] Its name came to seem bitterly ironic, since in reality it was now a territory dominated by a Pakistani bureaucracy that used coercive instruments—the police, army, and intelligence networks—to secure state-sponsored regimes' undemocratic authority.

Pakistan's collaboration with the Muslim Conference, a local political party which had supported the Pakistan movement even prior to the war of 1947–1948, allowed the party to control Azad Kashmir's domestic and foreign affairs. The Muslim Conference signed the Karachi agreement in 1949; Pakistan retained all important powers like defense, communications, negotiations with the United Nations Commission for India and Pakistan (UNCIP), and plebiscite activities, while only local matters remained within the purview of the Azad Kashmir administration.[20] Pakistan further strengthened its geostrategic position by taking direct control of Gilgit and Baltistan, the northern areas of the disputed state of Jammu and Kashmir that shared its borders with China, on the grounds that Azad Kashmir had failed to govern them due to scarce financial resources and poor communication systems.[21] Instead of giving the inhabitants of Gilgit and Baltistan a voice in shaping their political future, however, Pakistan administered the region with help of a "Political Agent" whose primary task was to prevent rebellions, frequently using violent and oppressive tactics.[22] As the United Nations, in the early post-partition decades, showed some serious interest in implementing the promised plebiscite, Pakistan decided not to fully integrate Gilgit and Baltistan in order to ensure a high vote count.

The new state of Pakistan, "bereft of a central state apparatus" after partition, relied on a "quickly assembled bureaucracy" to run the new nation-state.[23] In Azad Kashmir, the Ministry of Kashmir Affairs (MKA), established in January 1949 at Rawalpindi and composed of members of the federal bureaucracy, helped Pakistan administer Azad Kashmir. Within three years, the MKA reduced "the status of AJK government to that of a municipality" by granting the Joint Secretary of MKA the power to "pass final orders on appeals against orders passed by Secretaries and Heads of Departments in respect of government servants under their control, in all matters of appointments, promotion and disciplinary action."[24]

As the power of Azad Kashmir's government faded, the MKA treated Kashmiri politicians as second-class citizens, inciting internal rivalries and playing kingmaker by appointing and dismissing Azad Kashmir's presidents in quick succession.[25] The actors who shaped the course of Azad Kashmir competed for political power and benefits along ethnic, geographical, and clan lines as Jammuites, Mirpuris, Poonchis, and Kashmiris.[26] The MKA capitalized on *biradari* loyalties to fracture and thus conquer Azad Kashmiri leadership.

Soon after the drawing of the ceasefire line, tribal divisions pitted two rival political factions against each other. Sardar Ibrahim Khan, the first president of Azad Kashmir, confident of his massive support base (especially in his native Poonch), challenged MKA's domination and pushed for democracy and rights. Chaudhry Ghulam Abbas, a prominent leader of the Muslim Conference from Jammu city who had migrated to Azad Kashmir in 1947, was propped up by the MKA as the "supreme head" of the Muslim Conference. The "migrant" status of Abbas in Azad Kashmir, which meant he had no support at a grassroots level, made him fearful of being outvoted in any real election. To remain relevant in Azad Kashmir's politics, he subserviently followed the dictates of Pakistani bureaucrats. The MKA rewarded Abbas's "loyalty" with dictatorial powers, including right to nominate presidents and make all appointments. Not surprisingly under these circumstances, the "supreme head" strongly opposed an elected legislature, preferring to disempower his political rivals.[27] Abbas's political clout grew after 1948; the Pakistani government gave him complete power to distribute a subsistence income, almost one lakh Pakistani rupees, to unemployed Muslim Conference members who had migrated from India-administered Kashmir.[28] Abbas's supporters received a larger share of this money, while others depended on his charity. The dissonance in Kashmiri voices lessened their leverage to negotiate for more autonomy, and the MKA used their discontent to keep Kashmiri leaders subservient.

The tensions within the different strands of the Muslim Conference erupted in 1950 after Abbas, at the instigation of the MKA, dismissed Sardar Ibrahim Khan from the presidency of Azad Kashmir. In response, Khan's supporters, the Sudhans from the Rawalakot area of Poonch, led a revolt that lasted for several months. Pakistan declared martial law in Poonch and arrested almost five hundred Azad Kashmiris.[29] In response, Kashmiri political activists launched a civil disobedience agitation and denounced the dictatorial governance of the Pakistan-supported Abbas group. They demanded the reorganization of the government on democratic lines. A pamphlet entitled *Dictatorship in Azad Kashmir* written by Kashmiri activist Mir Abdul Aziz reminded people that their fight is for democracy, freedom, and the right of self-determination, rather than glorification of individuals or political groups. The author implored Pakistan to rise to the occasion and ensure that Kashmiris have real democracy and freedom.[30] However, Pakistan considered Azad Kashmir's electoral politics a distraction, and seemed interested in encouraging Azad Kashmiris to devote their lives to Kashmir's "liberation" from India. Thus, Pakistan failed to institute a formal democratic system with regular elections at national and provincial levels. For newly created Pakistan, the "imperative of constructing a central government from scratch outweighed the resources of the state," and the onset of the military dispute with India over Kashmir made Pakistan focus on asserting central authority over the provinces with the help of its fledgling administrative bureaucracy. Writing a new constitution was "delayed due to fierce disagreements on how political and economic power would be shared between the provinces."[31] Azad Kashmir's relationship with Pakistan deteriorated as the primary focus remained the plebiscite issue in the United Nations, rather than holding elections in theoretically "free" Kashmir.[32]

The inhabitants of Azad Kashmir also resented their economic dependence on Pakistan. The division of Jammu and Kashmir and the closure of major routes, especially the famous Jhelum Valley Road, which had allowed trade between the Kashmir Valley and the rest of India prior to partition, limited economic growth in Pakistan-administered Kashmir. From the outset, Azad Kashmir's topography, hilly and mountainous, made development difficult. Apart from water and forests, the region lacked natural resources that could fuel economic growth. Its poor soil and small landholdings made farming very unproductive.[33] Economic hardship forced many people in the Pahari-speaking districts of Kotli, Poonch, Rajouri, Bhimber, and Mirpur to migrate to the booming English industrial towns of Bradford, Birmingham, Manchester, and Luton.[34] Most migrants, however, retained close ties with the homeland and frequently visited their families. These Kashmiris, on the margins of society in Britain, saw themselves as temporary migrants rather than immigrants, and planned to return home to Azad Kashmir after saving their earnings.[35] Those who stayed in Azad Kashmir hoped for better state policies that would modernize their economy and bring new jobs.

The Pakistani state, however, struggling to handle Muslim refugees pouring in from India and maintain its own security, did not fund development in Azad Kashmir, creating deepening poverty, neglect, and stagnation. Many Azad Kashmiris believed that their poverty stemmed from Pakistan's failure to fully integrate Azad Kashmir, a circumstance which meant it was not entitled to the same budget reserved for other states. A pamphlet written by a Kashmiri political activist and circulated clandestinely among Pakistani bureaucrats in 1964 addressed the financial discrimination the region faced:

> If Azad Kashmiris were free, they could ask for a refund of customs and excise duty as was done by Afghanistan. If they were Pakistanis, they could have sought the same treatment as is meted out to other backward areas like the North West Frontier regions and Baluchistan.... Baluchistan, like Azad Kashmir, has an income of one crore of rupees. But Pakistan allows Baluchistan to spend 6 crores a year on current expenditures while it expects Azad Kashmir to be content with a subvention of 15 lakhs, although they [Pakistan] takes [*sic*] away from Azad Kashmir nearly 75 lakhs a year in terms of custom and excise duties. Similarly, the revenue of former N.W.F.P. is nearly eight crores and expenditure nearly 30 crores, the balance of expenditure being met by the more prosperous areas of Pakistan. As if this unfair treatment were not enough, the same disparity is visible in the development budget of Azad Kashmir.[36]

Financial neglect in the region accentuated Azad Kashmiris' feeling of political suppression and sparked public anger against the Pakistani bureaucracy, especially the MKA, anger which forced both the Kashmiri intelligentsia and local political groups to demand democratic rule.

Kashmiri journalists and intellectuals used the print media to question the Muslim Conference leaders' subservience and debate innovative ways to achieve political rights, economic emancipation, and cultural regeneration. Since no printing press existed within Azad Kashmir, Kashmiri journalists established publishing houses in other Pakistani cities to debate the challenges that confronted Azad Kashmiris.[37] Their newspaper articles circulated in Azad Kashmir, and many were republished in the Delhi-based *Voice of Kashmir*, a monthly journal edited by political activist Prem Nath Bazaz, a vocal supporter of Kashmiri self-determination. Azad Kashmiri activists aimed to give Kashmiris in the Valley living under oppressive India-sponsored state regimes an accurate picture of their political situation, in order to discourage romantic visions of Azad Kashmir as a free land. In the early 1950s, the Indian government's arrest and dismissal of Sheikh Abdullah, the prime minister of India-administered Kashmir, for resisting Kashmir's complete accession to India had stunned Azad Kashmiris and transformed Abdullah into a "hero." Thereafter, Abdullah's concept of an independent Kashmir fascinated the Kashmiri intelligentsia, who debated it in the weekly newspapers *Kashir* and *Hamara Kashmir*, both published from Rawalpindi.

G. N. Gilkar, the editor of *Hamara Kashmir* and one of the pioneers of Muslim political mobilization in 1931, felt that the way "freedom" had unfolded in divided Kashmir made a mockery of the countless sacrifices Kashmiris had made over the previous century. He suggested that Kashmiris declare themselves independent and "conclude treaties of friendship with their neighbors."[38] In one thought-provoking editorial, Sanaullah Butt, the editor of *Kashir*, pointed out that the perennial conflict in the region stemmed from the bitterness between India and Pakistan. The Kashmiri struggle for freedom, he argued, meant the "establishment of political structures in the state that could fit in with aspirations of the people." The end of Dogra rule did not mean that Kashmiris should accept the rule of a new tyrant, even of the same religious persuasion as the majority: "Tyranny in any shape or form is tyranny, whether the perpetrators are the Hindus or the Muslims." He pointed out that the two major political parties of Jammu and Kashmir—the National Conference and the Muslim Conference—had assured their supporters that the prosperity of the state depended on becoming part of India or Pakistan. However, as both countries had denied Kashmiris their rights, the parties' claims had proved hollow. Although supporting the idea of an independent Kashmir would be considered a "political crime" in Pakistan's official circles, the "demand of the masses" could not be ignored. Kashmiris would strive to attain "freedom and democracy," Butt argued, even though Kashmiri political elites would attempt to retain their power privileges.[39] These bold views led the Pakistani establishment to arrest Sanaullah Butt and eject him across the ceasefire line, a common punishment in the 1950s inflicted by both nations on those Kashmiris who questioned the status quo.[40]

The MKA's coercive methods did not prevent Azad Kashmiris from demanding that representatives of all political parties, classes, and communities living in the state be included in negotiations to find a solution. The much-anticipated plebiscite was delayed, increasing frustration. Plans put forward by United Nations representatives Sir Owen Dixon (May–September 1950) and Frank P. Graham (September 1951–February 1953) were unacceptable to both India and Pakistan, who could not reconcile their differences on the length of the demilitarization period and the size of the forces to be retained along of the ceasefire line after the cessation of hostilities.[41] In 1955, a deputation of Kashmiri Muslim leaders submitted a memorandum to the prime ministers of India and Pakistan, stating that Kashmiris wanted to protect their homeland from the "ambitions of land hungry politicians and evil designs of imperialists." They requested a joint declaration from both countries, ratified by the United Nations and "guaranteeing the future autonomy of Kashmir, before the plebiscite is held.[42] India and Pakistan ignored their demands.

The Muslim Conference's leadership in Azad Kashmir, involved in fractious internal politics, paid zero attention to ensuring political rights and civil liberties for all Azad Kashmiris instead of focusing primarily on personal power. In the late 1950s, this selfish approach having alienated its supporters, the party attempted to shift its focus away from "undemocratic" policies. It adopted a proactive approach to shake the status quo on Kashmiri self-determination and force the world community to notice the unresolved Kashmir issue. Since the early 1950s, rumors had circulated on both sides of divided Kashmir about Abdullah and Abbas forming an alliance to "conclude an internal settlement of the Kashmir question."[43] Although those plans never came to fruition, the Muslim Conference took advantage of the uproar in Azad Kashmir caused by the April 1958 rearrest of Sheikh Abdullah in India-administered Kashmir, only four months after his release from prison. Chaudhry Ghulam Abbas launched the Kashmir Liberation Movement (KLM), a "non-violent mass crossing of the ceasefire line by volunteers into Indian Kashmir, like the 'march on Goa' by Indian volunteers in 1955" to free it from Portuguese occupation.[44]

The KLM hoped to electrify both the state and the world by mobilizing thousands to cross the line of control, facing bullets and courting arrest in India-administered Kashmir. They believed that the people's movement would reveal the futility of the ceasefire line and force the international community to resolve the Kashmir issue. This movement gained momentum not only in Azad Kashmir, but also in Punjab province, as the slogan "Kashmir Chalo" (March to Kashmir) emerged in public meetings, gatherings, and processions.[45] The Pakistani government opposed this movement; Prime Minister Firoz Khan Noon announced on June 2, 1958, that "Pakistan would not hesitate to use force if necessary to prevent any breach of the cease-fire agreement." Several leaders of the KLM were arrested, including Ghulam Abbas and two former presidents of Azad Kashmir, Sardar Qayyum Khan and Colonel Sher Ahmed Khan. Almost "300 volunteers were dispersed by the police from the cease-fire line; only 10 succeeded in crossing into Jammu, where they were arrested and detained." The arrests ensured the failure of the KLM.[46]

The establishment of military rule in Pakistan following General Ayub Khan's October 1958 imposition of martial law transformed Azad Kashmir's politics. The military cultivated ties with new Azad Kashmiri leadership to displace the fractious Muslim Conference, hoping to stabilize the region. In 1961 now-President Ayub Khan, who had banned all political activity as part of bending the provinces to his will, introduced the tiered Basic Democracy (BD) system, a structure of limited and indirect representation composed of local councils at the union, sub-district, district, and provincial levels which assisted the administration in gaining legitimacy.[47] Under this system, local bodies elected renowned Kashmiri leader K. H. Khurshid, originally from the Valley, as the new president of Azad Jammu and Kashmir. For the first time "elections" took place in Azad Kashmir; however, this exercise did not lead to effectual democratization as the Muslim Conference leaders Abbas and Sardar Ibrahim Khan were debarred from participating in elections after being charged with corruption.[48]

Although limited, the "elections" in Azad Kashmir lent legitimacy to the Khurshid administration, which asserted itself against the domination of the MKA, hoping to make Azad Kashmir autonomous. In 1962, Khurshid and his cohorts formed a new political party, the Jammu Kashmir Liberation League (JKLL), which called for international "recognition of the Azad Jammu and Kashmir government as a revolutionary provisional successor government" of the deposed Dogra ruler and as the lawful government of the entire state.[49] The JKLL hoped to ensure that the Azad Kashmir government would be free to lead Kashmir's freedom movement without interference from Pakistan. At a press conference in Rawalpindi, Khurshid emphasized that "international treaties and obligations undertaken by Pakistan did not apply to Azad Kashmir, and declared that his government was not tied to the apron strings of any bloc or big power and would welcome aid from any country in 'the liberation of Kashmir from Indian military occupation.'"[50] The party aimed to mobilize Kashmiris to advocate for self-determination, casting a wide net as they suggested reuniting Pakistan-controlled Gilgit and Baltistan with Jammu and Kashmir.[51] In response, the MKA, disapproving of these "independent" views, curtailed Khurshid's powers.

Tensions increased as administration officials simply declined to obey the president's orders, ultimately leading to Khurshid's resignation and arrest in 1964.[52] Thereafter, the MKA subordinated Azad Kashmir's local government; acts in 1964 and 1968 downgraded the Azad Kashmir administration to municipal committee status, with members unable to pass laws or spend money without the approval of a Pakistani joint secretary and a Pakistan-appointed "chief advisor."[53] The premature departure of the first elected president, K. H. Khurshid, had a tremendous psychological impact on local politics. While Azad Kashmiri elites struggled for autonomy against the domination of the MKA, another strand of resistance now argued that political "freedom" could not be limited to the choice of joining either India or Pakistan. These voices focused on redefining the United Nations resolutions on Kashmiri self-determination to include the option of voting for an independent nation.

Dissent and Transnational community: Mirpur and the Independent Kashmir Movement

In Pakistan-administered Kashmir, the clan politics of the *biradaris* and their dealings with the MKA shaped their responses toward the future status of Azad Kashmir within Pakistan. The people of Azad Kashmir, especially the Sudhans and the Jat community, professed loyalty to their clan leaders, prominent members of the Muslim Conference who supported Kashmir's accession to Pakistan. Most Sudhans of Poonch, who had revolted in 1947, still believed that Kashmir should become a part of Pakistan, while also resisting the undemocratic policies of the MKA during the 1950s.[54] Similarly, many displaced Kashmiri Muslims from the Valley who had settled in Punjab after 1947 had integrated "culturally and emotionally" with Pakistan and held important positions in the military, bureaucracy, business, and industry.[55] However, some criticized the undemocratic politics of the Muslim Conference, leading to their tarring as "agents of Sheikh Abdullah" by the Azad Kashmir government.[56] These people, along with the Pahari-speaking Mirpuris from Mirpur and the Dadyal district of Azad Kashmir, became the staunchest critics of Pakistan's policies and advocates of an independent Kashmir. Mirpuris resented Pakistan not only because of its undemocratic practices, but also because Pakistani policy decisions had altered the social and economic landscape to their disadvantage, forcing many Mirpuris into economic migration.[57]

Abdul Khaliq Ansari, born in Mirpur, pioneered the independence movement in Pakistan-administered Kashmir. A lawyer by profession, Ansari was an active member of the National Conference prior to 1947 and considered Sheikh Abdullah his political leader. In the early 1950s, he worked with dissident Muslim Conference members to form the Awami Conference seeking social justice and complete independence.[58] Inspired by socialist ideals, Ansari asked Kashmiris to refrain from supporting accession to Pakistan, which meant joining a country that valued neither democracy nor an egalitarian society. Ansari complained that Pakistan's dominance over Azad Kashmir only benefited political elites, while the masses suffered economic ruin; the privileged few exercised power while Kashmiris who raised their voices against injustice suffered imprisonment.[59] To counter the influence of *biradari* politics, Ansari argued for Kashmir's unification and the importance of the province's residents claiming a Kashmiri, rather than *biradari*, identity.[60]

The proposed construction of the Mangla Dam across the river Jhelum in Mirpur became a rallying point for Ansari's political organization; organizing mass protests across *biradari* affiliations, he used the proposed dam as a means of highlighting Kashmir's unique identity.[61] The dam promised farmers across Pakistan, but especially in the Punjab, water to irrigate large areas of land across Pakistan. The proposed earth-filled dam, the third largest of its type in the world, would provide 40 percent of Pakistan's electricity and 50 percent of its water for year-round irrigation.[62] People in Mirpur worried about the plan, however, as the structure would be on disputed territory.

In August 1960, the Anti-Mangla Dam Front demonstrated, arguing that the project would destroy the lives of poor farmers in the area to be covered by the dam. However, the government dismissed these protests, assuring people that the construction would "usher an era of prosperity through the building of various industries and an irrigation system."[63] Activists pointed out that while Pakistan argued internationally for Kashmir's right of self-determination, it was treating Azad Kashmir's territory as its own by planning to construct a dam against the wishes of its people. Kashmiris criticized their own political elites, who had sanctioned the mutilation of land for the construction of the dam "in the name of Pakistan's government," despite Section 4 of the Jammu and Kashmir Alienation of Land Act, which prohibited the transfer of land to anyone who was not a state subject.[64] Such official orders, they argued, suggested that either the "Pakistan government had become a hereditary state subject or that the president of Azad Kashmir was an employee of Pakistan." When the dam was completed in 1966, 122 villages (including 65,000 acres of the most fertile land in the region) were submerged overnight, displacing more than 100,000 people.[65] The construction mutilated shrines and graveyards, and destroyed roads and infrastructure along with villages.[66] Though the dam was located in Kashmir, which bore the consequences of its construction, other Pakistani provinces reaped its benefits—excellent irrigation facilities and cheap electricity—causing many grievances among Mirpuris. A mass migration from Mirpur to Britain ensued, accelerating the development of anti-Pakistani sentiment in the transnational community as well as in Azad Kashmir.[67]

Displaced from their homeland, Mirpuri migrants struggled to integrate within British society. Despite the hardships that marred their lives, they provided each other with fellowship and support. They shared experiences of racial discrimination and marginalization as they intermingled in cafés that served South Asian food and played Bollywood music, and read (and wrote for) a new Kashmiri community print media. Urdu newspapers published in Bradford and Birmingham connected migrants with life in Kashmir, portraying their readers as "temporary labor whose future life, like the remittance money [they] sent home to Mirpur and other villages each month, ultimately belonged in

Kashmir."[68] If *biradari* networks resulted in fractured political strength at home, they strengthened community identity among the migrants abroad. Established migrants sponsored members of their clans and provided newcomers with meals and lodging. In turn, the new migrants, when settled, helped other members of the *biradari*. These kinship networks promoted internal group cohesion among British Kashmiris.[69]

The promise of self-determination resonated with Azad Kashmiris both at home and in the global spaces of migration; many believed that exercising this right would reverse their "lack of status" within Pakistan, which had placed them at a disadvantage in the disbursement of grants, subsidies, and funds. By the mid-1960s, the idea of self-determination promised to Kashmiris in the United Nations resolutions of 1948 had lost its international relevance. The international community's solutions to the Kashmir dispute now only considered ways to divide Kashmir's territory between India and Pakistan.[70] Great powers like the United States and Britain pressured both India and Pakistan to "find an honorable and equitable solution of the issue."[71]

Kashmiri hopes were not an international priority, a fact which became further apparent after the India–Pakistan war of 1965. The Tashkent Agreement which ended hostilities placed "Kashmir in cold storage," while both countries committed to "settle their disputes through peaceful means" and noninterference in the other's internal affairs.[72] Many Kashmiris felt that both Indian and Pakistani political leaders had continuously failed to listen to them. If no space for independent expression existed, Kashmiris had no choice but to align with the policies and agendas of one or the other of the nation-states that dominated their territory. While many accepted this reality, others objected and redefined self-determination, using a radical approach to challenge the territorial sovereignty of the involved nation-states.

The Advocates of Independence: Double Agents, Traitors, or Freedom Fighters?

Although India considers the line separating the two parts of Kashmir to be a sacred boundary that defines its territorial integrity, and Pakistan wants to transgress this line and claim the other side, the territory of Jammu and Kashmir remain a contested zone. For decades, however, people living in this liminal space defied the creation of borders within their own homeland, and crossed the ceasefire line to establish intellectual and political networks with their counterparts. South Asian scholarship has seen borderland insurgencies as the result of rival nation-states' machinations, as they aid and abet insurgents with a view to destabilizing and dismembering their neighbors. Indeed, the feelings of discontent brewing among the political dissidents from India-administered Kashmir made it easy for Pakistani intelligence to manipulate Kashmiri emotions of discontent to their political advantage. However, this section focuses on Kashmiri voices of resistance that attempted to regain their agency to challenge the hegemony of both India and Pakistan, and construct new strategies to end their marginalization.[73]

Disenchanted Kashmiri Muslims living in Pakistan-administered Kashmir merged their own political experiences with the ideas of resistance circulating in the Valley to build a forceful independence movement, seeking a freedom that evidently could not be found in the so-called Azad Kashmir while it remained dominated by Pakistani nationalist politics.[74] In April 1965, a group of political activists from different sub-regions of Jammu and Kashmir formed the Plebiscite Front AJK (Azad Jammu and Kashmir). Most of its leaders had migrated in 1947 from the western parts of Jammu province to Pakistan-administered Kashmir to escape communitarian violence. Under the leadership of Khaliq Ansari, they met at Sialkot, a border town near Jammu, and swore to unite both sides of Kashmir.[75]

Although the Plebiscite Front AJK drew inspiration from the Valley's Plebiscite Front, they defined self-determination differently. Instead of confining the options before potential voters to those defined by the 1949 United Nations resolutions, namely joining either India or Pakistan, the Plebiscite Front AJK advocated the "unlimited and unconditional right of self-determination," by which they meant that Kashmiris should have the right to choose independence from both nation-states for the entire state. This Plebiscite Front believed that Jammu and Kashmir belonged to Kashmiris, who had equal rights irrespective of caste, creed, or religion, and the inherent right to shape their future in accordance with their national aspirations.[76]

The plebiscite movement in Pakistan-administered Kashmir emphasized a Kashmiri identity rather than loyalty to clans and groups. Like Sheikh Abdullah's National Conference, the Plebiscite Front AJK was committed to secular values and promised to establish a socialist government. The members of the group criticized the use of school curriculums to instill a Pakistani identity among Azad Kashmiris. Textbooks written and published in Pakistan focused on Pakistani nationalist history at the expense of Kashmir's regional history. At Azad Kashmir school assemblies, children recited pledges promising that "Kashmir will become a part of Pakistan."[77] The Plebiscite Front AJK worried that students only learned about Pakistan's interpretation of the Kashmir conflict while ignoring Kashmiri expressions of pride in their homeland.

The party also rejected the postwar division of Jammu and Kashmir state, believing that the separation abrogated their right of self-determination. It aimed to replace the "external armies" stationed on both sides of the state with a state army "duly reorganized and adequately equipped." They further focused on promoting trade between the two sides and rebuilding human contact across the ceasefire line. The Front encouraged the two nation-states to open road links between the two sides of Kashmir and end "unwarranted, unjustified and oppressive restrictions on the movement of state nationals from one side of the cease-fire line to the other."[78]

The Plebiscite Front AJK became a home for many voices criticizing the moderate approach of Kashmiri politicians who worked closely with Pakistan. Prominent voices within the Plebiscite Front AJK, including Khaliq Ansari, called the Karachi Agreement of 1949 that gave Pakistan complete control over Gilgit and Baltistan a sell-out by mainstream Azad Kashmiri leadership. Ansari considered the Karachi Agreement a non-binding imposition because the wishes and aspirations of ordinary Kashmiris had not been taken into consideration. The Front demanded Gilgit and Baltistan's reunification with Azad Kashmir so that its inhabitants were not forced to live in a "police state" but would have due representation in democratic structures.[79]

In time, some members of the Front came to believe that political freedom was unobtainable through democratic or peaceful means. Instead, they advocated armed struggle to force the world community's intervention and to achieve the long-promised right of self-determination. Notable advocates of this idea included Maqbool Butt and Amanullah Khan. Born in the Astore area of Gilgit, Khan belonged to a family of traders who had migrated to Jammu in the 1920s. He went to school in the Valley and graduated from Sri Pratap College in Srinagar in 1952. The Dogra regime's denial of civil rights inspired Amanullah to join Sheikh Abdullah's anti-Dogra movement. After Kashmir's accession to India, however, the young man became disillusioned by continued political suppression in Kashmir. In 1952, he migrated to Pakistan and obtained a degree in law from Karachi University.[80] His political worldview in the 1960s and 1970s was shaped by the Palestinian and Algerian freedom movements and their diasporic leadership based in Pakistan. Khan kept company with Muhammad Kiloo, one of the leaders of the revolutionary Algerian National Liberation Front, who rejected all forms of imperialism and preferred armed struggles to end forced occupations. Conversations with Kiloo and access to Algerian revolutionary literature convinced Khan that Kashmir's freedom struggle had to be waged on three fronts with three distinct goals: dislodging "imperialist" India, winning

Kashmir's independence from Pakistan, and removing the pliant regimes that toed the political line of both nation-states.[81] Maqbool Butt, a prominent political activist who later emerged as the face of Kashmiri resistance, shared these ideas and considered guerrilla warfare the best instrument for Kashmir's liberation.[82]

In 1965, Khan and Butt, along with other like-minded Kashmiris, formed the Jammu and Kashmir National Liberation Front (popularly known as NLF), modeled on the Algerian revolutionary group Front de Libération Nationale (FLN). The NLF coordinated military, financial, and political activities across Kashmir. Its armed wing aimed to recruit guerrillas from both sides of the ceasefire line, train them, and initiate operations against armed forces in India-administered Kashmir, including ambushes of Indian army patrols and attacks on military installations. At the same time, the political wing worked to sway public opinion in favor of an armed struggle and to gain popular support for an independent Kashmir. The group collected funds and acquired arms and ammunition from the tribal areas of Pakistan.[83] The NLF wanted to operate independently from any official body in Pakistan. It received financial donations not only from rich Kashmiri businessmen based in Lahore and Karachi, but also from several Pakistani corporate groups who believed in their cause. While Amanullah Khan and other members of the organization popularized the idea of Kashmir's independence on a political front, his comrade Maqbool Butt gave practical shape to the armed freedom movement.

Throughout his public life, Maqbool Butt faced accusations by the Indian state of being a Pakistani agent and, by Pakistani authorities of being an Indian agent. Born to a peasant family in the Kupwara district of India-administered Kashmir on February 18, 1938, his perception of the meaning of "freedom" was shaped by his experience of poverty and class disparities.[84] Butt despised Kashmir's class-ridden organization which allowed only a select group to exercise power, revolting against this "unjust system" at a very young age.[85] In one of the letters, he narrated a humiliating childhood experience in which he, along with other village children, had to lie down in front of the car of a *jagirdar* or landlord while their parents begged for the remission of land revenue. As a student at a local elementary school, Butt refused to accept an award for his accomplishments unless the school authorities scrapped the established tradition of seating parents on separate sides of the assembly hall according to their wealth.[86] In common with Marxist-inspired radicals across the twentieth century's postcolonial landscape, revulsion against any form of injustice molded his political psyche.

As a graduate student at St. Joseph's College at Baramulla, Butt was actively involved in politics and, like hundreds of thousands of Kashmiris, considered Sheikh Abdullah's dismissal and imprisonment a grave injustice committed by an authoritarian India. He decried India's imposition of puppet regimes who added new laws to their armory of repression. Freedom from Dogra rule seemed meaningless, as a new form of authoritarianism had replaced earlier despotism. Butt organized political protests against these state regimes that suppressed free expression. To escape harassment and arrest, he secretly entered Pakistan-administered Kashmir in 1958; he completed his master's degree at Peshawar University and later worked as a journalist for the local newspaper *Anjaam.*[87] Butt's interest in Kashmir's freedom drew him closer to political personalities like K. H. Khurshid, who was demanding recognition of the Azad Jammu and Kashmir government as the lawful government of the entire state. When Khurshid's clash with the MKA in Islamabad led to his dismissal and arrest, Butt realized that conditions in Azad Kashmir bore a striking resemblance to those he had fled in the Valley—ordinary people were denied democratic participation and civil rights, while the powerful political elite acted as mouthpieces of the nation-state.[88]

Butt wanted not only to gain political freedom for Kashmir, but also to end social disparities that allowed elites to become rich at the expense of the poor. He envisioned a classless society, free from economic exploitation, in which poor people could live with dignity. For Butt, *aazadi* meant "not just getting rid of foreign occupation—but also to remove hunger, poverty, ignorance, and disease and to overcome economic and social deprivation."[89] "Freedom" entailed restoring Kashmiri dignity and ending the humiliations and hardships Kashmiris had endured for generations. Radicalized by the poverty and exploitation he witnessed on both sides of the ceasefire line, Butt's indignation about state-sponsored injustice, and his lack of faith that the international community or either nation-state would ever act to redress it, prompted him to imagine extreme methods for attaining his goals. The mid-1960s were marked by India's political suppression of the Valley's nonviolent plebiscite movement and the continuous detentions of its leaders, especially that of Sheikh Abdullah. During the 1965 war, meanwhile, Pakistan attempted to infiltrate Kashmir with guerillas; the entire planning of the operation occurred without Kashmiri input. Fed up with outside interference, Butt initiated a revolutionary struggle and called on Kashmiris to take the initiative in seizing their rights. "If a nation, struggling to attain freedom lacks the initiative to lead an independent movement, without interference from 'outside' forces," he argued, "then freedom would be unattainable. Unity and self-reliance among Kashmiris is the key to their freedom."[90]

If unity and self-reliance were to be the cause as well as the consequence of Kashmiri freedom, Butt believed they would have to be developed and encouraged among the victims of centuries of colonial regimes. Similar views were also articulated by Dr. Abdul Basit, a young Kashmiri lawyer whose family had migrated from the Valley to Pakistan in 1947. He had studied in the United States and worked as a barrister in London. Basit's book *Kashmir's War for Freedom*, popular among independence-minded Kashmiris, and published in the United Kingdom in the 1970s, was banned in Pakistan.[91] Basit envisioned that "freedom" would end a Kashmiri mentality of dependence on Pakistan and lay the basis for an independent state with immense strategic value. He believed that centuries of slavery had crushed Kashmiri initiative and self-confidence. The other communities within the subcontinent viewed Kashmiris with contempt because of their pacifist nature, and their subjugation had created a culture of dependence among Kashmiris, a mentality that had continued into the postcolonial era and been encouraged by both India and Pakistan. The armed struggle, Basit wrote, aimed to cultivate a new sense of self-reliance. Developing "a cohesive fighting force from a people whose entire history was devoid of organized armed struggle" would require planning and effort, but the armed struggle would change Kashmiris.[92] They would realize that they could be masters of their own destiny.[93]

Butt also believed that armed struggle was not only a practical way to gain freedom, but a tool to build self-reliance, a belief that formed the core of Butt's political philosophy. The communist revolutionary literature dominant in the 1950s and 1960s inspired Butt to initiate a Kashmiri struggle that he hoped would be on the model of that waged by guerilla movements in Southeast Asia and Latin America. A study of Mao Tse Tung's *On Guerrilla Warfare* convinced Butt that these tactics were the only way a nation inferior in arms and military equipment could win against a powerful aggressor. Similarly, the example of the Argentine Marxist revolutionary Che Guevara's activities during the 1959 Cuban Revolution inspired Butt to contemplate establishing small armed resistance units in the countryside. These units would engage in a covert war against India, building support among the rural peasantry while striking non-civilian targets in the cities.[94] Butt believed that breaking the chains of oppression and re-establishing "justice" and "truth" required teaching Kashmiris about the art of prolonged resistance; his soldiers needed to inculcate self-worth and courage among themselves and others, and learn how other struggling nations had risen in the cause of freedom.[95] Although peace and tranquillity in Kashmir remained an important part of his political discourse, Butt emphasized that "peace at the cost of just aspirations of Kashmiris whose life was overshadowed by constant terror and fear is no peace. To dream of such 'peace' is a mere corruption of mind. Indeed, arguing for such peace is asking to accept the death of aspirations."[96]

Butt's concern about dependency and self-determination drove his financial practices. He aimed to create a self-sufficient army: "soldiers of conscience," a group committed to Kashmir's freedom and ready to wage a prolonged fight.

Butt worried that certain elements in Pakistan wanted Kashmiris to define self-determination as accession to Pakistan. He claimed that NLF would consider as "friends" only those nations that offered practical help and support. To avoid furthering a dependent mentality, his organization refused financial aid or assistance from outside sources, projecting only that if Kashmiris did attain freedom, other nations struggling for self-determination would be welcome to come to their assistance—if there were no strings attached to such aid from sympathizers. Nations that threatened Butt's goal of an independent Kashmir would be enemies, regardless of their shared religious beliefs.[97]

In the late 1960s, Butt led a self-trained group of NLF activists to India-administered Kashmir to train future fighters for sabotage and to establish secret cells.[98] Some Valley youth had already begun to contemplate an armed revolt. Most came from educated middle-class families and had studied at professional colleges in Srinagar. Disillusioned by the Valley's lack of civil liberties and the moderate approach of resistance leadership, students in a number of schools and colleges organized resistance cells advocating an armed struggle. Like Butt, they believed that freedom was only possible if ordinary Kashmiris initiated an armed movement, instead of relying on Pakistan. While records of these organizations are sparse, the Jammu and Kashmir archives do hold a cyclostyled paper, "Red Kashmir," issued by the Al-Fatah party and outlining the organization's goals: enlist men, organize youth, attack civil and military installations, and snatch arms and ammunition.[99]

The revolutionary ideas of these Kashmiri youth challenged those of the nonviolent Plebiscite Front, bringing to the forefront tensions within Kashmiri discourses on freedom. The Plebiscite Front advised students to refrain from initating an armed resistence based on an Algerian-type struggle as it would not benefit Kashmiris. The student community, however, believed the plebiscite leaders to be stooges of the Indian government. In this political environment, Butt was able to ally with many known and unknown Kashmiri voices of resistance to spread the idea of an armed struggle; he succeeded in setting up several armed cells in the Valley.[100] To fund the growth of his organization, he also spearheaded a bank robbery which led to the death of an Indian intelligence officer and subsequently to his arrest. Charged with the murder and with being a Pakistani agent bent on destroying state security, he was sentenced to death.

However, within three months of his arrest, Butt escaped through a tunnel dug in secret with two other prisoners. Contemporary Kashmiri historian Yusuf Saraf described the popular reaction to the escape:

> It created a sensation and the truth remains it electrified the people who rejoiced at his brilliant escape and prayed for his safe return into Azad Kashmir. An inquiry committee was set up and a number of jail officers and guards were suspended. A cash reward of Rs. 10,000 was announced for his arrest. Thousands of posters with his photographs and repeating the government offer were circulated.[101]

Maqbool Butt, however, managed to escape from the Valley and return to Pakistan-administered Kashmir, whereupon the Pakistani government immediately arrested him to ensure that he was not acting at the behest of Indian security agencies. Butt, who had risked his life crossing the ceasefire line, was shattered by the severe treatment he received at the Black Fort at the hands of the Pakistani military during the course of his three-month imprisonment.[102] He later wrote that his reentry into Pakistan forced him to rethink several crucial matters related to Kashmir's freedom. For the first time, he found it difficult to distinguish between his "friends" and "enemies."[103] His arrest inspired protests among pro-independence groups in Pakistan-administered Kashmir.

Butt's dramatic escape from a death sentence in the Srinagar jail made him a hero among pro-independence political activists in Azad Kashmir.[104] In 1969, the members of the Plebiscite Front AJK elected him to their presidency. He organized political gatherings throughout Pakistan to teach people about the necessity of an armed struggle, portraying the state-sponsored regimes on both sides of Kashmir as "enemies of freedom," put in place by India and Pakistan to further their own political agendas. These governments lacked legitimacy, Butt argued; they had not only "mortgaged Kashmir's freedom for money and position in the government but had also denied people economic and social freedom."[105] Butt, like other Azad Kashmiri activists, worked to include Gilgit and Baltistan in Kashmir's freedom movement. He disputed Pakistan's claim to these areas and hoped to initiate a movement for the inclusion of these northern regions in Azad Kashmir.

Maqbool Butt's attempts to spread his vision of freedom received a setback in the late 1960s when a military coup crushed individual rights in Pakistan, with the regime assisted by the bureaucracy and intelligence departments. The Pakistani military regime viewed the independence-oriented NLF with apprehension and wanted to limit the group's freedom of action, if not subordinate it entirely to Pakistani foreign policy objectives. The NLF, in turn, tried hard to protect its autonomy against Pakistani interference. Nevertheless, the *Ganga* hijacking case of 1971 gave Pakistan an opening to control this movement.

In 1971, two young members of the NLF hijacked the Indian airplane *Ganga*, en route from Srinagar to Delhi, hoping to repeat the recent success of Palestinian activists in the so-called Dawson's Field hijackings. The hijackers demanded the release of thirty-six NLF members who were political prisoners. They also wanted a guarantee that New Delhi would not harm their own families.[106] Pakistani authorities convinced the hijackers to release the passengers and crew members of the *Ganga* and return them to India by road via Amritsar, whereupon the NLF, having lost its leverage, destroyed the plane. Initially, many Pakistanis celebrated the arrival of the *Ganga*, seeing the hijackers as champions of the Pakistani cause in Kashmir. Their enthusiasm did not last, however, as the hijacking occurred at a time when India–Pakistan relations had critical implications for the resolution of an ongoing civil unrest in Pakistan. In the general elections of 1970, the Awami League of East Pakistan had secured an absolute majority, while in West Pakistan the Pakistan People's Party won 81 of 138 seats. However, the Pakistani military regime refused to hand over power to these new political groups without assurances that the military and the bureaucracy would continue to dominate governance. This situation alienated the Bengali majority in East Pakistan.[107] New Delhi used the *Ganga* incident as a reason to ban Pakistani planes from Indian airspace at a time when East Pakistan was in open revolt. The loss of Indian air space, removing the quickest and easiest connection between the two parts of Pakistan, led in part to the Pakistani army's surrender and the independence of East Pakistan (now Bangladesh).

The Pakistani military regime argued that Indian intelligence agencies had manipulated the hijacking to dismember Pakistan.[108] Even a commission of inquiry appointed to investigate the incident confirmed that the hijacking had meant to spark a confrontation between India and Pakistan and to disrupt communication between the two wings of Pakistan. The report suggested that the Pakistani government should probe the "credentials" of everyone who argued for an independent Kashmir.[109] If the idea of an independent Kashmir was the handiwork of Indian intelligence agencies hoping to redefine "self-determination" toward independence, then this hope for "freedom" would not be for its own sake but to "weaken Kashmiri desire for accession to Pakistan." Kashmiri political activists who argued for an independent Kashmir were, according to this view, Indian agents who had "staged faked guerilla operations in India-held Kashmir to acquire hold on the minds of the Kashmiris on both sides of the ceasefire line."[110]

Pakistan's military regime considered the "independent" outlook of Kashmiri political activists a threat.[111] The "reorientation of the Kashmir dispute" meant that Kashmiris would associate self-determination with independence rather than accession to Pakistan. If this goal was achieved, Pakistan would have to give up its claims on Kashmir, an unthinkable option ever since the retention of Kashmir's territory had become an element of national identity during the post-partition war, and especially unthinkable in light of the very recent traumatic loss of East Pakistan.

Instead of only investigating the hijackers and their involvement with Indian intelligence, the Pakistani government arrested almost three hundred members of the NLF, including its entire high command, in connection with its investigation into the *Ganga*, alleging that every member had conspired with Indian intelligence agencies to destroy the Pakistani state. Many of these pro-independence activists were transferred to the interrogation center at the Shahi Qilla at Lahore, where they were tortured.[112] In Pakistan-administered Kashmir, people expressed extreme disappointment with how Pakistan's military regime had handled the Ganga hijacking case. Pro-independence Kashmiris noted that they had offered to cooperate fully with the Pakistani authorities in an inquiry to make certain that no "black sheep" had infiltrated their organization. "How could a Kashmiri freedom fighter not feel hurt and agitated by such ridiculous accusations?" Ansari wrote. To pro-independence groups in Pakistan-administered Kashmir, Pakistan's government had offended the sentiments of "freedom loving Kashmiris."[113]

After the 1972 formation of a democratic government in Pakistan, Pakistan's new prime minister Zulfikar Ali Bhutto established a tribunal to try the high command of the NLF. The pro-independence parties approved of this development, believing that the activists could prove their innocence.[114] Almost all who faced trial were Kashmiris originally from the Valley.[115] Pakistan charged them with providing strategic information to Indian intelligence by photographing and making maps of army movements and units, allegations the accused forcefully denied.[116] In a passionate statement at the Lahore High Court, Maqbool Butt tore apart propaganda from Pakistan's military regime that deliberately confused Kashmir's freedom fighters with agents of India. Butt traced this theory to the coincidence of the post-*Ganga* inquiry against the NLF with the breakdown of the negotiations between Pakistan's military leadership and the popularly elected Awami League of East Pakistan. The mass arrests of the NLF members had occurred in April 1971, when Yahya Khan's regime had ordered a military crackdown in East Pakistan. The Pakistani army's campaign against the Bengali resistance had left thousands dead and millions displaced. To shift public attention away from the loss of East Pakistan, Butt argued, the military regimes had blamed their failures on pro-independence Kashmiri political activists.[117]

Butt distinguished between military rulers and ordinary Pakistanis, arguing that that the latter supported the Kashmiri cause. He rejected the authority of the court before which he spoke, noting that it, and courts like it, had always stood as representatives of existing systems in defense against agents of change:

> If the struggle for freedom were to be stopped by court rulings there would hardly have been any free nation on the world today. If the evolution of civilization, democracy and freedom was to be prevented by the existing judicial and administrative system no revolution would have taken place from the beginning of history. Decisions about welfare and freedom of people are not made in existing courts, but the evolutionary process of human history gives the verdict of these governments. For the courts, themselves are the products of the system that these movements are aimed to change.... No one can stop me from claiming that every ruling power in Pakistan has exploited the Kashmir issue for the last twenty-five years for its lust for power and abused this issue to mislead the people of Pakistan who have and still do support the freedom of Kashmir.[118]

Butt declared passionately that far from being a clandestine agent of India or Pakistan, he was exclusively committed to the vision of an independent Kashmir.

> It is my faith that the dawn of freedom will fall in my country and the line of division will be trodden. This will be the time when facts about my life will come out. Only then I will get justice and this will be done in the court of history. That day my people will know the reality of allegations, by both Indian and Pakistani rulers against me, of being an agent of India and Pakistan. At present, I have no other choice but to give myself to the merciless hands of time and wait for the day when the darkness of discrimination and malice, cruelty and exploitation will be replaced by the light of justice. That day I will ask for justice![119]

Similar statements made by other NLF members mocked Pakistani references to Kashmiris as "cowards," incapable of attaining freedom on their own. The NLF activists blamed paralysis in the region on Pakistan's military regimes, which had crippled Kashmiri initiative in furtherance of their own political agendas.[120]

The trial against the top command of the NLF continued for three years. During the trial, the court examined over 1,900 witnesses, including the prominent Kashmiri leaders K. H. Khurshid, Khaliq Ansari, and Amanullah Khan, each of whom expressed their faith in the integrity of the accused and presented them as Kashmir's freedom fighters.[121] Ultimately, the tribunal acquitted all of the accused except the main hijacker, Hashim Qureshi, who was sentenced to prison for eighteen years for hijacking and having links with Indian intelligence agencies. The fallout from the extended inquiry and trial was complex.

The NLF movement lost steam in Pakistan-administered Kashmir, while the idea of an independent Kashmir became unacceptable in Pakistani political discourse. But although Pakistan's military regime clamped down on Kashmiris who advocated independence, the student community in Azad Kashmir still supported the unflinching resistance of Maqbool Butt and his cohorts to both India and Pakistan. The National Student Federation continued its activism, organizing protests to seek independence. In early 1970, students broke through police barriers to distribute a pro-independence pamphlet to a visiting delegation of Muslim leaders from around the Islamic world. To silence this opposition, the federal government arrested countless students under the Federal Security Act.[122]

In Britain, a group of migrants from Azad Kashmir, now living in the industrial towns of Bradford and Birmingham, helped pro-independence activists in their homeland by collecting funds for the legal defense of the Kashmiris in the *Ganga* trial. At the same time, they organized protests, demonstrations, and campaigns to counter the propaganda unleashed by Pakistan's military regimes, which portrayed the *Ganga* hijackers and their supporters as "double agents."[123] Leaflets and posters published in Britain circulated widely, though often clandestinely, in Pakistan and Pakistan-administered Kashmir, characterizing the accused instead as "freedom fighters" who had dedicated their lives to Kashmir.[124] Refusing to be tools of any "imperial power," transnational Kashmiris imagined alternatives in freeing Kashmir from both India and Pakistan.[125]

Interrogating Imperialism, Capitalism, and Socialism

The role of the Kashmiri transnational community in shaping Kashmiri resistance demonstrates again that "Kashmir" in the postcolonial era was not just a geographical entity but a political imaginary. For the transnational community, "Kashmir" transcended cultural and territorial definitions of identity and evoked a longing for a homeland. The exclusion and racism the Kashmiri transnational community experienced in its host society inspired diasporic residents to imagine a homeland free from political injustices and economic disparities. The end of the conflict in Kashmir, whether achieved through bilateral or international diplomacy, popular demonstrations, or a successful armed rebellion, would pave the way for exiles' and expatriates' return to the original "home."

The global political realities of the 1960s and 1970s shaped the worldview of these diasporic activists. A group of educated Kashmiris along with individuals working in factories in Birmingham in the early 1970s debated, discussed, and proposed practical strategies to free Kashmir. Exposure to the worldwide left-wing activist movements of the twentieth century—especially the International Marxist Group (IMG) in Britain, which drew from diverse intellectual currents like Maoism and Trotskyism—fascinated these Kashmiri activists. They attempted to replicate these ideas as they imagined a revolutionary vision for Kashmir. Throughout the 1970s, diasporic activists organized social events, debated politics in cafés, and distributed revolutionary literature and pamphlets. They raised awareness among their fellow British Kashmiris about the new currents sweeping the world and brainstormed about how Kashmiris could adapt, modify, or replicate these leftist movements in charting novel approaches for the region's liberation.

The first Kashmiri transnational organization, the United Kashmir Liberation Front (UKLF), was formed in the early 1970s by educated expatriates, along with a few factory workers in Birmingham, who hoped to provide intellectual direction for Kashmir's freedom.[126] Its founders, including Master Abdul Majid, Younus Taryaby, and Nazir Nazish, lived in a world split between the rival social and economic systems—capitalism and communism—propagated by two superpowers, the United States and the Soviet Union, who had drawn the entire world into Cold War politics. Their struggle for hegemony played out within proxy nations in Asia, Africa, and Latin America, many either recently decolonized or still struggling under the yoke of colonialism.

A majority of the people living in these colonized nations understood "freedom" not only as the end of foreign occupation, but as the initiation of a social revolution to end class disparities and economic inequalities. As a result, they equated capitalism with neocolonialism, a social system that ensured the dominance of the elites over the excluded majority.[127] The experiences of the working-class Kashmiri transnational community, both as a part of the excluded majority within their own homeland and as a community struggling against discrimination in British industrial centers, naturally aligned them more closely with socialist ideology. They absorbed the intellectual and political currents sweeping the world in the 1960s, especially the growing socialist activism on college campuses that not just called for opposition to all forms of imperialism but also advocated radical protest, direct action, and civil disobedience.

The British Kashmiri transnational community, closely tied to its homeland, saw how socialist revolutionary currents had even reached the shores of military-ruled Pakistan in the 1960s, seeping into the imagination of poets, writers, and intellectuals. In Pakistan, public discussions centered on the economic disparities and social discontent unleashed by the India–Pakistan war of 1965 and the growing industrialization that had created a wedge between economic growth and social development. Wealth polarization was ever more visible; twenty-two elite families "owned 66 percent of industrial assets, 79 percent of insurance and 80 percent of banking," while the rest struggled to make ends meet.[128] In response, students, trade union groups, and other leftists launched a series of protest movements and supported a new political party, the Pakistan People's Party (PPP), which promised not only reform and democratic change, but the creation of an egalitarian society. Surrounded by socialist ideologues, the PPP's charismatic leader Zulfiqar Ali Bhutto fused the concept of socialism with the "progressive aspects of Islam" to counter accusations from right-wing Islamist groups that socialism was "anti-Islam" and the PPP was an "atheist" party. For its part, the PPP "denounced the conservative religious" parties as "representatives of monopolist capitalism" and agents of backwardness and social and spiritual stagnation.[129] These debates in Pakistan's political discourse were a constant feature in the diasporic newspapers like the London weekly *Mashriq*, read by British Kashmiris as they contemplated the future of their homeland within the context of socialist principles and ideals.[130]

British Kashmiri activists' intellectual journeys forced them to reconcile their individual beliefs and religious identity with the revolutionary global concepts of socialism and communism. Younus Taryaby, raised in the conservative social milieu of Pakistan-administered Kashmir where the Muslim peasantry had been exploited by Hindu landlords for generations, perceived social inequalities through a communitarian lens. In Britain, Taryaby underwent a severe mental crisis while reconciling socialist and Islamic principles, especially after reading a series of articles in the *Mashriq* that debated the fatwa declaring socialists to be heretics, issued by more than one hundred religious scholars in Pakistan. Gradually, his thinking transformed on two levels. First, his personal observation of the discrimination endured by South Asian workers in Britain, regardless of their religious background, convinced him that "real" conflicts stemmed not from religious affiliation but from social and economic inequalities that allowed one class to dominate the other. Second, meetings with other left-leaning diasporic Kashmiris convinced him that religion, even devoid of political ideology, remained an effective tool in the hands of the elites, who skillfully created dissent among the poor using religious, ethnic, and tribal differences to suppress independent thinking and keep the poor subjugated.[131]

Nazir Nazish, inspired by the Marxist ideas, played a key role in transforming Taryaby's thinking. A teacher by profession, born and raised in the Dadyal area in Pakistan-administered Kashmir, Nazish wanted to understand new revolutionary ideas and ideologies. After his arrival in England, he met Tariq Ali, a prominent British Pakistani political activist who in the late 1960s was an active member of the IMG.[132] The party, affiliated with the Trotskyist Fourth International, condemned the class divisions and relationships characteristic of capitalist societies, especially elite domination of the working class. It agitated for a revolutionary transformation of societies, believing parliamentary subservience to big-business interests made it an instrument of capitalism.[133] The IMG believed that revolution would transform society; they supported not only struggles for national liberation and socialism, including the Chinese, Vietnamese, and the Cuban revolutions, but also the anti-bureaucratic struggles in Eastern Europe and labor movements in advanced capitalist countries. Nazish voraciously read revolutionary literature, especially the newspapers *Black Dwarf* (1968–70) and *Red Mole* (1970–3). Both elaborated on the ideas of Marxism and Trotskyism and devoted issues to global topics like the Bolivian diaries of Che Guevara, British imperialism in Ireland, the Vietnam War, and the Cuban revolution.[134] These articles inspired Nazish and likeminded Kashmiri expatriates to become actively involved in various protest campaigns organized by the IMG to show solidarity with the Vietnamese and Irish causes. And he became convinced that the only way forward for oppressed people was a revolutionary struggle.[135]

Transnational activists like Nazish and Taryaby distributed free copies of *Red Mole* among British Kashmiri laborers and organized public gatherings both to explain these new ideologies to their fellow workers and to contemplate the revolutionary implications for their homeland. In a series of pamphlets written between 1971 and 1973, the members of UKLF framed the search for Kashmir's freedom in "anti-imperialist and anti-capitalist terms."[136] Even though the old forms of colonialism no longer existed, they argued, a new form of economic imperialism had taken root—one that subjugated other nationalities and suppressed local cultures through intellectual control and physical subjugation. The party saw Kashmir's occupation as imperialism, now practiced by India and Pakistan rather than by Britain. Anticolonial movements in South Asia had not transferred power to the majority working classes. Instead, local elites retained their power beyond decolonization, using predatory capitalist economic practices to expand their riches while deploying the financial aid provided by the new nation-states to suppress worker–peasant resistance. Applying this integrated understanding of imperialism and capitalism to the political culture of Kashmir, expatriate political activists perceived India and Pakistan as imperial powers with no interest in the welfare of Kashmiris, looking only to ensure their domination over Kashmir's territory by co-opting political elites.[137]

The UKLF's manifesto, *Kashmir: India, Pakistan, or Independence*, called for a revolutionary movement to transform Kashmir's social and economic organization and lay the foundation for a prosperous and independent country of Jammu and Kashmir. The UKLF aimed to detach the Valley from India's control and establish a socialist government in free Kashmir. In one of their pamphlets, the UKLF taught Kashmiris that peasants, workers, and laborers would lead the revolutionary movement in Jammu and Kashmir. The UKLF sought to end the imperial domination of India and Pakistan and to eliminate the social and economic disparities in Kashmiri society. Imagining a revolutionary struggle that would overthrow imperial rule and capitalist domination, the party believed that initiating a revolution in Kashmir could topple the old structures of power and lay the basis for a new class-free society.[138]

Although the UKLF provided a theoretical vision for Kashmir's revolutionary struggle, the party members agreed that the Kashmiri transnational community could not bring about a revolution itself; they could only provide diplomatic and political support to a revolutionary party within Kashmir's territory. Constrained by distance, they worried about the lack of strictly revolutionary parties on both sides of the ceasefire line. The UKLF believed that every political party in Pakistan-administered Kashmir lacked sufficient revolutionary credentials. Even political groups like the Plebiscite Front that operated on both sides of divided Kashmir were, according to the UKLF, nationalist organizations that paid lip service to the idea of self-determination, but practiced a moderate politics that failed to bring any resolution to the dispute.[139] They decided that though the Plebiscite Front in Pakistan spoke of a socialist outlook, its failure to provide a clear-cut plan for a future socialist revolution meant that it would continue supporting existing feudal structures. Members of the UKLF were convinced that revolutionary combat, as they had seen in other international movements for liberation, was the only way to gain Kashmir's freedom.[140]

Imagining Alternatives with Revolutionary Metaphors

The members of the UKLF supported pro-independence revolutionaries in Azad Kashmir, but searched for a third option that would free them from dependence on Pakistan and allow them to chart a new route to free Kashmir. Inspired by international revolutionary movements, they initially imagined converting Kashmir into another Vietnam. The Kashmiri transnational community understood the experiences of the Vietnamese, who were struggling to end the occupation by the French and the Japanese. The agreement signed with the French at the 1954 Geneva Conference had stipulated a ceasefire for the peaceful withdrawal of French forces and the temporary division of Vietnam along the seventeenth parallel (which split the country into communist North Vietnam and noncommunist South Vietnam), a division similar to Kashmir's ceasefire line. The failure of the international community to uphold the agreement and to conduct a general democratic election in 1956, which would have reunited the country under one government, also resonated with the UKLF, which drew parallels with the proposed plebiscite in Kashmir. In the end, elections were held only in South Vietnam, rather than countrywide, because the United States feared a communist victory. The limited elections led South Vietnamese communist sympathizers, supported by North Vietnam, to establish the National Liberation Front, also known as the Viet Cong, as a guerilla force directed against South Vietnamese and eventually US troops.[141] To launch a struggle for the reunification of Jammu and Kashmir, the UKLF suggested setting up an analogous free government in Pakistan-administered Kashmir. As in Vietnam, Kashmiris would have their own army that would not only "protect the boundaries of Azad Kashmir but also free the Valley from bondage."[142]

While exploring these strategies for securing Kashmir's freedom, certain contradictions emerged within the political stance of the transnational UKLF. Some of its members expressed concern that although they considered the governments in Pakistan-administered Kashmir to be puppet regimes, they did not see how Kashmiris could gain their freedom without operating under Pakistan's control. Focused on setting the Valley free, they wanted to use Azad Kashmir as a base camp. They reiterated that only one solution could end the Kashmir conflict: erasing the ceasefire line and reunifying Jammu and Kashmir. But initially, they were less critical of Pakistan's role in Kashmir and considered Pakistan sympathetic to their demand for self-determination.[143] They changed their stance after the *Ganga* hijacking case.

Transnational activists like Younus Taryaby and Fazal Haq became convinced that Pakistan wanted to control Kashmir as much as India controlled the Valley. They argued that the transnational community should rethink its strategy for gaining Kashmir's freedom, since Pakistan would not support a fight for independent Kashmir. Abdul Basit's *Kashmir's War for Freedom*, which had inspired Maqbool Butt, also attracted these expatriate Kashmiris.[144] Basit's book provided the most compelling plan of action to attain Kashmir's freedom without dependence on Pakistan. Azad Kashmir made perfect sense as a "springboard of operations" from which to drive India's occupation army out of Kashmir, yet any attempt to restore sovereignty to its people entailed grave risks of "repressive reprisals on the model of Jordan's savage crackdown on Palestinian freedom-fighters."[145] Pakistan would view the rise of a self-sustaining liberation movement in Kashmir as a threat to its interests. The goal, Basit argued, should be to convince Pakistanis to think broadly and focus on the deeper regional challenges that faced them.

Basit wrote *Kashmir's War for Freedom* prior to the creation of Bangladesh, when tensions between the then East and West Pakistan had reached new heights. He addressed in detail the "widening emotional gap" between East Pakistan and Kashmir. In East Pakistan, the Kashmir conflict "did not resonate in the same existential way"[146] as it did among West Pakistanis, especially Punjabis. The politically aware in East Pakistan, Basit argued, resented West Pakistan's deep interest in Kashmir. Many Bengalis felt that West Pakistan placed too much importance on the Kashmir issue, while ignoring the grievances of East Pakistan. Given these political tensions, he argued that Pakistan should focus less on the Kashmir issue and, instead, divert its energies to mending relations with East Pakistan.[147]

To win the moral support of Pakistani citizens, Basit suggested, Kashmir's pro-independence groups should distribute literature and organize conferences to convince Pakistanis that Kashmiris were not agents of any outside country but members of a nation struggling to find its own voice in its quest for freedom. This approach would prevent the Pakistani political and military elite from unleashing its propaganda machinery to discredit them.[148] Basit's strategy focused on developing closer relations with the Chinese, seeking training in the art of prolonged resistance on the model of the response to Japanese occupation during the Second World War.[149]

Basit's vision remained a pipe dream, yet his ideas generated interest among the UKLF leaders, including Younus Taryaby and Master Abdul Majeed, who were contemplating new plans after the arrest and trial of pro-independence Kashmiris in Pakistan. Though convinced that freeing "India-occupied Kashmir" while based in "Pakistan-occupied Kashmir" was possible, Taryaby suggested an end to the "dual occupation" of Jammu and Kashmir, instead of only focusing on freeing the Valley from India. He also rejected the banner of "plebiscite," arguing that nation-states continuously dangled the possibility to keep Kashmiris subservient.

Playing the plebiscite card, according to Taryaby, meant marching to the tune of India or Pakistan.[150] However, others within the organization, including Nazir Nazish, considered it practical to support pro-plebiscite groups in Britain that had a support base in the South Asian subcontinent and could play an active role in initiating a movement for Kashmir's liberation. These tensions caused a split within the UKLF; while certain members supported a more moderate approach to Kashmir's freedom and continued to support an internationally backed plebiscite, others preferred a bold move, declaring both India and Pakistan as occupiers deserving a revolutionary anticolonial response.[151]

After the split within the UKLF, Younus Taryaby widened the movement to address the challenges faced by the Kashmiri community in Britain as well as those faced by the homeland. In the early 1960s, the Kashmiri working class had joined the Pakistan Workers Association (PWA) to fight racism and improve working conditions for South Asians in Britain. However, by the early 1970s many Kashmiri PWA members wanted to form an exclusively Kashmiri organization. An initial compromise led to the formation of the Pakistan-Kashmiri Workers Association, but this new group only survived for a year. Tensions erupted during debates on the future status of Kashmir; Pakistani workers supported Kashmiris when they discussed the "Indian occupation of Kashmir" but resented references to Pakistan as an "occupier." The Pakistani transnational community, in other words, wanted Kashmiris to continue their quest for self-determination if that meant accession to Pakistan, but not if it meant independence.[152] These conflicts motivated Younus Taryaby to establish the Kashmir Workers Association (KWA). Three core principles informed the party's agenda. First, it stood in solidarity with oppressed nations, especially those struggling against imperialism, capitalism, and foreign occupation. The party also wanted to end racism in Britain; addressing issues related to racism and organizing protest movements and demonstrations helped the KWA reach a wider audience than they did through revolutionary ideology alone. As a result, the KWA built alliances with other South Asian labor groups and with progressive whites, who then provided them moral support for their third goal, the "national liberation and expulsion of foreign forces from Kashmir."[153]

Despite its physical distance from the subcontinent, the KWA helped shape the trajectory of the armed struggle for Kashmiri independence. As the first Kashmiri diasporic organization that considered the demand for plebiscite a deliberate ploy to keep Kashmiris subservient, the KWA argued that the call for a plebiscite was merely a euphemism for "Kashmir Banega Pakistan" (Kashmir will become part of Pakistan).[154] The organization disaggregated the Kashmiri and Pakistani nationalist agendas, and radicalized the emergent Kashmiri struggle for independence. Nevertheless, it failed to take any practical steps to bring about a revolution in the homeland. Their inspirational ideas remained confined to discussions and debates and failed to generate a revolution in Kashmir.

The KWA was not the only Kashmiri expatriate organization seeking to establish a transnational political foothold. The Plebiscite Front of Britain's members belonged to the clan of Khaliq Ansari, the preeminent pro-independence Kashmiri political activist from Pakistan-administered Kashmir. Unlike members of the KWA, who drew on international communist revolutionary movements, the Ansari clan kept its distance from Marxist philosophy. The group believed in the prospect of a plebiscite as the ideal way to attain Kashmir's freedom, but also supported pro-independence Kashmiri exiles who arrived in Britain after the *Ganga* hijacking case of 1971.[155]

Several other Kashmiri transnational groups also emerged in the 1980s with different strategies for Kashmir's freedom. Some mirrored the mainstream political parties in the homeland that supported Kashmir's accession to Pakistan. At the same time, a group of Pahari-speaking Kashmiris originally from the Mirpur district of Azad Kashmir started the Kashmir National Identity Campaign (KNIC), and pushed for the "recognition of Kashmiris in Britain as a separate community from Pakistanis." Instead of equating Pahari-speaking Kashmiris with Punjabi- or Urdu-speaking Pakistanis, the group demanded the "dual recognition of Kashmiris as a separate ethnic group, and of Pahari as a separate language" to end British Kashmiri invisibility.[156] Their demands reveal the increasing disappointment of British Mirpuris with Pakistan for primarily prioritizing Kashmiris from the Valley while treating Azad Kashmiris in general and Mirpuris in particular as inconsequential and peripheral, despite the region contributing immensely to Pakistan's foreign exchange earnings through remittances. However, the KNIC goal of making a distinction between "Kashmiri" and "Pakistani" identity was rejected by pro-Pakistan Kashmiri transnational groups like the British branch of the Muslim Conference and the Pakistan–Kashmir United Forum that considered their campaign an ill-conceived move that could lead to deeper divisions within the Kashmiri discourses on freedom.[157] The sense of a transnational Kashmiri identity frayed as disagreements about strategy threatened to overwhelm the otherwise wide agreement on self-determination.

Integration with Pakistan? Twist in the Relationship between Pakistan and Azad Kashmir

Back on the South Asian subcontinent, the dismemberment of Pakistan and the creation of the new nation-state of Bangladesh in the early 1970s redefined the relationship between India and Pakistan, with overflowing consequences for the Kashmiri quest to attain self-determination. The Simla Agreement of 1972, meant to once again restore peace between India and Pakistan, stated that the Kashmir dispute, along with all other differences between the two countries, was a bilateral issue. Both nation-states agreed to respect the ceasefire line, referred to as the line of control. The notable absence of the much-touted principle of "self-determination" negated the long-promised plebiscite as a means of determining the region's future.[158] While there was no formal agreement to accept the ceasefire line as a permanent border between India and Pakistan, the implication of the agreement was that both nation-states "accepted the partition of Kashmir as *fait accompli*."[159] In the Valley, Sheikh Abdullah's Plebiscite Front, convinced of India's hegemonic domination, accepted the necessity of reconciliation with New Delhi and acknowledged the finality of Jammu and Kashmir's accession to India.[160]

In Azad Kashmir, the prime minister of Pakistan, Zulfiqar Ali Bhutto, restored democratic governance and brought the disputed region "closer" to the federal government, although Azad Kashmir was not formally a province of Pakistan. Earlier in the 1970s the PPP had established an Azad Kashmir branch to replicate the constitution and the federal parliamentary system of Pakistan. In June 1974, the Pakistani and Azad Kashmir governments announced an interim constitutional agreement, which was adopted by the Azad Kashmir legislative assembly on September 24, 1974.[161] The new act granted Azad Kashmir a legislative assembly including forty-two members directly elected by universal suffrage for a five-year term. Islamabad institutionalized its relationship with Azad Kashmir by establishing the Azad Kashmir Council. This body, headed by the prime minister of Pakistan, regulated contact between senior Pakistani government officials and Azad Kashmiris. Nevertheless, the constitution was officially only an interim measure until Azad Kashmir's status was resolved through the promised plebiscite. For the first time under this arrangement, Azad Kashmir received substantial financial assistance from Pakistan. The government's allocation increased from 16 million Pakistani rupees in 1971–2 to 120 million Pakistani rupees in 1975–6, satisfying mainstream politicians.[162] Azad Kashmiris who supported the realignment of relations with Pakistan hoped that the flow of funds to the region after two decades of neglect would promote economic development and prosperity.

Pro-independence groups, however, expressed displeasure with certain clauses of the new constitution. Ironically, the constitution insisted that all "Azad" Kashmiris seeking office should support and swear allegiance to Jammu and Kashmir's accession to Pakistan. It prohibited individuals and political parties in Azad Kashmir from participating in activities "prejudicial or detrimental to the ideology of the state's accession to Pakistan."[163] Pakistan's government, threatened by the regional discontent brewing in Sind, Khyber Pakhtunkhwa (NWFP), and Baluchistan, prohibited Azad Kashmiris from "self-determining" anything besides accession to Pakistan. The central government also equated the invoking of linguistic and cultural differences in pursuit of regional rights with sedition, passing a 1975 law prescribing seven years' imprisonment for any Pakistani claiming more than one nationality.[164]

Pro-independence Kashmiris like Khaliq Ansari criticized the political positions of both India and Pakistan after the signing of the Simla Agreement. Ansari believed that New Delhi and Islamabad had collaborated to illegitimately settle the Kashmir dispute not by allowing regional self-determination but by incorporating their respective parts of Jammu and Kashmir.[165] The NLF voiced similar concerns in its official newspaper, arguing that, as all clauses of the Simla Agreement contradicted the national interests of the Kashmiri people, they could not and would not abide by them: "Kashmiris stand fully absolved of the responsibilities, which the [Simla] agreement puts on the shoulders of its signatories," and would continue to struggle against usurpers "with greater momentum and deeper dedication" until they achieved freedom.[166] Under pressure from Islamabad, independence-minded Azad Kashmiris did curb revolutionary activity in the subcontinent during the 1970s, but continued to fight within the transnational space of the transnational community.

Territorial Nationalism and the Idea of Independent Kashmir

When political activists from Pakistan-administered Kashmir arrived in Britain after advocating for Kashmir's independence on the subcontinent, some of the tensions previously submerged by physical distance surfaced. After the NLF disintegrated due to the *Ganga* case in 1972, for example, Amanullah Khan traveled to Britain to mobilize the Kashmiri transnational community and continue the freedom struggle. Khan sought to unite different diasporic strands and articulate a common vision for Kashmir's freedom. Most followed his lead because of his active involvement in Kashmir's freedom struggle in the subcontinent, although some disagreed with him politically. The KWA suggested that the transnational community should advocate for revolution, rather than holding onto the goal of "plebiscite." To adopt a broad policy that could unite all Kashmiris, in 1977 Khan formed a separate political party, the Jammu and Kashmir Liberation Front (JKLF), to advocate for an independent Kashmir on a global level.[167]

To popularize the ideology of the JKLF among the Kashmiri transnational community, Khan published an illustrated Urdu/English weekly called *Voice of Kashmir*. Printed in Birmingham from 1977, the weekly provided Khan with a perfect medium for expounding his views on the Kashmir dispute. Filled with stories of the Palestinian and Algerian revolutionary struggles, the paper was intended to stir Kashmiris to launch an armed struggle for Kashmir's freedom. Article after article exhorted Kashmiri Muslims to emulate the courage and commitment of the Palestinian revolutionaries in seeking freedom. Khan credited Al-Fatah, a Palestinian political and military organization founded by Yasser Arafat in 1958, for drawing international attention to the Palestinian cause. Despite the challenge of reuniting and reviving the Palestinian identity among widely dispersed refugees, the Al-Fatah remained committed to initiating a Palestinian national movement. Kashmiri activists learned how the Palestinian organization had launched its own independence movement despite the efforts of successive Arab governments to dominate them. This struck a chord among Kashmiri political activists seeking to free themselves from Pakistan's hegemony in initiating their own movement for independence. They admired Al-Fatah's insistence on direct armed action to restore human dignity. Khan also expressed solidarity with the peoples of Rhodesia and South Africa fighting racism and the National Liberation Front of Eritrea resisting autocratic policies of their ruling regime. [168]

Drawing legitimacy for his own plans from these movements of self-determination, Khan emphasized that in the context of Kashmir, the nonviolent approach had failed. He now believed that armed struggle was the only way to attain freedom: "War for justice is more sacred than peace at the cost of justice. India and Pakistan may sign one thousand and one agreements about Kashmir that will not diminish our determination to fight for national emancipation."[169] The armed struggle would force India and Pakistan to realize their aspirations. To gain support among the transnational community, the JKLF constructed a new Kashmiri national flag and displayed a map of Kashmir in their publications.[170] The party also set up a pirate radio station, Sada-i-Kashmir (Voice of Kashmir), which transmitted revolutionary broadcasts to Kashmiris living in England and Scotland.[171]

In the late 1970s and 1980s, support in Britain for the JKLF's goal of an independent Kashmir grew steadily. JKLF leaders came from diverse class, social, and regional backgrounds, with many from middle-class and rural origins; very few, if any, came from the elite classes who dominated political power in Kashmir itself. As the JKLF's support base grew, it ushered in an era of diasporic mass politics, involving more people in the political movement for Kashmir's freedom. Though most concentrated in Britain, the JKLF published and distributed a series of pamphlets and newsletters among Kashmiri expatriates in Europe and the United States to seek their support for an independent Jammu and Kashmir state that would reunite India-administered Kashmir, Pakistan-administered Kashmir, and the northern regions of Gilgit and Baltistan. They conceived the united independent state as neutral, secular, and federal. A neutral Kashmir would have friendly relations with all major powers surrounding its boundaries, thus ensuring peace in the region, while a secular and federal Jammu and Kashmir would guarantee religious freedom and a voice for all parts of the new nation-state in shaping its future.[172]

JKLF leaders hoped not only to mobilize Kashmiris, but also to convince Indian and Pakistani public opinion that an independent Kashmir was in their national interest. The JKLF refuted its critics in the nationalist presses of India and Pakistan, who argued that granting independence to Jammu and Kashmir would strengthen other "separatist" movements in the subcontinent and lead to the balkanization of India and Pakistan. The JKLF, however, argued that Kashmir was *sui generis*.[173] The international dimensions of the Kashmir conflict and the United Nations endorsement of the Kashmiri right of self-determination set it apart from "freedom movements" in other dissident Indian states. Unlike those states, the JKLF activists claimed, the state of Jammu and Kashmir was constitutionally not a part of India or Pakistan; the United Nations recognized the state's constitutional status through its maps of the region, which clearly separated Jammu and Kashmir from India and Pakistan. Furthermore, independence for Kashmir was the only option that would not hurt the "national esteem" of either India or Pakistan. Pakistan would be content that, in Amanullah Khan's words, "Muslim majority Jammu and Kashmir has been freed from Indian occupation," while India would be "elated that region has not become a part of Pakistan."[174] The resolution of the Kashmir dispute would end wasted defense expenditures and both nations could focus instead on development and economic progress.

To win the support of the many cultural and linguistic communities that inhabited Jammu and Kashmir, JKLF promised "final freedom" to every person, "according to his or her choice to practice their religious, political, and economic principles." Ironically, however, this vision of a united, independent Jammu and Kashmir, like any nationalism, argued for a rigid, monolithic concept of sovereignty. The JKLF proposed a democratic form of government free from religious discrimination and based on economic equity and social equality. However, they added, no law would be enacted that contradicted Islam's basic principles. To appease its diverse sub-regions, the JKLF promised that independent Kashmir would have a federal parliamentary style of government to negotiate the political, linguistic, and religious demands of Kashmir's communities and sub-regions.[175] But the potential conflicts between majority preferences at the national level and at the local level illustrate the difficulty of creating a stable federal state in which one group's conception of "freedom" is not shared by all. And although the philosophy of the JKLF claimed to ensure religious freedom and federal governmental organization, it ignored the reality that many sub-regions and minorities within the state would prefer to be a part of India even if such guarantees were enforced.

The JKLF also sought to change the way the world community interpreted the Kashmir issue. Many nations viewed the conflict in Kashmir as a territorial dispute between two countries, because India and Pakistan had succeeded in "dressing the issue of Kashmir in a cloak of their own interest." The international community did not wish to embroil itself in controversy by meddling in a bilateral issue. The JKLF initiated a diplomatic effort through conferences, public conventions, and personal contact with ambassadors and foreign dignitaries to generate global awareness about Kashmiri views.[176] Meanwhile, independence politics had become a major topic of debate among British Kashmiris. While propagating their ideology in the global arena, the JKLF also mobilized the transnational community to seek the release of Kashmiri political activists imprisoned on the South Asian subcontinent because of their political beliefs.

In 1984, an underground transnational organization, the National Liberation Army, kidnapped an Indian diplomat to force India to negotiate for the release of Maqbool Butt, who had been sentenced to death for endangering the security of the country. When the Indian government refused to negotiate, the members of the National Liberation Army murdered their hostage.[177] After this incident, there was strong pressure from India on Britain to curtail the activities of Kashmiri pro-independence groups; increased surveillance of Kashmiri activists in Britain resulted, among other outcomes, in the 1985 arrest of Amanullah Khan.[178] Though Khan was held for fifteen months on charges of bomb making and other illegal activities, none could be proven in court. Despite his December 1986 acquittal, however, he was subsequently deported to Pakistan.

Khan's deportation opened a new chapter in Kashmir's resistance movement as, at the behest of the Pakistani intelligence agencies (the Inter-Services Intelligence, or ISI), his organization took advantage of the discontent in India-administered Kashmir to initiate an armed struggle across the ceasefire line. Even though the JKLF's dream of an independent Kashmir conflicted with the ISI's organizing principle of Kashmir's integration with Pakistan, the two groups successfully allied to execute a major revolt against India during the 1990s. Because any help from ISI meant carrying forward the Pakistani agenda in the Valley in the name of independence, a portion of the Kashmiri transnational community strongly disagreed with Khan's plans. This type of Pakistan-supported insurgency, they argued, resembled a proxy or puppet war more than the grassroots guerrilla warfare that had succeeded in Cuba and Vietnam, and could lead to civilian casualties. When Khan went ahead with his secret work with the ISI anyway, it caused a deep rift in the British JKLF. Many members resigned, believing that Khan had compromised the party's core ideology of a self-sustained struggle for independence.[179] However, Khan's plan would convince more Kashmiris, both in the transnational community and within the state's borders, in the late 1980s; the repressive political climate in India-administered Kashmir and the dramatic global transformations brought about by the end of Cold War set the stage for Kashmiri radicalization.

The armed insurgency of the 1990s led to harsh repercussions against Kashmiris in both India and Pakistan. The "border" became a bloodied place as countless Kashmiris searching for weapons died crossing the heavily militarized line of control, now "strictly monitored" with miles of army bunkers and armed patrols. The insurgency displaced Kashmiris who lived in the villages and towns close to the line of control, including Baramulla, Kupwara, Handwara, Karnah, and Poonch. Due to their proximity to the border and knowledge of the topography of the line of control, the Indian army blamed border villagers for guiding the insurgents to Azad Kashmir for guerrilla training. The villagers inhabiting these areas had been suspected of spying by both nation-states, even in times of relative peace, since the establishment of the ceasefire line. During the insurgency, their remoteness from media scrutiny allowed the Indian army to commit atrocities against the local population without fear of reprisal.[180]

In the early 1990s, thousands of Kashmiris from these towns and villages entered Azad Kashmir searching for a safe place for their families. Pakistan welcomed these refugees, whose presence reinforced Pakistan's claim that Indian control of Kashmir was illegitimate under international human rights law.[181] The refugees faced immense challenges, however. To ensure that they were not infiltrated with "Indian spies," Pakistani intelligence agencies questioned them before granting permission to stay in Azad Kashmir. Most of them had undertaken dangerous journeys through "tough and forested mountains under the cover of darkness" with their families, carrying no possessions. Initially living in tents, they were vulnerable to weather and disease. The displaced Kashmiris had no citizenship or identity cards and no jobs, surviving on a monthly stipend of 1,500 Pakistani rupees (14 US dollars) for a family; their children had no access to schools. Some refugees, especially those who spoke Koshur, struggled to adapt as a cultural minority in Azad Kashmir, where Pahari, Pothwari, or Gojari were the dominant languages. The local communities stigmatized them as the "other," and sometimes resented their presence amidst them.[182] Many of those who were physically able decided to join the insurgency against the Indian army, convinced that it was the only option that would enable them to return home.[183]

Even though the insurgency was being waged in India-administered Kashmir, the inhabitants of Azad Kashmir also bore the repercussions. Anam Zakariya asserts the areas close to the border, especially the Neelum Valley and its inhabitants, became the worst sufferers of the constant firing and shelling. The villagers constructed bunkers in their homes but found it difficult to lead a normal life. The bombing of the only school at the Neelum Valley excluded its young generation from gaining an education. It resulted in an "entire generation" being uneducated. The women of the Neelum Valley faced the brunt of the violence, while their menfolk worked in cities of Muzaffarabad, Karachi and Rawalpindi to make ends meet, and rejected the idea of *aazadi* and blamed the militants trained by the Pakistani establishment for creating havoc in their homes.[184]

Azad Kashmir became more important to Pakistan after the army decided to set up camps to train foreign fighters to fight jihad (holy war) against India, abandoning the JKLF rebels' vision for an independent Kashmir unbeholden to outside influences. The presence of these military installations created an aura of fear among Azad Kashmiris, who viewed them as effective tools to suppress internal dissent. The freedom of the press was curtailed, and journalists often faced intimidation and coercion if they threatened to publicize any issue contrary to Pakistan's supposed national interest. In a statement to Human Rights Watch, one anonymous Muzaffarabad journalist commented:

> We are caught between a rock and a hard place—unable to overthrow the Indian yoke there and at the mercy of Pakistani jihadis and the dreaded ISI here. But the problem is, we are all compromised. If the ISI calls me and asks me whether I spoke to you, I will probably tell them everything. That is the price to be paid to live in peace, if not in dignity.[185]

The rise of the insurgency in the Valley provided a pretext for the Pakistani army to control local administrative matters in Azad Kashmir and appoint ministers and administrative officials. Thus, the autonomy of the Azad Kashmir government eroded further, and local administration became inert on multiple fronts. The long-term consequences of these events include the response to the October 8, 2005, earthquake, which killed 75,000 people. When the local government failed to take control of the relief operation in an orderly manner, radical Islamist groups provided aid in some of the worst-affected villages.[186] The Islamists' penetration into this governmental role reveals the inability of the Azad Kashmir government to respond to local needs, while the failure of the Pakistani army to act in a timely manner during the crisis showed, in Human Rights Watch's words, that their "obsession with its notion of state security" meant "undermining human security."[187]

Pakistan has also strengthened its presence in the northern areas of Gilgit and Baltistan despite Azad Kashmiris' pleas to restore the territory of the former princely state of Jammu and Kashmir. In the early 1990s, when the movement for independence in the Valley was at its height, there was growing resentment in Gilgit and Baltistan both against Pakistan's hegemony and against Azad Kashmir's mainstream leaders, who had given Pakistan administrative control over the region in 1949, but not bothered to consult its inhabitants. Anam Zakaria asserts that the people of Gilgit and Baltistan also have no emotional attachment with the *aazadi* movement in India-administered Kashmir. In their perception it is a Valley-dominated movement that failed to include them in their quest for freedom.[188]

One nationalist party, the Balawaristan National Front (BNF), defined Gilgit and Baltistan as a nation "separate from both J&K and Pakistan and therefore entitled to national self-determination." The party's vision of the independent republic of Balawaristan included the Kargil district and certain sections of the Ladakh region in India-administered Kashmir. In a letter written to the secretary general of the United Nations in May 2016, the party leader Abdul Hamid Khan implored the United Nations to end their "apathy" toward "Pakistan occupied Gilgit and Baltistan." He bemoaned the absence of an independent judiciary and human rights organizations that allow the "Pakistani regime to violate all the civilized norms" and eliminate voices that challenge their unjust policies in the region.[189] However, other voices within Gilgit and Baltistan considered it prudent to forge connections with Azad Kashmiris and to jointly resist Pakistan's domination. In the early 1990s, residents of Gilgit and Baltistan filed a writ petition in the High Court of Azad Kashmir demanding that their region be considered a part of the Azad Jammu and Kashmir state with full representation in its legislative assembly. The High Court ruled in their favor, declaring Azad Kashmir's claim to Gilgit and Baltistan legal and directing the Pakistani government to merge these regions with Azad Jammu and Kashmir state.[190] However, Pakistan rejected the competence of the AJK court, considering the court's jurisdiction to be limited to Azad Kashmir and not applicable to the northern areas, which remained unincorporated.[191]

Instead, in 2009 Pakistan passed a series of reform measures under the Gilgit-Baltistan (Empowerment and Self-governance) Order. For the first time, a provision was made for setting up a twenty-four-member directly elected legislative assembly, headed by a chief minister, who did not, however, have the power to select his cabinet. The region was assigned its own governor, an appointee of Islamabad who held office at the pleasure of the Pakistani president, and who selected the chief minister's cabinet. These half-hearted reforms failed to satisfy the inhabitants of the region, who perceived them as another Pakistani attempt to deny them real constitutional rights. In a scathing letter to the prime minister of Pakistan, Malika Baltistani, the chairperson of the Gilgit Baltistan National Alliance, wrote: "What you have endowed upon us is a provincial set up but without a provincial status, a political system without political empowerment, a constitutional package without constitutional rights, a constitutional draft for Gilgit and Baltistan without the input or suggestions by Gilgitis and Baltis."[192] Since then, Pakistan has moved ahead with integrating Gilgit–Baltistan with its federal structure, provoking protests from Gilgit nationalists, Azad Kashmiris, and even the government of India.[193]

As the battle for territory consumes India and Pakistan, Kashmiris on both sides of the line of control hope for peace. A brief phase of forced diplomacy between India and Pakistan in the early twenty-first century raised hopes of demilitarization and an economic union between the two sides of Jammu and Kashmir, which would have reduced the line of control to a geographical demarcation. In the aftermath of 9/11, the US "war on terror" forced Pakistan to destroy militant organizations' safe havens in its territory. Pakistani president Pervez Musharraf initiated dialogue with India to resolve outstanding issues, including Kashmir. While this diplomacy ended in a stalemate, Kashmiris welcomed the confidence-building measures initiated by both countries. The opening of the Srinagar–Muzaffarabad road, the only year-round road connecting the two divided parts of Kashmir, for the first time in nearly six decades allowed families separated by the line of control to reconnect. Since 1947, Kashmiris had missed weddings and funerals due to the inability to secure visas, even though they were just a few hours away from their families. Kashmiris on both sides walked the "Peace Bridge," garlanding their loved ones with marigolds and offering plates of sweets, while billboards along the line of control read "Home to Home."[194] This fleeting peace was once again brought to a screeching halt after terrorist attacks by Pakistani nationals in metropolitan Mumbai in November 2008, which killed

164 Indian civilians. As part of its response, India re-increased its militarization of the Valley and doubled down on casting Kashmiri resistance as a manifestation of Pakistan-supported Islamist terrorism.

Kashmiris in the transnational community, however, continued to counter this narrative by drawing attention to the state violence unleashed in India-administered Kashmir. The portrayal of Kashmiri resistance as "terrorism," many argued, allowed India to avoid international scrutiny and implement the "draconian Armed Forces (Jammu and Kashmir) Special Powers Act (AFSPA) that gives soldiers the permission to shoot to kill with impunity."[195] Transnational Kashmiris initiated a diplomatic effort through conferences, public conventions, and personal contact with parliament members, ambassadors, and foreign dignitaries to generate global awareness about Kashmiri resistance as a movement for political justice and rights rather than Islamist terrorism. They organized marches and demonstrations, including the 2014 "Million March" in Britain, attended by hundreds of British and European Kashmiris to protest killings of civilians in India-administered Kashmir.[196] Despite their different visions for Kashmir's political future, whether independence, accession to India or Pakistan, or a peaceful division, the transnational community united to appeal for basic human rights in Kashmir.

Conclusion

Although its strength, tactics, and exact aims have varied over time, throughout Kashmir's postcolonial history Kashmiri voices of resistance in the region and in the transnational community have sought to reunite the two parts of Kashmir. Despite some Muslim activists' identification with Muslim-majority Pakistan, following the 1947 division of Kashmir along the ceasefire line India and Pakistan controlled their respective sides in markedly similar ways. India had always prevented the establishment of democratic governance in the Valley and, in a comparable way, Pakistan controlled Azad Kashmir by propping up puppet regimes. Governments were created and toppled one after another on orders from, respectively, Islamabad and New Delhi, leading Kashmiri political elites to believe that submission was the only way to remain in power. Meanwhile, the United Nations was unable to implement the promised "self-determination" plebiscite as the Kashmir conflict became entangled in Cold War politics. The failure of larger external entities to resolve the situation meant that Kashmiri voices of resistance tapped into ordinary residents' economic and social grievances, encouraging them to challenge the artificial and contingent divide and reveal the fallacy of separating peoples, families, and communities from each other.

As Kashmiris in the transnational community took the lead in changing international attitudes about political exclusion in their homeland, they maintained an emotional connection with Kashmir, which became not merely a geographical entity, but a territory both imagined and real in which true freedom was currently denied, but where a better future could be obtained through present-day sacrifice. Holding on to Kashmiri political identity rather than releasing it in favor of identification with their host society motivated expatriates to invest time and resources in generating greater political awareness around their "occupied" homeland. The transnational community, with its wide experiences abroad, drew inspiration from an assortment of global forms of resistance to legitimize their own claims to self-determination in their homeland. Their salience to the development of events in India-administered Kashmir lay in their ability to articulate and embody a coherent Kashmiri political identity, seeking to convince the international community that what was at issue in Kashmir was not a territorial dispute between two nuclear powers but a struggle between those powers and a people worthy of rights and freedom.

As this chapter has explored, the Kashmiri armed resistance of the 1960s and 1970s drew inspiration from the leftist guerilla movements popular in different parts of the world. However, in the final chapter, I shift my focus to the new global trends that defined the Kashmiri Muslim discourse on resistance in the 1980s and 1990s. The globalization of Islam, the Afghan war, and the fall of the Berlin Wall had a strong bearing on the political thinking of radicalized Kashmiris; they became convinced, unlike their immediate predecessors, that the armies of strong nations could be defeated by dedicated local populations, inspiring many to contemplate waging an armed struggle against India. In the Valley, meanwhile, the ideologies of secularism and socialism had lost relevance for Kashmiri Muslims, who now equated these concepts with forcible integration into India and failure of the government to bring about a socialist revolution in the aftermath of decolonization.

As disillusioned Kashmiris turned away from "secularism" and India, which had done little for them, the ideologues of political Islam took advantage of Kashmiri disillusionment to reshape the concept of "self-determination" in their own image. As they did so, India's repressive reaction to perceived violations of its territorial sovereignty drove many young Kashmiri Muslims into open revolt, and the religious identity gained preeminence in Kashmiri discourses on freedom.

Notes

1. Shams Rehman, *Maqbool Bhatt: The Life and Struggle of an Imprisoned Martyr*, Maqbool Bhat Foundation, http://www.maqboolbhat.com/index.php/record/185-maqbool-bhatt-the-life-and-struggle-of-an-imprisoned-kashmiri-martyr-c-shams-rehman, accessed December 28, 2019.
2. There were many strands of resistance in Kashmir. While some argued for an independent Kashmir, many others wanted Kashmir's mergence with Pakistan.
3. Roger Ballard, "The Kashmir Crisis: A View from Mirpur," *Economic and Political Weekly* 26, nos. 9–10 (March 2–9, 1991): 513–17.
4. Ballard, "The Kashmir Crisis."
5. Shams Rehman, *Azad Kashmir and the British Kashmiri Transnational Community* (Saarbrücken: VDM Verlag, 2011), 12–17.
6. Human Rights Watch, *With Friends Like These: Human Rights Violations in Azad Kashmir* 18, no. 12 (September 2006), 12.
7. Robinson, *Body of Victim, Body of Warrior*, 34–8.
8. Jeffrey Alan Kile, "An Unsettled State: The Birth of Transnational Community and Homeland in the Transnational Fight for Kashmir," Ph.D. dissertation, University of Berkeley, 2008, 269.
9. Ballard, "The Kashmir Crisis," 514–15.
10. P. N. Bazaz, *The History of Struggle for Freedom in Kashmir*, 636–7.
11. Zakaria, *Between the Great Divide*, 905–10.
12. Zakaria, *Between the Great Divide*, 598.
13. S. I. Khan, *The Kashmir Saga*, 116–17.
14. P. N. Bazaz, *The History of Struggle for Freedom in Kashmir*, 640.
15. S. I. Khan, *The Kashmir Saga*, 60–5.
16. Snedden, *The Untold Story of the People of Azad Kashmir*, 87.
17. S. I. Khan, *The Kashmir Saga*, 128–29.
18. Ershad Mahmud, "Status of AJK in Political Milieu," *Policy Perspectives* 3, no. 2 (July–December 2006): 105–23.
19. Muhammad Feyyaz, *Pakistan–Azad Jammu Kashmir: Politico-Legal Conflict* (Islamabad: Pakistan Institute of Legislative Development and Transparency, 2011), 11.
20. Mahmud, "Status of AJK in Political Milieu," 107.
21. Feyyaz, *Pakistan–Azad Jammu Kashmir*, 9–10.
22. Martin Sökefeld, "From Colonialism to Postcolonial Colonialism: Changing Modes of Domination in the Northern Areas of Pakistan," *The Journal of Asian Studies* 64, no. 4 (2005): 939–73.
23. Ayesha Jalal, *The Struggle for Pakistan: A Muslim Homeland and Global Politics* (Cambridge, MA: Harvard University Press, 2014), 60.
24. Mahmud, "Status of AJK in Political Milieu."

25. Snedden, *The Untold Story of the People of Azad Kashmir*, 90.
26. Snedden, *The Untold Story of the People of Azad Kashmir*, 117–21.
27. Mahmud, "Status of AJK in Political Milieu,"111–13.
28. Saraf, *Kashmiris Fight for Freedom*, Vol. 2, 1297–305.
29. Saraf, *Kashmiris Fight for Freedom*, Vol. 2, 1307–8.
30. P. N. Bazaz, *The History of Struggle for Freedom in Kashmir*, 650–4.
31. Jalal, *Democracy and Authoritarianism in South Asia*, 49–51.
32. For details, see Mirza Shafiq Hussain, *Azad Kashmir: Eak Siyasi Jayaza, 1947–1974* (Islamabad: Islamic Research Institute Press, 1990); Saraf, *Kashmiris Fight for Freedom.*
33. Snedden, *The Untold Story of the People of Azad Kashmir*, 163–7.
34. Rehman, *Azad Kashmir and British Kashmiri Transnational Community*, 186–7.
35. Interview with Daalat Ali, Birmingham, November 2010.
36. Basharat Ahmad Sheikh, "Azad Kashmir Needs Attention" (private archives of Shabbar Agha, Mirpur, Azad Kashmir).
37. Snedden, *The Untold Story of the People of Azad Kashmir*, 121.
38. Ghulam Nabi Gilkar, "Demand of Independent Kashmir," *Voice of Kashmir* 11, no. 2, Delhi: Kashmir Democratic Union (February 1955): 22–23.
39. Sanaullah Butt, "Why Independent Kashmir," *Voice of Kashmir* 11, no. 4, Delhi: Kashmir Democratic Union (April 1955): 16–17.
40. S. Butt, "Why Independent Kashmir," 16.
41. For details, see Lakhanpal, *Essential Documents and Notes on Kashmir Dispute,* 186–235.
42. Abdul Salam Yatu, "Take State People into Confidence," memorandum submitted to the Prime Ministers of India and Pakistan by Kashmir Kisan Mazdoor Conference, *Voice of Kashmir* 11, no. 4, Delhi: Kashmir Democratic Union (April 1955): 17.
43. Snedden, *The Untold Story of the People of Azad Kashmir*, 94.
44. "Political Developments in Azad Kashmir," *Keesing's Record of World Events* 7 (August 1961), Indian, Pakistani, 18290, http://web.stanford.edu/group/tomzgroup/pmwiki/uploads/1309-1961-08-xx-KS-a-RRW.pdf, accessed March 15, 2018.
45. Saraf, *Kashmiris Fight for Freedom*, Vol. 2, 1320–1.
46. "Political Developments in Azad Kashmir," *Keesing's Record of World Events.*
47. Jalal, *The Struggle for Pakistan*, 105–7.
48. Mahmud, *Status of AJK in Political Milieu*, 113.
49. "K. H. Khurshid's Death Anniversary," *Dawn*, March 11, 2011.
50. "Political Developments in Azad Kashmir," *Keesing's Record of World Events.*
51. K. H. Khurshid, *Jammu Kashmir Liberation League: Eak Jamat, Eak Tehreek* (Muzafarrabad: Markazai Publicity Board, 1982), 19–21.
52. Saraf, *Kashmiris Fight for Freedom*, Vol. 2, 1340–1.
53. Snedden, *The Untold Story of the People of Azad Kashmir*, 98.
54. Ballard, "The Kashmir Crisis."

55. International Crisis Group Asia Report, *Kashmir: The View from Islamabad* (Islamabad: International Crisis Group, December 4, 2003); Ballard, "The Kashmir Crisis," 513–17.
56. Unpublished autobiography of Khawaja Ghulam Naqui (private collection of Mahboob Ali, Srinagar); S. Butt, "Why Independent Kashmir," 16.
57. Ballard, "The Kashmir Crisis."
58. Interview with Abdul Khaliq Ansari on Skype, Mirpur, January 10, 2012.
59. Interview with Abdul Khaliq Ansari.
60. Rehman, *Azad Kashmir and the British Kashmiri Transnational Community*, 90.
61. Rehman, *Azad Kashmir and the British Kashmiri Transnational Community*, 148–52.
62. See *Mangla: A Study of Change and Development in Mirpur, Azad Jammu and Kashmir and Pakistan* (South Yorkshire: Development Education Centre, 1995).
63. Major Raja Abbas Khan, *Real Azad Kashmir*, 18–19 (personal archives of Agha Shabir, Mirpur).
64. Major R. A. Khan, *Real Azad Kashmir*, 25–6.
65. Kile, "An Unsettled State," 156.
66. Ballard, "The Kashmir Crisis."
67. For details, see Khalid Rahim, *My Father: A Kashmir Betrayed* (London: B.W.D Ltd., 1995).
68. Kile, "An Unsettled State," 161.
69. Interview with Shams Rehman, Manchester, November 2010.
70. *Studies for Kashmir Solution Based on Functional Arrangement*, SEA 70/1.
71. *Studies for Kashmir Solution Based on Functional Arrangement*, SEA 70/1.
72. Lamb, *Kashmir: A Disputed Legacy, 1846–1990*, 271.
73. For details, see Van Schendel, *The Bengal Borderland*.
74. Muhammad Rafq Khawaja, *Safaar-i-Hurriyat* (Mirpur: Kashir Publishers, 1997), 37.
75. Amanullah Khan, "The NLF," *Voice of Kashmir* 1, no. 2, Birmingham: Jammu Kashmir Liberation Front (September 1976): 6–9.
76. A. Khan, "The NLF," 6.
77. Abdul Khaliq Ansari, *Saach Kaah Doon Eah Brahman* (Mirpur: Jammu and Kashmir Liberation Front, 1986), 64–5; interview with Khaliq Ansari, January 2012, Mirpur.
78. Resolution submitted by the Jammu and Kashmir Plebiscite Front (for Azad Kashmir and Pakistan) at the State People's Convention at Srinagar in 1970, in Fazili, *Kashmir Predilection*, 184–5.
79. For details, see Ansari, *Saach Kaah Doon Eah Brahman*.
80. For details, see Amanullah Khan, *Jahd-i Musalsal: Amanullah K͟han kī K͟hvudnavisht Savaniḥ 'Umriu* (Rawalpindi: Self-published, 1992).
81. Amanullah Khan, "Algeria ki Jang-i-Aazadi," *Voice of Kashmir*, Birmingham: Jammu Kashmir Liberation Front (October 1976), 7–9.
82. A. Khan, "The NLF," 7.

83. A. Khan, "The NLF," 8.
84. Rehman, *Azad Kashmir and British Kashmiri Transnational Community*, 204–6.
85. Rehman, *Azad Kashmir and British Kashmiri Transnational Community*, 113–14.
86. Letter written by Maqbool Butt to Azra Mir, the daughter of G. M. Mir, the president of NLF, http://united-kashmir.blogspot.com/2008/06/shaoufarda-letters-of-maqbool-bhat.html, accessed January 14, 2018.
87. Rehman, *Azad Kashmir and British Kashmiri Transnational Community*, 205–6.
88. Khawaja, *Safaar-i-Hurriyat*, 39.
89. Shubh Mathur, *The Human Toll of the Kashmir Conflict: Grief and Courage in a South Asian Borderland* (New York: Palgrave Macmillan, 2016), 120.
90. Khawaja, *Safaar-i-Hurriyat*, 39–45.
91. Interview with Dr. Basit on Skype, Lahore, January 2011.
92. Fazal H. Dar, "Kashmir ki Jang-i-Azadi," a review in *Pakistan Forum* 2, no. 2 (November 1971): 8–10.
93. Abdul Basit, *Kashmir ki Jang Azadi* (personal collection of Dr. Abdul Basit, Lahore, February 2012), 211–15.
94. Kile, "An Unsettled State," 68.
95. Maqbool Butt, "Transcripts of Press Conference at Sialkot," November 1969, in Muhammad Rafiq Khawaja, *Safaar-i-Hurriyat* (Mirpur: Kashir Publishers, 1997), 217–32.
96. "Letter written by Maqbool Bhat to Akraam Ullah Jaswaal, a Plebiscite Front activist from Azad Kashmir, dated 2nd May, 1980," http://www.oocities.org/jklf-kashmir/mbletters.html#letter2, accessed October 15, 2013.
97. M. Butt, "Transcripts of Press Conference at Sialkot," 217–32.
98. "Notes on Arrest of Akhtar Ahmed Khan S/O Abdul Rashid Khan R/o Baghat Barzulla student 1 TDC, S.P. College and his associates on14.10.1968,"File No.15-120 A/ 1968, Reports on Student Cells in Kashmir, Home Department, Jammu and Kashmir Archives.
99. "A Brief Note on Sabotage Activities Recently Unearthed Cell Sponsored by Pakistan," File No.15-120 A/1968 Reports on Student Cells in Kashmir, Home Department, Jammu and Kashmir Archives.
100. During his stay at Srinagar, Maqbool Butt used the house of Waji Ahmad Andrabi as a hideout and met several Kashmiri leaders. See Malik, *Kashmir under the Shadow of Gun*, 44.
101. Saraf, *Kashmiris Fight for Freedom*, Vol. 2, 1379.
102. Rehman, *Azad Kashmir and British Kashmiri Transnational Community*, 117–18.
103. Khawaja, *Safaar-i-Hurriyat*, 115.
104. In the Valley, however, Maqbool Butt did not attain the same level of popularity until the 1980s.
105. Recording of the speech made by Maqbool Butt as the president of the Plebiscite Front, 1969 (private archives of Showkat Maqbool Butt, Muzaffarabad).

106. Lamb, *Kashmir: A Disputed Legacy, 1846–1990*, 291–3.
107. Jalal, *Democracy and Authoritarianism in South Asia*, 61–2.
108. *Judgment Copy of the Ganga Hijacking Case*, Lahore High Court, 1972 (personal collection of Dr. Abdul Basit, Lahore, February 2012), 4–5.
109. *Judgment Copy of the Ganga Hijacking Case*, 4–5.
110. *Judgment Copy of the Ganga Hijacking Case*, 9.
111. *Judgment Copy of the Ganga Hijacking Case*, 1–10.
112. See Mir Abdul Qayoom, *Tehreek-i-Azadi aur Nowkarshahi* (Lahore: Defense Committee, 1972); Mir Abdul Qayoom, *Ab Manzil Door Nahi* (Lahore: Defense Committee, 1972).
113. Abdul Khaliq Ansari, *Taqseem-i-Kashmir ki Saazish* (Mirpur: Kashir Advertising Printing Press, 2009), 80–1.
114. Ansari, *Taqseem-i-Kashmir ki Saazish*, 80–1.
115. Judgment Copy of the Ganga Hijacking Case, Lahore High Court, 1972 (personal collection of Dr. Abdul Basit, Lahore, February 2012), 9–10.
116. For examples of statements by the accused, see Muhammad Ashraf Qureshi, Court Statement in the Ganga Hijacking Case (Lahore: Defense Committee, 1972); Qayoom, *Tehreek-i-Azadi aur Nowkarshahi*; Qayoom, *Ab Manzil Door Nahi*.
117. Maqbool Butt's statement at the Lahore Court, *Kashmirwalla*, https://thekashmirwalla.com/2012/02/maqbool-butts-statement-in-lahore-court/, accessed September 15, 2014.
118. Maqbool Butt's statement at the Lahore Court.
119. Maqbool Butt's statement at the Lahore Court.
120. For details, see Mir Abdul Qayoom, *Tehreek-i-Azadi aur Nowkarshahi* (Lahore: Defense Committee, 1972).
121. A. Khan, *Jahd-i Musalsal*, 124.
122. Rehman, *Azad Kashmir and the British Kashmiri Transnational community*, 101–2.
123. Younus Taryaby, *Master Abdul Majd aur Bartanvi Kashmiriyon ki Inqalabi Jad-o-Jahad* (Birmingham: Alim-wa-Arfan Publishers, 2009), 128–35.
124. Kile, "An Unsettled State," 71.
125. Taryaby, *Master Abdul Majd aur Bartanvi Kashmiriyon ki Inqalabi Jad-o-Jahad*, 119–20.
126. Taryaby, *Master Abdul Majd aur Bartanvi Kashmiriyon ki Inqalabi Jad-o-Jahad*, 82–6.
127. Richard Saull, "Locating the Global South in the Theorisation of the Cold War: Capitalist Development, Social Revolution and Geopolitical Conflict," *Third World Quarterly* 26, no. 2 (2005): 253–80.
128. Lal Khan, *Pakistan's Other Story: The 1968–69 Revolution*, http://www.marxist.com/introduction-pakistans-other-story-1968-69-revolution.htm, accessed July 27, 2017.

129. Nadeem F. Paracha, "Riding the Arrow: The Ideological History of PPP," *Dawn*, June 7, 2012, https://www.dawn.com/news/724608/riding-the-arrow, accessed July 26, 2017.
130. Taryaby, *Master Abdul Majd aur Bartanvi Kashmiriyon ki Inqalabi Jad-o-Jahad*, 66–7.
131. Taryaby, *Master Abdul Majd aur Bartanvi Kashmiriyon ki Inqalabi Jad-o-Jahad*, 66–7.
132. Taryaby, *Master Abdul Majd aur Bartanvi Kashmiriyon ki Inqalabi Jad-o-Jahad*, 740–1.
133. David Bouchier, "Radical Ideologies and the Sociology of Knowledge: A Model for Comparative Analysis," *Sociology* 11, no. 1 (January 1977): 25–46.
134. "From Black Dwarf to Red Mole Archives," https://redmolerising.wordpress.com/2016/08/29/from-black-dwarf-to-red-mole/, accessed July 27, 2017.
135. Taryaby, *Master Abdul Majd aur Bartanvi Kashmiriyon ki Inqalabi Jad-o-Jahad*, 740–1.
136. Sökefeld, "The Kashmiri Diaspora in Britain and the Limits of Political Mobilization," 29.
137. Taryaby, *Master Abdul Majd aur Bartanvi Kashmiriyon ki Inqalabi Jad-o-Jahad*, 74–89, 104–5.
138. Taryaby, *Master Abdul Majd aur Bartanvi Kashmiriyon ki Inqalabi Jad-o-Jahad*, 66–90.
139. Taryaby, *Master Abdul Majd aur Bartanvi Kashmiriyon ki Inqalabi Jad-o-Jahad*, 74–83.
140. Taryaby, *Master Abdul Majd aur Bartanvi Kashmiriyon ki Inqalabi Jad-o-Jahad*, 74–83.
141. George C. Herring, "The Cold War and Vietnam," *OAH Magazine of History* 18, no. 5 (October 2004): 18–21.
142. Taryaby, *Master Abdul Majd aur Bartanvi Kashmiriyon ki Inqalabi Jad-o-Jahad*, 74–90, 104–27.
143. Taryaby, *Master Abdul Majd aur Bartanvi Kashmiriyon ki Inqalabi Jad-o-Jahad*, 119–20.
144. Taryaby, *Master Abdul Majd aur Bartanvi Kashmiriyon ki Inqalabi Jad-o-Jahad*, 123–7.
145. Dar, "Kashmir ki Jang-i-Azadi," 8–10.
146. Mumtaz Iqbal, "The 1965 War: The View from East," *Rediff News*, October 5, 2005.
147. Basit, *Kashmir ki Jang Azadi*, 211–15.
148. Basit, *Kashmir ki Jang Azadi*, 228–36.
149. Basit, *Kashmir ki Jang Azadi*, 211–15.
150. Taryaby, *Master Abdul Majd aur Bartanvi Kashmiriyon ki Inqalabi Jad-o-Jahad*, 125–7.

151. Taryaby, *Master Abdul Majd aur Bartanvi Kashmiriyon ki Inqalabi Jad-o-Jahad*, 248–9.
152. Taryaby, *Master Abdul Majd aur Bartanvi Kashmiriyon ki Inqalabi Jad-o-Jahad*, 248–9.
153. Taryaby, *Master Abdul Majd aur Bartanvi Kashmiriyon ki Inqalabi Jad-o-Jahad*, 363–4.
154. Kile, "An Unsettled State," 278.
155. Interview with Masoom Ansari, Birmingham, November 2011.
156. Alexander Evans, "Kashmir: A Tale of Two Valleys," *Asian Affairs* 36, no. 1 (2005): 35–47.
157. Kile, "An Unsettled State," 295–7.
158. Snedden, *The Untold Story of the People of Azad Kashmir*, 101.
159. Gowher Rizvi, "India, Pakistan and Kashmir Problem, 1947–1972," in Raju G. C. Thomas (ed.), *Perspectives on Kashmir: The Roots of Conflict in South Asia* (Boulder, CO: Westview Press, 1992), 73.
160. Ghulam Nabi Hagroo, "Fidelity Call to Muslims," *Motherland*, New Delhi, September 12, 1971.
161. Snedden, *The Untold Story of the People of Azad Kashmir*, 99–104.
162. Snedden, *The Untold Story of the People of Azad Kashmir*, 172.
163. Snedden, *The Untold Story of the People of Azad Kashmir*, 102.
164. Ayesha Jalal, "The Past as Present," in Maleeha Lodhi (ed.), *Pakistan Beyond the Crisis State* (Karachi: Oxford University Press, 2011), 11.
165. Interview with Abdul Khaliq Ansari on Skype, Mirpur, January 10, 2012.
166. Amanullah Khan, "The Simla Agreement," *Voice of Kashmir* 1, no. 1, Birmingham: Jammu and Kashmir National Liberation Front (August 1976): 8.
167. See A. Khan, *Jahd-i Musalsal*, 131–41.
168. Amanullah Khan, "Mere Kashmir Zara Jag," *Voice of Kashmir* 1, no. 2, Birmingham: Jammu Kashmir Liberation Front (September 1976): 19–22; Muzzamal Iqbal, "Is Terrorism by Freedom Fighters Justified," *Voice of Kashmir* 1, no. 4, Birmingham: Jammu Kashmir Liberation Front (November 1976): 10–11.
169. Amanullah Khan, "Peace? No! Freedom," *Voice of Kashmir* 1, no. 2, Birmingham: Jammu Kashmir Liberation Front (September 1976): 1.
170. A. Khan, "Peace? No! Freedom," 1.
171. Kile, "An Unsettled State," 40.
172. Amanullah Khan, *Free Kashmir* (Karachi: Central Printing Press, 1970), 133–44.
173. A. Khan, *Free Kashmir*, 133–44.
174. A. Khan, *Free Kashmir*, 133–44.
175. Amanullah Khan, *Ideology of an Independent Jammu and Kashmir* (Mirpur: NIKS Publishers, 1991), 26–8.
176. A. Khan, *Ideology of an Independent Jammu and Kashmir*, 26–8.
177. *Birmingham Post*, Birmingham, England, February 5, 1985.

178. Wajahat Ahmed, "Amanullah Khan: Life History of an Azadi Ideologue," *Kashmir Narrator*, May 30, 2016.
179. Taryaby, *Master Abdul Majd aur Bartanvi Kashmiriyon ki Inqalabi Jad-o-Jahad*, 663–90; Rehman, *Azad Kashmir and British Kashmiri Transnational Community*, 172.
180. Asad Hashim, "Kashmiri Refugees Living a Life on Hold," *Al-Jazeera*, September 18, 2013, https://www.aljazeera.com/indepth/features/2013/09/201391711186325937.html, accessed March 10, 2018.
181. In September 2017, the prime minister of "Azad" Kashmir, Farooq Haider, claimed that as many as 40,000 refugees had poured in from India-administered Kashmir since 1989. Zakaria, *Between the Great Divide*, 1271–2.
182. Zakaria, *Between the Great Divide*, 1313.
183. Human Rights Watch, *With Friends Like These*, 55–9.
184. Zakaria, *Between the Great Divide*, 1312–14.
185. Human Rights Watch, *With Friends Like These*, 22.
186. Shamineh S. Byramji, "The Pakistan Earthquake: An Agent of Social and Political Change," *Al Nakhla: The Fletcher School Online Journal for Issues related to Southwest Asia and Islamic Civilization* (Fall 2006), 1–11.
187. Human Rights Watch, *With Friends Like These*, 23.
188. Zakaria, *Between the Great Divide*, 3539.
189. "BNF Sends Letter to UN SG to Press for Protection of People of Gilgit-Baltistan," Underrepresented Nations and Peoples Organizations, May 17, 2016, https://unpo.org/article/19017, accessed December 2, 2019.
190. Martin Sökefeld, "At the Margins of Pakistan: Political Relationships between Gilgit-Baltistan and Azad Jammu and Kashmir," in Ravi Kalia (ed.), *Pakistan's Political Labyrinths* (New York: Routledge 2015), 174–88.
191. See *High Court of Judicature Azad Jammu and Kashmir: Verdict on Gilgit and Baltistan* (Mirpur: Kashmir Human Rights Forum, 1990).
192. Dr. Shabir Choudhry, *New Dimensions of the Kashmir Struggle* (Mirpur: Kashar Publications, 2009), 247–8.
193. Although India's official position has always been that the entire state of Jammu and Kashmir acceded to India in 1947 and Pakistan has no legal jurisdiction to occupy the territory, its recent protests stem from Gilgit and Baltistan's strategic value for Pakistan. The region is "the starting point of the China–Pakistan Economic Corridor (CPEC)," and the close partnership between China and Pakistan has resulted in joint development projects in the region. China's presence so close to disputed Kashmir has made India uncomfortable and it has declared Pakistan an "illegal occupant." Sabena Siddiqui, "Why Gilgit Baltistan Should Be a Province of Pakistan?" *Asia Times*, June 2, 2018, http://www.atimes.com/why-gilgit-baltistan-should-be-a-province-of-pakistan/, accessed July 2018.

194. Somini Sengupta, "Pakistan, India Span an Old Gap," *New York Times*, April 8, 2005, https://www.sfgate.com/politics/article/Pakistan-India-span-an-old-gap-Kashmiris-cross-2717147.php, accessed December 15, 2017.
195. Priyanka Mogul, "Kashmiri Killings: Young Kashmiris in UK Express Fears for the Future of Their Homeland," *International Press Foundation*, July 28, 2016, http://the-ipf.com/2016/07/28/kashmir-killings-kashmiri-youth-uk/, accessed March 2016.
196. Mina Sohail, "Situationer: Kashmir in the Spotlight," *Dawn*, October 29, 2014, https://www.dawn.com/news/1141038/situationer-kashmir-in-the-spotlight, accessed June 14, 2018.

6 *Jang-i-Aazadi* (War for Freedom)
Religion, Politics, and Resistance

Time went mad in villages and towns,
A macabre dance was there from dawn to dusk.
All, the young, the old and innocent brood,
Lost their peace, took to confined recesses.
Mothers saw their loved sons dying in their laps,
Whoever was found was driven to the gibbet,
Unknown phantoms engulfed sisters and brothers,
Children's fathers were taken to unknown places,
Doom overwhelmed every house of this land.

—Zarif Ahmad Zarif, "The Sparrow's Sorrow"[1]

Written by preeminent Kashmiri poet Zarif Ahmad Zarif, this verse captures the dismal situation in Kashmir after the armed insurgency of the late 1980s. This years-long fight between insurgents and the Indian state led to massive human rights violations in the Valley, whose inhabitants, regardless of their religious affiliation, bore the brunt of the war. The human tragedy that has since unfolded in Kashmir has impacted Kashmiri families, crystallized religious identities, and created a seemingly unbridgeable gap between its Hindu and Muslim communities, forever changing Kashmir's social and cultural landscape.

Most scholarship on the region views the Kashmir insurgency through the prism of Indian and Pakistani claims on the state, as a threat to the nation-states' strategic security.[2] Another strand of scholarship sees the insurgency as a reaction to India's failed democratic attempt to integrate Kashmiri Muslims.[3] Others portray it as an Islamist movement sponsored by Pakistan, or, more recently, as a manifestation of Islamic terrorism or jihad.[4] In this chapter, however, I unravel the complex ways religion and politics intertwined within Kashmiri discourse, differentiating between Kashmiri Muslim attachment to their religious and regional identity and the articulation of Islamist ideology by political groups that aimed to transform Kashmir into an Islamic state. This chapter asserts that Kashmiris' disillusionment with the compromise politics of their mainstream political leaders provided a space for the advocates of political Islam to reshape concepts of self-determination in their interest, providing new Islamic frames of reference to construct and internalize political identity. Indeed, the Islamists attempted to rewire Kashmiri mindsets to reject imported nationalist models and embrace politics as an inseparable part of the Islamic faith. Meanwhile, the anti-Muslim rhetoric of the Hindu right in India and its increasing political power enhanced the already existing fears of Kashmiri Muslims that Hindu nationalists would erase their religiously informed cultural identity. As these apprehensions crystallized Kashmiri Muslim consciousness in the 1980s, religious symbols emerged as mediums to articulate Kashmiri Muslim disenchantment with India. In the post-insurgency era, Muslim religious identity gained further preeminence in each political protest, leading to a dominant narrative that Kashmir was in the throes of an Islamist plot to destabilize "secular" India and eliminate the region's minorities. This depiction of Kashmiri resistance serves the nationalist perspectives of both rival nations; while Pakistan supported the Islamist groups who portrayed their struggle as a jihad (holy war) to integrate Kashmir with Pakistan, India was eager to delegitimize the entire movement by highlighting its Muslim character and presenting it as Islamist.

As has recently been common with other armed struggles, the Indian state labeled the violence of the armed rebellion in Kashmir "terrorism." Likewise, the Indian state moved to protect its territorial integrity by applying force against political resistance; however, the state directed its violence not only toward the insurgents, but also against the entire Kashmiri Muslim population, considered an "internal enemy" conspiring with Pakistan to create an Islamic state.[5] State suppression, however, generated not only fear but also greater awareness among Kashmiri Muslims of their religious identity, expressed in protest against the denial of their human rights. Ultimately, this chapter reveals how Kashmiri armed resistance during the early 1990s again brought the contested meaning of "freedom" into sharp relief, re-establishing the conflicting identities that have made the Kashmir issue so intractable. It demonstrates how contemporary Kashmiri youth, raised in a militarized state, are using new popular art forms and digital tools to engage in decades-old calls for "freedom" and "self-determination," putting their own spin on the discourses this book has explored.

The Intersection of Religion and Politics: Islamic Resurgence and Kashmiri Resistance

Political protests became more frequent in the Valley during the early 1980s, and protestors used religious slogans and symbols to express discontent with the misgovernance, corruption, and centralization of the Indian state. These protests raise key questions: What role did religion and religious identity play in Kashmiri Muslim alienation from India? Why were religious idioms important for Kashmiri Muslims expressing dissent against the Indian state? A close look at Kashmir's history reveals that religious identity has long been part of Kashmiri self-definition. As Mridu Rai has argued, in the princely state of Jammu and Kashmir, the Hinduization of political power by the Dogra Raj privileged the Hindu minority, while leaving the vast Muslim majority unrepresented in power-sharing arrangements and making religious institutions the only outlet for political expression.[6] In postcolonial India, the Muslim-majority character of Jammu and Kashmir played a crucial role in defining India's relationship with Kashmiri Muslims. Although the postcolonial Indian state claimed to be secular and divorced from religion, at the time of partition it rather ironically touted Kashmiri Muslim accession as an endorsement of these secular credentials.[7] However, when Kashmiri Muslims protested the Congress' centralization policy, India delegitimized these protests as anti-national.[8] While centralization politics provoked Kashmiri Muslims to reassert their religious identity as a means of voicing dissent, the growing power of Hindu rightist parties in India demanded forcible "nationalization" of Muslims and compounded Kashmiri Muslim insecurities.

The political chaos in post-independence Kashmir made Kashmiri Muslims vulnerable about their status in democratic India. They felt disappointed with Kashmiri leaders for their failure to rise above the personal desire for power and usher in real progress, social justice, and economic equity. As the fiber of Kashmiri society became bruised due to political injustices, rampant corruption, and nepotism, ordinary Kashmiris found comfort in religion. *The Kashmiri Mussulman*, written by G. H. Khan, a prominent Kashmiri intellectual, in the early 1970s, provides an in-depth analysis of the challenges before the Kashmiri Muslim community in the postcolonial era. Khan expresses concern about the political corruption, economic transformations, and patterns of social change that have altered the old existing values in Kashmir and created fissures between classes. He laments the presence of "professional priests" who exploit Islam for political ends and the "local leaders" who make it acceptable to gain wealth by immoral means.

In these transformative times, Khan worries that lack of spiritual guidance might plunge Kashmiris into the abysmal depths of immorality and vice. He advices Kashmiri Muslims to embrace their religious heritage and hold on to "the sublime moral and ethical values" enshrined in Islam to tide over these changing times.[9] Instead of blindly imitating the "unethical western concepts of materialism and capitalism," Kashmiri Muslims should embrace the "Islamic economic system," and act as trustees of their property by sharing their "superfluous" wealth with the poor and needy. The concept of "Islamic insurance," which encourages the rich to take care of the less privileged sections of the society, Khan believed, could unite the fragmented Kashmiri Muslim community. For individuals like Khan, religion as faith was important to tide over the tough political and economic times.

Kashmiri Muslim attachment to religious identity, however, must be separated from the ideology of the Islamist groups that emerged in the 1970s and that used political discontent to propagate their Islamic vision for Kashmir. The notion of an Islamic state in the Valley was the brainchild of the Jamaat-i-Islami, a party on the political fringes until the late 1970s. The Jamaat had struggled to expand its foothold in a society where most practiced Sufi-based Islam.[10] Since its creation in the 1940s, the Jamaat sought not only to implement its political reading of Islam in the Valley, but also worked to dislodge the power base of the National Conference. Abdullah's party had succeeded in popularizing its secular-socialist ideology among the masses by seeking support from shrine custodians, who held significant power over Kashmiri Muslim public opinion. In the 1950s and 1960s, in contrast with the National Conference, the Jamaat's "implicit challenge to popular Sufism" made it difficult for them to reach a wide audience of Kashmiri Muslims, who were emotionally attached to Islamic mystic traditions.[11] Realizing the futility of posing a direct challenge to these power structures, the Jamaat instead played a very long game while it attempted to popularize its ideology among a literate audience. Until the early 1970s, the party remained largely apolitical, focusing on creating a tightly knit and well-structured network of activists. Crucially, it established schools throughout the Valley, providing both religious and secular education. The Jamaat wanted to shape the "character and conduct" of every Kashmiri on "Islamic lines."[12] The aim was to train an army of educated Kashmiris, well-versed in the Jamaat's ideology, who would penetrate government departments and institutions and establish an Islamic state.[13]

The political journey of the Jamaat reveals the challenges the party endured to carve out a space in Kashmir's political landscape. In June 1970, the State People's Convention, organized by Abdullah to bring conflicting Kashmiri voices to debate workable solutions to the Kashmir conflict, gave the party an opportunity to place their political vision before a broader audience. The Jamaat, fearing reprisal from the Indian state, did not openly advocate for an Islamic state. Instead, party leadership demanded the removal of the term "secular-democratic state" from any future political solution for Jammu and Kashmir.

As India had embraced "secular nationalism" as a descriptor of its national identity, the Jamaat suggested a separate vision should be offered to Kashmiris, which would enable them to differentiate between Kashmir and India while exercising self-determination. The Jamaat's reservations about "secularism" plunged the convention into a heated debate about the concept's real meaning. Many expressed ignorance, relying on dictionaries and encyclopedias. Some equated the term with "being irreligious," while others defined it as "Indian secularism," an ideology imposed from above conflating secularism with nationalism, with the goal of assimilating minorities into mainstream India. Those who expressed reservations about "secularism," however, clarified their support for democratic institutions and the rights of minorities; they suggested replacing the term "secularism" with "non-communal democratic forces." Even after a heated debate, the convention failed to arrive at a consensus. However, the Jamaat's insistence on eliminating the term "secularism" from any blueprint for Kashmir's future political structures raised deep concerns. Several delegates interpreted the move as Jamaat's first step toward altering the political fabric of Kashmir and setting the stage for the gradual imposition of their political ideology. Kashmiri journalists and intellectuals, uncomfortable with the Jamaat's ultimate vision of creating an "authentic Islamic legal order through the political machinery of the modern nation-state,"[14] critiqued their exclusionary discourse.[15]

Following the convention, the Kashmiri Muslim journalist Shamim Ahmed Shamim, the editor of the weekly *Aaina*, emerged as a powerful voice openly disagreeing with the Jamaat. He considered the erasure of "secularism" from Kashmiri political vocabulary to be a dangerous move that could hurt minorities in both Kashmir and India. Although he admitted that communal riots in India had "hurt the soul of secularism," making Muslim citizens question the authenticity of "Indian secularism," the Jamaat's plan was not a solution. He considered the party's exclusionary ideology a mirror image of Hindu nationalist groups like the RSS. The Jamaat's advocacy for an Islamist state, Shamim worried, would only cement the Hindu right in India, inciting the RSS to increase harassment of Muslim minorities in their bid to create a Hindu state.[16]

The Jamaat, however, vociferously defended their political ideology. In Jamaat's perception, Indian Muslims might fare better in an openly Hindu state, possibly securing some concessions. The Jamaat envisioned a similar model for Kashmir:

an Islamic state with some safeguards for minorities.[17] Through their official mouthpiece, *Azan,* the Jamaat upped their criticism of the "mirage of India's secularism" and dismissed their critics as "irreligious." Mushtaq Kashmiri, a vocal advocate of Jamaat-i-Islami, wrote a scathing poem in the 1980s, critiquing the "false doctrine of secularism," and how it had ensnared Kashmiri Muslim minds, deviating them from *real* Islam.

> In this land every inhabitant is secular,
> Its mosques and its government, both are secular,
> The imams, the preachers, the *muftis* [clerics authorized to issue *fatwas*],
> Their nears and dears, they all are secular!
> The heart, the mind, and the prevailing culture,
> The sunlight and the evening star, all are secular
> In shrines and movie theaters alike
> Men and women, dress and act secular,
> The intellect of our intellectuals is corrupted
> We are all made fools [by] those who are secular
> This works for those who follow false doctrines
> For Islam, there is great harm in all talk [that is] secular,[18]

Jamaati activists perceived secularism as antithetical to their ideological goal of establishing a separate and distinctly Islamic political system. Ironically, while the Jamaat considered it essential for Kashmiri Muslims to live in a society governed by Islamic norms, the party was quite indifferent to the feelings of Kashmiri minorities, many of whom considered it unjust to prioritize one religion over the other.

The Jamaat's internal contradictions were also visible in their electoral politics. The party considered Kashmir a disputed territory and at every opportunity questioned the legitimacy of Indian control; however, they showed no qualms about participating in elections and forging an alliance with a party synonymous with accession to and integration into India. The Jamaat participated in elections throughout the 1960s at the local and the district levels.[19] However, in the 1972 elections it obtained a share in political power for the first time "apparently after an understanding" with the state Congress party to undermine the appeal of Sheikh Abdullah's Plebiscite Front, a "nationalist" party that challenged Kashmir's complete integration with India. The "understanding" guaranteed Jamaat success in five constituencies, allowing the Jamaat to expand its educational institutions, reach a wider audience, and even penetrate the civil services and police departments.[20] However, this unofficial understanding only lasted until the Congress declared Jamaat a banned organization in the wake of the national emergency imposed in Jammu and Kashmir. The ban on the Jamaat lasted from 1975 to 1977.

The Jamaat's critics questioned their participation in state elections, held under the auspices of the Indian constitution, accusing it of compromising its principles out of lust for political power. The Jamaat, however, believed that their strategic alliance with the Congress represented only the best available political strategy to place religious-minded Muslims in positions of power, from which seats they could ensure that Islamic principles were protected by the supposedly secular state. Ashiq Kashmiri, a prominent Jamaat voice, elaborated how party members in the legislative assembly fought hard to protect Islamic law from "secular" Muslim politicians. The Jamaat resisted any modification in Muslim personal law, no matter how minor. Their representatives questioned prioritizing customary law over Muslim law in matters of inheritance and penalizing individuals who failed to register their marriage certificates within three months. On the matter of the state's involvement in women's questions, the leaders of the Jamaat did not support demands for modification in the four-marriage option available to Muslim men, especially government officials. Jamaati members of the legislative assembly (MLAs) provided social and religious justification for allowing four marriages, claiming that these were not imposed on women but only entered into with their consent.[21] Party members took every opportunity to present themselves as defenders of Islam, surrounded by irreligious Muslims bent upon separating Kashmiris from their religious moorings.

Sheikh Abdullah's 1975 re-entry into mainstream politics proved a serious blow for the Jamaat, temporarily preventing it from further developing its social base in the Valley. Their enmity stemmed from Jamaat-organized mass protests against Abdullah's decision to give up the slogan of "self-determination" and sign an accord with New Delhi defining Kashmir as an integral part of India. The Jamaat labeled the Indira–Abdullah Accord of 1975 a "sell-out" and branded Abdullah a traitor who played with the sentiments of Kashmiri Muslims languishing in prison over their support of his movement for self-determination.[22]

Once the accord was signed, Indira Gandhi, the prime minister of India, had no patience for any kind of political pushback. She used the looming specter of a state emergency, declared throughout India, to accuse the Jamaat of spreading religious hatred, then banned the party and put its leadership behind bars. To cripple the Jamaat financially, the government ordered the closure of about 125 schools managed and run by the party, affecting 25,000 students and 550 teachers.[23] The Jamaat denied the charges of spreading religious hatred or preaching violence.

They argued that the idea that they were a "communal" party was deliberate propaganda launched by the mainstream Kashmiri political parties to prevent an Islamic movement from taking root. As proofs of their tolerant stance, articles in *Azan* referred to the Jamaat's constitution, which made their schools available to all without discrimination, and to the humanitarian relief their activists offered to both Hindu and Muslim victims of the Budgam earthquake. These expressions of the Jamaat's 'non-communal' nature, however, proved unsatisfactory to the Indian state; the ban on Jamaat continued until the Janata party came to power in India in 1977.[24]

Thereafter, the Jamaat focused on rebuilding its political position in the Valley and tried to discredit their Muslim political opponents as "communists"—"the enemies of Islam, bent upon removing religion from everyday lives of Kashmiris." They doubled down on this rhetoric after the hanging of Pakistan's prime minister Zulfikar Ali Bhutto in April 1979, when several of their houses, orchards, and other properties in south Kashmir, Baramulla, and Sopore were destroyed by vandals. Many Kashmiris believed the Jamaat-i-Islami in Pakistan was responsible for Bhutto's death, and organized protests which some saw as an ideal opportunity to express their wrath regarding Jamaat's condemnation of shrine worship.

The Jamaat, in turn, described the riots as a "well-planned conspiracy by their 'secular' rivals to eliminate Jamaat from the political map of Jammu and Kashmir." They accused the ruling National Conference of the complicity of taking no concrete action to stop the violence. To give hope to a "demoralized community," the Jamaat published a pamphlet, *Black April*, reminding their supporters to "remain steadfast in face of adversity." Kashmir's transformation from an irreligious to a religious society, the author wrote, would be "a long-drawn process," requiring "patience and a spirit of sacrifice;" the "enemies of Islam" would create roadblocks to stop the creation of an Islamic state.[25]

The global resurgence of Islamic identity in the 1970s, however, buttressed Islamist groups within Kashmir, providing them both moral support and economic sustenance. The Arab–Israeli War of 1973, which led to the Organization of Arab Petroleum Exporting Countries (OAPEC) oil embargo against Israel's Western allies gave Saudi Arabia unprecedented international financial power. The Saudis used petro-dollars to wield their influence around the world, but predominantly in Sunni-majority Muslim countries. They provided generous funds for the construction of mosques and the establishment of charitable institutions facilitating the export of Saudi Arabian Wahhabi Islam.[26] The Jamaat-i-Islami in Kashmir established close ties with Saudi Arabia and in due course received largesse in both cash and kind. With these resources at its disposal, the Jamaat built mosques and opened madrasas, introducing a much more conservative Sunni Islam to Kashmiri society. This sudden access to petro-dollars allowed the Jamaat to expand its support base in rural and urban areas.[27] The rising economy of Saudi Arabia encouraged many unemployed educated Kashmiri Muslims to migrate to the Middle East for better opportunities. These migrants sent financial remittances, but also brought home a more puritanical form of Islam. The spread of Wahhabism in Kashmir corresponded with a phenomenal rise in mosque attendance.

Azan published countless articles praising this growing Islamic consciousness, while critiquing communist and capitalist ideologies alike for their subjugation of the "non-western world." One article, "Islamic Movements and Kashmiri Muslims," expressed disdain for Muslim political elites in the Middle East who acted as stooges of the United States and Russia in their Cold War rivalry and placed the strategic interests of global powers before their own. The "forces of imperialism" sowed dissension in the Muslim world, keeping it weak, while the "imported secular models" failed to bring economic prosperity and political freedom. The author showered praise upon individuals like Maulana Mawdudi of the Jamaat-i-Islami, Ayatollah Khomeini of Iran, and Hassan al-Banna of Egypt, who had re-examined their own values and provided an alternative vision, free from foreign influence, to the Muslim world. At the same time, the author expressed disappointment with Kashmiri Muslims' apparent complete indifference toward these global Islamic trends. He blamed Kashmiri Muslim intellectuals for presenting Islamic movements in a negative light, and accused Muslim clerics tied to Sufi traditions of keeping Kashmiris ignorant about *real* Islam.[28]

An essential part of the Jamaat's agenda was educating Kashmiris to embrace politics as an inseparable part of the Islamic faith. To place Kashmir on the Islamic world map, the Jamaat organized a successful international convention attended by delegates from Kuwait, Iran, and the United Arab Emirates, including the Imam of the holy shrine of Mecca. Iranian religious scholars who visited Kashmir circulated literature about the success of the Islamic revolution in their homeland. In a show of Shia–Sunni unity, Ayatollah Khamenei, a Shia cleric and the current supreme leader of Iran, joined the Sunni Friday prayers at Srinagar's historic Jama Masjid. These activities cemented the Jamaat's claims to be Islam's representatives in Kashmir.[29]

The Jamaat also portrayed itself as a party that had never compromised on its principles, and targeted its rhetoric to fit Kashmiri Muslim fears of deliberate secularization; it expressed contempt for the corruption and nepotism of secular governments and promised to retain the Muslim-majority character of the state.

Wooing future voters, the party presented the National Conference as political stooges of New Delhi incapable of resolving issues faced by ordinary Kashmiris. Arguing that secularism, socialism, and capitalism had all failed to provide real freedom to ordinary people, the Jamaat instead advocated democracy as an integral part of Islamic political ideals.[30] The popularity of the Jamaat spread among educated Kashmiri youth, mostly from middle-class families, who were struggling against misgovernance and seeking an alternative politics to erase their hopelessness. The party wanted to translate the average Kashmiri's growing alienation from the National Conference and its increasingly autocratic ways into votes to establish an Islamic state.

The party's student wing, the Islami-Jami'at-i-Tulaba or the Islamic Union of Students, with a growing support base in educational institutions, decided to reframe "self-determination" in Islamic terms and transform the student community's political discontent into overt resistance.[31] The Jami'at established contacts with Islamist student movements in the rest of the Muslim world. Their goal was to highlight the significance of Islamic universalism and encourage Kashmiri Muslims to think of themselves as part of the worldwide Muslim community. Delighted with the success of the international Islamic convention at Srinagar, the Jami'at-i-Tulba planned an international Islamic conference in Srinagar on August 22, 1980, and invited prominent Muslim student organizations and scholars from around the world. The date coincided with the anniversary of the 1969 burning of a part of the Al-Aqsa mosque, located in Jerusalem, a major bone of contention between Israel and Palestine. Showing solidarity with Palestine, the Jami'at-i-Tulba believed, would allow Kashmiris to draw parallels with other resistance movements, while also making the Kashmir question visible in the Islamic world.[32]

The state government, however, feared that organizers could use this event to persuade the Muslim world to pressure India into granting Kashmiris the right of self-determination. Anticipating disruption, the government banned the conference. The Jamaat accused India of preventing Kashmiri Muslims from freely participating in religious conferences and activities, while the leaders of the Jami'at defied the ban and went ahead with preparations. The administration's response was heavy-handed. Police arrested both leaders and supporters of the Jamaat and the Jami'at under the notorious Public Safety Act, which specified detention for a maximum of two years in the case of persons acting in any manner "prejudicial to the security of the state."[33] The Jami'at railed against this decision, accusing India of targeting them because leaders feared that "Kashmir's movement for self-determination is morphing into an Islamic revolution," beyond their control, at a time when secular nationalist parties had failed to grant Kashmiris self-determination.[34]

In the 1980s, the Jami'at and Jamaat openly aligned themselves with other leaders—Nazir Ahmad Wani of Al-Fatah, Abdul Majid Pathan of the Youth League, and Azam Inqilabi of the Students' Islamic Organization, among others—who formed the Jammu and Kashmir People's League to keep alive the slogan of self-determination in the aftermath of the despised 1975 accord. Farooq Rehmani, a prominent leader of the People's League and sympathetic to the Jamaat, wrote scathing critiques of Abdullah, accusing him of betraying both his religion and the nation in pursuit of power. Abdullah used mosques and pulpits to seek support from the masses, Rehmani argued, but once he established a political foothold, he divorced "self-determination" from religion and intertwined it with the Western concepts of socialism, nationalism, and secularism. Kashmiris, who worshipped Abdullah, had lost track of Islam and its significance in attaining "true" self-determination. Kashmiri resistance, Rehmani believed, could only succeed if self-determination was understood in Islamic terms. For Rehmani and individuals like him, religion and political identity were inextricably intertwined; he had no patience with Muslims who asked Kashmiris to focus on "faith" as a matter separate from "politics."[35]

This revival of the concept of "self-determination" appealed to frustrated Kashmiri youth unhappy with the rigging of successive elections and a mounting economic crisis—especially coupled with the growing power of the aggressively anti-Muslim Hindu right in India. Discontented youth engaged with police in pitched street battles and chanted slogans against both India's and Kashmir's political leadership. A street accident in Srinagar in July 1980 demonstrated how these tensions could easily erupt into serious violence. An army jeep hit some civilians, causing serious injuries to at least three people. The driver tried to escape, but bystanders caught and handed him over to the state police. However, the army cantonment of the driver's battalion saw this action as a challenge to Indian might and power. Considering themselves above the law, battalion members rampaged through the streets of Srinagar, beating civilians, including women and children, with hockey sticks and rifle butts.[36] Even the Kashmiri police, including the superintendent of Srinagar, suffered injuries; they appeared inept against the wrath of the Indian army.[37] This incident generated significant anger, protests, and demonstrations throughout the Valley. It reinforced Kashmiri Muslims' feelings of subjugation and made them see the Indian army as an occupying force with no regard for their dignity.

The upheaval forced Sheikh Abdullah to order a commission of inquiry; however, the report was not made public for fear it could provoke further protests.[38]

This event drew many ordinary Kashmiris toward the anti-accord forces, who had adopted more extremist tones to instigate the youth to revolt against the denial of their human rights. In press statements, political activists condemned the Indian army as an occupying force and emphasized the emotional disconnect between Kashmir and India, which, they claimed, made it impossible for Kashmiris to embrace an Indian identity.[39]

At around this time Shabir Shah of Anantnag district emerged as a prominent face mobilizing the masses for "self-determination." Born in 1953, he belonged to a generation actively involved in Abdullah's plebiscite movement. As a teenager, he distributed posters and pamphlets for self-determination and was arrested several times. To negate India's claims that elections were a substitute for plebiscite, Shah asked Kashmiris not to participate in state assembly elections. Along with other political activists from the People's League, Jamaat, and Jami'at, he organized a campaign against the state licenses freely provided to set up liquor stores throughout Anantnag district in south Kashmir. The campaign condemned the state for "creating alcoholics" and disrupting Kashmir's social fabric. The activists justified picketing shops by pointing out that the consumption of liquor was against Islamic discipline. They considered the administration's liquor policy a deliberate move to drive Kashmiris away from their Muslim identity.[40] Shabir Shah also created problems for the state administration when he, along with other like-minded Kashmiris, protested the playing of a one-day international cricket match between India and the West Indies at Srinagar in 1983, due to the region's disputed nature. The match was broadcast all over the world, and the anti-India slogans chanted by Kashmiri protestors embarrassed the government, which, furious with Shabir Shah for submitting a memorandum to the captain of the West Indies cricket team requesting that the world community implement self-determination, arrested him.[41]

Arrests and detentions of resistance leaders did not calm Kashmir's passions. Simmering anger re-emerged openly in Srinagar during a 1985 screening of *Omar Mukhtar*, a movie about Libyan armed opposition to Italian colonial forces. In the film, a Libyan schoolteacher trains a group in guerilla warfare and launches successful attacks against Italian forces. However, after resisting the Italians for twenty years, the teacher is captured and executed by the colonial armies. This story resonated with Kashmiri youth; after the first night's show, the crowd left the theatre shouting freedom slogans and condemning National Conference leaders as traitors.[42]

This period of protests in India-administered Kashmir coincided with the dramatic global transformations brought about by the end of the Cold War, setting the stage for Kashmiri radicalization. The fall of the Berlin Wall in November 1989 and the unification of East and West Germany created hope that it might be possible to reunite Kashmir as well.[43] In neighboring Afghanistan, meanwhile, the Soviet–Afghan war fascinated Kashmiris. The success of the scrappy and resource-limited Afghan mujahideen against the powerful and well-armed Soviet Union made Kashmiris realize that strong nations could be defeated. Most significantly, the battle-hardened Afghan mujahideen created a gun culture in the South Asian subcontinent, making it easier to secure arms and ammunition, and inspiring Kashmiri youth to take a radical approach to alter the status quo.[44]

Although the global resurgence of Islam sustained the exclusionary view of the Jamaat, Kashmiri Muslims' growing awareness of religious identity was a reaction to the activities of Hindu right-wing groups in the state and the Hindu-majority politics of the Congress. As regional dissidence increased against the centralization policy of the Congress in the 1980s, the national party played the majoritarian card to rally Hindu votes. This led to an increased focus on religious identity among communities throughout India, while the state of Jammu and Kashmir was simultaneously engulfed within the nationwide communal upsurge caused by the temple–mosque controversy. In 1984, the Vishwa Hindu Parishad (VHP), a Hindu rightist group, announced a campaign to set up a temple in Ayodhya at a place that, according to them, had originally marked the birthplace of the Hindu god Ram before being usurped by the Babri mosque, built on the orders of the Mughal emperor Babur by his military commander Mir Baqi in the sixteenth century.[45] In 1986, the district court at Ayodhya decreed that the site was indeed that of a temple and granted Hindus permission to enter the mosque's premises for worship. Indian Muslims disputed this claim and organized massive protests; they expressed disappointment with the "secular" state for failing to protect the collective identity of the Muslim community.[46] Hindu rightist political parties, meanwhile, mobilized Hindus on the issue. The temple–mosque controversy generated a religious frenzy and led to an increase in communal riots all over India.

Agitations over the temple–mosque dispute enveloped the state of Jammu and Kashmir as well. While Jammu supported the temple, the Muslims within the Valley backed the mosque. The explosive potential of these agitations rocked the state in 1986, when the region became embroiled in riots pitting the Hindu and Muslim communities against each other. The trouble emerged after the chief minister of the state, G. M. Shah, issued instructions to open two prayer rooms next to a temple in Jammu's government secretariat to counteract the prolonged and repeated absences of the Muslim government officials from duty because of the obligation to regular prayers. This act caused deep resentment among Hindu devotees visiting the temple within the secretariat, who saw it as an attempt to set up a mosque next to a temple. The temple–mosque agitation in the rest of India reached a crisis point when the district court in Uttar Pradesh (Faizabad) passed down orders to the local authorities to unlock a place of worship claimed by Hindus as a temple and by Muslims as a mosque. The Babri Masjid Action Committee called for protests, which led to violence at several places in India. Muslims in the Valley also protested this decision; the police dealt with the protestors harshly, injuring almost fifty people.[47]

Communal trouble started in Jammu when the two communities staged two separate processions—one by Muslims protesting police excesses in Srinagar and the other by Hindus against the mosque inside Jammu's secretariat. Clashes between the two groups led to riots which destroyed Muslim properties and resulted in many injuries. The government ordered the evacuation of Muslim officials and their families from Jammu. When they reached the Valley, they narrated gruesome stories, making the political climate extremely volatile. The charged environment encouraged the communal elements within the Valley to take revenge and indulge in the loot and plunder of Kashmiri Hindu properties, mostly in south Kashmir.[48] These acts of aggression sharpened the Hindu minority's insecurity in the Valley.

The riots were politically engineered, but the government blamed them on Islamist groups. However, the Kashmiri Pandit Association exonerated the Jamaat from these communal incidents and held Shah's government, a coalition of the Congress and the National Conference, guilty of collaborating with anti-social elements.[49] As these riots occurred in south Kashmir, the bastion of the Congress Party, many believed they had been orchestrated by the Congress to remove G. M. Shah and impose governor's rule. Many individual Kashmiri Muslims expressed deep regrets about the riots; in some regions within the Valley, organizations cropped up to collect and contribute funds to rebuild the damaged temples. Additionally, a public interest litigation filed in the High Court by a Muslim lawyer proposed that the state allow a Liberalization of Arms Act for self-defense, create an anti-riot police force with representation from the minority community, and build a riot relief fund.[50] Despite these good-will gestures, communitarian tensions affected relations within and between regions in Jammu and Kashmir.

The situation worsened after New Delhi dismissed the state government due to its inability to prevent riots and declared governor's rule in the state. The new governor of the state, Jagmohan, had a reputation for religious bias, especially during his stint as chief executive of the Delhi Development Authority. As chief executive, he had evicted the entire Muslim population from Turkman Gate of Old Delhi.[51] The Kashmiri Muslims were extremely apprehensive about the treatment they would receive from a governor notorious for anti-Muslim bias. During his first term, Jagmohan revealed his antipathy for Article 370; he believed that if central laws were not extended to the state, the "isolationist, parochial and separatist forces" would threaten Indian integrity. To demolish Kashmir's special autonomous status within the union, he extended Article 249 of the Indian constitution to the state, empowering parliament to legislate on matters on the state list.[52]

Frustrations among politically excluded Kashmiris increased, especially after the National Conference leadership, under Farooq Abdullah, formed an electoral alliance with the new Indian prime minister, Rajiv Gandhi, in 1986, that brought Farooq Abdullah back to power. For many Kashmiris any alliance with the Congress meant siding with a political group that undermined democracy in the state, demanded the complete subordination of regional parties, and left no space for a separate Kashmiri identity.[53] The National Conference's critics perceived the Sheikh's family, including Farooq Abdullah, as "stooges of Delhi" who had operated to promote Indian interests since 1947.[54] The social base of the National Conference, especially in the rural areas which had been its strongholds, dwindled. Disillusionment with the National Conference set the stage for a new electoral coalition of religio-political groups, the Muslim United Front (MUF), who forged a common platform against the National Conference–Congress alliance.

The MUF came into existence in September 1986, when three religio-political organizations (Jamaat-i-Islami, Umaat-i-Islami, and Ithad-ul-Muslimeen) united to promote Islamic unity and to resist unwarranted political interference by the Indian government in the state's affairs.[55] Establishing their difference from the "undemocratic secular parties" that existed in the state, the MUF aimed to safeguard Kashmiri Muslim identity. Yet the three groups differed in their agendas and approaches. The Jamaat-i-Islami, a powerful group within the MUF, focused on highlighting the failures of secularism and socialism, proposing an Islamic state as the only viable option for stability. The party insisted that Kashmir's accession to India was not final and demanded self-determination.

The Umaat-i-Islamia of Qazi Nisar, an emerging politician from south Kashmir's Anantnag district who had aligned with the Congress in the 1983 elections to weaken Farooq Abdullah's National Conference, disagreed with the Jamaat's stand on self-determination. Nisar's Umaat had emerged as an independent body after the communal riots of February 1986. He became popular within his district after a successful agitation in response to the governor's decision to suspend the divisional commissioner and deputy superintendent police for their failure to prevent riots. Emerging as a defender of Muslim bureaucrats against what he considered deliberate discrimination enabled him to control important civilian and police departments, creating almost a parallel government in Anantnag district.[56] During his election campaign, he accused India of treating Kashmir as a colony, while making it clear that accession was not an issue—their struggle was against Brahmanical domination that denied Kashmiri Muslims equal rights in a Hindu-majority state.

The third group, Ithad-ul-Muslimeen, under Maulvi Abbas Ansari, a representative of the Shia minority community, made the restoration of democratic rights which Kashmiris had been deprived of since 1947 the central issue of his election campaign. Even though there were political schisms within the community, with many supporting the Congress Party, Shias united in supporting the MUF in the 1987 elections after the Congress refused to provide an electoral ticket to any Shia leader. Ansari's party focused on countering the spread of the Hindu rightist movement in Jammu, especially in the aftermath of the riots, when the Muslim community was asked to convert to Hinduism if they wished to remain in India.[57]

Besides these three Muslim organizations, the MUF initially also received support from Abdul Ghani Lone's People's Conference, a group that had fought on the Congress ticket in 1967, but later advocated complete internal autonomy. Former chief minister G. M. Shah of the Awami National Conference also expressed unity with the MUF. However, both parties' ideological differences with the Jamaat made it difficult for them to align with the MUF. The Jamaat was hesitant to include groups that had entered elections on a Congress or National Conference ticket, as they worried it would dilute the MUF stand. Kashmiri youth formed the bulk of the support base, particularly because the Jamaat had deeply penetrated educational institutions at every level. The class base was mainly the wealthy sections of society, especially rich peasants, orchard owners, and prosperous business groups.[58]

The MUF also received support from the Islamic Student League (ISL)—college students under the leadership of Shakeel Bakshi, a former teacher from a local school in Srinagar, who came together to counter the "intentional dilution of the Muslim culture" by Governor Jagmohan. ISL activists expressed deep concern about several issues: the governor's decision to ban the slaughter of sheep and sale of meat on Janamashtami day (a Hindu festival) in deference to Hindu sentiment, though no such ban existed in the rest of India; the imposition of the Hindi language and exclusion of Islamic Studies from the state curriculum; and the presence of video parlors where pornographic tapes were available, representing callous disregard of Kashmiri Muslim sensibilities.[59] Kashmiri Muslim fears that their regional and religious identity was under threat from both secular and communal elements within India was strengthened by the rise of political Hinduism in Jammu and the political repression unleashed against individuals who challenged the status quo in Kashmir.

As the MUF mobilized the masses on issues concerning the Muslim community, local newspaper editorials highlighted discriminatory treatment against Kashmiri Muslims in the service sector, especially in central departments like telecommunications and postal services—a century-old issue revived once again. Governor Jagmohan's decision to set up a Subordinate Service Selection Board, which decreased the number of selected Muslim candidates by nearly half, also generated anxiety among government employees about religious discrimination.[60] The popular press pointed out that while Kashmiri Hindus had the option of finding jobs in India and in central departments, Kashmiri Muslims were denied these opportunities. They pleaded with the government to provide jobs to Kashmiri Muslims in proportion to their numbers.[61]

Discussions in the Muslim community also centered on apprehensions about official moves to alter the state's Muslim-majority character. The governor's erosion of Article 370 created deep fears among Kashmiri Muslims. They worried his next step would be to unilaterally rescind the state-subject category that prevented "outsiders" from seeking employment or purchasing a property in Kashmir. Editorials raised red flags when census reports showed a reverse population trend among Muslims in Jammu and Kashmir as compared to other states within India. In 1961, the population of Muslims had stood at 68.3 percent; in 1971, it declined to 65.85 percent, and fell even further in 1981, to 64.19 percent.[62] A debate ensued on whether this was a real depiction of changes in the population ratio, or represented the manipulation of figures by the census department of India. The public particularly wanted answers for the sharp decline in the Muslim population in the non-Muslim-dominated areas of Jammu and Ladakh.

The MUF leaders' rhetoric presented elections as a contest between Islam and secularism, arguing that the secular politics of the Congress and the National Conference had merged to destroy Kashmir's special status. A major target was the dynastic politics of the National Conference that had "exploited uneducated Kashmiris in the past" and used the slogan of autonomy to win votes without following through. Their 1986 election campaign also sought to prevent what they called a "deep rooted conspiracy to destroy the Muslim-majority character of the state by the center."[63] The MUF accused Governor Jagmohan of issuing outsiders state-subject certificates to increase the state's non-Muslim population. Concerns about the import of non-Muslim outsiders were balanced by calls to increase the Muslim population. Qazi Nisar urged Muslims not to adopt India's family planning program, calling it un-Islamic and a subtle plot to further reduce the Muslim population of the state. The MUF pledged to enforce rigid rules regarding state citizenship and opposed granting state-subject certificates to West Pakistan refugees based in the Jammu region. They also promised public accountability for all political leaders, bureaucrats, and others at the helm of affairs.[64]

Since Kashmir's accession to India, all administrations had dealt harshly with Kashmiri youth who protested state policies. The MUF's popularity was built on its promise to create a free political atmosphere and protect civil liberties. The oppressive political climate of Kashmir, which the MUF promised to reverse, was once again captured best in fiction. In his short story "The Cattle Pound," Amin Kamil highlighted the postcolonial Kashmiri dilemma, as "democracy" bore a striking and deeply disturbing resemblance to the Dogra Raj's absolute monarchy. The story addresses a common Kashmiri problem: the indiscriminate arrests not only of agitators but also of innocent civilians. As the narrator inquires into the cause of some of these arbitrary arrests, a police officer responds that the government has ordered the arrest of individuals involved in protests. As the police cannot locate all the agitators, they arrest anyone they can lay their hands on to avoid being accused of dereliction of duty. This incident reminds the narrator of a similar story from the Dogra era. A few cows had stopped the motorcade of the maharaja and an order was issued to take all the wandering cows to the cattle pound. As the police could not locate the cows in question, however, they decided to take cows from a nearby cowshed to fulfill their obligations. The despotism of Dogra rule, to the author, seemed in sync with postcolonial Kashmir's arbitrary arrest sprees, which had become routine as Kashmiris battled misgovernance and police oppression.[65]

The print media also published articles about the role of the security agencies in pushing Kashmiri Muslims into the lap of extremism. A 1986 article by the Kashmiri political activist Ghulam Qadir Wani, narrating his stint in an interrogation center, provides insight into how the state negotiated with dissenting voices, denying them basic human rights to destroy their spirit of resistance. Wani's experience resonated with those of thousands of Kashmiri youth arrested for words or deeds influencing political protests against the established order. Although these individuals considered themselves political prisoners, the state framed them as terrorists and a threat to national security. Instead of providing them a chance to stand trial, the state detained them in interrogation centers, where they were often kept in complete isolation, disconnected from their families and loved ones, and endured days of torture. Wani described how the state fabricated names of nonexistent terrorist organizations to legitimize silencing agitators, as they protested political injustices and challenged the status quo of suppression.[66] Their only crime, he lamented, was to oppose fundamental political wrongs fostered and reinforced by the state's exploitative conditions. They aimed to transform their society into an order harmonious with the material and political needs of its members.

Kashmiri narratives of this period also expressed contempt for the intelligence agencies in the Valley that created a shadow of fear and made it impossible for Kashmiris to trust each other. Ordinary Kashmiris had to negotiate not only the network of Indian intelligence agencies, but also the state intelligence department, as both used every means to extract information. Although the central intelligence bureau's state unit, called the Subsidiary Intelligence Bureau, worked in every state of India, in Jammu and Kashmir every branch of intelligence (the Research ans Analysis Wing, or RAW, the Central Bureau of Investigation, or CBI, army intelligence, and BSF intelligence) was actively involved. Phones were frequently tapped, while intelligence agencies also induced young unemployed students to become agents and later used and abused them for their own agenda. People knew that these tactics created dissensions within communities and political groups to keep Kashmiri voices weak and fragmented, but they seemed powerless against the agencies. The Kashmiri youth who bore the brunt of these issues hoped that the MUF, if elected, would break these intelligence networks so that people could live freely without constant surveillance.[67]

The MUF's campaign made extensive use of Islamic symbolism, even inscribing Quranic verses on its political banners, thus promising protection of Muslim identity its main priority. The party's promises made it extremely popular in the Valley and in Jammu's enclaves of Kashmiri-speaking Muslims.[68] Most Kashmiri Muslims, if not all, who were disillusioned with the National Conference wanted to exercise their democratic right to bring a party of their choice, a party that would heed their grievances, to power. The MUF's growing popularity concerned Farooq Abdullah. Shortly before the elections, he brought charges against eight MUF leaders under the controversial Terrorist and Disruptive Activities (Prevention) Act (1987) (TADA) for "rousing religious sentiments of the people and demanding independence from Indian union."[69] Two weeks before the election, the government arrested six hundred MUF workers. Despite the MUF's gains in popularity, it lost in the elections. With the help of police and bureaucrats, the National Conference-Congress alliance subverted the democratic process; the MUF won only four seats, with the National Conference-Congress taking the rest.

Chaos and disorder broke out after the alliance took over as the new government. Public discourse highlighted Kashmiri Muslims' utter disappointment; they had lost all faith in ever having a government representative of the aspirations of Kashmiris.[70] The MUF demanded an investigation into allegations of electoral rigging, but, instead, the government gagged the opposition.[71] The police and security agencies made liberal use of formidable laws, especially the Jammu and Kashmir Public Safety Act (1978) and TADA, to curtail civil liberties and deny freedom of expression. People arrested under these acts could be placed in detention without trial for two years.[72]

No public or political space existed in which Kashmiris could exercise their legal rights as Indian citizens; every form of protest, even those related to administrative and economic issues, was suppressed with brutal force.[73] The government outlawed organizations and detained individuals found guilty of questioning India's sovereignty over any of its current territory.[74] In many cases, the state framed political dissenters as terrorists and a threat to the security of the state. Sometimes, the police attempted to intimidate political activists by arresting family members not directly involved in any protest. In April 1989, Shabir Shah called for "Kashmir Bandh," a general strike, to protest police atrocities. The *bandh* was a tremendous success, but when the police could not locate Shah himself, who was in hiding, they arrested his father and tortured him. A frail old man, the father could not endure torture and died. The police ordered the family to bury the body during the night hours to prevent further protests.[75] The indiscriminate repression faced by the strikers intensified existing anti-India sentiment among the Muslim community, convincing Kashmiri youth that the bullet would deliver where the ballot had failed.

The Cry of *Aazadi*: From Insurgency to Mass Resistance

After Kashmiris were prevented from channeling their grievances through a democratic system, Kashmiri protest entered a new phase. In 1988, increasing numbers of young men from towns and villages from across the Kashmir Valley crossed the line of control in search of weapons that would help them achieve their rights. The insurgency was initiated by a few individuals who raised the banner of freedom, "Aazadi," in Kashmir; they initially received only tacit support from the masses, but soon transformed their small insurgency into a mass movement for independence. Here I examine how the state repression intensified Kashmiri Muslim alienation, crystallizing old grievances while also creating new ones. Not even at the height of the Plebiscite Front's popularity in the 1960s had the estrangement of the Kashmiri Muslim population from India been so apparent. As India's territorial integrity took precedence over the state's responsibility to follow its constitutional commitments, and protect the fundamental rights of their Kashmiri citizens, the violence perpetrated by the state alienated and radicalized young Kashmiris while also making them more aware of their religious identity. *Aazadi* took a new meaning; the notion of "honor" intertwined with the elusive sentiment of freedom mobilizing hundreds of young Kashmiris to resist dehumanization and to restore their dignity.

The first generation of insurgents in the Valley emerged from prison cells and interrogation centers after enduring torture for contesting the results of the 1987 rigged elections. A common thread of disillusionment with democratic institutions ties the stories of five young Kashmiri MUF political activists, popularly known as the HAJY group after the first names of its four members, Hamid Sheikh, Ashfaq Majid Wani, Javed Mir, and Yasin Malik, who collectively initiated the armed insurgency in the Valley.[76] Ashfaq Wani, a brilliant student and athlete who had been denied admission to medical college because his parents could not afford the required bribe, was kept in solitary confinement for nine months for actively supporting the MUF, and released with cigarette burns all over his body.[77] Mohammed Yasin Malik, who had once been an active member of the Islamic Students Union, traced his growing political awareness to the incident, described earlier, during which the Indian army had rampaged against Srinagar's civilian population in retaliation for the arrest of army officers involved in a traffic accident. As an MUF activist, Yasin endured severe beatings during the 1987 protest demonstrations. While he was imprisoned, the authorities refused to give him medical help for a congenital heart issue. He later went on a hunger strike, which led to his release. After leaving jail, Yasin stated, "They [police] called me a Pakistani bastard. I told them I wanted my rights, my vote was stolen. I was not pro-Pakistani, but I have lost faith in India."[78] Similar experiences shared by Hamid Sheikh and Javed Mir motivated them, as these kinds of abuses had motivated an earlier generation of Kashmiris, to contemplate an armed struggle.

After their release from prison, the HAJY group went to Pakistan-administered Kashmir in search of training and weapons. While at Muzaffarabad, these young Kashmiris interacted with Amanullah Khan, head of the JKLF, a transnational party advocating for an independent Kashmir. Amanullah was searching for recruits to initiate an insurgency in the Valley in collaboration with the Pakistani intelligence agencies known as ISI. Even though the JKLF's political agenda differed from the ISI's stance on Kashmir's integration with Pakistan, Amanullah considered it prudent to collaborate with the ISI to wage a successful armed resistance in the Valley. Amanullah's lengthy conversations with disillusioned Kashmiris from the Valley convinced them that an independent Kashmir was an ideal solution to the problem of Indian repression.[79] Thereafter, Pakistani intelligence agencies provided training and weapons to the HAJY group, hoping to overthrow the Valley's established authority. When bombs exploded outside the Central Telegraph Office and at the Srinagar Club in July 1988, they sent a jolt down the spine of the political establishment, signalling that Kashmiri defiance had entered a new stage.

Localities in inner Srinagar city—Maisuma, Gawkadal, Khanyar, Batamaloo—with a prior history of resistance, especially during the Plebiscite Front movement, re-emerged as hotspots where unemployed Kashmiri youth were exposed to "fancy guns and sophisticated bombs" brought by the insurgents. Mostly inhabited by small traders, carpet weavers, handicraft artisans, butchers, and *waza*s, or chefs, these urban working-class neighborhoods had endured decades of corruption and nepotism. Resentful at being denied a voice in shaping Kashmir's political future and angry at the state propaganda that branded them "fundamentalists," the youth in these neighborhoods felt guns would give them a sense of security "against the arrests, detentions and midnight knocks" that had become a regular feature of their lives. Drawing inspiration from the Punjab insurgency of the 1980s that had demanded a separate state of Khalistan for the Sikh community and the Palestinian intifada brewing in the Middle East, the disgruntled youth gave code names to their *mohalla*s, or neighborhoods, titling them Khalistan, Akal Takht, and Palestine as they imagined recreating these places as zones of resistance.[80]

In public discourse, the JKLF insurgents were typically perceived as heroes, individuals willing to die to regain "Kashmiri dignity." Kashmiris celebrated the death of insurgents resisting the Indian army, seeing their actions as martyrdom for the greater cause of freedom. Kashmiri youth felt that they could challenge the negative stereotypes of Kashmiri character dominant in the travel narratives of the "other" that had always portrayed them as "cowards without dignity" who lacked the courage to fight for their rights. For these youths, the images of Kashmiris with guns inculcated a new feeling of empowerment and pride. One 1989 editorial published in the *Srinagar Times* emphasized that Kashmiri Muslims were neither cowards nor terrorists. The editorial framed current events with reference to the historical enslavement of Kashmiris by a series of foreign invaders who had destroyed their spirits through forced labor and derogatory treatment. This political suppression had continued in the postcolonial era, the editorial concluded. Despite stereotypes, the author argued, Kashmiris possessed resilience that had enabled them to adjust to their oppressive environment. The will to survive was itself an expression of Kashmiri courage. However, while earlier Kashmiri Muslims had simply survived under police repression, now Kashmiris were expressing dissent with newfound confidence. This resistance, the author claimed, was not terrorism, despite the insistence of state authorities on presenting Kashmiri dissent in an unfavorable light. The editorial suggested that the only way India could regain the confidence of Kashmiri Muslims was to treat them like the rest of its citizens.[81]

At the inception of the insurgency, some members of the Indian press agreed with this approach. An article published in the leading political journal *India Today*, for example, held the Indian government responsible for preventing extremism by ensuring democracy and civil liberties in Kashmir. The article emphasized the need to treat Kashmiris as "alienated youth" who could be "rehabilitated" with proper policies—as opposed to irredeemable criminals and terrorists. Continuing the current policy of suppression, the author feared, would reinforce feelings of discrimination and further alienate Kashmiri Muslims.[82] However, as Kashmir was a contested space claimed by Pakistan, India interpreted the resistance not as Kashmiri disillusionment with Indian policies, but an external conflict maneuvered by Pakistan to threaten India's territorial integrity. Once the insurgency gained steam, the Indian armed forces exercised a great degree of brutality against the "entire local population" whom they saw as "disloyal and traitorous, in bed with an enemy state."[83] Ahsan Butt asserts, "Pakistani support led to a more challenging fight, since it meant a stronger Kashmiri nationalist movement alongside the potential for a Pakistani invasion."[84] This explains India's tough line in handling Kashmiri rebellion, and the lack of empathy towards Kashmiri citizens.

During the beginning of the insurgency the Indian government, however, did not have a clear policy for handling the new wave of anger enveloping Kashmir. In December 1989, the JKLF insurgents gained visibility after kidnapping the daughter of Mufti Sayeed, the Indian home minister and a Kashmiri politician. The insurgents demanded the release of members of their organization who were in prison. However, before the insurgents could make any decision, the Indian government panicked and released the five imprisoned JKLF leaders. This event exposed the weakness of the Indian state and raised the morale of the insurgents.[85] Ordinary Kashmiris who considered the JKLF insurgents as freedom fighters, now erroneously believed that India would buckle under pressure and grant them freedom. Jubilant crowds rejoiced and danced in the streets of Srinagar and gathered at the mosques, which had always been centers of political mobilization in the Valley. Processions emerged from every locality in Srinagar as people marched toward the local United Nations office, where they submitted memorandums urging the world community to compel India to leave Kashmir. No one had anticipated this reaction. The Indian security forces appeared inept before these raw emotions of ordinary citizens, who had lost all fear in their newfound euphoria.[86]

Despite its release of the JKLF militants during the kidnapping incident, India decided to adopt a tough stance on Kashmir. In January 1990 the Indian government reappointed Jagmohan Malhotra, a member of the right-wing Hindu nationalist party BJP, to a second term as the governor of Jammu and Kashmir. Jagmohan's administrative policies aimed to crush resistance in every form, as he considered the "valley full of scorpions" where "inner and outer forces of terrorism had conspired to subvert the union and to seize power."[87] Thus, he used every weapon available to protect India's integrity, even if it came at the cost of innocent human lives. Governor Jagmohan gave the security agencies free rein to conduct house-to-house searches for individuals involved in protest demonstrations, and they arrested almost three hundred Kashmiri youth, mostly teenagers.[88] To intimidate civilians, the security forces used physical violence, beating and dragging these youths from their homes. Even the women who protested against these strong-arm methods were not spared.[89] Groups of demonstrators—men, women, and children—marched from Srinagar in the winter of 1990 to protest against this excessive use of force and alleged molestation of women. During a demonstration near Gawkadal Bridge in Srinagar city, Indian security forces opened fire on unarmed civilians, killing almost sixty protesters, including women and children.[90]

The indiscriminate use of bullets against protesting civilians changed the situation's tone; this was no longer a fight between insurgents and the security forces, but now pitted the latter against the entire Kashmiri Muslim population.[91] The insurgency's relationship with Pakistan made Kashmir a national security issue for India, and, as a result, the Indian state introduced draconian laws giving the military special powers to crush resistance. Besides extensively using the Jammu and Kashmir Public Safety Act to place citizens in detention for two years without trial, the governor introduced the Terrorist and Disruptive Activities (Prevention) Act (TADA). While Section 3 of TADA covered violent activity against the state, Section 4 made any speaking or writing about "cession" a crime punishable with a life sentence.[92]

In the summer of 1990, the governor passed two more acts that provided tremendous power to the police and the armed forces, and further curtailed Kashmiri freedom. Under the Jammu and Kashmir Disturbed Area Act of 1990, the governor declared the entire Kashmir Valley a "disturbed area," giving security forces the right to shoot any person who, according to them, was indulging in breach of public order. The forces also had the right to destroy any shelter or structure that they believed was a hideout for insurgents. The act also provided that legal proceedings could not be instituted against security forces with regard to any action taken by them to maintain law and order. The Armed Forces (Jammu and Kashmir) Special Powers Act (AFSPA), meanwhile, enabled India to deploy its armed forces in Kashmir.[93]

Although laws with identical provisions were also applicable in other parts of India, especially the northeast, only the Indian security forces had a right to implement these laws in the Valley. Kashmiri police, who were mostly Muslim, were deeply distrusted by the Indian state. In some instances, Kashmiri police officers were even shot if they questioned the army's conduct during search operations. Even though Section 6 of the Armed Forces Act stated that armed personnel had to hand over individuals taken into custody to the local police, that rule was never followed. Instead, security forces took the detained individuals to interrogation centers.[94] The simmering tensions between the state's police and the Indian army came to a boiling point in the winter of 1990, when two hundred state police personnel protested against Indian security forces for killing three of their colleagues.[95] Many police officers who had dedicated their lives in service to the state felt disillusioned in the new political climate as their religious affiliation evidently justified doubting their loyalty.[96]

The state-controlled machinery practiced torture to contain and eliminate organized dissent. A "long spell of state repression, in the form of extended curfews" without any provision for food supplies or medicine, cordon and search operations, beatings, rape, and shootings against public processions, created a deep divide between Kashmiri Muslims and the Indian state.[97] Men picked up during these raids were tortured with electric shocks and red-hot iron rods. The brutal methods of torture physically crippled the victims and left them mentally scarred. In some cases, people taken to the interrogation centers never returned home.[98]

The Indian security forces saw every Kashmiri as a "security threat" and failed to differenciate between militants and civilians. They subjected hospitals to regular searches and raids, and barred them from reporting any medical cases that implicated the state in human rights violations. Lawyers and journalists who exposed illegal detentions and custodial deaths faced constant threats.[99] Even government employees were disillusioned with the Indian state; they organized a three-month strike protesting state atrocities, bringing the entire administration to a standstill. In an interview with American journalist Mark Fineman, a local doctor lamented, "Look what the government has done. A bureaucrat is a suspect. An engineer is a suspect. A doctor is a suspect. A lawyer is a suspect. My God, a policeman is a suspect. If we are all suspects, then who is with them [the Indians]?"[100] Alienated Kashmiris representing different strata of society, including professionals, government servants, and state police, and not only unemployed youth, were now drawn to support the *tehreek* (movement).

While state repression of active insurgents increased, almost every house in the Valley had a story of humiliation to narrate—stories which have remained embedded in Kashmiri popular memory. For example, a retired government official recounted how soldiers forced him to lick off the JKLF symbol painted by a vandal on the wall of his house, then pushed him around when his tongue was too dry to continue. "I supported accession to India. But now they are victimizing us. It is because we are Muslims and they think we are *Pakistani Muslims*."[101] To undermine Kashmiri dignity in the border towns of Kupwara, Sopore, and Handwara, far away from the gaze of the press and media, the army used rape as a weapon of suppression. The early 1990s gang rape of women in the Kupwara village of Kunan Poshpora, along with several rape incidents reported by Amnesty International, highlighted the abduction of Kashmiri women and their abuse in captivity, hardening Kashmiri determination to win freedom at any price.[102]

As torture reached a new level, young Kashmiris embraced Aazadi to restore human dignity. Basharat Peer's autobiographical narrative *Curfewed Night* provides insight into how stories of rape, violence, and killings radicalized youth. Thousands of Kashmiri teenagers, deeply shaken by these atrocities, crawled past Indian army bunkers and trekked past Indian check posts to reach the mujahideen training camps in Pakistan-administered Kashmir. A new euphoria gripped the youth, as Peer wrote: "Fighting and dying for freedom was as desired as the first kiss on adolescent lips."[103] The government-sponsored radio and television remained silent at the growing Kashmiri Muslim resentment and instead focused on shining the spotlight on the captured Kashmiri militants crossing the line of control, with military style weapons and ammunition. They broadcast interviews of captured Kashmiri militants who expressed repentance at taking the path of resistance. Hundreds of young Kashmiris were killed at the line of control. In some cases, the army did not return their bodies to their families. *Al-Safa*, a local newspaper, in a scathing editorial criticized the mutilation and desecration of the dead militants by the Indian army, which they presented as India's "hatred" toward Kashmiri Muslims.[104]

As violence became a routine part of people's lives, young Kashmiris struggled to make sense of their new reality. In *The Collaborator*, Kashmiri novelist Mirza Waheed sketched the mental anguish and identity crisis that confronted young

Kashmiris as they struggled with their loyalties while trying to decide which path to take for freedom. The story's unnamed narrator is a nineteen-year-old son of the *sarpanch*, or headman, of Nowgam, a village close to the line of control, inhabited by the nomadic Gujjars. Even though his village is far from the mass uprising in Srinagar city, the army brands the border villagers as "guides" who help the insurgents cross the line of control due to their familiarity with the terrain. Harsh reprisals against the border villages radicalize even apolitical communities like the Gujjars, who then join the resistance. The narrator, however, is conflicted between obeying his father, who wants him to work for the Indian army, and his own desire to follow the footsteps of his friends and neighbors who feel compelled to resist the repressive state machinery and regain lost dignity. He decides to stay and work for an Indian captain, who makes him descend into the Valley to collect the identity cards and weapons of thousands of dead Kashmiris shot down by the Indian army while crossing the line of control into the Valley, after receiving military training in Pakistani-administered Kashmir; however, he is extremely unhappy. Each time the narrator collects these identity cards, he undergoes mental trauma, fearing he might come across the corpses of his childhood friends.[105] The novel provides insight into the dilemma faced by Kashmiri youth, torn between loyalty to their families and the need to align with their comrades against the violence unleashed by the state.

The Valley's civil society groups decided to pose a legal challenge to the "immoral and unconstitutional" conduct of the government of India. The former chief justice of the Jammu and Kashmir High Court, Bahauddin Farooqi, filed a writ petition demanding the nullification of proclamations enabling the state administration to assume arbitrary powers of arrest, detention, curfew, and house arrest. Farooqi wanted the Indian government to prosecute Governor Jagmohan for "acts of genocide, killings, oppression, and suppression committed on the people of the state and sufferings inflicted on them by him or under his orders."[106] In the Valley, the public debated manifestations of "violence," emphasizing that the mass upsurge was a reaction to "state violence." One newspaper editorial commented, "Violence [use of force] against violent forces [army or paramilitary] that represents an authority which has violated the basic rights of people by illegal and immoral methods cannot be termed violence." The local press portrayed the Kashmiri resistance as a struggle for justice and dignity that had been denied by the state and its coercive instruments, the army and intelligence services.[107]

Kashmiri journalists and intellectuals requested the international community to not remain silent about the extensive human rights violations by the Indian security forces. An editorial published in the *Al-Safa* requested the European powers to impose economic sanctions against India due to its poor human rights record against dissenting voices in Kashmir, Assam, and Punjab. The punitive actions by the global powers, the author hoped, would pressure India to end its suppressive policies.[108] On the other hand, the Indian press remained silent about human rights violations in Kashmir, and argued that allowing Kashmir independence would lead to a rise in Hindu fundamentalism, which in turn would lead to genocide against Muslim minorities in India. Few Indian intellectuals and journalists challenged the unrestrained power given to the military to deal with the insurgency.[109] The nationalist media dismissed stories of human rights violations published in the local newspapers as mere "allegations" or "fabrications" that could not be proved. Some justified army actions, noting that soldiers worked in a hostile environment, with the local administration against them.[110] This media policy reflected popular perceptions about Kashmir in India's nationalist imagination: an embodiment of the nation-state, the core of India's identity, and hence a non-negotiable issue.

In Kashmir, meanwhile, not every stratum of society supported the "movement for freedom." Class and religious divisions played a significant role in the differentiated responses of the elites, as compared to the working classes, toward the new political situation. While business groups were unhappy with the economic decline caused by political instability, the Kashmiri political elite, who had supported Kashmir's accession to India, were now considered traitors who had exploited Kashmir and Kashmiris for political gain. The open anger against formerly mainstream political groups, especially the National Conference and the Congress, was clearly visible during Sheikh Abdullah's 1989 death anniversary, which Kashmiris celebrated with firecrackers. The government placed armed guards outside Abdullah's burial ground, preventing people from desecrating the grave of Kashmir's once most revered leader, the Lion of Kashmir. The insurgents directed their wrath against groups or individuals who supported accession to India.[111]

Fearing persecution, the families of these political elites fled to India. One official estimated that 20,000 Muslim families from the Valley had migrated and "a large number of Muslims had been killed by security forces and militants."[112] Those that remained tried to win over the support of armed insurgents by disassociating from politics or offering donations. Although this approach allowed some elite Kashmiri Muslim families to survive in the Valley, the minorities, especially the Kashmiri Pandits, felt excluded and threatened in the new gun culture that forever changed communitarian relations in the Valley.

The Counter-narrative of *Aazadi*: Kashmiri Hindus and Displacement from the Homeland

The minority Hindu community of the Valley, which had always presented itself as a group of true Indian patriots wedded to their Indian identity, now found itself in an extreme dilemma as the *tehreek-i-aazadi* threatened their security. The community felt safer as a part of Hindu-majority India, as it feared political domination in Muslim-majority Kashmir. It had thus often opposed Kashmiri Muslim calls for self-determination, equating this with anti-nationalism. As Ayesha Jalal has argued, "the demands for Kashmiri self-determination were overborne by the delicate communal balance in the state." Hindu opposition to this demand had "foreclosed the possibility of the Indian Centre conceding the demand in any shape or form."[113] The polarized political positions that the two communities had adopted since 1947 reached a breaking point in the new political climate of the 1990s, when Kashmiri Muslims openly invoked anti-India slogans and demanded *aazadi*.

As the new valorization of armed resistance gripped the region, targeted killings of prominent members of the Kashmiri Hindu community whom the JKLF insurgents believed to be Indian intelligence agents sent shivers down the spine of the minority community. Stories of Kashmiri Pandits, branded as "informers," and killed in their own homes or in their alleys, and survived by grieving wives and children, had a tremendous impact on the psyche of the minority community. Their fears were heightened as religious slogans merged with the cry for independence emerging from the mosques of Kashmir. Certain militant groups even wrote threatening letters to the Kashmiri Hindu community, asking them to leave the Valley. In March 1990, the majority of Kashmiri Hindus left the Valley for "refugee" camps in and outside the Hindu-dominated sub-region of Jammu.[114]

This exodus of the Kashmiri Pandit community changed the relationship between communities and even created alternative versions of Kashmir's history. Most Pandits viewed their own forced exodus from the Valley as a deliberate Kashmiri Muslim plan to expunge the minority community in order to establish an Islamic theocratic state. Kashmir's Pandits lived in constant fear of the Muslim militants "who were bent on terrorizing them into leaving the Valley."[115] Their narratives expressed disappointment, anger, and resentment against the Kashmiri

Muslim community for their support of the "gun culture" that had led to their displacement.[116] In this violent and unstable atmosphere, rumors spread that the exodus of Kashmiri Hindus was the machinations of the state governor who planned to use unrestrained force to suppress Kashmiri Muslim resistance and thus viewed the presence of the Kashmiri Hindus in the neighborhoods as a hindrance to the army in quickly and efficiently carrying out its plan.[117] Many Kashmiri Muslims claimed to have "witnessed departing Pandits boarding vehicles organized by the state," and felt fearful about their own security.[118]

A senior Indian administrator, Wajahat Habibullah, posted in Kashmir at this critical juncture, denied the involvement of the government in a coordinated plan for Kashmiri Hindu departure. However, he emphasized that the state governor did little to stop the Pandits from leaving the Valley. Jagmohan remained adamant that he would not be able to offer protection to the Valley's widely dispersed Hindu community, and rejected Habibullah's suggestion to televise "the request of hundreds of Muslims to their Pandit compatriots not to leave the valley." Instead, the government reassured Pandits of their support in settling them in refugee camps in Jammu and paying the civil servants their salaries, if the community decided to leave.[119] Balraj Puri, an eminent political activist from Jammu, also emphasized the governor's indifference to restoring "inter-community relations." The joint committee formed by Puri along with the chief justice of the High Court, Mufti Bahauddin Farooqi, and Kashmiri Hindu leader, H. N. Jatto, to convince the Pandits to not leave the Valley received no support from the governor.[120] Undoubtedly, both at a state and at a communitarian level, very little was done to allay the fears of Kashmiri Hindus and offer them protection. As the issue of Kashmiri Hindu mass migrations became mired in controversy, the distrust between the two communities increased, enhancing insecurities and old existing fears about the "other."

Several displaced Kashmiri Pandits wrote autobiographies, novels, and poetry to record their experiences of violence and give their community an outlet to make sense of their forced "exile." Siddhartha Gigoo's *Garden of Solitude* captures the pain, anger, and helplessness that gripped the community during the early 1990s, as they abandoned their homes and tried to grapple with the loss of the familiar. The main character of the novel, Sridhar, a young Kashmiri Pandit growing up in a refugee camp in the hot humid plains of Jammu, observes his community struggling against the harsh environment while enduring sunstrokes, snake bites, and the stench of human excrement in their temporary shelters. The agony of seeing the older generation wait endlessly for peace to return so that they could return home breaks his heart. Eventually, as an adult, he returns to his old home in the Valley, and is greeted warmly by the new Muslim owners. In these familiar surroundings, he feels different. He witnesses the alteration in the fabric of the Kashmiri society as the new generation of Kashmiri Muslims seem unaware of the Pandit community's existence, despite it being an integral part of Kashmir. The erasure of their memories from the minds of young Kashmiri Muslims saddens Sridhar's heart as he wonders whether it will ever be possible to bridge the divide between the two communities.[121]

In exile, poetry also became a realm where displaced Kashmiri Hindu families memorialized past suffering and tied future generations to their traumatic history.[122] Many Kashmiri Hindus wrote in the vernacular, not only to re-establish their linguistic and cultural traditions, but also to express nostalgia for the "lost home" and past lives altered by new political currents:

> Neither bulbul chirps here, nor dove's cuckoo wakes me up
> Nor do hedge flies create a buzz through the grove
> There fairies sing in springs, there is the shade of Chinar
> Here sweltering heat and not a drop of water to drink
> There graveyards are being crammed, here pyres are blazing
> Men are disappearing, and almond orchards have stopped to blossom.[123]

In poetry, some Pandit voices questioned their exclusion from the discourses of freedom debated by Kashmiri Muslims, which had no space for their aspirations. Literary scholar Lalita Pandit critiqued the Kashmiri Muslim demand for freedom in the following verses:

> To the women who love them [insurgents]
> they tell nothing except that
> one day *Aazadi* will arrive
> at everyone's doorstep.
> Life will become prettier, more
> honourable, more pious.
> Who are these men?
> I would like to ask you.
> I would like to know
> why their dream of *Aazadi*
> excludes me, and my people.[124]

Interestingly, themes of omission, anger, and betrayal are absent from the narratives of those Kashmiri Pandits who stayed in the Valley and refused to migrate. Even though life was extremely difficult without the support of their own community, their stories emphasize human relationships that transgressed the religious divide, and highlighted the importance of building bridges between communities.[125]

Pandits' experience of displacement varied depending on their class status. While the urban elite found jobs in other parts of India, lower-middle-class Hindus, especially those from rural Kashmir, suffered the most, many living in abject poverty. The local communities into which they migrated saw their presence as a burden, generating ethnic tensions between the "refugees" and the host community.[126] Adding to the tension, Kashmiri Hindus from the Valley, mostly Brahmans, had their own social and religious practices that differed from the Hindus of Jammu. They wanted to retain their own cultural and linguistic traditions, which made it difficult for them to assimilate into Jammu society.[127] The Pandits' situation was further complicated by the indifference of Indian political parties, especially the Congress and the 1989–90 National Front government.[128] Kashmiri Pandits perceived themselves as "true patriots" who had "sacrificed greatly for their devotion to the Indian nation." As such, they saw the inability of the state to provide support in exile as a moral failure and a betrayal.[129] This vacuum was filled by Hindu rightist groups, who, while advocating for Kashmiri Pandits, preyed on their insecurities and further alienated them from Kashmiri Muslims.[130] The "extreme intolerance" of Kashmiri Muslims became a major talking point of right-wing political groups, who claimed that the Muslim-dominated Valley was waging an Islamic movement to secede from Hindu India. This stance legitimized India's use of force in Kashmir and delegitimized the demand for *aazadi* by branding it as Islamist fundamentalism.

Some Kashmiri Pandits adopted a radical approach and organized the "Panun Kashmir" (Our Own Kashmir) movement, demanding a homeland carved out from the Valley. Panun Kashmir claimed that the entire Valley had originally been inhabited by Hindus, giving them a right to it in the present. The movement argued that to prevent the total disintegration of India, Kashmiri Pandits "who have been driven out of Kashmir in the past" or "who were forced to leave on account of the terrorist violence in Kashmir" should be given their own separate homeland in the Valley. The movement's slogan was "Save Kashmiri Pandits, Save Kashmir, and Save India."[131] Kashmiri Hindus, according to its leaders, had borne the cross of Indian secularism for several decades and their presence had played a major role in the restoration of the Indian claim on Kashmir.[132] The organization warned India that restoring any form of autonomy to the state would indirectly mean conceding the creation of an Islamic state. As historian Mridu

Rai has argued, ironically, while "Panun Kashmir opposes demands for *Aazadi* as an illegitimate demand of Islamist separatists, their own territorial claims are no less separatist." The exclusionary nature of their organization was immediately visible from their maps, which depicted a Valley denuded of Muslim religious sites. As Rai argues, maps such as Panun Kashmir's are "fashioned to enable easy pleating into that of India, the status quo power in the Valley."[133]

Battling narratives of Kashmir's contested history revealed the widening chasm between the two communities; the most tragic aspect of Kashmir's history is that the ongoing trauma has created alternative memories. The violence and impoverishment endured by Kashmiri Muslims and Kashmiri Hindus, in which each sees the other as responsible for their misery, has made peaceful coexistence impossible. Agha Shahid Ali, a renowned Kashmiri-American poet, expresses this dichotomy in the following verses:

> At a certain point, I lost track of you.
> You needed me. You needed to perfect me.
> In your absence, you polished me into the enemy.
> Your history gets in the way of my memory.
> I am everything you lost. You can't forgive me.
> I am everything you lost. Your perfect Enemy.
> Your memory gets in the way of my memory.[134]

Indeed, the communities' mutual "othering" created animosities, segregated identities, and dissolved feelings of common belonging during the early years of the armed conflict. These communitarian divisions sharpened in the mid-1990s, especially after Pakistan hijacked the indigenous Kashmiri resistance and infiltrated Kashmir with foreign fighters who had their own motives and agendas.

The Islamization of *Aazadi*: Non-state Actors and Counterinsurgency

Pakistani support gave a religious tone to the armed insurgency in Kashmir, overshadowing the nationalist vision of an independent and united state of Jammu and Kashmir. Although Pakistan had supported the JKLF in initiating the insurgency in the Valley, Kashmiri support for the JKLF made Pakistan rethink its policy. Fearful that the independent ideology of the JKLF would sideline their interests in the Valley, Pakistan abandoned the JKLF and supported militant groups that would advocate Kashmir's accession to Pakistan.[135] The

Kashmiri Jamaat-i-Islami, which until the early 1980s had officially condemned violent means of attaining self-determination, now found it prudent to align with Pakistan in opposition to the JKLF's nationalism.[136] The idea of nationalism was anathema for the Jamaat, whose leaders believed that sovereignty resided with God rather than with any nation. Party literature expounded on the need to forgo the concept of territorial nationalism, and insisted on adopting an Islamist vision as a prerequisite for attaining true freedom.[137]

After the intervention of Pakistan in Kashmir post 1989, the Jamaat saw Kashmir as a part of the worldwide Muslim community, and its incorporation into the Muslim state of Pakistan as the first step toward eventual unity of all Muslims. Thereafter, the party provided a religious rationale for advocating Kashmir's accession to Pakistan, and defined the armed struggle against India as a holy war—a jihad.[138] Syed Ali Shah Geelani, the Jamaat's leading ideologue, elaborated on the contested concept of jihad in his writings.[139] Geelani moved away from the ethical understanding of the term, in which the war in question was a spiritual struggle to be human, toward an interpretation driven by the temporal realities of his times. The human rights violations that had alienated Kashmiris became the political justification for the Jamaat's support of armed jihad. Further, the Jamaat emphasized, the growing power of Hindu nationalist parties with their anti-Muslim bias made it impossible for Kashmiri Muslims to contemplate a future within India.

In the early 1990s, the Jamaat took center stage in the militant movement, and its armed wing, the Hizbul Mujahideen (HM), gave the jihad a practical shape. This powerful group, funded and supported by Pakistan's intelligence services, molded the insurgency to suit Pakistan's interests. The HM gained momentum in the Valley as it emerged as the most vocal critic of the 1991 Ekta Yatra, or unity march, led by the Hindu rightist political party BJP to unfurl the Indian flag at the historic Red Square in Srinagar city. The HM condemned this march, undertaken provocatively at the height of the insurgency, as a "Hindu expansionist and hegomonistic design to erase Kashmiri Muslim identity," and claimed that it waged jihad against such forces.[140]

At the same time, HM's motivational literature used state violence as a justification for mobilizing ordinary Kashmiris to join the armed resistance. This explains the support that the HM received in the rural areas of Kashmir; the HM explained the concept of (armed) jihad as an act that a person must undertake after becoming aware of a violation of human rights. Commenting on this period, anthropologist Cabeiri Robinson has argued that jihad in Kashmir was not a "collective fight for the sovereignty of the Islamic polity, but a personal struggle to establish the security of Muslim bodies against political violence, rape, and torture." She argues that the young Kashmiri men who joined the militant organizations were not recruited through traditional Islamic party networks or through indoctrination in traditional religious institutions. Most individuals who joined militant organizations were less concerned with the ideological outlook of parties or with the "defense of Muslim territorial sovereignty" and more with how jihad could protect Kashmiri human rights.[141]

Pakistan also nurtured several small Valley Islamist groups like the Allah Tigers, Al-Umar, and the Muslim Mujahedeen to fragment the support base of the JKLF and popularize the idea of waging an armed struggle along Islamic lines. To display their Islamic ideals, these militia groups ordered the closure of bars, cinemas, and video shops, even asking Kashmiri women to wear the burqa. While some Kashmiris readily embraced the outer manifestations of Islamic identity to show their support for the *tehreek*, or movement for freedom, others followed the armed groups' dictates out of fear. Advocates of religious policing wrote newspaper articles condemning those who questioned their rules for Muslim women's attire and providing their interpretation of the relevant Quranic verses.[142] In their perception, creating an "ideal Islamic society" was imperative for a successful freedom movement, in contrast to the JKLF's political agenda of creating an independent, but not necessarily exclusively Muslim, Kashmir.[143]

The JKLF's increasing marginalization in the Valley was accompanied by the suppression of the organization in Pakistan-administered Kashmir. Pakistan branded pro-independence Kashmiris "not only anti-Pakistan, but also against Islam" to delegitimize their claims.[144] On February 11, 1992, Amanullah Khan, the leader of the JKLF, planned and led a symbolic peaceful mass crossing of the border between Pakistan-administered Kashmir and India-administered Kashmir to prove the irrelevance of the line of control. The Indian government sealed off border villages and imposed a dawn to dusk curfew. On the Pakistani side of Kashmir, almost ten thousand people participated, despite crackdowns by the Pakistani army that led to seven deaths and many injuries.[145] This event inspired protests on both sides of divided Kashmir, while the global Kashmiri diaspora intensified its support for independence.

Pakistan, however, not only supported the HM in preference to the JKLF, but also encouraged its protégé to eliminate the JKLF cadre. In July 1994, the HM put prominent politician Qazi Nisar to death for his pro-independence sympathies, alienating thousands of his supporters who joined rallies and processions condemning Pakistan.[146] To build public opinion in their favor, the JKLF and HM leveled accusations at each other via the local newspapers, while converting towns and cities into battlegrounds. One editorial published in the daily *Al-Safa* expressed disappointment with armed militant organizations which allowed their ideological differences to overshadow the sacrifices made by ordinary Kashmiris, buried in the graveyards or still languishing in the jails. The author reminded the militant organizations that allowing the freedom struggle to fragment into bloody rivalry would harm their movement, especially since Kashmiri resistance had garnered international attention. This appeal for unity fell upon deaf ears as Kashmir became embroiled not only in an insurgency against India, but in a civil war between the armed militant groups, with the Pakistan-supported HM at an advantage over its rival.[147]

Kashmiri leaders who had advocated armed insurgency in the late 1980s were deeply disappointed by Pakistan's actions, as they came to believe that Pakistan had systematically undermined every political group that did not toe its pro-accession line. In one press conference, Javid Mir, a key member of the JKLF, criticized the Pakistani intelligence agencies for creating rifts among militant groups operating in the Valley. The JKLF secured weapons from smugglers operating in Afghanistan, Pakistan, and India after the ISI stopped funding them.[148] India also covertly encouraged the HM by targeting the JKLF in its crackdowns and allowing the HM to attack and decimate its rivals. In December 1991, the Committee for Initiative on Kashmir reported:

> Looking back at the history of Kashmir of the last two years, it seems as if the government of India was bent on pushing the Valley into the lap of pro-Pakistan militants in a diabolical game to create a marketable image of the enemy. It is easier to sell the pro-Pakistan militants as foreign enemies for public consumption and national sanction for the policy of repression than JKLF, which enjoys the reputation of fighting for *Aazadi* on both parts of Kashmir.[149]

Even though the JKLF-popularized slogan "Aazadi" maintained its relevance for ordinary Kashmiris, the rivalry with the HM, fully backed by the Jamaat and Pakistan's intelligence services, pushed the JKLF's armed wing to the fringes.

Kashmiri insurgency took a new turn in the mid-1990s after Pakistan infiltrated Kashmir with foreign fighters. The non-state actors that hijacked the Kashmir insurgency emerged from the battlefields of Afghanistan, benefiting from the funds that poured into Pakistan from Saudi Arabia and the United States to dismantle communism. Most of these militants trained in the Deobandi madrasas in the North West Frontier province, now renamed Khyber Pakhtunkhwa. Created by the Pakistani intelligence agencies, these schools indoctrinated students in sectarianism and intolerance toward all religions, especially Muslims who did not adhere to their bigoted and violent form of Islam. This religious extremism lured countless youth to die and kill in the name of jihad.[150]

After the end of the Afghan war, the ISI assisted foreign fighters from Afghanistan and other parts of the Islamic world in the creation of new militant groups committed to fighting the Indian army in the name of Islam. In 1994 the Pakistan-formed United Jihad Council brought militant groups like the Harkat-ul-Mujahideen (HuM), Lashkar-e-Taiba (LeT), Jaish-e-Mohammad (JeM), and the Harkat-ul-Jihad-e-Islami (HuJI) together on a common platform and coordinated their activities.[151] Gradually, these foreign groups grew to dominate the Valley, injecting "sectarianism and Wahabi tendencies into what had started as a freedom struggle with no specific religious agenda" and "sidelining the local militant groups like HM, who had a limited agenda of freeing Kashmir from India."[152]

The foreign militant groups claimed that waging a global jihad would lead to an Islamic state, where they could enforce puritanical Wahhabi Islam in Kashmir, showing no respect for Kashmir's indigenous Sufi-based Islam and its "idolatrous" practices of visiting shrines and holding local saints in esteem.[153] Their religious policing led to "covert resentment among thousands of Kashmiris."[154] The destruction by fire of the Chrar-i-Sharif shrine to the patron saint Nund Rishi, in disputed circumstances, caused deep anguish.[155] Foreign militants occupied the shrine in 1995 and accused the Indian army of destroying it in an attack to flush them out, while the army claimed that the militants had burned the 600-year-old wooden shrine.

Kashmiri Muslim voices expressed unhappiness with Pakistan's policy of fragmenting Kashmiri resistance and supporting anti-Sufi Islamist militant groups. Azam Inqilabi, the leader of Mahaz-i-Aazadi and an active supporter of Kashmiri self-determination since the 1960s, whose Muslim identity was a significant part of his outlook, expressed concern about "Pakistani demagogues" obsessed with gaining Kashmir's territory while being indifferent to Kashmiri aspirations. Pakistani regional conflicts and its mismanagement of the Kashmir issue, Inqilabi claimed, had altered Kashmiri perceptions about Pakistan.[156] Instead of pushing for Kashmir's accession to the Islamic Republic of Pakistan on the grounds of shared religious identity, Inqilabi presented a vision for an independent Islamic state of Kashmir, based on a social welfare system, that would inspire the entire Muslim world.[157] Just because the illusion that Pakistan was an interested and reliable protector of Kashmiri aspirations had shattered, however, did not mean that Kashmiris had reconciled with India, emotionally or politically.

In the mid-1990s, the Indian government launched a counterinsurgency operation in Kashmir to dismember the armed resistance. The army and the intelligence services created a band of militants, populated by ex-insurgents, drug dealers, and criminals, known as the Ikhwan-ul-Muslimoon, to spread terror among resistance supporters and sympathizers. The army also trained a few local youths in government camps and infiltrated militant organizations to incite clashes between them. The government-sponsored militants, under the patronage and protective cover of the Indian army and the Rashtriya Rifles (RR), tracked down and killed not only HM militants, but also Kashmiri lawyers, journalists, and medical workers who raised their voices against human rights violations.[158] The most notorious case was that of Jalil Andrabi, founder of the Kashmir Commission for Jurists and Kashmir's most respected human rights activist. During the height of India's counterinsurgency operations, Andrabi fearlessly exposed the human rights violations committed by the Indian army at an international level. In March 1996, he planned to attend the United Nations Human Rights Commission in Geneva, despite rumors that he was on the government's hit list. In its report *Jammu and Kashmir: Remembering Jalil Andrabi*, Amnesty International described his death:

> Jalil Andrabi was taken from his car by personnel of the 35 Rashtriya Rifles unit stationed at Badgam as he was driving home with his family. The group of paramilitaries was headed by a Sikh major and accompanied by renegades acting as "spotters," identifying passers-by.... On 27 March, the decomposed body of Jalil Andrabi was found in the Jhelum river. His hands were tied up and his face was mutilated....[159]

Even though the victims were picked up by uniformed men in the presence of family members, the security agencies denied having participated. The state-orchestrated counterinsurgency veiled its extralegal activities from the world community and blamed the killings on inter-group rivalries.[160]

Criminal elements from the 1970s and 1980s, including a racket of drug dealers, also joined the insurgency to make quick money. The criminalization of the movement made life unbearable for Kashmiris, as both anti-India and pro-India militants subjected civilians to intimidation and extortion.[161] Sometimes the militants made money by forcing people to pay fines for "family squabbles" or blamed innocent people for being police informers.[162] There were incidents of forcible marriages, rapes, and harassment.[163] In some cases, organized crime groups developed contacts with military and government officials to siphon off government funds. There was rampant corruption even among some security forces who saw their deployment in the Valley as a lucrative venture to mint money. Sometimes they colluded with timber smugglers to make profits, while some even sold back captured weapons and allowed border crossings at a price.[164] The atmosphere of violence and conflict facilitated these criminal acts, and greatly disillusioned Kashmiris against the armed insurgency. Yet families who had suffered the loss of their loved ones during the insurgency retained a soft spot for the *real mujahid*, the true fighter, lamenting the way fake insurgents or *nakli mujahid* had harmed a "just" cause.[165]

The cycle of violence created fatigue and war-weariness by the late 1990s. Popular exhaustion allowed India to claim that Kashmiris had only provided help to the militants under duress and out of fear of reprisals. Claiming it had crushed militancy in the Valley, after six years of governor's rule India decided to hold the 1996 elections in Jammu and Kashmir despite threats from militants. A call to boycott the elections also came from a separatist political group, the Hurriyat Conference, a conglomeration of more than thirty parties encompassing all major players who questioned Kashmir's accession to India and still demanded the right to self-determination. Yet Kashmiris voted: a 40 percent turnout in the 1996 elections dropped to 32 percent in the 2002 elections, but rose to 60 percent in the 2008 elections.[166]

The Indian media celebrated Kashmiri participation in elections as a political victory for India and Kashmiri Muslim reconciliation with Indian rule. However, Kashmiri narratives present the voting process as an elaborate drama directed by the Indian government with predetermined winners and losers, though a necessary action needed to maintain the façade of legitimacy. One political satire, Akhtar Mohiuddin's short story *The Elections*, exposes the charade of elections as every participant maneuvers the democratic process to his advantage. The puppet candidates exploit the people to seek votes, while the "self-seeking Kashmiris" willingly cast votes for "personal gains," despite being denied basic rights and liberties. Akhtar's story reveals his frustrations at being trapped in a broken system of farcical elections that fail to transform Kashmir or Kashmiri lives.[167]

In fact, participation in voting in no way meant that Kashmiri Muslims had forgotten the humiliations they had endured at the hands of the Indian paramilitary forces. Many Kashmiris in far-flung villages complained of military coercion and intimidation forcing them to the polls.[168] Only the presence of a blue ink mark on their finger, indicating that they had voted, saved them from harassment. For others, the "elected" state government, in their perception, was powerless to determine the future political arrangement of Jammu and Kashmir. The state government could, however, provide them with core necessities like roads, schools, health centers, and jobs. Therefore, it was worth participating in elections that would not bring freedom, but might bring basic economic stability.[169] The semblance of normalcy created by the introduction of the democratic process in the Valley could not, however, erase the increasing militarization of Kashmir, thus reinforcing the perception of India as an occupying power.

The Digital and Creative Roots of Kashmiri Protest

As Kashmir's landscape became dotted with bunkers, checkpoints, and armed personnel, the Indian military exercised special powers to carry out operations without adherence to laws and norms. The culture of immunity extended to state institutions, and the judiciary seemed ineffective in addressing human rights violations. The Indian state's dismissal of complaints against the military as "aberrations," reflects the prioritization of state sovereignty and national security over the government's responsibility to protect citizens and seek popular support. India considers elections in battle-ridden Kashmir sufficient to claim legitimacy in the region, conveniently ignoring that democracy requires dialogue and debate to be meaningful. Meanwhile, Kashmiri voices of resistance, frustrated at being negatively caricatured and their reality misrepresented, have restored their agency to redefine their struggle. This section explores the digital and creative stage of Kashmiri resistance that ultimately culminated in literary and artistic representations, as the new generation of Kashmiris born and raised during the height of the insurgency chose to create their own historical and cultural records, rather than having their stories represented by others.

The present generation of Kashmiri activists came of age during the transformative times of the post-9/11 world. The Al-Qaeda network's attack on the United States permanently changed the international community's perception of armed political movements, especially in the Islamic world, forcing young Kashmiris to rethink their strategies of resistance. After 9/11, the world developed zero tolerance for any non-state groups supporting the use of violence, even in a nationalist struggle. The international "war on terror" has focused on terrorist groups and the countries that supported them. India, which had accused Pakistan of cross-border terrorism for quite a while, was now able to convincingly present the Kashmiri insurgency as "Islamist terrorism" instigated by Pakistan. Under pressure from the United States, Pakistan froze the assets of militant groups and closed some training camps in Pakistan-administered Kashmir.[170]

In the Valley, separatist political groups now denounced violence as a mode of attaining freedom. Azam Inqilabi, formerly a prominent advocate of armed struggle for attaining self-determination, now pushed for a humanistic solution to the Kashmir conflict. Highlighting the mystic traditions of the Valley based on "humanity and compassion," Inqilabi blamed "fascist India" for pushing Kashmiris to extremism. Claiming to retrieve Kashmiri resistance from the "quagmire of mass violence," he asserted that Kashmiri separatist leaders firmly believed in finding a political solution to the Kashmir issue. However, he cautioned the global powers, including India and Pakistan, to pay heed to people's voices to prevent Islamist terrorist organizations from converting "Kashmir into an ideal hunting place" for new recruits.[171] As militant activity in the Valley dried up under both international and indigenous pressure, a new generation, born and raised during the height of the insurgency, found space to disassociate from armed resistance and embrace a civilian movement using modern technology and creative art to express dissent. Although religious identity has remained an important marker, these individuals used the tropes of "oppression" and "occupation" to protest, rather than invoking "Islam" or "Islamism."

The rallying point for Kashmiri youth is the militarization of Kashmir—the presence of bunkers, checkpoints, and extraordinary military powers that have made daily life unbearable. Kashmir's civilian population lives alongside approximately 600,000 to 700,000 Indian security forces armed with the draconian AFSPA. AFSPA provides them with unrestrained impunity, creating a legal basis for making war against locals. The armed forces are authorized to ignore the law during military operations intended to protect national security. The immunity enjoyed by the army under the act, which enables soldiers to kill even those merely suspected of insurgency, "camouflages the murderous assaults unleashed by its personnel against innocent members of the public."[172] A report published by the International People's Tribunal on Human Rights and Justice describes the situation:

> The Indian state's governance of Indian-administered Kashmir requires the use of discipline and death as techniques of social control. The structure of governance affiliated with militarization in Kashmir necessitates dispersed and intense forms of psychosocial regulation. As an established nation-state, India's objective has been to discipline and assimilate Kashmir into its territory. To do so has required the domestication of Kashmiri peoples through the selective use of discipline and death as regulatory mechanisms. Discipline is affected through military presence, surveillance, punishment, and fear. Death is disbursed through "extrajudicial" means and those authorized by law. Psychosocial control is exercised through the use of death and deception to discipline the living. Discipline rewards forgetting, isolation, and de-politicization.[173]

The tribunal estimated that between 1989 and 2009 "India's military and paramilitary forces in Kashmir have perpetrated more than 8,000 involuntary disappearances and 70,000 deaths, including through extrajudicial or 'fake encounter' executions, custodial brutality, and other means. Lawyers have reportedly filed 15,000 petitions since 1990, inquiring, largely unsuccessfully, into the location and health of detainees and the charges against them."[174] In *The Torture Trail*, prominent Kashmiri civil rights activist Parvez Imroz documented "1500 cases of people becoming impotent after their genitals were electrocuted and hundreds of [other] cases regarding the systematic use of sexual violence to humiliate Kashmiris."[175] These acts symbolize the presence of an empowered military. The state does not hold them accountable as it worries that enforcing accountability could affect the morale of the army.[176]

A report published by the International People's Tribunal for Human Rights and Justice in Indian administered Kashmir in 2012 provides a detailed exposition of the entrenched culture of impunity in the militarized Valley. It reveals the judicial branch in Jammu and Kashmir has rendered itself subservient to the power of the executive and thus condoned continuous human rights violations. Indian law "does not criminalize enforced disappearances which means it is unable to prosecute perpetrators of such crimes, thus depriving the people of appropriate instruments to force prosecution." The "hypocritical culture of structural impunity" in highly militarized Kashmir emerges from the Supreme Court judgment in the so-called Pathribal Fake Encounter Case. In the spring of 2000, unidentified gunmen entered the Chattisinghpora village in Anantnag district, killing thirty-six Sikhs. Within five days, the Indian army killed five persons in "Pathribal village in the same district, alleging that they were foreign terrorists who had perpetrated the massacre in Chattisinghpora." These killings, however, coincided with reports filed by five families whose kin went missing from the same village. The further investigation "revealed that the five persons killed were in fact ordinary villagers."[177]

In March 2000 the CBI filed a case against the 7 Rashtriya Rifles (RR), a battalion of the Indian army, accusing them of killing these five persons in "fake encounters." In the face of "damning evidence," the army decided to avoid court martial as chances of conviction were high, preferring regular criminal court and seeking protection for their officials under AFSPA. The state high court dismissed the petition, clarifying that the Criminal Procedure Code and AFSPA made it obligatory to seek permission from New Delhi before prosecuting any member of the Indian army in a regular criminal court. It further stated that AFSPA can only apply if "the alleged act is committed by the accused while acting or purporting to act in the discharge of his official duties." The army decided to take the issue before the Supreme Court. During the court proceedings, even though unmistakable evidence implicated the 7 RR battalion in the crime, the Supreme Court cited Section 7 of the AFSPA in its judgment to emphasize that the "court could not recognize prima facie case validity of this evidence as crimes" without prior sanction of the central government.[178]

It is clear that the central government is simply not interested in prosecuting these individuals. The implications of the Supreme Court judgment also impact cases in which individuals die in police custody or are killed in protest demonstrations. For example, Altaf Ahmad Sood from Boniyar village in Baramulla district was killed by the Central Industrial Security Force personnel while protesting power shortages near the local power station. Even though a magisterial inquiry concluded that the firing was unprovoked, the police filed a charge sheet avoiding the potential charge of murder. The state dismisses violations committed by the army as "aberrations or false allegations leveled to demoralize the armed forces or malign their image." To appease public unrest, the state orders compensatory relief rather than bring perpetrators to justice. As the report prepared by the International People's Tribunal on Human Rights and Justice in India-administered Kashmir points out, without addressing "individual criminal responsibility, monetary compensation is at best a palliative and at worst a bribe to buy silence."[179]

The advocates of national security dismiss human rights accusations against Indian soldiers as "frivolous charges" and consider the existing impunity granted under AFSPA imperative to prevent army casualties.[180] Their rhetoric underscores the dangers posed by local militants who operate within Kashmir's civilian population, making it difficult for the Indian army to differentiate between civilians and militants. Indeed, such arguments enable the state to evade taking any responsibility for protecting the life and liberty of its Kashmiri citizens.

The unwillingness of the Indian state to abide by its obligations to address human rights issues in Kashmir contradicts its own constitution that guarantees its citizens right to life and personal liberty. India also does not feel inclined to abide by the provisions of the Universal Declaration of Human Rights, which, along with basic rights and freedoms, guarantees individuals protection against torture and arbitrary arrests.[181] The indivisible nature of human rights limits state power to amend them.[182] However, India pitches the Kashmir issue as a threat to "state security," drawing from the international norms embedded in the concept of "state sovereignty" and giving the state the right to resort to violence to protect its territorial integrity. This legalistic view of sovereignty ignores the reality that sovereignty is not unilateral but represents a relationship between rulers and the ruled. Sovereignity is inherently about legitimacy that comes from being representative of aspirations at the social base. Without this elementary relationship, state sovereignty is a hollow idea.

The prolonged military oppression in Kashmir over the course of decades has convinced Kashmiris of their unequal status as Indian citizens, while reinforcing India's image as an occupying power. Pent-up anger and frustration against the Indian government and its unaccountable military bubbled over in a series of protests that rocked the Valley during the summer of 2008. Popular demonstrations in this period marked a significant shift in Kashmir's resistance history; Kashmiri youth pushed the mainstream Kashmiri leadership to the sidelines and utilized social media and cell phones to mobilize masses. This time the spark related to the agreement reached between the state and the Indian government to transfer land to the Amarnath Shrine Board to set up temporary facilities for Hindu pilgrims visiting the Amarnath caves. Kashmiri Muslims saw the land transfer as an encroachment on the state-subject category which prevents non-Kashmiris from buying land in Kashmir.[183] This law has always been a sensitive issue for Kashmiri Muslims, who interpret any change as the first step to altering the Muslim-majority character of the state. Kashmir's civilian population organized massive protests against the Amarnath land transfer.[184] Given the sensitivity of the issue, the mainstream elected government of Jammu and Kashmir sided with the masses and denounced the transfer decision.

This agitation in the Valley provoked a counter-agitation in Jammu, spearheaded by Hindu rightist parties and the Congress, who saw the Valley protests as a petty effort to deny Hindus basic amenities during their pilgrimage. To punish the Valley agitators, the counter-protestors in Jammu blocked the only highway that connects Kashmir to the rest of India. This economic blockade of the Valley led to an extreme shortage of medicines, petrol, and basic commodities, while the Kashmir fruit industry suffered as truckloads of fruit rotted because they could not reach Indian markets.[185] The separatist political group the Hurriyat Conference termed the blockade an "act of war" and organized a march to cross the line of control, intending to establish a direct trade link with Pakistan-administered Kashmir. Half a million Kashmiris joined the march, but the Indian army prevented them from crossing the line of control. Thereafter, thousands of Kashmiris defied curfew for months and marched in large processions, leading to killings and arrests of hundreds of Kashmiris who were kept in prison without trial.[186]

Inspired by the Palestinian Intifada, the new generation of Kashmiri Muslims, who felt pushed to the wall, defied the all-powerful Indian military with stones. Most of the *saang baze*, or stone pelters, have lived their entire lives in a war zone, surrounded by bunkers while enduring curfews, arrests, detentions, and humiliations. They come from different social and economic backgrounds but are united in their grievances against the Indian state. While some feel that stone-throwing might draw global attention to Kashmir's militarization, others perceive it as the only way to resist the armed might of the state; in the post-9/11 world, any other armed response would be labeled "terrorism" and draw international wrath. Although stone-pelting is not a peaceful form of protest, the protesters believe that "the very act of choosing stone as a weapon" places them on a "higher moral ground" than the army, who showers their demonstrations with bullets.[187] The Indian military dismissed these civilian protests as "agitational terrorism," and charged almost four hundred protesters under the Public Safety Act of 2009 for defiling "state honor." The Indian media, on the other hand, portrayed the stone-pelters as "paid agents" of separatist groups who disturbed law and order for money.[188]

The state government prevented the circulation of news stories highlighting this new wave of civilian resistance and banned cable news channels for "telecasting provocative speeches" by "secessionist" elements. However, the Kashmiri youth who had been using social media effectively as early as 2008 had observed the power of Facebook, Twitter, and YouTube as critical modes of protest.[189] A few years down the line, they witnessed similar tactics during the anti-regime demonstrations in the Middle East during the so-called Arab Spring of 2011. Egyptians also utilized social media to challenge biased state narratives and provide the world a window into their reality. As a result, online activism became an essential tool in Kashmiri mobilization. Several anonymous Facebook pages, like "Saang Baze-e-Kashmir" (Stone Pelters of Kashmir) and "Aalaw" (The Call), influenced public opinion and exposed police brutalities through text, videos, and photos. Facebook pages like "Today in History" and the digital newspaper the *Kashmir Walla* published updates about the experiences of civilians living in militarized Kashmir. These blogs publicize stories of Kashmiri "heroes" who resisted economic exploitation and political injustices in pre-partition Kashmir; they celebrate World Braille Day by posting images of blinded Kashmiris shot with pellet guns by Indian security forces; they memorialize the victims of massacres during the heyday of insurgency. Photographs of each victim with their names, date of birth, and date of death are posted on these blogs and Facebook pages to make visible the impact of state violence on individuals and communities.

Through these social networking sites, ordinary Kashmiris connect with their past, speaking not only to each other, but reaching the world.[190]

When social media was placed under state surveillance in the decades of the 2000s, music, graffiti, paintings, and posters proved the futility of censorship in the contemporary era. As in the past, Kashmiris today use indigenous entertainment forms to make their points when direct political statements are disallowed. Protest music is a form of nonviolent resistance that comments on the denial of human dignity and the injustices of militarization, and endorses resistance as the way to retain Kashmiri identity. However, young Kashmiris in an effort to reach the Western audience used English to unite around issues that touch their emotions and connect them with struggles around the globe through genres of protest music. Hip-hop, popular among the African-American community in the United States as a means of critiquing social injustice, inspired Kashmiri youth like Roushan Illahi, popularly known as M. C. Kash, who, inspired by the African-American rapper Tupac Shakur (2Pac), made his music a creative forum to protest "injustice, oppression, and falsehood."[191] Illahi's "I Protest," written in English, is an anthem for the civilian disobedience movement, exposing human rights violations in Kashmir, critiquing the complacency of the Kashmiri political establishment, and instigating Kashmiri youth to continue protests to gain *aazadi*:

> They say you run from darkness, all you seek is light
> But when the blood spills over, you will stand and fight
> Threads of deceit woven round a word of plebiscite
> By treacherous puppet politicians who have no soul inside
> My paradise is burning, with troops let loose within
> Who murder and rape, they hide behind a political shadow
> Can you hear the screams now see the revolution?
> Their bullets, our stones, don't talk restitution,
> Cuz the only solution is the resolution of freedom![192]

Illahi's songs questioned India's claim on Kashmir, making him a target for surveillance and harassment. However, Kashmiri students inspired by this song posted it on YouTube and Facebook hoping to connect with people enduring injustice around the globe.[193]

Art became a powerful tool for Kashmiris who desired to narrate their story to a wider audience and preserve "the memories of the past, negotiate the uncertainties of the present, and carve out a collective future."[194] Political cartoonist Malik Sajad recounted his own story of growing up in militarized Kashmir in his graphic novel *Munnu: A Boy from Kashmir*. His work mirrors American Jewish cartoonist

Art Spiegelman's retelling of his father's experiences in Nazi Germany in *Maus*. Spiegelman "shows the dehumanization of Jews by the Nazis in the form of mice, while the Germans are represented as cats." Sajad, in the same vein, portrays a Kashmiri as the *hangul*, the Kashmir stag, an endangered species, whose land, culture, and customs are being preyed upon by the army who are drawn in their human form.[195] Sajad, like other members of his generation, focused on themes of oppression and occupation to expose how the intensely militarized state of Jammu and Kashmir has denied its inhabitants human dignity. Another cartoonist, Mir Suhail, attempted to draw global attention to the cycle of violence in Kashmir by digitally manipulating famous Western "paintings like the 'Mona Lisa' by Leonardo da Vinci, 'Self-Portrait' by Vincent van Gogh, and 'The Scream' by Edvard Munch by placing bandages" on the subjects' eyes indicating blinding due to pellet guns used by the army against Kashmiri protestors.[196]

The mainstream Kashmiri leadership remains indifferent to Kashmiri feelings of "anger" and "betrayal," while focusing on retaining political power at any price. In the 2014 state elections, the People's Democratic Party (PDP), whose core ideology is "self-rule," entered an electoral alliance to form a government with the Hindu nationalist party the BJP, which stands for the erosion of Kashmir's special autonomous status within India.[197] Shortly after this alliance was formed, Hindu rightist groups like the RSS formed and funded organizations like the Kashmir Study Centre to challenge the constitutional validity of Article 35A of the Indian constitution, which bars non-citizens of Jammu and Kashmir from buying land in the state.

The Kashmir Study Centre characterized Article 35A "discriminatory" toward Kashmiri women and Hindu refugees. Article 35A puts Kashmiri women at a disadvantage, they argued, as it prevents them from inheriting property if they married "outsiders."[198] However, the Jammu and Kashmir High Court in the Susheela Sawhney case of 2002 had already decided that women from Jammu and Kashmir could retain the state-subject privileges regardless of their marital status.[199] Furthermore, the inability of the Hindu refugees from West Pakistan settled in Jammu and Kashmir from buying land in the state also irked the Hindu right activists. Although their rhetoric blasted the "special privileges" given to Jammu and Kashmir to "appease" its Muslim majority, the group conveniently ignored that India has also provided such constitutional protections to states in the northeast, though they "vary in degrees for historical reasons."[200] Like the Hindu refugees in Jammu and Kashmir, the Chakma Buddhist refugees that had arrived in Arunachal Pradesh from eastern Bangladesh in the 1960s also could not own land. The state of Arunachal Pradesh resisted New Delhi's attempt to erase their "special status" to accommodate the Chakma Buddhist refugees. In 2017, the Hindu nationalist government compromised and offered "conditional citizenship" to the Chakma refugees, with a proviso for "employment, educational and electoral rights" but stopped short of "granting land rights."[201] However, the Muslim-majority character of Jammu and Kashmir makes the Hindu nationalists eschew any kind of "compromise." Ending Article 35A, they believe, will resolve the Kashmir issue, as it will alter the state's demography and make Kashmir into a Hindu-majority area with a correspondingly greater attachment to the Indian state.

Kashmiri Muslims watch with helpless trepidation as "New India" is aggressively transforming into a Hindu state bent upon disenfranchising the Muslim community. The recent Citizenship Amendment Act (2019) promises citizenship to non-Muslim minorities who entered India as illegal immigrants from Pakistan, Afghanistan, and Bangladesh on the grounds of religious persecution, but ignores the persecuted Muslim minorities in the region. By making religion a litmus test for citizenship in "secular" India, Hindu nationalists plan to effectively turn 200 million Indian Muslims into second-class citizens.[202] At a national level, the spike in hate crimes and mob violence against religious minorities and the charges of sedition filed against Kashmiri Muslim students enrolled in national universities for expressing political dissent has convinced many Kashmiri Muslims that their aspirations have no space in an India under the spell of the populist Hindu nationalist party.[203] The deafening silence about Kashmir and Kashmiris even spills into the international arenas, which now insist on viewing Kashmiri resistance as an Islamist insurgency, rather than a struggle of people worthy of rights and dignity.

Conclusion

As religion intertwined with politics, the advocates of political Islam challenged the "secular" model of Kashmiri nationalists by highlighting their broken promises and failures to usher in *real* freedom. They cloaked self-determination in Islamic robes and forged transnational ties with other parts of the Islamic world, especially Saudi Arabia which provided them economic sustenance to extend their support base in rural and urban Kashmir. However, the growing Kashmiri Muslim awareness of their religious identity stemmed from the anti-Muslim rhetoric of the Hindu right and their growing demand for abrogating Kashmir's special status. Many Kashmiris endangered by the integrationist moves of India, constrained by economic resources, and excluded from political power felt insecure and aligned with groups and parties that promised to protect their religiously informed cultural identity.

In the post-insurgency era, India's prioritization of "territorialism" and omission of its constitutional commitment to protect the fundamental rights of its Kashmiri citizens has made Kashmiri Muslims, even those who are apolitical, more aware of their religious identity, while also convincing them of their unequal status as Indian citizens. Thus, in the tone and tenor of Kashmiri Muslim protests from the 1980s until quite recently, religious identity was often preeminent. However, the indigenous Muslim resistance in Kashmir primarily derives from a longstanding experience of state oppression and political injustices rather than from a desire to create an Islamic state in the region. The present-day Kashmiri resistance is a manifestation of long-standing Kashmiri aspirations for "freedom" from all symbols of oppression and occupation.

Notes

1. Extract from Zarif Ahmad Zarif's poem "The Sparrow's Sorrow," translated from the original by Shafi Shauq (private collection of Zarif Ahmad Zarif, Srinagar, 2012).
2. Ganguly, *The Crisis in Kashmir.*
3. Sumantra Bose, *Kashmir.*
4. Swami, *India, Pakistan and the Secret Jihad.*
5. Sumantra Bose, *Kashmir: Roots of Conflict, Paths to Peace*, 113.
6. Rai, *Hindu Rulers, Muslim Subjects.*
7. Rai, *Hindu Rulers, Muslim Subjects*, 296–7.
8. Jalal, *Democracy and Authoritarianism in South Asia*, 161–83.
9. G. H. Khan, *The Kashmiri Mussulman*, 152–81.
10. The foundation of the Jamaat-i-Islami in Jammu and Kashmir and its close affinity with Jamaat-i-Islami Pakistan are discussed in Chapter 3.
11. Sikand, "The Emergence and Development of the Jama'at-i-Islami of Jammu and Kashmir (1940s–1990)," 705–51.
12. M. A. Wani, *Muslim Religious Trends in Kashmir in Modern Times*, 72.
13. "Our Educational Objectives," *Azan*, Srinagar, July 1970.
14. SherAli Tareen, "Sayyid Abu'l-A'la Mawdudi," *Oxford Bibliographies*, May 25, 2011, https://www.oxfordbibliographies.com/view/document/obo-9780195390155/obo-9780195390155-0129.xml, accessed November 2019.
15. Ashiq Kashmiri, *Tahrik-i-Islami Jammu aur Kashmir, 1947–1980 Tak* (Vol. 2) (Srinagar: Markazi Maktaba-i-Jamat-i-Islami Jammu aur Kashmir, 1984), 264–8.
16. Kashmiri, *Tahrik-i-Islami Jammu aur Kashmir, 1947–1980 Tak*, 268–9.

17. Kashmiri, *Tahrik-i-Islami Jammu aur Kashmir, 1947–1980 Tak*, 269–71.
18. Extract from Mushtaq Kashmiri's poem "Secularism," *Azan*, January 10, 1980, translated here by Syed Taffazull Hussain, Srinagar, India.
19. Kashmiri, *Tahrik-i-Islami Jammu aur Kashmir, 1947–1980 Tak*, 243–51.
20. Qasim, *My Life and Times*, 132–3; Verma, *Jammu and Kashmir at the Political Crossroads*, 126.
21. Kashmiri, *Tahrik-i-Islami Jammu and Kashmir, 1947–1980 Tak*, 344–8.
22. "Is Sheikh Abdullah the Sole Leader of Kashmiris," *Azan*, Srinagar, February 5, 1973.
23. Yoginder Sikand, "The Emergence and Development of the Jama'at-i-Islami of Jammu and Kashmir (1940s–1990)," *Modern Asian Studies* 36, no. 3 (July 2002): 705–51.
24. Kashmiri, *Tahrik-i-Islami Jammu and Kashmir, 1947–1980 Tak*, 320–30.
25. Kashmiri, *Tahrik-i-Islami Jammu and Kashmir, 1947–1980 Tak*, 320–30.
26. Ayesha Jalal, "An Uncertain Trajectory: Islam's Contemporary Globalization," in Niall Ferguson et al. (eds.), *The Shock of the Global: The 1970s in Perspective* (Cambridge, MA: Harvard University Press, 2010), 326.
27. "Oil Nations Aid Jamaat," *Times of India*, New Delhi, September 2, 1980.
28. "Islamic Movements and Kashmiri Muslims," *Azan*, Srinagar, January 10, 1980.
29. Tabish Rafiq Mir, "Tracing the 'Kashmiri Spark' behind the Iranian Revolution," *Free Express Kashmir*, February 12, 2018, https://freepresskashmir.com/2018/02/12/tracing-the-kashmiri-spark-behind-the-iranian-revolution/, accessed January 10, 2019.
30. For details, see "National Conference se Nazriyati Ikhtilafat," *Azan*, Srinagar, May 21, 1981; "Zulum we Jabar ki Siyasat," *Azan*, Srinagar, September 4, 1980.
31. "Islami-Jami'at-i-Tulaba ke Nazim-i-Allah aur Sheikh Muhammad Abdullah," *Azan*, September 4, 1980.
32. "Magzooba Kashmir Mein Islami Inquilab ki Ahat," *Azan*, Srinagar, September 4, 1980.
33. Rehmani, *Azadi ki Talash*, 270–4.
34. Rehmani, *Azadi ki Talash*, 270–8.
35. Rehmani, *Azadi ki Talash*, 15–19.
36. Interview with Yasin Malik, Chairman of Jammu and Kashmir Liberation Front, June 2011, Srinagar.
37. S. Butt, *Uhad-Nama-Kashmir*, 136–9; Rehmani, *Azadi ki Talash*, 263–5.
38. Rehmani, *Azadi ki Talash*, 267–8.
39. *Times of India*, August 9, 1980.
40. Rehmani, *Azadi ki Talash*, 279–86.
41. A. Hussain, *Shabir Shah*.
42. "When a Movie Inspired Kashmir Rebellion," *Kashmir Newz*, September 15, 2009.
43. Sumantra Bose, *Kashmir: Roots of Conflict, Paths to Peace*, 111.

44. For details, see Schofield, *Kashmir in Conflict*, 176; Azam Inqilabi, *Masla-i-Kashmir aur Operation Balakote* (Mirpur: Lalazar Publishers, 1990).
45. Sumantra Bose, "Hindu Nationalism and Crisis of the Indian State: A Theoretical Perspective," in Sugata Bose and Ayesha Jalal (eds.), *Nationalism, Democracy and Development: State and Politics in India* (New Delhi: Oxford University Press, 1997), 104–64.
46. Nikhil Chakravartty, "The Communal Wind Blows," *Times of India*, New Delhi, May 3, 1987.
47. Gauri Bazaz, "February Riots in Jammu and Kashmir and Their Aftermath," *Radical Humanist* 50 (August 1986), 19–26.
48. G. Bazaz, "February Riots in Jammu and Kashmir and Their Aftermath."
49. Balraj Puri, "Communal Upsurge in J&K," *Times of India*, New Delhi, April 14, 1986.
50. "J&K Writ Plea on Arms Act Fails," *Times of India*, New Delhi, October 28, 1987.
51. V. Krishna Ananth, *India since Independence: Making Sense of Indian Politics* (New Delhi: Pearson, 2010), 171.
52. Jagmohan, *My Frozen Turbulence in Kashmir*, 351–2, 864.
53. Punjabi, "Kashmir: The Bruised Identity," 147.
54. "National Conference on Path of Ruin," *Chatan*, Srinagar, December 2, 1986.
55. "MUF ka Qayam," *Chatan*, Srinagar, September 2, 1986.
56. V. K. Dethe, "A Preacher to Watch," *Times of India*, New Delhi, July 12, 1986.
57. "Plebiscite: A Beautiful Betrayal," *Chatan*, Srinagar, August 8, 1986; P. S. Verma, "The Muslim United Front in Jammu and Kashmir (1987)," in S. Bhatnagar and Pradeep Kumar (eds.), *Regional Political Parties in India* (New Delhi: Ess Ess Publications, 1988), 185–201.
58. Verma, "The Muslim United Front in Jammu and Kashmir (1987)," 192–5.
59. Shakeel Bakshi, "Bharti Faujain aur Kashmiri Plebiscite," in Imtiyaz Hussain Raja (ed.), *Aazadi* (Mirpur: Kashmir Students Freedom Movement, 1989), 42–5.
60. Puri, *Kashmir towards Insurgency*, 37.
61. Ghulam Nabi Hagroo, "Dr. Farooq Abdullah: The Muslim Character of the State Is More Important Than Lust for Power," *Srinagar Times*, October 11, 1988.
62. Peerzada Arshad Hamid, "Counting Kashmiris," *Himal*, April 2011, http://www.himalmag.com/component/content/article/4355-counting-kashmiris.html, accessed November 4, 2013.
63. "Where Have 31 Thousand Muslims Gone?" *Chatan*, Srinagar, December 8, 1986.
64. V. K. Dethe, "A Preacher to Watch," *Times of India*, New Delhi, July 12, 1986.
65. H. S. Chandalia and Showkat Hussain Ittoo, *Tales of Anguish and Alienation: Short Stories of Kashmir*, http://www.academia.edu/8001953/Tales_of_Anguish_and_Alienation_Short_Stories_of_Kashmir, accessed February 28, 2018.
66. Ghulam Qadir Wani, "The Truth behind Al-Fath, Al Barq, and al-Jihad," *Chatan*, Srinagar, December 8, 1986.

67. Rehmani, *Azadi ki Talash*, 300–1; Udyan Sharma, "How Delhi Spies on Kashmir Politicians," *Sunday*, September 13, 1981.
68. Sumantra Bose, *Kashmir: Roots of Conflict, Paths to Peace*, 48.
69. "Eight Men Charged under Terrorist Act," *Indian Express*, New Delhi, March 9, 1987.
70. "Violent Government and Bureaucracy," *Srinagar Times*, September 15, 1988.
71. "MUF Tables Copies of Fake Votes," *Statesman*, Delhi, April 2, 1987.
72. G. Q. Wani, "The Truth behind Al-Fath, Al Barq, and al-Jihad."
73. Puri, *Kashmir towards Insurgency*, 54–8.
74. S. Butt, *Uhad-Nama-Kashmir*, 136–9
75. A. Hussain, *Shabir Shah*, 66–7.
76. Sumantra Bose, *Kashmir: Roots of Conflict, Paths to Peace*, 103.
77. "Martyrdom of Ashfaq Majid Wani," *Al-Safah*, Srinagar, April 8, 1990
78. Inderjit Badhwar, "Kashmir Valley of Tears," *India Today*, Delhi, May 31, 1989.
79. Interview with Yasin Malik, May 2011, Srinagar.
80. Inderjit Badhwar, "Kashmir Witnesses Dangerous Rise of Militancy as Violence Rocks Valley," *India Today*, Delhi, May 31, 1989.
81. "A Kashmiri Is Neither a Coward Nor a Terrorist," *Srinagar Times*, March 11, 1989.
82. Badhwar, "Kashmir Witnesses Dangerous Rise of Militancy as Violence Rocks Valley."
83. A. Butt, *Secession and Security*, 118.
84. A. Butt, *Secession and Security*, 118.
85. Sumantra Bose, *Kashmir: Roots of Conflcit, Paths to Peace*, 108.
86. Barbara Crossette, "Radicals Hearten Many in Kashmir," *New York Times*, December 15, 1989; "Startling Scenario in Kashmir," *India Today*, New Delhi, January 15, 1990.
87. Jagmohan, *My Frozen Turbulence*, 21.
88. Puri, *Kashmir towards Insurgency*, 60.
89. For details, see Khalid Hasan (ed.), *Kashmir Holocaust: The Case against India, Text of a Writ Petition Filed by Bahauddin Farooqi, Former Chief Justice of the Jammu and Kashmir High Court* (Lahore: Dotcare, 1992).
90. Lokshahi Hakk Sanghatana, *Blood in the Valley: Kashmir, Behind the Propaganda Curtain*, Issue 22 of Report (Institute of Kashmir Studies, Human Rights Division) (Bombay: Lokshahi Hakk Sanghatana, 1995). 64.
91. Puri, *Kashmir towards Insurgency*, 61.
92. Lokshahi Hakk Sanghatana, *Blood in the Valley*, 95–6.
93. Lokshahi Hakk Sanghatana, *Blood in the Valley*, 97–8.
94. Lokshahi Hakk Sanghatana, *Blood in the Valley*, 99.
95. Balraj Puri, *Kashmir towards Insurgency*, 61.
96. Shiraz Sidhva, "Brute Force," *Sunday*, Calcutta, May 13, 1990.
97. Behera, *Demystifying Kashmir*, 48.

98. Inam ul Haq and Muzafar Ahmad Dar, "Human Rights Violations in Kashmir," *European Academic Research* 2, no. 7 (October 2014), http://www.academia.edu/12938405/Human_Rights_Violations_in_Kashmir, accessed February 28, 2014.
99. Andhra Pradesh Civil Liberties Committee (APCLC), Committee for Protection of Democratic Rights (CPDR), Lok Shahi Hakk Saghatana (LHS), and Organisation for Protection of Democratic Rights (OPDR), *Undeclared War on Kashmir* (Bombay, August 1991), 20–4.
100. Mark Fineman, "Critical Test for India," *Los Angeles Times*, May 11, 1990, in A. R. Minhas and Mustahsan Aqil, *Kashmir: Cry Freedom* (Mirpur: Kashmir Record and Research Cell, 1991), 128–31.
101. Edward W. Desmond, "Sing a Song of Freedom," *New York Times*, May 14, 1990, in A. R. Minhas and Mustahsan Aqil, *Kashmir: Cry Freedom* (Mirpur: Kashmir Record and Research Cell, 1991), 139–41.
102. Muzamil Jaleel, "Konan Poshpora Mass Rape: 22 Years On, State Still Out to Scuttle Probe," *Indian Express*, June 11, 2013, https://indianexpress.com/article/india/latest-news/konan-poshpora-mass-rape-22-years-on-state-still-out-to-scuttle-probe/, accessed June 29, 2020.
103. Basharat Peer, *Curfewed Night* (New York: Scribner, 2010).
104. "Lashoon ki Sarhad," *Al-Safa*, Srinagar, July 31, 1990.
105. Mirza Waheed, *The Collaborator* (London: Viking Publishers, 2011).
106. For details, see Hasan, *Kashmir Holocaust*.
107. *Al-Safa*, Srinagar, March 20, 1990; *Srinagar Times*, July 12, 1990.
108. "Kashmiriyon ke Katal ka Jawaz," *Al-Safa*, March 9, 1993.
109. Ashok Mitra, "Kashmir: A Moral Issue," *The Telegraph*, Calcutta, May 16, 1990, in A. R. Minhas and Mustahsan Aqil, *Kashmir: Cry Freedom* (Mirpur: Kashmir Record and Research Cell, 1991), 144–5.
110. Anil Maheshwari, *Crescent over Kashmir: Politics of Mullaism* (New Delhi: Rupa & Co. 1993), 144–74.
111. T. Singh, *Kashmir*, 145; Schofield, *Kashmir in the Crossfire*, 238.
112. Puri, *Kashmir towards Insurgency*, 69.
113. Jalal, *Democracy and Authoritarianism in South Asia*, 179.
114. For details, see Maheshwari, *Crescent over Kashmir*, 229–93.
115. Maheshwari, *Crescent over Kashmir*, 175–202.
116. Kanhya L. Kaul, "The Destruction of Community: Violation of Their Human Rights," K. S. Dattatreya, "Homeland Slogan: A Historical View," in T. N. Kaul Papers, Printed Material, S. No. 8, 1-3 Instalments, Nehru Memorial Museum and Library, New Delhi, 44.
117. For details, see Hasan, *Kashmir Holocaust*, 36–7.
118. Azad Essa, "Kashmir: The Pandit Question," *Al-Jazeera*, August 1, 2011.
119. Essa, "Kashmir: The Pandit Question."

120. Puri, *Kashmir towards Insurgency*, 66.
121. Siddhartha Gigoo, *The Garden of Solitude* (New Delhi: Rupa & Co., 2011).
122. Basharat Shameem, "Kashmir's Exile Poetry: An Aesthetic of Loss," *CounterCurrents.org*, June 19, 2016, https://countercurrents.org/2016/06/kashmirs-exile-poetry-an-aesthetic-of-loss, accessed December 15, 2019.
123. Tasleem A. War and Naadiya Yaqoob Mir, "The Lost Homeland of Kashmiri Migrant Pandits," *Criterion: An International Journal in English* 3, no. 1 (March 2012), http://www.the-criterion.com/V3/n1/Naadiya.pdf, accessed January 15, 2018.
124. Extract from Lalita Pandit's poem "Azadi: 1989–1995," in *Sukeshi Has a Dream and Other Poems of Kashmir*, http://www.koausa.org/Books/Sukeshi/index.html, accessed December 19, 2017.
125. Azad Essa, "Kashmiri Pandits: Why We Never Fled?" *Al Jazeera*, August 2, 2011, http://www.aljazeera.com/indepth/spotlight/kashmirtheforgottenconflict/2011/07/201176134818984961.html, accessed December 15, 2017.
126. Charu Sawhney, "Internally Displaced Kashmiri Pandits: Negotiation and Access to Cultural Capital," *South Asia: Journal of South Asian Studies* 42, no. 6 (2019): 1062–77.
127. Letter written by K. L. Koul to local newspaper, *Al-Safa*, September 18, 1990.
128. Girilal Jain, "Callous Indifference towards Kashmiri Refugees," *Al-Safa*, April, 24, 1990.
129. Haley Duschinski, "'Survival Is Now Our Politics': Kashmiri Hindu Community Identity and the Politics of Homeland," *International Journal of Hindu Studies* 12, no. 1 (April 2008): 41–64.
130. Committee for Initiative on Kashmir, *Kashmir: A Land Ruled by the Gun* (New Delhi: Committee for Initiative on Kashmir, 1991), 14–15.
131. For details, see the official website of Panun Kashmir, http://www.panunkashmir.org/, accessed December 15, 2017.
132. Dr. Pradeep Mattoo, *Why Homeland for Kashmiri Pandits in Kashmir*? (Jammu: Press and Publicity Cell, 1993), 24.
133. Mridu Rai, "Making a Part Inalienable: Folding Kashmir into India's Imagination," in Sanjay Kak (ed.), *Until My Freedom Has Come: The New Intifada in Kashmir* (Chicago: Haymarket Books, 2011), 250–78.
134. Extract from Agha Shahid Ali's poem "Farewell," http://wonderingminstrels.blogspot.com/2002/12/farewell-agha-shahid-ali.html, accessed February 15, 2018.
135. Lokshahi Hakk Sanghatana, *Blood in the Valley*, 61–2.
136. Sikand, "The Emergence and Development of the Jama'at-i-Islami of Jammu and Kashmir (1940s–1990)," 705–51.
137. Behera, *Demystifying Kashmir*, 152–4.
138. Syed Ali Shah Geelani, *Rudad-i-Qafas* (Srinagar: Mizan Publications, 1993), 3.
139. Behera, *Demystifying Kashmir*, 152–4.

140. Murtaza Shibli, "Kashmir: Islam, Identity and Insurgency (with Case Study: Hizbul Mujahideen)," *Kashmir Affairs* (January 2009), 1–40.
141. Robinson, *Body of Victim, Body of Warrior*, 4–5, 178–9.
142. Mushtaq Kashmiri, "It's Sad That Kashmiri Muslims Demand Explanations about Veils," *Al-Safa*, July 10, 1990.
143. Raymond Whitaker, "Militants of Kashmir," *Al-Safa*, July 3, 1990.
144. Zakaria, *Between the Great Divide*, 3396.
145. Kesava Menon, "The Third Option: Idea of Independent Kashmir," *Frontline*, March 13, 1992; Ellis and Khan, "The Kashmiri Diaspora," 169–85.
146. O. N. Dhar, "No Longer a Kashmiri Insurgency," *The Hindu*, Chennai, January 18, 1996; Behera, *Demystifying Kashmir*, 164.
147. "Kashmir on the Verge of Civil War," *Al-Safa*, April 7, 1994.
148. "Interview with Javid Mir," *Al-Safa*, March 19, 1994.
149. Lokshahi Hakk Sanghatana, *Blood in the Valley*, 62–3.
150. Jalal, *Partisans of Allah*, 280–2.
151. Austrian Centre for Country of Origin & Asylum Research and Documentation, Pakistan-administered Kashmir, *Azad Kashmir and Gilgit-Baltistan* (Vienna: ACCORD, 2012), 38.
152. Jalal, *Partisans of Allah*, 280–2.
153. Behera, *Demystifying Kashmir*, 164–7.
154. Shibli, "Kashmir: Islam, Identity and Insurgency (with Case Study: Hizbul Mujahideen)," 24.
155. John F. Burns, "Muslim Shrine in Kashmir Is Destroyed," May 12, 1995, *New York Times*.
156. Azam Inqilabi, *Quest for Friends Not Masters* (Srinagar: Sho'aba Tasneef-o-Taleef J&K Mahaz-e-Azadi, 2004), https://docslide.com.br/documents/quest-for-friends-not-masters-vol-ii-complete-book.html, accessed January 15, 2018; Behera, *Demystifying Kashmir*, 165.
157. Azam Inqilabi, *Masla-i-Kashmir aur Operation Balakote* (Mirpur: Kashmir Publishers, 1990), 5–9.
158. Institute of Kashmir Studies, *Counter Insurgency in Kashmir* (Srinagar: Institute of Kashmir Studies, 1996), 1–10.
159. Kile, "An Unsettled State," 97.
160. Kile, "An Unsettled State," 22.
161. Schofield, *Kashmir in the Crossfire*, 267–8.
162. Harinder Baweja, "Mujahids, Once Worshipped as War Heroes, Are Now Unwelcome Visitors," *India Today*, May 31, 1992.
163. Schofield, *Kashmir in the Crossfire*, 267–8.
164. Prabhu Ghate, "Kashmir: The Dirty War," *Economic and Political Weekly* 37, no. 4 (January 26–February 1, 2002): 313–22.
165. Interview with Parveena Ahangar, the Chairperson of the Association of Parents of Disappeared Persons (APDP), May 2010.

166. Gautam Navlakha, "Jammu and Kashmir Elections: A Shift in Equations," *Economic and Political Weekly* 44, no. 3 (January 17–23, 2009): 10–12.
167. Akhtar Mohiuddin, "Elections: Kashmir Style," in Syed Taffazul Hussain (ed. and trans.), *Short Stories of Akhtar Mohiuddin* (Srinagar, 2015), 74–80.
168. Mushtaq Geelani, "Kashmir: A History Littered with Rigged Elections," *Media Monitors Network*, June 2011, https://www.mediamonitors.net/perspectives/kashmir-a-history-littered-with-rigged-elections/, accessed March 15, 2019.
169. Kak, *Until My Freedom Has Come*, 38–41.
170. Shahnawaz Khan, "Kashmir: Post 9/11," *Kashmir Newz*, September 11, 2006, http://www.kashmirnewz.com/n00035.html, accessed November 3, 2013.
171. Inqilabi, *Quest for Friends Not Masters*.
172. Anand Chakravarti, "Conscience of the Constitution and Violence of the Indian State," *South Asian Studies Forum*, January 15, 2013, http://www.academicroom.com/blogs/post/conscience-constitution-and-violence-indian-state-anand-chakravarti, accessed March 15, 2019.
173. Angana P. Chatterji, Parvez Imroz, and Gautam Navlakha (eds.), *Buried Evidence: Unknown, Unmarked, and Mass Graves in Indian-administered Kashmir* (Srinagar: International People's Tribunal on Human Rights and Justice in Indian-administered Kashmir, 2009), 9.
174. Chatterji, Imroz, and Navlakha, *Buried Evidence*, 10.
175. Julia Meszaros, "The Continued Silencing of Torture in Kashmir," *Huffington Post*, April 22, 2014, https://www.huffingtonpost.com/julia-meszaros/the-continued-silencing-kashmir_b_4821002.html, accessed June 15, 2016.
176. "SC to Hear Plea of Army Personnel Challenging Prosecution in AFSPA Areas," *Economic Times*, August 14, 2018.
177. For details, see Parvez Imroz, *Alleged Perpetrators: Stories of Impunity in Jammu and Kashmir* (Srinagar: International Peoples Tribunal for Human Rights and Justice in Indian Administered Kashmir, 2012); Syed Tassadque Hussain, *Kashmir: A Valley of Endless Sorrow* (Srinagar: Gulshan Books, 2015), 100–23.
178. Imroz, *Alleged Perpetrators*; S. T. Hussain, *Kashmir: A Valley of Endless Sorrow*, 100–23.
179. Imroz, *Alleged Perpetrators*, 8.
180. Amitabh Hoskote and Vishakha A. Hoskote, "The Debate on Armed Forces Special Powers Act," *International Journal of Current Research and Modern Education* 3, no. 1 (2018): 437–46.
181. Ravindran Daniel, "Human Rights Are Not Solely an Internal Matter," *The Hindu*, January 11, 2020.
182. "What Are Human Rights," United Nations Human Rights, https://www.ohchr.org/en/issues/pages/whatarehumanrights.aspx, accessed March 15, 2020.
183. Parvaiz Bukhari, "Summers of Unrest: Challenging India," in Sanjay Kak (ed.), *Until My Freedom Has Come: The New Intifada In Kashmir* (Chicago: Haymarket Books, 2011), 5–7.

184. Somini Sengupta, "Kashmir's Hindus and Muslims in Shrine Dispute," *New York Times*, August 8, 2008.
185. Sengupta, "Kashmir's Hindus and Muslims in Shrine Dispute."
186. Nagesh Rao, "Kashmir Repression Rewards Hindu Far Right," *SocialistWorker.org*, August 14, 2008.
187. Fahad Shah, *Of Occupation and Resistance* (New Delhi: Tranquebar Press, 2013), 2–5.
188. Shah, *Of Occupation and Resistance*, 2–5.
189. Shah, *Of Occupation and Resistance*, 2–5.
190. For details, see the following websites: "Today in History," https://www.facebook.com/groups/todayinhistorykashmir/; *Kashmir Walla*, http://thekashmirwalla.com/.
191. Shah, *Of Occupation and Resistance*, 5.
192. M. C. Kash, "I Protest," in Sanjay Kak (ed.), *Until My Freedom Has Come: The New Intifada in Kashmir* (Chicago: Haymarket Books, 2011), 110–11.
193. Aijaz Hussain, "Kashmir Rapper Uses Rhymes to Protest India Rule," in Sanjay Kak (ed.), *Until My Freedom Has Come: The New Intifada in Kashmir* (Chicago: Haymarket Books, 2011), 113–15.
194. Aaliya Anjum and Saiba Varma, "Curfewed in Kashmir: Voices from the Valley," in Sanjay Kak (ed.), *Until My Freedom Has Come: The New Intifada in Kashmir* (Chicago: Haymarket Books, 2011), 63.
195. Torsa Ghosal, "Munnu: A Boy from Kashmiir," review of *Munnu: A Boy from Kashmiir* by Malik Sajad, *South Asia Popular Culture* 14, nos. 1–2 (2016): 128–130.
196. Marta Vidal, "Kashmiris Turn to Art to Challenge the Indian Rule," *Al-Jazeera*, March 20, 2018; Abishek Saha, "Art as a Means of Resistance," *Hindustan Times*, August 11, 2016.
197. V. Kumara Swamy, "'The Seeds of Kashmiri Discontent and Alienation Were Sown When the PDP Allied with the BJP," *The Telegraph*, September 25, 2016, https://www.telegraphindia.com/7-days/39-the-seeds-of-kashmiri-discontent-and-alienation-were-sown-when-the-pdp-allied-with-the-bjp-39/cid/1315125.
198. "Jammu Kashmir Study Centre to Challenge Article 35A in Supreme Court," Vishwa Samvad Kendra Bharat, July 14, 2015.
199. Press Trust of India, "J&K Women Marrying Non-natives Don't Lose Residency Rights," *Business Standard*, January 22, 2019.
200. A. G. Noorani, "Article 35 Is Beyond Challenge," *Greater Kashmir*, August 14, 2015. For example: Article 371A and 371G of the Indian constitution bars the "parliament of India from making any law in respect of ownership and transfer of land" in the border states of Nagaland and Mizoram.
201. Rina Chandran, "Chakma Refugees to Get Citizenship after 50 Years in India, Not Land," *Reuters*, September 19, 2017.
202. Jeffrey Gettleman and Suhasini Raj, "India Steps toward Making Naturalization Harder for Muslims," *New York Times*, December 16, 2019.
203. Danish Pandit, "In India, Kashmiris Face Deepening Discrimination," *The Diplomat*, March 20, 2020.

Conclusion

He doesn't know whose land is this
Nor does he know whose land is that
As he limps on his lone limb
And a pair of crutches
Following his fearful flock...

While once he used to sprint
Wild spirited and free
And tame his wild flock
With a youthful yell

Unhindered across the mountains and meads...
A loud bang blows off his limbs...
Ah! He doesn't know
That Tiffin sized box is a landmine
Sown across the barbed line
That slices the heart of the land
He once roamed around freely

—Mohammad Zahid, "The Line of Control"[1]

Narrating the experiences of a wounded shepherd tending his flock in the meadows close to the "border," Kashmiri poet Mohammad Zahid captures the physical pain and emotional trauma caused by the arbitrary legal division of the former princely state of Jammu and Kashmir. At the same time, his verses illuminate the irrelevance of such borders in the Kashmiri psyche and the desire to transgress this divide, to "roam freely" in their homeland without the constraints and restrictions of its militarized landscape. In the aftermath of partition, as India and Pakistan laid claims to Kashmir's territory, Kashmiris struggled to come to grips with the ceasefire line and their own presence within the new political constructs of India and Pakistan.

But the division of Kashmir, like other partitions in the South Asian subcontinent, has failed to bring peace. Instead, the trauma of partition continues to unfold in Kashmir as both warring neighbors remain frozen in time, each claiming Kashmir as the cornerstone of its national identity. Its territory is a battleground for real and proxy wars between rival nations, who flex their military muscles and demonstrate their willingness to use force to protect what they perceive to be their national interests. In the power struggle between India and Pakistan, the concept of territorialism and national security has long taken precedence over the aspirations of Kashmiris and helped make managing the situation, rather than resolving it, the priority. Unless both countries break the mold of past practice and understand that any long-term political resolution in Kashmir will require less reliance on national security and militaristic methods and more on human security, there can be no lasting peace in the region. This book has shifted the focus away from the statist perceptions that construe Kashmir as a region under dispute between India and Pakistan. Instead, I have delved deeper into Kashmiri experiences across the last century to give voice to the shifting meanings of freedom across political and geographic spaces. This work reveals that Kashmiri imaginings have not been limited by the borders sketched by the nation-states but have long spilled outside its territorial contours, challenging imposed notions of sovereignty.

In the postcolonial era, the concept of Kashmiri-ness was not limited to its cultural definitions but extended into the political realm as diverse ethnic and linguistic communities from the former princely state identified with Kashmir and called themselves "Kashmiris." Kashmiris living in different geographical spaces appropriated the concept of "Kashmir" to imagine a homeland free from the territorial control of India and Pakistan, where future generations would be guaranteed political rights, economic equity, and social justice. A Kashmiri identity allowed the Muslim inhabitants of Jammu and Kashmir, regardless of their linguistic, cultural, or ethnic orientation, to establish distance from India and Pakistan. As Kashmir emerged as a site for the negotiation of rights, the legal category of the state-subject, introduced by the Dogra rulers in the 1920s and retained in the state constitutions by the postcolonial governments, became the legal basis of Kashmiri political identity. The state-subject category allowed only residents property ownership while recognizing all displaced state subjects as Kashmiris, a status that even allowed Kashmiris living in diasporic spaces to build a common identity around their "occupied" homeland.

Kashmiris remained active participants instead of powerless spectators in the political drama unfolding in their homeland, even though their participation was embedded in specific power relations. This is a story that finds big powers aligning with regional elites to limit Kashmiri freedom for their own political and financial benefit. Political elites who equated "freedom" with personal power played a significant role in immiserating the territory while suppressing a range of local voices with different visions. The complicity of local elites with the nation-states prevented consensual politics from taking root, creating fissures between classes and communities while New Delhi and Islamabad pulled the strings of puppet regimes on both sides of the ceasefire line to secure what they saw as their national interests. India "internationalized" the sovereignty dispute by filing a complaint with the United Nations against Pakistan-sponsored aggression in Kashmir. However, as Kashmir became embroiled in Cold War politics, India stymied every effort at United Nations intervention, creating a stalemate that prevented Kashmiris from exercising their political right of self-determination as promised by the Security Council resolutions of 1948. The unwillingness of India to "internationalize" the Kashmir issue encouraged the big powers to maintain the status quo, creating a space for India to pursue its centralization policy, integrating Kashmir and eroding its autonomy. Kashmiri autonomists who resisted the erosion of Article 370, which provided special status to Kashmir within the Indian union, were pushed to the political margins despite the legitimacy their support provided India at the time of accession.

Thereafter, the state-sponsored regimes were provided endless funds to create a class that would profess loyalty to India. These new political elites amassed wealth at the cost of the poor, suppressing dissent and crushing civil liberties at India's bidding. In their zeal to promote Indian "secularism" for national integration, elites showed disdain for religion, values, and ethics, transforming Kashmiri society and making wealth equivalent to respectability. The middle and poorer segments of Kashmiri society found it difficult to relate to either the secularism of the elites or their amoral form of democracy. Excluded from democratic structures, many Kashmiris clung more tightly to their religious identity. True democracy never flourished; instead rigged elections in India-administered Kashmir purported to demonstrate India's legitimate presence and Kashmiri acceptance of the Indian constitution.

Across the line of control in Pakistan-administered Kashmir, the Ministry of Kashmir Affairs, dominated by Pakistani bureaucrats, did not even maintain the charade of democracy, but appointed "prime ministers" and "presidents" who remained Pakistan's loyal supporters. Although Pakistan emerged as a vocal advocate for Kashmiri self-determination, this advocacy was hollow: it limited the meaning of this phrase to one choice, Kashmir's accession to Pakistan. Pakistan also established direct control of Gilgit and Baltistan, the northern areas of the former princely state of Jammu and Kashmir, to protect its strategic interests. Pakistan's focus remained gaining territorial control of the Valley to secure access to its economy-sustaining rivers. In the process, Azad Kashmir became a backwater with little attention paid to its economic and political development. The undemocratic misgovernance of Azad Kashmir in comparison with other parts of Pakistan caused deep disillusionment among Azad Kashmiris. Ordinary Kashmiris on both sides of divided Kashmir resented the patronage politics of corrupt and nepotistic pliant regimes that benefited certain social groups but excluded a clear majority from networks of rewards, subsidies, and contracts. Excluded Kashmiris, utterly disappointed with the way freedom had unfolded in the region, questioned the superior authority of India and Pakistan and emphasized that real sovereignty stems from the general will of the people.

As both nation-states rode roughshod over the political aspirations of the majority Kashmiri Muslim community, excluded Kashmiris articulated a resistance discourse and equated self-determination with the themes of political justice, human dignity, and economic self-reliance, ideas inherent in their regional mystical literature and oral traditions, which they adapted to suit the needs of their deteriorating economic and political landscape. The concepts of *haq* (rights), *insaf* (justice), and *izzat* (dignity) wove through political discourses about self-determination and appealed to the emotions of ordinary Kashmiris who craved an era of justice, rights, and good governance—the unfulfilled ideals of freedom that had defined their resistance against the Dogra monarchy. The advocates of self-determination reinterpreted the Kashmir conflict as not simply a territorial dispute between India and Pakistan but as a human problem that affected countless Kashmiris separated from their families across the ceasefire line. As the new legal procedures of permits and passports made it almost impossible for separated families to reconnect, ordinary Kashmiris supported self-determination to erase the artificial divide and promote human-to-human contact. In their perception, Kashmir's unification would reopen old trade routes and promote economic self-sufficiency.

Kashmiri Muslim articulations of self-determination, expressed as a nonviolent demand intended as a democratic right for all inhabitants of the state, failed to impress some of the territory's non-Muslim minorities, if not all. Some vocal Kashmiri Hindus emerged as powerful voices condemning New Delhi's autocratic handling of Kashmir, yet others felt more secure in Hindu-majority India and rejected "self-determination" as a secessionist slogan meant to entrench majority (Muslim) rule in Jammu and Kashmir. As the majority and the minority clashed over conflicting understandings of self-determination, the state turned the spotlight on the diverse minorities within Jammu and Kashmir that wanted complete integration with India. Most of the non-Muslim minorities in Jammu and Kashmir had resented post-partition developments that allowed the largely Muslim Valley to dominate Kashmiri politics. Their anxieties multiplied after the new Kashmiri Muslim leadership took populist administrative measures, like land confiscation and the abolition of the monarchy, that threatened to disadvantage them. Feelings of underdevelopment, marginalization, and political exclusion in Jammu and Ladakh widened sub-regional tensions, while making it increasingly difficult to find common ground on the question of Kashmiri self-determination. By the 1960s it was increasingly clear that the politicization of "self-determination" and its repudiation by the minority community would ensure the maintenance of the Indian-dominated status quo. Thereafter, excluded Kashmiris decided to adopt a forceful approach to make their voices heard in the corridors of power. Kashmiri Muslim resistance, I have argued, stemmed from the undemocratic and exploitative political system that suppressed civil liberties and practiced coercion, intimidation, and harassment of political dissenters. The silence of the world community, which viewed Kashmir primarily through the binary lens of the India–Pakistan conflict, made Kashmiris activists imagine new strategies to gain visibility.

Debates on Kashmiri self-determination were not confined within the territorial contours of the nation-states or the region; Kashmiris forged interregional and diasporic connections to challenge the sovereignty of nation-states, in the process reimagining the very idea of Kashmir itself. In the postcolonial era, I have argued, "Kashmir" became not just a territorial space, a breathtaking landscape coveted by powerful nation-states, but a site for Kashmiris to assert and contest their rights and culture. Kashmir's history of subjugation at the hands of a series of tyrannical dynasties embedded it in the popular imagination as a brutalized landscape, which added a greater significance to Kashmiri yearnings for emancipation, good governance, and economic freedom. Even prior to partition, those Kashmiris who migrated to other parts of India to escape the stark reality of their poverty-stricken lives retained an emotional affinity with Kashmir. In the early twentieth century, these expatriate Kashmiris articulated a discourse that built pride in Kashmir's history and aimed to uplift Kashmiri culture, community, and identity. The links between these expatriates and the homeland in the colonial era reveal that Kashmiri identity transcended cultural and territorial definitions, stemming rather from a sense of belonging to the homeland. Kashmiri diasporic voices penetrated the international community's indifference toward Kashmir:

by asserting a transnationally informed and stable sense of political identity, the transnational activists gave specific, practical shape to the generalized notions of freedom in broad circulation. While Kashmiris in the South Asian subcontinent feared retaliation from a coercive state machinery, expatriate Kashmiris, far away from the stifling political atmosphere of the homeland, found it feasible to debate the possibility of radical resistance to ultimately unite the two divided parts of Kashmir.

In the late 1980s, transnational actors working in collaboration with local Kashmiri youth who had lost faith in Indian democracy initiated an armed resistance that transformed into a mass uprising. To protect its territorial integrity, Indian security forces transformed Kashmir into an armed military camp and occupied every nook and cranny of the Valley. Kashmir's extensive militarization, which persists today, has created an image of India as a new colonial occupier, bent upon exercising extreme force to induce submission. In the name of national security, the state has imposed draconian laws that grant the security forces immunity to suppress dissent. The military does not limit its special powers to combating insurgency, but extends it into criminal acts, sexual violence, and murder. Even the judiciary is complicit in these institutionalized human rights violations, as it does not want to hold Indian soldiers accountable for criminal acts due to fears about military morale.

The militarization of Kashmir has produced a landscape of widows and half-widows (whose husbands have disappeared and are presumed deceased) living in conditions of extreme insecurity and subject to social surveillance and sexual abuse. The Indian state continues to dismiss Kashmiri Muslim protests as "agitational terrorism" to justify violent clampdowns on street protesters. At any sign of resistance, the government places the Valley under curfew, stops the publication of local newspapers, and even cuts off phones and internet connections. Ironically, while it frames retaining territorial control as a vital constitutional mandate, India's Kashmir policy demonstrates a complete disregard for its own constitutional requirements and commitment to civil liberties. The freedoms and fundamental rights guaranteed in the Indian constitution are not extended to its Kashmiri citizens. Indian democracy seems a fraud in the region, as no real effort is made to engage dissenting voices in a political dialogue to find a real solution to the violence that pervades Kashmir.

In the international arena, India continues to delegitimize Kashmiri Muslim civilian resistance as an Islamist terrorist movement initiated at the behest of Pakistan. Statist narratives highlight the mass exodus of Kashmiri Hindus from the Valley to stress the exclusive nature of Kashmiri Muslim resistance. In a post-

9/11 world wary of any armed insurrection in a Muslim-dominated region, much of the international community has been willing to accept the characterization of Kashmiri civilian resistance as "Islamist terrorism." Scholarly circles also reinforce such narratives, revealing a tendency to view the Kashmir struggle exclusively through the lens of religious identity, rather than acknowledging political dysfunctions and the mundane socioeconomic factors that provoke resistance. This book does not deny the importance of religious identity in understanding Kashmiri Muslim protests, but has engaged with the socioeconomic transformations that altered relationships within and between communities, complicating questions of identity and religious belonging. As social structures transformed in postcolonial Kashmir, a result of economic changes that altered the internal composition of the Kashmiri Muslim community, it generated insecurity about religious identity. The Kashmiri Muslim middle class saw the imposition of Indian secularism, eliding differences in the name of national integration, as a threat to their religiously informed cultural identity. With the subsequent rise of Hindu nationalism in India, Kashmiri Muslims found it difficult to differentiate between the politics of the openly Hindu rightist parties that wanted Kashmir's complete integration and the Congress Party that preached secularism but used majoritarian mobilization techniques to win electoral support. Kashmiri Muslims increasingly felt that their regional and religious identity was under threat from both secular and communal elements within India. As the "secular" approach of regional political elites failed to usher in real freedom, Kashmiri Muslims expressed their political grievances in religious tones. Islamist parties in the Valley tapped into Muslim grievances about the mainstream leaders who collaborated with India to integrate Kashmir, seeking to convince Kashmiris to shun nationalism and secularism as these had failed to resolve their social and economic issues. These Islamist political groups received succor from the global Islamic movements that swept the world in the 1970s—Saudi Arabia's exportation of Wahhabi Islam, the Islamic Revolution in Iran, and the Afghan war—which encouraged many Muslims to embrace the outer symbols of their religious identity in political protests.

As the present wave of Hindu nationalism sweeps India, fostering intolerance and hate toward minorities, the claims of Islamists that India is not a secular nation, but a Hindu state bent upon erasing Muslim culture and identity, gain credence. As I conclude this book in the late autumn of 2019, Kashmiri Muslims are watching with despair as the Hindu right blatantly shreds democratic norms, occupying and hoping to assimilate Kashmir in its own image. These religious nationalists consider Kashmir a part of Hinduism's glorious past, an abode of gods and goddesses, which therefore needs to be firmly stitched into the fabric of mother India. For decades, the Rashtriya Swayamsevak Sangh (RSS), the militant branch of Hindu nationalists, has imagined "recreating" a Hindu Kashmir, erasing its Muslim-majority character and using their land to absorb Hindus. Since independence and partition, they have pushed for the abolition of Kashmir's special status to incorporate the territory into an Indian national identity defined by Hindutva. This far-right Hindu nationalist vision ultimately came to fruition after their political wing, the Bhartiya Janata Party (BJP), won a thumping majority in the May 2019 general elections, allowing them to claim a mandate for a hard line on Kashmir.

In August 2019, the far-right BJP aggressively exercised its power, in the name of territorial nationalism and integration, to unilaterally abolish Kashmir's autonomous status, the basis of Kashmir's provisional accession to India. These Hindu nationalist ideologues crafted an elaborate plan that included withdrawing support from the local coalition government and declaring President's rule in Jammu and Kashmir. Thereafter, the BJP made up an intelligence report that Kashmiri militants planned to attack Hindu pilgrims to the holy Amarnath cave. At New Delhi's instruction, all Hindus left the Valley, while military reinforcements entered Kashmir. On August 4, at midnight, India cut all means of communication in Kashmir and declared a curfew. The next day both houses of the Indian parliament removed statehood from Jammu and Kashmir, and partitioned it into two union territories, Jammu and Kashmir in the west and Ladakh in the east, to be directly administered by New Delhi. Indians celebrated Kashmir's "integration," while conveniently ignoring the undemocratic forced nature of the acquisition of Kashmir, attained after the arrest of all mainstream pro-Indian Kashmiri politicians, the imposition of a complete communication blackout, and therefore the muting of seven million Kashmiri voices.[2]

The Hindu nationalists defended "integration" as a means of ushering in economic development and ending a Kashmiri separatist mentality. Kashmir's special status and restrictions on land ownership, the BJP supporters argued, prevented Kashmiris from feeling themselves one with India, and stopped private corporate investment, which kept Kashmir economically backward. Yet in past decades the Jammu and Kashmir government has always offered ninety-year renewable leases to private companies interested in investing in Kashmir. Behind the "integration" ploy of the Hindu nationalists lay the larger agenda of abolishing Article 35A of the Indian constitution, which authorizes the Jammu and Kashmir legislature to define its permanent residents and provide them special rights and privileges. The state-subject issue has long irked Hindu nationalists. BJP activists have long launched petitions in the Supreme Court challenging the validity of Article 35A, while others pushed for abrogating the article through a presidential order. However, such actions posed legal problems. Some constitutional experts, like A. G. Noorani, consider revocation of Article 35A illegal, as it was not inserted by a presidential order but at the recommendation of Kashmir's Constituent Assembly. As this assembly was dissolved in 1957, it is legally impossible to amend or delete the article. Additionally, as the state-subject category is a part of the Jammu and Kashmir constitution, it cannot be eliminated by a presidential order. However, the new Hindu nationalist government, with complete disregard for legal and constitutional constraints, has now abolished Article 35A without any input from Kashmiris. As *New India* is emerging into an authoritarian Hindu state, it is undermining the pluralistic democracy and asymmetric federal arrangements that defined India's relationship with several other states in the Indian union.

The abrogation of Article 35A has reignited Kashmiri Muslims' primal fear, the systematic annihilation of their majority status and the conversion of their homeland into Hindu settlements—a long-standing Hindu nationalist policy. Kashmiri Muslims envision their homeland being transformed into something resembling Israel's settlements in the West Bank and Gaza. They fear Hindu settlements could be strategically placed in the very centers of Kashmiri-populated areas to facilitate military and territorial control. Kashmiri Muslims dread the obliteration of their religiously informed cultural identity through tactics resembling China's toward the Uighurs of Xinjiang. The possibility of detention centers jamming Hindutva's ideology and culture into "de-radicalized" Kashmiris looms psychologically large.[3] Although as I write, the practical repercussions of ending Kashmir's special status have yet to unfold, the change in Kashmir's legal status will almost undoubtedly reduce Kashmiri Muslims to a disenfranchised minority and circumvent their political aspirations.

Once again, history might repeat itself. The Indian colonial enterprise will search for local collaborators and networks, promising power and economic prosperity, just as they did in 1953 after the undemocratic removal of Abdullah. If Kashmiri elites compromise for economic gains or sell their lands to settlers for unprecedented profits, this will potentially enhance tensions and civil strife. It may perpetuate civil violence, and India might adapt the counterinsurgency strategy of the 1990s, when it nurtured civilian militia groups to eliminate "traitors," creating the impression that Kashmiris were killing Kashmiris. Such colonial impulses, however, will not bring a final resolution. India cannot deny Kashmiris basic civil and human rights forever, nor can it erase the psychological appeal of a Kashmiri Muslim political identity that is embedded in their history. India's decision will only push the region into a spiral of violence.

Meanwhile, it should be noted that Pakistan's intelligence has not been an innocent bystander to the bloodshed unfolding across the "border," but has long manipulated Kashmiri Muslim resentment of India to its own political advantage. To wage a proxy war against India, they supplied arms and ammunition to the indigenous militia groups that stood for Kashmir's independence, but had no qualms about crushing these independence groups once the call for freedom mobilized Kashmiris and turned an armed insurgency into a popular revolt. Fearful that Kashmiris might support independence rather than accession to Pakistan, intelligence agencies lent a religious tone to the armed insurgency by supporting indigenous Islamist groups that had advocated for Kashmir's accession to Pakistan. As militancy gained strength in the Valley, Pakistan sidelined these indigenous Islamist militant groups and infiltrated the area with foreign jihadi groups from the battlefields of Afghanistan. These groups destroyed the essence of Kashmiri resistance—based on ideas of political justice, human dignity, and economic equity—and injected pro-Wahhabi doctrines, reinterpreting the Kashmiri struggle in global Islamist terms.

The Pakistani government has always been obsessed with Kashmir, to the point that it supported foreign Islamist groups in these proxy battles even when this was to the nation-state's own detriment. However, at present Pakistan is in a tight spot, unsure how to proceed after India stripped India-administered Kashmir of its autonomy. The United States has downgraded its traditional ties with Islamabad, and suspended security assistance due to Pakistan's support for various Islamist militant groups fighting US troops in Afghanistan. Pakistan is struggling financially. The Financial Action Task Force, the Paris-based group that monitors terrorism, has placed it on the "grey list," making it impossible for the state to secure international loans. Pakistan cannot afford the cost of a full-fledged war, nor can it use militant groups as proxies amid the threat of international sanctions. Even though Pakistan is helping the United States end its war in Afghanistan by encouraging the Taliban to negotiate, the United States has remained silent on the Kashmir issue.[4] The present administration in Washington is not willing to upset India, their close ally against China. The Muslim countries of the Middle East have also preferred to ignore Kashmir, looking to secure business investments in India. India has been emboldened by a weak Pakistan with little international support. Forcibly integrating Kashmir gives India complete control over the river waters that sustain Pakistan, a scarce resource in South Asia that India can use to gain regional hegemony. As India at present is feeling invincible, it is bent upon reducing rebellious Kashmiri Muslims to submission. Acting more like an authoritarian state, rather than a true democracy, India has removed Kashmiris from any political conversation while it rewrites India's constitution to erase Kashmir's special status—the basis of its political partnership with India. Young Kashmiris reeling from the aftereffects of militarization feel outraged at a brutal state power that dehumanizes them in its zeal to retain territorial control. The occupation of Kashmir, accomplished with complete disregard for its people's aspirations, is thus very likely to enhance Kashmiri Muslims' sense of their difference from India and reinvigorate the spirit of *aazadi* I have traced in this book.

Over seventy years have passed since partition, yet Kashmir remains embedded in the nationalist psyches of India and Pakistan. As we retrace these decades, the most important voices do not belong to the leaders of either nation-state, whose policies have only complicated the lives for millions of ordinary people. The overt and covert wars have left several generations of Kashmiris emotionally and physically scarred as they grapple with feelings of loss and frustration, unable to lead peaceful, normal lives. The idea of territorial nationalism that has gripped the nation-states of India and Pakistan has failed to bring stability to the South Asian subcontinent. India and Pakistan have prioritized state sovereignty, and in the process, have presumed that nation-states have inherent rights and protections. They forget that the government can receive sovereignty only if the people choose to grant it. In other words, states can impose raw power to enforce their will on alienated populations, but an illegitimate government is not divinely entitled to sovereign rights. India's failure to protect the fundamental rights of Kashmiri Muslim citizens reflects its disregard for its own constitution. The state justifies intimidating and harassing dissenting political opinions as necessary to protect its national security, citing risks of belligerent external enemies inciting internal violent protests against the country. This also raises the question of whether states that are at war with their own citizens and practice human rights violations have a right to claim legitimacy. The silence of the international community about human rights violations in the Valley is largely due to India's successful efforts in framing the Kashmir conflict as a state-security issue. As international law permits state violence to protect a nation's territorial integrity, India is eager to limit the reach of a human rights lens on the conflict. But while abuses of human rights may not have moved the international community to action, and while these policies may have strengthened India's grip on the territory, ongoing Kashmiri protests and resistance will continue to call India's legitimacy into question.

To bring reality to the much-awaited Kashmiri dream of freedom and restore a semblance of stability in the region, it is imperative to dismantle all forms of nationalism—Indian, Pakistani, and Kashmiri—and take a novel approach, one that neither replicates the territorialization of the nation-states nor seeks to erase differences for the sake of sameness. There can be no peace in Kashmir until the majority and the minorities strive to identify shared values and bridge political, cultural, and religious differences. The responsibility for appeasing the apprehensions of the Kashmiri Pandit community lies with the majority Muslim community; in turn, Kashmiri Hindus must avoid the traps of the Hindu nationalist parties who sow fear and prevent peaceful coexistence. Only when the tropes of occupation and submission are erased from Kashmir's political and geographical landscape, and priority is given to humans rather than territory, will it be possible to heal the wounds of the past and move toward a better future. This vision, a Kashmiri imagining of real peace, is captured by the renowned Kashmiri American poet Agha Shahid Ali envisioning a homeland free from soldiers, where Hindu and Muslim inhabitants will come together to mend broken bonds and rebuild a strong society:

> We shall meet again, in Srinagar
> By the gates of the Villa of the Peace
> our hands blossoming into fists
> till the soldiers return the keys
> and disappear, again we'll enter
> our last world, the first that vanished,
> in our absence from the broken city.
> We'll tear our shirts for tourniquets
> and bind the open thorns, warm the ivy into roses. Quick, by the pomegranate—the bird will say—Humankind can bear everything![5]

Endnotes

1. Extract from Mohammad Zahid's poem "The Line of Control," in *The Pheromone Trail* (Srinagar: Cyberwit.net, 2013), 77.
2. Arundhati Roy, "The Silence Is the Loudest Sound," *New York Times*, August 15, 2019.
3. James Griffiths, "In Seeking to Control Kashmir, Modi May Look to China's Actions in Xinjiang and Tibet," *CNN*, August 8, 2019.
4. Maria Abi-Habib, "Pakistan Runs Out of Options as India Tightens Grip on Kashmir," *New York Times*, August 9, 2019.
5. Extract from Agha Shahid Ali's poem "A Pastoral," in *The Country without a Post Office* (New Delhi: Orient Longman Ltd., 2013), 23–4.

Select Bibliography

ARCHIVAL DOCUMENTS

Jammu State Archives, Jammu

General Department Records
Political Department Records
Home Department Records

National Archives of India, New Delhi

Foreign and Political Department Records
Ministry of States Records
Ministry of Information and Broadcasting Records
Ministry of Finance Records
Ministry of Home Affairs Records

Nehru Memorial Museum and Library, New Delhi

All India Congress Committee Papers
B. P. L. Bedi, Transcripts of Interview
Jayaprakash Narayan Papers
J. B. Kripalani Papers
Mridula Sarabhai Papers
S. P. Mookerjee Papers
T. N. Kaul Papers

India Office Records and Private Papers, British Library, London

Crown Representative's Residency Records
Foreign and Political Department Records
Mss.Eur.D.704. Political Note on Kashmir Problem

National Archives, Kew, UK

Cabinet Office and Predecessors Records

Dominion Office and Commonwealth Relations Office Records
Foreign Office and Foreign and Commonwealth Office Records

OFFICIAL DOCUMENTS

Department of Information, Government of Jammu and Kashmir. *Jammu and Kashmir Agrarian Reforms Act of 1976*. 1976.

Development Education Centre, South Yorkshire. *Mangla: A Study of Change and Development in Mirpur, Azad Jammu and Kashmir and Pakistan*. Sheffield: DECSY, 1995.

Glancy, B. J. *Report of the Commission Appointed under the Order of His Highness, the Maharajah Bahadur dated 12th November 1931 to Enquire into Grievances and Complaints*. Jammu: Ranbir Govt. Press, 1933.

Government of Jammu and Kashmir. *A Report: Four Years*. Srinagar, 1951.

———. *Five Months: Account of the Work Done by the Jammu and Kashmir Government under Prime Minister Bakhshi Ghulam Mohammad*. 1954.

———. *Crisis in Kashmir Explained*. 1953.

———. *The Second Five Year Plan: A Supplement*. 1957.

———. *The Third Five Year Plan: A Supplement*. 1961.

———. *Ayyangar Committee Report of the Commission of Inquiry to Enquire into Charges of Misconduct against Bakshi Ghulam Muhammad*. 1967.

———. *Saxena Report on State's Crusade against Corruption*. 1984.

———. *Kashmir Festival*. 1956.

———. *Report of the Committee of Economic Reforms* [*Godbole Committee Report*]. 1998.

———. *"My Blood Your Sweat," Text of Speech by Chief Minister Sheikh Muhammad Abdullah on 14 May 1975*. 1975.

———. *Report of the Jammu and Kashmir Commission of Inquiry* [*Gajendragadkar Committee Report*]. 1968.

———. *An Account of Activities of First Three Years of Sheikh Abdullah's Government*. 1951.

———. *Land Reforms: A Review of Working of the Land Reforms with Special Reference to Big Landed Estate Abolition Act in Jammu and Kashmir State*. 1952.

———. *In Ninety Days: A Brief Account of Agrarian Reforms Launched by Sheikh Muhammad Abdullah's Government*. 1948.

———. *Jammu and Kashmir Constituent Assembly Debates*. 1952–1955.

———. *Jammu and Kashmir Legislative Assembly Debates*, 1956–1980.

Government of India. *White Paper on Jammu and Kashmir*. New Delhi, 1948.

———. *Twelve Months War in Kashmir*. New Delhi, 1948.

Government of Pakistan. *White Paper on Jammu and Kashmir Dispute*. Islamabad, 1977.

Kashmir Bureau of Information. *Jammu Situation: Nehru–Mookerjee–Abdullah Correspondence: January–February*. 1953.

Ministry of Information and Broadcasting, Government of Jammu and Kashmir. *Aid from India*. 1955.

National Council of Applied Economic Research, *The Techno-Economic Survey of Jammu and Kashmir*. New Delhi, 1969.

Planning Commission of India. *State Development Report: Jammu and Kashmir*. New Delhi, 2003.

Real Side of the Picture, Memorandum Presented by the Muslim Citizens of Kashmir to Mr. Y. B. Chavan, the Home Minister of India. Srinagar, 1956.

Newspapers

Aina
Al-safa
Azan
Chatan
Hamdard
India Today
Indian Express
Kashmir Times
Khalid
Khidmat
Mahaz
Martand
New York Times
Times of India
Voice of Kashmir (Birmingham)
Voice of Kashmir (Delhi)

Urdu Sources

Abbas, Chaudhry Ghulam. *Kashmakash*. Lahore: Urdu Academy, 1951.

Abdullah, Muhammad. *Aatish-i-Chinar*. Srinagar: Ali Muhammad and Sons, 1985.

Afaqi, Sabir. *Iqbal Aur Kashmir*. Lahore: Iqbal Academy, 1977.

Akhtar, Safir. *Kashmir: Azadi ki Jad-o-Jehad*. Islamabad: Institute of Policy Studies, 1990.

Ansari, Abdul Khaliq. *Saach Kaah Doon Eah Brahman*. Mirpur: Jammu and Kashmir Liberation Front, 1986.

———. *Taqseem-i-Kashmir ki Saazish*. Mirpur: Kashir Advertising Printing Press, 2009.

Assad, Muhammad Saeed. *Shora-i-Farda*. Mirpur: National Institute of Kashmir Studies, 2001.

Butt, Maqbool Ahmed. *Court Statement of Maqbool Butt.* Lahore: Defense Committee, 1972.

Butt, Sanaullah. *Uhad-Nama-Kashmir.* Srinagar: Ali Muhammad and Sons, 1996.

Fauq, Muhammad-ud-din. *Mashir-i-Kashmir.* Lahore: Zafar Brothers, 1911.

———. *Tarikh-i-Aqwam-i-Kashmir.* Srinagar: Chinar Publishing House. 1996.

———. *Shabab-e-Kashmir.* Srinagar: Gulshan Publishers,1984.

Geelani, Syed Ali Shah. *Rudad-i-Qafas.* Srinagar: Mizan Publications, 1993.

Hashmi, Mahmood. *Kashmir Udas Hai: Personal Diary of 1947.* Lahore: Nasharan-i-Tajran Khutub, 1994.

Hussain, Mirza Shafiq. *Azad Kashmir: Eak Siyasi Jayaza, 1947–1974.* Islamabad: Islamic Research Institute Press, 1990.

———. *Kashmiri Musalmanon ki Siyasi Jad-o-Jahad, 1931–1939.* Srinagar: Gulshan Publications, 1991.

Inqilabi, Azam. *Masla-i-Kashmir aur Operation Balakote.* Mirpur: Kashmir Publishers, 1990.

Ishaq, Munshi Muhammad. *Nidai-i-Haq.* Srinagar: Kashmir Book Foundation, 2014.

———. *Nidai-i-Haq.* Srinagar: Self-published, 1969. Personal archives of Munshi Ghulam Hasan.

Kashmiri, Ashiq. *Tahrik-i-Islami Jammu aur Kashmir: 1947–1970* (Vol. 2). Srinagar: Markazi Maktaba-i-Jamat-i-Islami Jammu aur Kashmir, 1984.

Khan, Abid Hussain. *Sheikh Abdullah ki Zindigi ki Khuli Kitab.* Hyderabad: Muhammad Printing Press, 1980.

Khan, Amanullah. "Mere Kashmir Zara Jag." *Voice of Kashmir* 1, no. 2, Birmingham: Jammu Kashmir Liberation Front (September 1976).

———. "Peace? No! Freedom." *Voice of Kashmir* 1, no. 2, Birmingham: Jammu Kashmir Liberation Front (September 1976).

———. *Jahd-i Musalsal: Amānullāh K͟hān kī K͟hvudnavisht Savāniḥ 'Umrī.* Rawalpindi: Self-published, 1992.

———. "The NLF." *Voice of Kashmir* 1, no. 2, Birmingham: Jammu Kashmir Liberation Front (September 1976).

Khawaja, Muhammad Rafiq. *Safaar-i-Hurriyat.* Mirpur: Kashir Publishers, 1997.

Khurshid, K. H. *Jammu Kashmir Liberation League: Eak Jamat, Eak Tehreek.* Muzaffarabad: Markazi Publicity Board, 1982.

Mohiuddin, Akhtar. *Jahanumukh Panun Panun Naar.* Srinagar: Nishat Publications, 1975.

Qari, Saifuddin. *Vadi-i-Pukar.* Srinagar: Markaz-i-Makhtab-i-Jamaat-i-Islami, 1979.

Qasim, Mir. *Dastan-i-Hiyat.* Delhi: Idārah-yi Adabiyāt, 1990.

Qayoom, Mir Abdul. *Ab Manzil Door Nahi.* Lahore: Defense Committee, 1972.

———. *Tehreek-i-Azaadi aur Nowkarshahi.* Lahore: Defense Committee, 1972.

Qureshi, Muhammad Ashraf. *Court Statement in the Ganga Hijacking Case.* Lahore: Defense Committee, 1972.

Qurrat-ul-Ain. *Aina Numa: Collection of Shamim Ahmed Shamim's speeches in the State Legislative Assembly and Indian Parliament.* Srinagar: TFC Publications, 2004.

Rehmani, Muhammad Farooq. *Azadi ki Talash*. Srinagar: Aflakh Publishers,1982.
———. *Sheikh Abdullah ke Naqoosh*. Srinagar: Gulshan Publications, 1988.
Sadruddin, Mujahid. "Raishumari: Hamari Tahreek." *Khalid-i-Jadid*, Srinagar, October 2, 1955.
Shah, Molvi Atiqullah. *Serat-ul-Waizeen*. Lahore: Rifai Aam Press, 1910.
Shamim, Shamim Ahmed. "Tazleel ke Dag." *Aina*, Srinagar, November 5, 1967.
Taryaby, Younus. *Master Abdul Majd aur Bartanvi Kashmiriyon ki Inqalabi Jad-o-Jahad*. Birmingham: Alim-wa-Arfan Publishers, 2009.
Taseer, Rashid. *Tehrik-i-Hurriyat-i-Kashmir*, Vol.1. Srinagar: Ali Brothers, 1973.

English Sources

Abdullah, Farooq. *My Dismissal*. New Delhi: Vikas Publishing House, 1985.
Abdullah, Muhammad. *The Kashmir Conspiracy Case*. Srinagar: Legal Defense Committee, 1959.
Abdullah, Sheikh Muhammad. *Flames of the Chinar: An Autobiography*. Translated from the Urdu by Khushwant Singh. New Delhi: Penguin Books, 1993.
———. *Jammu and Kashmir: A Human Problem*. Srinagar: Jammu and Kashmir Plebiscite Front, 1965.
———. *New Kashmir*. New Delhi: Kashmir Bureau of Information, 1951.
———. *Why Self-Determination?* Srinagar: Jammu and Kashmir Plebiscite Front, 1959.
———. *Former Prime Minister of Kashmir Appeals from Behind the Prison Walls*. Washington, DC: Information Division, Embassy of Pakistan, 1957.
———. *The Blazing Chinar: An Autobiography*. Translated from Urdu by Mohammad Amin. Srinagar: Gulshan Books, 2013.
Ahmad, Imtiaz and Helmut Reinfeld. *Lived Islam in South Asia*. New Delhi: Social Science Press, 2003.
Ahmad, Nafis. *The Jan Sangh and the Muslims*. New Delhi: Sarmodhya Virodhyi Committee,1964.
Aitchinson, C. U. (ed.). *A Collection of Treaties, Engagements and Sanads: Relating to India and Neighbouring Territories*, Vol. 12. Nendeln: Liechtenstein, 1973.
Akbar, M. J. *India: The Siege Within*. England: Penguin Books, 1985.
Akthar, Shaheen. *Elections in Indian-held Kashmir: 1951–1999*. Srinagar: Regional Studies, 2001.
Al-Ali, Nadje and Khalid Koser. *New Approaches to Migration? Transnational Communities and Transformations of Home*. London: Routledge, 2002.
Ali, Agha Shahid. *The Country without a Post Office*. New Delhi: Orient Longman Ltd, 2013.
Ali, Nasreen. "Kashmiri Nationalism: Beyond the Nation State." *South Asia Research* 22, no. 2 (September 2002): 145–60.
Ali, Nisar. *Agricultural Development and Income Distribution in Kashmir*. New Delhi: Rima Publishing House, 1985.

Anand, Adarsh Sein. *The Constitution of Jammu and Kashmir: Its Developments and Comments*. New Delhi: Universal Book Traders, 1994.

Andhra Pradesh Civil Liberties Committee (APCLC), Committee for Protection of Democratic Rights (CPDR), Lok Shahi Hakk Saghatana (LHS), and Organisation for Protection of Democratic Rights (OPDR). *Undeclared War on Kashmir*. Bombay, August 1991.

Ballard, Roger. "The Kashmir Crisis: A View from Mirpur." *Economic and Political Weekly* 26, nos. 9–10 (March 2–9, 1991): 513–17.

Bayly, C. A. *Origins of Nationality in South Asia*. New Delhi: Oxford University Press, 1998.

Bazaz, Gauri. "February Riots in Jammu and Kashmir and Their Aftermath." *Radical Humanist* 50 (August 1986).

Bazaz, Nagin. *Ahead of His Times: Prem Nath Bazaz—His Life and Works*. Delhi: Sterling Publishers, 1983.

Bazaz, Prem Nath. *Democracy through Intimidation and Terror: The Untold Story of Kashmir's Politics*. New Delhi: Heritage, 1978.

———. *The History of Struggle for Freedom in Kashmir*. Srinagar: Gulshan Publications, 2003.

———. *Inside Kashmir*. Mirpur: Verinag Publishers, 1987.

———. *Jammu Kashmir Kissan Mazdoor Conference: A Short History*. Rawalpindi: Kissan Mazdoor Publishing Bureau, 1946.

———. *Kashmir in Crucible*. New Delhi: Pamposh Publications, 1967.

———. *Kashmir Pandit Agitation and Its Aftermath*. New Delhi: Pamposh Publications, 1967.

———. *Azad Kashmir: A Democratic-Socialist Conception*. Lahore: Ferozsons Publications, 1950.

Beg, Aziz. *Captive Kashmir*. Lahore: Allied Business Corporation, 1957.

Beg, Mirza Muhammad Afzal. *On Way to Golden Harvests*. Jammu: Land Reforms Officer. 1951.

———. *The Kashmir Conspiracy Case: Reports*. Srinagar: Legal Defense Committee, 1961.

———. "Land Reforms in J&K." *Mainstream* 15 (July 1976).

———. *Report of the Land Compensation Committee* (Srinagar: Jammu and Kashmir Government, 1952.

———. *White Paper on Constitutional Relationship of Kashmir with India*. Srinagar: Jammu and Kashmir Plebiscite Front, 1964.

Behera, Navnita Chadha. *Demystifying Kashmir*. Washington, DC: Brookings Institute Press, 2006.

Beig, M. Siddiq. *Kashmiri Short Stories*. Srinagar: Crown Printing Press, 1997.

Bhat, Ram Krishen Kaul. *Political and Constitutional Development of the Jammu and Kashmir State*. Delhi: Seema Publications, 1984.

Bhatnagar, S. and Pradeep Kumar (eds.). *Regional Political Parties in India*. New Delhi: Ess Ess Publications, 1988.

Bhattacharjea, Ajit. *Kashmir: The Wounded Valley.* New Delhi: UBS Publishers, 1994.

Birdwood, Lord. *Two Nations and Kashmir.* London: Hale, 1956.

Bose, Sugata. *A Hundred Horizons.* Cambridge, MA: Harvard University Press, 2006.

Bose, Sugata and Ayesha Jalal (eds.). *Nationalism, Democracy and Development.* New Delhi: Oxford University Press, 1997.

Bose, Sumantra. *The Challenge in Kashmir: Democracy, Self-Determination and a Just Peace.* New Delhi: Sage, 1997.

———. *Kashmir: Roots of Conflict, Paths to Peace.* New Delhi: Vistaar Publications, 2003.

Brecher, Michael. *The Struggle for Kashmir.* New York: Oxford University Press, 1953.

Butt, Ahsan. *Secession and Security: Explaining State Strategy against Separatists.* Ithaca: Cornell University Press, 2017.

Butt, Sanaullah. *Kashmir in Flames: An Untold Story of Kashmir's Political Affairs.* Srinagar: Ali Mohammad & Sons, 1981.

———. "Why Independent Kashmir." *Voice of Kashmir* 11, no. 4, New Delhi: Kashmir Democratic Union (April 1955).

Chatterji, Angana, Parvez Imroz, and Gautam Navlakha (eds.). *Buried Evidence: Unknown, Unmarked, and Mass Graves in Indian-administered Kashmir.* Srinagar: International People's Tribunal on Human Rights and Justice in Indian-administered Kashmir, 2009.

Chatterji, Joya. "Fashioning of a Frontier: The Radcliffe Line and Bengal's Border Landscape." *Modern Asian Studies* 33, no. 1 (1999): 185–242.

Copland, Ian. "Islam and Political Mobilization in Kashmir, 1931–34." *Pacific Affairs* 54, no. 2 (Summer, 1981): 228–59.

Das, Durga (ed.). *Sardar Patel's Correspondence, 1945–50*, Vol. 1. Ahmedabad: Navajivan Publishing House, 1971.

Das Gupta, Jyoti Bhushan. *Jammu and Kashmir.* The Hague: Martinus Nijhoff, 1968.

Digby, William. *Condemned Unheard.* New Delhi: Asian Educational Services, 1940.

Drabu, Haseeb A. *J&K Economy: Reform and Reconstruction.* New Delhi: Asia Development Bank, 2004.

Duschinski, Haley. "Destiny Effects: Militarization, State Power, and Punitive Containment in Kashmir Valley." *Anthropological Quarterly* 82, no. 3 (2009): 691–717.

———. "'Survival Is Now Our Politics': Kashmiri Hindu Community Identity and the Politics of Homeland." *International Journal of Hindu Studies* 12, no. 1 (April 2008): 41–64.

Ellis, Patricia and Zafar Khan. "The Kashmiri Diaspora: Influences in Kashmir." In Nadje Al-Ali and Khalid Koser (eds.), *New Approaches to Migration? Transnational Communities and Transformations of Home.* London: Routledge, 2002, 169–82.

Fazili, Manzoor. *Kashmir Predilection.* Srinagar: Gulshan Publishers, 1988.

———. *Socialist Ideas and Movements in Kashmir.* New Delhi: Eureka Publications, 1980.

Fayaz, Farooq. *Kashmir Folklore: A Study in Historical Perspective.* Srinagar: Gulshan Books, 2008.

Feyyaz, Muhammad. *Pakistan–Azad Jammu Kashmir: Politico-Legal Conflict.* Islamabad: Pakistan Institute of Legislative Development and Transparency, 2011.

Gadru, S. N. *Kashmir Papers: British Intervention in Kashmir.* Srinagar: Freethought Literature Company, 1973.

Ganguly, Sumit. *The Crisis in Kashmir: Portents of War, Hopes of Peace.* Cambridge: Cambridge University Press, 1997.

Gigoo, Siddhartha. *The Garden of Solitude.* New Delhi: Rupa Publications, 2011.

Gilani, Syed Manzoor Hussain. *The Constitution of Azad Jammu and Kashmir.* Islamabad: National Book Foundation, 2008.

Gilkar, Ghulam Nabi, "Demand of Independent Kashmir." *Voice of Kashmir* 11, no. 2, New Delhi: Kashmir Democratic Union (February 1955).

Giyas-Ud-Din, Peer. *Understanding the Kashmiri Insurgency.* New Delhi: Anmol Publications, 1992.

Gopal, S. (ed.). *Selected Works of Jawaharlal Nehru*, Vol. 4. New Delhi: Jawaharlal Memorial Fund, 1986.

Gundevia, Y. D. *The Testament of Abdullah.* New Delhi: Palit & Palit, 1974.

Gunjoo, P. N. *Portrait of Sheikh Muhammad Abdullah.* Srinagar, 1964.

Gupta, N. S. and Amarjit Singh. *Agricultural Development of States in India*, Vol. 1. New Delhi: Seema Publications, 1979.

Gupta, S. P. *Planning and Development in India.* New Delhi: Allied Publishers, 1989.

Gupta, Sisir. *Kashmir A Study in India Pakistan Relations.* New York: Asia Publishing House, 1966.

Hasan, Khalid (ed.). *Kashmir Holocaust: The Case against India, Text of a Writ Petition Filed by Bahauddin Farooqi, Former Chief Justice of the Jammu and Kashmir High Court.* Lahore: Dotcare, 1992.

Hasan, Mohibbul. *Kashmir under the Sultans.* Srinagar: Ali Muhammad and Sons, 1974.

Hassnain, F. M. *British Policy towards Kashmir (1846–1921).* New Delhi: Sterling Publishers, 1974.

———. *Freedom Struggle in Kashmir.* New Delhi: Rima Publishing House, 1988.

Human Rights Watch. *With Friends Like These: Human Rights Violations in Azad Kashmir* 18, no. 12 (September 2006).

Hussain, Altaf. *Shabir Shah: A Living Legend in Kashmir History.* Srinagar: Noble Publishing House, 1994.

Hussain, Syed Taffazull. *Sheikh Abdullah: A Biography—The Crucial Period, 1905–1939.* Srinagar: Woodclay, 2009.

——— (ed. and trans.). *Topical Poems of Mehjoor.* Srinagar: Self-published, 2016.

Hussain, Syed Tassadque. *Kashmir: A Valley of Endless Sorrow.* Srinagar: Gulshan Books, 2015.

Hussain, Zakir. *Indian Muslim Leaders Memorandum on Kashmir.* New Delhi: Aligarh Muslim University, 1951.

Imroz, Parvez. *Alleged Perpetrators: Stories of Impunity in Jammu and Kashmir.* Srinagar: International Peoples Tribunal for Human Rights and Justice in Indian Administered Kashmir, 2012.

Inqilabi, Azam. *Quest for Friends Not Masters.* Srinagar: Sho'aba Tasneef-o-Taleef J&K Mahaz-e-Azadi, 2004. https://docslide.com.br/documents/quest-for-friends-not-masters-vol-ii-complete-book.html, accessed January 15, 2018.

Institute of Kashmir Studies, *Counter-Insurgency in Kashmir.* Srinagar: Institute of Kashmir Studies, 1996.

Iqbal, Muhammad. *Javid Nama.* Translated by Arthur J. Arberry. London: George Allen, 1966.

Jacquemont, Victor. *Letters from India, 1829–1832.* London: Macmillan and Co., 1936.

Jagmohan. *My Frozen Turbulence in Kashmir.* New Delhi: Allied Publishers, 1991.

Jalal, Ayesha. *Democracy and Authoritarianism in South Asia: A Comparative and Historical Perspective.* Cambridge: Cambridge University Press, 1995.

———. *Partisans of Allah: Jihad in South Asia.* Cambridge, MA: Harvard University Press, 2008.

———. *Self and Sovereignty: Individual and Community in South Asian Islam since 1850.* New Delhi: Oxford University Press, 2001.

———. *The Struggle for Pakistan: A Muslim Homeland and Global Politics.* Cambridge, MA: Harvard University Press, 2014.

Kabir, Ananya Jahanara. *The Territory of Desire: Representing the Valley of Kashmir.* Minneapolis: University of Minnesota Press, 2009.

Kak, Sanjay (ed.). *Until My Freedom Has Come: The New Intifada in Kashmir.* Chicago: Haymarket Books, 2011.

Kak, Subhash. *The Secrets of Ishber.* New Delhi: Vitasta Publications, 1996.

Kaul, Shridhar and Kaul, H. N. *Ladakh through the Ages: Towards a New Identity.* New Delhi: Indus Publishing, 1992.

Kaul, T. N. (ed.). *Gems of Kashmiri Literature.* New Delhi: Sanchar Publishing House, 1996.

Khan, Amanullah. "Maqbool Butt Arrested by Indians Again." *Voice of Kashmir* 1, no. 1, Birmingham: Jammu and Kashmir National Liberation Front (August 1977).

———. "The Simla Agreement." *Voice of Kashmir* 1, no. 1, Birmingham: Jammu and and Kashmir National Liberation Front (August 1977).

Khan, Ghulam Hassan. *Freedom Movement in Kashmir, 1931–1940.* New Delhi: Light & Life Publishers, 1980.

———. "Kashmir's Educational System." Unpublished pamphlet, Srinagar, 1968. Personal collection of Mrs. Khan, Srinagar.

———. *The Kashmiri Mussulman.* Srinagar: Faleh-E-Eam Press, 1973.

———. *Government and Politics of Jammu and Kashmir.* Srinagar: Self-published, 1988.

———. *Ideological Foundations of Freedom Movement in Jammu and Kashmir.* Delhi: Bhavana Prakashan, 2000.

Khan, Ishaq. *Perspectives on Kashmir: Historical Dimensions.* Srinagar: Gulshan Publishers, 1983.

Khan, Mohammad Ayub. *Friends Not Masters.* London: Oxford University Press, 1967.

Khan, Mohammad Ishaq. *Kashmir's Transition to Islam: The Role of Muslim Rishis.* New Delhi: Manohar Publications, 1994.

Khan, Sardar Ibrahim. *The Kashmir Saga.* Lahore: Ripon Printing Press, 1965.

Kohli, Atul. *Democracy and Discontent: India's Growing Crisis of Governability.* Cambridge: Cambridge University Press, 1990.

Korbel, Josef. *Danger in Kashmir.* Princeton: Princeton University Press, 1954.

Kotru, Nil Kanth. *Lal Ded: Her Life and Sayings.* Srinagar: Utpal Publications, 1989.

Kshemendra. *Three Satires from Ancient Kashmir.* Delhi: Penguin Books, 2011.

Ladejinsky, Wolf Isaac. "Land Reform Observations in Kashmir". In Louis J. Ladejinsky (ed.), *The Selected Papers of Wolf Ladejinsky, Agrarian Reforms an Unfinished Business.* New York: Oxford University Press, 1977, 178–89.

Lakhanpal, P. L. *Essential Documents and Notes on Kashmir Dispute.* Delhi: International Books, 1968.

Lamb, Alastair. *Kashmir: Birth of Tragedy.* Hertingfordbury: Roxford Books, 1992.

———. *Kashmir: A Disputed Legacy.* Karachi: Oxford University Press, 1992.

Lawrence, Walter. *The Valley of Kashmir.* Srinagar: Kesar Publishers, 1967.

Little, Richard and Mark Wickham-Jones. *New Labour's Foreign Policy: A New Moral Crusade?* Manchester: Manchester University Press, 2000.

Lokshahi Hakk Sanghatana. *Blood in the Valley: Kashmir, Behind the Propaganda Curtain*, Issue 22 of Report (Institute of Kashmir Studies, Human Rights Division). Bombay: Lokshahi Hakk Sanghatana, 1995.

Low, D. A. *Political Inheritance of Pakistan.* Basingstoke: Macmillan, 1991.

Ludden, David. "Spatial Inequity and National Territory: Remapping 1905 in Bengal and Assam." *Modern Asian Studies* 46, no. 3 (2012): 483–525.

Ludsin, Hallie. "Returning Sovereignty to the People." *Vanderbilt Journal of Transnational Law* 46, no. 1 (January 2013).

Madhok, Balraj. *Jammu, Kashmir and Ladakh: Problem and Solution.* New Delhi, 1987.

Mahajan, M. C. *Looking Back: An Autobiography of M. C. Mahajan.* Bombay: Asia Publishing House 1963.

Mahjoor, Ghulam Ahmad. *Kuliyat-i-Mahjoor.* Srinagar: J and K Cultural Academy, 1970.

Malik, Iffat. *Kashmir: Ethnic Conflict International Dispute.* Karachi: Oxford University Press, 2002.

Malik, Rao Farman Ali. *Kashmir under the Shadow of Gun.* New Delhi: Uppal Publishing House, 2012.

Manela, Erez. *The Wilsonian Moment: Self-Determination and the International Origins of Anticolonial Nationalism.* Oxford: Oxford University Press, 2007.

Manjapra, Kris. *Age of Entanglement: German and Indian Intellectuals across Empire.* Cambridge, MA: Harvard University Press, 2014.

———. *M. N. Roy: Marxism and Colonial Cosmopolitanism.* Delhi: Routledge, 2010.

Mathur, Shubh. *The Human Toll of the Kashmir Conflict: Grief and Courage in a South Asian Borderland.* New York: Palgrave Macmillan, 2016.

Mattoo, Pradeep. *Why Homeland for Kashmiri Pandits in Kashmir?* Jammu: Press and Publicity Cell, 1993.

Mattu, Bahauddin. *Rishinamah.* Srinagar: Academy of Art, Culture and Languages, 1982.

Mazower, Mark. *No Enchanted Palace: The End of Empire and Ideological Origins of the United Nations.* Princeton: Princeton University Press, 2008.

Menon, V. P. *The Story of Integration of Indian States.* New York: Macmillian, 1956.

Mir, G. M. *Geographical Realities of Jammu and Kashmir.* Yorkshire: United Kashmir Publishers, 2000.

Misri, M. L. and M. S. Bhat. *Poverty, Planning and Economic Change in Jammu and Kashmir.* Delhi: Vikas Publishing House, 1994.

Mitchell, Timothy. *Carbon Democracy: Political Power in the Age of Oil.* London: Verso, 2011.

Mohiuddin, Akhtar. *Seven One Nine Seven Nine and Other Stories.* Srinagar: Gulshan Publishers, 2009.

———. *Looking into the Heart of Life.* Srinagar: Book Bank, 2010.

Moorcroft, William. *Travels in the Himalayan Provinces of Hindustan and the Panjab, in Ladakh and Kashmir, in Peshawar, Kabul, Kunduz, and Bokhara from 1819 to 1825,* Vol. 1. London: William Clowes and Sons, 1841.

Mullik, B. N. *Kashmir: My Years with Nehru.* New Delhi: Allied Publishers, 1971.

Najar, G. R. *Kashmir Accord 1975: A Political Analysis.* Srinagar: Gulshan Publications, 1988.

Naqash, Nasir A. and G. M. Shan. *Kashmir: From Crisis to Crisis.* Delhi: APH Publications, 1997.

Navlakha, Gautam. "Jammu and Kashmir Elections: A Shift in Equations." *Economic and Political Weekly* 44, no. 3 (January 17–23, 2009): 10–12.

Noorani, A. G. *Article 370: A Constitutional History of Jammu and Kashmir.* New Delhi: Oxford University Press, 2011.

———. *The Kashmir Question.* Bombay: Manaktalas, 1964.

Peer, Basharat. *Curfewed Night.* New York: Scribner, 2010.

Prakash, Siddhartha. "The Political Economy of Kashmir since 1947." *Contemporary South Asia* 9, no. 3 (2000).

Puri, Balraj. "Budgets of the First and Second Five Year Plans: Revenue Receipts and Expenditure." *Kashmir Affairs* 3, no. 9 (January–February 1961).

———."Central Aid to Kashmir." *Kashmir Affairs* 13, no. 9 (January–February 1961).

———. *Communism in Kashmir.* Calcutta: Institute of Social and Political Studies, 1961.

———. "Congress I: Short-Sighted Game." *Economic and Political Weekly* 18, no. 49 (December 3, 1983).
———. "A General View of Galloping but Lopsided Economy." *Kashmir Affairs* 3, no. 9 (January–February 1961).
———. *Jammu: A Clue to Kashmir Jammu—A Simmering Tangle.* New Delhi: Photoflash Press, 1966.
———. *Jammu and Kashmir: Triumph and Tragedy of Indian Federalism.* New Delhi: Sterling Publishers, 1981.
———. "Jammu's Quest for Identity." *Economic and Political Weekly* 19, no. 41 (October 13, 1984): 1772–3.
———. "Kashmir's Indebtedness to the Center." *Kashmir Affairs* 4 no. 11 (May–June 1961).
———. *Kashmir towards Insurgency.* New Delhi: Orient Longman, 1993.
———. "More Money and Less Restrictions on Spending." *Kashmir Affairs* 4, no. 11 (May–June 1961).
———. *Simmering Volcano: Study of Jammu's Relations with Kashmir.* New Delhi: Sterling Publishers, 1983.
Pyarelal. *Mahatma Gandhi: The Last Phase*, Vol. 2. Ahmedabad: Navajivan, 1958.
Qasim, Mir. *My Life and Times.* New Delhi: Allied Publishers, 1992.
Rahim, Khalid. *My Father: A Kashmir Betrayed.* London: B. W. D Ltd., 1995.
Rai, Mridu. *Hindu Rulers, Muslim Subjects: Islam, Rights and History of Kashmir.* New Delhi: Permanent Black, 2004.
Raina, N. N. *Kashmir Politics and Imperialist Manoeuvres, 1846–1980.* New Delhi: Patriot Publishers, 1998.
Raina, Triloki Nath. *An Anthology of Modern Kashmiri Verse (1930–1960).* Poona: Sangam Press, 1972.
———. *The Best of Mahjoor: Selections from Mahjoor's Kashmiri Poems.* Srinagar: J&K Academy of Art, Culture and Languages, 1989.
Ramaswamy, Sumathi. *The Goddess and the Nation: Mapping Mother India.* Durham, NC: Duke University Press, 2010.
Ramnath, Maia. *Haj to Utopia: How the Ghadar Movement Charted Global Radicalism and Attempted to Overthrow the British Empire.* Berkeley: University of California Press, 2011.
Rehman, Shams. *Azad Kashmir and the British Kashmiri Transnational Community.* Saarbrücken: VDM Verlag, 2011.
Robinson, Cabeiri. *Body of Victim, Body of Warrior: Refugee Families and the Making of Kashmiri Jihadists.* Berkeley, University of California Press, 2013.
Saqi, Moti Lal. *Kulliyat-i- Shaikh al Alam.* Srinagar: Jammu and Kashmir Cultural Academy, 1985.
Saraf, Yusuf. *Kashmir's Fight for Freedom*, Vols. 1 and 2. Lahore: Ferozsons Publications, 1977.

Sathu, Jagannath. *Behind the Iron Curtain in Kashmir*. Delhi: Kashmir Democratic Union, 1952.

Saull, Richard. "Locating the Global South in the Theorisation of the Cold War: Capitalist Development, Social Revolution and Geopolitical Conflict." *Third World Quarterly* 26, no. 2 (2005).

Schonberg, Baron Erich von. *Travels in India and Kashmir*, Vol. 2. London: Hurst & Blackett, 1853.

Schofield, Victoria. *Kashmir in the Crossfire*. London: I. B. Tauris & Co. 1996.

Sen, Sudhir. *A Richer Harvest: New Horizons for Developing Countries*. Maryknoll, NY: Orbis Books, 1974.

Shah, Fahad. *Of Occupation and Resistance*. New Delhi: Tranquebar Press, 2013.

Sharma, M. L. and R. K. Punia (eds.). *Land Reforms in India: Achievements, Problems and Prospects*. Delhi: Ajanta Publications, 1989.

Sharma, Suresh K. and S. R. Bakshi (eds.). *Sheikh Abdullah and Kashmir*. New Delhi: Anmol Publications, 1995.

Shibli, Murtaza, "Kashmir: Islam, Identity and Insurgency, with Case Study: Hizbul Mujahideen." *Kashmir Affairs*, January 2009.

Sikand, Yoginder. "The Changing Course of the Kashmiri Struggle: From National Liberation to Islamist Jihad?" *Muslim World* 21, nos. 1–2 (March, 2001): 229–56.

———. "The Emergence and Development of the Jama'at-i-Islami of Jammu and Kashmir (1940s–1990)." *Modern Asian Studies* 36, no. 3 (2002): 705–51.

Singh, Tavleen. *Kashmir: A Tragedy of Errors*. New Delhi: Viking Publishers, 1995.

Sisson, Richard and Leo E. Rose. *War and Secession: Pakistan, India, and the Creation of Bangladesh*. Berkeley: University of California Press, 1990.

Snedden, Christopher. *The Untold Story of the People of Azad Kashmir*. New York: Columbia University Press, 2012.

Sökefeld, Martin. "The Kashmiri Diaspora in Britain and the Limits of Political Mobilization." In Astrid Wonneberger, Mijal Gandelsman-Trier and Hauke Dorsch (eds.), *Migration Networks Skills*. Hamburg: Transcript-Verlag, 2016, 23–46.

Soz, Saifuddin. *Why Autonomy for Kashmir?* New Delhi: India Centre for Asian Studies, 1995.

Stein, M. A. *Kalhana, Rajatarangini*, Vol 1. Westminster: Archibald Constable and Company, 1900.

Sufi, G. M. D. *Kashir: Being a History of Kashmir*, Vol 2. New Delhi: Light and Life Publishers, 1974.

Swami, Praveen. *India, Pakistan and the Secret Jihad: The Covert War in Kashmir, 1947–2004*. London: Routledge, 2007.

Tejani, Shabnum. *Indian Secularism: A Social and Intellectual History, 1890–1950*. Indiana: Indiana University Press, 2008.

Teng, Mohan Krishen. *Kashmir: Article 370*. New Delhi: Vikas Publishing House, 1990.

Thomas, Ragu G. C. (ed.). *Perspectives on Kashmir: The Roots of Conflict in South Asia*. Boulder, CO: Westview Press, 1992.

Thorner, Daniel. "The Kashmir Land Reforms: Some Personal Impressions." *The Economic Weekly* (September 12, 1953): 999–1002.

Troll, Christian (ed.). *Muslim Shrines in India: Their Character, History and Significance*. Delhi: Oxford University Press, 1992.

Van Schendel, Willem. *The Bengal Borderland*. London: Anthem, 2005.

Vashishth, Satish. *Sheikh Abdullah: Then and Now*. Delhi: Maulik, Sahitya Prakashan,1968.

Verma, P. S. *Jammu and Kashmir at Political Crossroads*. New Delhi: Vikas Publishing House, 1994.

Vigne, G. T. *Travels in Kashmir, Ladakh, Iskardo*, 2 Vols. New Delhi: Sagar Publications, 1981.

Visram, Rozina. *Ayahs, Lascars and Princes*. London: Pluto Press Limited, 1986.

Waheed, Mirza. *The Collaborator*. London: Viking Publishers, 2011.

Wakhlu, Khem Lata and O. N. Wakhlu. *Kidnapped: 45 Days with Militants in Kashmir*. Delhi: Konark, 1993.

Warikoo, K. (ed.). *Religion and Security in South and Central Asia*. London: Routledge, 2014.

Widmalm, Sten. "The Rise and Fall of Democracy in Jammu and Kashmir." *Asian Survey* 37, no. 11 (November 1997): 1005–30 .

Wingate, A. *Preliminary Report of Settlement Operations in Kashmir and Jammu*. Lahore: W. Ball & Co., 1888.

Wirsing, Robert G. *Kashmir in the Shadow of War: Regional Rivalries in a Nuclear Age*. London: Routledge, 2003.

Yasin, Mohammad and Abdul Qaiyum Rafiqi (eds.). *History of the Freedom Struggle in Jammu & Kashmir*. New Delhi: Light and Life, 1980.

Yatu, Abdul Salam. "Take State People into Confidence," memorandum submitted to the Prime Ministers of India and Pakistan by Kashmir Kisan Mazdoor Conference. *Voice of Kashmir* 11, no. 4, Delhi: Kashmir Democratic Union (April 1955).

Zahid, Mohammad. *The Pheromone Trail*. Srinagar: Cyberwit.net, 2013.

Zahid, Z. H. (ed.). *Jinnah Papers: Quaid-i-Azam Mohammad Ali Jinnah Papers: Prelude to Pakistan, 20 February–2 June 1947*. Islamabad: National Archives of Pakistan, 1993.

Zakaria, Aman. *Between the Great Divide: A Journey into Pakistan-Administered Kashmir* Delhi: Harper Collins, 2018.

Zutshi, Chitralekha (ed.). *Kashmir: History, Politics, Representation*. Cambridge: Cambridge University Press, 2018.

———. *Languages of Belonging: Islam, Regional Identity, and the Making of Kashmir*. New York: Oxford University Press, 2004.

Dissertations

Javid-ul-Aziz. "Economic History of Modern Kashmir with Special Reference to Agriculture." Ph.D. dissertation, Kashmir University, 2010.

Kile, Jeffrey Alan. "An Unsettled State: The Birth of Transnational Community and Homeland in the Transnational Fight for Kashmir." Ph.D. dissertation, University of Berkeley, 2008.

Lockwood, David. "The 'Lion of Kashmir': Sheikh Mohammed Abdullah and the Dispute over the Relationship between Jammu and Kashmir State and the Indian Union." Ph.D. dissertation, Johns Hopkins University, 1971.

Websites

Amnesty International, "Document—India: Impunity Must End in Jammu and Kashmir." April 2001. https://www.amnesty.org/en/documents/asa20/023/2001/en/, accessed March 10, 2019.

Essa, Azad. "Kashmiri Pandits: Why We Never Fled?" *Al Jazeera*, August 2, 2011. https://www.aljazeera.com/news/2011/8/2/kashmiri-pandits-why-we-never-fled-kashmir, accessed December 5, 2019.

Khan, Shahnawaz. "Kashmir: Post 9/11." *Kashmir Newz*, September 11, 2006. http://www.kashmirnewz.com/n00035.html, accessed November 3, 2013.

Letter written by Maqbool Butt to Akraam Ullah Jaswaal, a Plebiscite Front activist from Azad Kashmir, dated May 2, 1980. https://bloodiedrivers.wordpress.com/2015/04/30/maqbool-bhats-letter-to-akraam-ullah-jaswaal/, accessed October 15, 2013.

Letter written by Maqbool Butt to Azra Mir, the daughter of G. M. Mir, the president of NLF. http://united-kashmir.blogspot.com/2008/06/shaoufarda-letters-of-maqbool-bhat.html, accessed January 14, 2018.

Maqbool Butt statement at the Lahore High Court. https://thekashmirwalla.com/2012/02/maqbool-butts-statement-in-lahore-court/.

Pandit, Lalita. "Azadi: 1989–1995." In *Sukeshi Has a Dream and Other Poems of Kashmir*. http://www.koausa.org/Books/Sukeshi/poem2.html, accessed December 19, 2017.

"Shaheed-i-Kashmir, Maqbool Butt Foundation." http://maqboolbhat.com/.

Sheikh, Junaid. "More Cracks Open in Hurriyat." *New Indian Express*, July 8, 2012. http://newindianexpress.com/thesundaystandard/article561155.ece, accessed November 3, 2013.

Text of the Simla Agreement, 1972. http://www.stimson.org/research-pages/simla-agreement/, accessed June 15, 2018.

Vijay, Tarun. "Kashmir's 'Azadi' with the Tricolor." August 23, 2010. https://timesofindia.indiatimes.com/blogs/indus-calling/kashmir-s-azadi-with-the/, accessed August 14, 2017.

Pamphlets

Ali, Sadiq and Madhu Limaye. *Report on Kashmir.* New Delhi: Praja Socialist Publication, 1954.

All Jammu and Kashmir Praja Parishad. *Jammu Fights against Separatism, Communalism, and Totalitarianism.* New Delhi, 1952.

Ayar, Abdul Ghaffar. *Sher-i- Kashmir on Unity.* Srinagar: n.d.

Bazaz, Prem Nath. *Azad Kashmir: A Democratic-Socialist Conception.* Lahore: Ferozsons Publications, 1950.

———. *Does India defend Freedom or Fascism in Kashmir?* Delhi: Kashmir Democratic Union, 1952.

———. *Economic Chaos in Kashmir.* New Delhi: Kashmir Democratic Union, 1952.

Bedi, B. P. L. and Freda Bedi. *Sheikh Abdullah: His Life and Ideals.* Srinagar, 1949.

Bhan, Mona. *Pandit Rughonath Vaishnavi Annual Lecture.* Srinagar, July 2016.

Bhartiya Jana Sangh. *Kashmir Problem and Jammu Satyagraha.* Delhi, 1952.

Butt, Maqbool. *People's Movement in Kashmir: A Strategy, Press Conference of Maqbool Butt, Sialkot, 1969.* Mirpur: Mahaz-Rai Shumari, 1985.

Dogra, J. N. "The Great Betrayal: Independent Kashmir Demanded." New Delhi: Hind Union Press, 1949.

General Secretary, Jammu and Kashmir National Conference. *Democracy a Casualty in Jammu and Kashmir.* Srinagar, 1986.

Hussain, Zakir. *Indian Muslim Leaders Memorandum on Kashmir.* New Delhi: Aligarh Muslim University, 1951.

Iqbal, Muzzamal. "Is Terrorism by Freedom Fighters Justified?" *Voice of Kashmir* 1, no. 4, Birmingham: Jammu Kashmir Liberation Front (November 1976).

Ishaq, Munshi Muhammad. *Choudhveen Sadi* [Fourteenth Century]. Srinagar: Self-published, 1950.

Khan, Amanullah. *Al-Fatah Aur Kashmiri Nawjawan* [Al-Fatah and Kashmiri Youth]. Karachi: Jammu and Kashmir Plebiscite Front, 1969.

———. *Maqbool Butt and Jammu Kashmir Liberation Front.* Muzaffarabad: Jammu Kashmir Liberation Front, n.d.

———. *Free Kashmir.* Karachi: Central Printing Press, 1970.

———. "Global Movements for Self-Determination." *Voice of Kashmir* 1, no. 1, Birmingham: Jammu and Kashmir National Liberation Front (August 1976).

———. *Ideology of an Independent Jammu and Kashmir.* Mirpur: NIKS Publishers, 1991.

———. "Peace? No! Freedom." *Voice of Kashmir* 1, no. 2, Birmingham: Jammu Kashmir Liberation Front (September, 1976).

Mahaz-i-Raishumari Ka Ehlan Haq, No. 1. Star Press, Srinagar, 1956.

Roudad. *Annual Session of All India Muslim Kashmir Conference.* Lahore: Steam Press, 1925.

Vaishnavi, Raghunath. *Voice of Suppressed Kashmiris.* New Delhi: Kashmir Democratic Union, 1952.

Private Collections

Ali, Daalat. Private collection including newspaper cuttings and pamphlets. Birmingham.

Ali, Mehboob. Private collections of Khwaja Ghulam Naqui, autobiography. Srinagar.

Ansari, Masoom. Private collections of newspapers and pamphlets of Jammu Kashmir Liberation Front. Birmingham.

Basit, Dr. Abdul. Private collections of court documents, proscribed books and pamphlets. Lahore.

Bazaz, Bushan, Private collection of Prem Nath Bazaz. New Delhi.

Ishaq, Munshi Muhammad. Private papers of Munshi Ishaq, including letters, pamphlets and photographs. Srinagar.

Khan, G. H. Private Collection including pamphlets, letters, manuscripts and newspaper cuttings. Barzulla, Srinagar.

Mujahid, Shabir. Private collection including newspaper cuttings and pamphlets. Srinagar.

Shabbar, Agha. Private collection including newspaper cuttings and pamphlets. Mirpur.

Index

Abbas, Chaudhry Ghulam, 41, 48, 53–4, 59, 244, 248
Abdullah, Begum, 198
Abdullah, Farooq, 147–8, 202, 221–3, 306, 310
Abdullah, Sheikh Muhammad, 3, 37–44, 47–60, 62–5, 69*n*21, 72*n*89, 78–82, 86–7, 89–90, 92–4, 96, 99–105, 109–20, 130*n*198, 132, 134–7, 140–1, 144, 146–7, 149, 153, 155, 157–8, 161, 163–6, 172, 177*n*41, 185–7, 189–94, 196–203, 206–7, 212–24, 226, 236*n*161, 239, 246, 248, 250, 253–56, 272, 295, 297–8, 302–3, 306, 310, 319, 341*n*31, 357
  against integrationist forces, 116
  arrest, 203
  in National Conference, 143
  limiting the jurisdiction of India's central government, 99
  political views on partition, 62–3
  would nullify the state subject category, 117
Action Committee, 153–4
  Awami, 204
  Babri Masjid, 305
  Buddhist, 228
  Hindu, 209
  Muslim, 198, 202, 204
  West-Pakistani Refugees, 220
administrative, Kashmir
  acceptability, 5, 172
  anti-corruption campaigns, 148
  complications, 92
  inefficiency, 86
  measures, 353
  officials, 87, 278
  services, 143
  zone, 107
Afghanistan, 246, 304, 327–8, 339, 358
agrarian reforms, 104–11, 140, 163, 224
  deep resentment in Jammu, 109
  empowered a section of the Kashmiri peasantry, 107
  exempted fruit farms, 108
  manipulated revenue records, 108
  no compensation, 106
*ahli-i-tiqadi*s, 163
Ahmad, Bashir-ud-din Mahmud, 40
Ahmadiyyas, 40, 42
Ahrars, 40
Akal Takht, 313
Akali Dal, 112
Akbar, Sofi, 193
Aksai Chin, 203
Al-Fatah, 211, 214, 217, 258, 302
  commitment towards Palestinian national movement, 274
  on guerilla warfare in Kashmir, 212
Algeria, 19, 189, 202–3, 208, 239, 254, 258, 274
Algerian National Liberation Front, 254
Ali, Agha Shahid, 2–3, 20*n*1, 324, 360
alienation
  from India, 2–3, 294
  from National Conference, 301
  of Kashmiri Muslims, 28, 212, 294, 301, 311

Aligarh Muslim University, 37
All India Kashmir Muslim Committee, 40–1
All India Kashmir Muslim Conference, 31, 33, 40
All India States People's Conference, 47
All Jammu and Kashmir Muslim Conference, 242
All State Kashmiri Pandit Conference, 59
Allah Tigers, 326
Al-Qaeda, 331
Al-Umar, 326
Amarnath Shrine Board, 335
Amnesty International, 16, 317
Anantnag, 58, 162–3, 215–16, 303, 306–7, 333
Anantnag Degree College, 216
Andrabi, Jalil, 329
Anglo-Sikh wars of 1846, 27
Anjuman-i-Tabligh-ul-Islam, 155
Anjumun-i-Kashmir-Mussalmanan-i-Lahore, 31
Anjumun-i-Nusrat-ul-Islam, 33
Ansari, Abdul Khaliq, 250, 253–4, 262, 271, 273, 285*n*77
Ansari, Maulvi Abbas, 307
Arab–Israeli War of 1973, 299
Arafat, Yasser, 274
Armed Forces (Jammu and Kashmir) Special Powers Act (AFSPA), 281, 316, 332–4
Article (Indian Constitution)
  35A, 8, 103, 226, 338–9, 356–7
  249, 306
  275, 138
  306A, 100
  356, 145, 201
  370, 11, 100–1, 103, 137, 148, 166, 172, 201, 215, 218, 220–2, 224–5, 306, 308, 351
  371, 11
  371A, 11, 22*n*26
Arunachal Pradesh, 12, 172, 338–9
Ashai, G. M., 114
Ashraf, K. M., 45
Assam, 15, 172, 221, 319
Audit Report of 1962, 144
Auquaf-i-Islamia, 155
Awami League, 260–1
Awami Mahaz, 216
Awami National Conference, 307
Awami Raj, 80, 89, 120
Awami Socialist Conference, 191
Ayyangar Committee Report (1967), 141, 177*n*46
Ayyangar, N. Gopalaswami, 100, 141, 144
aazadi (*azadi*), 256, 278–9, 311–20, 323–31, 337
  counter-narrative of, 320–4
  demand by Kashmiris, 2, 4
  digital and creative roots of, 331–9
  Islamization of, 324–31
Azad Kashmir, 188, 214, 221, 229, 239–40, 250–1, 253–4, 256, 259, 263, 267–9, 277–80, 352
  accommodation and resistance in, 240–9
  as a base camp, 268
  dominated by Pakistani nationalist politics, 253
  feelings of political suppression, 246
  for guerilla training, 256
  involved in fractious internal politics, 248
  legislative assembly, 272, 279
  Pakistan and, relationship between, 271–3
  provisional government, 242
  puppet regimes, 281
  and self-determination promise, 252
Azad Kashmir Army, 241
Azad Kashmir movement, 95, 241–2
Azad Muslim Conference, 42, 202
Azad, Abdul Ahad, 61
Azad, Maulana Abdul Kalam, 119
Aziz, Mir Abdul, 245

Babri Masjid Action Committee, 305
backward classes, 166, 168, 182*n*160

Baghdad Pact, 187
Bakshi Brothers Corporation, 141
Bakshi, Rashid 153
Bakshi, Shakeel, 307
Bakula, Kushok, 110
Baluchistan, 246, 273
Balawaristan National Front (BNF), 279
Baltistan, 6, 243, 249, 254, 259, 275, 279–80, 290*n*193, 352
Bandung, 189
Bangladesh, 146, 260, 269, 271–2, 338–9
Baramulla, 204, 215, 255, 277, 299, 334
Basic Democracy (BD) system, 248–9
Basic Principles Committee, 101, 118
Basit, Abdul, 256–7
Batamaloo, 204, 313
Bazaz, Prem Nath, 43, 45–6, 51, 53, 57, 62, 94, 169, 187–8, 192, 208, 234*n*101, 102, 246
Bedi, B. P. L., 45, 81
Bedi, Freda, 45
Beg, Mirza Afzal, 102, 193, 215, 218
belonging(s), 8, 18, 31, 35, 65, 77–9, 85–6, 90–1, 97–8, 102, 104, 111, 120, 167, 241, 324, 353
  community, 14
  to different sub-regions, 41
  to either India or Pakistan, 64, 120
  to the homeland, 353
  political, 5, 17
  religious, 7, 355
  with the undivided territory of Jammu and Kashmir, 8, 241
Berlin Wall, 304
Bhan, D. N., 187
Bharatiya Janata Party (BJP), 228, 315, 338
  Ekta Yatra in 1991, 325
  victory in 2019 general elections, 356
Bhat, M. S., 160
Bhutto, Zulfikar Ali, 261, 265, 299, 272
Big Landed Estate Abolition Act, 106
biradari, 241, 244, 250–2
Birmingham, 245, 251, 263–4, 274
British paramountcy, 6, 60–1
bodhisattva, 26
border(s), 5–6, 10–13, 35, 40, 65, 67, 97–8, 199, 203, 205, 220, 229, 238, 242–3, 253, 272, 277–8, 317–18, 326, 330, 349–50, 358
  artificial, 2–3, 78, 83
  with China, 243
  within their homeland, 252
  in the Kashmiri psyche, 349
  of the nation-states, 3
  to reconnect communities, 83
Brinckman, Arthur, 30
Britain, 13, 17, 41, 99, 146, 229, 239–40, 245, 251–2, 263–6, 270–1, 273–6, 281
Buddhist, 4, 19, 26, 47, 95, 110, 224, 227–8
Budgam, 204, 299
Bukhari, Maulana Qasim, 155
bureaucracy, 108, 250, 259–60
  administrative, 245
  central, 170
  corrupt, 29
  Hindu, 28
  Pakistani, 12, 96, 229, 239, 243
Burma Ordinance of 1818, 40
business groups, 38, 47, 307, 319
Butt, Maqbool, 238, 254–5, 259, 261, 263, 269, 276, 286*n*104, 286*n*105, 287*n*117

Cabinet Mission, 58, 185
capitalism, 57–8, 263–7, 270, 295, 301
cease-fire line, 248, 254
central assistance
  Kashmir received a larger share, 138
  drove economic growth, 139
Central Reserve Police Force (CRPF), 210–11
centralization, 12–14, 93, 115, 133, 148, 166, 171, 187, 192, 217–25, 294, 304, 351

Chavan, Y. B., 169
Chenab river, 12
China, 11, 42, 243, 357–8
  challenged India's sovereignty in Aksai Chin region, 203
China–Pakistan Economic Corridor (CPEC), 290*n*193
Chrar-i-Sharif shrine, 328
citizen(s), 102, 104, 112, 135, 151, 158, 167–8, 170, 206, 219, 244
  Kashmiri, 8, 16, 312, 314, 334, 340, 354
  Indian, 17, 84, 91, 103, 154, 219–21, 311, 335, 340
  Pakistani, 221, 269
  Indian Muslims, 93, 339
Citizenship Amendment Act (2019), 339
civil liberties, 82, 95, 112, 144, 186, 191–2, 194, 205–7, 211, 226, 248, 258, 309, 311, 314, 351, 353–4
Civil Service Recruitment Board, 35
Cold War, 94, 187, 192, 203, 264, 277, 281, 300, 303, 351
collaborators, 5, 18, 134–48, 154, 167, 172, 357
commercialization of agriculture, 157–74
Committee for Initiative on Kashmir (1991), 327
Committee on Economic Reforms report (1998), 173
communalism, 44, 51–2, 57–8, 62, 116, 197, 206
communism, 19, 43, 67, 264–5, 327
communists influence on Kashmir, 55–60
Comparative statistics of the central assistance (as percentage of total outlay), 138
coercive state machinery, 354
Constituent Assembly (Indian), 11
  adopted Hindi as official language, 92
  debate on princely states, 100
constituent assembly of Jammu and Kashmir, 11, 65, 92, 100–3, 106, 109, 112, 114, 118, 137–8, 187, 193, 195, 199, 201, 220, 357
corruption, 34, 105, 136, 141–5, 147–8, 165–6, 169, 172, 174, 209, 219, 224, 249, 257, 294, 300, 313, 329
counterinsurgency, 324–31
Criminal Procedure Code, 333
Cuba, 208, 257, 266, 277
culture of immunity extended to state institutions, 331
Cyprus, 189

Dal Lake, 148
Debt Reconciliation Board, 107
decolonization, 10–11, 18, 20*n*3, 25, 77–90, 240, 266, 282
Delhi Agreement of 1952, 103–4
Delhi Development Authority, 305
demography, 9, 91, 221, 226, 339
Devanagari–Persian script controversy, 52–3, 92
Dhar, D. P., 205
diaspora, 326
  Mirpuri migrants, 251
  Pakistan–Kashmir United Forum, 271
  shared experiences of racial discrimination, 251
Directive Principles of State Policy, 92
Distressed Debtors Relief Act of 1950, 107
Dixon, Sir Owen, 118, 247
Dogra maharaja, 6–8, 28, 34–44, 47–8, 52–3, 58–9, 64–6, 78–9, 81, 89, 93, 101–2, 105, 108–10, 113, 125*n*93, 132, 134, 136, 144, 185, 188–90, 195–7, 201, 206, 219, 227, 240–2, 247, 249, 254, 256, 294, 309, 350, 352
  durbars (or court sessions), 34
  forced labor, 28, 313
  maharaja, 6–8, 28, 34, 41, 66, 78–9, 102, 125*n*93, 219, 241
  religious discrimination, 28, 36, 275, 308

misgovernance in Kashmir, 30
The Treaty of Amritsar, 27, 59
dominance, 28, 110, 115, 133, 158, 201, 217, 228, 250, 264

economic emancipation, 56, 95, 174, 246
education, 102, 143, 148–9, 151–2, 157, 164, 166–7, 175, 189, 278, 295
among Muslims, 155, 209
to gain social advancement, 163
at all levels a priority, 137
Sharp Education Commission, 33
educational enrollments, in Jammu and Kashmir, 170–1
Egypt, 45, 300, 336
elections, 9, 41, 47, 101, 109, 159, 163, 195–6, 200–1, 212, 214, 216, 218, 222, 229, 245, 260, 268, 297, 302–3, 306–7, 310, 329, 331, 338, 351, 356
as a contest between Islam and secularism, 308
in Jammu and Kashmir, 330
rigged, 9, 186–7, 312, 351
Enemy Agents Act, 205
English East India Company, 6
En-lai, Chou, 203
exodus of the Kashmiri Pandit community, 320

famine of 1877–8, 29
Fani, Pitambar Nath Dhar, 187
Farooq, Mirwaiz, 202, 216, 222
Farooqi, Mufti, 318, 321
fascism, 57
Fauq, Muhammad-ud-din, 31–3, 35
financial integration, 14, 103–4, 137–9, 141, 149
folk tales (*kath*), 29
folk theatre (*band-pathar*), 29
Forest Department, 142–3
Fotedar, Shiv Narayan, 59
Franchise Commission, 42–3
Free Thinkers Association, 55
Front de Libération Nationale (Algerian revolutionary group), 255
fundamental rights, 16, 103–4, 108, 190, 206, 312, 340, 354, 359

gaba (rug), 215
Gajendragadkar Commission, 168–9, 182*n*161, 183*n*162, 183*n*163, 236*n*178, 236*n*179, 237*n*192
Gandhi, Indira, 146, 206, 214, 219, 221–3, 298
Gandhi, Mohandas, 79, 105, 111, 123*n*55
Gandhi, Rajiv, 306
Ganga hijacking case, 259, 261, 268, 271, 273
Gawkadal, 39, 313, 315
German reunification (1990), 22*n*25
Gilgit, 6, 243, 249, 254, 259, 275, 279–80, 290*n*193, 352
Gilgit-Baltistan Empowerment and Self-Governance Order, 280
Gilkar, G. N., 247
Glancy Commission (1931), 41, 43
global resurgence of Islam, 299–300
government employees, in Jammu and Kashmir, 171
Graham, Frank P., 93, 247
Great Depression of 1930s, 39, 46
grievances, 17, 30, 33, 38, 54, 143, 169, 209, 211, 228, 281, 310, 311, 355
against the Indian state, 336
among Mirpuris, 251
cultural, 67
economic, 136, 165
of East Pakistan, 269
stemmed from the corruption, 169
valley dominated administration, 227
with the National Conference, 145, 147

Habibullah, Wajahat, 321
HAJY group, 312–13
Hamdani, Mirwaiz Ghulam Nabi, 42, 190
Hamdani, Sayyid Ali, 32

Handoo, Parmeshwari, 209–10
Handwara, 85, 277, 317
haq (rights), 10, 19, 194, 352
Harkat-ul-Jihad-e-Islami (HuJI), 328
Harkat-ul-Mujahideen (HuM), 328
Hashmi, Mahmood, 80
Hassan al-Banna, 300
Hazratbal mosque, 50, 89–90, 153–4, 196, 198
Hazratbal Robbery Case, 212
Henderson, Loy, 117
Hereditary State Subject Act, 21*n*14
Hindu Mahasabha, 112
Hindu nationalism, 51, 94, 114, 186–7, 190, 237*n*188, 355
Hindutva, 227, 237*n*188, 356–7
Hizbul Mujahideen (HM), 325–9
Holy Relic Agitation, 154–5, 198, 202
Home Guard, 80
homeland, 2, 5–9, 11–12, 19–20, 23*n*30, 25, 29–32, 44, 62, 80, 98–9, 110, 153, 185, 203, 207, 221, 239–40, 245, 247, 251–3, 263–6, 270–1, 282, 300, 320–4, 349–350, 353–4, 357, 360
humanism, 26, 49, 57, 95, 190
human rights, 15–16, 20, 82, 277, 279, 281, 292–3, 303, 309, 316, 318–19, 325–6, 329, 331–4, 337, 354, 359
Human Rights Watch, 278–9

identity, 3, 5–10, 11–19, 32, 35, 78. 84, 91, 326, 328, 332, 339–40, 350–1, 353
  among Azad Kashmiris, 253
  among the migrants, 252
  cultural, 17, 91–2, 94, 150, 156, 175, 228, 293, 340, 355, 357
  Islamic, 156, 299, 326
  Kashmiri, 6–7, 13, 31–2, 35, 78, 166, 211, 217, 223, 241, 253, 271, 306, 337, 350, 353
  of Indian Muslims, 92, 156
  of Ladakhis, 228
  of the National Conference, 221
  political, 7–9, 17, 102–3, 153, 241, 282, 293, 302, 350, 354, 357
  regional, 96, 293
ideology of, 49, 51, 85, 96, 155–7, 162, 194–5, 219, 270, 273, 276–7, 293
  Islamists, 13, 15, 19, 149, 158
  National Conference, 82
  revolutionary, 270
  a self-sustained struggle, 277
  socialist, 18, 264–5, 295
Illahi, Roushan (known as M. C. Kash), 337
Imroz, Parvez, 333
Iran, 32, 300
India-administered Kashmir, 12, 16, 81, 84, 96–7, 102–3, 120, 187, 208, 229, 238–9, 243–4, 246, 248, 253, 255, 275–9, 281–2, 303–4, 326, 334, 351, 358
Indian Airlines Corporation, 169
Indian Maintenance of Public Order Act, 214
Indian National Congress, 40, 46, 48, 53, 78, 217
Indian Union, 8, 61, 64, 99–101, 110–11, 113, 144, 152, 198, 310, 351, 357
India–Pakistan–Kashmir confederation, 202
India–Pakistan war
  1965, 204–5, 212, 252, 256, 265
  1971, 146, 214
Indira–Abdullah Accord of 1975, 215, 222, 298
Indus Waters Treaty of 1960, 173–4
Inqilabi, Azam, 331–2
insaaf (justice), 10, 19, 194, 223, 352
insurgency, 2, 13, 15, 19–20, 22*n*28, 171, 252–3, 277–8, 292–3, 311–20, 331–2, 336, 339
integrate, 3, 13, 61, 91, 94, 111–14, 117, 133–34, 174, 184, 187, 198, 201, 224–5, 243, 246, 251, 293, 355
  Azad Kashmir, 243, 246
  culturally and emotionally, 226, 250

financially, 133
Gilgit Baltistan, 280
Kashmiri Muslims, 3, 292
only Jammu and Ladakh, 113
with India, 61, 228
within British society, 251
Integrated Rural Development Programme (IRDP), 165
intelligence, 3, 13, 32, 79, 81–3, 93, 101, 114, 119, 135, 140, 154, 159, 198, 205, 243, 253, 258–9, 260–1, 263
agencies in the Valley, 310
created rifts among militant groups, 327
Inter-Services Intelligence (ISI), 276–7, 312, 327–8
networks, 276
Subsidiary Intelligence Bureau, 310
Intensive Agricultural Area Programme (IAAP), 159
internal legitimacy flows from sovereignty in the people, concept of, 15
International Marxist Group (IMG), Britain, 264, 266
International People's Tribunal on Human Rights and Justice, 332–3
Inter-Services Intelligence (ISI), 276–7, 312, 327–8
Iqbal, Muhammad, 31–2, 37
Ishaq, Munshi Muhammad, 89, 193, 204
Islam role in Kashmiri resistance, 13–19, 294–311
Islamia High School, 33
Islamic Caliphate, 13
Islamic resurgence, 294–311
Islamic Student League (ISL), 307
Islami-Jami'at-i-Tulaba (or Islamic Union of Students), 301
Islamist, 4, 13, 19, 149, 157–8, 165, 214, 279, 281, 293, 295–6, 299, 301, 305, 355
fundamentalism, 323
groups, 15–16, 18, 134, 265, 279, 293, 295, 299, 305, 326, 358
insurgency, 339
separatists, 324
sponsored by Pakistan, 292
state, 296
student movements, 301
terrorism, 4, 16, 281, 331, 355
Ithad-ul-Muslimeen, 306–7
izzat (human dignity), 10, 19, 194, 223, 352

Jacquemont, Victor, 27
jagir, 66, 108–9
jagirdar (landlord), 56, 255
jagirdari land grant system, 104, 109
Jaish-e-Mohammad (JeM), 328
Jamaat-i-Islami, 155–7, 163, 214, 216, 295, 297, 299–300, 306, 325, 340*n*10
prioritizing Muslim law, 298
reservations about "secularism," 296
strategic alliance with the Congress, 298
to dislodge the power base of the National Conference, 295
Jama Masjid, 33, 38, 42, 136, 216, 300
Jammu and Kashmir Agrarian Reforms of 1972, 161–2
Jammu and Kashmir Civil Service Rules of 1956, 168
Jammu and Kashmir Disturbed Area Act of 1990, 315–16
Jammu and Kashmir Ingress Control Act 1948, 84
Jammu and Kashmir Kissan Conference, 58
Jammu and Kashmir Liberation Front (JKLF), 222, 273–8, 312–15, 317, 320, 324–7
an independent Kashmir, 273–8, 312
and diplomatic effort, 276
and religious freedom, 275–6
and secret work with ISI, 277
insurgents, 313–14, 320
Jammu and Kashmir Motor Vehicles Act of 1941, 142
Jammu and Kashmir People's League, 302

Jammu and Kashmir Preventive Corruption Act, 143–4
Jammu and Kashmir Preventive Detention Act, 214
Jammu and Kashmir Public Safety Act (1978), 311, 315
Jammu Autonomy Forum, 225
Jammu Kashmir Liberation League (JKLL), 249
Jan Sangh, 112–13, 154
Jatto, H. N., 321
Lower Jhelum Hydroelectric Project (LJHP), 173
Jhelum river, 12
Jhelum Valley Road, 30–1, 86, 145–6, 199, 245
jihad (holy war), 4, 20, 278, 292–3, 325–6, 328
Jinnah, Muhammad Ali, 54–5, 61, 63
  indifference to the National Conference, 64
  support for the Muslim Conference, 55

Kalhana *Rajatarangini* (River of Kings), 25–6
Kamil, Amin, 151, 309
Karachi, 255, 278
Karachi agreement of 1949, 243, 254
Karachi University, 254
Karra, Ghulam Mohiuddin, 189–90
Karnah, 277
Kashmir Civil Services, 145, 167
Kashmir Conspiracy Case, 198
Kashmir Democratic Union (KDU), 188–90, 192
Kashmir for Kashmiris movement, 8, 34, 102
Kashmiri Muslims, 2–3, 6–11, 13–15, 17–20, 28, 30–40, 43–5, 50, 52, 63–5, 78–9, 86, 88, 90–9, 101–3, 106, 109–12, 114–17, 119–20, 136, 144–5, 149, 153–6, 168–70, 184–8, 190–1, 193, 197–9, 201, 204, 208–13, 215, 219, 221–4, 226, 229, 238–9, 247, 250, 253, 274, 282, 292–8, 300–2, 304–17, 319–25, 328, 330, 335–6, 339–40, 352–5, 357–9
  about India's secular credentials, 92
  as suspects to be kept under surveillance, 93
  based in Punjab, 31
  equate democracy with authoritarianism, 208
  excluded from structures of power, 144
  expressions of attachment to religious identity, 15
  insistent on the state-subject category's retention, 9
  invoked self-determination, 186
  resented New Delhi's interference, 166
  transgressed the ceasefire line, 238
Kashmir Liberation Movement (KLM), 248
Kashmir National Identity Campaign (KNIC), 271
Kashmir Socialist party, 81
Kashmir Study Centre, 338
Kashmir Workers Association (KWA), 270–1, 273
Kashmir Youth League, 45, 55, 206, 302
Kashmiri Pandit Agitation, 209–11, 305
Kashmiri Pandits, 21*n*14, 34, 37, 43–5, 48, 51–3, 57, 59, 81, 105–6, 169, 209–11, 320–3, 360
  disassociated from the National Conference, 53
  experience of displacement, 323
  felt excluded and threatened, 320
  in state-services, 44, 225
Kashmiri, Mushtaq, 297
Kashmiriyat, 5–10, 78
Khalistan, 313
Khamenei, Ayatollah, 300
Khan, Amanullah, 254–5, 262, 273, 275–6, 312, 326
Khan, Chaudhry Hamidullah, 48
Khan, G. H., 146, 152, 170

Khan, General Ayub, 200, 248
Khan, Maulana Zafar Ali, 59
Khan, Mohammad Ishaq, 20*n*6
Khan, Sardar Muhammad Ibrahim, 242–4
Khan, Sardar Qayyum, 248
Khan, Yahya, 261
Khan, Zafar, 8, 21*n*16
Khanqah-i-Mohalla, 38
Khanyar, 40, 313
Khomeini, Ayatollah, 300
Khurshid, K. H., 65, 249, 256, 262
Khyber Pakhtunkhwa, 78, 242, 273, 327
Kilam, Pandit Jialal, 51
Kissan Mazdoor Conference, 81
Kripalani, Acharya, 115–16, 119

Ladakh, 6, 104–13, 118, 182*n*161, 203, 224–8, 279, 308, 353, 356
Ladakhi Buddhist Association, developed relationship with Hindu right parties in India, 228
Lal Chowk (or the Red Square), 153, 198, 207
Laleshwari (known as Lal Ded or Lalla), 26
Land Commission Committee (1963), 159
Lashkar-e-Taiba (LeT), 328
Lawrence, Walter R., 21*n*7, 30
legalistic view of sovereignty, 334–5
line of control, 2, 11–12, 85, 146, 202, 229, 239, 248, 272, 277, 280, 311, 317–18, 326, 335, 351
Lippman, Walter, 212
loans from India to Jammu and Kashmir government, 87, 137, 139, 172–3, 175, 176*n*20
Lohia, Dr. Ram Manohar, 191
Lone, Abdul Ghani, 145
Lower Jhelum Hydroelectric Project (LJHP), 173
loyalty, 18, 41–2, 77–8, 90, 93, 96, 109, 111, 170, 244, 250, 253, 316, 318, 351
  of Abdullah, 114
  of Bakshi's government, 135
  of Kashmiri Hindus, 105
  of Kashmiri Muslims, 78
  to Congress, 223
  to India, 223, 351
  to the maharaja, 41

Madhok, Balraj, 154, 226
Maharaj Gunj market, 38
Mahaz-i-Aazadi, 328
Mahjoor, Ghulam Ahmad, 24, 56, 68*n*1, 77, 88–9, 98–9
Maisuma, 39, 313
Majid, Master Abdul, 264
Majoritarian card to rally Hindu votes, 304
maktab, 37
Malhotra, Jagmohan, 23*n*32, 148, 305–9, 315, 321
Malik, Mohammed Yasin, 312
Mangla Dam, 250–1
Manto, Saadat Hasan, 98
Martand, 226
marusi (ancestral) land, 107
Masoodi, Maulana, 193
Mawdudi, Maulana, 155, 300
Mazdoor Sabha, 46
Mehta, Asoka, 191
Menon, V. P., 61
migrations, 29, 65–6, 109, 229, 240, 251–2, 321, 354
  to Britain, 229
  in Dogra period, 29–30
  economic, 250
  of Hindus and Sikhs, 91
  to Middle East, 300
  to Pakistan, 66
  riot-driven, 91
Milad-ul-Nabi festival, 50
militarization of Kashmir, 15–16, 20, 281, 331–2, 336–7, 354, 359
Million March (2014), Britain, 281
Ministry of Kashmir Affairs (MKA), 243–4, 246–7, 249–50, 256

Ministry of States, 61, 84–5
Mir, Javed, 312
Miraj-ul-Alam, 50
Mirpur, 40, 54, 66, 240–1, 244–5, 250–2, 271
mobilization, 6, 192–9, 336
  political, 17–18, 27, 38, 43–4, 50, 56, 189, 247, 314
  in favor of freedom, 27
  majoritarian, 222, 355
  regional, 43
Moe-e-Muqaddas, 153
Mohiuddin, Akhtar, 191
Mookerjee, Syama Prasad, 112–13
Moorcroft, William, 27
Mother India, 10–11, 356
Mountbatten, Lord (Governor General of India), 67, 125*n*93, 195
  special session of Chamber of Princes, 60–1
Muhammad, Bakshi Ghulam, 82, 119, 130*n*206, 134, 141, 144, 149, 154, 187, 190
  lacked legitimacy, 134
  subdue Kashmiri discontent, 135
  to align with India, 136
mujawaza (grain procurement), 136–7
Mullik, B. N., 93, 119
Musharraf, Pervez, 280
Muslim Conference, 33, 37, 41–57, 59, 64–5, 70*n*39, 80–1, 85, 136, 187, 202, 241–4, 246–50, 271
Muslim League, 46–7, 51, 54–5, 58–9, 61–5, 95
Muslim Mujahedeen, 326
Muslim United Front (MUF), 306–12
  elections as a contest between Islam and secularism, 308
  resist unwarranted political interference, 306
  safeguard Kashmiri Muslim identity, 306
Muzaffarabad, 97, 240–1, 278, 280, 312
Nagaland, 12, 22*n*26
Narayan, Jayaprakash, 191, 206, 213
National Assembly, 56, 101
National Conference, 48–9, 51–60, 62–5, 78–81, 86–8, 90, 92, 94–5, 101, 103, 106–7, 109–10, 112–16, 118–19, 134–5, 143, 145, 153, 156, 160, 162, 164–6, 185, 190, 193, 197, 201, 215, 217–18, 220–3, 226–7, 242, 247, 250, 253, 295, 299, 301, 303, 305–6, 308, 310, 319
  administrative policies, 104
  agrarian reforms in 1950s, 224
  collaborative politics, 120
  demand for autonomy, 111
  Home Guard, 80
  and minority reservations on administrative policies of, 104–11
National Demand manifesto of Muslim Conference, 47–8, 51, 53
National Front government (1989–90), 323
National Hydel Power Corporation (NHPC), 173
National Liberation Army, 276
National Liberation Front (NLF), 254–5, 258–63, 268, 273–4
  activists in India-administered Kashmir, 260
  hijacked the Indian airplane *Ganga*, 260
  on the Algerian revolutionary group, 255
  to operate independently, 255
  to recruit guerillas, 255
National Rural Employment Programme (NREP), 165
national security, 3–4, 16, 60, 144, 203, 309, 315, 331–2, 334, 350, 354, 359
nationalism, 13, 57, 43, 50, 52–3, 58, 62, 67, 302, 360
  Hindu, 94, 114, 186, 190, 237*n*188, 355
  militant, 225
  regional, 7

secular, 14, 18, 45, 51, 91, 148, 150, 156, 296
territorial, 3, 10, 13, 120, 240, 273–81, 325, 356, 359
Western ideologies of, 25, 36
nationalist ideology, 49–50
nationalization of Muslims, 294
Nawabs of Dacca, 32
Naya Kashmir (or New Kashmir Manifesto), 56–7, 62–3, 79, 95, 104, 133
Nazish, Nazir, 264, 266, 270
Neelum Valley, 278
Nehru, Jawaharlal, 11, 46–7, 54, 59–61, 63–5, 67, 79, 81, 94, 100, 103, 110, 112–13, 115, 118, 143, 186–7, 199–200, 216, 220
and Abdullah, 64, 103, 112–13
leading the All India States People's Conference, 47
pledged to consult the Kashmiri people, 79
support for Quit Kashmir, 59
nepotism, 105, 142, 166, 169, 172, 174, 209, 219, 224, 294, 300, 313
New Kashmiri Bookshop, 55
negotiations, 7, 100, 103, 200, 204, 212, 215–16, 243, 247, 261
between Pakistan's military leadership, 261
for rights, 7, 229
with legitimate Kashmiri leaders, 212
with New Delhi, 215
with the Dogra state, 6
with the United Nations Commission for India and Pakistan, 243
Nisar, Qazi, 306, 309, 326
Noon, Firoz Khan, 248
Noorani, A. G., 201, 219, 357
Noor-ud-Din, Sheikh (or Nund Rishi), 26, 328
North-West Frontier Province (now Khyber Pakhtunkhwa), 66, 78, 246, 273, 327
nouveau riche, 133, 141–2, 149–50, 171
number of government employees in Jammu and Kashmir, 1978–88, 171
online activism, tool in Kashmiri mobilization, 336

Operation Gibraltar, 203
Organization of Arab Petroleum Exporting Countries (OAPEC), 299

Pakistan People's Party (PPP), 260, 265, 272
Pakistan-administered Kashmir, 2, 8, 12–13, 19, 80, 96–7, 187–8, 199, 208, 219–21, 229, 239–41, 245, 250, 253, 259, 261, 263, 265–8, 271, 273, 275, 312, 317, 326, 331, 351
Pakistan Workers Association (PWA), 270
Palestine, 19, 239, 301, 313
Pandit, Lalita, 322
Pandits' experience of displacement, 323
Panun Kashmir (Our Own Kashmir) movement, 323–4
partition of India, 3
and sovereignty dispute, 60–7
Patel, Sardar Vallabhbhai, 61, 93, 100, 109, 114
Pathribal Fake Encounter Case, 333
patronage politics, 141, 143, 174, 352
Peace Brigade, 135, 153, 191, 196–7
peasants, 28–30, 34, 39–41, 49, 55–8, 66, 79, 81, 103, 106–8, 110, 133, 136, 140, 158, 160–1, 163, 165, 169, 193, 215, 255, 257, 265–7, 307
People's Democratic Party (PDP), 338
People's League, 223, 302–3
Permanent Resettlement Bill, 220
Persian, 52, 92
plebiscite, 9–10, 18–19, 77, 84, 87, 90, 93, 97, 99–101, 110–14, 118, 120, 135, 153, 184–7, 190–2, 205, 211–12, 215, 218, 224, 238, 242–3, 245, 247, 269–73
movement, 192–9, 221, 223, 239, 253, 256, 303

politics of, 199–204
self-determination, 281
Plebiscite Front, 18, 140, 144–5, 163, 165, 192–5, 198–9, 204–5, 208, 213–17, 253–4, 258–9, 267, 271–2, 285*n*78, 286*n*105, 297, 311, 313
Plebiscite Front AJK (Azad Jammu and Kashmir), 253–4, 259
Persian, 52, 92
pirs, 28, 169
Political Conference, 189–90, 193, 199, 204
political economy, 18, 120, 132, 134
political elites, Kashmiri, 4–5
political legitimacy, 5, 38, 172
Poonch, 54, 66, 83, 113, 237*n*187, 240–1, 244–5, 277
Poonch Revolt, 241–2, 250
popular sovereignty, 15, 56, 120
pradhanmantri, 155
Praja Parishad, 81, 93–4, 109, 115, 118, 128*n*163, 190
and autonomy of Kashmir and plebiscite, 111–14
organize a *satyagraha*, 112
support from Hindu rightist parties, 112
Praja Socialist Party (PSP), 191–2
Prasad, Dr. Rajendra, 112
Prevention of Unlawful Activities Bill, 205
Preventive Detention Act, 205, 214
Preventive Detention Law (1955), 190
princely states of Jammu and Kashmir, 3, 5–6, 8, 18, 24–5, 27, 30, 32–3, 40, 47, 49, 54, 59–61, 65–6, 77, 99–100, 102, 104, 146, 190, 196, 199, 224, 239–41, 279, 294, 349–50, 352
Prophet Solomon, 5
protest music, 337
Public Safety Act of 2009, 336
Public Safety Ordinance Act, 119, 219
Public Service Commission, 167
Public Works Department (PWD), 142, 177*n*41
Punjab, 25, 27, 30–1, 33, 35, 40–1, 44, 53, 59, 65–6, 71*n*67, 86, 112, 145, 158, 174, 221, 248, 250–1, 313, 319
1891 census report, 29
East, 86
West, 83, 85, 87, 91, 226
Punjabi Hindus, 34, 38, 52, 102
Puri, Balraj, 143, 225, 321

Qadir, Abdul, 38
Qasim, Syed Mir, 161
Quit Kashmir movement, 58–9, 101, 189
Quran, 36–7, 49, 155, 196–7, 310, 326
Qureshi, Fazal Haq, 211

Radhakrishnan, Dr. S., 199
radical humanism, 57
Radio Kashmir, 118
rahdari system, 29
Raina, Niranjan Nath, 55
Ranbirsinghpura, 116
rashtrapati, 154
Rashtriya Rifles (RR), 329, 333
Rashtriya Swayamsevak Sangh (RSS), 65, 91, 104, 111, 123*n*55, 228, 296, 338, 356
Rawalpindi, 85–6, 145–6, 243, 246, 249, 278
rayat-nama, 102
Raza-Pathar, 29
Reading Room Party, 35, 37–8
revenue, 27–30, 37, 42, 86–7, 108, 137–40, 146–7, 160–1, 164–5, 173, 255
corporate tax, 147
for debt payments, 173
of former N.W.F.P., 246
from land grants, 28
increase, and balance the budget, 86
refugees, 7, 65, 83, 91, 93, 96, 117, 188, 220–1, 226, 239, 245, 274, 277–8, 309, 320–1, 323, 338–9
Chakma Buddhists, 338–9
Kashmiri Hindus (Pandits), 34, 105
Kashmiri Muslim, 7

West-Pakistan, 220
regional dissidence, 19, 147, 166, 217–24, 304
Rehmani, Farooq, 223, 302
religious bigotry, 61
religious minorities, 104, 197, 339
Report of the Basic Principles Committee, 101
Rishis, 158
definition of freedom, 26–7
Roy, M. N., 74*n*143, 190
rural, 49–50, 55–6, 58, 106–8, 132, 137, 168, 175, 226, 257, 274, 300, 306, 323, 325, 339
constituencies, 162
development projects, 158
elites, 133, 149, 169, 157–4
middle class, 163
orchardists, 162
poverty, 158, 164
–urban tensions, 18, 157–65, 174
Russia, 56, 62, 189, 300

Sadar-i-Riyasat, 103, 145
Sadiq, G. M., 46, 126*n*103, 130*n*198, 144–5, 201, 205, 209
discretionary powers, 209
emotional integration, 144
extended Article 356, 201
sadr-i-riyasat (governor), 154
Sajad, Malik, 337–8
Sanatan Dharma Young Men's Association, 43
Sarabhai, Mridula, 143, 193
*sarmayadar*s (moneylenders), 107–8
*sarpanch*es (village officials), 108
Sathu, J. N., 187
satiric ballads (*ladisha*s), 29
Savarkar, V. D., 237*n*188
Sayeed, Mufti, 314
secularism, 13–15, 18, 25, 47, 50, 82, 91–3, 105, 115–16, 134, 148–57, 166, 175, 192, 197, 209, 282, 296–7, 301–2, 306, 308, 323, 351, 355
self-determination, notion of, 10, 13, 15, 19, 33, 113–14, 133, 140, 144, 146, 155, 175, 184, 194–9, 202, 204, 222–3, 239–40, 245, 249, 251–4, 257–8, 260, 267–8, 270–3, 275, 279, 281–2, 293, 296, 298, 301, 303, 306, 320, 325, 330, 332, 339, 351–3
Chinese support for, 203
evolution of, 185–93
exercise in parts, 12
in Jammu and Ladakh, 224–8
Kashmiri expressions of, 9, 55–60, 63–4, 79, 90, 93–5, 98, 165, 229, 248, 302, 320, 328
Kashmiri Muslims invoke, 13, 320
and student activism, 204–17
UN promise of, 111, 185
Shah Hamdan shrine, Srinagar, 2
Shah, G. M., 147, 223–4, 304–5, 307
Shah, Mirwaiz Rasool, 33
Shah, Mirwaiz Yusuf, 41–2, 54, 202
Shah, Shabir, 303, 311
Shakur, Tupac (2Pac), 337
Shamim, Shamim Ahmed, 158, 167, 180n108, 206–7, 211, 296
Sharp Education Commission, 33
Sheikh, Hamid, 312
Sher-i-Kashmir (Lion of Kashmir), 120
Shia, 307
Shia–Sunni unity, 300
Sikh conquest of 1819, 27
Sikkim, 12, 22*n*26
Sikri Commission of 1979, 228
Simla Agreement of 1972, 272–3
Singh, Karan, 119
Singh, Maharaja Gulab, 21*n*14, 102
Singh, Maharaja Hari, 21*n*14, 61, 67, 107
Singh, Maharaja Pratap, 52
Sino-Pakistani alliance, 203
social justice, 10, 13, 44, 46, 56, 60–1, 79, 95, 144, 175, 191, 250, 294, 350
social transformations in urban Kashmir, 148–57

social structures, 18, 31, 134, 149, 355
socialism, 19, 25, 36, 43–4, 47, 67, 134, 143, 263–7, 282, 301–2, 306
Socialist Party of India, 115
Sopore, 162–3, 193, 195, 216, 299, 317
South-East Asia Treaty Organization (SEATO), 187
Soviet Union, 187
Soviet–Afghan war, 304
Srinagar, 2, 28, 33, 35, 37–8, 40, 43, 46–7, 59, 65, 80–1, 97, 101, 107, 113, 136, 141, 149, 153, 168, 193, 202, 204–5, 207, 209–10, 216, 222–4, 227, 258–60, 300–3, 305, 307, 312–15
  Reading Room party, 35
Staff Selection Commission, 169
state legitimacy, 15, 20
State People's Convention (1968), 212–14, 226, 295
state sovereignty, 3, 12, 16, 20, 331, 334–5, 359
state-subject category, 8–9, 11, 102–3, 219, 241, 308, 335, 350, 357
  basis of political identity, 7–8
  introduced by the Dogras, 7, 219, 241, 350
  only residents private ownership, 350
  part of the Jammu and Kashmir constitution, 357
  reinforced Kashmir's unique position, 8
stone-pelting, 336
Student Federation, 55, 263
Students' Revolutionary Council, 211
Study Circle, 55
sub-regional tensions, 104, 224, 353
  appeasing Kashmir, 225
  autonomy for sub-regions, 225
  Durbar Move agitation, 227
  excluded Jammu from power-sharing arrangements, 225
  Ladakhi Buddhists distrusted, 228
Subsidiary Intelligence Bureau, 310
subsidy(ies), 28, 87, 133, 136–9, 141, 158, 160, 164–5, 173–4, 196, 252, 352
Sufi-based Islam, 156, 158, 295, 328
support base, 15, 31, 33, 53, 55, 65, 89, 111–12, 135–6, 141, 156, 158, 165, 193, 200, 219, 226, 244, 270, 274, 300–1, 307, 326, 339
  of the Plebiscite Front, 193–4
  of the Congress, 200
  of the JKLF, 326
Supreme Court of India, 103–4, 137, 168, 333–4, 356

Taqdeer-i-Kashmir (Fate of Kashmir) pamphlet, 194
Taryaby, Younus, 264–6, 268–70
Tashkent Agreement (1966), 204, 252
tehreek-i-aazadi, 2, 320
Tenancy Amendment Acts (1955 and 1962), 160
territorial integrity, 2, 12, 15–16, 67, 114, 152, 252, 293, 312, 314–15, 334, 354, 359
territoriality, 3, 19
territorialization, 10–13
Terrorist and Disruptive Activities (Prevention) Act (1987) (TADA), 310–11, 315
transnationalism, 5, 7–8, 10–13, 16–17, 19, 23*n*30, 229, 239–41, 250–2, 263–4, 266–8, 270–1, 273–4, 276–7, 281–2, 312, 339, 354
transnational networks, 10–13
Treaty of Amritsar, 27, 59
tribal invasion of 1947, 60–7, 80, 104, 242
true Muslim, definition of, 26

Umaat-i-Islami, 306
unemployment among Kashmiri youth, 166–74
United Jihad Council, 328
United Kashmir Liberation Front (UKLF), 264, 266–70

United Nations, 9–10, 16, 79, 82, 93, 95–9, 114, 117, 186–7, 193, 200, 207–8, 224, 240, 243, 245, 247, 249, 253, 275, 279, 281, 314, 351
  plebiscite promise by, 77, 100, 111
United Nations Commission for India and Pakistan (UNCIP), 243
United Nations Human Rights Commission, 329
United Nations Security Council, 86, 101, 192, 242
  interpretation on India's withdrawal of plebiscite, 192
  resolution of 1948, 185, 252
United States, 99, 117, 187, 197, 203, 252, 257, 264, 268, 275, 300, 327, 331, 337, 358
Universal Declaration of Human Rights, 334
Urdu, 16, 31, 52, 59, 92, 154, 190, 251, 271, 274
urban, valley, 18, 28–9, 33–4, 39–40, 42, 49, 53, 55, 65, 86, 111, 132–3, 136–9, 148–50, 157–9, 163–5, 168, 174–5, 193, 226, 300, 323, 339
  decadence, 150
  middle-class businessmen, 200
  poor, 34
  trading spaces, 39
  working class neighborhoods, 313

Vaishnavi, Pandit Raghunath, 190, 199
Vakil, Molvi Muhammad Abdullah, 35
valorization of armed resistance, 320
Vietnam, 19, 239, 266, 268, 277
Vishwa Hindu Parishad (VHP), 304

Wahhabi Islam in Kashmir, 328
Wani, Ashfaq Majid, 312
Wani, Nazir Ahmad, 211
War Council, 198
wazir-i-azam (chief minister), 154
Wilson, Woodrow, 9
Women's College, 216
World Braille Day, 336
World War
  First, 9, 34, 66
  Second, 55, 66, 269
women, 39, 149–50, 159, 204, 297, 302, 317, 326, 338
  battalion of, 80
  at a disadvantage, 338
  imposed on, 298
  from Maisuma and Gawkadal, 39
  molestation of, 315
  of the Neelum Valley, 278
  protested against, 315
  rights of, 56

Yachu, Sham Lal, 190
Yatu, Abdul Salam, 58
Young Men's Muslim Association (YMMA), 35, 41
Youth League, 45, 55, 206, 302
Yuvak Sabha, 48
  Roti Agitation, 43

Zaghloul, Saad, 45
Zahid, Mohammad, 349
Zain-ul-abidin, Sultan (known as Bud Shah or great king), 31–2
Zarif, Zarif Ahmad, 292
Zehgeer, Ghulam Rasool, 211

For EU product safety concerns, contact us at Calle de José Abascal, 56–1°, 28003 Madrid, Spain or eugpsr@cambridge.org.

www.ingramcontent.com/pod-product-compliance
Ingram Content Group UK Ltd.
Pitfield, Milton Keynes, MK11 3LW, UK
UKHW010248140625
459647UK00013BA/1735